The Cultural Turn in U.S. History

Past, Present, and Future

Edited by James W. Cook,
Lawrence B. Glickman,
and Michael O'Malley

The University of Chicago Press
Chicago and London

James W. Cook is associate professor of history and American culture at the University of Michigan. Lawrence B. Glickman is professor of history at the University of South Carolina. Michael O'Malley is associate professor of history at George Mason University.

The University of Chicago Press, Chicago 60637
The University of Chicago Press, Ltd., London
© 2008 by The University of Chicago
All rights reserved. Published 2008
Printed in the United States of America

17 16 15 14 13 12 11 10 09 08   1 2 3 4 5

ISBN-13: 978-0-226-11506-1 (cloth)
ISBN-13: 978-0-226-11507-8 (paper)
ISBN-10: 0-226-11506-2 (cloth)
ISBN-10: 0-226-11507-0 (paper)

Library of Congress Cataloging-in-Publication Data

The cultural turn in U.S. history : past, present, and future / edited by James W. Cook, Lawrence B. Glickman, and Michael O'Malley.
     p. cm.
   Includes bibliographical references and index.
   ISBN-13: 978-0-226-11506-1 (cloth : alk. paper)
   ISBN-10: 0-226-11506-2 (cloth : alk. paper)
   ISBN-13: 978-0-226-11507-8 (pbk. : alk. paper)
   ISBN-10: 0-226-11507-0 (pbk. : alk. paper)
1. United States—Civilization—Historiography. 2. Popular culture—United States—Historiography. 3. United States—Race relations—Historiography. 4. United States—Social conditions—Historiography. 5. United States—Historiography. I. Cook, James W., 1966– II. Glickman, Lawrence B., 1963– III. O'Malley, Michael.
   E169.1.C8425 2008
   973.072—dc22

                                                      2008028285

For Lawrence W. Levine,
1933–2006

CONTENTS

ACKNOWLEDGMENTS

This project began in September 2005 with "The State of Cultural History," a national conference in honor of Lawrence W. Levine. Our first debts are to the people at George Mason University who helped to make that event possible: the late Roy Rosenzweig, who spearheaded the organization, fund-raising, and planning; Mike O'Malley, who designed the conference Web site; and Olivia Ryan, who juggled many of the logistics. We also thank the paper presenters, commentators, panel chairs, and more than two hundred registered attendees who brought their energy and ideas to the larger conversation.

One of the great joys of the conference was the participation of Larry Levine's extended family, many of whom traveled great distances to be with us. We are especially grateful to Cornelia Levine for bringing everyone together and speaking on Larry's behalf, and to Leon Litwack for his gracious and insightful opening remarks.

Our thanks, too, to all of the authors who worked with us to produce this volume, a group of scholars that cuts across multiple generations and many locations within the cultural turn.

At the University of Chicago Press, our special thanks go to Robert Devens, a superb editor whose enthusiasm and wise counsel guided us at every stage; and to Emilie Sandoz, who was enormously helpful in pulling everything together. Two anonymous press readers read the manuscript and offered extensive critical feedback.

On a more personal level, a number of individuals lived with and supported this book:

Jay Cook acknowledges Rita Chin and Oliver Chin Cook (who arrived just in time to help celebrate the book's completion).

Larry Glickman acknowledges Jill Frank.

And Mike O'Malley acknowledges Roy Rosenzweig, friend and colleague, and Kathleen Trainor.

Finally, our heartfelt thanks go to our teacher and friend, Larry Levine, who passed away in fall 2006. Sadly, by the time of the conference Larry was too ill to make the long trip from Berkeley, California, to Arlington, Virginia. As this volume makes clear, however, his rich ideas and passion for history have continued to reverberate across the discipline.

PART I

Introduction

ONE

Twelve Propositions for a History
of U.S. Cultural History

JAMES W. COOK AND LAWRENCE B. GLICKMAN

This volume was born of our belief that the time is ripe for a broad assessment of U.S. cultural history. Since the mid-1970s, at least, cultural historians working on a wide range of topics have stretched, deepened, and dramatically transformed our sense of the nation's past. And if one includes the important body of historical scholarship produced under the banner of American studies, the U.S. field would feature a lineage that actually precedes the "new cultural history" by more than three or four decades. Yet these same signs of innovation, breadth, and longevity have often pushed against neat and easy categorization. With a few notable exceptions, U.S. cultural historians have tended to prioritize new research over methodological reflection, leaving the important work of field assessment to their Europeanist colleagues (who in turn have often defined their own trajectories as "cultural history" writ large).[1]

By calling for a dedicated history of the U.S. field, we do not mean to suggest that it can be easily disentangled from parallel projects in other national contexts (a comparative question to which we return later). Nor has the U.S. field lacked tough and useful debates about its own working methods. Yet these more explicit conversations about historiography have tended to cluster around particular topics—from consumerism, popular culture, and the concept of cultural hegemony to working-class life, moral problems, and the cultures of the cold war—rather than the larger enterprise of cultural history itself.[2] Even today, as some commentators have begun to speculate on a methodological future "beyond the cultural turn," we still lack a clear sense of what, exactly, the U.S. field *was* for much of the past century.[3]

In this introductory chapter, we look backward and forward, and also meditate on the current state of U.S. cultural history. In looking backward, we attempt to sort through the multiple strands of questioning that first coalesced into a recognizable disciplinary project, now often described as the "cultural turn." This story is one that currently exists only in bits and pieces, and is largely unknown even by many of the field's practitioners. We begin with the conviction that any speculations on the future need to be grounded in a much longer, broader, and more comparative view of the field's complex development.

At the same time, we want to look forward by tracing some of the field's current and future contours. Now that cultural history has come to occupy a central disciplinary position, how should we think about its once controversial efforts to make language, identity, perception, and meaning-making primary objects of historical analysis? Are these efforts best understood as the momentary correctives of older blind spots? Or have they fostered more lasting and productive projects?

———

As an object of analysis, U.S. cultural history presents a number of built-in challenges. One is the field's remarkable diversity, a pattern well illustrated by the roster of contributors to this volume. Some of us began our careers in social, intellectual, labor, gender, and African American history and only slowly gravitated toward cultural history as a self-description. Others of us went to graduate school specifically to train in American studies or U.S. cultural history and have spent much of our careers working within well-established national networks. Much the same can be said about our current institutional locations. Some of us were hired in American studies programs and now teach (at least part of the time) in history departments, whereas others have spent much of their history careers pushing toward more interdisciplinary modes of teaching, research, and writing. Over half of us currently hold joint appointments.

These complex conjunctures point to one of the field's defining features. Although we see ourselves as engaged in common analytical problems and source types, none of us would insist upon a fixed or finished method for "doing" cultural history. Nor would we insist on any one definition of "culture," a notoriously slippery concept whose multiple meanings have long thwarted strict categorical precision.[4] Of course, this very flexibility runs the risk of producing a kind of Rashomon effect, with each cultural historian telling a different story about the field's origins and foundational practices. We begin, then, with twelve propositions for assembling a more coherent history of U.S. cultural history. We offer these propositions not as a comprehensive chronicle—something that would require much more than a single introductory essay—but as multiple angles of approach on a large and shifting target.

Proposition One: The new cultural history was, in fact, a relatively late development

This initial proposition will no doubt strike some readers as counterintuitive. After all, the phrase "new cultural history" did not achieve common currency until at least the late 1980s.[5] And since that time, most leading commentators, especially on the European side, have described it as a specific response to major intellectual shock waves from the previous decade. Some have pointed to the growing disenchantment with quantitative analysis that led many "new social historians" to push for alternative ways of accessing the subjective experiences and perceptions of nonelites. Others have emphasized the budding historical interest in symbolic systems and rituals of meaning-making, projects commonly associated with the anthropological writings of Mary Douglas, Victor Turner, and above all, Clifford Geertz. Still others have highlighted Michel Foucault's efforts to explicate the microworkings of power through shifting patterns of discourse.[6]

We too see these developments as crucial and in this chapter attempt to trace some of their distinctive American resonances. But first we want to challenge the more basic notion of the "new cultural history" as a methodological starting point. On the European side, such a periodization would elide dozens of pioneering efforts by French Annalistes such as Lucien Febvre, British neo-Marxists such as Eric Hobsbawm and E. P. Thompson, and American Europeanists such as Natalie Davis, Carl Schorske, and Robert Darnton. On the U.S. side, by contrast, it would neglect a vast body of postwar scholarship (largely but not exclusively within American studies) that sought to historicize dominant patterns of language, imagery, and collective perception three or four decades before the arrival of Geertz and Foucault.[7]

The problems of periodization become more pronounced when we examine some of the very first investments in culture.[8] Often forgotten now is the fact that something called cultural history was periodically prominent in the U.S. field before World War II, practiced by some of the country's most important historians. As Harry Elmer Barnes noted in 1922, summing up the goals of the "New American history," our nation's past "can by no means be restricted to a record of political and military development. The most notable American achievements have been non-political in character." In particular, Barnes singled out "psychological and cultural elements" as the key alternatives to political and military history.[9]

These early developments were shaped by a number of broader innovations in the social sciences. Among the most crucial was the pioneering anthropological work of Franz Boas from the late 1910s through the 1930s. "After Boas," explained the eminent sociologist Robert Lynd, culture came to be understood not so much as a racialized set of evolutionary traits but as "the ways that people inhabiting a common geographic area . . . do things . . . the ways they think and feel about things."[10] It was also during this period that some of the best-known literary and humanistic definitions from the nineteenth century began to give way. Matthew Arnold's rarified notion of culture as "the best which has been thought and said," for example, was now increasingly supplanted by the longstanding German emphasis on "the totality of ideas in a society, popular as well as scholarly—in other words, low as well as high culture."[11]

In the U.S. field, the major historiographical innovator during the 1930s was Caroline Ware, who launched a series of new research projects on previously "neglected" topics such as documentary photography, folklore, and popular music. To promote her "bottom-up" vision of U.S. history, Ware organized dozens of panels at the American Historical Association meeting in 1939. And in 1940 she edited a major AHA-sponsored volume based on those sessions, *The Cultural Approach to History*.[12] This volume received widespread critical attention from many leading scholars, including Melville J. Herskovits, Charles Beard, and Crane Brinton.[13] One contemporary reviewer, using language that many of us assume only arose in the late 1960s, noted that "many of the writers" begin from the proposition that "history should concern itself with the inarticulate masses, their lives, languages, loves, etc."[14] Whereas previous historians had focused primarily on society's "intellectual and political leaders," the goal now was to understand "processes of change" that affected "the multitude."[15]

For Ware, in particular, these goals were part of an explicitly "integral" approach to the study of history, as well as a more socially conscious orientation in an age of "mass unemployment" and "the degradation of totalitarian war." "The historian of today," she concluded, "no longer secure within the framework of nineteenth-century Western European assumptions, needs new intellectual tools with which to view his society."[16]

Looking back on these efforts four decades later, one contributor to Ware's volume, the eminent business historian Thomas Cochran, wondered why such a promising body of research had not become "synonymous with history" (which is what Cochran and many of his colleagues had hoped and predicted during early 1940s).[17] The prominent anthropologist Ruth Benedict shared Cochran's view, writing to Ware in April 1941: "I have been reading 'The Cultural Approach to History' and I am delighted with your introduction. . . . I believe it will stimulate much valuable historical work; perhaps, even, in ten years, it will be possible to get out a really definitive collection of historical studies of the kind you call for."[18]

From our own vantage point, it is easier to see that Ware's innovative projects of the late 1930s were alternatively ignored, recast, or unselfconsciously absorbed by the dominant groups of political, intellectual, and social historians that soon followed, a pattern that led many self-described culturalists of the 1970s and 1980s to assume they were entering into wholly uncharted territory.[19] As Donald Kelley observed in a 1996 review essay, the "most recent phase of cultural history has not paid much attention to its antecedents."[20]

As a first step, then, it seems important to recast the "new cultural history" of the late 1980s in more precise terms: not as a wholly distinctive historiographical phenomenon, or as the field itself, but as one major development within a much longer twentieth-century trajectory.

Proposition Two: The broad historical interest in culture
that first took root during the 1930s did not simply disappear
in the years following World War II

Once again, our genealogical instincts may seem to fly in the face of conventional wisdom. Previous discussions of Ware's career, for example, have generally characterized her postwar influence as less significant, not least because Ware herself pursued a series of very different professional projects, including government service, consumer activism, and teaching social work classes at Howard University.[21] Likewise, most general surveys have described the postwar years as dominated by the "presidential synthesis" and "consensus history"—two projects that seem to have little in common with the bottom-up perspectives, popular sources, and pluralistic models running through Ware's 1940 volume.

To some extent, these characterizations are accurate. Few today would argue that something called U.S. cultural history constituted a dominant, or even particularly coherent, *field* during the late 1940s and 1950s. Fewer still would insist on tracing direct lines of influence between Ware's cultural approach and the more pervasive cultural turn that began to take shape three or four decades later. One could argue, in fact, that it was directly in opposition to the presidential synthesis and consensus historiography—with their conventional emphases on elite white men, high-level diplomacy, electoral politics, and ideological continuity—that many of the subsequent innovators in U.S. cultural history positioned themselves.[22]

Still, this familiar trajectory can be qualified and sharpened in a number of ways. One has to do with consensus history itself. As Robert Berkhofer first noted, it was precisely by applying prewar social science's more expansive concept of culture to American politics that so-called consensus scholars such as Richard Hofstadter, Daniel Boorstin, and David Potter sought to explain the relative absence of socioeconomic conflict in U.S. history.[23] The specific models varied from author to author and text to text. In the *American Political Tradition* (1948), for example, Hofstadter referred to "common climates of opinion" and "bounded horizons" of political debate, whereas Potter's *Peoples of Plenty* (1954) emphasized the "traits," "values," and "behavioral patterns" central to the formation of "national character."[24] For our purposes, however, the most notable feature of this scholarship was less its internal variations than its broader tendency to treat political questions in cultural terms. Potter, in particular, was quite explicit about his conceptual debts, applauding Ware's *Cultural Approach* for "breaking new ground" in the "broader relationship between history and the behavioral sciences."[25] By the mid-1950s, moreover, Hofstadter began to focus more squarely on the problems of "status politics" and "symbolic analysis"—two lines of questioning that, as Daniel Signal has argued, shared a number of affinities with Geertz's later reconceptualization of ideology as a "cultural system."[26]

Another important qualification involves the postwar rise of American studies. By the mid-1950s, this increasingly national "movement" (which generated its own journal, professional association, conferences, and degree programs) had become the second major location for analyzing culture in historical terms. But whereas consensus historians understood culture as the ideological wellspring of American politics, American studies scholars such as Henry Nash Smith, R. W. B. Lewis, John William Ward, and Leo Marx focused their attention on shifting patterns of representation, a move specifically designed to bridge the gap separating formalist analyses of "individual works of art" and broader historical treatments of their "social setting."[27]

The hybrid work that followed was a major challenge to U.S. historians, not just as competing claims to particular source types but also at the more fundamental levels of concepts and epistemologies. For Smith and his colleagues, much of the point of American studies was to complicate U.S. historiography's conventional tendency to treat aesthetic forms as straightforward "reflections" of social, political, or economic developments. And in this sense, at least, one could argue that the American studies boom of the 1950s was not so much an extension of Ware's "cultural approach" but a vehicle for its displacement, offering postwar scholars interested in shifting patterns of representation an alternative register in which to engage some of the era's most widely discussed historical issues (e.g., the significance of the West in the popular imagination).

In our view, however, these methodological contrasts should not overshadow the era's most notable long-term development, namely, the crosscutting dialogues around culture that began to take shape in multiple disciplinary quadrants. By the early 1960s, that is to say, U.S. historians regularly cited leading works in American studies and vice versa. English professors such as Perry Miller, Howard Mumford Jones, and John Cawelti published historical studies of Puritanism, Jeffersonianism, and the self-made man, while history professors such as Merle Curti and William R. Taylor wrote about patterns of representation in nineteenth-century fiction.[28] Henry Nash Smith was alternatively described as both the founder of the American studies movement and one of the nation's leading cultural historians. And virtually everyone in these circles had something to say about the new critiques of mass culture launched (both within and outside of academia) by H. L. Menken, Robert Merton, Theodore Adorno, Dwight MacDonald, and David Riesman.

Not surprisingly, these postwar conversations often generated sharp debates. Social scientists liked to complain about American studies scholars' somewhat fuzzy conceptualization of the relation between "mythic constructions" and "empirical facts," an issue that left unresolved the fundamental question of causality.[29] American studies scholars, in turn, defended their "unscientific method" by pointing to some of the analytical blind spots in quantitative studies of literature, music, and film—many of which categorized (and counted) complex works of art according to their core "messages."[30] As Smith argued in one of his best-known essays, the aesthetic "content" in such studies was far "too rudimentary" in conceptualization; "it is . . . a factor [understood as] common to large numbers of works, which means a factor that is very far from exhausting the particularity of even a simple work of art. We need a method that can give us access to meanings beyond the range of such a systematic simplification—meanings that are not, so to speak, homogenized."[31]

Should these postwar debates be understood as part of the larger genealogy of U.S. cultural history? In our view, the answer is yes, not least because prominent postwar historians began to describe them as such. A good example is David Brion Davis's 1968 *American Historical Review* essay, "Recent Directions in American Cultural History." For Davis, postwar historical studies by Arthur O. Lovejoy, Walter Houghton, and John Higham formed key branches of the family tree, but so too did leading American studies titles such as Smith's *Virgin Land*, Lewis's *The American Adam*, and Charles Sanford's *The Quest for Paradise*. Also revealing was Davis's strategic juxtaposition of a recent work in American studies (Leo Marx's *Machine in the Garden*, 1964) with another in history (William R. Taylor's *Cavalier and Yankee*, 1961) to build his central arguments: first, that the best cultural history work necessarily incorporates *all* of these analytical registers; and second, that the field as a whole was now becoming increasingly sensitive to the "inner contradictions" and "conflicting values" that have often divided American culture.[32]

In this last respect, especially, Davis's essay looked ahead to the more "contested" models of culture that began to emerge during the 1970s and 1980s (a topic to which we will return). Ultimately, though, the most important lesson of the postwar period probably has less to do with fixing the precise moment—or problematic—in which the field began to achieve some degree of methodological coherence than acknowledging the intensely polyglot character of the larger project. As Davis's essay made clear, U.S. cultural history was something of a mess during the 1950s and 1960s, practiced in bits and pieces across a wide variety of scholarly locations. But perhaps that's the key lesson. What we now describe as the field's conventional eclecticism was at least a decade or two old when Davis began to sort it out.

Proposition Three: More recent varieties of U.S. cultural history have regularly encompassed a wide range of "culture concepts"

In one sense, of course, this proposition only adds to the problems of categorization.[33] Just as no two cultural historians would describe the field's chronological parameters in precisely the same way, neither would they map its core concepts according to a perfectly consistent set of definitions. What follows here, then, should be understood not as a rigid or comprehensive taxonomy of the field at large but as a starting point for more careful and complex readings of individual works.

CULTURE DEFINED AS ARTISTIC EXPRESSION In this formulation, culture has generally signified a movement (e.g., Impressionism), an idiom (e.g., blues), a mode of display (e.g., P. T. Barnum's three-ring spectacles), or a set of critical categories (e.g., Clement Greenberg's antipodes of "avant-garde" and "kitsch").[34] Somewhat ironically, the best recent genealogies of European cultural history have ignored artistic expression almost entirely, a pattern that may reflect older materialist prejudices against any notion of culture as set apart from "ordinary" experience.[35] On the U.S. side, however, such social and epistemological separations have held far less sway. In fact, one of the distinctive features of pioneering U.S. studies such as David Brion Davis's *Homicide in American Fiction* (1957), Alan Trachtenberg's *Brooklyn Bridge* (1965), David Grimsted's *Melodrama Unveiled* (1968), Nathan Huggins's *Harlem Renaissance* (1971), Neil Harris's *Humbug* (1972), and Ann Douglass's *Feminization of American Culture* (1978) was the desire to track their subjects across the conventional boundaries separating intellectual, cultural, and social history; representation and politics; art and ideas; high and low.[36]

CULTURE DEFINED AS THE LARGER MATRIX OF COMMERCIAL INSTITUTIONS AND STRUCTURES IN WHICH ARTISTIC FORMS ARE PRODUCED AND CONSUMED In this formulation (a reworking of the previous concept), new styles and genres have been understood as inseparable from questions of commodification, standardization, promotion, distribution, and regulation. Some of the earliest work in this mode (e.g., Max Horkheimer and Theodore Adorno's midcentury writings on the "culture industry") presented the impacts of capitalism somewhat monolithically: as part of a longer declension story in which modern American consumers found themselves increasingly manipulated or alienated from the growing numbers of cultural products all around them.[37] By the mid-1980s, however, leading scholars (both in the United States and Europe) had begun to reconceptualize the relation between producers and consumers in more nuanced and dialectical terms. Where previous critics had spoken of "unending sameness" and "captains of consciousness," the trend now was toward more localized studies of "cultural appropriation" and "strategic positions to be won or lost."[38]

CULTURE DEFINED AS ANY SOCIAL OR INSTITUTIONAL SPHERE IN WHICH COLLECTIVE FORMS OF MEANING ARE MADE, ENFORCED, AND CONTESTED This much broader formulation includes explicitly cultural sites of production such as theaters, museums, publishing houses, amusement parks, and film studios, but also artisan workshops, abolitionist conventions, middle-class parlors, boxing rings, and secondary schools—in short, any institution that generates its own norms, values, rituals, and representations. Not surprisingly, older boundaries separating different forms of social life and ideological expression have been especially permeable here. Indeed, much of the point of this formulation was to explicate "culture" and "context" as mutually constitutive—as two sides of the same historical process.[39]

CULTURE DEFINED AS A COMMON SET OF BELIEFS, CUSTOMS, VALUES, AND RITUALS—A.K.A. THE "ANTHROPOLOGICAL" CONCEPT OF CULTURE As we have seen, one early version of this formulation achieved currency just before World War II. And in the years that followed, it continued to resonate (somewhat abstractly) in many local and community studies—as a "whole way of life" or as "tradition" itself. Starting in the 1960s and 1970s, however, new waves of social and labor historians began to recast the community-based culture concept in the more specific register of "agency." Driving this shift was the desire to explore the subjective and experiential dimensions of culture, as well as a political imperative to take seriously the vernacular expressions and consumption habits of subjugated peoples (peasants, slaves, industrial workers, and the like) who left behind few written records. In the new formulations, culture generally functioned as a "resource," as a font of oppositional "consciousness," as a "unifying force," or as a mode of "infrapolitics."[40]

CULTURE DEFINED AS A SEMIOTIC OR DISCURSIVE SYSTEM In this formulation, "culture" has generally referred to signifying practices that could be "read like a text" or excavated via dominant patterns of "discourse."[41] Often, too, these modes of questioning have been described as "postmodern" in orientation and European in origin.[42] Yet many of the same critical impulses lay at the heart of the postwar American studies movement, especially in its efforts to explicate "those mediating forms which organize, define, and subdue the details of experience."[43]

By acknowledging these domestic precedents, we do not mean to ignore or downplay the innovations that followed. Henry Nash Smith's introductory remarks from *Virgin Land* provide a useful touchstone. In

1950, Smith defined the core American studies concepts of "myths" and "symbols" in two basic ways: as "intellectual constructions" that "fuse concept and emotion" and as "collective representations." But he also argued (in the very next sentence) that such "products of the imagination" should be set apart from "empirical facts." Myths and symbols, in this view, existed on a "different plane" from external "reality."[44]

For late twentieth-century scholars following in the wake of Geertz and Foucault, by contrast, sharp analytical distinctions between representation and reality became increasingly difficult to sustain. Where Smith had gestured somewhat vaguely toward the impact of representations on "practical affairs," growing numbers of Americanists now began to emphasize the constitutive power of words and symbols in shaping the very parameters of what could be thought, said, imagined, and experienced. In many cases, moreover, these explicitly "productive" dimensions of language and imagery became the crucial springboards for exploring new kinds of collective identities: from the "white" self-identifications of antebellum artisans and the "civilizing" discourses articulated by late nineteenth-century reformers, to the interwoven cultural tropes of "good wives, nasty wenches, and anxious patriarchs" that shaped social life and law in colonial Virginia.[45]

CULTURE DEFINED AS TRANSNATIONAL OR GLOBAL CIRCULATION This last formulation has emerged from a number of overlapping projects. One of the most fundamental was the desire to challenge the notion of a singular American "mind," "character," or "culture"—three master tropes from the postwar period that were sometimes used to celebrate American exceptionalism and to privilege white middle-class viewpoints. That these critiques often surfaced in the contexts of immigration history and ethnic studies was hardly coincidental.[46] For those working on questions of national belonging, the historical movement of peoples and cultures was not a shiny new idea fostered by world systems theory or the information age. It was the central problematic for much of the field.

Over time, however, this body of work has expanded and overlapped with two related projects: one on the transnational circulation of art, ideas, and politics; and another on U.S. empire and global capitalism. In the first instance, the goal was to account for cultural practices and intellectual debates never wholly contained by nation states—from the multiple forms of black artistic expression that have moved across the Atlantic diaspora to the transnational intellectual and political exchanges fundamental to so many of the twentieth century's saving ideas (such as

Social Democracy and Pan-Africanism).[47] In the second cluster of work, by contrast, the emphasis has been on the expanding systems of commerce, colonialism, and communications through which much of the cultural traffic actually *moved*. Perhaps inevitably, this last formulation has involved a more systems-oriented vocabulary than some of its predecessors. Whereas immigration historians had emphasized the circulation of specific individuals, groups, and traditions, much of the new work has sought to explicate the conduits themselves: from the "chains" of commodities to the "webs" of communication to the "networks" of colonial rule.[48]

> *Proposition Four: In actual practice, most cultural*
> *historians have sought to work* across *these concepts,*
> *often combining them in new and productive ways*

Consider, for example, Lawrence Levine's *Black Culture and Black Consciousness* (1977), one of the seminal works in the U.S. field. At first glance, Levine's epic study seems to fit neatly within an anthropological conception of culture. Through much of the book, orally transmitted customs, values, and rituals serve as the primary entry points into a collective "black consciousness," while classic ethnographic works by Herskovits, Malinowski, and Lévi-Strauss appear regularly in the footnotes. Yet for anyone familiar with Levine's meticulous readings of antebellum folk tales—or his extended discussion of "the rise of secular song"—it would be hard to describe this book as something other than a study of black aesthetics. Indeed, part of what made *Black Culture and Black Consciousness* so fresh and exciting during the late 1970s was precisely its insistence that the history of African American vernacular expression required both the functionalist tools of cultural anthropology and the formalist scrutiny previously reserved for canonical works of art.[49]

Similar arguments could be made about many of the best-known works in the U.S. field over the past thirty years. Was Karen Halttunen's *Confidence Men and Painted Women* (1982) an innovative study of middle-class cultural rituals in parlors, ballrooms, and cemeteries or a more discursive analysis of antebellum notions of sincerity and theatricality? Should Susan G. Davis's *Parades and Power* (1986) be viewed as a community history of artisan culture in nineteenth-century Philadelphia or as a semiotic analysis of their public protests? Was Janice Radway's *Reading the Romance* (1984) an institutional history of a major publishing industry or a more localized reception study of women's reading habits?

In actual practice, of course, the methodological strands running through these distinctions cannot be neatly or easily separated. And over time, the strands have only become more entangled. Our view, in fact, is many (if not most) of the field's landmark works achieved their broad resonance precisely by *combining* culture concepts in powerful new ways.

Proposition Five: Previous confusion surrounding the parameters of cultural history has stemmed in part from a long-running tendency to elide the field in more general U.S. surveys

The pattern here is surprisingly extensive. In 1981, the editors of the *Journal of Interdisciplinary History* devoted two entire volumes to the topic "The New History: The 1980s and Beyond." Painting a broad canvas of the cutting edge of the profession, the editors solicited articles on myriad topics, including political, economic, family, population, and intellectual history, as well as the history of science, biography, and quantification. At this early juncture, however, cultural history was not included.[50] The following year, "The Promise of American History," a special issue of the influential journal *Reviews in American History*, similarly omitted cultural history in its analysis of the state of the U.S. field.

In 1990, Eric Foner's important edited collection, *The New American History* (a volume specifically designed to register the U.S. field's multicultural expansion), offered no extended discussion of culture in thirteen different review essays. The second (1997) edition, significantly, contained a wide-ranging essay by Thomas Bender titled "Intellectual and Cultural History." But even here, the move was somewhat circumscribed. As the title suggests, cultural history was now grouped with, and partially subsumed by, a related field; and in terms of longer genealogies, the category of "cultural" analysis emerged here only as one of four seedbeds for intellectual history. Louis Masur's 1998 volume, *The Challenge of American History*, similarly examined cultural methods only as subtopics of dedicated essays on colonial history, narrative history, urban history, ethno-racial history, and visual studies.[51]

Over time, this pattern has produced an increasingly untenable disjuncture: even as many leading Americanists now point to "the cultural turn" as the major historiographical development of the late twentieth century, new waves of U.S. surveys continue to offer little acknowledgment that cultural history actually *happened*.[52] In our view, however, the real problem is not so much the contents of journals or the contours of essay collections as their concomitant silences on questions of transmissions and influence. What we still lack, in other words, is a clear sense of how the growing interest in culture over the past three decades grew out of and ultimately transformed many of the core fields in U.S. history. It is to these more comparative questions of historiographical impact and change that we now turn.

Proposition Six: Many of the seedbeds of U.S. cultural history can be found in the work of those who first identified themselves as specialists in other fields

Consider, for example, the generational cohort of Herbert Gutman, Warren Susman, Nathan Huggins, Lawrence Levine, and Carroll Smith-Rosenberg, five scholars we would group together as cultural historians *avant la lettre*. During the late 1950s and 1960s, these scholars often described themselves (or were described by others) in relation to some other methodological rubric, be it labor history (Gutman), intellectual history (Susman), social history (Huggins), political history (Levine), or women's history (Smith-Rosenberg).[53] Yet their forward positions within each of these fields suggest a number of structural similarities.

On a very basic level, all five scholars moved toward culture as part of a larger departure from the main currents of postwar U.S. historiography. None of them, for example, evinced much interest in the tools of quantitative social science. Nor did they favor the rubrics of big events history (such as elections, treaties, and wars). Rather, all five began to argue that the nation's most compelling dramas required an analytical register more sensitive to the contingencies of individual perception, language, imagery, and day-to-day experience.[54] They also shared the conviction that a more capacious—and contested—understanding of American culture was central to the larger process of expansion. By redefining the boundaries of the nation's cultural life to include workers, non-elite consumers, racial/ethnic minorities, and women, they simultaneously refuted long-running assumptions about *whose* histories were worthy of serious consideration.

Their shared commitments to culture as a historical motor, furthermore, sometimes put them in marginal or ambiguous positions vis-à-vis their original areas of training. In Levine's case, this led to feelings of "loneliness" and "isolation" as he embarked upon an eleven-year study of black popular culture, while for Gutman it meant serving as "the spokesman" for a new mode of working-class history "that as yet had no name."[55] It also required them to articulate more precisely the limits of historiographical practice in neighboring fields. In 1976, for example, Gutman described the conventional tendency to align his work with "the new social history" as both "pleasing" and "disturbing," noting that "much in the new social history soundly examines greatly neglected but important aspects of past working-class experience. But too much of it is narrowly classificatory, too narrowly statistical and behavioral." Culturally specific beliefs, habits, customs, and experiences, he now argued, were the essential missing pieces for "explaining" (rather than merely "describing") the "regularities" of American working-class life.[56]

Similarly, Smith-Rosenberg's autobiographical introduction to *Disorderly Conduct* ("Hearing Women's Words") described her approach as an evolving effort to transcend the constraints of her graduate training. Starting from a "traditional social historian's" emphasis on public life and institutional structures during the late 1960s, she increasingly turned to the private thoughts and writings of nineteenth-century women to add a more "experiential component." These discussions of "the every day," in turn, opened up new historiographical registers: first, by endowing "census data with the warmth of emotional reality"; and second, by allowing her to "test the accuracy" of Victorian era "prescriptive material" against "what people actually did." She also began to argue that both the "language" of emotional intimacy and the "categories" of social relations required a new set of analytical tools. Whereas earlier historians might have understood "friendship," "love," "domesticity," and "licentiousness" as straightforward behavioral descriptors, Smith-Rosenberg now turned her focus to the "shared systems of signs or symbolic languages rooted in, and expressive of, social relationships and social experiences."[57]

There are, of course, limits to how far one should take this sort of generational synthesis. For Susman, Huggins, and Smith-Rosenberg, "neglected" or "non-elite" forms of culture generally meant commercial products, published sources, and middle-class correspondence, whereas Gutman and Levine used the very same terms to describe the orally transmitted habits, customs, values, and artistic expressions of workers and slaves. One can also point to obvious differences in the theoretical tools used to access and explain these things. Whereas Gutman and Levine developed their understandings of culture via anthropology and folklore, Smith-Rosenberg, in her somewhat later interventions, included the more explicitly linguistic and semiotic approaches of Bakhtin, Barthes, and Foucault. Susman, by contrast, was particularly attuned to the social scientific literatures on U.S. consumerism, while Huggins sought to bridge previously separate scholarly discourses on the intellectual history and civil rights politics of the 1920s and 1930s.

Ultimately, though, it was this cohort's collective efforts to put culture at the center of analysis that mattered most. For those of us who followed, this was the pivotal generation of scholars who assembled the new sets of questions, sources, and narrative practices around which a larger field of U.S. cultural history began to constitute itself.

Proposition Seven: Some of the most important debates from this period involved historians loosely or explicitly identified with the New Left

Central to these debates was the pathbreaking work of the British literary scholar Raymond Williams, the American anthropologist Sidney Mintz, and the British and American labor historians E. P. Thompson and Herbert Gutman, all leading influences on the slightly younger New Left generation, which came of age during the 1960s and 1970s. Williams was especially important for challenging the vulgar Marxist base/superstructure model in which culture generally functioned as an epiphenomenon (or mere reflection) of deeper economic realities.[58] Also crucial was Thompson's emphasis on culture as the key to understanding the "experience" of class in history. "Class consciousness," he argued in a crucial passage from *The Making of the English Working Class* (1963), "is the way in which these experiences are handled in cultural terms: embodied in traditions, value-systems, ideas and institutional forms."[59] Americanist practitioners of the new social and labor histories quickly followed suit, shifting their understanding of culture (in Michael Denning's wry formulation) from "sweetness and light to customs and morals."[60]

For Gutman, following Mintz, culture was above all a "resource" in working-class struggles. He generally located these struggles in particular communities, which were (again following Mintz) the "arena" in which the experiences of class played themselves out. In this way, the "community study" became the conventional monographic framework of the new social and labor histories, thanks in good measure to Gutman's place-centered approach to labor history as well as the broad influence of pioneering social histories, such as Stephen Thernstom's influential work on mobility in a New England town.[61]

Community, in these works, signified two things. It was a distinct locale (such as the shoe-making town of Lynn, Massachusetts, about which four important books were written), and it stood for the solidarity of working people within those towns and cities.[62] Communities were seen as embodying culture in Gutman's sense: as a resource and bulwark in the larger class struggle. Scholars emphasized the unique cultures of working-class communities across a wide variety of locales, describing them as social as opposed to individualistic, mutually supportive rather than competitive, and characterized by "rough" amusements rather than middle-class rituals of respectability.[63] By the late 1980s, Leon Fink noted that the "culturalist thrust," with its emphasis on the defense of both the labor process and the working-class community, had become the "central paradigm" of the new labor history.[64]

These patterns, in our view, can be understood as part of a broader New Left celebration of community-based values and politics. By shifting their focus to more localized and quotidian forms of agency, new labor historians paralleled the simultaneous New Left turn toward community-based, rather than electoral, politics.[65] As the Port Huron Statement, the founding document of Students for a Democratic Society (SDS), noted, "politics has the function of bringing people out of isolation and into community." Several years earlier, Rev. Martin Luther King Jr. claimed that the country was witnessing the "creation of the beloved community" during the Montgomery bus boycott.[66]

As New Leftists worked to create truer and more vital forms of collectivity in their own time through localized organizing projects and the development of a new style of community-based politics, they simultaneously sought to recover much earlier working-class struggles of the sort that Gutman was so effective at unearthing.[67] The renegade sociologist C. Wright Mills's famous "Letter to the New Left" (1960) is often remembered today for its call to young progressives to reject the "labor metaphysic." But Mills also claimed that the working class must be studied "freshly" and with an emphasis on the "agency" of workers.[68] Many New Left historians found that freshness in the oppositional cultures of working-class communities. Here, after all, was a homegrown alternative to the inexorable advance of late capitalism, an alternative that put forth the values of mutualism and the public good that New Leftists so valued.[69]

By the 1980s, however, some within these circles believed that their colleagues had gone too far. Despite more than a decade's worth of efforts to politicize culture, critics increasingly condemned what they now called "culturalism," largely on the grounds that however one tried to interpret it, culture was not power. The critics also charged that the new emphasis on culture had become a distraction from the questions that mattered most in working-class history. They spoke of the "tyranny of culturalism" and a "creeping culturalism." The "cultural approach," some declared, "had floundered."[70]

For self-identified cultural historians, however, the fundamental problem with the "culturalism" of the new social and labor histories lay in its limits rather than its excesses. Even the so-called culturalist wings among the new labor and social historians, those who expanded the meaning of the political to include the cultural, tended to treat it in somewhat circumscribed and instrumentalist terms.[71] Many suggested, for example, that their investment in culture was delimited by their broader political vision. As Ira Berlin has written of Gutman's lack of interest in culture per se, "Outside the terrain of class struggle, such cultural baggage appeared merely as a collection of antiquarian curiosities; within that context, it was a powerful instrument of class warfare."[72] Similarly, another key mentor to the culturalist wing of new social and labor historians (albeit one with a very different approach), the pioneering British cultural studies scholar Stuart Hall, famously said that his interest in popular culture was primarily as a "place where socialism might be constituted. This is why 'popular culture' matters. Otherwise, to tell you the truth, I don't give a damn about it."[73]

In this way, new social and labor historians were momentarily at the forefront of the cultural turn but soon became critical targets during the late 1980s.[74] Good examples of this transition can be found in a pair of seminal essays first published in *International Labor and Working-Class History:* Joan Scott's "On Language, Gender, and Working-Class History" (1987) and Michael Denning's "The End of Mass Culture" (1990). Both of these essays pushed labor historians to bring the insights of cultural history and cultural studies more directly to bear on their scholarship. Scott suggested to labor historians that linguistic analysis provided a way to more fully and accurately incorporate gender as a central category of analysis, whereas Denning urged them to see mass culture not as alien to working-class life but as the very landscape in which modern politics and culture were necessarily bound.[75]

Key words within social and labor history similarly became theoretical points of departure for some of the most innovative work in cultural history: from Jackson Lears's 1985 meditation on "cultural hegemony" and Joan Scott's 1991 challenge to the "evidence of experience" to Daniel Rodgers's 1992 conceptual analysis of "republicanism" and Walter Johnson's 2003 reevaluation of "agency" as the master trope of slavery studies. Each of these essays took a generally discursive and critical approach, decrying the limitations and begged questions of previous methodological formulations.[76] A central target of Scott's critique, for example, was the new labor history's somewhat narrow conceptualizations of "difference," a category, she argued, that could benefit from more careful investigations of language, identity, and perception.[77] After some labor historians responded to these provocations by arguing that the real world of "experience" trumped theory, Scott began to question the category of experience itself, arguing that "it is not individuals who have experience but subjects who are constituted through experience. Experience in this definition . . . becomes not the origin of our explanation, not the authoritative (because seen or felt) evidence that grounds what is known, but rather that which we seek to explain."[78]

In retrospect, it is notable that so many of the seminal articles in late twentieth-century cultural history were published in journals of social and labor history. These were two of the primary fields that revived cultural analysis during the 1970s. But in the view of many scholars who subsequently migrated to cultural history, they were also fields that ultimately served to constrain it.

Proposition Eight: The unifying trope of a "cultural turn" needs to be understood not as the evolution of a single method but as a weaving together of innovations from a variety of disciplinary locations

We have already pointed to some of the innovations brought forth from various disciplinary locations, such as the "myth and symbol" school of American studies, or the "culturalist" wing of the new labor history. Here, we argue more broadly that most if not *all* of the traditional fields in U.S. history experienced their own particular "turns" to culture. And in virtually every case, the disciplinary locations mattered deeply for how the surrounding debates unfolded.

In U.S. intellectual history, for example, much of the discussion of the late 1970s involved a growing crisis of confidence around the question of how broadly to conceptualize the province of ideas.[79] As John Higham explained in the opening pages of *New Directions in American Intellectual History* (1979), "the quest for national definition" that had driven many of the leading intellectual histories of the postwar period proved "devastatingly" brief: "In a few years of the early and midsixties what was called 'consensus history' suddenly lost credibility. . . . Simultaneously, in sociology, anthropology, and history, two working assumptions that were closely related to the idea of national character came under withering attack: first, the assumption that societies tend to be integrated, and second, that a shared culture maintains that integration."[80]

The result, Higham concluded, was a growing bifurcation between the "levels of consciousness" studied by intellectual historians. Some continued to focus on the "clearly articulated beliefs" of philosophers and scientists, a body of thought "amenable to formal exegesis," whereas others now began to emphasize "the less refined level of consciousness the French have taught us to call collective mentalites." By 1979, these levels of consciousness were already associated with a more circumscribed sphere of intellectual activity (what David Hollinger referred to as "communities of discourse") as well as a new set of methodological tools. Anthropology's insights on the "meanings expressed in symbol, ritual, and language," Higham noted, were quickly outpacing "the heuristic insights of literary critics" and "psychologists in the Freudian tradition." Clifford Geertz, he quipped, was the volume's "patron saint."[81]

For other leading Americanists, however, this splitting of consciousness into distinctive social and epistemological domains proved less than fully satisfying. Richard Fox and Jackson Lears's widely influential 1983 collection on U.S. consumerism is a good case in point.[82] Whereas previous intellectual historians might have offered a synoptic lineage of theories of capitalist development (or divided this complex subject into formal policymaking and popular attitudes), Fox and Lears framed their anthology around the more capacious notion of a "culture of consumption." This conceptual shift from "intellect" to "culture" did not amount to a wholesale jettisoning of elite ideas. As Fox and Lears argued in the volume's introduction, "to discover how consumption became a cultural ideal, a hegemonic 'way of seeing,' requires looking at powerful individuals and institutions who conceived, formulated, and preached that ideal or way of seeing."[83] Still, their larger project tracked a surprisingly broad range of "individuals and institutions" involved in the hegemonizing. Henry James and John D. Rockefeller Jr. were part of the process. But so too were dozens of lesser-known advertising executives, bank presidents, Protestant ministers, newspaper reporters, poll makers, and policy wonks.

In women's history, by contrast, much of the debate during this period focused on the central categories of analysis. By the mid-1970s, many leading figures in the field had begun to shift their attention from "women" (previously understood as a demographic and historical group) to "gender," a more expansive category that now signified social and cultural rather than biological constructions of sexual difference. This shift also signaled a growing interest in "masculinity" on much the same terms: as a historically specific set of cultural norms and social relations as opposed to natural traits and immutable forms of "patriarchy."[84]

As in the other fields we've surveyed, these innovations were neither universally applauded nor wholly accepted. Some feminist scholars viewed the shift from women to gender as a problematic retreat from the more concrete work of explicating and fighting male oppression.[85] Others, especially feminists of color, argued that the broader category of gender continued to mask long-running normative assumptions of "women" as white, middle class, and often detached from the world of work.[86] Still others began to argue that the rapidly proliferating body of work on gender-as-cultural-construct could not be neatly separated from related categories such as race, class, and sexuality.[87] By the mid-1990s, in fact, the core insight that such categories were "mutually constituted" (in both ideology and social relations) had become an article of faith for most U.S. cultural historians.

On one level, then, it is helpful to think of the "cultural turn" in latitudinal terms: as a series of interrelated debates in adjoining fields, each with its own particular vectors and points of emphasis. But one can also track this process across the career trajectories of individual scholars. Consider, for example, Paul E. Johnson, a leading practitioner of the new social history whose work has become increasingly "cultural" over time. In *A Shopkeeper's Millennium: Society and Revivals in Rochester, New York, 1815–1837* (1978), Johnson approached his topic through a series of sophisticated quantitative analyses and a strong emphasis on class relations. The book's opening chapter, titled "Economy," had an organizational framework designed to suggest the determinative impact of material conditions in shaping the era's great battles over religious beliefs and moral values.[88]

To the extent that he drew explicitly on theory, Johnson utilized the statistical methods common to his cohort as well as a mostly sociological model of "social control" descended from Durkheim. And despite the fact that Johnson later described his project as a study of "Rochester's culture wars of the 1820s and 1830s," he did not actually *use* the word "culture" in *A Shopkeeper's Millennium*.[89] Topics that we might now define as squarely within the bailiwick of cultural history (such as drinking, the circus, and other forms of popular amusement) Johnson grouped together under the chapter heading "Society."

By contrast, Johnson's most recent book, *Sam Patch, the Famous Jumper* (2003), focuses on a single Rhode Island mill worker-cum-waterfall daredevil. At first glance, this book shares a number of obvious similarities with his earlier study. Beyond the common geographic locations (both books are set in small northeastern cities of the early nineteenth century), Johnson employs many of the same sources to examine the effects of industrialization on one of the nation's first proletarianized families. But *Sam Patch* is less the product of the author "listening" to the historically "inarticulate" (Patch, after all, did not leave much information about his life, and the only statement attributed to him is drawn from a newspaperman's paraphrase) than a rigorous series of "readings" of the meanings of Patch's public gestures in relation to contemporary debates about popular amusements, aesthetics, and celebrity. In stark contrast to the community-based approach of *Shopkeeper's Millennium*, in *Sam Patch* Johnson places his protagonist's individual daredevilry at the center, treating each death-defying leap as a kind of oppositional performance art through which we can glimpse the struggles of thousands of anonymous mill workers who left behind no written records.

This new emphasis on subaltern agency and consciousness was not unrelated to Johnson's earlier questions about "social control." Indeed, it is only in defiance of the "rational amusements" and "languages of progress" championed by bourgeois reformers that Patch's public gestures accrue their deeper social and ideological significance. More accurately, then, we might say that *Sam Patch* employs many of the conventional tools of late twentieth-century cultural history—thick description, discourse analysis, close readings of visual imagery, a more performative model of selfhood, the narrative structure of microhistory, and so forth— to expand what can be known about the day-to-day struggles of those caught in the vortex of nineteenth-century industrialization.[90] And in *this* sense, especially, the trajectory to *Sam Patch* was typical of its period. Like many of his colleagues trained in social, labor, African American, women's, intellectual, and religious history during the 1960s and 1970s, Johnson came to culture not out of disinterest with the questions in his earlier work but as an alternative way of framing and answering them.

Proposition Nine: As growing numbers of younger scholars embraced cultural history from the outset, the specific terms of debate began to shift once again

During the late 1980s and 1990s, that is to say, a new generation of historians came to culture not through some other rubric, such as social, labor, intellectual, or woman's history (many of whose innovations from the 1970s they now took for granted), but as a more explicit starting point. They also began to notice broader historiographical patterns largely unobserved by the earlier celebrants and critics of culture, including a certain sameness of conceptual emphasis. To some extent, these new critiques echoed earlier concerns about the proliferation of "community studies." But whereas previous commentators such as Eric Foner had feared an incoherent "patchwork" of "diverse values and identities among working people," with no "coherent overview of labor's historical development," many cultural historians of the late 1980s and 1990s perceived the problem as one of structural redundancy.[91] Again and again, the localized exploration of non-elite customs, habits, and traditions seemed to produce much the same forms of "community-building," "consciousness," and "agency."

New waves of cultural historians also began to question some of the core stylistic values of the earlier scholarship, especially its conventional hostility to narrative. For earlier generations of social and labor historians, in particular, narrative history had represented (in Eric Monkkonen's words) a denial of "complexity," a demand "for a return to simpler times and simpler tales, for a world no longer mired in . . . opacity."[92] By the mid-1980s, however, growing numbers of Americanists in a variety of fields were beginning to challenge the notion that effective storytelling and incisive analysis were mutually exclusive.[93] One of the earliest examples was Nick Salvatore's 1982 prize-winning biography of Eugene V. Debs, a work published by the University of Illinois Press in its influential Working-Class in American History series.[94] But the trend quickly expanded to include a wider range of historiographical experiments.

In some cases, these experiments involved the presentation of an odd or improbable episode—an eighteenth-century printer's joke about a riotous massacre of cats, for example; or the surprising tendency of antebellum blackface troupes to quote Shakespeare before working-class audiences—which, in turn, became the very problem that the cultural historian sought to unpack, contextualize, and explicate.[95] In other cases, however, it was precisely the plurality and variability of *competing* stories that generated the analytical sparks. Narrative, that is to say, now began to serve not merely as a delivery system for arguments and evidence but also (and more specifically) as a dedicated field of analysis for those increasingly sensitive to the complexities of language, rhetoric, perception, and memory.[96]

Over time, these manifold efforts to rethink the fundamental forms of historical writing enabled a much wider range of scholars—from ethnoculturalists to quantifiers, feminist historians of gender to Marxist historians of workers—to embrace the cultural turn as a forward position. In many cases, too, these migrations to culture were accompanied by new conceptualizations of power, especially among somewhat younger scholars, such as Robin Kelley, Tera Hunter, and Kimberly Phillips, all of whom published new studies during the 1990s that productively transcended the conventional boundaries separating African American, social, labor, and gender history. All three scholars, that is to say, remapped the conventional parameters of black "struggle" by following their subjects across a wide variety of social and institutional domains: from domestic work, tenant farming, religion, and public health to Harlem dance halls, interracial vice districts, and the more autonomous spaces of rural "jook joints."[97]

Building upon the theoretical insights of James C. Scott, moreover, these studies made it easier to appreciate the "hidden transcripts" and "infrapolitical" moments within black working-class life, moments that might not have passed muster as orthodox expressions of Thompsonian "class consciousness" a decade or two earlier, but that nevertheless shed crucial new light on the cultural expressions, thoughts, and aspirations of non-elite African Americans. As Kelley noted in a key passage from his 1994 study *Race Rebels*, the larger goal was to excavate a "dissident political culture" carried out both "off stage" (in the autonomous cultural spaces constructed by and for working-class blacks) as well as "on stage" (through countless "unorganized, clandestine, and evasive" acts that only suggested the "appearance of consent"). That the political valence and intent of such acts should remain partially "invisible" was, of course, entirely "by design."[98]

Broadly speaking, then, we might describe the 1990s as a period of ongoing experimentation and innovation. But this was also a period during which some of the older shared identifications became more tenuous and complex. An important case in point is the December 1992 forum on "popular culture and its audiences" that appeared in the pages of the *American Historical Review*. The location here was significant: not since Caroline Ware's pioneering work of the prewar period had a collective project in U.S. cultural history received such high-level support from the discipline's national organization. By the time of publication, moreover, all four of the *AHR* forum's participants—Lawrence Levine, Robin Kelley, Natalie Davis, and Jackson Lears—had become (or were quickly becoming) major figures in the field.[99]

What transpired in print, however, can hardly be described as a simple exercise in collective self-congratulation. In the forum's lead essay, Levine emphasized his ongoing struggles to convince skeptical colleagues that twentieth-century entertainment products (such as radio programs and Hollywood films) might be read as something more than evidence of the profit-making schemes and marketing formulas of corporate producers. In stark contrast to the earlier praise bestowed upon *Black Culture and Black Consciousness*, he noted, "I have learned unmistakably . . . that this time around there will be no easy acceptance, that popular culture is seen as the antithesis of folk culture: not as emanating from within the community but created—often artificially by people with pecuniary or ideological motives—for the community, or rather for the masses who no longer had an organic community capable of producing culture." In response, Levine emphasized the creativity and efficacy of consumer choices. "Modernity," he acknowledged, "dealt a blow to artisanship in culture. . . . But to say this is not to say that, as a result, people have been rendered passive, hopeless consumers. What people *can* do and *do* do is to refashion the objects created for them to fit their own values, needs, and expectations."[100]

This concept of refashioning was itself a subtle variation on the older theme of "culture-as-resource," now updated to include the localized consumption practices and meaning-making strategies of those who had little hand in the production of mass entertainments. Throughout the essay, Levine was explicit about the methodological connections to his earlier work on slave vernaculars, noting that "my intention is to explore the degree to which popular culture functions in ways similar to folk culture and acts as a form of folklore for people living in urban industrial societies."[101]

For the two younger scholars on the forum, however, this leap across the threshold of mass production was riddled with potential problems. Kelley, for instance, questioned the wisdom of projecting "folk" concepts into new commercial contexts, arguing that this move often equates degrees of "marginalization" and "distance from commercial influence" with some putative notion of "authenticity."[102] Kelley also questioned Levine's broader assumption that the work of "refashioning" typically leads in progressive directions:

Although I agree with his point that people actively make meaning out of popular culture (which also means revising and jettisoning narratives or representations that are unacceptable), his discussion sometimes seems too celebratory. By focusing on the audience versus producer dichotomy rather than race, gender, and class hierarchies *within* popular culture audiences, and by placing too much emphasis on the autonomy of "the folk," Levine misses an opportunity to illustrate how popular culture can simultaneously subvert and reproduce hegemony.[103]

Lears, by contrast, took issue with Levine's larger approach to the issue of "consumer choice." The fundamental problem, in Lears's view, was not that twentieth-century audiences were simply duped or manipulated by corporate producers, but that the rhetoric of choice-as-agency was itself a recapitulation of one of the fundamental tenets of neoclassical economics: the notion that "sovereign consumers" maximize "their gratification through freedom of choice" and meet "their needs rationally in the cultural marketplace."[104] The choices at stake, Lears argued further, were far from equal and could only be assessed critically by including more structural questions about who controls the flow of goods to the point of purchase: "What difference did it make, for example, that some groups or classes had the capital to mass produce and mass market cultural forms, while other groups had to make the best of what they bought— reinterpreting, rejecting, reinventing texts creatively and even subversively sometimes, but still basically stuck with what they were sold?"[105]

For those of us who read and learned from these exchanges, a number of larger conclusions began to take shape. One was that the initial work of field building had now given way to difficult but nonetheless crucial differences of opinion—differences that were in many ways inevitable given our multiple modes of training and diverse trajectories into the field. Like many leading culturalists of his generational cohort, Levine came to the question of vernacular expression via cultural anthropology, which meant that he also tended to ground localized acts of meaning-making squarely within the fabric of experience.[106] Popular artifacts, in this view, were "good to think with."[107] And for Levine, writing good history meant never assuming that one's subjects were incapable of recognizing the same "hegemonizing" forces subsequently identified by professional intellectuals.[108]

By 1992, however, this ground-level mode of historicizing was merely one of many powerful ways of conceptualizing popular/mass culture. For Lears, who had spent much of his career explicating capitalism's manifold impacts on rhetoric and ideology, the functionalist theories of postwar social scientists were themselves deeply suspect because they tended to reproduce the "therapeutic" rationales so essential to modern consumerism—each rational "choice" leading to satisfied needs and meaningful outcomes. To question the assumptions at work in this model, he insisted, was not to ignore the creativity of ordinary consumers. Rather, it was the crucial first step toward imagining a better and more capacious set of choices, as well as a model of analysis in which the self-justifications and "agenda-setting powers" of corporate capital were more plainly visible.

Kelley, too, was deeply interested in such questions, but from the somewhat different angle of cultural studies. One consequence of this distinction was Kelley's more explicit focus on key words, categories, and questions of identity. "A cultural studies approach," he explained, "would insist that terms like 'folk,' 'authentic,' and 'traditional' are socially constructed categories that have something to do with the reproduction of race, class, and gender hierarchies and the policing of the boundaries of modernism."[109] Kelley also called for more careful attention to the expanding distribution fostered by the rise of mass media, a process that enabled modern consumers to "experience a common heritage with people they have never seen" and "acquire memories of a past to which they have no geographic or biological connection."[110]

Looking back on these debates, it is easier to see them as one of the major watersheds in the cultural turn: a pivotal moment in which leading practitioners began to argue with each other over competing visions of the field, as opposed to defending themselves from skeptical colleagues in other specialties. But of course that's what happens to fields as they diversify and prosper. Latent tensions in the foundational concepts become more pronounced. And the concepts themselves quickly proliferate. Which is why cultural history remained such an exciting place to be during the 1990s, even as the field began to look more and more like the disciplinary center.

Proposition Ten: Over the past three decades, many U.S. cultural historians have developed new understandings of politics as central components of their methodological projects

Starting in the 1980s, cultural historians often reacted against what they saw as the narrow approach of traditional political history in terms of sources, topics and methodology. A good number of them also criticized what they viewed as the too-easy linkage between politics and history made by some of the new social and labor historians, in which history from the bottom up was frequently understood as the moral equivalent of New Left politics. These politics, as Roy Rosenzweig explained in a recent interview about the motivations of his graduate school cohort, "shaped their work in history. They were looking for connections between politics and history and looking for ways to 'use' the past. They saw direct connections between doing 'history from the bottom up' or 'social history' and the politics of the 1960s." Rosenzweig agreed with his interlocutor, however, that his later works (on the history of Central Park, on historical memory, and in public history, among other topics) "resist easy classification."[111]

The same was true for many cultural historians who came of age during the mid-1980s and beyond, for whom the relation between politics and historical practice was perhaps less direct or obvious than it was for many of their predecessors. Brought up in an age of political cynicism, when the traditional Left vision of social democracy no longer seemed entirely viable, and schooled in the works of Michel Foucault, some of these scholars increasingly problematized the very meanings and functions of intellectual engagements with politics. In good postmodern fashion, they also learned to display "incredulity to metanarratives," questioning the straightforwardly deterministic assumptions crafted by older generations of social, political, and labor historians.[112] The widely cited work of the "new historicist" literary scholar Walter Benn Michaels, for example, warned against pigeonholing complex works of fiction as "for" or "against" capitalism and aimed instead to show the ways in which transformations in the economy affected the narratives styles of seemingly radical authors, such as Theodore Dreiser and Frank Norris. Leo Marx, a founding figure of American studies, praised Michaels' "subtle" approach and highlighted its "unschematic conception of the convergence of literature and power."[113]

A similar shift was evident in *The New American Studies*, an influential collection of essays reprinted from one of the leading journals of the cultural turn, *Representations*. Phillip Fisher, the editor of the collection, pointed to the authors' shared interest in "rhetorics" as opposed to "myth" (the earlier focal point of American studies), as well as their tendency to cast this concept in the plural (as opposed to the more singular and monolithic understandings of "American culture" from the postwar decades). Studying rhetorics, according to Fisher, involved the close analysis of "words, formulas, images, and ideological units of meaning within politics." He also highlighted a new focus on contestation and paradox, which in turn "reveals interests and exclusions." Fisher labeled this approach the "politics of culture."[114]

Although they sought to complicate the relationship between history and politics, those who took the cultural turn during the late 1980s and 1990s did not deny that there was a crucial connection between the two. Indeed, most new cultural historians also drew from the view, promulgated by new social and labor historians, that culture was, to use a favored metaphor, "contested terrain," but now reconfigured in terms of what James Scott has called "infrapolitics," a domain of quotidian struggle practiced largely outside of the realm of elections and elite policymakers. One index of the ongoing importance of these questions is the growing popularity of "cultural politics," a phrase rarely used before the late 1980s but which has since appeared in dozens of book titles.[115] A book series of that name was initiated by the University of Minnesota Press in 1990, and *Cultural Politics: An International Journal* was begun in 2005. Cultural politics was also one of the central concepts (often paired with "aesthetic ideologies") at the heart of Michael Denning's influential 1998 book, *The Cultural Front*, which sought to expand our conception of art's relation to politics in the twentieth century. Demonstrating that working-class cultural production (disseminated by diverse ethnic and racial groups) was central to New Deal politics, Denning viewed politics and culture as overlapping categories, since the positions taken by cultural workers on social issues and the aesthetic forms they developed had important political meanings.[116]

Somewhat paradoxically, many of those who use cultural politics as a standard catchphrase treat politics implicitly. For example, *Keywords for American Cultural Studies* (a reference work published in 2007) contains no dedicated discussion of politics as a category of analysis, although politics is implicit in almost all of the sixty-four entries, such as those on citizenship, corporations, and capitalism.[117] By contrast, the second edition of *The Cultural Studies Reader,* published in 1999, added a section on politics, which was not part of first edition, published in 1993. This section included two articles on the relationship between culture and public policy, a topic discussed in several of the essays in this book as well. In his introduction to the 1999 edition, Simon During noted a growing "acceptance of the state hitherto unknown in cultural studies."[118]

Significantly, many of the cultural historians who have fueled these developments have combined two approaches previously seen as antagonistic. On the one hand, they have adopted the concern with paradox, ambiguity, and irony that characterized the worldview of mid-twentieth-century "consensus historians." These scholars, as we have seen, countered the conflict-ridden worldview of the early twentieth-century "progressive historians," emphasizing unity through social science categories such as "national character," or *the* American mind. In this sense, they used culture to explain politics; indeed, one could say that Richard Hofstadter, Bernard Bailyn, John William Ward, and Daniel Boorstin invented the idea of "political culture."[119]

On the other hand, more recent practitioners of the cultural turn have espoused an increasingly conflictual and multifaceted conception of politics, emphasizing power differentials operating along the axes of class, race, ethnicity, gender, and sexuality. For most of these scholars, political history is comprised not merely of grassroots practices and phenomena—as it was for many of the new social and labor historians. Nor do they understand political consciousness as singular or unitary—as it was for many of the earlier consensus historians.[120] Rather, in current practice, identity itself has become a central object of political struggle.

Recent scholars have also stressed conflict at the epistemological level by highlighting the construction of normative categories as a fundamentally political process. Saul Cornell, for example, has emphasized that denaturalization, dehierarchalization, and demystification are among the central tasks of today's politically conscious historian.[121] In this sense, many of those practicing cultural history today have been far more circumspect about making broad and confident claims about the political efficacy of their work. Yet the larger shift has not been without its rewards and insights. On the most basic level, recent cultural historians have dramatically expanded the definition of what counts as "political." In the process, they have also created new forms of cross-talk and symbiosis between cultural and political history. For many of us, the older certainties of the new social, political, and labor histories have given way to a pair of open questions: "what is *cultural* about politics and what is *political* about culture."[122]

Proposition Eleven: As long as there has been a cultural turn, the adjacent fields of European and U.S. cultural history have alternatively merged and diverged in significant ways

The first half of this proposition becomes easier to grasp as soon as we acknowledge some of the shared concerns running through many of the fields' landmark texts. One can point, for example, to the roughly contemporaneous interests in subaltern thought, ritual, and agency that informed both Natalie Zemon Davis's *Society and Culture in Modern France* (1975) and Lawrence Levine's *Black Culture and Black Consciousness* (1977). Or the parallel efforts to unpack dominant categories of collective identity in Joan Scott's *Gender and the Politics of History* (1989) and

David Roediger's *Wages of Whiteness* (1991). Or the shared sensitivity to shifting modes of urban perception that guided Judith Walkowitz's *City of Dreadful Delight* (1992) and John Kasson's *Rudeness and Civility* (1990). Or the new emphasis on transnational circulation that began to crystallize in Paul Gilroy's *The Black Atlantic* (1993) and George Lipsitz's *Dangerous Crossroads* (1994). Or the cross-cutting debates around historical memory running through John Gillis's *Commemorations* (1995) and Edward Linenthal and Tom Engelhardt's *History Wars* (1996).

In many cases, moreover, the theoretical discussions driving these projects have dovetailed in recognizable ways. A prominent example is Clifford Geertz's work in symbolic anthropology, which appeared in the footnotes of dozens of important cultural histories during the 1980s: from William Sewell's *Work and Revolution in France* (1980), Robert Darnton's *The Great Cat Massacre* (1984), and Lynn Hunt's *Politics, Culture, and Class in the French Revolution* (1984) to Rhys Isaac's *The Transformation of Virginia* (1982), Roy Rosenzweig's *Eight Hours for What We Will* (1983), and Susan Davis's *Parades and Power* (1986).[123] But Geertz was hardly exceptional in this regard. In fact, one could easily construct similar genealogies vis-à-vis Antonio Gramsci on hegemony, Theodor Adorno on the culture industry, Mikhail Bakhtin on carnival, Michel Foucault on discourse, Walter Benjamin on the flaneur, Edward Said on Orientalism, and Pierre Nora on sites of memory—all key concepts that have regularly migrated back and forth across fields.[124]

This migration does not mean, however, that the fields have simply mirrored one another. On the European side, for example, one can point to an earlier set of engagements with the psychological and cultural dimensions of colonialism, a pattern deriving (at least in part) from the pathbreaking work of postcolonial scholars such as Frantz Fanon, Léopold Senghor, Aimé Césaire, C. L. R. James, and Stuart Hall.[125] On the U.S. side, by contrast, one can trace a wider spectrum of research around the problem of consumerism, an issue that goes back at least as far as the early 1980s (to the work of Warren Susman, Jackson Lears, Roland Marchand, and Daniel Horowitz), and which more recently has generated rich new studies on topics ranging from the "free produce" campaigns of antebellum abolitionists to the New Deal politics of the "citizen consumer."[126]

When we turn from clusters of work to institutional histories (or more precisely, to their interrelation), the contrasts become sharper and more complex. Consider, for example, the central cases of American studies and British cultural studies. By the early 1950s, American studies had become a full-blown "movement," with its own national journal (*Ameri-*

can Quarterly), professional organization (the American Studies Association), and degree programs across a number of leading universities and colleges (such as Harvard, Yale, Penn, Minnesota, and Amherst). British cultural studies, by contrast, first emerged in a poorly funded postgraduate research center (the Centre for Contemporary Cultural Studies, founded in 1964 at the University of Birmingham) and a "house journal" (*Working Papers in Cultural Studies*) that was quite explicit about the "incomplete" and "tentative" character of the larger enterprise.[127]

These institutional contrasts likewise corresponded to basic differences in political outlooks and modes of questioning. Especially early on, American studies gathered momentum in an ideological climate of American exceptionalism, while British cultural studies emerged from a series of debates among prominent New Left intellectuals over the future of Marxist cultural theory. And whereas American studies defined itself as an effort to work across the disciplinary boundaries separating literature and history, British cultural studies sought a "materialist" mode of cultural analysis that might better account for "the dialectic between agency and conditions."[128] Not surprisingly, this last goal pushed in a very different direction than the earlier American studies problematics. Indeed, if American studies conceived its foundational project as the excavation of distinctively national forms of mind, character, and culture, early British cultural studies emphasized "cultures, not Culture," and more precisely, the "necessary struggle, tension and conflict between cultures . . . the struggles betweens 'ways of life' rather than the evolution of 'a way of life.'"[129]

Once again, however, it seems important not to overstate the analytical divide separating these two projects. Frequently forgotten today is the fact that the exceptionalist impulses running through much of postwar American studies often coexisted with a more critical emphasis on the *power* of representations to shape collective perception—myth, in short, as something closer to a dominant ideology than a straightforward celebration of cultural taproots.[130] And in this respect, at least, works in American studies such as Smith's *Virgin Land* or Marx's *Machine in the Garden* can still seem surprisingly prescient, pointing ahead to much later British cultural studies interrogations of the popular cultural "ground" upon which collective "common sense" is forged. On the British side, to be sure, this "radically new" way of theorizing the popular grew out of a particular intellectual conjuncture: namely, Gramsci's writings on the concept of hegemony, which exerted a powerful influence on early works in British cultural studies such as *Resistance through Rituals* (1976),

Policing the Crisis (1978), and *The Empire Strikes Back* (1982).[131] Even here, though, it would be a mistake the draw the contrast too sharply. By the mid-1980s, few continental theorists were more widely invoked by U.S. cultural historians than Gramsci. And in many cases, those pushing the debates forward were either trained or teaching in American studies departments.[132]

Our final area of comparison involves a recent trio of historiographical studies on the European side: Victoria E. Bonnell and Lynn Hunt, eds., *Beyond the Cultural Turn* (1999); William Sewell, *Logics of History* (2005); and Geoff Eley, *A Crooked Line* (2005). In each case, these works proceed autobiographically: from the exciting intellectual and political possibilities of the "new social history"; to a growing sense that social history's emphasis on quantitative categories and material conditions had become inadequate for explaining the deeper subtleties of human perception and localized meaning-making; and finally, to the rise of a "new cultural history" designed to address some of the blinds spots. Not surprisingly, each book offers a slightly different mix of antecedents and historiographical motors. Sewell, for example, emphasizes cultural anthropology and the French Annalistes as the key influences driving his own transition from social to cultural history, whereas Eley emphasizes Foucault's work on discourse, the impact of British cultural studies, and the deconstructed identity categories developed by Joan Scott.

What really stands out in these narratives, however, are the multiple points of convergence. All three studies pivot their narratives on a crisis of confidence among New Left historians and hail the cultural turn as a useful corrective to the rigid "determinisms" and "totalizing logics" of 1970s social science. All three studies, furthermore, cite Hunt's 1989 edited volume, *The New Cultural History*, as the critical juncture at which an eclectic jumble of interpretive modes began to crystallize into a more clearly recognizable historical field. Finally, all three studies register a growing ambivalence vis-à-vis the cultural turn—at least in its narrower, deconstructive forms of the late 1980s and 1990s. Indeed, much of the point of these studies is to insist that the now conventional tools of cultural history—thick description, linguistic analysis, the interrogation of identity categories, and so forth—need to be reconnected to socioeconomic structures and the lived realities of class.

In our view, these recent efforts to move beyond the antinomies of social and cultural history represent a welcome intervention. Yet we would also insist that there are crucial differences between the European and U.S. trajectories—differences that matter deeply for how one conceptualizes the broader turn to culture. Consider, for example, the respective positions of class and race within each field. Sewell and Eley, in particular, present class as the central category of analysis. Both single out the British neo-Marxist historiography of Eric Hobsbawm, E. P. Thompson, and Christopher Hill as foundational. Both draw intellectual lineages from the political revolts of 1968 to the renewed interest in "history from below" during the 1970s. And both trace the origins of a "new cultural history" to the pivotal moment when many social historians began to doubt the deterministic power of social structures and material conditions.

On the U.S. side, by contrast, it is simply impossible to tell this story apart from race. Here again, Levine's *Black Culture and Black Consciousness* is instructive. Initiated during the mid-1960s, while Levine himself was actively involved in the civil rights movement, *Black Culture and Black Consciousness* wrestles with many of the same problematics highlighted by Sewell and Eley. It is a "history from below" that explicitly sought out new ways of conceptualizing subaltern thought, experience, and agency. But it did so from a very different set of personal and intellectual vantage points. As Walter Johnson has recently argued, the strong rhetorical emphasis on self-determination in Levine's work had obvious affinities with the era's civil rights politics.[133] And the "determinisms" against which Levine framed his argument generally came in the form of psychoanalytic theories of victimization (e.g., Stanley Elkins's somewhat earlier claim that the antebellum plantation had constituted a "total institution").[134]

Much the same kind of argument can be made about the work on identity categories that began to emerge during the mid-1980s. On the European side, one of the earliest interventions was Gareth Stedman Jones's *Languages of Class* (1983), an important but controversial book that Eley describes as an "early stalking horse for . . . the linguistic turn."[135] Although Jones's work was widely discussed and cited by Americanists, it would be difficult to argue for an obviously parallel case—in part, because the debates around class never quite achieved the same depth and centrality in U.S. historiography.[136] If we shift the focus to race, however, the patterns look very different. Only three years after the publication of *Languages of Class*, Michael Omi and Howard Winant's *Racial Formation in the United States* (1986) performed a similar kind of maneuver by describing race (a category that had long been understood as self-evidently tied to skin color and other forms of physiology) as an ideological construct traceable across shifting patterns of discourse. And over the next decade, this new way of thinking about race quickly became a sign of the times, extending from Alexander Saxton's *Rise and Fall of the White Republic* (1990), Thomas Almagauer's *Racial Fault Lines* (1994), and Kathleen Brown's *Good Wives, Nasty Wenches, and Anxious Patriarchs* (1996) to Neil Foley's *The White Scourge* (1997), Philip Deloria's *Playing Indian* (1997), and Robert Lee's *Orientals* (1999).

At this point, we suspect, some readers may want to insist on a pair of qualifications: first, that much of the work has argued for race and class (as well as gender and sexuality) as interwoven categories of analysis; and second, that this pattern was partially anticipated and informed by a number of seminal works in British cultural studies, such as Stuart Hall's "Race, Articulation and Societies Structured in Dominance" (1980) and Paul Gilroy's *There Ain't No Black in the Union Jack* (1987). We readily agree on both counts. But we also suggest that these wrinkles are entirely consistent with our central argument: namely, that the U.S. and European trajectories have regularly merged and diverged. Which also means that any history of cultural history that limits itself to a single geographic field runs the risk of missing a lot.

Proposition Twelve: As cultural history has moved to the center
of the discipline, the question of what is and what is not
cultural history has become increasingly complex

Consider, for example, Walter Johnson's history of the antebellum slave market, *Soul by Soul* (1999). In terms of the book's narrative arc (the transposition of human beings into chattel) and collection of sources (such as probate inventories, tax records, and notarized acts of sale), there is little that can be described as strictly or obviously cultural. The slaves in Johnson's story do not spin tales, tell jokes, or sing more than a few short verses. The only institution that receives much focused attention is the slave market itself.

Yet in many other respects *Soul by Soul* exemplifies one of the major developments in recent historiography: the proliferation of cultural interpretations of topics previously understood as squarely within the province of other historical fields. Johnson's sophisticated treatment of the buying and selling of slaves is a good case in point. For much of the late twentieth century, historians of the antebellum South might have analyzed such practices exclusively through quantitative or statistical measures, or by some criterion of economic necessity. Historiographical debate might have turned on the bottom-line question of slavery's profitability, which, in turn, might have been used to construct a much larger argument for or against the inevitability of the Civil War.

In Johnson's hands, by contrast, these market-driven questions about the profitability of slaves ultimately reveal more subtle cultural motives, rationales, and payoffs. In recording their financial transactions in human property, slaveholders simultaneously "make themselves" and their "social worlds." In writing to relatives about "making a start" in the slave market, they "translate" the "productive and reproductive labor" of their slaves into "images of their own upward progress." And in computing the "necessity" of individual purchases, they do more than simply respond to structural and economic pressures. More accurately, Johnson argues, slaveholders "objectified their desires into necessities," thereby "giving cultural meaning to the economy in people upon which their lives (or at least their livelihoods) depended."[137]

Over the past few years, this impulse for mixing subjects, sources, and modes of questioning has made it increasingly difficult to draw sharp boundaries around cultural history. One thinks, for example, of Mary Renda's recent study of the U.S. military occupation in Haiti, or John Stauffer's chronicle of interracial abolitionism, or Scott Sandage's work on failed nineteenth-century businessmen, or Sarah Igo's treatment of modern survey research—all innovative histories that have applied the tools of cultural analysis to an increasingly broad swath of the American past.[138] Paradoxically, this pattern of expansion has led some commentators to suggest the field's impending obsolescence. If "we are all culturalists now" (as one recent formulation has it), why bother with a dedicated field called cultural history? If the field's "heuristic work" is now largely complete, perhaps the "family of inquiries" known as cultural history will simply ripple across the disciplinary pond and fade away.[139]

In our view, there are a number of problems with this line of speculation. One is that the recent migrations of cultural methods have never signaled universal acceptance. Even today, more than a few of our colleagues continue to view culture as the proper concern of some *other* discipline—be it literature, anthropology, American studies, art history, gender studies, or cultural studies. Another basic problem is the implicit assumption of a finite collection of cultural approaches, when in fact the larger process of cross-pollination always cuts in multiple directions. Much of the best recent work, that is to say, has provoked new modes of questioning in other fields even as it has forced a reconsideration of what, exactly, counts *as* cultural history among self-identified practitioners.

This pattern is not entirely new. During the mid-1970s, for example, when Carroll Smith-Rosenberg turned her attention to the "mythic constructs" and "experiential components" of Victorian gender relations, she also remapped the conventional thresholds separating women's, social, religious, and urban history. Likewise, during the late 1980s and early 1990s, when Alexander Saxton and David Roediger began to explicate the racialized languages of "wage slavery" favored by antebellum artisans, they simultaneously challenged prevailing certainties about what an innovative history of the market revolution might entail. What U.S. historians have defined as cultural, in other words, has always been in flux to one degree or another. So if there seems to be ongoing confusion today about the field's conventional thresholds, that confusion probably has more to do with the volume of studies than the basic impulse for methodological stretching.

Finally, we question the somewhat counterintuitive calculus that equates broad disciplinary impact with fragmentation and decline. From our own vantage points, the sheer numbers of books, articles, dissertations, and graduate applications in cultural history show few signs of flagging. But they raise a critical issue: what will the next waves look like as the field's normative boundaries and epistemological centers continue to move? It is to these complex—and still open—questions about the future of U.S. cultural history that the remaining sections of this volume are addressed.

NOTES

For their critical feedback on this essay, the authors thank Michael O'Malley, Daniel Rodgers, Ann Fabian, Gina Morantz-Sanchez, and Nan Enstad.

1.   Important exceptions include David Brion Davis, "Some Recent Directions in American Cultural History," *American Historical Review* 73 (February 1968), 696–707; Lawrence W. Levine, "The Historian and the Culture Gap," in *The Historian's Workshop*, ed. L. P. Curtis Jr. (New York: Knopf, 1970); and Levine, "The Unpredictable Past," *American Historical Review* 94 (June 1989); Jackson Lears and Richard Fox, introduction to *The Power of Culture* (Chicago: University of Chicago Press, 1993); Michael Denning, "The Socioanalysis of Culture: Rethinking the Cultural Turn," in *Culture in the Age of Three Worlds*, by M. Denning (London: Verso, 2004); Jean-Christophe Agnew, "Lawrence Levine and the Opening of American History," *Journal of American History* 93 (December 2006); and Daniel Wickberg, "What Is the History of Sensibilities? On Cultural Histories, Old and New," *American Historical Review* 112, no. 3 (June 2007): 661–84. The best assessments of the "cultural turn" by Europeanists include the following work: Roger Chartier, *Cultural History* (Ithaca, NY: Cornell University Press, 1988); Peter Novick, *That Noble Dream* (New York: Cambridge University Press, 1988),

pt. 4; Lynn Hunt, ed., *The New Cultural History* (Berkeley: University of California Press, 1989); Robert Darnton, *The Kiss of Lamourette* (New York: Norton, 1990); Peter Burke, *Varieties of Cultural History* (Cambridge, MA: Polity Press, 1997); and Burke, *What Is Cultural History?* (Cambridge, MA: Polity Press, 2004); William H. Sewell Jr., *Logics of History* (Chicago: University of Chicago Press, 2005); and Geoff Eley, *A Crooked Line* (Ann Arbor: University of Michigan Press, 2005).

2.   Topic-specific discussions of methodology have generally appeared in review essays, edited collections, and journal forums. Important review essays include Jackson Lears, "The Concept of Cultural Hegemony: Problems and Possibilities," *American Historical Review* 90 (June 1985): 567–93; Thomas Bender, "Wholes and Parts: The Need for Synthesis in American History," *Journal of American History* 73 (June 1986): 120–36; Michael Kammen, *American Culture, American Tastes* (New York: Knopf, 1999), 3–26. Prominent edited collections include Daniel Walker Howe, ed., *Victorian America* (Philadelphia: University of Pennsylvania Press, 1976); Richard W. Fox and Jackson Lears, eds., *The Culture of Consumption* (New York: Pantheon, 1983); Michael Frisch and Daniel Walkowitz, eds., *Working-Class America* (Urbana: University of Illinois Press, 1983); Lary May, ed., *Recasting America: Culture and Politics in the Age of Cold War* (Chicago: University of Chicago Press, 1989); Richard Butsch, ed., *For Fun and Profit* (Philadelphia: Temple University Press, 1990); William R. Taylor, ed., *Inventing Times Square* (Baltimore: Johns Hopkins University Press, 1991); James Gilbert, Amy Gilman, Donald Scott, and Joan Scott, eds., *The Mythmaking Frame of Mind* (Belmont, CA: Wadsworth, 1993); Amy Kaplan and Donald Pease, eds., *Cultures of United States Imperialism* (Durham, NC: Duke University Press, 1993); Francis Couvares, ed., *Movie Censorship and American Culture* (Washington, DC: Smithsonian Institution Press, 1996); Karen Halttunen and Lewis Perry, eds., *Moral Problems in American Life* (Ithaca, NY: Cornell University Press, 1998); Susan Strasser, Charles McGovern, and Matthias Judt, eds., *Getting and Spending* (New York: Cambridge University Press, 1998); Reinhold Wagnleitner and Elaine Tyler May, eds., *"Here, There, and Everywhere": The Foreign Politics of American Popular Culture* (Hanover, NH: University Press of New England, 2000); Burton Bledstein and Robert D. Johnston, eds., *The Middling Sorts* (New York: Routledge, 2001). Major journal debates include those in the *Journal of American History* 74 (June 1987), with essays by David Thelen, Nell Irvin Painter, Richard Wightman Fox, Roy Rosenzweig, and Thomas Bender on the problems of synthesis; *Journal of American History* 75 (June 1988), with essays by Leon Fink, John Patrick Diggins, Jackson Lears, George Lipsitz, and Mary Jo and Paul Buhle on the issue of hegemony; *International Labor and Working-Class History* 38 (Spring 1990), with essays by Michael Denning, Janice Radway, Luisa Passerini, William R. Taylor, and Adelheid von Saldern on theories of mass culture; *American Historical Review* (December 1992), with essays by Lawrence Levine, Robin Kelley, Natalie Davis, and Jackson Lears on the question of how to use popular culture as historical evidence.

3.   Victoria Bonnell and Lynn Hunt, eds., *Beyond the Cultural Turn* (Berkeley: University of California Press, 1999).

4.   The classic statement on this issue comes from Raymond Williams, who described "culture as one of the two or three most complicated words in the English language." Williams, *Keywords* (New York: Oxford University Press, 1983). See also Williams, *Culture and Society* (New York: Columbia University Press, 1958); Larry Brownstein, "A Reappraisal of the Concept of 'Culture,'" *Social Epistemology* 9,

no. 4 (1995): 311–51; George Steinmetz, *State/Culture: State Formation after the Cultural Turn* (Ithaca, NY: Cornell University Press, 1999), 4–8; and William H. Sewell Jr., "The Concept(s) of Culture," in Bonnell and Hunt, *Beyond the Cultural Turn,* 35–61. Two of the best and earliest discussions of culture concepts on the U.S. side can be found in Warren Susman, *Culture as History* (New York: Pantheon, 1984); and Lawrence W. Levine, *Highbrow/Lowbrow: The Emergence of Cultural Hierarchy in America* (Cambridge: Harvard University Press, 1988).

5.   Most scholars associate the origins of this phrase with Lynn Hunt's edited collection of the same name, first published in 1989.

6.   See Hunt, *New Cultural History;* Joyce Appleby, Lynn Hunt, and Margaret Jacob, *Telling the Truth about History* (New York: Norton, 1994); Sewell, *Logics of History;* and Eley, *Crooked Line.* For an early survey of the influence of symbolic anthropology, see Ronald Walters, "Signs of the Times: Clifford Geertz and Historians," *Social Research* 47 (Autumn 1980): 537–56.

7.   Henry Nash Smith, *Virgin Land: The American West as Symbol and Myth* (Cambridge: Harvard University Press, 1950); John William Ward, *Andrew Jackson: Symbol for an Age* (New York: Oxford University Press, 1955); R. W. B. Lewis, *The American Adam* (Chicago: University of Chicago Press, 1959); Charles L. Sanford, *The Quest for Paradise* (Urbana: University of Illinois Press, 1961); William R. Taylor, *Cavalier and Yankee* (New York: W. H. Allen, 1963); Leo Marx, *The Machine in the Garden* (New York: Oxford University Press, 1964); Alan Trachtenberg, *Brooklyn Bridge* (Chicago: University of Chicago Press, 1965); and Winthrop Jordan, *White over Black* (Chapel Hill: University of North Carolina Press, 1968). Clifford Geertz develops the concept of "thick description" in *The Interpretation of Culture* (New York: Basic Books, 1973), 3–30. Michel Foucault's notion of "discourse" can be traced through a number of major works. See, especially, Foucault, *The Order of Things* (New York: Vintage, 1973); *Language, Counter-Memory, Practice* (Ithaca, NY: Cornell University Press, 1977); *Discipline and Punish* (New York: Vintage, 1979); and *Power/Knowledge* (New York: Pantheon, 1980).

8.   We refer here to the U.S. field. On the European side, the historical analysis of culture goes back at least as far as Jacob Burckhardt's *Civilization of the Renaissance in Italy* (1867). For a helpful overview of European developments from the eighteenth through the twentieth centuries, see Donald Kelley, "The Old Cultural History," *History of the Human Sciences* 9 (1996): 101–26.

9.   Harry Elmer Barnes, "The New American History," *New Republic,* July 26, 1922, 259–60.

10.   For an excellent overview of the interwar fascination with culture, see John S. Gilkeson Jr., "The Domestication of 'Culture' in Interwar America, 1919–1941," in *The Estate of Social Knowledge,* ed. JoAnne Brown and David K. van Keuren (Baltimore: Johns Hopkins University Press, 1991), 153–74; the quotation from Robert Lynd is at 153. Boas's most prominent students included Margaret Mead and Ruth Benedict, whose 1934 work, *Patterns of Culture,* provided the most systematic explanation of Boas's holistic, nonracialized model.

11.   Robert F. Berkhofer, "Clio and the Culture Concept in Historiography," in *The Idea of Culture in the Social Sciences,* ed. Louis Schneider and Charles M. Bonjean (Cambridge: Cambridge University Press, 1973), 82. Warren Susman has similarly argued that this "special sense" of culture was one of the era's distinguishing intellectual features: "In sketching this structure [of the 1930s], no fact is more significant than the general and even popular discovery of the concept of culture.

Obviously, the idea of culture was anything but new in the 1930s, but there is a special sense in which the idea became widespread in the period. What had been discovered was 'the inescapable interrelatedness of . . . things so that culture could no longer be considered what Matthew Arnold and the intellectuals of previous generations had often meant—the knowledge of the highest achievements of men and art through history" (Susman, *Culture as History*, 153).

12. Our focus here is on early culturalists working specifically within the field of U.S. history. But it's important to note that Ware was not alone during the 1930s. Indeed, one could easily construct a parallel story in the emerging field of American studies featuring Constance Rourke and F. O. Matthiessen, both of whom published foundational works on early American culture around the very same moment as Ware's 1940 essay collection. On Rourke's contributions, see Joan Shelley Rubin, *Constance Rourke and American Culture* (Chapel Hill: University of North Carolina Press, 1980).

13. Caroline F. Ware, ed., *The Cultural Approach to History* (New York: Columbia University Press, 1940). Ware used the phrase "bottom up" on pp. 73 and 273; another contributor to the volume, Constance McLaughlin Green, also used it on p. 275. For discussion of the volume's reception, see Gilkeson, "Domestication of 'Culture.'"

14. William L. Kolb, review of *The Cultural Approach to History* by Caroline Ware, *American Sociological Review* 7 (February 1942): 122–25, quotation at 123. We do not mean to suggest that the reception of Ware's *Cultural Approach to History* was uniformly positive. For a more hostile response, see the May 1941 issue of the *Historical Bulletin*.

15. Ware, *Cultural Approach to History*, 8.

16. Ibid, 9–10.

17. Thomas Cochran, "Forty Years of the Cultural Approach to History," presidential address to the Business History Association, 1980; http://www.hnet.org/~business/bhcweb/publications/BEHprint/v009/p0001-p0012.pdf (accessed February 11, 2008).

18. Private correspondence, as quoted in Ellen Fitzpatrick, "Caroline F. Ware and the Cultural Approach to History," *American Quarterly* 43, no. 2 (June, 1991): 192.

19. An interesting case here is that of Merle Curti, one of the contributors to Ware's 1940 AHA volume and the author—three years later—of the first modern synthesis of U.S. intellectual history, *The Growth of American Thought* (New York: Harper and Row, 1943). In retrospect, Curti's remarkably broad range of topics—which included the penny press, birth control, the YMCA, and the Ku Klux Klan, as well as numerous popular authors, such as George Lippard, Bruce Barton, and Huey Long—suggests some obvious methodological affinities with Ware's cultural approach. One can see continuities, as well, in Curti's opening statements on methodology: "The interrelationships between the growth of thought and the whole social milieu seem to be so close and have been so frequently neglected that this study of American life has tried consistently to relate that growth to the whole complex environment. It is thus not a history of American thought, but a social history of American thought, and to some extent a socio-economic history of American thought" (x).

20. Kelley, "Old Cultural History," 116. In this essay, Kelley argues that Ware's *Cultural Approach to History* has been "unacknowledged." Fitzpatrick makes a similar point when she notes that social and labor historians of the 1960s and 1970s

"reflected little, if any, recognition of the 1930s cultural approach." Fitzpatrick, "Ware and the Cultural Approach to History," 193. See also Ellen Fitzpatrick, *History's Memory: Writing Americas Past, 1880–1980*, new ed. (Cambridge: Harvard University Press, 2004), 186–87; Ian Tyrell, *Historians in Public: The Practice of American History, 1890–1970* (Chicago: University of Chicago Press, 2005).

21. Fitzpatrick, "Ware and the Cultural Approach to History," 193–94. One result, as Fitzpatrick notes, was that "no cadre of graduate students existed to carry on Ware's work and reputation" (193).

22. For a sophisticated and early example, see Levine, "Historian and the Culture Gap." We return to this issue in proposition 6.

23. Berkhofer, "Clio and the Culture Concept in Historiography," 75, 88–89.

24. Richard Hofstadter, *The American Political Tradition* (New York: Knopf, 1948), vii–viii; David Potter, *People of Plenty* (Chicago: University of Chicago Press, 1954), xiii–xxvii.

25. Potter, *People of Plenty*, xxi. Another important exception to the postwar pattern of historiographical forgetting was Herbert Gutman, who twice cited Ware's 1924 labor study, *Early New England Cotton Manufacture*, in his own *Work, Culture, and Society in Industrializing America* (New York: Vintage, 1976), 28n21, 29n22. By the 1970s, however, Gutman's theoretical citations on "culture" focused more specifically on the work of Sidney Mintz, Clifford Geertz, and E. P. Thompson.

26. Daniel Joseph Signal, "Beyond Consensus: Richard Hofstadter and American Historiography," *American Historical Review*, 89, no. 4 (October 1984): esp. 988–1003. See Clifford Geertz, "Ideology as a Cultural System," in *Ideology and Discontent*, ed. David E. Apter (London: Free Press of Glencoe, 1964), for Geertz's reconceptualization. On Hofstadter's shifting methods, see the following: Christopher Lasch, foreword to *The American Political Tradition*, by Richard Hofstadter (1948; repr., New York: Knopf, 1973); Michael Kazin, "Hofstadter Lives: Political Culture and Temperament in the Work of an American Historian," *Reviews in American History* 27 (June 1999): 334–48; and David S. Brown, *Richard Hofstadter: An Intellectual Biography* (Chicago: University of Chicago Press, 2006).

27. See, for example, Henry Nash Smith's two prefaces in *Virgin Land* (1950; repr., Cambridge: Harvard University Press, 1970); Joesph J. Kwiat and Mary Turpie, eds., *Studies in American Culture* (Minneapolis: University of Minnesota Press, 1960); Leo Marx, "American Studies: A Defense of an Unscientific Method," *New Literary History* 1, no. 1 (October 1969): 75–90; Barry Shank, "The Continuing Embarrassment of Culture: From the Culture Concept to Cultural Studies," *American Studies* 38, no. 2 (Summer 1997); Lucy Maddox, ed., *Locating American Studies: The Evolution of a Discipline* (Baltimore: Johns Hopkins University Press, 1999).

28. Perry Miller, *The New England Mind* (Cambridge: Harvard University Press, 1953); Howard Mumford Jones, *Jeffersonianism and the American Novel* (New York: Teachers College, 1966); John Cawelti, *Apostles of the Self-Made Man* (Chicago: University of Chicago Press, 1965); Curti, *Growth of American Thought*; Taylor, *Cavalier and Yankee*. This pattern was mirrored in the cross-disciplinary training and appointments of many of the postwar period's most innovative Americanists. John William Ward is a prime example. As Barry O'Connell explained, Ward "earned his B.A. in American History and Literature from Harvard in 1947 and went on for his doctorate in English at the University of Minnesota. Immediately upon receiving his final degree in 1953 he joined the faculty in English at Prince-

ton University. He taught there until 1964, first in English, then in History and as chair of their special program in American Civilization. He began his long association with Amherst College in 1964 when he accepted a chair in History and American Studies." O'Connell, "In Memoriam: John William Ward," *American Quarterly* 38, no. 3 (1986): 496. Similarly, Perry Miller became Professor of American Literature at Harvard in 1946 but was often described as the leading U.S. intellectual historian of the mid-twentieth century. Many of his best-known students (e.g., Bernard Bailyn and Edmund Morgan) were historians, as well.

29. Shank, "Continuing Embarrassment of Culture," 99. The most carefully developed argument along these lines came somewhat later. See Bruce Kuklick, "Myth and Symbol in American Studies," *American Quarterly* 24, no. 4 (October 1972).

30. Henry Nash Smith, "Can 'American Studies' Develop a Method?" *American Quarterly* 9, no. 2, pt. 2 (Summer 1957); Marx, "American Studies."

31. Smith, "Can 'American Studies' Develop a Method?" 204–5.

32. Davis, "Recent Directions," 700, 703. An interesting parallel example is Richard Sykes, "American Studies and the Concept of Culture," *American Quarterly* 15, no. 2, pt. 2 (Summer 1963): S253–S270, which similarly mixes texts from multiple disciplines.

33. The useful phrase "culture concepts" has a long history across much of the social sciences. See, for example, Sykes, "American Studies and the Concept of Culture"; John William Ward, "History and the Concept of Culture," in *Red, White, and Blue*, by W. Ward (New York: Oxford University Press, 1969); Berkhofer, "Clio and the Culture Concept in Historiography"; Sewell, "Concept(s) of Culture."

34. Clement Greenberg, *Art and Culture* (Boston: Beacon Press, 1961). As this list suggests, we use the term "artistic expression" in the broadest possible sense—as a category encompassing both elite and non-elite forms.

35. The most sophisticated discussion of this issue can be found in the work of Raymond Williams. See, for example, Williams, "Culture Is Ordinary," in *Resources of Hope*, ed. Robin Gable (London: Verso, 1989).

36. Space constraints dictate that we can only point to some of the earliest and most widely influential examples for each of the culture concepts in the pages that follow. Other important studies in the arts and ideas tradition include John Cawelti, *Apostles of the Self-Made Man* (1965); Neil Harris, *The Artist in American Society* (1966); Robert Toll, *Blacking Up* (1974); John Kasson, *Civilizing the Machine* (1976); Jackson Lears, *No Place of Grace* (1981); David Levering Lewis, *When Harlem Was in Vogue* (1981); Michael Rogin, *Subversive Genealogy* (1983); Mary Kelley, *Private Women, Public Stage* (1984); and Jean-Christophe Agnew, *Worlds Apart* (1986).

37. See, for example, Max Horkheimer and Theodore Adorno's landmark essay, "The Culture Industry: Enlightenment as Mass Deception," first published as chap. 4 in *Dialectic of Enlightenment* (Amsterdam: Querido, 1947). Other prominent examples of this pattern can be found in Bernard Rosenberg and David Manning White, eds., *Mass Culture: The Popular Arts in America* (New York: Free Press, 1957); and Norman Jacobs, ed., *Culture for the Millions? Mass Media in Modern Society* (Princeton: Van Nostrand, 1961). For an important early exception, see David Riesman, "Listening to Popular Music," *American Quarterly* 2 (1950): 359–71.

38. The first quotations in this sentence are from Adorno and Horkheimer, *Dialectic of Enlightenment* ("unending sameness"); and Stuart Ewen, *Captains of Consciousness: Advertising and the Social Roots of the Consumer Culture* (New York: McGraw-Hill, 1976). The other concepts in quotations ("cultural appropriation" and "strategic

positions to be won or lost") come from one of the foundational texts in British cultural studies: Stuart Hall, "Notes on Deconstructing the Popular" (1979), in *People's History and Socialist Theory*, ed. Raphael Samuel (London: Routledge and Kegan Paul, 1981). See also Michael Denning, "The End of Mass Culture," *International Labor and Working-Class History* 37 (Spring 1990): 4–18, which describes Hall's essay as foundational for the new scholarly consensus on mass culture that began to take shape during the mid-1980s. Prominent early examples of this approach include Janice Radway, *Reading the Romance* (1984); Michael Denning, *Mechanic Accents* (1987); Andrew Ross, *No Respect* (1989); George Lipsitz, *Time Passages* (1990); Richard Butsch, ed., *For Fun and Profit* (1990); Miriam Hansen, *Babel and Babylon* (1991); Robert Allen, *Horrible Prettiness* (1991); Eric Lott, *Love and Theft* (1993); and Richard Ohmann, *Selling Culture* (1996).

39. See, for example, Daniel Rodgers, *The Work Ethic in Industrial America* (1974); Burton Bledstein, *The Culture of Professionalism* (1976); Ronald Walters, *The Antislavery Appeal* (1976); Paul Boyer, *Urban Masses and Moral Order* (1978); Lewis Erenberg, *Steppin' Out* (1981); Emily Rosenberg, *Spreading the American Dream* (1982); Robert Rydell, *All the World's a Fair* (1984); Karen Halttunen, *Confidence Men and Painted Women* (1984); Elliott Gorn, *The Manly Art* (1986); Kathy Peiss, *Cheap Amusements* (1986); and Elaine Tyler May, *Homeward Bound* (1988).

40. These quotations come from Gutman, *Work, Culture, and Society*; Lawrence W. Levine, *Black Culture and Black Consciousness* (New York: Oxford University Press, 1977); Lizabeth Cohen, *Making a New Deal* (New York: Cambridge University Press, 1990); and Robin D. G. Kelley, *Race Rebels: Culture, Politics, and the Black Working Class* (New York: Free Press, 1994), respectively. On the American side, the theoretical lineage goes back at least to Sydney Mintz's pathbreaking work of the early 1970s. See, for example, Mintz's foreword to *Afro-American Anthropology: Contemporary Perspectives*, ed. Norman Whitten and John Szwed (New York: Free Press, 1970), 1–16; and Mintz, "Toward an Afro-American History," *Journal of World History* 13 (1971): 317–33. One can see the conceptual apparatus coming together (and migrating to other U.S. fields) in Gutman's long footnote on culture as "resource" in *Work, Culture, and Society*, 17n14. Beyond Mintz, those to whom Gutman owed conceptual debts included Eric Wolf, Zygmunt Bauman, Clifford Geertz, and E. P. Thompson (who was thanked as the central influence on the work as a whole). Other major examples in this mode include Albert Raboteau, *Slave Religion* (1980); Roy Rosenzweig, *Eight Hours for What We Will* (1983); Charles Joyner, *Down by the Riverside* (1983); Francis Couvares, *The Remaking of Pittsburgh* (1984); Deborah Gray White, *Ar'n't I a Woman* (1985); Christine Stansell, *City of Women* (1986); Sterling Stuckey, *Slave Culture* (1987); Richard Stott, *Workers in the Metropolis* (1990); and George Sanchez, *Becoming Mexican American* (1993).

41. The two terms in quotations here come from Geertz, *Interpretation of Culture* ("read like a text"), and Foucault, *Order of Things* ("discourse"). See n. 7 for additional key citations.

42. See, for example, Appleby, Hunt, and Jacob, *Telling the Truth about History*.

43. On this issue, see especially Alan Trachtenberg, "Myth and Symbol," *Massachusetts Review* 25 (Winter 1984): 667.

44. Smith, *Virgin Land* (1950), xi. The subsequent critiques and revisions of Smith's 1950 methodological statements were often launched by those from within the early American studies movement. See, for example, Smith, "Can American Stud-

ies Develop a Method?"; and Smith, 1969 preface to *Virgin Land* (1970), vii–x; Marx, "American Studies"; and Trachtenberg, "Myth and Symbol."

45. For early semiotic analyses in American studies, see Smith, *Virgin Land* (1950); Leo Marx, *The Machine in the Garden* (1964); Alan Trachtenberg, *Brooklyn Bridge* (1965); Richard Slotkin, *Regeneration through Violence* (1974); and Robert Berkhofer, *The White Man's Indian* (1978). Pathbreaking cultural histories that treated signs and language as central topics include Rhys Isaac, *The Transformation of Virginia* (1982); Carroll Smith-Rosenberg, *Disorderly Conduct* (1985); Susan G. Davis, *Parades and Power* (1986); Lawrence Levine, *Highbrow/Lowbrow* (1989); David Roediger, *Wages of Whiteness* (1991); Gail Bederman; *Manliness and Civilization* (1995); and Kathleen Brown, *Good Wives, Nasty Wenches, and Anxious Patriarchs*, (1996).

46. See, for example, John Higham, "The Cult of the 'American Consensus': Homogenizing our History," *Commentary* 27 (February 1959): 93–100; Levine, "Historian and the Culture Gap"; John P. Diggins, "Consciousness and Ideology in American History: The Burden of Daniel J. Boorstin," *American Historical Review* 76 (February 1971): 99–118; Ronald Takaki, *Strangers from a Distant Shore* (Boston: Little Brown, 1989); Kaplan and Pease, *Cultures of United States Imperialism;* David Gutierrez, *Walls and Mirrors* (Berkeley: University of California Press, 1995); K. Scott Wong, "The Transformation of Culture: Three Chinese Views of America," *American Quarterly* 48, no. 2 (June 1996); Lisa Lowe, *Immigrant Acts* (Durham, NC: Duke University Press, 1996); Jose David Saldivar, *Border Matters* (Berkeley: University of California Press, 1997); and John Carlos Rowe, ed., *Post-Nationalist American Studies* (Berkeley: University of California Press, 2000).

47. On black cultural circulation, see, for example, Robert Farris Thompson, *Flash of the Spirit* (New York: Random House, 1983); Henry Louis Gates Jr., *The Signifying Monkey* (New York: Oxford University Press, 1988); Paul Gilroy, *The Black Atlantic* (Cambridge: Harvard University Press, 1993); George Lipsitz, *Dangerous Crossroads* (London: Verso, 1994); Joseph Roach, *Cities of the Dead* (New York: Columbia University Press, 1996); Hazel Carby, *Cultures in Babylon* (London, Verso, 1999); Brent Edwards, *The Practice of Diaspora* (Cambridge: Harvard University Press, 2003); and Penny Von Eschen, *Satchmo Blows up the World* (Cambridge: Harvard University Press, 2004). On the intellectual exchanges that informed the concepts of Social Democracy and Pan-Africanism, see especially James Kloppenberg, *Uncertain Victory* (New York: Oxford University Press, 1986); Daniel Rodgers, *Atlantic Crossings* (Cambridge: Harvard University Press, 1998); Robin Kelley, *Freedom Dreams* (New York: Beacon Press, 2002); and Kevin Gaines, *American Africans in Ghana* (Chapel Hill: University of North Carolina, 2006).

48. See, for example, Arjun Appadurai, *Modernity at Large: Cultural Dimensions of Globalization* (Minneapolis: University of Minnesota Press, 1996); Edward Herman and Robert McChesney, *The Global Media* (London: Cassell, 1997); Frederic Jameson and Masao Miyoshi, *The Cultures of Globalization* (Durham, NC: Duke University Press, 1998); David Held, Anthony G. McGrew, David Goldblatt, and Jonathan Perraton, *Global Transformations: Politics, Economics and Culture* (London: Polity Press, 1999); Denning, *Culture in the Age of Three Worlds;* Pascale Casanova, *The World Republic of Letters* (Cambridge: Harvard University Press, 2004); Franco Moretti, *Graphs, Maps, Trees* (London: Verso, 2005); and Donald Sassoon, *The Culture of the Europeans* (New York: Harper Collins, 2006).

49. In Levine's hands, spirituals, folk tales, work songs, and jokes emerged as both

powerful social tools (for living) and complex representational forms (whose stylistic conventions required their own modes of questioning).

50. The closest approximation to a cultural history essay was a piece on "anthropology and history."

51. Louis P. Masur, ed., *The Challenge of American History* (Baltimore: Johns Hopkins University Press, 1999). This, too, grew out of a special issue of *Reviews in American History* published in March 1998. The essays we have in mind here were written by Kathleen Brown, James Goodman, Timothy Gilfoyle, David Hollinger, and George H. Roeder Jr., respectively.

52. See, for example, Howard Sitkoff, ed., *Perspectives on Modern America* (New York: Oxford University Press, 2001); and Melvyn Stokes, ed., *The State of U.S. History* (New York: Berg, 2002). For recent commentary on the movement of cultural history to the center of the U.S. field, see "The Practice of History," *Journal of American History* 90 (September 2003): 577–91. The commentators in this roundtable included Drew Gilpin Faust, Hendrik Hartog, David Hollinger, Akira Iriye, Patricia Nelson Limerick, Nell Irvin Painter, David Roediger, Mary Ryan, and Alan Taylor.

53. The rubrics in this list refer to the field of training and dissertation topic of each scholar. We base our claim of a generational cohort on the years in which they received their Ph.D.'s: Susman, 1958; Gutman, 1959; Huggins, 1962; Levine, 1962; and Smith-Rosenberg, 1968.

54. Levine's 1971 essay "The Historian and the Culture Gap" is a prime example of this shift. But one can also see the larger pattern at work in the introductions to Gutman's *Work, Culture, and Society;* Susman's *Culture as History;* Huggins's *Harlem Renaissance* (New York: Oxford University Press, 1971); Levine's *Black Culture and Black Consciousness;* and Smith-Rosenberg's *Disorderly Conduct: Visions of Gender in Victorian America* (New York: Knopf, 1985).

55. The Levine quotation is from his introduction to *The Unpredictable Past: Explorations in American Cultural History* (New York: Oxford University Press, 1993), 6. The description of Gutman's working methods comes from Ira Berlin, "Introduction: Herbert Gutman and the American Working Class," in *Power and Culture: Essays on the American Working Class* by Herbert Gutman (New York: Pantheon, 1987), 17. It is noteworthy that both assessments were written during the late 1980s, at a point when the field divisions were somewhat clearer and easier to describe.

56. Gutman, *Work, Culture, and Society,* xii.

57. Smith-Rosenberg, *Disorderly Conduct,* 22, 29, 43. Much the same self-consciousness about combining and transcending older historiographical approaches runs through all of these scholars' work from the late 1960s and 1970s. See, for example, the acknowledgments to *Harlem Renaissance* in which Huggins thanks Henry May for teaching him about "the 1920s and American intellectual history," Kenneth Stampp for his inspiration in "Afro-American history," and Oscar Handlin for "opening his mind to social and cultural history" (ix). Or Susman's introductory remarks to *Culture as History* about the specific type of "cultural conflict" he hoped to explicate: "Historians, to be sure, have readily seen and studied other basic cultural conflicts in American history: between classes, between regions and sections, between urban and rural worlds, between native and immigrant populations, between races and ethnic groups, and more recently between genders considered as cultural groups. These essays propose another kind of cultural

conflict that offers additional perspectives on such work, and that, I believe, can help explain much of the dynamic conflict over values in our century"(xx).

58. Raymond Williams, "Base and Superstructure in Marxist Cultural Theory," *New Left Review* (November–December 1973). This essay was reprinted in a number of places. See, for example, Raymond Williams, *Postmodernism, Materialism and Culture* (New York: Verso, 1980).

59. E. P. Thompson, *The Making of the English Working Class* (London: Victor Golancz, 1963), 10.

60. Denning, "Socioanalysis of Culture," 77. Williams's and Thompson's powerful influence on U.S. historians is a complex story that we can only begin to point to here. For more detailed genealogies of New Left historiography on the U.S. side, see the following (in addition to Denning): David Brody, "The Old Labor History and the New: In Search of an American Working Class," *Labor History* 20 (1979): 111–26; Mike Davis, "Why the U.S. Working Class Is Different," *New Left Review* 123 (1980): 3–46; David Montgomery, "To Study the People: The American Working Class," *Labor History* 21 (1980): 485–512; and Frisch and Walkowitz, *Working-Class America*. Major U.S. histories of the working class that explicitly acknowledge Williams's and Thompson's influence include Roy Rosenzweig, *Eight Hours for What We Will* (1983); Francis Couvares, *The Remaking of Pittsburgh* (1984); and Christine Stansell, *City of Women* (1986). Interesting transitional cases here are George Lipsitz, *Class and Culture in Cold War America* (1981), and Kathy Peiss, *Cheap Amusements* (1986), both of which pushed the new labor history toward a more explicit focus on leisure and consumption. For helpful genealogies of New Left historiography on the European side, see Sewell, *Logics of History*, and Eley, *Crooked Line*.

61. In 1988, Christopher Johnson noted that the "detailed local study to illuminate the world of ordinary people" was the characteristic form of labor history. Johnson, "Back to Politics: Some Recent Work in North American Labor History, a Review Article," *Comparative Studies in Society and History* 30 (October 1988): 804–19, quotation at 806. Stephen Thernstrom, *Poverty and Progress: Social Mobility in a Nineteenth Century City* (Cambridge: Harvard University Press, 1964). For a good example of Gutman's conceptual impact even among quantitative social and labor historians, see Tamara Hareven, *Family Time and Industrial Time* (New York: Cambridge University Press, 1982), 418n2.

62. Studies of Lynn include Mary H. Blewett, *Men, Women, and Work: Class, Gender, and Protest in the New England Shoe Industry, 1780–1910* (Urbana: University of Illinois Press, 1990); John T. Cumbler, *Working-Class Community in Industrial America: Work, Leisure, and Struggle in Two Industrial Cities, 1880–1930* (Westport, CT: Greenwood Press, 1979); Alan Dawley, *Class and Community: The Industrial Revolution in Lynn* (Cambridge: Harvard University Press, 1976); and Paul G. Faler, *Mechanics and Manufacturers in the Early Industrial Revolution: Lynn, Massachusetts, 1780–1860* (Albany: State University of New York Press, 1981). See also Alan Dawley and Paul Faler, "Working Class Culture and Politics the Industrial Revolution: Sources of Loyalism and Revolution," *Journal of Social History* 9 (1976): 466–80.

63. See, for example, Bruce Laurie, "Nothing on Compulsion: Life Styles of Philadelphia Artisans, 1820–1850," *Labor History* 15 (Summer 1974).

64. Leon Fink, "Looking Backward: Reflections on Workers' Culture and the Conceptual Dilemmas of the New Labor History," in *Perspectives in American Labor*

History, ed. Alice Kessler-Harris and J. Carroll Moody (De Kalb: Northern Illinois University Press, 1989), 13. Mari Jo Buhle and Paul Buhle likewise noted in 1988 that the cultural turn in labor history was built on a long history: "Behind what we now call a 'cultural approach' to United States labor history stands a long and complex scholarly evolution." Buhle and Buhle, "The New Labor History at the Cultural Crossroads," *Journal of American History* 75 (June 1988): 151–57, quotation at 151.

65. For a survey that is a good measure more sympathetic to the "old labor history" than are most of the new labor historians, see Brody, "Old Labor History and the New."

66. The Port Huron Statement is quoted in James Miller, *Democracy in the Streets: From Port Huron to the Siege of Chicago* (New York: Simon and Schuster, 1988), 333. King is quoted in Charles Marsh, *The Beloved Community: How Faith Shapes Social Justice, from the Civil Rights Movement to Today* (New York: Basic Books, 2005), 206.

67. See, for example, Wini Breines, *Community and Organization in the New Left: 1962–1968* (New York: Praeger, 1982), which includes a chapter titled "Politics as Community"; and Jennifer Frost, *"An Interracial Movement of the Poor": Community Organizing and the New Left in the 1960s* (New York: New York University Press, 2001).

68. C. Wright Mills, "Letter to the New Left," *New Left Review,* no. 5 (September–October 1960).

69. See, for example, Sean Wilentz and responses, "Against Exceptionalism: Class Consciousness and the American Labor Movement," *International Labor and Working-Class History* 26 (1984): 1–36.

70. The quotations in this sentence are from, respectively, Howard Kimeldorf, "Bringing the Unions Back in (or Why We Need a New Old Labor History)," *Labor History* 32 (1991): 91–103; Johnson, "Back to Politics," 805; Alice Kessler-Harris, "A New Agenda for American Labor History: A Gendered Analysis and the Question of Class," in Kessler-Harris and Moody, *Perspectives in American Labor History,* 220. See also, for more general critiques of the "culturalist" bent of social history, Tony Judt, "A Clown in Regal Purple: Social History and the Historians," *History Workshop Journal* 7 (1979): 66–94; Elizabeth Fox Genovese and Eugene D. Genovese, "The Political Crisis of Social History: A Marxist Perspective," *Journal of Social History* (1976): 205–21; and Geoff Eley and Keith Nield, "Why Does Social History Ignore Politics?" *Social History* 5 (1980): 249–72.

71. We take this to be Alice Kessler-Harris's point when she writes, "in the end, we never struggled with the meaning of culture" ("New Agenda for American Labor History," 222).

72. Berlin, introduction to *Power and Culture,* 37.

73. This passage from Stuart Hall, "Notes on Deconstructing the Popular" (1979), was widely quoted. See, for example, Andrew Ross, "Giving Culture Hell: A Response to Catherine Gallagher," *Social Text* 30 (1992): 98.

74. "Ironically, labor historians played major roles in both the emergence and opposition to the cultural turn in the United States," notes Daniel J. Walkowitz in "The Cultural Turn and a New Social History: Folk Dance and the Renovation of Class in Social History," *Journal of Social History* 39 (2006): 51.

75. Joan Scott, "On Language, Gender, and Working-Class History," *International Labor and Working-Class History* 31 (Spring 1987): 1–13; Denning, "End of Mass Culture."

76. Lears, "Concept of Cultural Hegemony"; Joan Scott, "The Evidence of Experience," *Critical Inquiry* (Summer 1991): 781; Daniel T. Rodgers, "Republicanism: The Career of a Concept," *Journal of American History* 79 (June 1992) 11–38; Walter Johnson, "On Agency," *Journal of Social History*, 37(2003): 113–24.

77. Scott, "Language, Gender, and Working-Class History." For critical responses to Scott that emphasized the physical reality of class, see Bryan Palmer, "Response to Joan Scott," *International Labor and Working-Class History* 31 (Spring 1987): 14–23; and Dick Geary, "Labour History, the 'Linguistic Turn,' and Postmodernism," *Contemporary European History* 3 (2000): 445–62. Scott, "Evidence of Experience,", 781.

78. Scott, "Evidence of Experience," 779–80.

79. A key intervention in this regard was John Higham and Paul Conkin, eds., *New Directions in American Intellectual History* (Baltimore: Johns Hopkins University Press, 1979). Significantly, two of the volume's best-known essays—Neil Harris's "Iconography and Intellectual History: The Half-Tone Effect," and Warren Susman's "'Personality' and the Making of Twentieth-Century Culture"—are now considered foundational works in U.S. cultural history. For an intriguing representation of the "crisis" within late 1970s intellectual history, see Arthur Schlesinger Jr.'s essay in which he notes a general "flight" from synthesizing concepts such as "national character" and "the liberal tradition," as well as a growing consensus that anthropological conceptions of culture might serve as intellectual history's "salvation." Schlesinger, "Review Essay/Intellectual History: A Time for Despair?" *Journal of American History* 66 (March 1980): 888–93. For an additional view that cuts across U.S. and European historiography, see Robert Darnton, "Intellectual and Cultural History," in *The Past before Us: Contemporary Historical Writing in the United States*, ed. Michael Kammen (Ithaca, NY: Cornell University Press, 1980).

80. John Higham, introduction to Higham and Conkin, *New Directions in American Intellectual History*, xii. "Intellectual historians," Higham was quick to add, "had by no means ranged themselves solidly" behind these assumptions. "Some had been among the leading critics of the consensus approach; most were sensitive to its limitations" (xii).

81. Ibid., xv–xvi. Our point here is simply to chronicle one of the most important subdisciplinary debates that pushed in the direction of cultural history as an independent field of analysis. For helpful assessments of cultural and intellectual histories' symbiotic relationships, see Thomas Berber, "Intellectual and Cultural History," in *The New American History*, ed. Eric Foner (Philadelphia: Temple University Press, 1997); and Casey Nelson Blake, "Culturalist Approaches to Intellectual History," in *A Companion to American Cultural History*, ed. Karen Halttunen (New York: Wiley-Blackwell, 2008).

82. Fox and Lears, *Culture of Consumption*.

83. Ibid., x.

84. The literature on these issues is too vast to summarize here. For explicit theoretical discussions and historiographical surveys, see especially Joan Scott, "Gender: A Useful Category of Historical Analysis," *American Historical Review* 91, no. 5 (1986): 1053–75; Mary Poovey, "Feminism and Deconstruction," *Feminist Studies* 14, no. 1 (1988): 51–65; the issue of *Gender and History* 1, no. 1 (1989): 1–6, 7–30; Louise Newman, "Critical Theory and the History of Women: What's at Stake in Deconstructing Women's History," *Journal of Women's History* 2, no. 3 (1991); and

Newman, "Gender History/Women's History: Is Feminist Scholarship Losing Its Critical Edge," *Journal of Women's History* 5, no. 1 (1993): 89–128.

85. For prominent discussions of these debates, see Ann Sitow, Christine Stansell, and Sharon Thompson, *Powers of Desire: The Politics of Sexuality* (Boston: Monthly Review Press, 1983); Judith Bennett, " Feminism and History," *Gender and History* 1, no. 3 (1989): 252–72; and Elizabeth Fox Genovese, *Feminism without Illusions* (Chapel Hill: University of North Carolina Press, 1991).

86. Here again, the paper trail is enormous. For pathbreaking historical studies, see the following: Paula Giddings, *Where and When I Enter* (New York: Bantam, 1984); Deborah Gray White, *Ar'n't I a Woman* (New York: Norton, 1985); Jacqueline Jones, *Labor of Love, Labor of Sorrow* (New York: Basic Books, 1985); Evelyn Nawanko Glenn, *Issei, Nisei, War Bride* (Philadelphia: Temple University Press, 1986); and Darlene Clark Hine, *Black Women in White* (Bloomington: Indiana University Press, 1989). See also Evelyn Brooks Higginbotham, "Beyond the Sound of Silence: Afro-American Women's History," *Gender and History* 1, no. 1 (1989): 50–67. For multicultural critiques from within feminism, see Bell Hooks, *Ain't I a Woman?* (Boston: South End Press, 1981); Gloria T. Hull, Patricia Bell Scott, and Barbara Smith, eds., *All the Women Are White, All the Blacks Are Men, But Some of Us Are Brave* (Old Westbury, NY: Feminist Press, 1981); Cherrie Moraga and Gloria Anzaldua, eds., *This Bridge Called My Back* (New York: Kitchen Table, Women of Color Press 1983); Patricia Hill Collins, *Black Feminist Thought* (London: Routledge, 1990); and Chandra Talpade Mohanty, Ann Russo, and Lourdes Torres, eds., *Third World Women and the Politics of Feminism* (Bloomington: Indiana University Press, 1991).

87. On this question, see especially Elsa Barkley Brown, "Womanist Consciousness: Maggie Lena Walker and the Independent Order of Saint Luke," *Signs* 14 (Spring 1989): 610–33; Evelyn Brooks Higginbotham, "African-American Women's History and the Metalanguage of Race," *Signs* 17, no. 2 (1992): 251–74; Gail Bederman, *Manliness and Civilization: A Cultural History of Gender and Race in the United States, 1880–1917* (Chicago: University of Chicago Press, 1995); and Kathleen M. Brown, *Good Wives, Nasty Wenches, and Anxious Patriarchs: Gender, Race and Power in Colonial Virginia* (Chapel Hill: University of North Carolina Press, 1996).

88. It is in precisely this sense that many 1970s historians spoke of tracing the "social origins" of seemingly non-economic topics (such as religious revivals). In the twenty-fifth-anniversary edition of the book, Johnson, referring to both the tone and the methods he employed, noted that "much of this way of doing history is over with now." Paul E. Johnson, *A Shopkeeper's Millennium: Society and Revivals in Rochester, New York, 1815–1837* (1978; repr., New York: Hill and Wang, 2004), xv.

89. Paul E. Johnson, *Sam Patch, the Famous Jumper* (New York: Hill and Wang, 2003), 228n13.

90. Not surprisingly, *Sam Patch* also draws upon a much wider range of theoretical insights, moving through scholarly literatures on celebrity, the sublime, parades, and visual culture as well as the work of many foundational thinkers in European cultural theory such as Walter Benjamin, Michel de Certeau, and Terry Eagleton.

91. As quoted in Kessler-Harris, "New Agenda for American Labor History," 224. See also Bender, "Wholes and Parts."

92. Eric H. Monkkonen, "Resurgence of Narrative History" (letter), *New York Times Book Review*, September 5, 1982, 21.

93. The case was beautifully made in William Cronon, "A Place for Stories: Nature,

History, and Narrative," *Journal of American History* 78 (March 1992): 1347–76. See also Sarah Maza, "Stories in History: Cultural Narratives in Recent Works in European History," *American Historical Review* 101 (December 1996): 1493–1515; and John Demos, "History Can Be Literary," *New York Times,* December 30, 1998, A17.

94. Nick Salvatore, *Eugene V. Debs: Citizen and Socialist* (Urbana: University of Illinois Press, 1982). Significantly, this book was published the same year as Monkkonen's critique of narrative history. For additional evidence of how the tide was shifting, see Melvyn Dubofsky's review of *Eugene V. Debs,* which singled out the "warm grace, power, and feeling" of the prose while emphasizing the analytical richness of Salvatore's account. Dubofsky, review, *American Historical Review* 88 (December 1983): 1336–37. A few years later, Salvatore went on to publish one of the earliest and most successful "microhistories" by an Americanist: *We All Got History: The Memory Books of Amos Webber* (New York: Times Books, 1996).

95. These examples come from Robert Darnton, *The Great Cat Massacre and Other Episodes in French Cultural History* (New York: Basic Books, 1984); and Lawrence W. Levine, "William Shakespeare and the American People: A Study in Cultural Transformation," *American Historical Review* 89, no. 1 (February 1984): 34–66.

96. One important wellspring here was the historiographical work of Hayden White: *Metahistory: The Historical Imagination in Nineteenth-Century Europe* (Baltimore: Johns Hopkins University Press, 1973); *Tropics of Discourse: Essays in Cultural Criticism* (Baltimore: Johns Hopkins University Press, 1978); and *The Content of the Form: Narrative Discourse and Historical Representation* (Baltimore: Johns Hopkins University Press, 1987). But one can also point to a number of innovative cultural histories that put these ideas into practice. See, for example, Natalie Zemon Davis, *The Return of Martin Guerre* (Cambridge: Harvard University Press, 1983); and Davis, *Fiction in the Archives* (Palo Alto, CA: Stanford University Press, 1987); Simon Schama, *Dead Certainties* (New York: Knopf, 1991); John Demos, *The Unredeemed Captive* (New York: Knopf, 1994); and Richard Wightman Fox, *Trials of Intimacy* (Chicago: University of Chicago Press, 1999).

97. Kelley, *Race Rebels;* Tera W. Hunter, *To `Joy My Freedom: Southern Black Women's Lives and Labors after the Civil War* (Cambridge: Harvard University Press, 1997); Kimberley L. Phillips, *Alabama North: African-American Migrants, Community, and Working-Class Activism in Cleveland, 1915–45* (Urbana: University of Illinois Press, 1999). For commentary on the innovative breadth of these studies, see, for example, Deborah Gray White's review of *To `Joy My Freedom,* in which she describes Hunter's work as "a sophisticated blend of labor, social and cultural history." White, review, *Journal of American History* 85 (June 1998): 290–91.

98. Kelley, *Race Rebels,* 7–8. James C. Scott, *Weapons of the Weak: Everyday Forms of Peasant Resistance* (New Haven: Yale University Press, 1985); and James C. Scott, *Domination and the Arts of Resistance* (New Haven: Yale University Press, 1990). The goal here, as Kelley argues, was an expansion (as opposed to a supercession) of earlier historical understandings of "the political": "Like Scott, I use the concept of infrapolitics to describe the daily confrontations, evasive actions, and stifled thoughts that often inform political movements. I am not suggesting that the realm of infrapolitics is any more or less important or effective than what we traditionally understand to be politics. Instead, I want to suggest that the political history of oppressed people cannot be understood without reference to infrapolitics, for these daily acts have a cumulative effect on power relations" (8).

99. At this point, Levine held the Margaret Byrne Chair of U.S. History at the University of California–Berkeley, had been a MacArthur Foundation fellow, and was the newly elected president of the Organization of American Historians. Similarly, Davis held an endowed chair at Princeton University and was a former president of the American Historical Association (1988–89). Lears and Kelley were at somewhat earlier stages in their careers, but each had already developed a considerable national reputation as a leader in his respective specialty. On the back cover of Kelley's 1994 book *Race Rebels*, for example, Cornel West described Kelley "as the preeminent historian of black popular culture writing today."

100. Lawrence Levine, "The Folklore of Industrial Society," *American Historical Review* 97, no. 5 (December 1992): 1370, 1373. U.S. cultural historians were not the only ones arguing about methodological questions during these years. For tough debates on the European side, see, for example, Roger Chartier, "Texts, Symbols, and Frenchness," *Journal of Modern History* 57, no. 4 (December 1985): 682–95; Robert Darnton, "The Symbolic Element in History," *Journal of Modern History* 58, no. 1 (March 1986): 218–34; James Fernandez, "Historians Tell Tales: Of Cartesian Cats and Gallic Cockfights," *Journal of Modern History* 60, no. 1 (March 1988): 113–27; Dominick LaCapra, "Chartier, Darnton, and the Great Symbol Massacre," *Journal of Modern History* 60, no. 1 (March 1988): 95–112; and Harold Mah, "Suppressing the Text: The Metaphysics of Ethnographic History in Darnton's Great Cat Massacre," *History Workshop Journal* 31 (1991): 1–20.

101. Levine, "Folklore of Industrial Society," 1372.

102. Robin D. G. Kelley, "Notes on Deconstructing the Folk," *American Historical Review* 97, no. 5 (December 1992): 1402–3.

103. Ibid., 1404–5 (our emphasis).

104. T. J. Jackson Lears, "Making Fun of Popular Culture," *American Historical Review* 97, no. 5 (December 1992): 1419.

105. Ibid., 1422–23. In the next sentence, Lears put the point more strongly: "Levine remains oblivious to the fundamental fact of cultural power: not its capacity to manipulate consciousness but its existence as a set of givens that form the boundaries of what the less powerful can do or can even (sometimes) imagine doing." (1423). Kelley made a similar point: "The question of power and access to the tools of production (as opposed to the receptacles and spaces for consumption) is surprisingly absent from Levine's discussion. . . . Although Levine cites test screenings and audience surveys as examples of consumers shaping popular film, this is not the same as having a direct voice in cultural production from inception to completion. Subordinate groups, especially in the period Levine is writing about, generally did not have access to the production of radio, television, and film in the same way they had access to churches, local clubhouses, and street corners" ("Notes on Deconstructing the Folk," 1404).

106. See, for example, Natalie Zemon Davis, *Society and Culture in Early Modern France* (Palo Alto, CA: Stanford University Press, 1975); Rhys Isaac, *The Transformation of Virginia, 1744–1790* (Chapel Hill: University of North Carolina Press, 1982); and Charles Joyner, *Down by the Riverside: A South Carolina Slave Community* (Urbana: University of Illinois Press, 1983). Along these lines, it is noteworthy that Davis was by far the least critical respondent to Levine's essay in the December 1992 *AHR*.

107. The phrase "good to think with" comes from the cultural anthropologist Claude Lévi-Strauss. For an extended discussion of the phrase's resonances in Euro-

pean cultural history of the 1970s and early 1980s, see Darnton, *Great Cat Massacre*, 3–7.

108. This historiographical rule of thumb applied equally to pre-industrial slave communities and twentieth-century consumers of commercial entertainment. Indeed, it was in just this spirit of taking seriously the localized reception practices of mass audiences that Levine argued: "We need more empirical research like that done by Herbert Gans in the Italian working-class homes of Boston's West End in the 1950s. Although the television was on constantly, actual viewing was highly selective and was structured to filter out themes inimical to the life of the peer group" ("Folklore of Industrial Society," 1380). In this sense, Levine's approach to the study of popular culture shared certain affinities with the eminent British social historian E. P. Thompson, who described his work as an effort to "rescue" the lost customs, values, and political choices of early modern workers from "the enormous condescension of posterity" (*Making of the English Working Class*, 12). The "condescension" that Thompson had in mind here derived in large part from the "prevailing orthodoxies" of postwar scholars, many of whom, he argued, treat the "great majority of working people" as "passive victims of laissez faire" or as "the data for statistical studies" (11).

109. Kelley, "Notes on Deconstructing the Folk," 1402. Such an approach, Kelley noted, had been essential to Stuart Hall's pathbreaking analysis in "Notes on Deconstructing the Popular" (1979), as well as to Levine's previous book, *Highbrow/Lowbrow: The Emergence of Cultural Hierarchy in America* (1988). For additional discussion of this facet of Levine's scholarship, see Nan Enstad's essay in the present volume.

110. Kelley, "Notes on Deconstructing the Folk," 1403–4. Kelley's quotations here drew heavily on George Lipsitz's important 1990 collection, *Time Passages: Collective Memory and American Popular Culture*.

111. "History Frontiers: An Interview with Roy Rosenzweig by John H. Summers," *Left History* 7, no. 1 (Spring 2000); http://www.yorku.ca/lefthist/online/interview/rosenzweig.html (accessed November 3, 2006). A similar view was expressed by a labor historian in the mid-1980s: "Many of us ventured into labor history for political reasons . . . it was part of the whole project of changing something in the sixties" (as quoted in Kessler-Harris, "New Agenda for American Labor History," 221).

112. Simon During spoke of the decline of the "social-democratic power bloc." See Simon During, introduction to *The Cultural Studies Reader*, 2nd ed., ed. S. During (London: Routledge, 1999), 16. The quotation is from Jean-François Lyotard, *The Postmodern Condition: A Report on Knowledge*, trans. Geoff Bennington and Brian Massumi (Minneapolis: University of Minnesota Press, 1984).

113. Walter Benn Michaels, *The Gold Standard and the Logic of Naturalism: American Literature at the Turn of the Century* (Berkeley: University of California Press, 1987). This book was the second volume in the influential series The New Historicism: Studies in Cultural Poetics, edited by Stephen Greenblatt. Marx's comments appear on the University of California Press's Web site page for the book.

114. Phillip Fisher, introduction to *The New American Studies: Essays from Representations*, ed. P. Fisher (Berkeley: University of California Press, 1991), quotations at vii, xix. Michaels's piece in the collection is "An American Tragedy: Or the Promise of American Life," 171–98.

115. See Jerold M. Starr, ed., *Cultural Politics: Radical Movements in Modern History* (New

York: Praeger, 1985). See, for example, Sara Ahmed, *The Cultural Politics of Emotion* (Edinburgh: Edinburgh University Press, 2004); James L. Watson and Melissa L. Caldwell, eds., *The Cultural Politics of Food and Eating: A Reader* (Malden, MA: Blackwell, 2005); Julia V. Emberly, *The Cultural Politics of Fur* (Ithaca, NY: Cornell University Press, 1997); Keith Albert Sandifer, *The Cultural Politics of Sugar: Caribbean Slavery and Narratives of Colonialism* (New York: Cambridge University Press, 2000). One early exception is a 1985 volume on art, but it had a different conception of cultural politics than it subsequently connoted.

116. Michael Denning, *The Cultural Front: The Laboring of American Culture in the Twentieth Century* (London: Verso, 1998), see esp. chap. 2. See also Waldo E. Martin Jr., *No Coward Soldiers: Black Cultural Politics and Postwar America* (Cambridge: Harvard University Press, 2005).

117. Bruce Burgett and Glenn Hendler, ed., *Keywords for American Cultural Studies* (New York: New York University Press, 2007). Another book of cultural keywords also omitted politics as a central category. See Tony Bennett, Lawrence Grossberg, and Meaghan Morris, eds., *New Keywords: A Revised Vocabulary of Culture and Society* (New York: Wiley, 2005).

118. The new section of During, *Cultural Studies Reader*, 2nd ed., titled "Culture-Political Economy and Policy," included two articles: Tony Bennett, "Putting Policy in Cultural Studies"; and Nicholas Garnham, "Political Economy and Cultural Studies." The quotation is from During's introduction (17).

119. For two deft assessments of Hofstadter's contributions to the concept of political culture, see Signal , "Beyond Consensus"; and Kazin, "Hofstadter Lives."

120. See, for example, "From Culture Concept to Cultural Studies," a special issue of *American Studies* 38 (Summer 1997).

121. Many of the ideas in this paragraph are influenced by two important articles by Robert Berkhofer Jr.: "Clio and the Culture Concept in Historiography"; and "A New Context for American Studies," *American Quarterly* 41 (1989): 558–613. Saul Cornell, "Moving beyond the Great Story: Postmodern Possibilities, Postmodern Problems," *American Quarterly* 50 (1998): 349–57.

122. John Armitage, Ryan Bishop, and Douglas Kellner, "Introducing Cultural Politics," *Cultural Politics: An International Journal* 1 (March 2005): 1.

123. As early as 1980, Ronald Walters noted this trend in "Signs of the Times: Clifford Geertz and Historians." Four years later, Daniel Signal half-jokingly described Geertz as cited "so often by historians that it has become something of a professional embarrassment" ("Beyond Consensus," 998). This does not mean, however, that cultural historians of the period simply embraced Geertz in precisely the same way. Darnton and Chartier, for example, conducted a fairly heated debate on the question of Geertz's influence in a pair of essays. See Chartier, "Texts, Symbols, and Frenchness"; and Darnton, "Symbolic Element in History."

124. In 1989, for example, Lynn Hunt described the resonance of Foucault's theoretical work as "undeniably tremendous" among recent Europeanists. Hunt, "Introduction: History, Culture, and Text," in *New Cultural History*, 9. Yet the pattern was hardly restricted to Hunt's own field. Indeed, for much of the next decade, Foucault was a regular presence in scores of U.S. cultural histories, including Michael O'Malley, *Keeping Watch* (1990); Eric Lott, *Love and Theft* (1993); Elizabeth Lunbeck, *The Psychiatric Persuasion* (1994); Gail Bederman, *Manliness and Civilization* (1995); George Chauncey, *Gay New York* (1995); Michael Meranze, *Laboratories of Virtue* (1996); and Kathleen Brown, *Good Wives, Nasty Wenches, and Anxious Patri-*

archs (1996). This does not mean, however, that U.S. historians' engagements with Foucault began during the early 1990s. See, for example, David J. Rothman, *The Discovery of the Asylum* (Boston: Little, Brown, 1971); and Edmund Morgan, *American Slavery, American Freedom* (New York: Norton, 1975).

125. For general introductions to this long-running body of work, see Frederick Cooper and Ann Stoler, eds., *Tensions of Empire* (Berkeley: University of California Press, 1997), esp. 1–56; and Frederick Cooper, *Colonialism in Question* (Berkeley: University of California Press, 2005), esp. 33–55. Also helpful is Bill Schwartz's interview with Stuart Hall, "Breaking Bread with History: C. L. R. James and the Black Jacobins," *History Workshop Journal* (1998). By the early 1990s, a major surge of work on the U.S. side was taking shape, as well. See, for example, Pease and Kaplan, *Cultures of United States Imperialism.*

126. On antebellum "free produce" campaigns, see Lawrence Glickman, "'Buy for the Sake of the Slave': Abolitionism and the Origins of American Consumer Activism," *American Quarterly* 57 (December 2004): 889–912. For the origins of the "citizen consumer," see Lizabeth Cohen, *A Consumer's Republic: The Politics of Mass Consumption in Postwar America* (New York: Knopf, 2003). Other recent U.S. studies in this area include Gary Cross, *Kid's Stuff* (Cambridge: Harvard University Press, 1997); and Cross, *An All-Consuming Century* (New York: Columbia University Press, 2000); Strasser, McGovern, and Judt, *Getting and Spending;* Grace Hale, *Making Whiteness* (New York: Pantheon, 1998); Nan Enstad, *Ladies of Labor, Girls of Adventure* (New York: Columbia University Press, 1999); Elizabeth Chin, *Purchasing Power* (Minneapolis: University of Minneapolis Press, 2001); Christina Klein, *Cold War Orientalism: Asia in the Middlebrow Imagination, 1945–1961* (Berkeley: University of California Press, 2003); T. H. Breen, *The Marketplace of Revolution* (New York: Oxford University Press, 2004); and Charles McGovern, *Sold American* (Chapel Hill: University of North Carolina Press, 2006). Key works on the European side include Rosalind Williams, *Dream Worlds* (Berkeley: University of California Press, 1982); Thomas Richards, *The Commodity Culture of Victorian England* (Palo Alto, CA: Stanford University Press, 1990); Roy Porter and John Brewer, eds., *Consumption and the World of Goods* (New York: Routledge, 1993); Anne McClintock, *Imperial Leather* (New York: Routledge, 1995); Victoria De Grazia and Ellen Furlough, eds., *The Sex of Things* (Berkeley: University of California Press, 1996); Erika Rappaport, *Shopping for Pleasure* (Princeton: Princeton University Press, 2000); and Victoria De Grazia, *Irresistible Empire* (Cambridge: Harvard University Press, 2005).

127. On these contrasting histories, see Michael Denning, "The Special American Conditions," *American Quarterly* 38, no. 3 (1986); and Shank, "Continuing Embarrassment of Culture." Also helpful on the U.S. side are the individual histories of American studies programs at Yale, the University of Pennsylvania, the University of Minnesota, and Amherst College (among others) in *American Quarterly* 22, no. 2, pt. 2 (Summer 1970); and Maddox, *Locating American Studies.* On the British side, see Stuart Hall, "Cultural Studies and the Centre: Some Problematics and Problems," in *Culture, Media, Language: Working Papers in Cultural Studies, 1971–1979,* ed. Stuart Hall, Dorothy Hobson, Andrew Lowe, and Paul Willis (London: Unwin Hyman, 1980); Hall, "Cultural Studies: Two Paradigms," in *Culture, Ideology, and Social Process: A Reader,* ed. T. Bennett, G. Martin, C. Mercer, and J. Woollacott (London: Batsford Academic and Educational in association with the Open University Press, 1981); Richard Johnson, "What Is Cultural Stud-

ies Anyway?" *Social Text* 16 (Winter 1986–87): 38–80; and Stuart Hall, "Cultural Studies and Its Theoretical Legacies," in *Cultural Studies,* ed. Larry Grossberg, Cary Nelson, and Paula Treichler (New York: Routledge, 1992). For quotations, see Hall, "Cultural Studies and the Centre," 15–16.

128. Hall, "Cultural Studies and the Centre," 24.

129. Ibid., 20. Much of Hall's language here came from Thompson's *Making of the English Working Class.*

130. In Denning's genealogy (which builds on Trachtenberg's retrospective essay, "Myth and Symbol"), this less celebratory mode would form part of the "critical" American studies tradition that achieved an early "focus" in the work of F. O. Matthiessen. Denning, "Special American Conditions."

131. Denning, "Special American Conditions," 40.

132. Prominent examples include Lears, "Concept of Cultural Hegemony" (1985); George Lipsitz, "The Struggle for Hegemony," *Journal of American History* 75 (June 1988): 144–66; Buhle and Buhle, "New Labor History at the Cultural Crossroads" (1988); and Denning, "End of Mass Culture" (first published in 1990, but written for a 1988 conference).

133. Johnson, " On Agency."

134. Stanley Elkins, *Slavery: A Problem in American Institutional and Intellectual Life* (Chicago: University of Chicago Press, 1959).

135. Eley, *Crooked Line,* 93.

136. For early examples of U.S. historians' reactions to Jones's work, see Frisch and Walkowitz, *Working-Class America.*

137. Walter Johnson, *Soul by Soul: Life Inside the Antebellum Slave Market* (Cambridge: Harvard University Press, 1999), 83–86.

138. Mary Renda, *Taking Haiti: Military Occupation and the Culture of U.S. Imperialism* (Chapel Hill: University of North Carolina Press, 2001); John Stauffer, *The Black Hearts of Men* (Cambridge: Harvard University Press, 2001); Scott Sandage, *Born Losers: A History of Failure* (Cambridge: Harvard University Press, 2005); Sarah E. Igo, *The Averaged American: Surveys, Citizens, and the Making of a Mass Public* (Cambridge: Harvard University Press, 2007). Further evidence of this pattern can be found in many of the most interesting and important U.S. histories from the past few years. See, for example, Leigh Eric Schmidt, *Hearing Things: Religion, Illusion, and the American Enlightenment* (Cambridge: Harvard University Press, 2000); Bruce Dorsey, *Reforming Men and Women: Gender in the Antebellum City* (Ithaca, NY: Cornell University Press, 2002); Klein, *Cold War Orientalism;* Barry Shank, *A Token of My Affection: Greeting Cards and American Business Culture* (New York: Columbia University Press, 2004); Amy Greenberg, *Manifest Manhood and the Antebellum American Empire* (New York: Cambridge University Press, 2005); and David Henkin, *The Postal Age: The Emergence of Modern Communications in Nineteenth-Century America* (Chicago: University of Chicago Press, 2007). A related but somewhat less serious development can be found in the growing numbers of trade titles on unconventional topics describing themselves as "cultural histories." See, for example, Jim Dawson, *Who Cut the Cheese: A Cultural History of the Fart* (Berkeley: Ten Speed Press, 1999); and Andy Lechter, *Shroom: A Cultural History of the Magic Mushroom* (New York: Ecco, 2007).

139. These speculations were ventured by Hollinger, "Practice of History," 588–90.

PART II

Practicing Cultural History

MICHAEL O'MALLEY

These essays originated in "The State of Cultural History: A Conference in Honor of Lawrence Levine" in September 2005. Levine's work always stressed empathy—the capacity to reach a state of understanding that takes one past or outside oneself. In that aspect it helped to launch one of the key historiographical projects that Cook and Glickman make clear in the introduction, namely, cultural history's strong roots in the "new social history" and in the New Left, with a shared concern for neglected subjects and peoples, for the real lives of the less powerful and the subaltern. This line of work, coming to the fore with Levine's generation in the 1960s and 1970s, tended to seek an empathic bond with the past, an experience of understanding that builds a bridge of meaning between the historian, the reader, and the subject.

As Cook and Glickman also show, however, equally strong roots of cultural history grew from the discursive approach introduced by postmodernism and cultural studies in the 1980s. At its most extreme, postmodern theory looked suspiciously on empathy, seeing it as a false, self-serving construct, recapitulating colonial appropriation and the minstrel show. This line of thinking cast suspicion on histories that tried to recover the unmediated voice of others, or to speak for subaltern or neglected groups, tending to see the groups themselves as discursive formulations, as socially constructed, and to see the act of speaking for as a kind of ventriloquism. In the chapters that follow, eight practicing historians navigate this tension in cultural history, between what might be called empathic and discursive approaches.

Of the eight chapters, arranged simply in chronological order, Eric Avila's "Turning Structure into Culture: Reclaiming the Freeway in San Diego's Chicano Park" most clearly reflects the new social history tradi-

tion. Avila details the ways a Chicano community, long shut out of formal politics, mobilized to make its own use of a freeway project forced
on it by local authorities. Avila describes how a self-conscious, historically grounded Chicano identity emerged out of efforts to turn the space
beneath the freeway into a community park; in turn, he demonstrates
the crucial role culture plays in mobilizing communities for political
action. Avila's chapter conveys a strong sense of empathy for a marginal-
ized community; similarly, Ann Fabian's "A Native among the Headhunters" follows the extraordinary career of William Brooks, a Pacific Coast
Chinook made to travel during the Jacksonian era as both an anthropological oddity and a model of Christian missionary success. Fabian's
chapter uses the framework of cultural history to blend genres of history
that usually stand apart. She uses empathy for the complex human story
of William Brooks to build a thickly textured, rich picture of the ways
religion, science, and the market intersected. Elliot Gorn also focuses on
one person to describe how historical fact, commercial representation,
and popular memory came together to create the myth of John Dillinger.
In Gorn's "Re-membering John Dillinger," the famous gangster lives as
both a real man and literally a legend in his own time. Gorn's account of
the Dillinger legend demonstrates another source of cultural history, the
early American studies tradition, fascinated with myth and symbol and
seeking a distinctively American culture or character in the myths built
around the facts of actual lives.

Another historian with strong roots in American studies, John Kasson, extends this approach in "Behind Shirley Temple's Smile." Kasson
follows Temple's career to dramatize how Americans in the 1930s felt
about both childhood and the labor market. While treating Temple as
an exploited laborer, a worker in the culture industry but in every real
sense a worker, he also brings the tools of literary analysis and visual
culture to bear on her films. The result shows clearly how culture encodes
and obscures power relations; desiring Temple to be "genuine" and "real,"
Americans tended to miss the actual nature of the work she did and the
people she did it for. Waldo Martin's "Be Real Black for Me" also considers the problem of authenticity in commercial culture, but from a different angle and with a different set of questions. Martin takes a single song
recorded by Donny Hathaway and Roberta Flack and, by building its multiple social, aesthetic, and political contexts, suggests the issues at stake
in the creation of an "authentic" black identity during the late 1960s and
1970s. Martin explores the meaning of "authentic" in the age of cultural
history—"authentic" is a constructed identity, yet African Americans have

always maintained a specific set of traditions and practices—not set in stone or formalized in law, but articulated in a dialogue with commerce and culture.

Money, race, authenticity, and the market are at play in "The Envelope, Please," from Shane White, Stephen Garton, Stephen Robertson, and Graham White. Their chapter concerns a subject cultural historians have long been fascinated by, the confidence man. The authors turn their attention to Harlem of the 1920s, and to confidence games African Americans ran on each other and on others. Drawing on an extraordinary and to this point untapped trove of material, the local district attorney's closed case files in the New York City Municipal Archives, they show confidence men, to paraphrase Clifford Geertz, "telling us stories about ourselves." "Black confidence tricksters" they write, "were particularly adept at sensing the fault lines in the society and in an individual's makeup." Their strategies and ploys, even as glimpsed here filtered through the imperatives and documents of law enforcement, are at least as rich and evocative as the poems, novels, and paintings of the Harlem Renaissance. By bringing to bear on criminal proceedings some of the techniques historians of culture developed to treat literary works, White, Garton, Robertson, and White demonstrate the broad empirical and interpretive range of the best cultural history.

My own chapter, "Rags, Blacking, and Paper Soldiers," along with Elaine Tyler May's—probably the most thoroughly discursive of the chapters in this section—looks at the issue of authenticity but without a clear human subject. My subject is instead the anxieties and contradictions American felt about greenback dollars and African American soldiers during the Civil War, and the ways they adopted essentialist theories of both race and money to ease those anxieties. It treats "race' and "money" as parallel systems of rhetoric, parallel ways of looking at the world. Elaine May similarly takes a broad view: her subject in "Gimme Shelter: Do-It-Yourself Defense and the Politics of Fear" is the culture of political fear and its role in shaping the explosive growth of the suburbs in the 1950s. Historians have long noted the growth of the suburbs and their segregated character; May takes a unique view in linking that racism to the cold war culture of anticommunism and nuclear anxiety. Like my own essay, it takes apparently dissimilar debates about communism, nuclear weapons, and racial integration and treats them as crucial to understanding our present political state.

Although there may be a tension in cultural history between empathic and discursive approaches, none of these essays stands at an extreme.

Both May and I want to connect the discourses of fear, race, and money to present-day political effects on actual people, particularly on those cast as subaltern by racist traditions. And neither Avila nor Martin, with an interest in the traditions and customs of specific communities, imagines his subjects as unmediated or "unconstructed." None of these chapters is either so purely discursive as to lose sight of the historical actors it describes, or so purely tied to the authenticity of the subject that it speaks without awareness of that subject's historical construction. While the tension between the empathic and the discursive continues, tension is productive, not destructive, and it needs no resolution. The essays collected in this section share a concern with the politics of the present, and a concern with the ways power works on ordinary people—which has always been the hallmark of the best work in any genre of history.

TWO

A Native among the Headhunters

ANN FABIAN

574. Indian of the CALAPOOYAH tribe of Oregon: artificially compressed.
Man, aetat. 50. F.A. 68°. I.C. 91.

*Catalogue of Human Crania in the Collection of the Academy of Natural Sciences
of Philadelphia*

December 1838

It was a chilly December day, but Philadelphia's naturalists were excited.
Especially, the city's skull collectors. A man with a flat head was in town.
Jason Lee (1803–1845), a Methodist minister who had been working
out in Oregon, had come East with a young Chinook man, a Christian
convert with a remarkable artificially flattened skull. Word went around
the scientific community that Lee and his flat-headed student, William
Brooks, would entertain visitors while they were staying with Dr. William
Blanding (1773–1857), a man still remembered for his work on American turtles. Brooks was personable, spoke English well, and didn't mind
being quizzed about his head or poked and measured.

By December, Brooks was used to dealing with Americans who were
curious about his skull. All that fall, Brooks and Lee had been preaching
to Methodist congregations up and down the East Coast, trying to raise
money for the small American settlement in Oregon's Willamette Valley.
Brooks must have remembered a time when the children he knew who
had been nursed by good mothers all had skulls like his—pushed flat on
top by cradleboards. But now he was with people who liked their heads
round. Crowds turned out to hear Lee describe his work at the mission

and to listen to Brooks talk about his Christian faith, yet many admitted they were simply curious and wanted to get a look at Brooks's head. They wondered if the man was as strange as his skull.

Philadelphia's curiosity was a special case. In that city, curiosity was "never prurient and aimless," a resident said. Informed curiosity was one piece of the enlightened intellectual culture that characterized Philadelphia, a city that many of America's best-known students of nature called home. Their cultivated curiosity distinguished Philadelphians from their sensation-hungry neighbors. By the late 1830s, New York was the country's financial capital, and Boston its literary center. But Philadelphia boasted America's best doctors and its leading scientific and medical societies, legacies of a Quaker tradition that discouraged ambitious Philadelphians from careers as lawyers and ministers. In Philadelphia, young men studied medicine instead, and some went on to become amateur naturalists. They created scientific societies, where they got together to compare notes on fossils and turtles, on strange weather and visiting Indians. These scientific men were interested in meeting William Brooks.[1]

Philadelphia was an orderly city, and some early nineteenth-century visitors liked it better than New York. Philadelphia's streets ran up from the river, "straight as a string," one man said, and they were lined with neat brick houses. Some people thought the grid was tiresome, but straight streets made it easy for visitors like Lee and Brooks to get around. Philadelphia seemed clean, since there weren't any pigs snuffling through garbage on the main streets. Men washed the streets with water piped up from the Schuylkill River. In the winter, city sweepers were out as soon as the snow stopped, and streets buzzed with life even on cold December days. Bundled against a bitter chill, caught up in the throng of pedestrians, Brooks and Lee made their way along the snowy streets and into a hothouse of American scientific curiosity.[2]

Herpetologist Blanding invited friends over to meet the young man: a genial Scottish phrenologist George Combe (1788–1858; fig. 2.1), an ornithologist John Kirk Townsend (1809–1851; fig. 2.2), a retired Indian agent and collector of Indian portraits Col. Thomas L. McKenney (1785–1859), and the craniologist Samuel George Morton (1799–1851; fig. 2.3), who was just then finishing up his big book of American skulls, Crania Americana: or, A Comparative View of the Skulls of Various Aboriginal Nations of North and South America, the volume that many consider the cornerstone of the intellectual enterprise known as scientific racism.

It must have been a strange meeting all around. A young native man in a big city, hustled into a stuffy drawing room, surrounded by six white

Samuel George Morton

Fig. 2.1. George Combe (1788–1858).
Print Collection, Miriam and Ira D. Wallach
Division of Art, Prints and Photographs, The
New York Public Library, Astor, Lenox and
Tilden Foundations.

Fig. 2.2. John Kirk Townsend (1809–1851).
Oregon Historical Society, image no. OrHi 648.

Fig. 2.3. Samuel George Morton
(1799–1851). Emmet Collection,
Miriam and Ira D. Wallach Divi-
sion of Art, Prints and Photographs,
The New York Public Library, Astor,
Lenox and Tilden Foundations.

men in white shirts, black silk ties, and black coats. They exchanged glances. This had all happened before; hundreds of native visitors had been ushered through meetings with curious white men. But this meeting bristled with a new curiosity about skulls. These were the high-water years for American interest in phrenology, and they were also the years when a small group began to work out the idea that differences among the races of men could be set down as differences in the shapes and sizes of skulls. The skull, like the gene today, promised to be the bottom line of difference. The white men in the group—the missionary, the craniologist, the phrenologist, and the collector of portraits—were thinking about race and skulls. And they were thinking about themselves as a new kind of American community; they were coming to see themselves as professional men of science who shared an understanding about how to go about discovering the laws and principles of nature.[3]

Did Brooks notice that he was surrounded by a distinctly "high-browed" group of men? The artists who painted these men's portraits or took their photographs knew that the light that glinted off their foreheads (or maybe it was the deep parts of receding hairlines) made the men appear intelligent to contemporaries, many of whom had at least a passing knowledge of phrenology. A phrenologist's map located all the intellectual features right there at the front of the brain.[4] When they looked at Brooks, the white men must have felt especially intelligent, comparing their high-browed selves to this young and definitely "low-browed" Indian.

Each of these men needed Brooks. Jason Lee (fig. 2.4) needed him to help prove to Methodist elders that despite the terrible epidemics that were killing native peoples in Oregon faster than they could be brought to Christ, there were still souls enough to make efforts at conversion worth the cost. Brooks's displays of piety could also help Lee quiet rumors spreading among some East Coast Methodists that he was out in Oregon for worldly profits. Lee needed Brooks's soul; the others wanted his head. Skull collectors, like Combe and Morton, and even the ornithologist Townsend, bargained hard when they saw a chance to get a distorted skull, objects particularly prized by gentlemen collectors. Skulls that had been altered by human hands stood out in cabinets of curiosities; they were interesting, easy to distinguish among a mass of dead heads. They were true curiosities, suspended neatly between nature and art, body parts and works of art.

When Morton met Brooks, he had been collecting skulls for almost a decade, but he wanted more skulls that had been intentionally deformed. When he sent out materials promoting *Crania Americana*, he promised

Fig. 2.4. Jason Lee (1803–1845).
Oregon Historical Society, image no. OrHi 8342.

subscribers especially detailed descriptions of the "extraordinary distortions of the skull, caused by mechanical contrivances." "In fact, the author's materials in this department are probably more complete than those in the possession of any other person; and will enable him to satisfy the reader on a point that has long been a subject of doubt and controversy."[5]

The points of doubt were actually many. How malleable were infant skulls? How much could a mother shape the head of a child? What if skulls were man-made (or woman-made) things? If skulls could be molded by mothers and midwives, how sure could he be that skull shape registered natural differences among men? Some of Morton's critics argued that the "characteristic diversities" of skulls were the "mere result of artificial causes originating in long perpetuated customs and nursery usages." The shape of a skull, in other words, was a product of culture, not nature. If this were the case, the craniologist's faith in the skull as the clear and certain marker of racial difference might just be misplaced. Morton needed to find the traces of the natural shape preserved in a distorted skull like that of William Brooks.[6]

Phrenologists, like Combe, had their own issues to settle. He wanted to believe that people who flattened the skulls of infants were actually instinctive phrenologists, manipulating baby heads to cultivate faculties they wanted to see develop in adults. He would never know for sure until he could get hold of a flattened skull, preferably one with a fresh brain.

For cultural historians, Brooks's story offers a prize of a different sort. Most histories of scientific racism that focus on the skull work of those in Morton's circle examine conversations among learned white men. These aspiring American scientists discussed the shortcomings of others but gave little thought to the human lives behind the objects they studied.

Brooks's presence complicates this picture. Brooks gives a life and face to a skull and invites us to consider the long chains of historical accidents that brought a man so close to becoming a specimen. We also have a trace of Brooks's ideas. Methodists and naturalists wrote about their meetings with the unusual young man and recorded some of his criticisms of the white world. Brooks's recovered voice, however distorted by translation, provides a treasure for our own postcolonial cabinets of curiosities.[7]

William Brooks, the Flathead Indian

After meeting him at Dr. Blanding's house, Col. Thomas L. McKenney invited Brooks to sit for a portrait. This likeness of Brooks appears in the second of McKenney's three-volume *History of the Indian Tribes of North*

Fig. 2.5. Stumanu/William Brooks.
Smithsonian Institution Libraries,
Washington, D.C.

America. In the lithograph taken from the portrait, Brooks looks every bit the native man from the West, with his flattened head and his shoulders wrapped in a beautiful Chilkat blanket. McKenney called him "Stum-a-nu. A flat head boy," thinking that identity preferable in a book of Indian portraits to "William Brooks, a Christian Man."

Title and blanket hint that the picture is not entirely honest. McKenney and his colleague Judge James Hall wanted to publish a collection of portraits of native people still in touch with lives unchanged by contact with Europeans or Americans. Certainly they deceived themselves, pretending that a man like Brooks traveling to the Atlantic seaboard would arrive uncontaminated by white influences, but they celebrated whatever authentic elements they could find, publishing portraits of men and women painted up and dressed in native garments. Many of their sitters were leaders on diplomatic missions to Washington, D.C., and they are elegant in their portraits.

Brooks is less formal. He was an ordinary young man, not an important tribal leader. To make him look more eye-catching, McKenney and his artist (scholars aren't sure who painted the picture) dressed the young in a striking Tlingit blanket. Brooks's costume had nothing to do his Chinook people. The blanket had come from southeastern Alaska. Tribesmen, European traders, and American collectors prized these blankets; they were the kinds of things that belonged to wealthy chiefs, certainly not the wearing apparel for young Chinook orphans growing up on the banks of the Columbia River. Lee probably brought the blanket east with him from Oregon, figuring it would be a good prop for his fund-raising sermons, since it was an object that virtually shouted its exotic origins in the Far West. One Methodist congregant recalled Lee exhibiting "a curiously wrought blanket" that "was spun and wove in an ingenious manner, very thick and covered with hieroglyphs."[8]

McKenney also recorded a version of Brooks's life. Brooks, who had grown comfortable in English during his two or three years among the missionaries, told McKenney that his father had died when he was two and that an uncle had raised him, his younger brother, and his sister. The uncle taught him to fish and to steer a canoe. Although his people had been dealing with Europeans and Americans for a generation or more, Brooks recalled for McKenney a world in which the patterns of traditional life—babies strapped to cradleboards, young men fishing for smelt and salmon and trading the surplus for horses and weapons with people who lived farther inland—still prevailed. Perhaps to match his smiling portrait, Brooks spun a tale of Chinook life in the 1820s that was connected to the white world but not yet ravaged by rum or by the epidemic diseases that would forever alter his world.[9]

The balance was delicate, and the boy's life changed when his uncle died in an epidemic of "intermittent fever" that devastated the villages along the Columbia River in the early 1830s. Demographers believe that the disease (probably a strain of malaria particularly deadly to the native peoples) cut the population of Chinookan and Kalapuyan people by a staggering 88 percent. Lewis and Clark estimated the population at around 15,000 in 1805. By 1841, barely 2,000 people were left alive. Biological destruction pulled the culture down with it. The orphaned children sought shelter with whites, turning first to Dr. John McLoughlin, chief factor of the Hudson Bay Company, the most powerful white man in the region and an unhappy witness to the fever's "dreadful havoc" on native families.[10]

It was McLoughlin who sent the children on to Jason Lee's recently established Methodist mission and school on the Willamette River, a project McLoughlin supported. Lee was a dedicated Methodist and, as an acquaintance wrote, "a tall and powerful man, who looks as though he were well calculated to buffet difficulties in a wild country." But Lee had a hard time balancing the earthly needs of settling the wild country with the spiritual expectations of a Methodist mission board in New York. Pious New Yorkers worried that Lee's work was more about settling Oregon for this world than sending converts to the next. His mission was too secular, they feared, and Oregon's population too sparse to justify the expense.[11]

Telling Brooks's story, McKenney noted that the native children were particularly valuable members of the struggling mission settlement, since farmhands and Indian souls were equally scarce in this recently devastated, thinly settled country. "The special providence of God has, already, seemed to throw upon our care three poor Flathead orphans; one, a lad of fourteen or fifteen years of age, who is quite serviceable in several ways," the mission teacher reported to eastern readers in 1835. "These children came to us almost naked, in a very filthy state, and covered with vermin. . . . J. Lee cleansed them from their vermin, so that they do not now appear like the same children they were when they first came."[12]

Lee assigned the children tasks to help assure their material and spiritual well-being, and Stumanu "quickly showed a great fondness, as well as an aptitude, for learning, was industrious and useful on the farm, and won esteem by the most amiable qualities of temper." According to McKenney, he also possessed "what was remarkable in an Indian, a decidedly mechanical genius, and excelled in the construction of tools and implements, and in the imitation of any simple articles of furniture that came under his notice, so that the mission family were fully repaid for the expense of his education and subsistence by his labour." Stumanu received food and clothing in exchange for his labor and earned a new name when Jason Lee baptized him in memory of a Massachusetts clergyman. In the same way, Stumanu's sister Kye-a-tah became "Lucy Hedding." These given names made them part of the "Christian family," although they erased the children's immediate family ties and perhaps their ancestral associations as well.[13]

These children were remarkable if only because they survived and stayed healthy enough to contribute to the mission enterprise. The missionaries kept a sort of "grim ledger" of disease and defection that lists the many children who died or ran away before they had earned enough to pay the costs of even a simple coffin. Fifty-two pupils showed up during the school's first four years; at least eight of them died, and others ran away or were taken away by their parents. Stumanu and his siblings had nowhere else to go.[14]

These were children who lived between worlds, straddling identities that must have pulled hard in different directions. Although the missionaries baptized the children and gave them new names, forbade them to speak their native language, and taught them to read and spell in English, to sing Methodist hymns, and to plow and plant, they nevertheless admitted advantages in having the children retain some of their native skills. Lee set out to produce a generation of native farmers, but one of his colleagues was pleased by a boy who spent "the forenoon in hunting (by which we are supplied with some animal food every day) and the afternoon in learning to read." Closer to Lee's project, to raise money in the East, the missionary needed "William Brooks" still to appear to be "Stumanu," both Christian convert and flat-headed "savage."

William Brooks lived and worked at the mission school for about two years between 1836 and 1838. His sister did not do as well. Missionaries reported that the girl died of scrofula (a vague description of any number of diseases, including tuberculosis, whose symptoms included swollen lymph glands) in October 1837, when she was about fourteen. "We took her to Vancouver for the benefit of medical advice," wrote one missionary. "She tarried a few weeks, but was discontented and homesick. She arrived on Friday and died on the following Thursday."[15]

After his sister's death, William's life changed again when the Reverend Lee took him along on a fund-raising tour in the East. *"Duty,"* Lee wrote in his journal, "required me to leave *home* and *wife* and *friends* and retrace my steps to the land of civilization." He headed east, hoping to recruit "a mission steward or business agent, two carpenters, a cabinetmaker, a blacksmith, and two farmers." Some say he also needed to persuade the faithful that the mission was a spiritual enterprise and not only the spearhead of American secular settlement in the Oregon territory. Of course, it is hard in retrospect to separate the two; as most native people had learned, secular settlement often followed close on the heels of missionary work.[16]

Most reports describe Lee as a man dedicated, in some sense, to the welfare of the native peoples he imagined he served. Lee sometimes advocated for intermarriage that would keep Indian blood running in the veins of all Oregonians. But Lee's financial backers insisted on more tangible evidence of the mission's effectiveness in bringing native souls into the Christian fold, so Lee brought east "two Indian boys—Wm. Brooks (a Chinook) and Thomas Adams," as well as the three mixed-race sons of a Hudson Bay Company employee, William McKay.[17]

Lee and the five boys set out from the mission in the spring, leaving behind Lee's pregnant wife, a white woman he had married somewhat dutifully eight months earlier. She died in childbirth as the little group headed east. The sad news reached Lee while the party was resting at a Methodist mission among the Shawnee on the Missouri frontier. Lee paused to mourn the passing of his wife and newborn son, but a journal he kept during those weeks hints at the trip's pleasures. Lee boasted that he and Brooks each brought down a buffalo. Lee killed his with his third shot. "Wm. also killed one," he wrote. "We thought we did very well, as there were but seven buffaloe, and so many old hunters, considering this was our first trial."[18]

Lee soldiered on east and dropped McKay's boys at their appointed schools (two of them at his alma mater, Wilbraham Academy in Massachusetts). He kept Brooks and Adams with him to help him raise money—the three of them representing Methodist success in the mixed-race mission out West. The two Indian men attracted large crowds as Lee sermonized up and down the eastern seaboard in the winter of 1838–39. Many of these easterners would have been accustomed to seeing visiting delegations of Native Americans. Some prominent native spokesmen discussed the politics and culture of white America with visitors who stopped by their hotel rooms. But again these were often chiefs, diplomats, and defeated warriors. Brooks and Adams were different; they were ordinary young men, remarkable mostly for their flattened heads. Lee quickly learned that there was money to be made for his settlement at just those points where the sermon shaded into a show of curiosities, where piety mixed with popular entertainment. Congregants liked seeing Adams and Brooks.[19]

The Methodists also worked them hard. Lee remembered Brooks addressing large audiences, night after night, and then staying around to answer their "innumerable questions." Sleep gave him some relief, but it was "a small portion of the time, for the good friends where we lodged seemed often to forget that we needed rest, or at least they seldom thought of it till twelve or one o'clock, even when we had to start at four or five in the morning."[20]

On the exhausting trip, Brooks seems to have grown confident expressing criticisms of white civilization and deft at avoiding the objectification
of both skull hunters and Methodist congregants. Skull-collector Morton
complimented his accent and his grammar, and the young man pleased
other potential supporters with his good table manners, apparent piety,
and striking speeches. Lee recalled, "Seldom did he arise to address a
congregation without bringing forward something new and striking that
he had not mentioned in any previous address; so that, contrary to what
might be expected, his daily communications, instead of becoming stale
and tiresome to me, by their tame monotony, were always interesting,
and sometimes delightful, pathetic, and thrilling, even beyond anything
I had dared to hope from him."[21]

It is hard to know what Brooks thought of Lee's addresses, because
our sense of him comes with so many layers of Methodist mediation. Lee
gave Brooks a pulpit, because he was an effective fundraiser, but Brooks
took advantage of his time in the pulpit to needle his hosts for hypocrisy.
Perhaps he tried to break the stale monotony of some of his patron's sermons by incorporating into his own speeches observations on the people and things that impressed or amused him on their tour of the East.
Accounts mention Brooks's skill with his audiences and suggest that he
liked expressing his opinions.

Methodist publications describe him addressing audiences in his native
language and then in English. On December 31, 1838, Brooks made his
first speech in English. Lee later admitted that he "of course, expected a
failure. But I was agreeably disappointed." One observer noted, "His tears
spoke with resistless eloquence." Brooks also made audiences laugh, or
as Lee put it, "excited the risibles." He "spoke with much feeling" about
the death of Mrs. Lee, his teacher, to a congregation in Connecticut and
so aroused the sympathies of an audience in Massachusetts that workers
from a shoe factory presented him with a new pair of boots. At each stop,
he moved audiences to open their purses, and Lee kept a running tally
of the contributions. One contemporary figured that Lee and the young
converts secured for the mission the sizeable sum of $40,000 (close to a
million dollars in today's money, if we can trust the accounts), along with
the tools they needed to construct a gristmill and a sawmill.[22]

Early in 1839, three or four months after Lee and Brooks had arrived
in the East, Methodist journals reported that the young man had begun
to wonder aloud "at the wickedness he saw." In his "somewhat ambiguous
English," he chastised those who saw the mission in Oregon as only the
beachhead of a secular settlement. Brooks was proof that good Christian

work was going on out in Oregon, and his presence helped quiet some of Lee's critics, who suspected him of just such worldly ambition. Brooks also made observations of his own. He was particularly struck by a blind man he met in Baltimore. "He's colored man—he belongs to our Church. He can't read, he can't see nothing, but he sees Jesus Christ. Children, you say that old blind man, colored man, miserable—but he be very happy. O, I love that old man, because he love Jesus Christ."[23]

Brooks denounced the white men who sold rum to Indians. Rum sellers carried death over the Rockies. "White men settled there about twenty-five years ago. Indians great many years ago never died very fast. But since settlement white men, they have died every hour. They give them rum—everything that is bad. I tell you one thing I want you to put down on paper, that *I don't want any wild Yankee there.*"[24]

And he didn't much like the "rude and wicked" children who insulted him, staring and laughing as he walked by. With some saucy questioners, however, he apparently joked about his flattened head. Several Methodist chroniclers recorded the story of a woman who asked Brooks about his skull, "rallying him somewhat on the curiosity of the fashion. William replied, 'All people have his fashion. The Chinese make little his foot. Indian make flat his head. You,' looking at her waist and putting his hand to his, 'make small here.' She at once decided if his head was flat, his wit was sharp." Or so the story goes.[25]

The little anecdote leads back to Philadelphia in the winter of 1838, to the new things that Brooks would have encountered during his visit, and to subjects that would have been on the minds of Americans. As he walked the streets, Brooks noticed women's waists cinched by whalebone corsets, but there was only one place he would have seen the bound feet of a wealthy Chinese woman, even if he had run into Chinese sailors from time to time back in Oregon. On Christmas Eve 1838, just about the time Lee and Brooks arrived in the city, China merchant Nathan Dunn opened his collection of "Ten Thousand Chinese Things" on the ground floor of Peale's Philadelphia Museum. I have not been able to prove that Brooks was among the 8,000 visitors who walked through Dunn's great lacquered gate and into "China in miniature" during the exhibit's first week. But whether Brooks saw it or not, the exhibition was the talk of all Philadelphia during the winter of 1838–39.

Phrenologist Combe did go to the exhibit and reported that "a survey of this museum approaches closely to a visit to China." The collection included dozens of dioramas, life-size clay figures posed in lifelike scenes meant to capture everyday life in China. Merchants, mandarins, literati, beggars, boat women, barbers, blacksmiths, jugglers, and shoe-makers performed their ordinary tasks. There were three hundred cases filled with Chinese things: lacquered boxes, printed books, porcelain tea-cups, cushions, vases, hats, candles, shells, birds, fish, a thirteen-foot boa constrictor, and hundreds of paintings—portraits and landscapes. One exhibit would have particularly interested visitors curious about manipu-lated bodies. Dunn displayed "the bandaging of the feet"; "golden lilies," he said they were called. "Civilized" Philadelphians perhaps shuddered, but Dunn did not judge. "This is, no doubt, an absurd, cruel and wicked practice; but those who dwell in glass houses should not throw stones." Bound feet marked rank in China, "just as small and white hands are with us deemed proof of gentility."[26]

Dunn's collection gave Philadelphians a glimpse of the world behind the China trade that was making a handful of their neighbors very rich. New wealth pricked local curiosity. The opium trade was making some men very wealthy. But Nathan Dunn made his fortune in China with-out trafficking in narcotics. The exhibit expressed his appreciation for the beauty of China's material culture and the skill of Chinese manufacture. When the excitement around the Philadelphia show faded, Dunn packed the collection off to London, where it drew crowds whose interest in China was sparked by the start of the Opium Wars.[27]

Brooks's comment about bound feet suggests that he might have drawn slightly different lessons from the show. During the 1830s, many Americans, including the naturalists who came out to meet Brooks, were trying to figure just who they were by exploring who they were not. Com-parison could take the form of vicious racism. But sometimes curiosity and comparison spawned a gentler cultural relativism. By needling his audiences about their cinched waists, Brooks tried to tease Americans in this direction. "All people have his fashion," as Brooks put it. Bound feet actually damaged women's health less than tight stays, Dunn wrote. Brooks knew that his distorted skull had not damaged his health or that of his kinsmen. And he may have recalled that, like bound feet, it served to distinguish him as superior to the round-headed captives, servants, or slaves living among his flat-headed people.

Abstracting the Skull

In December 1838, the odyssey Brooks had begun among the Oregon Methodists crossed into the territory of the Philadelphia naturalists. Brooks's wit seemed sharp to Morton too, and he thought Brooks had "more mental acuteness than any Indian I had seen." The craniologist also reported that Brooks was "communicative, cheerful, and well mannered." To look at Brooks, Morton said, one would notice his "marked Indian features, a broad face, high cheek bones, large mouth, tumid lips, a large nose, depressed at the nostrils, considerable width between the eyes, which, however, were not obliquely placed, a short stature and a robust person."[28]

Brooks "cheerfully consented" to let the good doctor measure his head. Morton recorded a longitudinal diameter of 7.5 inches, parietal diameter of 6.9 inches, frontal diameter of 6.1 inches, breadth between the cheek bones of 6.1 inches, and a facial angle of about 7.3 degrees, although he could not guess at the skull's capacity. If this patient man knew that Morton coveted his skull, if he thought for a moment that he had wandered unwittingly into a land of headhunters, he did not let on. But Morton let slip that "what most delighted me in this young man, was the fact that his head was as much distorted by mechanical compression as any skull of his tribe in my possession, and presented the very counterpart" to the skull from the Northwest Calapooyah tribe pictured in his book (fig. 2.6).[29]

Morton had purchased the Calapooyah skull he imagined as Brooks's counterpart from John Kirk Townsend, the ornithologist who was part of the group at Dr. Blanding's house. Morton reported that Townsend "knew this young man . . . in his own country, and they recognized each other when they met in Philadelphia." But given Townsend's account of his skull-collecting adventures in the West, the meeting may have been awkward for both men.[30]

Townsend came from a good Quaker family with a long-standing interest in science and medicine. He and his brothers were all trained to be dentists, but Townsend is best remembered today as an ornithologist who labored unhappily in the shadow of the great John James Audubon. Townsend said he sold ninety-three preserved birds to Audubon but complained that America's more famous birdman did not give him the credit he deserved. Townsend thought of publishing his own book on American ornithology, but after a brief stint stuffing birds for $3.00 a day at the National Institute (the Smithsonian's precursor), he went back to taking care of teeth.[31]

In spring 1834, when he headed off on his great adventure in the American West, he was young and enthusiastic and not yet twenty-five years old. He took a steamboat from Pittsburgh out to St. Louis and joined an expedition organized by Boston ice merchant Nathaniel J. Wyeth, who

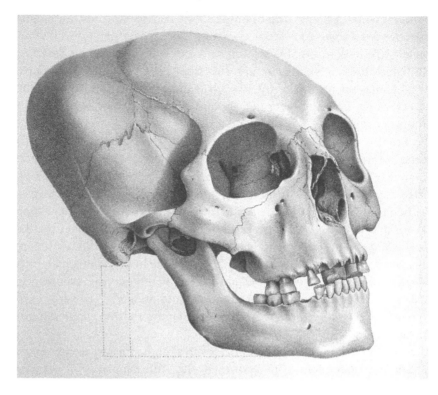

Fig. 2.6. Calapooyah skull.

planned to set up a fur-trading operation on the Pacific coast. Townsend made his way west on foot, walking slowly, looking at the countryside, and collecting specimens. Here was his chance to leave his name in the annals of science. If he were lucky, he could christen a new species, although he found that the continent's remaining naming opportunities were limited to rodents and a few birds. He took the opportunities that came his way and named a shrew mole, a meadow mouse, a marmot, a ground squirrel, a great-eared bat, a hare, a gopher, a thrush, a sandpiper, a cormorant, and a warbler after himself. He "honored," as he put it, a species of water ouzel "with the name of my excellent friend Doctor Samuel George Morton, of Philadelphia."[32]

Seeing Townsend again, Brooks may have remembered that in Oregon the ornithologist had been nearly as avid a collector of skulls as he had been a student of birds, reptiles, and rodents. Townsend penned for eastern readers an often-reprinted description of the cradleboards used to flatten infant skulls. He also recognized that skull gathering could be more than an intellectual enterprise. Townsend boasted to Morton that he was so determined to keep his promise to bring back some skulls to Philadelphia that he risked his life to rob an Indian burial place in Oregon, sneaking off with a reeking pack of human remains.[33]

Townsend's reports, set down in his *Narrative of a Journey across the Rocky Mountains*, provide some good details on the work of skull collectors. He found the people of the Columbia River region "shrewd and observant," as did most European and American visitors, and he concluded that skull flattening did not harm the intellect. He described how mothers carried infants in a "sort of cradle . . . formed by excavating a pine log to the depth of eight or ten inches." They lined the cradles with "a bed of little grass mats" and placed a child in it, but then they tied a "little boss of tightly plaited and woven grass . . . to the forehead, and secured [it] by a cord to the loops at the side. The infant is thus suffered to remain from four to eight months, or until the sutures of the skull have in some measure united, and the bone become solid and firm. It is seldom or never taken from the cradle, except in case of severe illness, until the flattening process is completed."[34]

A skull properly flattened, Townsend observed, remained the mark of a child well raised. And with that thought in mind, he may have noted that William Brooks's flattened head registered his mother's plans for her child's good future among his own people. His flattened head leaves evidence that she believed in the rightness of her people's customs, culture, and rituals. Even as the world along the Columbia was changing, she flattened her babies' heads to make them her own, to make them members of her tribe. Grown-up tribal leaders had flattened skulls; captives and slaves—individuals taken from other tribes—did not, their unflattened heads marking them permanently as outsiders, inferiors in these strongly hierarchical societies. As one midcentury observer noted, "The Flathead tribes are in the constant habit of making slaves of the Roundheaded Indians; but no slave is allowed to flatten or otherwise modify the form of her child's head, that being the badge of Flathead aristocracy."[35]

Still, Townsend found skull flatteners somewhat less than human. He admitted he was frightened and disgusted by a young child recently removed from a cradleboard—a child that remains an "it" in his account: "Although I felt a kind of chill creep over me from the contemplation of such dire deformity, yet there was something so stark-staring, and absolutely queer in the physiognomy, that I could not repress a smile; and when the mother amused the little object and made it laugh, it looked so irresistibly, so terribly ludicrous, that I and those who were with me, burst into a simultaneous roar, which frightened it and made it cry, in which predicament it looked much less horrible than it had before."[36]

Such a strange practice piqued the skull hunter's curiosity, and Townsend was among the collectors who benefited, indirectly, from the diseases that decimated the people of the Northwest Coast in the early 1830s. He explained to Morton that it was "rather a perilous business to procure indian sculls in this country. The natives are so jealous of you that they watch you very closely while you are wandering near their mausoleums & instant & sanguinary vengeance would fall upon the luckless [k]night who should presume to interfere with their sacred relics." "Great secrecy is observed in all their burial ceremonies, partly from fear of Europeans," an English traveler commented.[37]

History, meanwhile, appeared to be on the side of skull collectors. "I have succeeded in hooking one," Townsend continued, "& no doubt in the course of the winter, I shall get more. There is an epidemic raging among them which carries them off so fast that the cemeteries will soon lack watches. I don't rejoice in the prospect of the death of the poor creatures certainly, but then you know it will be very convenient for my purposes."[38]

Townsend encountered a people so devastated by disease that the living could no longer bury the dead, let alone keep watch over corpses and newly buried bodies. What he saw was a culture pushed to its limits. It would survive for a time in Stumanu's flattened head, but the lice-covered children were left orphans of a devastated world. Depopulation along the Columbia "has been truly fearful," he wrote. Witnesses to the effects of "intermittent fever" told him of devastated villages. One man remembered counting "no less than sixteen dead, men and women, lying unburied and festering in the sun in front of their habitations." And he added a horrifying description: "Within the houses all were sick; not one had escaped the contagion; upwards of a hundred individuals, men, women, and children, were writhing in agony on the floors of the houses, with no one to render them any assistance. Some were in the dying struggle, and clenching with convulsive grasp of death their disease-worn companion, shrieked and howled in the last sharp agony." The scenes Townsend described were etched in Brooks's mind as childhood memories.[39]

Escalating death rates strained traditional ways, making it difficult for people, even those skilled at adapting to new ways, to follow customary mourning and burial practices. Townsend recognized that proper disposition of the dead helped to anchor a people in place and in time. He knew that conquest (and conversion to Christianity) destroyed these spatial and temporal connections. Skull hunters had their own small parts to play in this drama of destruction. Brooks's reshaped head may have been an expression of his mother's faith in the future; Brooks's proper care for his mother's dead body would have helped carry his people's past into that future. But events in Brooks's life in the troubled 1830s destroyed connections with the past as surely as they demolished the roads to the future his mother may have imagined for her children.

Townsend left us descriptions of the skull collector's part in the dramas of this changing world. He recorded the risks collectors ran as they encountered resistance from people determined to defend customary ways. "I have been very anxious to procure the skulls of some of these Indians," Townsend wrote in his narrative, "and should have been willing so far as I alone was concerned, to encounter some risk to effect my object, but I have refrained on account of the difficulty in which the ship and crew would be involved, if the sacrilege should be discovered; a prejudice might thus be excited against our little colony which would not soon be overcome, and might prove a serious injury."[40]

Although disease was an ally, Townsend liked to imagine himself a brave collector, particularly as native peoples stepped up their efforts to protect corpses from scientific collectors. They hid bodies or watched over them more carefully. As challenges mounted, the collector's relish grew. Townsend described in detail one particular adventure on February 3, 1836. "During a visit to Fort William, last week, I saw, as I wandered through the forest . . . a canoe, deposited, as is usual, in the branches of a tree, some fourteen feet from the ground. Knowing that it contained the body of an Indian, I ascended to it for the purpose of abstracting the skull." Instead of a dried skeleton, Townsend found "a perfect, embalmed body of a young female, in a state of preservation equal to any which I had seen from the catacombs of Thebes." He was determined to have this mummy and returned that night, "at the witching hour of twelve"—a particularly nice touch in this account of a "scientific" grave robber—armed with a rope. He lowered the body to the ground and carried it off to his waiting canoe. "On arriving at the fort," he continued, "I deposited my prize in the store house, and sewed around it a large Indian mat, to give it the appearance of a bale of guns."[41]

This is not the end of the story. He needed to get the body to Vancouver so he could ship it east. He knew the Indians he had hired to paddle his canoe would not be happy to have the body as cargo, and so he asked the commander of the fort to stow it "under the hatches of a little schooner, which was running twice a week between the two forts." The commander did not oblige. Instead, he sent Townsend a note, explaining that "the brother of the deceased" had come to the fort to complain that his sister's grave had been disturbed. He "had been in the habit of visiting the tomb of his sister every year. He had now come for that purpose . . . and his keen eye had detected the intrusion of a stranger on the spot hallowed to him by many successive pilgrimages. The canoe of his sister was tenantless, and he knew the spoiler to have been a white man, by the tracks upon the beach, which did not incline inward like those of an Indian."[42]

The commander preferred not to risk the wrath of locals and returned the body to the mourning man along "with a present of several blankets, to prevent the circumstance from operating upon his mind to the prejudice of the white people. The grieving Indian took the body of his sister upon his shoulders, and as he walked away, grief got the better of his stoicism, and the sound of his weeping was heard long after he had entered the forest."[43] The weeping man cuts a fine sentimental figure in Townsend's account, but such tender moments did not deter his grave robbing nor cut into his notions that skulls were good things to sell. Townsend's cool ability to work with the dead helped him imagine himself as a "scientist," a word just then making its way into the American vocabulary to describe a career like the one Townsend fancied for himself before he went back to dentistry. It is worth noting too that his weeping man knew precisely where his sister was buried. Her body anchored her family, her people, in a time and a place.[44]

Townsend headed home to Philadelphia, taking a long trip by sea to Hawaii and around Cape Horn. He stopped long enough in Oahu to pick up the skulls of a ten-year-old girl and a forty-year-old man, which he sold to Morton. In a final tally of skulls, craniologist Morton thanked the ornithologist for these, for the skull of the Calapooyah, and for the heads of a chief, a child, and a slave, and for a cradleboard like the one Brooks's mother had used to flatten his head. And Townsend gave Morton two signed receipts for $25, recording the value of the skulls he had "hooked" in Oregon (as he put it to Morton) at $50 on the Philadelphia market.[45]

"The brains of these Flat-headed Indians"

We don't know if Townsend recounted his Oregon exploits when he met William Brooks again in Philadelphia. Or if Morton showed Brooks the Calapooyah skull he thought "his very counterpart." But just a few months after that January meeting, Brooks's skull became the object of a squabble among the East Coast intelligentsia.

In the final paragraph of his biography of the Flathead man, McKenney reports that "on the eve of the departure of the Rev. Mr. Lee to the scene of his labours on the Wallamette, Stumanu, flushed with the prospect of once more mingling with his kindred and friends, and gratified with all he had seen of the white man's capacity and powers was taken suddenly ill, in New York, and after a short but severe attack, died on the 29th of May, 1839." The editors of the *New York Herald* noted among the dead "on Wednesday, 29th inst., Wm Brooks, a native Flathead Indian, aged about 20 years."[46]

Jason Lee diagnosed Brooks's last illness as a mix of pleurisy, "congestive fever," and typhus, but again, it was likely tuberculosis that killed him. Methodist histories report that Lee watched over William Brooks in his last illness with "the care of a father." Shortly before he died, these histories report, Brooks told Lee that "'I want to go home.' 'What home?' said Mr. Lee; 'your home in Oregon?' 'No; my heavenly home.'"[47]

Did such a conversation ever take place? Perhaps. Or it may be that William Brooks on his deathbed has been made to serve the purposes of a pious fable, selected for a part in the Sunday school books handed out to Methodist children in the 1840s and 1850s. Or maybe Brooks's thoughts mixed the images offered by McKenney and Lee. Maybe he died, as McKenney put it, "flushed with the prospect of once more mingling with his kindred and friends," but picturing that meeting in Lee's Christian heaven come alive with native dead.[48]

Indeed, Lee's account of Brooks's Christianity is laced with images of death, suggesting that the new religion offered Brooks some real means to cope with the devastating experiences of his childhood in Oregon. Brooks clearly associated white presence with the escalating death rates among his people. "Indians great many years ago never died very fast. But since settlement white men, they have died every hour," as he put it. Fortunately for Brooks, Christianity gave him new some ways to think about the troubling new pace of death. Christianity's promise of everlasting life caught his attention first. As Brooks explained, "suppose one man believe in Jesus Christ and love Jesus Christ, by and by, when he die, he live with him in heaven; he never die a second death."[49]

The phrase "second death," repeated in so many of Brooks's speeches, must have had a particular power for one who had seen so many "first deaths." Conversion to Christianity provided Brooks with emotional tools to deal with death, just as it provided a metaphoric language to address eastern congregations. "I never go back again in the darkness heart. I pray more and more, and I go on. All time I thinking about those poor Indians dying in second death. I cannot sleep every night." He passed those sleepless nights contemplating a "representation of Christ upon the cross," which he hung in front of his bed. "I can't give it to you," he told one young woman who asked to have it as a souvenir of her encounter with the unusual youth. "I must carry it out among those poor Indians, and always show them Jesus Christ died for them, and then they will believe." Christian beliefs gave Brooks solace as he faced his own first death.[50]

The Philadelphia *North American* covered the New York funeral of this "estimable youth, beloved by all who were acquainted with him. But the best of all is, he died an experienced Christian." "The corpse was taken to the Greene-st. church on Thursday, and an address delivered on the occasion by Rev. Dr. Bangs." Brooks's body was buried in New York City near the Bedford Street M.E. Church. And there it likely remained until 1910, when the city of New York extended Seventh Avenue south of Bedford Street and moved the buried bodies out to Queens.[51]

In most life histories, these scenes would end the story: a eulogy by Lee, the assurance that "one native Indian, at least, of Oregon, is saved, as the fruit of missionary labor," and a corpse buried in a graveyard.[52] But given William Brooks's encounter with skull collector Morton, his agent Townsend, and the traveling phrenologist George Combe, one has to ask at least about the material afterlife of his body. Lee coveted his soul; others, perhaps Morton, but certainly Combe, coveted his head.

Although his role in this story of Stumanu/William Brooks has an unpleasant air, particularly when we hear him complaining that he could not get the dead youth's skull for his collection, Combe is not the most villainous figure among the race makers of the American 1830s. It is true that he helped promote Morton's skull work, but he dissented from the worst racist implications of American craniology and sometimes tried to turn his phrenological audiences against slavery. Combe was one of twelve children of an Edinburgh brewer who had urged his son to study law. The way Combe described it, he became a phrenologist because he wanted a career in which he could help people and become a famous writer. Strange as it seems, he saw a better chance for good works and literary fame in phrenology than in law.

At the turn of the nineteenth century, phrenology swept through European intellectual circles as serious brain science. Its basic idea was that the brain was the organ of the mind, that ideas originated in the brain and not in an immaterial soul. Following this insight into the biology of thought, phrenologists tried to locate mental qualities in different areas of the brain. In serious phrenology, we catch a glimpse of early exploration in a physical science of the mind and early efforts at understanding cranial location, but popularizers soon extended phrenology's reach to reading character traits. American practitioners traveled the country with trunks of skulls picked up from executioners and casts of heads of famous men. They traced the sins of notorious criminals and the accomplishments of great men in contours of their skulls. Then they ran their trained fingers over the skulls of the living, discovering latent talents and dangerous tendencies in their paying customers.

Combe took up phrenology not to make money, he said, but with a hunger to understand the human brain. After watching a brain dissection in Edinburgh, Combe was certain phrenology was a key to understanding the natural history of man and that the phrenologist's map of the brain offered a chart for reformers determined to improve humanity. In other words, Combe, although a promoter of phrenology, was a serious naturalist, not the kind of fortune-teller or carnival charlatan associated with phrenology by the middle years of the nineteenth century.[53]

In spring 1839, Combe was about midway through his "phrenological tour" of the United States, a trip meant to complete the journey begun by the great German phrenologist Johann Spurzheim, who had died suddenly of typhoid fever in Boston in 1832. When Combe, Lee, and the young Chinook men crossed paths late in fall 1838, Combe had been in the United States for fifteen months, lecturing on phrenology, visiting schools, cemeteries, asylums, and prisons, and observing American society, sometimes critically. He befriended such New England luminaries as the historian George Bancroft and the educator Horace Mann (who was so impressed by the Scotsman that he named his next son George Combe Mann).

In Philadelphia, Combe visited Morton's skull collection, and the two men became friends. Combe promised to help Morton finish his skull book, volunteering to write an afterward for *Crania Americana*, although Morton did not share Combe's complete confidence in phrenology as the way to analyze human skulls. Combe assured Morton that his endorsement would help sell the book to phrenologists in Europe. He also thought he could get the book good reviews in scientific journals.

Mostly, Combe was pleased to find American audiences still receptive to practices of skull reading that their educated European counterparts had begun to abandon. He found Americans who thought phrenology could be useful in an unsettled social landscape, where it was sometimes necessary to "read" the characters of strangers they met. Traveling around the United States, Combe played the part of an amateur neurologist, meeting with prodigies like the deaf and blind Laura Bridgman and examining the heads of people with strange complaints: a man who could no longer see colors, a policeman who had gone suddenly mute on a cold night in Harrisburg, and a New York child who was mentally healthy but missing a portion of the skull she damaged after she fell from an open window.[54]

Little wonder, then, that the flattened heads of William Brooks and his friend Thomas Adams excited Combe's curiosity. Late in May 1839, Combe met up again with Jason Lee. Brooks was too ill for an interview, but the minister introduced Combe to Adams. Combe found Adams "intelligent, ready and fluent" on things that demanded only "observation." On questions that required "the aid of Comparison and Causality, he was dull, unintelligent, and destitute equally of ideas and language." "The organs of Destructiveness, Acquisitiveness, Secretiveness, Self-Esteem, Love of Approbation, and Firmness, were very large; those of Combativeness, Philoprogenitiveness, and Adhesiveness, deficient. It was difficult to estimate the size of the moral organs, they were so displaced," he wrote.[55]

What did Combe expect readers to learn from this description? That here was a destructive, secretive young man, with good self-esteem but little love for fighting or children? He reassured Lee that head flattening displaced but did not destroy the convolutions of the brain. The man's brain was bent, he said, like the spine of a hunchback, but he had not lost his capacity to appreciate the word of God. Still, Combe surmised that manipulating the skull seemed to have damaged the mental faculties of comparison.

Had the Scotsman listened to Brooks's words to the Methodist woman rather than looking at his companion's head, he might have noticed that Brooks in fact had an acute gift for comparative observation. He had given the woman a perfect cross-cultural comparison—feet, waist, head. Combe admitted that he could not figure out precisely how head flattening changed the brain, and so he asked Lee "to carry a cast of a normal European brain with him, when he returned to his station, and to beg the medical officer of the Fur Company . . . to examine carefully the brains of these Flat-headed Indians after death, and report minutely the differences in the size and distribution of the convolutions."[56]

It bothered the phrenologist that a brain closer at hand had eluded him. Shortly after he left New York, Combe read an announcement of William Brooks's death, and he was frustrated that he had not been able to arrange to dissect the Indian's brain.

If Brooks had ever intended to preserve his body intact, like the mummified young woman Townsend had seen in Oregon, then he had a little bit of luck at the end of his short, death-filled life. A doctor by the name of David Meredith Reese attended Brooks in his last illness. Physician-in-chief of Bellevue Hospital, Reese was a cranky, outspoken, obnoxious man, a passionate advocate for the American Colonization Society's plans to send freed slaves and free African Americans to settle in Africa, and a dyspeptic opponent of things he considered popular fads. He campaigned against the extreme passions he dubbed "the humbugs of New-York." These included "quackery in general," "ultra temperance," "ultra abolition," and, in his mind, as bad as the rest, phrenology—a pure humbug that had somehow seduced otherwise intelligent men and women.

Reese wondered how sensible people could believe the absurd proposition that the soft stuff of the brain molded the hard matter of the skull, creating the palpable bumps that phrenologists "read" for signs of the true nature of the inner man. Adherents insisted that when "an organ increases, the skull yields by absorption at the spot against which it lies, and then, by a general growth over it, accommodates the development and displays it externally." The idea was ridiculous, Reese thought.

Vanity, not logic, explained phrenology's appeal. He was sorry to report that "men and women of reason and religion, who eschew fortune-telling, witchcraft, and astrology . . . submit their own heads, and those of their sons and daughters, to these fortune-tellers, who itinerate through the country like other strolling mountebanks, for the purpose of living without labour, by practising upon public gullibility." Phrenologists flattered clients, showering them with compliments about their fine internal characteristics.[57]

This fight over phrenology protected the corpse of William Brooks. To Combe's great distress, Reese "allowed this young man to be buried without examining his brain, or at least without reporting on it, or calling in the aid of phrenologists to do so." Reese was fighting charlatans, he said. But Combe pushed back, insisting that anyone really interested in uncovering the truth would study this rare head. "It is strange that those who are so confident that phrenology is a 'humbug' should be so averse to producing evidence by which alone it can be proved to be so. The condition of the brain in a Flat-headed Indian is an interesting and unknown fact in physiology, and any medical man who has the means of throwing light on it, and neglects to use them, is not a friend to his own profession or to general science."[58]

If Reese was not a friend to medicine and science, perhaps in the end the cranky man was a friend to William Brooks, who had come from a people with a high regard for the cultural importance of bodies of dead kin. Although Brooks's body was not handled as it would have been at home in Oregon, it was at least interred according to the customs of his adopted religion. That must have been preferable to Brooks to falling into the hands of even so amiable a body snatcher as George Combe or so avid a skull collector as Samuel Morton.

That Morton assembled a skull collection his acquaintances called an "American Golgotha"—shelves overflowing with a thousand human skulls—tells us that others who may have hoped to keep their heads were not as lucky as William Brooks.[59]

Seeing the Dead

Why go back to this story now? There are several threads to pull from the story of William Brooks's encounter with Philadelphia's headhunters. We know that Morton's work on skulls helped give theories about racial difference a "scientific" stamp and that his race science reached far beyond his Philadelphia circle, adding intellectual muscle to slaveholder resolve, and, when slavery was abolished, helping to shore up decades of discriminatory policies. But from Brooks we know that Morton and his friends did not hatch their race theories in a vacuum. Indeed, scientific racism was built in part on the ruins of Brooks's crumbling world, a world that though remote was part of the complex cultural landscape of the early nineteenth-century United States.

Brooks came close to becoming a specimen in a scientific collection, but he was a remarkably resourceful young man. He made his way gracefully through a rapidly changing world full of people with ideas about how to use his head, his body, his soul, and his story. Combe thought his brain might help restore legitimacy to phrenology; McKenney thought including a native from the far West might interest a few more buyers in his slow-moving collection of Indian portraits; Townsend thought his skull might sell for good money in eastern markets; and Lee thought that Brooks's simple Christian homilies might help convince eastern Methodists that the mission in Oregon was worth supporting.

For Morton, the man with the flattened head forced him to ask questions that went to the heart of his work on skulls and race. Did skulls carry nature's marks of racial difference? Or could nature's marks be blurred by culture? Morton hoped to keep nature separate from culture so he could argue that his culture's hierarchy of races carried the stamp of nature's authority. But what if skulls were products of culture, nearly as easy to manipulate as costumes and face paint? Brooks's head and its Calapooyah counterpart might bring down his system or they might just be the anomalies he needed to establish the natural range of the races.

Morton's work was meant to shore up the differences among the races, but when he began to build his theory from skulls he conjured humanity's common mortality. The scientists of Morton's generation were of many minds about death, and when they described themselves "abstracting" native skulls without flinching, as Townsend did, they distinguished themselves from their ordinary, superstitious, contemporaries—white neighbors and Native Americans. Yet, like their middle-class contemporaries, they were sentimental about their own bodies. They staged elaborate funerals and bought plots in the country's new garden cemeteries, where their dead bodies and marble headstones helped make permanent their claim on the landscape.

William Brooks's people in out Oregon lost their claim on the landscape and, in the rash of epidemics of the 1830s, lost their ability to handle the dead. Townsend described a people so decimated by disease that they could not follow customary burial practices. He witnessed a biological devastation that nearly took a culture down with it. In the ruins, Lee's Christian lessons actually offered young William Brooks some tools to deal with all the dying. It is true that Brooks and other young Indians learned to make simple wooden coffins in the mission's workshop, but from eastern pulpits Brooks described a Christian religion that protected him from "second death," perhaps offering a way to cut his emotional losses by half. But if he embraced Christianity as a means to cope with death, race science almost trumped religion at the end. William Brooks became a Christian, but when he died he became Stumanu again, more valuable for his Indian body than his Christian soul.[60]

NOTES

1.   Charles D. Meigs, *A Memoir of Samuel Morton, M.D., Late President of the Academy of Natural Sciences of Philadelphia* (Philadelphia: T. K. and P. G. Collins, Printers, 1851), 7. On the place of curiosity in the development of natural history, see Susan Scott Parrish, *American Curiosity: Cultures of Natural History in the Colonial British Atlantic World* (Chapel Hill: University of North Carolina Press, 2006),

57–64; and Lorraine Daston and Katharine Park, *Wonders and the Order of Nature: 1150–1750* (New York: Zone Books, 2001), 311–28.

2. George Combe, *Notes on the United States of North America during a Phrenological Visit in 1838-9-40* (Philadelphia: Carey and Hart, 1841), 1:176, 182–83. George Wilson Pierson, *Tocqueville and Beaumont in America* (New York: Oxford University Press, 1938), 458.

3. Dana D. Nelson, "'No Cold or Empty Heart': Polygenesis, Scientific Professionalization, and the Unfinished Business of Male Sentimentalism," *Differences* 11, no. 3 (1999–2000): 47.

4. Charles Colbert, *A Measure of Perfection: Phrenology and the Fine Arts in America* (Chapel Hill: University of North Carolina Press, 1997).

5. "Prospectus," *Journal of Belles Lettres*, February 27, 1838, 9.

6. Daniel Wilson, "Illustrations of the Significance of Certain Ancient British Skull Forms," *Canadian Journal*, March 1863, 22.

7. This essay could not have been written without the work of Stephen Jay Gould, *The Mismeasure of Man* (New York: Norton, 1996); George Fredrickson, *The Black Image in the White Mind: The Debate on Afro-American Character and Destiny, 1817–1914* (Middletown, CT: Wesleyan University Press, 1971); William Stanton, *The Leopard's Spots: Scientific Attitudes toward Race in America, 1815–1859* (Chicago: University of Chicago Press, 1960); and Reginald Horsman, *Race and Manifest Destiny: The Origins of American Racial Anglo-Saxonism* (Cambridge: Harvard University Press, 1981). I have tried to build on this work, heeding the caution of Mia Bay, *The White Image in the Black Mind: African American Ideas about White People, 1830–1925* (New York: Oxford University Press, 2000), that too much of the writing on race works from the point of view of white people. I have also borrowed from work on agency of "racialized" performers, in particular, Benjamin Reiss, *The Showman and the Slave: Race, Death and Memory in Barnum's America* (Cambridge: Harvard University Press, 2001); James Cook, *The Arts of Deception: Playing with Fraud in the Age of Barnum* (Cambridge: Harvard University Press, 2001); L. G. Moses, *Wild West Shows and the Images of American Indians, 1883–1933* (Albuquerque: University of New Mexico Press, 1999); and Philip J. Deloria, *Indians in Unexpected Places* (Lawrence: University Press of Kansas, 2005).

8. The portrait of Stumanu does not appear in the "Catalogue of Known Works" in Andrew J. Cosentino, *The Painting of Charles Bird King (1785–1862)* (Washington, DC: Smithsonian Institution Press, 1977), 121–206. In their 1934 edition of McKenney and Hall's *Indian Tribes of North America*, Frederick Webb Hodge and David I. Bushnell Jr. list the artist as "unknown" and note that the portrait is not mentioned in William J. Rhees, *An Account of the Smithsonian Institution, Its Founder, Building, Operations, etc., Prepared from the Reports of Prof. Henry to the Regents, and Other Authentic Sources* (Washington, DC: Thomas M'Gill, printer, 1859), 55–58. F. W. Hodge, introduction to *The Indian Tribes of North America with Biographical Sketches and Anecdotes of the Principal Chiefs*, 3 vols., by Thomas L. McKenney and James Hall (repr., Edinburgh: John Grant, 1934), 1:xlvi–liii, 2:287n8. On the blanket, see George T. Emmons, "The Chilkat Blanket, with Notes on the Blanket Design by Franz Boas," *Memoirs of the American Museum of Natural History* 3, no. 4 (1907): 329–401; and Cheryl Samuel, *The Chilkat Dancing Blanket* (Norman: University of Oklahoma Press, 1989). The contemporary observation appears in "Oregon Mission Concluded," *Boston Recorder* 24 (February 15, 1839): 26.

9. Thomas L. McKenney and James Hall, *History of the Indian Tribes of North America,*

vol. 2 (Philadelphia: F. W. Greenough, 1838). McKenney conceived his portrait gallery in the 1820s, when he was working for the U.S. government. Prominent native visitors to Washington impressed him, and he commissioned artist Charles Bird King to paint portraits of diplomats who showed up to negotiate treaties and settle land cessions. He moved to Philadelphia in the 1830s and set about publishing the collection of pictures. McKenney pictured a series running through twenty numbers, each containing six portraits and thirty pages of text. When the first number appeared in 1837, he had signed up some 1,250 subscribers, names enough to raise the substantial sum of $150,000. But the times were not auspicious for the ambitious project, and McKenney's fortunes, along with those of his printers and many of his subscribers, were upended by the severe economic depression that hit the country in 1837. By the time the project limped to completion in 1844, it had run through five different publishers and cut deeply into the fortunes of its authors. See Herman J. Viola, *The Indian Legacy of Charles Bird King* (Washington, DC: Smithsonian Institution Press; and New York: Doubleday, 1976); and Herman J. Viola, *Thomas L. McKenney: Architect of America's Early Indian Policy, 1816–1830* (Chicago: Sage Books, 1974).

10. Robert Boyd, *The Coming of the Spirit of Pestilence: Introduced Infectious Diseases and Population Decline among Northwest Coast Indians, 1774–1874* (Vancouver: UBC Press, 1999), 84–115; Herbert C. Taylor Jr. and Lester L. Hoaglin Jr., "The 'Intermittent Fever' Epidemic of the 1830's on the Lower Columbia River," *Ethnohistory* 9 (Spring 1962): 160–78; Sherburne Cook, "The Epidemic of 1830–1833 in California and Oregon," *University of California Publications in American Archaeology and Ethnography* 43, no. 3 (1955): 303–25; and Robert H. Ruby and John A. Brown, *The Chinook Indians: Traders of the Lower Columbia River* (Norman: University of Oklahoma Press, 1976): 185–200.

11. John Kirk Townsend, *Narrative of a Journey across the Rocky Mountains to the Columbia River and a Visit to the Sandwich Islands, Chili, &c., with a Scientific Appendix* (1839; repr., Corvallis: Oregon State University Press, 1999), 12.

12. Cyrus Shepard, letter of January 10, 1835, printed in *Zion's Herald* 6 (October 28, 1835): 170, and quoted in Cornelius J. Brosnan, *Jason Lee, Prophet of the New Oregon* (1932; repr., Rutland, VT: Academy Books, 1985): 76.

13. McKenney and Hall, *Indian Tribes of North America* (1838 ed.), 2:157; Shepard, as quoted in Brosnan, *Jason Lee*, 76; and Cyrus Shepard, letter from the Oregon Mission, *Zion's Herald* 8 (July 19, 1837): 8, 29. On Lucy Hedding's death, see Gustavus Hines, *A Voyage Round the World with a History of the Oregon Mission* (Buffalo: G. H. Derby, 1850), 17.

14. Historian Gray H. Whaley gives us the "grim ledger," describing missionary efforts to balance the costs of feeding and clothing children against their productive activities. Gray H. Whaley, "'Trophies' for God: Native Mortality, Racial Ideology, and the Methodist Mission of Lower Oregon, 1834–1844," *Oregon Historical Quarterly* (Spring 2006): para. 32; http://www.historycooperative.org/journals/ohq/107.1/whaley.html (accessed December 1, 2006).

15. Claude E. Schaeffer, "William Brooks, Chinook Publicist," *Oregon Historical Quarterly* 64 (1963): 41–54; Robert Moulton Gatke, "The First Indian School of the Pacific Northwest," *Oregon Historical Quarterly* 23 (1922): 70–83; Robert H. Ruby and John A. Brown, *Indians of the Pacific Northwest* (Norman: University of Oklahoma Press, 1981), 71; Shepard, letter from the Oregon Mission; and Whaley, "'Trophies' for God," para. 36.

16. "Diary of Rev. Jason Lee," *Quarterly of the Oregon Historical Society* 17 (December 1916): 405, 416.
17. Brosnan, *Jason Lee*, 93, 97; and Whaley, "'Trophies' for God," para. 42.
18. Hine, *Voyage Round the World*, 31; "Diary of Rev. Jason Lee," 425.
19. Thomas Adams fell ill along the journey and recuperated in Peoria, Illinois, before rejoining Lee and Brooks in spring 1839. Brosnan, *Jason Lee*, 100.
20. Jason Lee, "Some Farther Account of Wm. Brooks, the Flathead Indian," *Western Christian Advocate*, 6 (October 18, 1839): 104; Brosnan, *Jason Lee*, 104; H. K Hines, *Missionary History of the Pacific Northwest, Containing the Wonderful Story of Jason Lee* (Portland: H. K. Hines, 1899), 194; and Robert J. Loewenberg, *Equality on the Oregon Frontier: Jason Lee and the Methodist Mission* (Seattle: University of Washington Press, 1976).
21. *Christian Advocate and Journal* 14 (October 4, 1839): 25, as quoted in Brosnan, *Jason Lee*, 111.
22. *Christian Advocate and Journal* 13 (February 15, 1839): 102; (March 1, 1839): 109; and 14 (October 4, 1839): 25; as quoted in Brosnan, *Jason Lee*, 110, 111, 114, 116; *Zion's Herald* 10 (February 13, 1839): 26, as quoted in Brosnan, *Jason Lee*, 118; and Hines, *Voyage Round the World*, 37.
23. *Oregonian and Indian's Advocate* 1 (January 1839): 125–27, as quoted in Brosnan, *Jason Lee*, 121; *Zion's Herald* 10 (February 13, 1839): 27, as quoted in Brosnan, *Jason Lee*, 112.
24. "Oregon Mission Concluded," *Boston Recorder* 24 (February 15, 1839): 26.
25. *Christian Advocate and Journal* 14 (October 4, 1839): 25, as quoted in Brosnan, *Jason Lee*, 113; *Oregonian and Indian's Advocate* 1 (January 1839): 125–27, as quoted in Brosnan, *Jason Lee*, 121; Hines, *Missionary History*, 197; the anecdote also appears in Rev. A. Atwood, *The Conquerors: Historical Sketches of the American Settlement of the Oregon Country* (1907), 73n.
26. *"Ten Thousand Chinese Things": A Descriptive Catalogue of the Chinese Collection in Philadelphia with Miscellaneous Remarks upon the Manners and Customs, Trade and Government of the Celestial Empire* (Philadelphia: Printed for the Proprietor, 1839); Combe, *Notes on the United States*, 1:189–90; James Silk Buckingham, *Eastern and Western States of America* (London: Fisher, Son and Co., 1842), 2:55, 64; "Chinese Museum," *Niles National Register*, February 16, 1839, 5, abridges a report on the collection that appeared in Benjamin Silliman's *American Journal of Science and the Arts* in January 1839.
27. Jonathan Goldstein, *Philadelphia and the China Trade, 1682–1846: Commercial, Cultural, and Attitudinal Effects* (University Park: Pennsylvania State University Press, 1978), 50–78; *"Ten Thousand Chinese Things,"* 15–16.
28. Samuel George Morton, *Crania Americana: or, A Comparative View of the Skulls of Various Aboriginal Nations of North and South America* (Philadelphia: J. Dobson, 1839), 206.
29. Ibid. Other craniologists did not find their subjects so cooperative. "It is no easy thing to obtain actual measurements of Indians' heads," wrote Daniel Wilson, a Scottish historian, ethnographer, and craniologist working in his adopted Canada. "I have seen an Indian not only resist every attempt that could be ventured on, backed by arguments of the most practical kind; but on solicitation being pressed too urgently, he trembled, and manifested the strongest signs of fear, not unaccompanied with anger, such as made a retreat prudent." Daniel Wilson,

On the Supposed Prevalence of One Cranial Type throughout the American Aborigines (Edinburgh: Neill and Company, 1858), 19.

30. Morton, *Crania Americana*, 206.
31. In the end, it was his bird work that did him in. Townsend died in 1851 at the age of forty-two, poisoned by the arsenic in the powder he had developed to preserve dead birds. Curators knew the hazards of their work. As one packing slip warned, "The immense quantity of arsenic and corrosive sublimate necessary for their preservation requires, respectively, that very great caution should be observed, and that the handling and arrangements should be under either the immediate inspection or personal attention of one fully adequate to all the details connected with this subject. *In the hands of inexperienced persons, death might be the result.*" And so it was for Townsend, an experienced man but a careless one. G. Brown Goode, "The Genesis of the National Museum," *Annual Report of the Board of Regents of the Smithsonian Institution* (Washington, DC: GPO, 1892), 304, 349.
32. Townsend, *Narrative of a Journey*, 256.
33. Morton, *Crania Americana*, 206, 213; "reeking pack" is in Henry S. Patterson, "Memoir of the Life and Scientific Labors of Samuel George Morton," in *Types of Mankind: or, Ethnological Researches*, ed. J. C. Nott and George R. Gliddon (Philadelphia: Lippincott, Grambo and Co., 1855), xxix.
34. Townsend, *Narrative of a Journey*, 176. Matthias Weaver, an Ohio-born artist who sketched skulls for Morton, had a low opinion of Townsend's book. He described him as a "bold sort of a chap but not much of a writer." "Diary of Mathias Weaver," May 21, 1840, manuscript, Ohio Historical Society.
35. The comment on aristocracy is from Wilson, "Illustrations of Certain Ancient British Skull Forms," 25.
36. Townsend, Narrative of a Journey, 176–77. This account was reprinted as "Flathead Indians," Family Magazine 3 (1835–36): 451.
37. Townsend to Morton, September 20, 1835, Samuel George Morton Papers, American Philosophical Society (APS). Edward Belcher, *Narrative of a Voyage Round the World, Performed in Her Majesty's Ship Sulphur during the Years 1836–1842* (London: Henry Colburn, Publisher, 1843), 1:292.
38. Townsend to Morton, September 20, 1835, Samuel George Morton Papers.
39. Townsend, *Narrative of a Journey*, 232.
40. Ibid., 181.
41. On native efforts to protect the dead, see Belcher, *Narrative of a Voyage Round the World;* Townsend, *Narrative of a Journey*, 236–37.
42. Townsend, *Narrative of a Journey*, 237.
43. Ibid.
44. I am borrowing an idea about place and burial from Robert Pogue Harrison, *The Dominion of the Dead* (Chicago: University of Chicago Press, 2003), 18–24.
45. Townsend, *Narrative of a Journey*, 236–37, also 180–81: Morton, *Crania Americana*, 207–15; J. Aitken Meigs, *Catalogue of Human Crania, in the Collection of the Academy of Natural Sciences of Philadelphia* (Philadelphia: J. B. Lippincott, 1857), 54–55, 57, 63–64. "Receipts for *Crania Americana*, 1837–42," Rare Books, Manuscripts Collection, Princeton University Library.
46. McKenney and Hall, *Indian Tribes of North America* (1838 ed.), 2:158; *New York Herald*, May 30, 1839.
47. Hines, *Missionary History*, 196–97.

48. Although most of his examples are drawn from an earlier period, Erik R. Seeman offers an insightful interpretation of deathbed scenes. See Seeman, "Reading Indians' Death Bed Scenes: Ethnohistorical and Representational Approaches," *Journal of American History* 88, no. 1 (June 2001): 17–47. See also Laura M. Stevens, "The Christian Origins of the Vanishing Indian," in *Mortal Remains: Death in Early America*, ed. Nancy Isenberg and Andrew Burstein (Philadelphia: University of Pennsylvania Press, 2003), 17–31.
49. Lee, "Some Farther Account of Wm. Brooks," 104.
50. Ibid.; Whaley, "'Trophies' for God," paras. 17–23.
51. *North American*, as quoted in Brosnan, 140–41n.
52. Ibid.
53. On phrenology, see Colbert, *Measure of Perfection;* and Roger Cooter, *The Cultural Meaning of Popular Science: Phrenology and the Organization of Consent in Nineteenth-Century Britain* (Cambridge: Cambridge University Press, 1984).
54. Combe, *Notes on the United States*, 2:205–6 (Bridgman), 1:301 (color), 1:244–45 (policeman), 2:43–45 (damaged skull). On Combe, see Anthony Walsh, "George Combe: A Portrait of a Heretofore Generally Unknown Behaviorist," *Journal of the History of the Behavioral Sciences* (1971): 269–78.
55. Combe, *Notes on the United States*, 2:48–49.
56. Ibid., 2:49–50.
57. David Meredith Reese, *Humbugs of New York: Being a Remonstrance against Popular Delusions* (New York: J. S. Taylor, 1838), 64, 69; "Dr. Buchanan in Florida," *American Phrenological Journal* 2 (December 1, 1839): 139.
58. Combe, *Notes on the United States*, 2:50n.
59. Skulls and bones of thousands of ordinary Native Americans wound up in collections in Philadelphia, Cambridge, and Washington. Bodies of well-known figures such as William Brooks have their own distinct histories. See, for example, Orin Starn, *Ishi's Brain: In Search of America's Last "Wild" Indian* (New York: Norton, 2004); Kenn Harper, *Give Me My Father's Body: The Life of Minik, the New York Eskimo* (South Royalton, VT: Steerforth Press, 1986); Patricia R. Wickman, *Osceola's Legacy* (Tuscaloosa: University of Alabama Press, 1991); and of course the ongoing speculation about the whereabouts of Geronimo's skull.
60. Whaley, "'Trophies' for God," para. 32. On the use of bodies—dead and alive—to construct scientific and cultural authority, see Londa Schiebinger, *Nature's Body: Gender in the Making of Modern Science* (Boston: Beacon Press, 1993); Ruth Richardson, *Death, Dissection, and the Destitute* (Chicago: University of Chicago Press, 1987); and Michael Sappol, *A Traffic in Dead Bodies: Anatomy and Social Identity in Nineteenth-Century America* (Princeton: Princeton University Press, 2002). On burial practices and European conquest, see Claudio Lomnitz, *Death and the Idea of Mexico* (New York: Zone Books, 2005), 195; and Zine Mugabine, "Siminians, Savages, Skulls, and Sex: Science and Colonial Militarism in Nineteenth-Century South Africa," in *Race, Nature, and the Politics of Difference*, ed. Donald S. Moore, Jake Kosek, and Anand Pandian (Durham, NC: Duke University Press, 2003), 99–121.

THREE

Rags, Blacking, and Paper Soldiers: Money and Race in the Civil War

MICHAEL O'MALLEY

Once let the black man get upon his person the brass letter "U.S.," let him get an eagle on his button, and a musket on his shoulder and bullets in his pocket, there is no power on earth that can deny that he has earned the right to citizenship.

FREDERICK DOUGLASS, address at a meeting for the promotion of colored enlistments, Philadelphia, July 6, 1863

Lincoln had trouble financing the Civil War. Most northerners disliked slavery, but they generally disliked Negroes even more, and they liked taxes least of all. Lincoln's administration had tried twice to levy taxes to finance the war, with insufficient results. Bond sales had also realized less than hoped. Further taxing the Union to raise money for a war that might free slaves looked like a sure political mistake. So in 1862 the federal government resorted to an old strategy, authorizing the Treasury to print and release legal tender paper money. The words "legal tender" meant no one could legally refuse to take the green-backed bills in payment—if you sold munitions or pickled beef to the government, you took your pay in greenbacks. If you offered a supplier greenbacks in return, he took greenbacks and liked it. Soldiers took their pay in greenbacks as well. By 1865, $450 million worth of greenbacks passed for "real money" throughout the North. To put it simply, the greenbacks allowed Lincoln to finance the unpopular war.[1]

Yet greenbacks never enjoyed complete acceptance: a long tradition in American thinking about money regarded legal tender paper notes as evil, a cheat and a fraud. They made value out of nothing by mere proclamation. They confused the symbol (printed paper) with the real thing it stood for (gold or other precious metals). For those who loved paper money, one satirist argued, "words are things . . . not only things, but important and valuable things . . . I might even say *better* than things."[2] Advocates of gold argued that no one could simply declare a thing to be money by fiat—only something with real, intrinsic value could serve as money. "I would as soon provide Chinese wooden guns for the army as paper money alone for the army," Vermont congressman Elbridge Gerry Spaulding declared.[3] Paper money seemed absurd, immoral, like calling white black or good bad or declaring rain was actually snow or glass was diamond. Wartime expediency made greenbacks acceptable to these critics for a time, but only marginally. "We may regret the necessity," wrote the *New York Herald*, "but we cannot deny that it exists."[4]

This chapter explores the semantic confusion between greenback dollars and "negro soldiers," and the debate about the value of each during the Civil War. In it I argue that mid-nineteenth-century American culture constantly undermined its own market promises; it offered the possibility of self-making, self-creation, but then withdrew that promise behind fantasies of intrinsic or essential value. When they talked about greenbacks, those on all sides of the question tended to use what we see as racialized language: sometimes subtly, more often quite explicitly, they conflated money and race.

Before what we call the cultural turn in history, few historians noticed this common language.[5] Most historians treated the money debate, and economic questions generally, as distinct from other kinds of historical questions, as if economics, like physics or biology, lived under a set of specific laws or rules that formed the only proper frame for speaking about money issues. Both the political left and right treated money as a science, as something "lawful." Since both Karl Marx and, say, Milton Friedman descended intellectually from Adam Smith, both the left and right tended to see human beings as economic actors having a stable, objectively knowable interest they sought to maximize through exchange. True, Friedman and Marx might agree that people, blinded by rhetoric, did not always *see* their real interests, but those interests existed, concrete and authentic, nevertheless. Economics often entered history as a kind of metanarrative, a trump card, or if you will, a bottom line of meaning. Let me give two simple, well-known examples. In Charles Beard's famous account, the rhetoric of the American Revolution was "really about" debt and credit relations. And in Richard Hofstadter's work, the Populists' reliance on anti-Semitic language demonstrated mostly "the paranoid style" and their pathological inability to see their "real interests."[6] In this tradition, the rhetoric surrounding money screened the real story like a magician's sleight of hand conceals a silver coin.

Cultural history, though, tended to focus on the sleight of hand itself. As a student of Lawrence Levine in the 1980s, I learned that tricksters' tales, or Shakespeare's parodies, were not shadows of the "real" substance of history—they *were* the real substance of history. Inflected by the new social history of the 1960s and 1970s, Levine regarded the rhetoric of ordinary people as evidence of their determination to make the world sensible. Rhetoric was not smokescreen or a veil over the real; rhetoric, what ordinary people said and sang and joked about, was the real. For so many cultural historians, Clifford Geertz seemed to sum up this approach: there was no real, no bottom line, that rhetoric merely reflected; there was only re-presentation, only rhetoric or gesture.[7] A market, in this logic, was not the real manifestation of natural laws of exchange; it was itself rhetoric, a text, a representation of ideas about exchange, difference, and its meaning.[8]

What we tend to call postmodernism argued further that the subject of history, the "man" history studied, was itself simply another representation. In Foucault, *homo economicus* was not the revelation of a universal truth about human beings but simply a rhetorical construction, a discourse about what people might be and how they acted. In this line of thinking, no one has a real interest, they only have discourses about who they are and what their interests should or could be. And further, in this line of thinking there is no human subject, no person to "get in touch with," empathize with, or know; there is only rhetoric or discourse.[9]

The shared language of race and money marks the point at which two discursive systems, two bodies of knowledge, two ways of speaking and representing the world, collapsed into each other. This collapse suggests the instability of ideas about both race and money, and the instability of the line that makes them distinct from each other. This instability then suggests a larger uneasiness in American culture about exchange itself, and beyond that about the symbolic systems that underpinned liberal individualism, with its promises of freedom in self-fashioning.

Money markets, economies, are systems of symbolic exchange, like speech or writing and reading; they are representations of meaning, representations of the relative value of things and ideas. "Coin a phrase," and if it has "the ring of truth" it then passes, and gains or loses value over time. Human reproduction, genetic exchange itself, is also a system of symbolic exchange, in which differences between people are measured and compared and their meaning negotiated. Although the result—the child—is a real person, it can only be understood in symbolic terms, through language and gesture. It can only express itself, its acts can only gain meaning, in symbolic terms. Race offers one way to give meaning to human exchange, to give meaning to difference. Money is another. Money is shorthand for what the difference between two things *means*, just as race is shorthand for what the difference between two people means. Both race and money are signs of what difference means, but neither fully comprehends or accurately describes the world and its variety. Both symbolic systems pretend a solidity, a naturalness, that they cannot maintain: they are unstable.[10]

If money serves as a primary sign of what difference means (and what sameness means as well), then money itself must remain stable. Otherwise the system of making sense of difference collapses. If money itself has no fixed character, then how do any of us make sense of difference? When money seems unstable, people cast about for other signs of what difference means, other standards of value—like the idea of race. Conversely, in periods when the apparent stability of racial hierarchies comes into question, arguments about the gold standard reappear with renewed force.

This chapter turns on a core of revulsion at how "the market" proclaims freedom but also works against it; how it thwarts human desire for self-determination and presses crushingly arbitrary symbolic meanings like race onto human beings as if the words themselves were as lawful as gravity. Exchange and negotiation are the essence of culture: exchange produces new possibilities, new identities, new meanings. Far from rejecting the market, this chapter condemns the market for repeatedly failing to live up to its promises; indeed; this chapter argues that market individualism, as we commonly understand it, can never live up to its promises. The shared language of race and money reveals the ambivalence Americans felt about the market, and about the identities it both assigned and erased.

When Lincoln issued greenbacks, he entered into a debate with a long history. If one faction in American politics hated paper money and resisted it in any form, another faction argued hotly for more paper money, lots of money, to stimulate the economy. Our money, this argument went, is merely a convenience, something we all agree to accept. All value comes from labor, not from nature, and paper money represents our labor, or our potential labor, and so we can call anything money. If all agree to take it, all will prosper.

The argument for paper had waxed and waned in different periods leading up to the Civil War. Although all the colonies experimented with paper money, some more successfully than others, the memory of inflated Continental dollars made paper money suspect. Calls for paper money echoed in Shays' Rebellion: they appeared theoretically in the work of H. C. Carey and in practice through "wildcat" banking and the more than eight thousand kinds of money that circulated before the Civil War. The labor theory of value played a central role in American political philosophy, especially the philosophy of Lincoln's Republican Party. Wealth came from productive labor. Money only symbolized labor and value—it was not value itself.[11]

As the war continued and the North prospered, support for paper money probably rose. By 1863, voters were even writing and singing popular songs about the greenbacks—songs like this one, "How Are You Greenbacks?":

> We're coming father A-bram, one hundred thousand more
> Five hundred presses printing us from morn till night is o'er
> Like Maggie you will see us start and scatter thro' the land
> To pay the soldiers or release the border contraband.[12]

A hundred thousand greenbacks, coming like troops to help the Union cause: Bryant's Minstrels, a famous blackface company, performed this song in 1863 (fig. 3.1). In the next few pages we follow this song closely, as its performance takes us deeper into the puzzle of money and the problem of the real.

To understand this song—and many similar songs and poems from the same period—we need to explore the relation between money and race. Bryant's players would cover their faces with greasepaint or burnt cork, and take their turns on the stage as one of up to a dozen stock characters, all grotesquely styled parodies of African Americans. The minstrel's music—in the hands of gifted composers like Stephen Foster—drew on the songs slaves sang and used many of the same instruments slaves played, especially the banjo. Typically dressed in comically ragged clothes, minstrels danced in imitations of slave performances. Their accents mocked the accents they might have heard from African Americans on the streets, docks, and taverns. This odd spectacle dominated

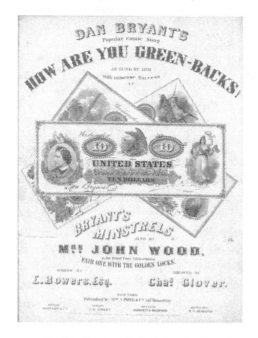

Fig. 3.1. Sheet music for "How Are You
Green-backs." Historic American Sheet Music,
Music B-1071, Duke University Rare Book,
Manuscript, and Special Collections Library.

American entertainment and made its leading practitioners rich, at least
in the short term. By the time of the Civil War, the minstrel show was the
most popular form of entertainment in America; it would remain popular well into the twentieth century.

Although clearly a viciously racist instrument of oppression, the minstrel shows presented an extraordinarily complex package of attitudes,
obsessions, phobias, and desires. Minstrel shows provided a venue for
forbidden longings; they fostered political satire; they reflected the cre-
olizing half-impulse, the "love and theft," so pronounced in American
popular culture.[13] They reflected the market's contradictory tendency
to erode meaning and to shore it up at the same time.[14] Minstrel shows
typically included patriotic songs and satirical ditties, like the one quoted
here, on contemporary politics. In the minstrel context, the song's comment on the money question seems especially pointed. Imitating poverty's rags, the white minstrels "passed" for black. Minstrels were a symbol
of the real (black) thing: counterfeits, but worth more than the original
they passed for.

"How Are You Greenbacks?" continued: "We're coming, Father Abram, one hundred thousand more, / And cash was ne'er so easily evok'd from rags before." Printers used rags to make the high-quality paper for greenbacks. They turned rags into cash. Critics of paper money frequently called it "rag money" or "rag currency"—an "accursed load of Rags and Blacking," as one revolutionary era critic put it.[15] They used the word to make paper money seem worn, feckless, valueless, like cast-off trash— "a currency no better than unwashed paper rags."[16] The term implied overcirculation, objects or goods used until all value had been wrung from them: it implied that value waned as it strayed too far from the original or moved too promiscuously from person to person. The minstrel himself was a popular fake, a symbol, a ragged counterfeit, so paper money seemed a particularly appropriate and popular subject for minstrel commentary.[17]

Paper money, its enemies repeatedly charged, "evoked cash from rags." Legal tender made valueless rag paper into valuable cash by a sort of magic. "Let the public believe that a smutted rag is money, it is money," scoffed a critic in 1858: "a sort of financial biology, which made, at night, the thing conjured for, the thing that was seen."[18] Those who favored "hard money" saw greenbacks as a violation of natural law, artificial: "paper-money banking," wrote Andrew Jackson's adviser William Gouge, created "an *artificial* inequality of wealth," as men of dubious character puffed themselves up on paper money.[19] The inequalities of wealth produced by a gold economy Gouge saw as "natural" and just: paper money, "miserable, ragged, and loathsome trash," destabilized the social order.[20] "Everything of fixed value will lose [its] value" if "vagabond" paper money circulates, insisted one Ohio congressman.[21] The *New York Herald* compared those who argued for paper money to real estate brokers, who, "with a few strokes of the pen convert a rickety old farm house . . . into an elegant villa surrounded by a spacious lawn," or theatrical managers, whose "genius renders a beggarly account of empty boxes into a crowded and fashionable house."[22] Thomas Nast later caricatured paper money as "the Rag Baby," a doll its owners treat as real.[23] An imposter, greenbacks papered over reality with dangerous illusions. They made it hard to know the real from the symbolic. In the mouth of a white performer, dolled up in greasepaint to look black, "How Are You Greenbacks?" took on a double meaning. It described not just how greenbacks symbolized wealth but also how Bryant's Minstrels dressed in rags to evoke slavery, to symbolize black people, and thereby earned cash.

The song also expressed popular ambivalence about greenbacks and more generally about the problem of value itself. The lyric continued, "cash was never so easily e-voked from rags before / To line the fat contractor's purse, or purchase transport craft / whose rotten hulks shall sink before the winds begin to waft." Now the song's initial enthusiasm for greenbacks seems even less sure: they are described as lining the corrupt contractor's purse, and so greenbacks are associated with men of doubtful character. Or even worse, greenbacks buy shoddy, "counterfeit" supplies, and what looks like a seaworthy craft collapses at the dock. Greenbacks were "a common legalized cheat that promises what he never performs, and lives by palming off counters." Greenbacks, like the minstrels themselves, please the eye; they perform impressive effects, but they are rotten beneath the surface, "counter-feit representative[s] of silver and gold."[24]

Counterfeiting posed a staggering problem to antebellum Americans. Before the National Banking Act of 1863 largely eliminated the practice, individual local banks could issue their own paper money. In the antebellum decades, literally thousands of different kinds of paper money circulated throughout the United States. Paper money issued by a well-known, well-established bank circulated at face value—it bought one dollar's worth of goods. A paper dollar from a shaky, distant, or poorly regarded bank, however, circulated at a discount. It bought perhaps eighty cents worth of goods, perhaps less. If the paper money moved far enough away from the bank that issued it, it might become completely worthless. Nearly every antebellum transaction involved not just questions of price, or judgments of the character of the parties involved, but also a long calculation of whether the money involved was "real" and how much it might actually be worth.[25]

A remarkable example of the financial system's loose, open character appears in the memoirs of escaped slave and author William Wells Brown. On a tour of Europe, Brown visited the Bank of England. The "monster building of gold and silver" reminded him oddly of his first days in freedom, in Monroe, Michigan, in 1835. He arrived in Monroe destitute, Brown recalled, and tried to get work in the shop of a local barber. The barber refused, but Brown managed to set himself up in business across the street, with a gaudy sign proclaiming him "Fashionable Hairdresser from New York, Emperor of the West." That he had never visited New York proved no deterrent, and soon, he claims, he had captured all the local business.[26]

Brown continues: "At this time, money matters in the Western States were in a sad condition. Any person who could raise a small amount of money was permitted to establish a bank, and allowed to issue notes for four times the sum raised." Banks were started all over the western states, Brown asserts, and the country flooded with worthless paper. "Notes from 6 to 75 cents in value," he explains, "were called 'Shinplasters.' I have often seen persons with large rolls of these bills, the whole not amounting to more than five dollars." Many antebellum businesses issued shinplasters or "token" money of their own: "transportation companies of all sorts—bridges, toll roads, ferry companies, and municipal enterprises—issued token currencies." In Georgia alone, between 1810 and 1866, "more than fifteen hundred varieties of currency of this type circulated."[27]

And in Michigan as well: one evening, Brown relates, a customer tells him "Emperor, you seem to be doing a thriving business. You should do as other business men, issue your Shinplasters." "From that moment," Brown recalled, "I began to think seriously of becoming a banker." Brown visited a local printer, chose the decorations for his shinplasters, and shortly received a roll of paper money worth twenty dollars. "At first my notes did not take well," he reported; "they were too new, and viewed with a suspicious eye. But through the assistance of my customers, and a good deal of exertion on my own part, my bills were soon in circulation; and nearly all the money received in return for my notes was spent in fitting up and decorating my shop."

Before long, however, a rival barber sent a series of men to Brown's shop, each bearing a large roll of Brown's shinplasters and each demanding some better form of money in return. A friend tells him: "You must act as all bankers do in this part of the country. . . . When your notes are brought to you, you must redeem them, and then send them out and get other money for them; and, with the latter, you can keep cashing your own Shinplasters." Brown took the advice and "immediately commenced putting in circulation the notes which I had just redeemed, and my efforts were crowned with so much success, that before I slept that night my 'Shinplasters' were again in circulation, and my bank once more on a sound basis."

A truly remarkable story—here Brown, a mixed-race fugitive slave, manages to set himself up in business in the raw West, issue his own paper money, and get people to take it. Backed solely by his own exertions, his skill at barbering, and his skill at self-representation—his face value, we might say—he prints his own paper bills to finance his shop tools. Brown, an abolitionist, a man acutely aware of the force of racism, presents this narrative with no mention whatsoever of race: it is as if the negotiability of value in Monroe, Michigan, has also opened up the meaning of race itself for renegotiation. He is like his own paper money, perfectly good if all agree to take it.[28]

A similar, although highly critical, linking of loose money and loose racial hierarchy appears in Robert Bird's satirical novel of 1839, *The Adventures of Robin Day*. In the novel country swain Robin, through a series of comic blunders, ends up a wandering fugitive with but a few paper notes to his name. Arriving in Philadelphia, he is immediately knocked down by "a blow from the wheelbarrow of a black porter; who, counting up from behind, whistling Yankee Doodle . . . tumbled me into a lot of pottery arranged along the pavement." Incensed, Robin starts after the porter, but "the dealer in washbowls and pattipans seizing me by the collar," demands that Robin pay for the damage to his shop.[29]

Robin hands him a five-dollar bill, but the merchant replies that the note was "a New Jersey note [and] like the bills of all New Jersey banks, at a discount"; he "refused to receive it, unless I allowed him an additional half-dollar by way of premium." Robin is about to pay "when a decent looking man stepped forward, inveighed against the roguery of the fellow," and "swore that New Jersey bank-bills were never at a discount, but always at a par." The stranger gives the merchant a dollar bill "of some Philadelphia bank" and hands Robin "four others as change; which being done, he clapped my Jersey note into his own pocket, and walked off." But Robin discovers, "about five minutes afterwards, that the four bills given me by the good-natured stranger were counterfeit, and my liberal gentleman a rascally swindler."

The misadventures continue: "I had not well got over the anger I had been thrown into by the assault of the porter, when it was my fate to encounter another blackamoor, a strapping tatterdemalion" who blocks his way. "I very naturally expected would get out of the way," but instead "he stalked against me, as if entirely ignorant of my presence, or quite indifferent to it; and I was, in a twinkling, laid upon my back." Two minutes later, Robin relates, "I encountered a similar accident; a third negro running against me with a violence that pitched me into a cellar; where was a cooper making cedar barrels or churns, one of which I had the satisfaction to demolish." "The coloured gentlemen of Philadelphia," Robin concludes, were "the true aristocracy of the town, or, at least, of the streets thereof." "The insolence of the black republicans" astonishes Robin, as does the submissiveness of whites. In Bird's satire, Philadelphia's dangers take the form of ambiguous money and impudent Negroes out of place.

Within three pages Bird links a loose and untrustworthy money supply to an inverted racial hierarchy—bad money equals black people out of place, and instability of both financial and social values.

It is precisely this kind of slipperiness that so exhilarated proponents of paper and so infuriated their conservative opponents. Paper money empowered the ambitious and the unscrupulous; it blurred the line between the two. As one of Robin Day's companions, a rogue who masquerades as a ship's captain, puts it later in the novel, "we must put on some kind of character, my skillagallee, hoist some sort of colours, split me; and if they happen to be false ones, where's the difference? Since not a lubberly rascal of us all ever sails under his own bunting." Brown, the imperial hairdresser not from New York, made up his persona as he made up his money; it was as real as he could maintain it to be. In Philadelphia, Robin unhappily encountered the equivalent of Emperor Brown, assuming the right to self-representation in the market.

In the daily life of the antebellum economy, the difference between representation and reality seemed impossible to establish. According to some estimates, at times more than 40 percent of the money in circulation before the Civil War was counterfeit.[30] To protect themselves, merchants subscribed to "counterfeit detectors"—weekly, biweekly, or monthly lists of banknotes that described a bank's paper money and rated the bank's character. Merchants typically needed more than one such periodical: the publishers of counterfeit detectors regularly accused their competitors of "puffing" the reputations of crooked bankers who bribed them. Herman Melville satirized the problem in *The Confidence Man*. When an elderly steamboat passenger receives some unfamiliar bills in change, he rushes to his "counterfeit detector" to examine "a three dollar bill on the Vicksburgh Trust and Insurance Banking Company." His "counterfeit detector," he mutters to himself, "says, among fifty other things, that, if a good bill, it must have, thickened here and there into the substance of the paper, little wavy spots of red; and it says they must have a kind of silky feel, being made by the lint of a red silk handkerchief stirred up in the paper-maker's vat." "Very well," says his traveling companion, who may in fact be the confidence man of the title. But no, says the old man: "that sign is not always to be relied on; for some good bills get so worn, the red marks get rubbed out. And that's the case with my bill here—see how old it is—or else it's a counterfeit, or else—I don't see right—or else—dear, dear me—I don't know what else to think."[31]

"Proves what I've always thought," says his companion: "that much of the want of confidence, in these days, is owing to these Counterfeit Detectors you see on every desk and counter. Puts people up to suspecting good bills." But the old man grabs a magnifying glass and continues reading his detector. "If the bill is good, it must have in one corner, mixed in with the vignette, the figure of a goose, very small, indeed, all but microscopic . . . not observable, even if magnified, unless the attention is directed to it." "Pore over it as I will," he says, "I can't see this goose." "Then throw that Detector away," says the stranger; "don't you see what a wild-goose chase it has led you?" But the passage ends with the old man poring over the bill into the small of the evening. These accounts dramatize money's close relations to both the democratic promise and the danger of self-making.

Hard money advocates cringed at the ambiguity and uncertainty of a paper money economy, at the thin line between counterfeit and real, especially when race entered the equation. *DeBow's Review*, the leading journal of the slave South, called paper money "that disease which taints all American blood, the paper money disease."[32] Economists frequently used the metaphor of blood to describe money. In this model, money circulated like the blood of the nation. "The currency of a country is to the community," John C. Calhoun wrote in 1837, "what the blood is to the body . . . indispensable to all the functions of life."[33] In these metaphors, paper money "debased" or corrupted the nation's blood. In 1860 *DeBow's Review* called gold money "natural," "God's money," and insisted that "all attempts to depreciate it by alloy, or to compel the use of a paper or any other substitute, have resulted in disastrous failure. . . . The surgeon or the anatomist who attempts to invent a substitute for the blood, is not a whit more presumptuous and charlatanic than the statesman who endeavors to force into circulation any other currency in place of the precious metals." "Money is as necessary to the social body as blood to the natural body," the writer continued: gold is "nature's currency."[34]

The language of blood in race echoed the language of value. "A community suffering incessant blood-disturbance," claimed a text on "blood admixture," "will exhibit social activity, though, if the disturbing element is very base, a corresponding depreciation of its absolute value will ensue."[35] The inferiority of the Negro, *DeBow's Review* concluded, "has been put to the severest test, by every possible ordeal, in war and in peace, in times past and times present, and, like gold, seven times tried in the fire, has proved itself to be genuine."[36] Slaveholders needed the difference between black and white to be "good as gold," because the southern economy depended on racial slavery. *DeBow's* insisted that paper money could only work when founded on unambiguously stable "real" commodities. Let that basis for redemption be made clear, "and who can doubt that a bank note will be a species of property as substantial and as enduring as an acre of land, as a negro, a house, or a mortgage upon any of those?"[37] As Walter Johnson points out, "slaves were regularly used as collateral in credit transaction; indeed, rather than giving an IOU when they borrowed money, many slaveholders simply wrote out a bill of sale for a slave who would actually be transferred only if they failed to pay their debt."[38] Slaves played the role of gold in economic exchange because, like gold, they were imagined to have an essential value that was both in the economy and outside it, beyond negotiation.

Of course the value of slaves was anything *but* stable: their value fluctuated along with their color—as even Josiah Nott argued: "A small trace of white blood in the negro improves him in intelligence and morality; and an equally small trace of negro blood, as in the quadroon, will protect such individual against the deadly influence of climates which the pure white-man cannot endure"[39] Miscegenation "improves" the Negro, but not so much that it erases the fiction of racial difference. The "isolated cases of negro smartness in this country prove" only "the value of a Caucasian admixture," claimed an article in *DeBow's*, suggesting that the value of Negroes was not fixed but negotiable. But it continued: "nature has marked, by unerring lines, the distinction between the species, and her tokens cannot be wiped out, by either the sophistry of the negrophilist, or the cant of the fanatic."[40] The contradiction is unmistakeable, and not surprisingly, *DeBow's* consistently attacked "amalgamation" as an evil, ignoring when it could the fact that in slave markets, color mattered—the darkness or lightness of the slave's skin inflated or lowered the price, depending on the circumstances.[41] When *DeBow's* published on money, it treated money as a kind of fixed natural fact, just as it treated racial difference. "Money and man are coeval and congenital as an institution," claimed a history of money; "[money's] uses came from heaven, was taught to man by his Maker. . . . Money is natural, and nature expelled today will return tomorrow."[42] Money "returned" in a different form than the writer hoped; it returned as a solvent that renegotiated and dissolved social distinctions, and it returned as the evidence of racial "amalgamation."

Paper money helped the entrepreneur, the man on the make. Having lots of paper money in circulation caused inflation but lowered interest rates and made credit easier to get, as William Wells Brown described. In this line of thinking, money represented nothing more than our common potential. It symbolized not some fantasy of "natural value" but the work all citizens did: "the value of money perpetually depends upon its power to represent value and not upon its material"[43] Debates about money merged with debates about the nature of character, about the difference between appearance and reality.

Whig and later Republican Party thinkers argued that paper money would democratize wealth. Dreams, ambitions were themselves a speculation, an imitation; making them come true required faith and vision. An ambitious man imitated the thing he hoped to become, the value he hoped to acquire. If ambitious men and women pooled their resources, founded a bank, and issued paper money, faith in their future partly backed the notes. If they could persuade others to accept their paper money, using the money to buy, say, building materials, they might make their dreams of prosperity into a reality. Thus could people "make themselves" through their own efforts.[44]

Republican editor Horace Greeley wrote: "An extraordinary proportion of our young men aspire to position, consideration, fortune, and expect to achieve these by Trade, or in some department of Productive Industry. Born poor, they seek independence through the use of Credit. . . . To a community thus suffused with the spirit of aspiration, of adventure, of industrial and commercial enterprise, the use of Paper Money is as natural as breathing."[45] If only gold served as money, Greeley and others argued, individual initiative strangled. And those who had gold could charge exorbitant interest rates to profit from someone else's work. Instead of imagining a "natural" economy, governed by intrinsic value and natural law, paper money advocates tended to see money, and the economy, as a social creation. In this line of thinking, money, wealth, *even identity itself* were mutable things, not values fixed by nature. They resulted from labor and will, not some accident of birth or creation.

Inevitably, in this line of thinking, the race question reasserts itself. The song "How Are You Greenbacks?" mentions Greeley several times. As editor of the *New York Tribune*, Greeley linked abundant paper money to the common man's desire for—and right to—self-advancement. The value of greenbacks, according to the song, depends on the soldier's commitment to the Union cause and the leadership that directs it:

> We're willing, Father A-bram, one hundred thousand more
> Should help our Uncle Samuel to Prosecute the war

> But then we want a chieftan true, one who can lead the van
> Geo. B McClellan, you all know, he is the very man.

McClellan, then enjoying great popularity, later ran for president on a "hard money," specie platform. "How Are You Greenbacks?" continues:

> We're coming, Father A-bram, One hundred thousand more
> To march with gleaming bayonets upon the traitor's shore
> But you must give us generals on whom we can depend
> And not let paper generals, drive off our faithful men.

The subject has shifted: it began as the greenbacks themselves, but the song now refers to Union soldiers. These verses make the greenbacks and the soldiers who take them in pay analogous. Both rush to the aid of Lincoln and the nation, but they need leaders of more than "paper." "How are you greenbacks?" the song asks, and the answer seems to be "only as good as our leaders and our willingness to fight": only as good as the Union itself. In the 1870s, the greenback and the scarred veteran frequently appeared as one, as in this 1878 campaign poem:

> O, Greenback, veteran of the years!
> Thou crippled soldier of the war!
> Baptized with blood and wet with tears.
> To-day thou art without a scar.
> Thou stood upon the picket line
> Wherever hissing bullets flew. . . .
> Thou stormed the forts; thou sped the ships;
> Thou dealt the gunboat's timely blow;
> Thou forged the cannon angry lips
> That screamed a welcome to the foe.
> Thanks, Greenback! Veteran of the years!
> Thou crippled hero of the war!
> To-day thy last wound disappears—
>   Thou standest forth without a scar![46]

In this poem the worn greenback and the weary soldiers who spent it come together. The greenbacks literally embody the citizens—they symbolize the loyal soldiers who fought for the Union cause, wounded as the soldiers they supported, crippled by political opposition. The greenbacks, then, represent not intrinsic value or natural aristocracy but rather labor, sacrifice, and patriotism. Service to the nation gave both greenbacks and veterans their value—they made themselves great. But how much value could service, and individual effort, actually confer?

One of the great questions of the war focused on African American soldiers: what would their service earn them? Bryant's minstrel tune "How Are You Greenbacks?" raised the question itself in its last few verses. Again the subject—the "we" that's coming—shifts. It concludes by literally identifying the greenbacks with African American soldiers:

> We're coming, Father A-bram, Nine hundred thousand strong
> With nine hundred thousand darkies, sure the traitors can't last long
> With Corporal Cuff, and Sergeant Pomp, to lead us in the melee
> And at their head, without a red, Our Brigadier General Greely.

In the first verse, greenbacks announced their own coming. Later, the (white) soldiers used the same language. Finally, the soldiers have become African Americans, newly issued like greenbacks themselves. Now the issues of money's value and the value of racial identity begin to come together as well. Mirroring the white public's ambivalence about "colored troops," on one level the song links African Americans in the patriotic celebration of the Union cause. On another, it points again to uneasiness about value and character. Some "inflation" seems to have occurred: "nine hundred thousand darkies" instead of the "one hundred thousand" men and greenbacks of earlier verses. Cuff and especially Pomp were common, mocking nicknames for African Americans, stock characters used in the minstrel show. Is the song praising their service to the Union or mocking it as false, "paper" value?

Critics of Lincoln's decision to enlist African Americans in the Union army claimed that it raised "colored" soldiers to a level of equality with whites; they argued that blacks lacked the basic qualities of discipline, courage, and intelligence necessary for battle. They saw the soldiers as inflated, valueless. An 1862 song attacking Lincoln criticized the "fractional currency"—paper notes in amounts of less than one dollar—that the North also issued during the war. These "Shin-plasters sure were bad enough," the song argued:

> That is when Rebels used them;
> And well the Nigger-worshippers,
> In consequence abused them,

But now to cap the climax, of
Our manifold disasters,
We've had to come to one and two
And three cent *sticking plasters.*

What next I wonder? Nigger troops
Or some such abomination;
As Niggers being our equals in
The states and in the nation.[47]

This verse sees African American soldiers, oddly, as the next logical step after the issue of "cheap" fractional paper currency. The progression superficially makes little sense—what do "colored troops" have to do with paper money? But the author clearly saw a connection between purely representational currency, a piece of paper named "three cents," and the representation of African Americans as equal citizens through the Union uniform.[48]

Other opponents of African American enlistment scorned the appearance of African Americans in uniform, "strutting up and down Pennsylvania avenue, and aping the port and gait of their illustrious prototype,"[49] in terms that inverted the minstrel show itself. In the minstrel show, white minstrels "aped" *their* prototype, African Americans—the whites strutting across the stage in raggedy costume. Their mimicry made them money, turned "rags into cash," even as it blurred the line between the real and the symbol. Popular commentary on "colored troops" focused on the soldiers as imitations of whites. Would this "imitation" lead to equality—would they become the things they imitated—or remain a valueless counterfeit?

"The Colored Brigade," another song written and published shortly after the enlistment of African Americans, reflected this ambivalence:

O when we meet de enemy I s'pec we make 'em stare,
I tink he'll catch a tartar when he meets de woolly hair;
We'll fight while we are able, and in greenbacks we'll be paid,
And soon I'll be a colonel in de colored brigade.

Chor.—A colonel, a colonel, in de darkey brigade,
And soon I'll be a colonel in de colored brigade.

The song's other stanzas refer favorably to African Americans' service in the Revolutionary War and with Jackson in 1812; it states: "Now some folks tink de darkey for the fighting wasn't made, / We'll show dem what's de matter in de colored brigade." But it points—"soon I'll be a colonel"— to inflated rank and argues:

> Some say dey lub de darkey and dey want him to be free,
> I s'pec dey only fooling and dey better let him be;
> For him dey'd break dis Union which de're forefadders had made,
> Worth more dan twenty millions ob de colored brigade.[50]

In this verse the Union is worth more than paper money and colored soldiers. It serves as the gold behind the linguistic and social exchange the song initiates.

"Great things are expected from this new principle of military amalgamation," commented the *Herald:* "Whether it will change the Ethiop's skin to white or convert the white man's skin to black remains to be tested."[51] The *Herald* wondered, or pretended to wonder, just how much the uniform— the representation of citizenship—might change its wearer's basic character. Would African American soldiers become the things they "imitated"?

Others more clearly saw African American soldiers as like the greenbacks themselves: a counterfeit. "For finance, issue Greenbacks; for war, Blackbacks," one critic of the administration argued.[52] Just as greenbacks could never acquire a value they intrinsically lacked, so African Americans would remain of doubtful value no matter their clothes. "How Are You Greenbacks?" concluded:

> We're coming, Father A-bram, Nine hundred thousand more
> With the greatest fighting hero, that lives upon our shore
> He fought in all the battle won, and shed his blood most freely
> But he's fought them all with the Tribune, and his name in Gen'l Greely.

Lampooning Greeley as a paper general whose battles all take place in the flat world of print representation, the song also mocks the African American soldier's contribution to the war, or at least devalues it to the level of paper. "How Are You Greenbacks?" begins with an image of printing presses patriotically turning out paper money and, as Bryant's Minstrels would have performed it on stage, ends with an image of minstrel characters, dressed as soldiers, comically marching behind their paper general. It makes an explicit link between the possibility of racial equality and the philosophy of paper money.

Other attacks on Lincoln and paper money made the same connec-

Fig. 3.2. Lyrics for "Who Will Care for Old Abe Now."
America Singing: Nineteenth-Century Song Sheets,
Rare Book and Special Collections Division,
Library of Congress.

tion, in explicitly racist terms. These attacks came most clearly in material written for the presidential campaign of 1864. "Jokes, Niggers, Greenbacks—all play'd out," mocked the first verse of the song "Who Will Care for Old Abe Now?" (fig. 3.2). McClellan stood for the return of gold, the song continued. "When 'Little Mac' is in the White House, / . . . / Greenbacks will vanish—Gold come down![53] "We're fighting for the nigger now," went another song:

> I calculate of niggers we soon shall have our fill,
> With Abe's proclamation and the nigger army bill.
> Who would not be a soldier for the Union to fight?
> For, Abe's made the nigger the equal of the white.

This song, titled "I Am Fighting for the Nigger," also claimed that the soldier "must be loyal, and his officers obey, / Though he lives on mouldy biscuit, and fights without his pay. . . . / Though he waits six months for Green-Backs, worth forty-five per cent." The song treats greenbacks, elevated to a position of equality with gold they cannot sustain, as part of the same mentality that has elevated African Americans to a counterfeit equality. It concluded that "when old Jeff Davis is captured, paid up you may be: / If you do not mind the money, don't you set the nigger free."[54] For Lincoln's opponents, the return to gold meant the return to racial hierarchy, whereas paper money meant freedom for slaves: "Oh! we want no . . . 'Greenbacks,' such as Chase used to utter." Another campaign song went: "We want no more rank niggers near the White House frying pan; / Nor to sit at the head of the table![55] This song treated greenbacks as part of a general scheme to upset the "natural" order of things. A third campaign song chided those who, "while worshipping the nigger, they'd let the Union slide." It concluded that under McClellan, "we'll *chase* away all greenbacks, and gather in our gold, / And then we will prosper, as in the days of old."[56] In the waning days of the war the *Charleston Mercury* denounced the northern economy, the "negro bogus National Banks," and their paper money, now flooding the South.[57] All these critics linked paper money to a confusion of the line between thing and symbol, black and white. Paper money had helped depreciate the white man while it inflated the black; it had destabilized not just financial value but the differences between things and people.

The *New York Herald* argued that the issue of greenbacks had served only to further the cause of the "niggerheads," who wanted to make a war for abolition. Referring partly to the issue of greenbacks, the *Herald* wrote: "Accursed be that infernal abolition fanaticism which has rendered them necessary. . . . The arts of the niggerheads have made volunteers and money equally scarce. Consequently it was necessary to pass the Conscription bill and issue more paper money."[58] "Negro-worshipers," it contended, have pushed through a policy of financial inflation. In depreciating the currency they have also depreciated the value of white men.[59] Another Democratic campaign document of 1864 compared paper money to "amalgamation, selection by affinity, polygamy, community of property and all the other disgusting and ruinous theories of depraved minds" and went on to compare those who wanted paper money with "stock jobbers, negro fanatics, bubble blowers, [and] broken-down wildcat [banknote] distributors." These arguments treat the ideal of racial equality, or even just the idea of some modest political considerations for African Americans, as akin to wild financial speculations, to inflation of blacks and depreciation of whites, to miscegenation, and to a general confusion of the symbol for the real thing. *The Great Paper Bubble* went on to compare greenbacks to a bad medical experiment, a transfusion of "cow's blood" into a human, resulting in madness and death.[60]

Grasping for optimism toward the end of the war, the *Charleston Mercury* imagined improvements in confederate finances. "Our currency," the *Mercury* claimed, "under the salutary provisions of the last Congress, must grow better and better daily, while that of the enemy, under the absorption of gold, the augmenting expenses of the government, and the increasing issues of promises to pay [i.e., greenbacks], must grow worse and worse." The *Mercury* then linked currency to the Confederate army's better blood: "Our army, like our currency, will grow better every day, led as it will be by the warm, young blood of the country pouring into it all the time its vivifying ardor," while "the army of the enemy . . . will soon contain nothing better than negroes, European mercenaries, substitutes, and conscripts too worthless to pay. . . . Thus our currency and our army are improving and theirs deteriorating."[61] The similarity of economic and racial language is unmistakable here. "Base" blood "depreciated the "absolute value" of a civilization that allowed it to circulate, in the same way that circulating paper money debased the nation's financial blood.

The money debate shows the intense contradictory desires at the heart of American culture. Attracted to, even obsessed with, the possibilities for self-transformation and the freedom to remake themselves, these same sources also express the opposite desire—the desire for fixed values and an unshakeable "natural" order. On the minstrel stage, those conflicts flashed when the topics of money and race came together. If the greenback represented the aspiring citizen's desire to get ahead, the greenback also suggested the possibility of a world in which people might simply declare themselves whatever they liked—the aspiring Negro might declare himself equal, or at least erase the "value" of the difference between white and black. The minstrel show toyed with that very idea, allowing its white audience to simultaneously blur the line between white and black and reinforce it. It sent bewilderingly mixed messages about both value and character.

As they watched whites "ape the port and gait" of "their prototype" on the minstrel stage, white audiences scorned African Americans in uniform as "paper soldiers" lacking real value. But they also celebrated the way labor and sacrifice could create value from paper, the way representation could become reality. American debates about the character of money continually restaged this conflict between limitless dreams of self-making and the security of a fixed, essential character. Neither money nor race is real: both are representations of difference and what it means, representations of what we are and what we might become. In the years following the Civil War, Americans retreated from the promises of both paper money and racial equality, and endorsed both hard currency and fierce racial segregation. The promise of market freedom and self-making never entirely went away, but it lived and lives in a setting of contradiction.

Today, for example, the most enthusiastic proponents of the "free market" almost invariably insist on "natural law" and natural hierarchy in human affairs. The libertarian Cato Institute, for example, seeks "alternatives to discretionary government fiat money that are consistent with individual freedom and a money of stable value," including "gold or other commodity standards."[62] It also commits itself to "a natural law and natural rights tradition that recognizes discoverable, rational standards for justice above and beyond the decisions of earthly governments"; Cato finds the sources for these concepts in, not surprisingly, Herbert Spencer and William Graham Sumner.[63] Spencer's insistence on a "natural" basis for human inequality needs no explanation; Sumner, the *Journal of Libertarian Studies* notes approvingly, "rejected the moralistic, equalitarian, and atomistic dogmas upon which democracy rested, he was not in favor of extending the suffrage to ex-slaves or to women."[64] "Moralistic, equalitarian" dogmas have no "natural law" basis. But a theory of "natural differences" and natural law confines individuals within the prison of their presumed "nature." Cato offers a model of freedom that, as the popular phrase has it, "isn't free." Like gold in a vault, the idea of racial difference has anchored the flights of American freedom: American freedom has been paid for by the gold standard of racial difference.

NOTES

1. Bray Hammond, *Sovereignty and an Empty Purse: Banks and Politics in the Civil War* (Princeton, 1957); Richard Franklin Bensel, *Yankee Leviathan: The Origins of Central State Authority in America, 1859–1877* (Cambridge, MA, 1990), chaps. 3–4.

2. John Pendelton Kennedy, *Annals of Quodlibet* (Philadelphia, 1840; repr., Saddle River, NJ, 1970), 58–59.

3. Elbridge Gerry Spaulding, *A Resource of War—The Credit of the Government Made Immediately Available* (Buffalo, NY, 1869), 63.

4. *New York Herald*, March 6, 1863.

5. Bensel, *Yankee Leviathan*, although an estimable account of the political economy

of the Civil War and Reconstruction, largely ignores rhetoric and its meaning. Those working in the tradition of Hofstadter—for example, Irwin Unger, *The Greenback Era* (Princeton, 1964); Robert Sharkey, *Money, Class and Party: An Economic Study of Civil War and Reconstruction*, Studies in Historical and Political Science (Baltimore, 1959); and Bray Hammond, *Banks and Politics in America* (1957; repr., Princeton, 1991)—had an eye for rhetorical flourish but treated racialized language as a sign of failure to understand the "real issues." More recently James Livingston, *Pragmatism and the Political Economy of Cultural Revolution* (New York, 1994), acknowledges the presence of racial rhetoric but sees it as a sign of backwardness in paper money forces and largely ignores it in gold bugs. Robin Einhorn, *American Taxation, American Slavery* (Chicago, 2006), talks about taxation with verve and originality but ignores the burning question of what medium the taxes were to be paid in. Mathew Frye Jacobson, *Barbarian Virtues* (New York, 2001), more completely integrates the rhetoric that orthodox economists used with the policies the rhetoric supported. Walter T. K. Nugent, *Money and American Society, 1865–1880* (New York, 1968), called attention to the linkage between gold and the Anglo-Saxon race.

6. Charles A. Beard, *An Economic Interpretation of the Constitution of the United States* (1913; repr., New York, 2004); Richard Hofstadter, *The Age of Reform* (New York, 1955), 60–93; and Hofstadter, *The Paranoid Style in American Politics* (New York, 1965).

7. Clifford Geertz, *The Interpretation of Cultures* (1973; repr, New York, 2000).

8. The literature on artifice, imposture, and illusion in popular culture is now extensive. The author was an undergraduate student of Miles Orvell, author of *The Real Thing* (Chapel Hill, NC, 1989). Other crucial books include Karen Halttunen, *Confidence Men and Painted Women* (New Haven, CT, 1986); John Kasson, *Rudeness and Civility* (New York, 1991); Kasson, *Houdini, Tarzan and the Perfect Man* (New York, 2002); James Cook, *The Arts of Deception* (Cambridge, MA); David Waldstreicher, *Runaway America* (New York, 2005); Jackson Lears, *No Place of Grace* (Chicago, 1994); Lears, *Fables of Abundance* (New York, 1995); Philip Deloria, *Playing Indian* (New Haven, CT, 1999).

9. Michel Foucault, *The Order of Things* (1970; repr., New York, 1994).

10. John Joseph Goux, *Symbolic Economies* (Ithaca, NY, 1990); David Graeber, *Toward an Anthropological Theory of Value* (London, 2001); Marc Shell, *Money, Language and Thought* (Baltimore, MD, 1991); Shell, *Art and Money* (Chicago, 1995); Viviana Zelizer, *The Social Meaning of Money* (Princeton, NJ, 1997); Walter Benn Michaels, *The Gold Standard and the Logic of Naturalism* (Berkeley, 1987).

11. Benjamin Franklin, "A Modest Inquiry into the Nature and Necessity of a Paper Currency" (1729), in *Documentary History of Banking and Currency in the United States*, vol. 1, ed. Herman E. Kroos (New York, 1963); Daniel Walker Howe, *The Political Culture of the American Whigs* (Chicago, 1979); Hammond, *Banks and Politics*. Good histories of antebellum banking tend at the moment to be motivated by libertarian politics. See, for examples, Howard Bodenhorn, *A History of Banking in Antebellum America* (Cambridge, 2000); Milton Friedman and Anna Schwartz, *A Monetary History of the United States, 1867–1960* (Princeton, NJ, 1963); Murray N. Rothbard, *A History of Money and Banking in the United States* (Auburn, AL, 2002); Lawrence Schweikart, *Banking in the American South: From the Age of Jackson to Reconstruction* (Baton Rouge, LA, 1978). For a fascinating account of the era of multiple currencies, see William H. Dillistin, *Bank Note Reporters and Coun-*

terfeit Detectors, 1826–1866 (New York, 1949); and David Henkin, *City Reading: Written Words and Public Spaces in Antebellum New York* (New York, 1998), chap. 4.

12. E. Bowers and Charles W. Glover, "How Are You Greenbacks?" (New York, 1863), in Historic American Sheet Music, 1850–1920 (from Duke University), American Memory Web site, Library of Congress; http://memory.loc gov.

13. The extensive literature on the minstrel show and its ambiguities includes Eric Lott, *Love and Theft* (New York, 1995); Michael Paul Rogin, *Blackface, White Noise: Jewish Immigrants in the Hollywood Melting Pot* (Berkeley, 1998); James Cook, *The Arts of Deception: Playing with Fraud in the Age of Barnum* (New York, 2001); and Cook, "Dancing across the Color Line," *Common-Place* 4, no. 1 (October 2003), http://www.common-place.org/vol-04/no-01/cook/; David R. Roediger, *The Wages of Whiteness: Race and the Making of the American Working Class* (New York, 1991), chap. 4.

14. See Cook, "Dancing across the Color Line"; Jacobson, *Barbarian Virtues* 15, 37.

15. *Pennsylvania Gazette*, September 20, 1786.

16. Stephen D. Carpenter, *Logic of History: Five Hundred Political Texts; Being Concentrated Extracts of Abolitionism; also, Results, of Slavery Agitation and Emancipation; Together with Sundry Chapters on Despotism, Usurpations and Their Frauds* (Madison, WI, 1864), 325.

17. On gold and circulation, see Michaels, *Gold Standard and the Logic of Naturalism*; and Henkin, *City Reading*, chap. 4.

18. Joseph G. Baldwin, *The Flush Times of Alabama and Mississippi: A Series of Sketches* (New York, 1858), 82.

19. William Gouge, "A Short History of Paper-Money and Banking in the United States" (1833), in *Documentary History of Banking and Currency in the United States*, ed. Herman E. Kroos (New York, 1983), 2:40. See also Benjamin G. Rader, "William M. Gouge: Jacksonian Economic Theorist," *Pennsylvania History* 30 (October 1963): 443–53.

20. "Monopoly and Paper Money," *United States Democratic Review* 35, no. 6 (June 1855): 440.

21. George Pendleton, as quoted in Alexander Harris, *A Review of the Political Conflict in America, from the Commencement of the Anti-Slavery Agitation to the Close of Southern Reconstruction* (New York, 1876), 250.

22. *New York Herald*, October 18, 1862.

23. David A. Wells, *Robinson Crusoe's Money* (New York, 1876), 97.

24. "Monopoly and Paper Money," 440.

25. See, for example, the account in Henkin, *City Reading*, chap. 4.

26. William Wells Brown, *Three Years in Europe; or, Places I Have Seen and People I Have Met. By W. Wells Brown, a Fugitive Slave* (London, 1852), 97–105. In the following paragraphs, all quotations of Brown are from this volume.

27. Schweikart, *Banking in the American South*, 80.

28. Slave narratives often emphasized the difference between the negotiability the market promised and that same market's determination to fix race in place as a distinct and nonnegotiable value. See Michael O'Malley, "Intrinsic Value to Its Species: Slave Narratives and the Colonial Economy," manuscript; and for examples see Olaudah Equiano, *The Interesting Narrative of the Life of Olaudah Equiano*, in *The Classic Slave Narratives*, ed. Henry Louis Gates (New York, 1987), passim; Venture Smith, *A Narrative of the Life and Adventures of Venture, a Native of Africa: But Resident above Sixty Years in the United States of America. Related by Himself* (New

London, CT, 1798), 971; Frederick Douglass, *Narrative of the Life of Frederick Douglass*, in Gates, *Classic Slave Narratives*, 312–13, 325.

29. Robert Montgomery Bird, *Adventures of Robin Day* (Philadelphia, 1839), 123–25. In the following paragraphs, all quotations of Bird are from this volume.

30. See Stephen Mihm, *A Nation of Counterfeiters: Capitalists, Con Men, and the Making of the United States* (Cambridge, MA, 2007); David R. Johnson, *Illegal Tender: Counterfeiting and the Secret Service in Nineteenth-Century America* (Washington, DC, 1995); Lyn Glaser, *Counterfeiting in America* (New York, 1968), 104–5; Murray T. Bloom, *Money of Their Own* (1957; repr., Port Clinton, OH, 1982), 101–3.

31. Herman Melville, *The Confidence Man: His Masquerade* (1857; repr., New York, 1984), 1108–10. In the following paragraphs, all quotations of Melville are from this volume.

32. "Fiscal History of Texas," *DeBow's Review: Agricultural, Commercial, Industrial Progress and Resources* 14, no. 4 (April 1853): 380–86.

33. John C. Calhoun, as quoted in Lacy K. Ford, *Origins of Southern Radicalism: The South Carolina Upcountry, 1800–1860* (New York, 1988), 93.

34. "Money as an Institution," *DeBow's Review* 29, no. 1 (July 1860): 21–25.

35. John William Draper, *Thoughts on the Future Civil Policy of America* (New York, 1866).

36. "Canaan Identified with the Ethiopian," *Southern Quarterly Review* 2, no. 4 (October 1842): 375.

37. "Basis of Commercial Credit," *DeBow's Review* 16, no. 1 (January 1854): 79.

38. Walter Johnson, *Soul by Soul: Life inside the Antebellum Slave Market* (Cambridge, MA, 1999), 25–26.

39. Josiah Clark Nott, *Types of Mankind: or, Ethnological Researches, Based upon the Ancient Monuments, Paintings, Sculptures, and Crania of Races, and upon Their Natural, Geographical, Philological and Biblical History* (Philadelphia, 1855), 68.

40. L. S. M., "Negro-Mania," *DeBow's Review* 12, no. 5 (May 1852): 519–20.

41. Johnson, *Soul by Soul*, 140–41.

42. "Money as an Institution," 22.

43. Edward Kellogg, *Labor and Other Capital* (1849), as quoted in W. A. Berkey, *The Money Question* (Grand Rapids, MI, 1876), 30.

44. Unger, *Greenback Era*, 50–58; Nugent, *Money and American Society*; Walter T. K. Nugent, *The Money Question during Reconstruction* (New York, 1967); and Rodney J. Morrison, "Henry C. Carey and American Economic Development," in *Transactions of the American Philosophical Society*, vol. 76 (Philadelphia, 1986). See also Lawrence Goodwyn, *Democratic Promise: The Populist Movement in America* (New York, 1974); Gretchen Ritter, *Goldbugs and Greenbacks: The Antimonopoly Tradition and the Politics of Finance in America* (Cambridge, 1997).

45. Horace Greeley, *Essays Designed to Elucidate the Science of Political Economy* (New York, 1869), 68. Greeley had some reservations about a purely "irredeemable" paper currency but was vague about what backed paper money if not gold. He wrote: "Between the bigotry which regards all Paper Money as virtually counterfeit, and the folly which would enrich a people by burying them in shinplasters, there is a happy medium" (*Essays*, 80).

46. W. A. Croffut, "Bourbon Ballads (Songs for the Stump): An Extra Edition, No. 52," American Memory Web site, Library of Congress.

47. Author unknown, "The Broker's 'Stamp Act'" (July 1862), American Memory Web site, Library of Congress.

48. The song mentions Benjamin Butler, the "beast" of New Orleans, the well-known political supporter of paper money widely disdained for his enlistment of "contraband" escaped slaves into the Union army. Butler also earned the South's rage for his famous "general order no. 28" in May 1862. Resenting the continued hostility of New Orleans women, Butler declared in this order that "as the officers and soldiers of the United States have been subject to repeated insult from the women (calling themselves ladies) of New Orleans, in return for the most scrupulous non-interference and courtesy on our part, it is ordered that hereafter when any female shall, by word, gesture, or movement, insult or show contempt for any officer or soldier of the United States, she shall be regarded and held liable to be treated as a woman of the town plying her avocation." In effect, Butler labeled otherwise respectable women "prostitutes" and had them arrested. The order made him infamous, and in Reconstruction his support of both greenbacks and racial equality would make him a favorite target.

49. *New York Herald*, May 22, 1863.

50. "The Colored Brigade" (Philadelphia, n.d.), American Memory Web site, Library of Congress

51. *New York Herald*, May 22, 1863.

52. *Atlas and Argus* (Albany), January 19, 1863, as quoted in Forrest G. Wood, *The Black Scare: The Racist Response to Emancipation Reconstruction and Reconstruction* (Berkeley, 1970), 44.

53. J. M. H. De Marsan, "Who Will Care for Old Abe Now? A Parody" (New York, 1864).

54. William Kiernan, "I Am Fighting for the Nigger" (New York, n.d.), American Memory Web site, Library of Congress.

55. J. F. Feeks, "Shouting Our Battle-Cry, 'McClellan,'" in *From the Democratic Presidential Campaign Songster* (New York, 1864).

56. John A. McSorley, "McClellan Campaign Song" (New York, 1864), American Memory Web site, Library of Congress.

57. *Charleston Mercury*, November 3, 1864.

58. *New York Herald*, March 6, 1863.

59. *New York Herald*, January 27, 1863; see also December 23, 1862: "The abolition radicals, then, and their managing agents in the Cabinet and the War Office, are responsible, in their disorganizing schemes and intrigues, for all the follies, failures and disasters of the war, including a derangement of our financial affairs and a depreciated paper currency."

60. Alexander Delmar, *The Great Paper Bubble, or, The Coming Financial Explosion* (New York, 1864), 54, 30.

61. *Charleston Mercury*, March 22, 1864.

62. Cato Institute, "Monetary and Banking Policy," http://www.cato.org/research/banking/index.html.

63. Brian Doherty, "The Roots of Modern Libertarian Ideas," in *Cato Policy Report*, March/April 2007, http://www.cato.org/pubs/policy_report/pr-index.html.

64. H. A. Scott Trask, "William Graham Sumner: Against Democracy, Plutocracy, and Imperialism," *Journal of Libertarian Studies* 18, no. 4 (Fall 2004): 8.

FOUR

The Envelope, Please

SHANE WHITE, STEPHEN GARTON, STEPHEN
ROBERTSON, AND GRAHAM WHITE

As was so often the case in Harlem, it began on Lenox, up near
127th Street. On a clear evening in late September 1930, John Scott, a
small-time swindler, mingled with a crowd being addressed by a series
of black orators. From this distance, it is difficult to know why Scott singled out James Skerritt as his mark; probably he did so because Skerritt
appeared to be unaccompanied, and looked at once morose and reasonably prosperous. Sidling up to Skerritt, Scott observed that the orator, to
whom both of them were listening, put him in mind of "Marcus Garvey
that got sent back to Jamaica," to which Skerritt replied that "this man
is talking something beneficial to the colored race, isn't he?" Scott then
attempted to lift Skerritt's spirits, suggesting that he knew how to make
Skerritt's blues go away. Skerritt muttered miserably that he would like
"to go some place to find out my troubles," whereupon Scott assured him
that he knew of someone who could help. The two men arranged to meet
the following evening at nine o'clock on the corner of 98th Street and
Amsterdam, at which point, Scott promised, he would introduce Skerritt to a "great man," who could give us "insight on misfortune." All now
depended on the great man's performance.

People who met con man Walter Hall, a.k.a. Paul Hall, the "great
man" in question, did not easily forget him; he had a presence that even
the passage of three-quarters of a century, and the necessity of our reliance on dry details long buried in a dusty case file, cannot dim. In early
November, when Robert Santangelo, the deputy assistant district attorney, closely questioned John Scott, Santangelo seemed particularly interested in Hall's appearance. In part this was because Hall had not as yet
been apprehended, but mostly Santangelo's interest seems to have been
prompted by expectations as to how a black con man should look, expec-

tations that Hall easily satisfied. Hall was thirty-two years old, weighed about 170 pounds, and was roughly the same height as Patrolman Michael McCarthy, who was also present in the small interview room at 137 Center Street. He had a knife scar in the middle of his forehead, was clean shaven, possessed thick lips but not very thick eyebrows, prominent ears, sharp eyes, and a round face. Scott also described Hall as being very dark complexioned, with kinky hair that was fashioned into "African curls." Only occasionally, Santangelo learned, did Hall exchange his trademark gray suit for a brown one. Were Hall's suits "baggy fitting or snappy"? Santangelo asked. "Close fitting," Scott replied. Scott further informed Santangelo that Hall always wore shoes with elevated heels, silk shirts that were either white or blue, a soft hat, and tweed overcoat. He was, however, never seen in a bow tie. Santangelo lingered over the subject of Hall's ties, asking "What are they, loud?" to which Scott replied, "very loud." The deputy assistant district attorney then wanted to know whether Hall had any gold teeth. Scott was certain that Hall "has plenty of gold in his mouth." Unquestionably, the "great man" was a sharp dresser who looked good and knew it.[1]

Hall also knew how to stage a performance. As soon as he met Scott, his accomplice, and Skerritt, the mark, the following night in September, he told them that he was a "great master" and that "I can do anything with spiritual power." It turned out the luckless Skerritt's wife had run away from him, taking some of his money as well. "Do what I tell you," intoned Hall. "Go ahead and buy a pad, two envelopes and a pound of rice and you sleep with them under your pillow until tomorrow; then you see me to-morrow at twelve o'clock and you'll see wonders performed." The three met at the same place the following day, and when Hall opened one of the envelopes, it turned out to contain that morning's winning clearing house number (released at ten o'clock). Hall then said: "you see that I'm a great man," and announced: "I want to bless you. You have curses on you. I want to change your whole life." Hall instructed Skerritt to "go to the bank and draw out every cent you have in the bank and bring it to me in hundred dollar bills, hundreds and fifties." With the bait having been taken, and the hook set, it was only a question now of landing the catch.

All three black men went downtown to the Union Dime Savings Bank at Sixth Avenue and 40th Street. Hall and Scott waited at a discreet distance while Skerritt withdrew $1,130, and when the hapless Skerritt emerged from the bank they rejoined him. Hall then said, "All right now, let's get a cab and go for the water, I have blessing to do, I have to bless you." The three men left the cab at 92nd and Riverside Drive and walked toward the Hudson, where the following exchange between the con man, Hall, and his dupe, Skerritt, ensued:

> "Have you all the money?"
> "Yes."
> "Now, do you believe in me?"
> "Yes.
> "Do you want to do what I tell you to do?"
> "Yes. All right."
> "You carry out my instructions and you'll succeed; your wife will come back to you on her knees and beg your humble pardon."

After these words had been spoken, Hall, Scott, and Skerritt sat on a bench near the water and prayed together. Hall then told Skerritt to count his money, place it in an envelope, and put the envelope in his pocket. After that the three men walked down to a sandy spit, where Hall took the envelope from Skerritt, tied a weight to it, and ordered Skerritt to throw the envelope containing his money into the water. As soon as the ripples had disappeared, Hall instructed his two companions to "walk back with me," warning, somewhat unoriginally, that if they looked back they would turn into pillars of salt. Once back at the park bench, Scott— our witness to these proceedings—did what he had been told to do and departed, leaving Hall and Skerritt quietly talking. Not only had the catch been beached; it had also been scaled, gutted, and tossed in the pan— and still the mark had no idea that he had been taken for every dollar he had managed to scrape together in this world.

For all his success in ultimately securing the convictions of both Hall and Scott, little about the case could have afforded Deputy Assistant District Attorney Santangelo much satisfaction. Probably embarrassed by the course of events and quite possibly still wary of Hall, Skerritt, the victim, was of no help. He denied that he was a spiritualist, and infuriated a disbelieving Santangelo by spinning a story about his withdrawing $1,130 from a bank way back in July, catching a cab with two men whom he had never seen before, getting out with them at 97th Street, some forty blocks from where he lived, being bashed on the back of his head by Hall, and subsequently being robbed by Scott, who had taken the money from his pocket. Scott, who was dealt with separately and sentenced to fifteen to thirty years in state prison, also proved to be a difficult witness for the state as it attempted to make its case against Hall. Concerned with the facts as only someone from the DA's office could be and anxious to tidy up the case, Santangelo plugged away, closely questioning Scott about the switching of the envelopes. It turned out, though, that Scott was even more literal-minded than was the deputy assistant district attorney. He may have reluctantly conceded that Hall did have a second envelope and that the one with the money in it was not thrown into the water, but he refused to admit that he had seen Hall's sleight of hand. "I couldn't see the switch," he stated. "The switching of the hand was swifter than the eyes." And that was an epitaph that Hall or any con man, black or white, could live with. Having given every indication that he would testify for the prosecution, Scott then refused to do so. It is difficult not to conclude that Hall was the sort of Harlem denizen whom one did not cross. In the end, Santangelo had to cut a deal with Hall, who pleaded to second degree grand larceny, in essence thereby acquiescing to Skerritt's unlikely story. Hall was sentenced to only two and a half years in state prison.[2] It was all very messy. But then this was Harlem, and above 125th Street things were seldom straightforward.

The occupation of confidence man has a long and venerable history among African Americans. Under slavery, the nature of the institution itself meant that slaves, from an early age, learned that their survival depended on their ability to deceive and to dissemble, to mask their feelings and thoughts from owners, overseers, and indeed any white person. What was demanded by the circumstances of slavery was further reinforced by the importance in black culture of the "man of words"—a tradition, which can be traced back to Africa, of placing a high value on verbal agility. "Puttin' on ole Massa" was a way of life for blacks held in slavery.[3] But if slavery was the school that honed these skills to a razor-sharp edge, it was freedom that revealed new vistas for their exploitation. For the first time, in the early decades of the nineteenth century in the North, large numbers of African Americans became free, and that meant things would never be quite the same again. In the 1820s and 1830s, cities such as New York and Philadelphia were alive with blacks who lived off their wits and linguistic skills. Those who did so in the contexts of abolition, the black church, and the incipient civil rights movement have been well served by historians. Not so those former slaves and children of slaves for whom the ability to talk well had opened up a whole new range of barely legal and sometimes plainly illegal possibilities in the rapidly expanding urban centers of the Northeast.

African Americans were hardly alone in seeking to make a living as confidence men in this era. In the world of strangers created by rapid urbanization, middle-class Americans worried about confidence men preying on those newly arrived in the city. Practitioners of various cons filled urban courts. A rich historical literature, beginning with Karen Halttunen's *Confidence Men and Painted Women*, has probed these fears about fraud and the etiquette manuals, urban guidebooks, and other mechanisms developed as defenses against deception.[4] But this literature has far less to say about cons as a feature of everyday life than it does about confidence men as a cultural force, and it makes no mention of African Americans.[5]

In the accounts of cons that filled the early nineteenth-century press, it was the notorious practice of "burning" that, in the 1820s and 1830s at least, was particularly associated with African Americans. What usually happened was that a black would strike up a conversation with the white mark, ask him if he could change a note, or whether he would hold the money for a bet, entice him into an alley, and there fleece him, either through sleight of hand or simply by grabbing his wallet and running. In March 1838, for example, as Mr. Nelson from Vermont came out of the New York exchange building, he was lured into an alley by a black man and relieved of all of his cash, a transaction that, the *Journal of Commerce* pointed out, was a "trick" that "had been often and extensively practiced in this city, and was called 'burning.'" The trick may have been common, but it was also surprisingly successful. A reporter for the *Evening Star* wondered "how any person of common sense can be so easily duped by a vile set of loafing black swindlers," but the writer was blinded by prejudice.[6] Many of these black burners were very good at their trade. Take Reuben Moore, for example, who has left traces of a long and mostly successful career as a burner in both Philadelphia and New York during the 1820s and 1830s. Denominated by the *Public Ledger* the "prince of petty swindlers," Moore was little short of brilliant at enticing his mark into a backstreet, tempting him by the prospect of easy money, convincing him "to bet on the drawing of cards, and by the aid of an accomplice, . . . fleec[ing] him of his money."[7] Stories about whites being duped by wily blacks circulated through the cities. In New York of the 1820s and 1830s, the occupation of "scouring," roughly equivalent nowadays to dry cleaning, was dominated by African Americans. On one occasion, so went a popular story, a guest at a city hotel, on encountering a black thief walking down the corridor heavily laden with an armload of coats, asked, "What are you doing with those coats, you black rascal?" "I'm jist `gwine to take `em home to scour `em," the black adroitly replied. "Oh, you are, ha?" said the guest, "well, here take mine and scour it too."[8] The stories that were retold most often may have been about country bumpkins from Vermont or upper-class fools, but whether the *Evening Star*'s reporter could credit it or not, the full panoply of white citizenry was capable of being gulled by smooth-tongued black burners.

It was not just whites who were the victims of these fast-talking black con men. Recently freed African Americans may have had severely limited opportunities to make a living, but still there was much more money in their pockets than ever there had been while they were slaves, a fact that did not go unnoticed. Unscrupulous blacks preyed on their unsuspecting fellows: one sold fake lottery tickets to old African American women; another, falsely claiming to be a slave trying to raise sufficient money to manumit himself, solicited contributions from the unwary.[9] Time after time, black con men exhibited an unerring instinct for finding the jugular, for baring the concerns and vulnerabilities of their compatriots. A black New Yorker obtained a list of African Philadelphians who had migrated to Haiti, forged letters from the émigrés back to their friends in which they gave glowing accounts of their new home, and then charged each of the "recipients" 37.5 cents for postage. As the *New York Evening Post* reported, the poor blacks, anxious for news of their friends, "seized on [the letters] with avidity." For the forgers, the scheme was a "gainful trade" for some weeks, until the scam was uncovered.[10] Much the same pattern, in which black con men preyed desultorily on either black or white victims, persisted for decades.

What transformed almost every aspect of African American life in New York was the emergence, in the early decades of the twentieth century, of Harlem as the city's black center. Hitherto, blacks had lived in scattered clusters in such neighborhoods as the Five Points, the Tenderloin, and San Juan Hill. But from the early 1900s, migrants from the southern United States and the West Indies, as well as blacks living downtown, poured into Harlem, making it the area of first choice for the city's black residents. The population mushroomed from a handful, early in the twentieth century, to near 200,000 by 1930. To be sure, there were still many whites living in the area, but Harlem seemed somehow to be separate. By the 1920s, it had become the Negro metropolis.

There was a fragility to Harlem; expansion at an exponential rate and the need to incorporate the thousands of migrants who arrived every month inevitably brought disruption and tension. There was also discrimination against blacks in virtually all facets of human existence— that, after all, was what had necessitated the creation of Harlem in the first place. Still, by the 1920s there was an almost palpable frisson of excitement in the air. In Harlem, it seemed, blacks could be themselves without having to worry too much about who was watching—a situation that not a few denizens of the black metropolis took advantage of with considerable flair and style. Garveyites in their finery and followers of all manner of other organizations paraded up and down Harlem streets; Hubert Fauntleroy Julian parachuted into Harlem wearing a skintight scarlet outfit and playing a saxophone; Bill "Bojangles" Robinson engaged in races with strapping young men in which he ran backward; over 100,000 Harlem residents jammed 137th Street outside Mother A.M.E. Zion Church on the occasion of Florence Mills's funeral. Freed from the social constrictions and suffocating poverty of the southern United States and the West Indies, African Americans flocked to Harlem to fashion themselves anew. Many did still earn their living by the sweat of their brow, albeit at better rates of pay, but some managed to become writers, newspaper reporters, boxers, and painters, while others secured a decent education and a path into a profession, and Hubert Julian, the Black Eagle, as he liked to be known, became an aviator, parachutist, and celebrity.[11] Harlem in the 1920s was a place where, it seemed, anything was possible. It was a perfect milieu in which a con artist could work.

Coincidentally, the years in which Harlem became the Negro Mecca—roughly from the beginning of World War I to the middle of the 1920s—were also, in American society generally, the Golden Age of the con. According to Luc Sante, who borrowed the idea from David Maurer's classic *The Big Con* (1940), the "short con" involved taking the mark for all the money he or she was carrying, whereas the "big con" sent the mark home to get whatever money he or she possessed. Other commentators confused the issue by insisting that any con games except the "rag," the "wire," and the "payoff" were short cons. (These were specific schemes probably only known today through the 1973 film *The Sting*, which was inspired by Maurer's *The Big Con*.) However, skilled operators often "put the send" (or prompted the mark to go home or to the bank to get more money) into short cons.[12] Technically speaking then, almost all Harlem cons, such as, for example, that involving John Scott and Walter Hall, outlined at the beginning of the chapter, were short cons into which the con artist had "put the send."

Regardless of these semantic difficulties, the fact remains that the cons perpetrated by African Americans were part of the myriad small dramas that made up everyday life in Harlem in the 1920s, and as such they are a valuable source for historians. Black confidence tricksters were particularly adept at sensing the fault lines in the society and in an individual's makeup. The stories they told relied on, and played with, the culture of their fellow blacks, and the cruel elegance of their schemes laid bare the fears and foibles of their victims. In their own way, the confidence men and women, and their schemes, were often as creative—and sometimes more revealing of the culture of Harlem's citizenry—as were the much-studied poetry, short stories, and novels of the Harlem Renaissance itself.[13] The particular value of cons, then, is that they take us beyond the conventional emphasis on black elites and respectable behavior, into a Harlem with which we are less familiar; out of the editorial offices, churches, and nightclubs and onto the streets; past a preoccupation with black struggles against white authorities, to relations among African Americans; and from a world neatly divided into the respectable and the criminal and into one in which, by necessity, many slid easily between licit and illicit behavior.

Occasionally, Harlem blacks chose whites as their targets. One black man took out an insurance policy on his apartment, only to have a mysterious fire gut the place a few hours later. In early August 1925, the management of the Cigar Stores Company of America had a flier printed which all employees were instructed to read and then to sign on the reverse side. The flier detailed what it called a "new trick" whereby "a colored man," claiming to be a Pullman porter, would order a considerable quantity of cigars and cigarettes, and ask to have them delivered to Grand Central Station. Once at the station, the black con man would take the package and either step with it onto a departing train or claim to be going to get the money to pay for the package, only to disappear through a door, never to be seen again. The flier warned every employee that "YOU ARE PERSONALLY RESPONSIBLE FOR LOSSES OF THIS KIND." Perhaps the threat prompted the desired level of vigilance: later that month Frank Jones, who lived on Lenox Avenue, was caught fleeing Grand Central with $105 worth of cigars and cigarettes in his possession.[14]

The closest thing to a classic "big con" that we found in Harlem, a case that occurred in 1927 and that the *New York Age* described as "one of the slickest confidence games in the history of the local police," also involved a white victim. In January, Samuel Gordon approached Louis Hackner, the white proprietor of Colonial Tailors, Inc., on Seventh Avenue, stating that he was a jeweler and that he desired to rent desk space and a show window in a store nearby. A deal was quickly struck; Gordon leased a part of Hackner's store and soon became a "familiar figure around the tailor shop." About a month later, Gordon began disappearing for several days at a time, but whenever he returned he would "triumphantly" announce that he had made $150 or more by buying and selling stolen jewelry. The absences became more frequent and, Gordon's "profits" grew larger and larger. Finally, Hackner asked to be included in some of these deals, to be given the chance to make some money. "No you stick to your trade and I'll stick to mine," Gordon tartly responded. Eventually, however, Gordon relented and included Hackner in one of his illicit transactions, which netted the white tailor $100. Then, in June 1927, Gordon told Hackner that he had the chance to buy $100,000 worth of platinum for $25,000 in cash, but that if Hackner were to be included in the deal he would need to contribute as much money as he could lay his hands on. In the event, Hackner and his wife were able to raise $9,300. A large trunk was delivered to the shop out of which Gordon took a piece of platinum. He gave the platinum to Hackner and told him to have it appraised by a jeweler. When Hackner was satisfied that the metal was in fact platinum, he handed Gordon the money. At Gordon's suggestion, they checked the trunk in at Grand Central Station for safekeeping, where it was to remain until the contents could be sold. From this point on, Gordon's absences became more and more frequent, but when he did turn up he kept on assuring Hackner that the market for platinum was not favorable at the moment. When, after several weeks, Gordon failed to appear, Hackner reclaimed the trunk from Grand Central, only to discover that it was different from the one he and Gordon had deposited and that this one was empty. (Gordon had switched tickets when the two men had gone down to the station.) Hackner went to the police. When, three years later, Gordon was apprehended in Brooklyn, he refused to divulge the whereabouts of the missing money. The only consolation for Hackner, as the *Age* pointed out, was that Gordon was going to do "a long stretch in prison."[15]

Such cases, however, were relatively unusual. Almost invariably the cons perpetrated by blacks that we found in the district attorney's records and in the black newspapers of the 1920s involved victims who were black[16]—an almost complete reversal of the way things had been in the first half of the nineteenth century. The change reflected the fact that, by the 1920s, Harlem was large enough and wealthy enough to support its own population of con men. Cons were also facilitated by the composition of Harlem's population: the migrants from throughout the South mingled with West Indians and African Americans born in the North, creating a world of strangers much like the populations of nineteenth-century cities in which the first generation of urban confidence men had flourished. By the 1920s, whites, increasingly able to rely on a stranger's location in the city to establish her or his identity, no longer faced such levels of anonymity.[17] But as countless commentators lamented, the racial segregation of blacks in Harlem threw all segments of the black population together, denying middle-class African Americans in particular the ability to separate and thereby identify themselves. The residential separation of blacks and whites also reduced and changed the character of everyday encounters between the races, diminishing African Americans' opportunities to con whites.

If "burning" was the bread and butter of African New Yorker con men in the 1820s and 1830s, in Harlem, a century later, the pocketbook game fulfilled much the same function. As with most effective cons, the pocketbook, or lemon pool, game was simple. A pair of con men would make sure that the mark had seen one or the other of them pick up a wallet from the street. The mark would then be hooked by the promise that he or she would share in the proceeds of the bulging wallet. First, however, the mark would have to produce his or her own money, either as a show of good faith or in order that a large-denomination bill could be changed. Once the con men had got the mark talking, and the victim had been fixated on the promise of easy money, the con was virtually a foregone conclusion. Almost inevitably, the hook would be set, the mark would hand the money over, and the swindler quietly disappear. The pocketbook game was an old one; the *New York Age* noted in July 1923 that it was "a swindle that has been exposed so many times it seems impossible for an intelligent person not to have heard of it." But, as the reporter also acknowledged, "operators of this game are finding a fertile field here in Harlem."[18] The fact that this con should have worked so well reveals something of the texture of everyday life in the dynamically expanding black metropolis.

Early on the morning of August 16, 1924, Minnie Fuller, a housewife of 126 West 137th Street in Harlem, went to the chicken market. Later, at about nine thirty, as she neared the corner of Seventh Avenue and 137th Street, on her way home, James Darrell, a thirty-two-year-old native of the Bahamas, approached her. Darrell told Fuller that his name was Jones and that he had come from Monroe, North Carolina, to try to find his sister, who had been knocked down by a car. The sister was now staying with a hairdresser somewhere on Seventh Avenue, but, Darrell told his mark, he had lost the envelope on which her name and address were written. A bemused Fuller told Darrell that she "didn't know any [hairdressers], but there was quite a few." Darrell then told Fuller that he had only just arrived in the city, that he needed a place to stay, and that he could pay $3 for lodging. Fuller declared that she had a room and that "since you are here, a stranger, and looking for your sister, you can have the room at one dollar a night." As soon as he saw the furnished room, on the second floor of Fuller's house, Darrell agreed to rent it. He then asked Fuller to give him directions to the post office so that he could write a letter back to North Carolina to obtain the address of the hairdresser. The pair stood on the front stoop, the center of much of Harlem's life in the summer months, and Fuller began pointing out the way to the post office, when suddenly Darrell said, "Do you see that man . . . did you see him pick it up, see him pick up the pocketbook." It turned out that the man who had picked up the pocketbook was a friend of Darrell's, and Darrell called him across and told him that "he must whack up," or share the contents of the pocketbook. Darrell then ushered everyone inside Fuller's house, where they encountered a problem: in order to divide up the money they needed to change a thousand dollar bill. If Fuller could help them, the two men promised her $500. Fuller had no money in the house, but she volunteered to go to her aunt's place on 122nd Street, where she borrowed $215. On her return, however, she was informed that this was not enough to change the bill. All three then caught a taxi down to Columbus Circle, where Fuller went into the Gotham Bank and withdrew $900 from her account. The three of them then caught a cab back to Harlem Hospital, where, after promising Fuller that she would get her $1,115 back and $500 more as well, Darrell's accomplice went off with the pocketbook and all of Fuller's money, still, supposedly, in search of change. After a short while, Darrell also melted away. It was only then that it slowly began to dawn on Minnie Fuller that she had been robbed. Fifteen months later, Fuller saw Darrell on the corner of 133rd Street and Lenox Avenue and had him arrested.[19]

When Deputy Assistant District Attorney William Dodge asked Minnie Fuller, "Didn't you think this strange, that a strange man whom you [had] never seen before would ask you to go to the bank and get $900 to give him for the purpose of making change?" he was merely voicing the commonsense reaction of someone who had not been present when the con was worked, who had not experienced the beguiling words and manner of the black con man. Nor did Fuller's answer—that "I never give it a thought. I never seen my mistake until it was done"—do justice to James Darrell's expertise. Minnie Fuller's husband, Matthew, worked on a boat on the Colony Line, was only in Harlem every other day, and at the time of the robbery he was in Providence, Rhode Island. Darrell took advantage of the fact that Fuller was a woman, alone in her house, and of her generous spirit, to keep her constantly on the wrong foot. Fuller's protestation to Darrell that "you can't bring that man in my house because he [is] a stranger," was simply brushed aside, as the con man insisted that his accomplice was a friend. A relentless patter of conversation and questioning kept Minnie Fuller off balance. Time and again, in her interview with Dodge, she testified that the two black con men had her in a dreadful state. "They never left me alone," Fuller told the DA's representative. "They just talked. I was so nervous I didn't know what to do." And later: "They got me so nervous at all I really didn't know myself." And later still: "I was so bewildered I wasn't myself."[20] But, of course, more was involved, for as the New York Age and others were fond of pointing out, "You cant trim a 'sucker' unless he's got larceny in his heart."[21] Darrell and his accomplice tantalized Fuller with the possibility of making a lot of money very quickly, indeed so much money so quickly that there can be little doubt that she knew the law was, at the very least, being bent, and that someone somewhere was going to lose a large amount of cash. Fuller simply did not suspect that it was she who was the one being duped. It was a powerful and practiced combination, more than potent enough to induce Minnie Fuller voluntarily to hand over the savings of a lifetime.

Minnie Fuller was but one of hundreds of Harlemites who lost sums of money—ranging from a small amount to thousands of dollars—to the notorious pocketbook game. For years, black con men wreaked havoc on the lives of their marks, in situations where, for the usually cash-strapped inhabitants of Harlem, even the loss of a few dollars could be little short of devastating. According to the Amsterdam News in 1923, a Mrs. Brown, stung to the tune of $50 that she had withdrawn from her bank account at the urging of a glib-tongued practitioner of the pocketbook game, sobbed out her story to the authorities, with tears coursing her cheeks.[22] On occasion, the damage was long-lasting, effectively, as in the case of Minnie Fuller, ruining lives. Fuller's neighbor, Rebecca Walker, told the authorities that immediately after the robbery, Minnie Fuller had "looked so strange and so all-excited" and had said to her neighbor, "Mrs. Walker I am nearly crazy." Sixteen months later, Fuller told the deputy assistant district attorney that, until that awful day in August 1924, her health had been good. But the con men had "just wrecked my life. I have been sick almost ever since, almost lost my mind."[23]

"When you feel someone tap you on the shoulder and ask you if you saw that man going down the street drop his wallet," the New York Age cautioned in December 1927, "BEWARE!" "Nine out of ten times the men are 'con' men, preying on any unsuspecting person," and the inevitable result would be that "someone's hard earned savings are stolen."[24] Yet for all the warnings in the press, the scam continued to work. When asked whether she had ever before been conned, Minnie Fuller replied, "never heard of it before in my life, never even heard of it," and there were plenty more unsuspecting Harlem residents who fell into the same category. In October 1929, the *New York Age* claimed that two detectives, Henry Bauerschmidt and John Crosby of the West 135th Street police station, had, in the previous ten months, arrested more than seventy people for the dropped pocketbook game. A year later, the *Age* reported that, during two days at the Harlem and West Side courts, six men charged with "being artists in that ancient and highly skilled profession of pocketbook swindling."[25]

In most cases, the victims of the pocketbook game were female. Pairs of black con men cruised Harlem streets, particularly hovering around the markets or churches, looking to target respectable black women who were out alone, and who often had saved some money. Appreciating the role that such women typically played in running the extensive network of rooms and beds for rent that housed Harlem's teeming population of new arrivals, the con men struck up a conversation with their intended victim, using their size and masculinity to cow the victim into doing what she was told.[26] On a Sunday morning in September 1925, Lucille Wright was crossing Seventh Avenue on her way back from church when a pair of strangers asked her "if she knew a good Christian home where they might lodge." The two men explained that they had just arrived from the South and wished to avoid being robbed. Wright, who had been in the same situation herself only two years previously, talked cheerfully to the men as she and they walked down 136th Street. Suddenly, one of the men stopped and picked up something from the sidewalk. "Did you see him pick up that pocketbook?" the other asked. Less than twenty-four hours later, Lucille Wright, having handed over the $28 in her possession and the $474 she had withdrawn from her bank earlier that morning, was waiting on the corner of 137th Street and Eighth Avenue for the men to return with her own money and her share of the $2,000 supposedly contained in the wallet. As the *Age* noted a few days later, "She might still be waiting there for all they know or care."[27]

Almost invariably the perpetrators of the pocketbook game were male. The exceptions were rare. Indeed, in June 1927, when twenty-six-year-old Mamie Reynolds was apprehended, after having convinced a Mrs. Mealy Daniels that there was $3,000 in a pocketbook and that for $228, which Daniels willingly handed over, the hapless housewife would be entitled to a share, the *Amsterdam News* claimed that Reynolds was "the first woman ever arraigned in Harlem Court charged with the [pocketbook] crime."[28] As the records of the New York courts show, it was hardly the case that there was a shortage of black women with larceny in their hearts. It seems, rather, that the pocketbook game was not a crime with which many women felt comfortable. We found only one case in our reading of the district attorney's records in which a black woman was a principal, but, interestingly, that case broke new ground in relation to where it occurred. In March 1930, Ethel Gaynor, a housemaid, was browsing through Gimbel's, the department store on Sixth Avenue and 33rd Street, when she was approached by another black woman. Department stores in New York at this time were not particularly welcoming to African Americans, a circumstance that probably made it easier for the con woman to start a conversation. She asked her mark whether she knew of a "nice place to live" and also whether she knew of "a safe place to deposit her money." Then, having drawn Gaynor's attention to a black man who had just picked up a pocketbook, she called the man over and engaged him in conversation. As the rather dry court document stated, "the said urgings of said man & woman caused deponent to go to her house get the money, & money on deposit in the bank amounting to $147 in all, which said man & woman assured deponent they must see before they would share the $4000," which, they convinced Gaynor, was in the pocketbook. Yet for all the newness of the location at which these con artists put their ploy into action, there was still something amateurish about this pair: rather than seeking to persuade Gaynor to hand over her money, they simply snatched it from her and ran off into the crowd.[29]

Most of the other popular Harlem cons centered around an envelope, or sometimes a handkerchief, into which the mark was induced to place his or her money. Later, when the victim opened the envelope, he or she found that it contained only cut-up newspaper. This was yet another simple con, and at its heart lay the envelope switch. For instance, a con man would pick an unsuspecting woman who had just made a withdrawal from a bank for her employer, approach her, and warn her that carrying the payroll in her handbag was a risky thing to do but that he could offer some advice. He would then produce an envelope, tell the woman to put the money into it, and then show her how to conceal the envelope in her coat so that she would avoid being held up. On her return to the office, of course, the woman discovered that there was no money in the envelope.[30]

At about lunchtime on September 15, 1925, Rupert Blackman, a janitor at a building on Broadway down near Wall Street and a sometime preacher at various Harlem missions, was sitting on a bench in St. Nicholas Park opposite his residence on West 137th Street, when he was approached by seventy-year-old John Ellison. "I am just from the south and my father died and left me a lot of money and I have $2000 in my pocket," the stranger told Blackman. Seemingly little more than a country bumpkin with too much money, the con man was able easily to talk Blackman into taking a bet: if Blackman would show Ellison that he had $1,000, Ellison would give him $200. They proceeded to the Empire Savings Bank on 125th Street, where Blackman withdrew $1,000. Outside the bank Ellison told Blackman to give him the money, which, as Blackman later ruefully admitted, "I like a good fellow gave him the thousand dollars." The con man then said, "I'll take my two hundred dollars and your thousand dollars and put it in this envelope," which he then put in Blackman's shirt, next to his skin. Of course, when Blackman went back in the bank to deposit the money, he discovered that the envelope contained only newspaper. As Blackman later told the deputy assistant district attorney in a somewhat resigned fashion, "I saved this money for ten years."[31]

For aficionados of the art, virtually all of the cons perpetrated in Harlem in the 1920s were short cons into which the operators had put the "send," or had convinced the mark to go away and come back with more money. On occasion, though, that "send" was more than a trip around the corner to the mark's home or to a bank; indeed, it could be truly spectacular—further testimony to how convincing a con man's spiel could be. In October 1927, the *Amsterdam News* printed a story of a con that the reporter described as "astounding." A pair of men convinced William Shorts to take care of $1,500 for one of them, asking him to deposit the money in a Harlem bank. First, however, Shorts was to provide $1,500 as security. Because Shorts had little money with him in New York, the pair paid his bus fare to Virginia, from whence he had come, and where he could obtain the required sum. On Shorts's return, the three men met and the $3,000 was put inside an envelope, but, of course, when Shorts arrived at the bank in Harlem, he found to his horror that the envelope contained only newspaper.[32] Unfortunately, newspapers' spare accounts of such cons tend to cause readers, then and now, to raise their eyebrows and wonder at the credulity of those who being deceived. Prosecutors were no more sympathetic to marks than were black newspaper reporters, but the district attorney's case files include statements from victims and other witnesses that, despite being shaped by the questions asked by deputy assistant district attorneys, provide a better sense of how the mark was conned, and of how the con was embedded in Harlem life.[33] And of course it is the details of the con men's successful patter, their sense of which stories would fly in the black metropolis, that laid bare the beliefs, fears, and sometimes naiveté of ordinary residents of Harlem.

Early on a Saturday evening in November 1930, John Richardson, unemployed and just twenty-two years old, was strolling along Eighth Avenue, between 127th and 128th streets, when he was accosted by George Webb. Webb claimed to be from Mississippi and sought Richardson's assistance in finding his uncle. While they were talking, Henry Geter walked by, and Webb called him over to enlist his help. Apparently Webb's father had died and left $1,700 to Webb's uncle, a fact that Webb demonstrated by flashing a roll of notes he had in his pocket. Geter quickly warned Webb, his fellow conspirator, that "you should not show money like that because some one might knock you over the head and take it away and it is a good thing you met this gentleman and I." Webb then explained why he was carrying the money with him: "My white folks in Mississippi told me not to deposit my money in the bank in New York" because "the white folks will take some money out of it every month." Geter objected that this was not so, that in fact the bank would "add interest to your money every three months." Six weeks later, when the assistant district attorney questioned Richardson, he asked the victim whether he had contributed anything to the conversation at all. Richardson replied that he "just stood there and listened for a while." Webb and Geter kept up a nonstop patter. Webb refused to believe that whites would pay interest on a black's money in a bank account and argued that "colored folks in Harlem haven't got no money or no place to stay and said they live in basements and holes and have not got any clothes to wear." Geter countered by pointing out that he had on good clothes and pulled a dollar bill out of his pocket to demonstrate that he was not a bum. He then turned to the mark and said, "Perhaps Mr. Richardson has some money too to show that he is not a bum either." Richardson only had fifty cents in his pocket, but he blurted out, "I have got money otherwise." It turned out that the money was in two bank accounts, but, of course, Webb, the supposedly artless Mississippian, had never seen a bank book, which he kept referring to as a "money tablet." Indeed, Webb offered to pay twenty-five dollars to anyone who would show him a bank book. Here Geter took Richardson aside and muttered, "Mr. Richardson you might show him the bank book and let him give you twenty-five dollars because he is so dumb he will give it to anybody if you do not accept it." Once Richardson had, as he thought, made some easy money, he was keen to make more and agreed to meet the pair of con men on the following Monday morning on a Harlem street corner in order to help Webb deposit his money in a bank account. As they traveled to the bank about thirty-six hours later, Webb kept on voicing his skepticism: they were trying "to April fool him," for "colored folks have no money in white folks' bank," and Richardson's bank books were only grocery bill books. Webb then stated that he would pay $100 if someone could "prove to me they can draw money out of the white folks money house without being locked up." Richardson then proceeded to take $70 out of his account at the North River Savings Bank on 34th Street and $79 out of his account at the Greenwich Savings Bank at 36th Street and Broadway. Now satisfied, Webb turned to the mark and said, "Mr. Richardson you take my money to the bank and make the deposit." But first, for safety's sake, Webb insisted that Richardson put his money with Webb's money inside a handkerchief. Once all the money was secure in the handkerchief, Webb placed the handkerchief underneath Richardson's shirt and told him to go and make the deposit, after which they would all meet up again at the subway station at 135th Street and Lenox Avenue. Of course, as soon as Richardson unwrapped the handkerchief in the bank, he discovered nothing but newspaper. Although the pair of con men were caught and pleaded to petit larceny, Richardson never saw a cent of his $149 again.[34]

If stories of lost relatives and of white-owned banks refusing to accept deposits revealed something of the anomie of Harlem in the 1920s (an inevitable effect, perhaps, of the whirling eddies of human movement that constituted the Great Migration), even more instructive were stories of those con men who pretended to be African conjurors and fortune-tellers. Here, the con artists were exploiting a rich tradition in black culture that can be traced back to Africa.[35] Undoubtedly there were conjurors and fortune-tellers in the North during slavery times, but finding material about them is difficult. In the early decades of the nineteenth century, however, as large numbers of now free blacks became an obvious presence in the dynamically expanding northern cities, there was a seeming efflorescence of such arts, one that left a clear, if largely unnoticed, impression on the historical record.

Some of this activity occurred solely among members of the African American population. It appears, for example, that the principal market for magic paraphernalia in the northern cities was among blacks. In August 1824, the *New York Spectator* reprinted the case of a black man in Philadelphia, named Johnson, who had stolen a completely black cat from a neighbor. Although Johnson had borrowed the cat allegedly to rub it on his scrofulous neck, he had instead boiled it, skimmed off the fat, and made candles from it, candles he sold for the extravagant price of fifty cents each. He claimed that, when lit, the candles would ensure that anyone asleep in the house would stay that way. The newspaper writer remembered a similar case of two years' earlier. Johnson had been selling small phials of Black Cat Fat, which, if secreted on the body, made a person invisible. Believing this to be true, a sixteen-year-old black, who patently remained visible to an irate storekeeper, was caught stealing in the storekeeper's shop and sentenced to two years in prison.[36]

The potential market for black fortune-tellers extended beyond the black population. Here was one of those occasions when white and black cultures comfortably converged, where many white New Yorkers had no trouble believing that some blacks had special powers. In 1826, the *National Advocate* reported that "a black prophet, who had let his wool grow for ten years so as to give himself a venerable appearance," had recently opened "a shop of fortune telling" near Canal Street in New York, where he was doing a roaring trade. Young ladies flocked uptown to hear about sweethearts, "widows to catch a word of husbands," and married ladies to learn of the prospects of their daughters and sons.[37] Contemporaries' opinions were divided as to the benefits, or otherwise, to be obtained from black fortune-tellers and their ilk—stories in newspapers fairly dripped sarcasm—yet ordinary whites and blacks continued to seek out such clairvoyants.

In effect, black fortune-tellers had become cultural brokers. On the one hand, fortune-tellers, knowing a good deal about the doings of African New Yorkers, occasionally helped the police to recover stolen property. On the other hand, one can almost hear the tom-toms of deepest Africa reverberating in the heads of the white women who went to Canal Street to learn their children's destiny. Arguably, there was more than an element of the con involved in the way in which the Canal Street fortune-teller and the purveyor of black cat fat made their living, although it is important to place these supposedly prescient practitioners in their cultural context. There can, however, be no doubt about the nature of the activities of some of the other conjurors and fortune-tellers who were, purely and simply, confidence men and women.

Three-quarters of a century later, this home-grown New York strain of religious and magical belief was considerably reinforced by the massive infusion of migrants from the southern United States and the West Indies. In ways that were not always welcomed by the older inhabitants, these new New Yorkers changed the culture of Harlem forever. Alarmed by some of the newcomers' cultural practices, the city's African American newspapers repeatedly fulminated against, among other things, the flourishing trade in charms, potions, and various so-called spiritual services, castigating "credulous dupes" for buying this material and the police for not rounding up "these money-hunting necromancers." In December 1919, the *New York Age* editorialized that New York City was the only possible rival to the South as a field for "fakers," particularly root doctors and fortune-tellers. Four years later, the same paper complained that Harlem was "being afflicted with a recrudescence of fortune tellers, clairvoyants, and other sharpers and fakers of the same class." Anyone who trusted the "weird and dark mysticisms" practiced by these salesmen and women, could, for example, purchase a powder potent enough to bring back a wandering lover, or remove the obstacles in the way of "unconsummated desire," and "it will cost only $25 or more if the victim appears prosperous." Much of this material was sold on the street by hucksters, but early in the 1920s, numerous drug stores started to spring up along Lenox Avenue.[38] In September 1931, the *Interstate Tattler* complained of the "jungle superstition" that continued "to bleed white" believers in the charms and mystic talismans that were sold by the "hobo street vendors in dark Harlem." The paper went on to relate the story of Alberta Simmons, who paid $52 in a series of small amounts to one of these salesmen, who had promised to reunite her with her missing husband. After vials of mystic ointment had had no noticeable effect, the charlatan gave the woman some white and gold "mystic threads," instructing her to sew them in the form of a cross on the husband's undergarments, since they were "guaranteed to unite practically anything that was separated." A few months later, the *Tattler* editorialized that "we do, indeed, disgrace ourselves in practically every community where great numbers of colored people live, through the insidious practice of fortune telling, 'readings,' spell casting, and mediumism."[39]

One of the more obvious manifestations of such spiritual beliefs in Harlem in the 1920s surrounded the novel gambling craze known as the "numbers." The history of the numbers went back at least to the early years of the nineteenth century, when it was known as "insuring the lottery" or "policy," essentially a matter of allowing the gambler to bet that a certain number between 0 and 999 would be on the lottery's winning ticket. By the 1830s and 1840s, the "corrupting mania" of policy was particularly associated with African Americans. In 1845, the *National Police Gazette* estimated that nine-tenths of New York's black population of some 10,000 had fallen victim to policy's addictive powers.[40] Two years later the editor of a small black newspaper estimated that the city's blacks, although only about 3 percent of the total population, accounted for a quarter of the $10,000 gambled on policy every day.[41] A large part of the appeal of this form of gambling consisted in the fact that the wager could be as little as a penny, but the return for a hit was often on the order of 400 or 500 to 1. In one form or another, policy continued into the twentieth century. On or about 1920, someone—reputedly Casper Holstein, a prominent Harlem figure well known for his charitable activities—hit on the idea of computing the winning number from two of the numbers released at ten o'clock every morning by the Clearing House, a financial district entity that oversaw the transfer of money between banks and other institutions.[42] To all intents and purposes, these numbers— typically they were of eight or nine digits—could not be manipulated by crooked operators. Many cities, including Chicago, continued to run policy wheels, but in New York this new form of playing the numbers spread like a wildfire through Harlem. Evidence of the ubiquity of the numbers game was everywhere. In May 1924, a story in the *Age* stated that "the casual stroller along Harlem thoroughfares can hear, without conscious effort at eavesdropping, comment from almost every group of two or more which he might pass concerning some phase of the 'Numbers' playing game." A few months later the same paper noted that the playing of the numbers game by the inhabitants of Harlem had "assumed tremendous proportions." Indeed, men and women from all ranks of life were addicted to it. The *Age* estimated that the take from numbers in Harlem in 1926 was $20,000,000, and the vast bulk of that staggering sum would have come from wagers of less than a dime.[43]

Most of that talk on Harlem streets related to the question of how one could pick the winning number, and all manner of stratagems were concocted to bring about this result. Church members wrote down the numbers of the hymns, or of verses taken from the Scripture reading at Sunday service, and bet on them. In March 1930, an episode of the radio serial *Amos 'n' Andy* mentioned that a phone call made by Amos to his girlfriend in Chicago had cost $2.45; the result was a small plunge on the number 245. (Strangely enough, 245 hit the following day.)[44] Many players used dream books, which enabled them to convert a dream into a number. These books were available all over Harlem and earned sizeable profits for their publishers. When, in 1930, a Harlem resident sued a Philadelphia pair, claiming that they were pirating his H.P. and Lucky Star dream books, he asked for $50,000 in damages. Droves of Harlem residents consulted various spiritual guides, desperate for the edge that would score them a hit. In March 1925, a young black janitress explained to an *Age* reporter that "I certainly do believe in spiritualism." She paid a fifty-cent fee for each visit to her spiritualist preacher, who dispensed advice about the numbers. "I couldn't possibly live on the pay I get as a janitress, and what I win on the 'numbers' helps me to get along." The advice she had obtained had been good, the woman declared, and "I am ahead of the 'numbers' game right now." In 1927, a supposed clairvoyant known as the Gig Lady (a gig was a three-digit number) lurked around New York, Chicago, and other northern cities, selling lucky numbers that would supposedly hit in a few days for five dollars each. When she set up shop on the South Side of Chicago in December of that year, over three hundred people tried to get into her flat on Indiana Avenue. Of course, what aided these charlatans was the fact that numbers gambling was illegal, ensuring that those who were ripped off had no practical legal recourse.[45]

The other obvious manifestation of Harlemites' spiritual beliefs was in the field of medicine. Undoubtedly there was merit in some of the natural remedies promulgated by various sellers of nostrums, but this view was not taken by the black newspapers (which were, however, happy enough to run advertisements on behalf of some seemingly dubious people). "Harlem Infested with Pest of Quacks, Medical, Fortune Telling and Spiritualists" blared one front-page headline in the *Age* in August 1923. The story went on to complain about "snake and root doctors," who were "thriving on newly arrived migrants who are ready victims," and to protest that these "charlatans" were each doing so to the tune of two or three hundred dollars a week.[46] Pieces about the horrible consequences of the actions of some of these "pseudo doctors," as the *Age* called them, peppered the black newspapers. In 1928, a British West African had treated a three-year-old, who was suffering from tetanus, by rubbing the boy's limbs while "muttering in an unintelligible manner." According to the *Age*, for this he charged $180. The boy died soon after. In 1930, the *Amsterdam News* reported on an almost penniless Bertha Jones, who had managed to scrape together $10 to pay a Joshua Anderson on the promise that he would prevent her husband from going blind. Anderson came with a "professional air" and an "imposing-looking black bag," as she later told the court, but his ensuing actions surprised her. After placing a "gay turban" on his head, he took out of his bag a "celluloid donkey and also a celluloid monkey, and, finally a pencil to which was attached a skull and cross-bones," and carefully placed them on the floor. Anderson then offered up prayers to the "powers," asking that the man's sight be restored. The prayers proved ineffectual.[47]

The healing powers of persons known as "African doctors" provided the basis for confidence schemes designed to defraud Harlem residents, often at moments when they were particularly vulnerable. In June 1930, Emily Sibblies confided to Daphnie Smith, whom she had met a month earlier, that her boyfriend was sick. Smith recommended that Sibblies consult an "African doctor," who could cure her friend by use of spiritualistic powers. The two women went to a spiritualistic church at 433 Edgecomb Avenue, where they met the African, one Freddie Green. Green and Smith lit some candles, after which Green spoke in a language that Sibblies did not understand but that Green explained was "the African language." Green then told Sibblies that she must withdraw all her money from the bank, assuring her, all the while, that she would get it back. On Sibblies' return, she placed her $411 in an envelope supplied by Green. As Sibblies was depositing the money, Smith noticed a ring—later valued at $85—on Sibblies' finger, whereupon she announced that if the ring were taken off and placed in a bowl, the spirits would effect the cure much faster. Green then told Sibblies that the money and the ring had to be left with him for three days, and that it was imperative that she and Smith should leave the church, walk three blocks, and then separate and not see one another for two weeks. The boyfriend's condition did not change. Daphnie Smith was quickly arrested, and the ring was found in a box in her room. She pleaded guilty to petit larceny. Green was arrested in May 1932, two years after commission of the crime, but by this time, hardly surprisingly, given the transience of many of Harlem's residents, no one could find Emily Sibblies, and all charges against Green were dropped. Sibblies never saw her money again.[48]

The harming traditions of conjure—and here we must remember that use of its supposed powers to cause pain and affliction has a history that goes back to slavery—were also particularly amenable to attempts at extortion.[49] In August 1930, an Audrey Dayrell, a native of the British West Indies, passed word to Lillian Tweed, a factory worker, that her life was in danger. Tweed went with her cousin to Dayrell's apartment on 127th Street, where Dayrell informed her mark that evil spirits were about to cause her sudden death. For $200, however, Dayrell would "charm the evil spirits away." Once the money had been delivered, Dayrell, according to the *Amsterdam News*, "darkened the room and went through a weird ceremony of prayer and chanting." Tweed was sworn to silence, but, in the event, was unable to resist talking about what happened. When Dayrell heard of this, she summoned Tweed, informed her that the spirits were very angry, and extorted another $200 from her. A while later, Tweed was visited by two men, who told her they had been sent by the spirits to kill her. In total, Dayrell mulcted some $1,140 from her victim. According to the deputy assistant district attorney's penciled notes of the case, scribbled on yellow legal paper, Dayrell also extorted more than $1,100 from three other victims. The deputy assistant district attorney's jottings, which formed the basis of his address to the jury, convey something of his outrage: "the evidence in this case discloses a type of racket which exists in this city," he believed, so there was no need to waste time persuading the jury that this kind of larceny was "particularly mean & vicious." Its victims were "ignorant & superstitious," fearing "death & sickness," with the constant threat of "catastrophe over their heads." Dayrell was convicted of grand larceny in the second degree and sentenced to eighteen months to three years in the state prison.[50]

On the whole, however, it was only occasionally that fraudulent conjurors and fortune-tellers used the stick rather than the carrot. Typically, an "African's" supposed spiritual powers were employed in cons that offered the prospect of the mark making a large amount of money. Even the most establishment of Harlem figures were duped by con men, who proved remarkably adept at finding their mark's vulnerabilities. Henry Warner, variously described by black newspapers as "a well-to-do and respected Harlem realtor" and a "hard-headed businessman," fell victim to the "voodoo hidden gold" swindle. In April 1928, one of Warner's tenants told the realtor that a man named Bolancia, an African who communicated with the dead, had been at a séance with "a departed Indian," at which he learned that Warner's father, who had died when Warner was six years old, "knew of a pot of gold in which he was anxious to have his son share." It was explained to Warner that in order to obtain the money, $10,000 would have to "pass" on the scene. Warner could contribute only $5,000, and the others agreed that this would entitle him to one-half of the spoils. A few days later, the three men drove out to a lot in a deserted part of Queens that Warner had up for sale. The con man measured the lot with a tape and then pointed to a spot where members of the group should begin digging. After a while the shovel hit something—according to the *Amsterdam News*, it was a tin box; according to the *New York Age*, somewhat implausibly, a concrete one. Both newspapers agreed, however, as to the wording on the top of the box—"$300,000 in gold, 1776, R.I.P." For the prophecy to be fulfilled, the money first had to pass. Bolancia pulled out a roll of small notes—"large enough to choke a horse," according to the *Age*—and this money was added to Warner's five crisp thousand-dollar bills before being put into an envelope. The envelope was then waved over the box as "the pretended African muttered a strange incantation." He and Warner opened the box and found a few gold coins on the top layer, at which point Bolancia warned that they must not proceed any further because "the spirits would be displeased if they hurried the procedure." The con men handed the envelope to Warner for safekeeping, and the three men drove back to the city. Warner let them off at 125th and Lenox and that was the last he saw of them. When they did not turn up the next morning, he hastily opened the envelope, only to find nothing but slips of paper.[51]

Throughout the 1920s, Arthur Millwood, a.k.a. Jake Williams, who had been born in the British West Indies, made a career of exploiting the spiritual beliefs of his fellow black citizens. In August 1924, Louis Blenman, a laborer originally from Barbados, was returning from the Carpentier–Tunney fight at the Polo Grounds when two men, one of whom was Millwood, began to talk with him about the bout. Millwood and his companion confided to Blenman that they had made a great deal of money by following the advice of Prof. Balenger, a native African, who possessed "supernatural powers and was their financial adviser." Balenger had been brought to America by "some prominent men of Wall street," who took up most of his time, but, because Blenman was their friend, they agreed to introduce him to the professor. The following day the three men met the African, and Blenman's interest was sufficiently piqued for him to go to his bank at 116th and Madison and withdraw his and his wife's life savings of $675. On the men's return to the professor's house, Blenman was induced, "after some more tricks," according to the *New York Age*, to leave his money on the table, while the three men went to the Hudson, where Blenman was told to "throw a coin in the water and shake his hands three times." Soon after the group had returned to the house there was a heavy knock on the door and a loud voice demanded that it be opened in the name of the law. A seemingly flustered Balenger ushered everyone behind a curtain, whereupon the fake policeman entered, arrested Balenger, and very obviously pocketed the money on the table as he left. Although Millwood eventually served a stint in the penitentiary, Blenman never saw his $675 again.[52]

According to Millwood's police-department criminal record, he was convicted again in July 1927 for "Grand Larceny, Con Game." And then, over the course of several months in the first half of 1930, Millwood and a new accomplice, Victor Davis, originally from Cuba, fleeced several Harlem residents of somewhere in excess of $10,000. It was, a writer in the *Amsterdam News* commented, "an amazing story of superstition and simple credulity," but once again the newspaper exaggerated how unusual the case was and underestimated how convincing the glib-tongued Millwood had been as he sold his scam. Millwood and Davis were caught and charged with mulcting Olive Dean, a laundress living on West 119th Street, of $2,311; the two policemen concerned told the *Age* that this was "one of the most important arrests of their career." Victor Davis had entered into conversation with Olive Dean and told her that he had just won $13,000, thanks to the assistance of a Hindu priest. The following day the Hindu priest, in reality Millwood, who needed Davis as an interpreter as he could not speak English, came and visited Dean. Millwood took out a sheet of paper, after which he "went into alleged religious rites, holding the paper over a lighted burner on the gas range." Before long, some writing appeared:

My Dear Daughter: You can trust these men. They will make you wealthy. Do as they say. (signed)

YOUR DEAR DEAD MOTHER.

Dean was then instructed to withdraw all of her money from the bank in order that the serial numbers on the bills could be written down; if given this information, the Hindu priest would be able to work out the next day's winning policy number. The con men then placed the $2,311 in an envelope, performed another religious ceremony, tied the envelope to the woman's back, and left, warning her not to move herself or the envelope for two hours. Just to be safe, Olive Dean waited three hours before stirring. Needless to say, the envelope contained only newspaper.

The arrest of Millwood and Davis brought to light a series of other cases. Herbert Reid, an expressman of West 127th Street, had been approached by Millwood, who claimed to know "a certain African who was making white men rich." As if to demonstrate their versatility, it was Davis, on this occasion, who posed as the African, claiming to be in contact with Reid's dead father. Reid dutifully went off to the Union Dime Savings Bank, where he withdrew $1,450. On his return, Millwood took note of the serial numbers on the notes in order, so he said, to work out the winning policy number. Reid was told to wait two and a half hours with the envelope on his back, but in fact he delayed until the following morning, at which point his wife opened the envelope and emptied out nothing but strips of newspaper. According to the *Age* and the *Amsterdam News*, other victims of the pair of con men included David Brown, who lost $853, Elmer Jordan, who lost $2,537, and Abraham Harris, who was swindled out of $4,000. The *Age* included a brief note in its story to the effect that Henry Warner, victim of the voodoo hidden-gold swindle, had also identified Millwood and Davis as the perpetrators of the scam that, two years previously, had relieved the Harlem realtor of $5000.[53]

The recovery of some of the long-forgotten stories of black con artists allows us to begin to view the Harlem of the 1920s from a perspective different than that offered by writers of the Harlem Renaissance or by activities of black leaders and performers. In many ways, Harlem was the Promised Land. Not only were wages higher there than in the South, but the disapproving white boss man was nowhere to be seen. As the sums of money detailed in many of the recounted cases show, numerous ordinary residents of Harlem were able to accumulate savings, often surprisingly large amounts of money. For many, Harlem embodied the way freedom was meant to be, and evidence of black success was everywhere—in the rich, such as Madame C. J. Walker and her daughter A'Lelia, or Casper Holstein; in the famous, including Jack Johnson, Paul Robeson, Florence Mills, and W. E. B. DuBois; and even in the denizens of that new category, the black celebrity, famous for little more than being famous, as seen, for instance, in the person of aviator and parachutist Hubert Julian. All these, and many more, cut a broad and obvious swath through the black metropolis. On Sunday mornings, and most especially on Easter Sunday, the full panoply of Harlem society, resplendent in its finery, was on display, as men and women strolled the avenues and streets, going to and from Harlem's churches. But for all that there was an underside to the African American dream. It may have been possible for black men and women to be successful in ways that had never before seemed credible, but that success was still hard won, and for many the dream went unrealized. Harlem was an unforgiving place, and preying around the edges of the dream were those who were ever ready to give aspiring migrants from the South or from the West Indies a "helping hand." Arguably, it was the possibility, indeed probability, of failure that instilled a hardness and an edginess to the urban black culture that emerged in Harlem in the 1920s.

The best way to comprehend the undoubted success of Harlem's con artists in gulling their compatriots to part voluntarily with so much money is to view their activities alongside those associated with the numbers racket, a form of gambling endemic in the 1920s and key to understanding ordinary Harlemites' everyday life. The numbers business, and stories about it, pervaded the black metropolis. Black numbers bankers were an obvious and notorious presence, whether cruising the streets in $12,000 cars to pick up the betting slips every morning or buying houses for $45,000 in cash.[54] Numbers bankers and runners eagerly publicized the stories of ordinary men and women who had "hit" and had won a few hundred dollars or more. For many Harlem blacks who played the numbers, the game seemed less a matter of random chance and more a working out of their destiny. All that was needed was some form of guidance that would allow the signs somehow embedded in their lives to be properly read. Here, of course, was an opening a mile wide for dishonest men and women. But more was involved than that. There was also a widespread belief that the system was rigged and that if one knew the right people and could get inside information, it was possible to make a lot of money quickly. This kind of thinking applied not just to the playing of numbers but to financial matters generally and was part of the reason that con men's spiels about someone or other being an adviser to whites, or to the denizens of Wall Street, were often effective with their black marks. From this distance, much of what the con artists said as they mesmerized their dupes appears impossibly artificial, obviously false. It seems to us, however, that many of those who were fooled were also aware of this plasticity, but nevertheless thought that this was the way in which the world worked, and that for once they would not be victims but would have the opportunity to be on the inside and to become rich at someone else's expense. It was more than a coincidence that the craze for numbers took off in the 1920s, a time when so many confidence men and women walked Harlem's streets looking for easy pickings.

Finally, is there anything more to say about those envelopes in our title? Perhaps. In late 1925 and early 1926, stationery stores suddenly started springing up all over Harlem. Quite a few of them were part of what the *Age* described as a "chain," controlled by Hyman Kassell, a particularly unsavory character and formerly one of Harlem's "king bootleggers." Everyone knew that stationery stores, many of which were concentrated along Lenox and Seventh avenues, the most popular thoroughfares in Harlem for strolling, were fronts for the collection of numbers slips from black men, women, and often children, hoping for a hit. Reportedly, the proprietors of some of these stationery stores were making in excess of $400 a week in commission on the numbers transactions taking place on their premises.[55] In fact, however, what was occurring was a turf battle for control of Harlem's immensely lucrative numbers racket, one in which the black bankers who worked the streets were slowly and surely being forced out by the white bankers who operated out of cigar stores, stationery stores, and the like. But clearly these stationery stores must have managed to do some legitimate business as well. After all, *someone* must have been selling all those envelopes to blacks in Harlem.

NOTES

We are extremely grateful to the Australian Research Council for a generous Discovery Grant for the project Black Metropolis: Harlem, 1915–1930, for 2003–7; the grant has funded the research and given us the time to write this chapter. We thank as well the staff at the Municipal Archives of the City of New York, particularly Ken Cobb and Leonora Gidlund, for all their assistance. Also, we thank the editors of this volume and the readers for the University of Chicago Press for their helpful comments.

1. For the importance of clothing and style in African American culture, see Shane White and Graham White, *Stylin': African American Expressive Culture from Its Beginnings to the Zoot Suit* (Ithaca, NY: Cornell University Press, 1998).

2. *James Skerritt v. Walter Hall* (1930), no.183749, District Attorney's Closed Case Files (DACCF), Municipal Archives of the City of New York, NY.

3. The best account of slave culture remains Lawrence W. Levine, *Black Culture and Black Consciousness: Afro-American Folk Thought from Slavery to Freedom* (New York: Oxford University Press, 1977).

4. Karen Halttunen, *Confidence Men and Painted Women* (New Haven: Yale University Press, 1982); Elaine Abelson, *When Ladies Go-a-Thieving: Middle-Class Shoplifters in the Victorian Department Store* (New York: Oxford University Press, 1989); John Kasson, *Rudeness and Civility* (New York: Hill and Wang, 1990); Jackson Lears, *Fables of Abundance: A Cultural History of Advertising in America* (New York: Basic Books, 1994); and James Cook, *Arts of Deception: Playing with Fraud in the Age of Barnum* (Cambridge: Harvard University Press, 2001).

5. Just as this chapter was being finished, Timothy J. Gilfoyle, *A Pickpocket's Tale: The Underworld of Nineteenth-Century New York* (New York: Norton, 2006), was published. Gilfoyle locates his protagonist, George Appo, in New York life, but, hardly surprisingly given Appo's Chinese origins, is little concerned with African Americans.

6. *Journal of Commerce*, March 22, 1838; *Evening Star*, August 11, 1838. See also *New York Daily Express*, August 11, 1838.

7. *Public Ledger*, February 16, 1837. On Reuben Moore, see Shane White, *Stories of Freedom in Black New York* (Cambridge: Harvard University Press, 2002), 179–81.

8. A. Greene, *A Glance at New York: Embracing the City Government* (New York: A. Greene, 1837), 67–68.

9. *New York Evening Post*, March 12, 1830; *Public Ledger*, December 31, 1836.

10. *New York Evening Post,* May 25, 1825.

11. On Julian, see Colonel Hubert Julian, *Black Eagle,* as told to John Bulloch (London: Jarrolds Publishers, 1964).

12. David W, Maurer, *The Big Con: The Story of the Confidence Man,* with an introduction by Luc Sante (1940; repr., New York: Anchor Books, 1999), x–xiii and passim.

13. For an interesting point of comparison, particularly the way in which confidence men took advantage of a society in disarray, see Sheila Fitzpatrick, "The World of Ostap Bender: Soviet Confidence Men in the Stalin Period," *Slavic Review* 61 (Fall 2002): 535–57.

14. *Frank Whitmore v. Frank Jones* (1925), no.161565, DACCF.

15. *New York Age,* October 25, 1930. Occasionally scams involved multiple victims. In 1928, the *Age* published details of a con involving James Henry in which between 150 and 200 residents of Harlem were paying Henry from 25 cents to $1.50 a week as premiums for a health insurance company that did not exist. He managed to run this scheme for at least two years before he was caught and arrested. See *New York Age,* November 17, 1928.

16. Thus far we have waded through all the cases for Manhattan in the district attorney's closed case files for the years 1916, 1917, 1920, 1925, 1928, and 1930—a considerable amount of paper. We have scanned all cases that were clearly identified as involving African Americans.

17. Halttunen, *Confidence Men,* 37–39.

18. *New York Age,* July 28, 1923.

19. Harlem was of a size that made it possible for a person to avoid being found if he or she so desired. But only for so long. Several of the cases discussed in this chapter involved situations in which the con man was seen on Harlem streets months or even years later and arrested. Of course by the time of the arrest, witnesses often had moved on, which caused the case to be dropped. Harlem, then, contained a large concentration of African Americans, but there were distinct limitations to the anonymity provided by the black metropolis.

20. *Minnie Fuller v. James Darrell* (1925), no. 162714, DACCF. For a brief newspaper account, with the names spelled incorrectly (court reporters often got the names wrong), see *Amsterdam News,* December 2, 1925.

21. See, for example, *New York Age,* April 12, 1930.

22. *New York Age,* July 28, 1923.In this case "Brown" was a pseudonym used to protect the victim.

23. *Minnie Fuller v. James Darrell.*

24. *New York Age,* December 31, 1927.

25. *New York Age,* October 26, 1929; *Amsterdam News,* October 29, 1930.

26. For an excellent account of the central role that women played in northern black communities, see Victoria W. Wolcott, *Remaking Respectability: African American Women in Interwar Detroit* (Chapel Hill: University of North Carolina Press, 2001).

27. *Amsterdam News,* September 23, 1925.

28. *Amsterdam News,* June 29, 1927.

29. *Ethel Gaynor v. Fred Jasper* (1930), no.182837, DACCF.

30. *New York Age,* December 31, 1927.

31. *Rupert Blackman v. John Ellison* (1925), no. 162138, DACCF. For a brief newspaper account of this crime, see *New York Age,* October 24, 1925.

32. *Amsterdam News*, October 5, 1927.

33. For a discussion of how to approach legal records as a source for cultural history, see Stephen Robertson, "What's Law Got to Do with It: Sexual Histories and Legal Records," *Journal of the History of Sexuality* 14 (January/April 2005): 161–85.

34. *Richardson v. Geter & Webb* (1930), no. 183993, DACCF.

35. See Yvonne P. Chireau, *Black Magic: Religion and the African American Conjuring Tradition* (Berkeley: University of California Press, 2003). On the role of Africa in black life in the 1920s, see Clare Corbould, "Making African Americans, 1919–1936," (Ph.D. diss., University of Sydney, 2005).

36. *New York Spectator*, August 13, 1824.

37. *National Advocate*, March 3, 1826.

38. *New York Age*, December 13, 1919; February 10, 1923.

39. *Interstate Tattler*, September 24, 1931; December 3, 1931. For an account of an *Age* investigation into a man, and his wiles, as he conned black women by offering to "make men support them, or rid them of men whom they couldn't quit, or bring back men who had deserted women," see *New York Age*, June 27, 1925.

40. *National Police Gazette*, October 11, 1845

41. The figures come from the "colored editor" of a newspaper named the *Ram's Horn;* they were reprinted in the *National Police Gazette*, March 20, 1847.

42. The historiography of "numbers" is lackluster, with few historians moving much beyond the remarkable Gustav Carlson, "Numbers Gambling: A Study of a Culture Complex" (Ph.D. diss., University of Michigan, 1940). By far the best recent treatment is Victoria W. Wolcott, "The Culture of the Informal Economy: Numbers Runners in Inter-War Detroit," *Radical History Review* 69 (1997): 46–75. Some of those myths of origin are rehearsed in Rufus Schatzberg and Robert J. Kelly, *African American Organized Crime: A Social History* (New Brunswick, NJ: Rutgers University Press, 1997), 66–68. For broader studies of gambling in American culture, see Ann Fabian, *Card Sharps, Dream Books, and Bucket Shops: Gambling in Nineteenth-Century America* (Ithaca, NY: Cornell University Press, 1990); and Jackson Lears, *Something for Nothing: Luck in America* (New York: Penguin, 2003). Our version of numbers in Harlem—Shane White, Stephen Garton, Stephen Robertson, and Graham White, "When Black Kings and Queens Ruled in Harlem"—is as yet unpublished.

43. *New York Age*, May 17, 1924; December 6, 1924. The *Age* estimated in 1926 that $75,000 a day was going to numbers bankers. See *New York Age*, June 12, 1926.

44. Letter to the editor, *New York Age*, July 31, 1926; *New York Age*, March 8, 1930.

45. *New York Age*, December 20, 1930; March 7, 1925; *Chicago Defender*, December 3, 1927. On dream books, see Fabian, *Card Sharps*, 142–50.

46. *New York Age*, August 23, 1923.

47. *Amsterdam News*, September 26, 1928; October 29, 1930.

48. *Emily Sibblies v. Daphnie Smith* (1930), no. 183004, DACCF.

49. On the harming traditions, see Chireau, *Black Magic*, 59–90 and passim.

50. *Lillian Tweed v. Audrey Dayrell* (1930), no. 184167, DACCF; *Amsterdam News*, November 12, 1930.

51. *New York Age*, May 19, 1928; *Amsterdam News*, September 25, 1929; *New York Age*, September 28, 1929.

52. *New York Age*, September 6, 1924.

53. *Herbert Reid v. Orville Milwood* (1930), no. 182456, DACCF (his name is spelled Milwood in the DA's files and Millwood in the newspapers); *Artemus Green v. Ver-

non Mullett (1930), no. 183114, DACCF (the papers dealing with Millwood are misfiled in this case file); *Amsterdam News,* June 16, 1930; *New York Age,* July 19, 1930. It seems likely that Rudolph Fisher heard about this and similar cases from the newspapers or by word of mouth when he was writing *The Conjure-Man Dies: A Mystery Tale of Dark Harlem* (1932).

54. *New York Age,* June 28, 1924; March 7, 1925.
55. *New York Age,* March 6, 1926; November 20, 1926.

FIVE

Re-membering John Dillinger

ELLIOTT J. GORN

Decades after the crime wave he initiated broke over America, John Dillinger remained a famous man. That fame took many forms—feature-length films, nostalgic magazine articles, Dillinger Day parades in towns where he and his gang had robbed banks. One memory held on with particular tenacity:

Joseph Snurr from Hagerstown, Pennsylvania, wrote to the Smithsonian Institution in May 1974 asking whether the story he had heard for years was true, "that John Dillinger's sexual organs were thirty-six inches long during an erection." Was it accurate that Dillinger's equipment killed several women during intercourse? And was this singular instrument in the Smithsonian's collections? Was it really preserved in alcohol for the benefit of researchers or was all of this just a myth?[1]

Snurr was not alone in contacting the Smithsonian about "this nationally famous story," as another correspondent put it. The editors of the *Book of Lists*, urged on by letters from their readers, enquired of the Smithsonian whether the object in question might not be added to the "Preserved Human Parts" section in the new edition of their reference book.[2]

The volume of mail that came to the Smithsonian on this topic is surprising. The size of a man's private parts, after all, is a delicate subject. In the spirit of pure research, a student from San Antonio wrote that she was completing an undergraduate paper for which she needed to know if the Smithsonian held "any of Mr. Dillinger's personal belongings, especially anything unusual." A writer from Westwood, New Jersey, asked rather delicately if the museum's exhibits centered "on a particular part of [Dillinger's] anatomy." Another from Durham, North Carolina, wrote that he learned of the Smithsonian story from *Playboy* magazine, but added that he wondered if the story was true, given the "filthy reputation" of that publication. One woman admitted that she was "embarrassed" to write but determined to settle a household dispute. Most asked about the legendary object as circumspectly as they could.[3]

One individual from Evanston, Illinois, wrote with an officiousness that had the ring of a university memorandum: "I understand the possible confidential nature of your position in this matter because of the potential controversy associated with this situation." He went on to say that he had heard about Dillinger's penis from "several serious, independent, and usually reliable sources" and that at least two of those sources placed the object in question at the Smithsonian, although not on public display. Trying to coax a candid response, he assured his correspondents that he had "chosen to avoid bringing into this probe any third party which may tend to publicize such rumors."[4]

Not everyone was so circumspect. One writer requested a photo of "the famous rod." Others simply asked where it was displayed so they might come and get a look. One can imagine the conversation that led to a brief and straight-forward query—Do you have it, and if so, where?—signed with elegant simplicity by "The Regular Customers of this Bar." Many correspondents asked for the dimensions of the item in question.[5]

Of course, the letters' very existence betrays doubt about the object's reality, or at least its presence at the Smithsonian. A medical research associate from the University of Alabama, Birmingham, wrote that Dillinger's penis was the subject of recurrent party debate. A woman from Jamaica Plain, Massachusetts, wanted to settle, among friends, the truth or falsehood of this "extraordinary vital organ." One query, written by the president of a financial services corporation in Palm Beach, Florida, was sure he had seen Dillinger's dick, but he didn't remember if it was at the Smithsonian or at FBI headquarters, so he asked for clarification.[6]

In fact, legend identified several venues as the final resting place of Dillinger's manhood. In "A Quiz You Can't Refuse," a little test for gangster buffs published in *Playboy* in 1991, the question was asked, "Which place keeps insisting it does not have Dillinger's prodigious pecker pickled in formaldehyde?" The possible answers were (a) the National Museum of Health and Medicine in Washington, D.C.; (b) the Smithsonian Institution; (c) the Mutter Museum in Philadelphia; and (d) the Cook County, Illinois, coroner's office. According to compiler William J. Helmer, the correct answer was all of the above, although the Smithsonian was the most frequently mentioned venue. (I know of one historian, by the way, who heard, as a young man, that it lay in a jar of formaldehyde on J. Edgar Hoover's desk.) [7]

The Smithsonian took pains to deny that it ever had anything to do with Dillinger's member. A boilerplate memo from the Division of Medical Sciences stated in 1971 that the museum did not possess any part of his anatomy and that "we have never had an exhibit on Dillinger, nor do we have anatomical specimens in our medical collection." Twenty years later, Museum Specialist Judy Chelnick composed a new memo for general circulation, noting that "this particular rumor has been running rampant for years" and denying that the Smithsonian or any other institution she knew of had any part of Dillinger's body. In 1991, the museum's Public Inquiry Mail Service sent out over a hundred copies of the denial. But the calls and letters kept coming. Ms. Chelnick, who continues to work in the Division of Medicine and Science, says that she enjoys urging callers to be explicit: "now, what exactly about John Dillinger interests you?"[8]

The Smithsonian story is part of a larger chronicle in folklore and popular culture. In Indiana, where Dillinger was born and raised, anecdotes are still told of small towns where he and his gang allegedly hid out after bank robberies. A common theme of the Dillinger legendry is that he did not in fact die in front of Chicago's Biograph Theater on July 22, 1934, but that once again the FBI got the wrong man. (After several failed attempts to capture Dillinger resulted in a number of dead and wounded civilians, Will Rogers commented that the only way the feds were likely to capture him was if he happened to stand near some innocent bystander and was shot accidentally.) Stories circulated about chance meetings with the famous outlaw, both when he was on the lam and after his alleged death. Other legends described the ghosts of those killed during holdups haunting the scenes of their deaths. Near Crown Point, Indiana, where Dillinger broke out of prison in early March 1934, locals referred to a road that ran by a desolate farm as "the Big Mary Road." Dillinger hid out at that farm, people said, harbored by a lover named Mary. Cops who drove by at night often saw Big Mary's ghost glaring at them.[9]

The legends continue to this day. I was told recently by the owners of a New Carlisle, Ohio, candle shop, housed in the building where Dillinger was said to have pulled his first bank job, that the place is haunted; they call the ghost John. On Sheridan Road, in Chicago's Uptown neighborhood, is the building where his body was laid out for burial; it was a funeral home back then but has since become a Native American social service center. That building too was said to be haunted, and only the efforts of an Episcopal bishop, then an Indian holy man, quieted things down. For the past several years, Dillinger buffs have gathered on Lincoln Avenue every July 22 to follow a bagpiper across the street to the alley where he fell; there, some say, lights flicker and cool breezes blow on the hour of his death.[10]

Still, the legends often come back to Dillinger's "prodigious pecker." In Indiana, one man believed that the reason the Woman in Red betrayed Dillinger was because they were lovers and she just couldn't take it any more. Another Hoosier claimed that Dillinger was known as Wailing Willy, but although his penis was twenty-three inches long flaccid, he was not a great lover because whenever he got an erection he would pass out from lack of blood to his brain. One man recalled that in junior high school in Washington, D.C., during the 1950s, he had heard that the dick was so big and powerful that Dillinger had to strap it down to his leg for fear of it ripping through his pants.[11]

Such stories, of course, are not so much about John Dillinger as they are about how he is remembered; to study him is to think not just about history but about memory. Midwestern newspapers run stories every year on the anniversary of Dillinger's death. Hollywood has made several feature-length films based on his life—the most famous starring Warren Oates in 1973—and more are planned. There were radio programs through the 1950s and television documentaries since then; serious poets have written about his exploits, artists have painted and sketched him, short stories and novels fill in details where research fails, and even small museums have been created to memorialize him. He is prominently featured on many Web sites, and Dillinger memorabilia are always for sale. One rapper even goes by the name Das Dillinger, and a punk band calls itself the Dillinger Escape Plan.[12]

What is this all about? How and why did a man whose claim to fame was robbing banks and breaking out of prisons become the subject of rural folklore, of urban legend, and of a seventy-year-long tradition in popular culture? This chapter grows out of a larger book project that will take up issues of history and memory, of gender and masculinity, of the Great Depression and its impact, of crime and punishment. Here, I hope merely to speculate a little about John Dillinger and American culture.

———

Dillinger, it is sometimes said, was the last American outlaw; newspapers compared him more often to Jesse James than Al Capone. Note that the immigrant Capone was usually referred to as a gangster, as are black and Latino youths in the drug trade today, but the native-born Dillinger was just as likely to be called an outlaw, a desperado, a badman. "Gangster" implies the city, "outlaw" resonates with open spaces; the former has valances of darker races and ethnicities, the latter is associated with white, heartland individuals. "Outlaw" is a term from the West of the imagination, and although outlaws are the "bad guys," they are also part of America's deepest myths.

John Herbert Dillinger was born in 1903 in Indianapolis and lived in that city until age sixteen, when his father left a tiny grocery store for a one-man farm in Mooresville, about twenty-five miles southwest of town. Farming had been in the family's history. Mathias Dillinger (the family pronounced the name with a hard *g*) was an Alsatian immigrant who came to Indiana in the mid-nineteenth century. His son, John W. Dillinger, was born in 1864 and raised on a farm. Father and son moved to Indianapolis in the early 1890s, and both became laborers. Before moving, however, John W. Dillinger married Mary Ellen "Mollie" Lancaster; their daughter Audrey was born in 1889. By the time John Herbert Dillinger was born in 1903, John Senior had acquired the grocery store and a little house on middling—with a push—Cooper Street.[13]

Various theories have been invoked to explain Dillinger's turn to crime—the early loss of his mother, the inconsistent child-rearing techniques of his father and elder sister, resentment toward his stepmother, whom Dillinger Senior married in 1912. All of this is pure speculation, but even the things that we know for sure are not very helpful. Lots of people lose a parent at a young age but do not become felons. We know that Johnny was an indifferent student (although he liked to read) but a good athlete; as a young adult during the early 1920s he played shortstop for a semipro team in nearby Martinsville. He might have been a bit high-spirited, but he was not thought of as a troubled kid. He left school around the time the family moved to Mooresville, and he drifted through a series of jobs as an upholsterer, a machinist, a furniture factory worker. He joined the navy, went AWOL, and was discharged. In 1924, at age twenty-one, he married Beryl Hovius, the young daughter of a local farm family.[14]

Dillinger was not a model citizen in the chamber of commerce or American Legion mold, but neither did he appear bound for criminal stardom as he reached full manhood. In his late teens he allegedly stole a car, although no one filed charges. Perhaps there were other petty infractions that did not get reported. He seems to have missed the excitement of the city, and certainly Mooresville bored him. He spent much of his time hanging around the local pool hall and took a particular liking to an older man, an ex-convict named Ed Singleton. Together, they planned a stickup, and their victim was an elderly local grocer, Frank Morgan. They accosted Morgan one night as he walked home with his store's receipts. Dillinger hit him on the head with a heavy bolt, but the old man did not go down. They wrestled, the gun Dillinger carried discharged (after it fell from his hand, he claimed), and the bullet ricocheted down the street. Both Dillinger and Singleton fled the scene, but local police soon picked them up. Dillinger's father urged his son to make a clean breast of it, to eschew an attorney, admit his crimes, and beg the court's mercy. Singleton, however, hired a lawyer who argued that Dillinger had masterminded the whole affair. Dillinger drew ten to twenty years in the Indiana State Reformatory in Pendleton, and he served a total of nine; Singleton served two. Those sympathetic to Dillinger often invoked the injustice of this outcome to explain his turn to serious crime.[15]

Prison was the formative influence in Dillinger's life. His records indicate that he was in trouble often with the guards, mostly for petty stuff like gambling and disorderly conduct but also for an escape attempt. Five years into his term, Beryl divorced him. Shortly thereafter, he was transferred from the Pendleton facility to the much tougher state prison in Michigan City. Clearly it was in prison that he thought about crime as a career. He spent his time among serious felons, many of whom became the core of the Dillinger gang after they got out.[16]

Dillinger entered the state correctional system in September 1924 and came out in May 1933, just a month shy of his thirtieth birthday. He had served nine long years—virtually his entire adulthood up to that time—before Indiana governor Paul McNutt signed parole papers. Back in Mooresville, Dillinger Senior had been circulating a petition for his son's release, and dozens of his neighbors signed it, including the local preacher, and even Frank Morgan, the man who Dillinger tried to beat out of his grocery receipts. The parole board also found very persuasive a plea for clemency from Judge J. W. Williams, the man who had sentenced Dillinger to prison nine years earlier. The illness of Dillinger's stepmother gave added weight to the cause. Johnny got home just moments after she passed away. He told his father that he was determined to make it in the straight world, but given how events played out over the next year, his sincerity is more than a little suspect.[17]

The America into which Dillinger reemerged was radically changed: commercial radio had been a novelty in 1924 but now was pervasive; film had been very popular albeit entirely silent in 1924, but now Hollywood cranked out hundreds of big talking pictures each year and showed them in grand movie palaces; automobiles, common in 1924, were ubiquitous by 1933. Most important, of course, the prosperity of postwar America had given way to the Great Depression. Indeed, the year 1933 saw the very depths of the depression, with a quarter of America's working population unemployed, banks failing by the thousands, and citizens losing their possessions to bill collectors. When Dillinger walked out of Michigan City, the New Deal was still in its first hundred days.[18]

Quietly, Dillinger began a series of robberies. In later years, there were reports of small heists that he may or may not have been involved in—at a tavern, at a thread mill—but the first big effort came on June 10, less than three weeks after his release from prison, when he robbed the bank in New Carlisle, Ohio, of $10,000. A month later, on July 16, he and another man robbed a bank in Daleville, Indiana, of $3,000. Although his name was not mentioned in the newspapers, it is clear from their descriptions that it was Dillinger. A clerk described the holdup man as 5 feet 7 inches tall, thin, well dressed, with a scar on his upper lip. Equally important was Dillinger's singular coolness—"This is a stickup; get me the money, honey," he said to the teller; when she froze, he vaulted over the counter and began scooping up cash, an athletic move he repeated several times, earning himself the nickname "the jackrabbit."[19]

Dillinger was very active during the next two months. He linked up with veteran criminals such as Harry Copeland and Sam Goldstein, and led shifting groups of them into banks in Montpelier, Indiana, Bluffton, Ohio, and Indianapolis (where they made off with $25,000). He also found a girlfriend during these months, Mary Longnaker of Dayton, Ohio. Together, they visited Dillinger's family in Mooresville; they also spent time in Chicago at the Century of Progress World's Fair and (the kiss of death) at Wrigley Field to watch Cubs' games.[20]

While Dillinger was incarcerated at Michigan City, he and some of his friends had worked in the prison's shirt-making facility. Sometime in mid-September 1933, he managed to smuggle guns into the plant in boxes of thread; a few days later, ten of his cronies—among them, Harry Pierpont, Charles Mackley, Russell Clark, and John Hamilton—shot their way out of the Indiana State Prison. In those intervening days, however, Dillinger himself was arrested and charged with the Bluffton robbery. On October 12, five of the escaped convicts entered the jail where Dillinger was being held in Lima, Ohio. They told Sheriff Jesse Sarber that they had been sent to remand his prisoner back to Indiana. When Sarber asked to see their credentials, they shot him to death, unlocked Dillinger's cell, and freed him. Two days later, Dillinger and two of the others raided an

Auburn, Indiana, police station, making off with Thompson machine guns and bulletproof vests; a week later, they grabbed more equipment at the Peru, Indiana, armory.[21]

In late October, Governor McNutt, the same man who had signed Dillinger's parole papers, called out the National Guard, but the gang had already fled to Chicago. The jobs got bigger now—the gang took $75,000 in Greencastle, Indiana, then another $25,000 in Racine, Wisconsin. Dillinger had a new girlfriend too, a Menominee Indian named Evelyn "Billie" Frechette. She had been raised on the reservation and married a Wisconsin man who ended up in Leavenworth Federal Prison; then she moved to Chicago to work in restaurants and night clubs. Pat Cherrington, Harry Pierpont's girlfriend, had introduced Billie to Johnnie, and from all accounts they fell in love. Billie certainly was game for the life she entered, aiding her lover by finding apartments, scouting banks, purchasing cars—the sort of interactions with the straight world that wives and sweethearts of robbers often performed. She even participated in shoot-outs and high-speed chases. There were also other women involved with the gang now, and Chicago police included two of these girlfriends or molls on their public enemies list. In fact, the entire gang comprised the list's top ten, with John Dillinger ranked number one.[22]

Still, the story to date was a local one, much as the roughly simultaneous chronicle of Bonnie and Clyde was a matter of interest mostly in the Southwest. (Bonnie and Clyde, incidentally, remained largely a local story until the eponymous 1967 movie.) Even the escape of the ten convicts from the state penitentiary, though it attracted national press, did not bring sustained attention to the Dillinger gang. They were certainly professionals; they knew how to case a job, obtain information about banks, map a proper getaway. They had underworld connections that helped them find safe havens and learn of new opportunities, although they were not part of a syndicate of the sort that Al Capone had run for years. They were bold and thorough, if not particularly innovative. They exploited the new technologies of crime—Thompson machine guns, powerful cars, good roads—and did so with excellent advance planning. They paid attention to details, such as keeping tubs of roofing nails on hand to throw at the tires of pursuing cars. From Ohio to Wisconsin, they certainly got people's attention, but they were a local law-enforcement problem. J. Edgar Hoover and his Division of Investigation remained aloof from the case.[23]

The Dillinger gang finished out the year by heading to Florida, renting a fancy waterfront house, and celebrating the New Year by firing off machine guns on Daytona Beach. From there they split up. Billie Frechette went back to Wisconsin to visit her family, the rest of the gang went to Tucson, Arizona, but Dillinger and John Hamilton, most sources agree, headed north, where on January 15 they held up the First National Bank of East Chicago. In the process, Hamilton was wounded, while Dillinger returned police officer William O'Malley's fire and killed him, the first and only casualty directly attributed to him throughout the entire crime spree. (Dillinger always denied that he shot O'Malley, that he was even in East Chicago that day, but he added that any man under fire would shoot back.) A few days later, Billie met Dillinger with a new car, they found a safe place for Hamilton to recuperate, and then they headed to Tucson.[24]

Their luck evaporated altogether ten days later when Tucson police arrested the whole bunch of them. Dillinger was flown back in irons to northern Indiana to stand trial for O'Malley's death. His accomplices Charles Mackley, Russell Clark, and Harry Pierpont were remanded to Ohio for Sheriff Sarber's murder.[25]

Now the real story begins. Dillinger was brought to the Lake County jail in Crown Point, Indiana, about fifty miles southeast of Chicago, where he posed for photographs with prosecutor Robert G. Estill and Lake County sheriff Lillian Holley. These photos were splashed across front pages all over America, and newsreel versions filled silver screens. There is Dillinger, smiling, looking at the camera out of the corner of his eye, his hand resting familiarly on Estill's shoulder, and the prosecutor and sheriff seeming to smile in complicity with their prisoner (see fig. 5.1). The photographs proved doubly embarrassing when they were reprinted a month later below headlines announcing Dillinger's escape, just a few days before his trial date. Someone had passed him a wooden gun, and it looked real enough that he used it to disarm several guards, free another prisoner (whom newspapers referred to as "negro Herbert Youngblood"), steal the sheriff's car from the garage across the street, take an auto mechanic hostage for a few miles, and drive to Chicago, singing "Git Along Little Doggies" and "The Last Roundup."[26]

Stealing the car and crossing state lines gave the Justice Department's Division of Investigation (soon to be the Federal Bureau of Investigation) jurisdiction over the case under the Dyer Act. The FBI had been following the Dillinger gang for a while anyway but had refrained from getting involved; now it could resist no longer, difficult as a fugitive hunt might prove to be. J. Edgar Hoover and John Dillinger were a remarkable pair: the former, straight-arrow, ambitious, moralistic, driven; the latter, at least in his public persona, easygoing, cool, always smiling sidelong at

Fig. 5.1. Shortly after being sent back to Crown Point, Indiana, for trial, John Dillinger posed with Lake County prosecutor Robert Estill and Sheriff Lillian Holley. Newspapers across the United States published the photos, and film versions of this scene appeared on newsreels in thousands of movie theaters.

the camera. Dillinger was, as several reporters noted, the Harry Houdini of bank robbers. At the very least he had the gift of being several places at once, for newspapers reported countless sightings of him over the next several months.[27]

With Mackley, Pierpont, and Clark securely behind bars (the former two would be executed in a matter of months, the latter given a life sentence), a second Dillinger gang formed. This time the crew included the truly sociopathic Lester Gillis, better known as Baby Face Nelson. He had been born near Chicago's stockyards of immigrant parents and grew up a foot soldier in the Chicago underworld, a man with a violent temper and a taste for blood. Within a few days of Dillinger's escape from Crown

Point, the gang robbed the Security National Bank in Sioux Falls, South Dakota, of almost $50,000. A week later, they took another $50,000 from the first National Bank in Mason City, Iowa. The gang not only stole more now, but the robberies grew spectacular. They often involved taking hostages as human shields, high-speed chases, and gun battles.[28]

Dillinger was slightly wounded in Mason City, and he and Billie disappeared into Saint Paul, Minnesota. (Tips came into the Bureau that the two had gone to New York City, and believing that they had found Frechette, federal agents picked up a woman who turned out to be Mrs. Chico Marx.) At the end of March, the G-men discovered the Saint Paul hideout and surrounded it, but Dillinger managed to blast his way out with a Thompson machine gun, while Frechette drove the getaway car. Just a week after the Saint Paul shoot-out, right under the feds' noses at the height of the manhunt, Billie and Johnnie were in Mooresville for a family reunion, where Dillinger introduced her as his wife. Despite the surveillance that the Dillinger family had learned to live with, they all enjoyed a big supper together, and even stepped outside for photographs, including one of Johnnie brandishing his wooden pistol and Thompson machine gun. One day after leaving Mooresville, however, in a State Street tavern in downtown Chicago, the FBI captured Billie, and Dillinger himself just got away. She was charged with harboring a fugitive, tried in Saint Paul, and sentenced to two years in prison and a $2,000 fine. Friends talked Dillinger out of trying to rescue her.[29]

Since Tucson, Dillinger had been on the front page of newspapers across America, but nothing topped the spectacular story of April 22, when the FBI surrounded the gang at the Little Bohemia lodge near Rhinelander, in northern Wisconsin. Acting on a tip, chief of the investigation in Chicago, Melvin Purvis—an ambitious, wealthy, aristocratic little man, one of Hoover's favorites—commandeered airplanes and flew two dozen agents into the area, then drove in the cold to surround the lodge by nightfall. The gang got wind of the trap (the feds started firing prematurely, and at the wrong people) and slipped out a back window. At daybreak, the G-men moved in and captured three women who ran with the gang and were still inside the lodge. Hoover's men had managed to kill one civilian and wound two others. Baby Face Nelson exacted the same toll on the federal agents before disappearing into the woods. Everyone else escaped in one of the most humiliating episodes in FBI history.[30]

By the beginning of May and for the next several weeks, the feds were clueless as to Dillinger's whereabouts; agents even searched the SS *Duch-*

ess of York on a tip that he was headed to Scotland. Meanwhile, Dillinger's notoriety had an impact well beyond the newspaper headlines. The new Hayes Commission, charged with cleaning up Hollywood, made it an explicit part of its agenda that movies no longer glorify crime and criminals, and they singled out Dillinger as someone who must not be romanticized on screen. Moreover, Attorney General Homer Cummings helped craft and bring before Congress a new omnibus crime bill. In pushing for passage, the Justice Department repeatedly cited the depredations of the Dillinger gang as evidence that a federal crackdown on felons was overdue. Congress passed ten of the bill's twelve provisions, supporting Franklin Roosevelt's "New Deal on Crime."[31]

Five state governors posted a $5,000 reward for Dillinger's capture at the end of May, and the federal government upped the ante with $10,000 more. But Dillinger and his partner Homer Van Meter were undergoing plastic surgery in a back room at the Chicago home of a mob-connected bar owner. Meanwhile, the feds threw all of their resources into finding Dillinger. Internal memoranda reveal tangled efforts to gain information from underworld snitches, as well as relentless wiretapping and interrogation of witnesses. Three weeks after his surgery, Dillinger met a new woman, Polly Hamilton, a waitress who also worked occasionally for Dillinger's friend, brothel keeper Anna Sage. Dillinger and Hamilton began to date, although she claimed later that she did not know who he really was. They celebrated Dillinger's thirty-first birthday together on June 22, just as he was named America's first Public Enemy Number One. The gang's last stickup proved a disaster: although they got away with $30,000 from a bank in South Bend, Indiana, one policeman died and four citizens were wounded.[32]

Dillinger must have known that the noose was tightening. Despite a new mustache, plastic surgery, fake glasses, and a change of hair color, he was still recognizable to anyone who had seen the wanted posters, newsreels, and photographs that were everywhere across America. But it was not some random bystander who brought him down. His friend Anna Sage was in trouble with federal authorities for her work running brothels. A Rumanian immigrant born Ana Cumpanis, she was told that leading the feds to Dillinger might help prevent her deportation. Dillinger had been staying in an apartment she owned on Halstead Street. She met with Special Agent Melvin Purvis, on the night of July 21, and agreed to let him know of Dillinger's whereabouts. Accompanying Sage was a friend who also stood to gain from Dillinger's demise. There is reason to believe that Sergeant Martin Zarkovich of the East Chicago police had aided Dillinger's escape from Crown Point and had even helped him hide out, but now big rewards and a fear that the fugitive might give evidence against the notoriously corrupt Zarkovich and his brother officers made Dillinger worth more dead than alive.[33]

The next day, as Chicago sweltered, Sage phoned Purvis to say that she, Dillinger, and Polly Hamilton were going to a movie at the air-conditioned Biograph Theater on Lincoln Avenue, that she would be wearing a brightly colored skirt. Dillinger loved movies, especially cop films, and playing that night was *Manhattan Melodrama* with Clark Gable in the role of Blackie Gallagher, a suave gangster, and William Powell playing Gallagher's boyhood friend, now a prosecuting attorney. Blackie, in the end, went to the electric chair. Sage, Hamilton, and Dillinger came out of the theater around 10:30, and federal agents along with officers of the East Chicago police department were waiting. Purvis lit his cigar, a signal for the G-men to close in. When Dillinger realized what was happening, he crouched, took a step or two down Lincoln Avenue, then started breaking left toward the alley that led back to Halstead Street. He was gunned down with shots through his back and neck, one bullet exiting through his cheek. In the official version, Dillinger had his gun out and so the shooting was justified. Other eyewitnesses said they saw no gun.[34]

Lincoln Avenue was a mob scene that night, as hundreds, perhaps thousands of people poured into the street. Newsreel cameras captured smiling Chicagoans in front of the Biograph, holding up newspapers with block headlines declaring the death of Public Enemy Number One. It was said that men dipped their handkerchiefs and women the hems of their skirts in Dillinger's blood on the sidewalk where he fell. Newspapers across America lead with his death the next morning, and soon papers in London and Bogotá, Beijing and Melbourne, featured prominent stories. Melvin Purvis found himself an instant celebrity. The excitement lasted for days. The Cook County Morgue was jammed on July 23 with "morbid curiosity seekers," as newspapers called; so was McReady's Funeral Home in Uptown a day later. Finally the elder John Dillinger and Johnnie's half brother Hubert were allowed to drive their kinsman back home. They had a wake for Johnnie in Mooresville and buried him beside his mother in the Crownhill Cemetery in Indianapolis. The FBI revealed that Dillinger had only seven dollars in his pocket, underscoring Hoover's mantra that "Crime does not pay." But other sources claimed that he was carrying thousands of dollars, that the money was lifted from his body, and that his death had more to do with corrupt police in East Chicago than the G-men's efficiency. Incidentally, Will Rogers' remark about Dillinger getting too close to innocent bystanders proved prophetic: two women suffered gunshot wounds, and they were eventually compensated by an act of Congress. One final point: the Woman in Red, as Anna Sage came to be known, was soon deported.[35]

———

Much of the Dillinger story has been well told by journalists such as Brian Burrough and Dillinger researchers like Joe Pinkston and Ellen Poulsen. There are certainly disagreements over details and larger issues too—did Dillinger carve the Crown Point gun himself or was it smuggled to him, and if so, by whom? Was Dillinger even present in East Chicago when Officer O'Malley was killed? Were banks complicit in their own robberies in order to collect insurance money? Was young Johnnie Dillinger a budding criminal just waiting to bloom, or did prison make him into a hardened felon?

Beyond the factual details, I am trying to understand how and why we remember the story. Why do parts of it get retold, forgotten, changed? How does historical context matter? Certainly the Dillinger story had resonance beyond the era of the Great Depression, but it was during that calamity that the large contours of its telling were set. As national newspaper coverage increased from the beginning of 1934 until Dillinger's death, the number of letters written to the president, the first lady, and the attorney general also multiplied. Many writers simply urged officials to do something about this menace. Some volunteered advice—for example, seize Dillinger's father, then capture Johnnie when he came to the rescue. Other individuals offered their services; several were willing to act as bounty hunters, bringing the fugitive in for a fee. But many writers were sympathetic to Dillinger and his gang. More than a few suggested that a man who could avoid police traps for so long obviously was smart and his talents should not be wasted. Others openly condemned the banks that Dillinger robbed and asked how he was any worse than the bank owners who seemed to be robbing people legally. Some of the letters were explicit in their class sympathies. Indeed, the Dillinger story became a venue in which large ideas about economic fairness and social justice were discussed.[36]

In this general sense, the sociologist Paul Kooistra is right: Dillinger was one in a long line of American Robin Hoods, rural bandits of legend who defied authorities and stood with the poor. But it was not so simple. Kooistra suggests that the Robin Hood tradition in America depended on rural settings, economic crises, and social dislocations. Stories about

Dillinger constantly invoked the Indiana countryside, and Dillinger himself was often referred to as a farm boy, but in fact he was raised mostly in the city, robbed banks in cities, hid out in cities. Moreover, although the Great Depression is important for understanding Dillinger, newspapers did not often invoke Robin Hood's name, and Dillinger was rarely depicted in oral tradition or in print as a public benefactor. The Dillinger of legend was portrayed not as taking care of others but as using whatever means necessary to take care of himself. So although the story invoked notions of class justice, expressed the presence of rural solidarity in Mooresville, and even reveled in the idea of oppressive institutions being put in their place, it fit the Robin Hood paradigm imperfectly. The Dillinger gang stole from the rich and gave to themselves; Americans knew it, and that was all right with many of them.[37]

Ideas about authority, particularly federal authority, were also projected onto this story. The expansion of the Bureau of Investigation and adoption of the omnibus crime bill were important policy initiatives of the new Roosevelt administration. Beyond that, J. Edgar Hoover made the Dillinger story into the FBI's founding myth. Richard Gid Powers has documented the Bureau's efforts to publicize its own efficiency and teamwork. Hoover was ever vigilant about his agency's image, and bringing down Dillinger was always presented—in film, newsreels, and newspapers—as a triumph of scientific investigation and sophisticated police work. In fact, one way to think about the Dillinger story was as a satisfying example of institutions working well, even as the economy collapsed. In the midst of social cataclysm, law enforcement agencies set their goal and met it, and they did so using sophisticated techniques like fingerprinting and ballistics analysis (see fig. 5.2). Even more than mere efficiency, here was a satisfying restoration of moral authority. The constantly repeated phrase "Crime does not pay" speaks to the importance of a predictable world in which honesty is rewarded and success is the fruit of walking the straight and narrow. In this reading of the story, all the photos of Dillinger's dead body were palpable evidence that another popular phrase from the newsreels—"You can't get away with it"—described absolute reality.[38]

Claire Bond Potter has argued convincingly that Dillinger's was the most spectacular story in an era that featured Bonnie and Clyde, Machine Gun Kelly, Pretty Boy Floyd, Baby Face Nelson, and the Karpis Gang. All were brought to heel in the early 1930s, and their depredations formed the justification not just for stronger federal policies but for a whole new ideology of federal power. The war on crime, Potter argues, was funda-

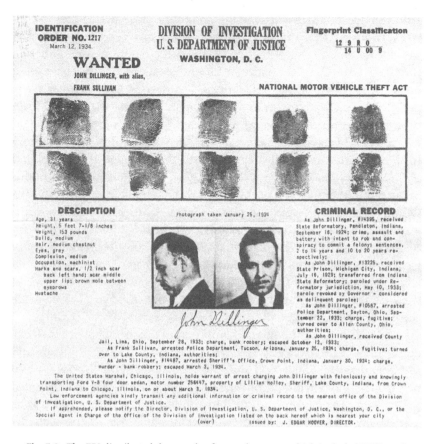

Fig. 5.2. The FBI distributed thousands of wanted posters, which included Dillinger's mug shot and fingerprints.

mental to the New Deal. The message emanating from law enforcement, the justice department, the attorney general, and finally the president was that only a federal government armed with new laws, armed with new agencies, and just plain armed (FBI agents did not routinely carry weapons until they were in the midst of the Dillinger manhunt) could protect the American people from those who would endanger lives and steal property. Of course the battles against criminals deflected attention away from the larger failures of Depression-era America to secure the health and welfare of its citizens. But the war on crime—on outlaws like Dillinger—was an important propaganda and policy victory, part of a larger vision of a newly centralized state.[39]

Powers and Potter are on to something important: Dillinger helped dramatize the need for interstate crime fighting, and his depredations were enlisted to justify whole new uses and even ideologies of federal power. But focusing on the triumph of the state over the bad guys does not quite capture the emotional power of crime stories. G-men, even heroic G-men like Melvin Purvis, were kind of boring. Historian David Ruth explores the appeal of criminals and argues that they were refashioned in popular culture during the 1920s and 1930s to represent models of style. Gangsters on the screen and in magazines were consummate consumers of liquor, cars, clothes—of the good life. As they were projected onto popular media, felons became harbingers of the new culture of leisure, pleasure, and sex, of risk taking, danger, and excitement. Of course these projections worked in reverse too—life imitated art. Dillinger died at a movie house having just watched a film about two boyhood chums, one who became a prosecutor and the other a major criminal. Yes, crime did not pay: Blackie Gallagher went to the chair in the end, but he went in style, with an air of defiance. To give another example, when the Dillinger gang was picked up in Arizona, it was photographs in a detective magazine that gave them away—exactly the sort of magazine that Dillinger ordered while in prison. In fact, several people who knew him commented that Dillinger loved to read about himself in the newspapers. What was it like for this man from a modest background who spent his adulthood behind bars to go into a crowded theater and see his own image projected a hundred times larger than life? Was Dillinger's year-long spree at least in part a playing up to expectations that he learned at the movies? Certainly he dressed stylishly, just like Hollywood's criminals. There was even talk toward the end of his life that he wanted to contact screenwriters to help turn his story into a movie. And much like the movies, Dillinger's wild year—which was so minutely covered and widely reported—was one big denial of life's bleak anonymity.[40]

That anonymity was very much about class. If Ruth is right, then the story of America's public enemies was a kind of dialogue between the 1920s and the 1930s. When we look at the great early gangster films, or for that matter at photographs of the celebrity felons from the 1930s, we can easily forget that the Great Depression, not the Roaring Twenties, was their social backdrop. Criminals like Dillinger came mostly from modest backgrounds, but it is significant that images of them emphasized fancy clothes and powerful cars. They were simply seizing all of the goods that American culture had blandished during the 1920s and taken away in the 1930s. Yet there was an outrageousness in the culture of crime—and here I mean real people like Dillinger as well as fictional criminals—that parodied America's love for displays of wealth. Cars, for example, facilitated bank robberies, because big, powerful, expensive cars were most useful in a getaway. But they were also symbols of wealth—wealth that most felons could never acquire in the straight world. Cars too were emblems of freedom, of the open road, and of course the Dillinger gang's exploits can be seen as one big road trip. That freedom must have been immensely appealing to those whose lives had been characterized by confinement—the confinement of prison, of limited means, of small-town life. Not just the likes of the Dillinger gang but law-abiding citizens too who read about celebrity felons' exploits in the newspapers must have found it exhilarating to ponder the untrammeled freedom of America's new highways, highways designed to facilitate commerce and progress, yet here enlisted in the cause of larceny.

Which brings us to something hard to define—the tone or style of the whole Dillinger episode. The photographs of Dillinger reveal a facet of the story not quite captured anywhere else. He is often smiling. More than smiling, laughing. His life was in mortal danger, but he clearly was having fun as he rested his hand on the prosecutor's shoulder or posed with the wooden gun that sprang him from the Crown Point Jail (see fig. 5.3). It was the same nonchalance that let him sing "Git Along Little Doggies" as he drove the sheriff's car to Chicago, the same coolness that brought him back for a family visit to Mooresville in the midst of the FBI manhunt, the same chutzpah that allowed him—one of the most recognizable men in America—to walk out of a crowded movie theater onto a busy street with a woman on each arm. Seen from this point of view, the tone of the story is quite opposite that propagated by authorities, especially the FBI. To Hoover's stentorian "Crime does not pay," Dillinger winked and asked, "Says who?" His playfulness mocked the serious business of law enforcement, a bulwark of the ideology of solid work, steady habits, and virtuous success. The laughing Dillinger eluding the law not only enraged the likes of J. Edgar Hoover but undermined the hierarchy that claimed to buttress a just society.[41]

Paradoxically, the Dillinger story was also filled with violence. This was one bloody binge. Judging from the newspaper accounts, people were fascinated with descriptions of stakeouts and shoot-outs. They were frightened but also captivated by descriptions of Thompson machine guns spewing death. For much of the public, the shoot-outs were more than just nihilistic violence; they also signified anger at financial institutions. The Dillinger gang robbed banks and attacked those who protected them. By the time the Dillinger story reached public awareness, something like ten thousand banks had closed their doors due to the Great Depression,

Fig. 5.3. John Dillinger poses in front of his family home
in Mooresville, Indiana, with a Thompson machine gun
and the fake wooden pistol he used to break out of the
Crown Point jail.

wiping out the resources of thousands of businesses and millions of individuals. Of course those who died during the gang's yearlong rampage
were far removed from the causes of the economic cataclysm. But the
anger directed against institutions that supposedly ensured Americans'
welfare was widespread, and fantasies of retributive violence must have
been appealing. At least that message comes through strongly in letters
written to government officials.[42]

But how do we reconcile hot rage on the one hand and cool nonchalance on the other? What is most compelling in the Dillinger story
is how it held seemingly conflicted feelings together. When we think of
the story this way—that it was less about a particular moral lesson than
about observing contradictory impulses and emotions at play—then we
get deeper into its possible meanings.

For example, one arc of the story was the hoary old assumption about
the virtues of the country and the corruptions of the city. Dillinger's

father was a central character here. The strongest representations of Old John are on newsreel footage, where he plows behind a horse on his one-man farm in Mooresville, or in newspaper stories where he says with terse love that Johnny was always a good boy, or in photographs where we can read his weathered face and quiet suffering, where his hat and suspenders and shirt tell us all we need to know of the hard but honest life of a farmer. Such nostalgia ignored the fact that Americans for decades fled the countryside and poured into the cities. Chicago, where Dillinger met his end, was known as the rawest and toughest of them all, at least from the end of the Civil War through the Great Depression. Cities kindled desires, sometimes fulfilled them, and the Dillinger story was all about desire—for sex, for money, for the open road, for freedom. Old John represented our nostalgia for the land, for the old ways, for stability; he embodied our obeisance to hard work and sober self-control, which, we like to think, built America. Johnnie left all of that behind him, much as Americans rushed to do precisely the same, to escape the drudgery, boredom, and narrowness of farm and village in a quest for money and for intense experience.[43]

Or consider the importance of women in the story. On the one hand, Dillinger was an outlaw, a bandit, a badman. He even sang cowboy songs as he escaped the law. It made sense that one of his lovers was an Indian. Billie was always depicted as pretty wild. Her photographs reveal an attractive woman who took care to highlight that attractiveness by the way she dressed and made herself up in public. Newspaper accounts called her things like "the Indian beauty," noted that she liked to drink, and depicted her as a "loose" woman. Indeed, the whole story was steamy for America in the 1930s. From the Michigan City prison break forward, the women associated with the Dillinger gang were much in the news. Dillinger himself was arrested at his first girlfriend's home, traveled openly with Billie Frechette, and was killed leaving the Biograph Theater with a notoriously promiscuous woman on each arm, one of whom was the Woman in Red, as Anna Sage was forever after known. On the one hand, the story was deeply homo-social—men with guns faced death together and trusted their very lives to each other. On the other the story was filled with lusty heterosexual liaisons. Both themes ran deeply contrary to notions of the stable nuclear family, which was at pains to survive the Depression.[44]

Dillinger's was also a white, heartland story. True, there were minorities at the margins: Herbert Youngblood, an African American prisoner who escaped from Crown Point with Dillinger, though he was never part of the gang and was killed shortly after the breakout; and two Jews, Samuel Goldstein, a veteran felon who pulled a few early jobs with Dillinger and then disappeared into prison, and Jessie Levy, who unsuccessfully defended Clark, Mackley, and Pierpont after they were remanded to Ohio. But mostly the story centered on middle America, which made it far different from most of the urban gangster stories that filled the newspapers in the late 1920s and early 1930s—stories of Italians and Jews and Irish and African Americans warring against the police and sometimes against each other over various forms of organized vice. Dillinger, by contrast, was the last outlaw, the modern Jesse James; he was a free man under the open sky, with only his guns and his buddies. Much of the appeal of Dillinger's story came from the fact that these men—these white men from the American heartland—were not soldiering on despite the Depression but were hanging out. And instead of being dutiful wives caring for dutiful husbands, the women flaunted their attraction to outlaws and were openly part of the urban underworld. Rather than men and women cleaving to the sheltering safety of home, these individuals took to the road; in fact, they took everything they could lay their hands on.

Which brings us back to Dillinger's private parts. The day after his death, several newspapers published a photo from the morgue suggesting that he had an enormous erection under the sheet covering his body (fig. 5.4). Probably, however, it was just his hand, hovering over his midsection in rigor mortis, or perhaps part of the mechanism that raised and lowered the autopsy table. Realizing how sexually evocative the picture was, some editors reprinted it the next day with the towering structure airbrushed out. That's not all that was missing. Over the next few days came a series of stories: that Dillinger's brain had been taken during the autopsy, then that the autopsy report itself was lost; his gun too was nowhere to be found, and all the money he'd stolen in the past few months was also gone. Missing items were everywhere.[45]

Still, the stories about Dillinger's penis and its appropriation by the feds apparently were not in circulation during his lifetime, or in the years immediately after his death. The earliest I've found evidence of anyone claiming to remember the Smithsonian story was in the 1950s, and the tale only gained wide currency in the next decade, more than a generation after the outlaw's demise. Certainly the Smithsonian legend was a fitting metaphor for the 1960s and 1970s, an era when male fantasies of sexual fulfillment, of breaking through social constraints, of personal indulgence all found heightened expression in popular culture. And this was

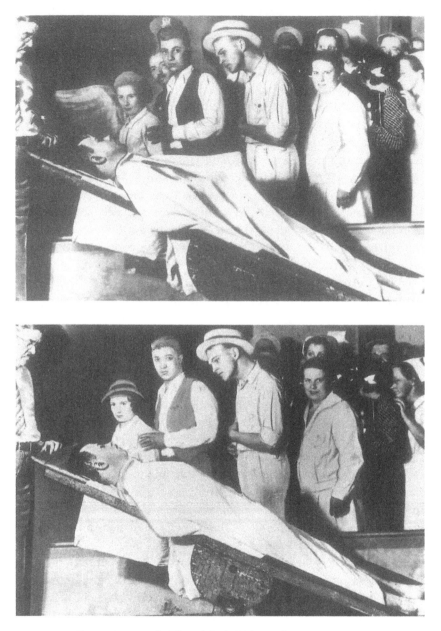

Fig. 5.4. Images of Dillinger's body in the Cook County Morgue,
distributed the day after his death.

primarily a *male* story—men told it to other men. Although no one ever made the connection at the time, Dillinger in some ways fit the bill as the sort of cool, attractive outsider Norman Mailer later described when he coined the phrase "the white negro" to describe the disaffection of many American men from mainstream culture. Looked at one way, the letters to the Smithsonian suggested that many Americans sought a palpable record of Dillinger's mythic capacities, preserved in the nation's repository of memory. Of course, even as the legend evoked fantasies of male sexual prowess, it also questioned their legitimacy. What could better symbolize the uneasiness, the ambivalence with Dillinger's alleged sexual potency than death and castration, with his manhood, in the end, safely pickled in formaldehyde and stashed away in the federal labyrinth?[46]

If the Smithsonian legend was a product of postwar desires and fears, the sexualization of Dillinger was nonetheless there from the beginning. The legend of his enormous member a generation after his death extended and literalized the widely reported fact that sex was central to the story and that women were attracted to him. He was, after all, betrayed by the Woman in Red, an image redolent of easy virtue, erotic pleasure, leading to sexual treachery. Or as one newsman put it, "Dillinger died as he lived—in a hail of bullets and a welter of blood. He died with a smile on his lips and a woman on each arm." Many newspapers even predicted before his death that his "weakness" for women would be his downfall, and they repeated it alongside photographs of Anna Sage, Billie Frechette, and Polly Hamilton after he died. Even without the legendary organ, the Dillinger of legend was tied to fantasies of untrammeled masculinity, of sex and violence.[47]

Dillinger's wild year was a response, in part, to ideals of masculinity that were problematic during the best of times and that were failing terribly during the Great Depression. In a society historically divided by class and race, the old model of manhood defined by working hard, getting ahead, providing for a family, and so forth was difficult enough. Even the newer consumerist version enshrined during the prosperous 1920s— masculinity as style, enhanced by accoutrements like cars, clothes, and leisure pursuits—grew not just unattainable for many people but hollow. With the odds of failure dramatically increased by the social crisis of the 1930s, the desire to break free of convention and return to elemental notions of masculinity must have fascinated countless men, alarmed others, and perhaps epitomized some combination of the two for more still. Dillinger, it seemed, made up the rules, lived by his own code, decided to take whatever he wanted that life had denied him.

Let Dillinger and Hoover stand for Id and Superego. There was reassurance, of course, in the thought that America's chief law enforcement officer always "got his man." The feds stopped the crime menace, and more, Dillinger's death brought expiation for those who had indulged fantasies of sex and violence. But at the level of guilty pleasure, or literature, or myth, or legend—whatever this story was and is—the key was the tension between the two poles, the play of opposites, the game of social ideals at war with each other. Dillinger was so bold, so outrageous, so self-assured that, in the vernacular of the culture, he must have been well endowed. By contrast, his story reminded us then and reminds us now of how average we are in the dailiness of our lives. Like all good stories, it reveals something of the audience as well as the subject. In this sense, the Dillinger chronicles are as much about us as him. It is about us looking at him, even though he is beyond the grave, a fake wooden pistol in one hand, a Thompson submachine gun in the other, and a smile on his face that says he knows something we don't know.[48]

NOTES

1. Joseph Snurr to the Director of Scientific Research Dept., May 15, 1974, Dillinger Letters file, Division of Medical Sciences, Smithsonian Institution (hereafter SIDL). The Dillinger Letters file contains a few dozen in total, all from the early 1970s through the early 1990s, plus office memoranda and clippings such as an article from *Playboy.* Judith Chelnick kindly allowed me access to the file.
2. Laurel Overman, Associate Editor, *The Book of Lists,* to Western History Curator, July 13, 1978, SIDL.
3. Patsy Jo Masonhall, San Antonio, to Smithsonian, September 5, 1974; Mr. W. E. Wright, Westwood, NJ, to Smithsonian, March 28, 1973; Brian Gaston to Smithsonian, March 4, 1975; Mrs. James Reynolds, North Chili, NY, to Office of the Secretary, Smithsonian, January 29, 1992; all in SIDL.
4. Robert Zumstein, Evanston, IL, to Smithsonian, August 29, 1973, SIDL.
5. Jack H. to Med. Sci., Smithsonian, n.d.; Jeff Sacks, Washington, DC, to Office of Exhibits, Smithsonian, April 15, 1988; Linda Raffel, New Dorm, Alfred University, to Smithsonian, September 25, 1973; A. Rolff, Houston, TX, to Smithsonian, n.d.; Gary Simpson, Reese Hall, University of Tennessee, to Smithsonian, n.d.; "The Regular Customers of this Bar," to whom it may concern, December 24, 1974; all in SIDL.
6. James H. Griggs, Birmingham, AL, to Smithsonian, May 18, 1973; Elizabeth Vieux, Jamaica Plain, MA, to Curator, Smithsonian, October 20, 1973; John R. Smith, Palm Beach, FL, to unnamed correspondent, Smithsonian, n.d.; all in SIDL.
7. William J. Helmer, "A Quiz You Can't Refuse," *Playboy,* March 1991, no pages numbers visible, copy, SIDL. For an interesting discussion of human remains, real and fictive, in the National Museum of Health and Medicine of the Armed

Forces Institute of Pathology, see Paul S. Sledzik and Lenore T. Barbian, "From Privates to Presidents: Past and Present Memoirs from the Anatomical Collections of the National Museum of Health and Medicine," in *Human Remains: Conservation, Retrieval, and Analysis*, ed. Emily Williams, proceedings of a conference held in Williamsburg, VA, November 7–11, 1999, BAR International Series 934 (n.p., 2001).

8. For example, in the early 1970s, the Smithsonian's Division of Medical Sciences sent out memos to all who enquired about Dillinger that read in part, "The Smithsonian Institution does not have any part of the anatomy of John Dillinger. We have never had an exhibit on Dillinger, nor do we have anatomical specimens in our medical collection." Twenty years later, the Smithsonian felt the need to send out another memo, which read, "The National Museum of American History does not have nor do we know of any other museum or institution that has any part of the anatomy of John Dillinger" (SIDL).

9. Several of these legends are collected in Ronald L. Baker, *Hoosier Folk Legends* (Bloomington: Indiana University Press, 1984), 155–64. Others mentioned here are from the Dillinger file in the University of California, Berkeley, Folklore Archive, kept by the Folklore Program, Kroeber Hall. The archive consists mainly of items collected over the years by students taking introductory folklore classes. For the contention that Dillinger did not die in front of Chicago's Biograph Theater on July 22, 1934, see Jay Robert Nash, *Dillinger: Dead or Alive* (Chicago: Regnery Publishing, 1970). Will Rogers' syndicated column, "Will Rogers Says," can be found, for example, in the *Newark* (OH) *Advocate*, April 24, 1934, 1.

10. Because this subject exists in the fugitive realms of folklore and popular culture, it only makes sense that the Internet would also be packed with lore about John Dillinger. The commemoration of Dillinger's death in Chicago (which I've personally attended in recent years) was originally organized by the John Dillinger Died for You Society, founded by William J. Helmer and Rick Mattix, two assiduous and thorough researchers of the criminal underworld. For the annual observance, see http://www.ghosttours.com/press/dillinger/htm.

11. "No. 181, Why the Lady in Red Betrayed Dillinger" and "No. 182, Dillinger's Long Penis in the Smithsonian," in Baker, *Hoosier Folk Legends*, 161–62; Hal Kirshbaum, "Legend—Personal," February 25, 1969, Dillinger file, UC Berkeley Folklore Archive.

12. Media materials on Dillinger are voluminous. The largest single repository is the Library of Congress. The folk music division, for example, has a dozen or so songs on sheet music, mostly recorded around the time of his death; the film division has feature-length movies and documentaries; the sound recordings division has several radio programs from the 1930s through 1950s. For the first half of 1934, the Dillinger gang was featured often in newsreels, distributed by Hearst, Universal, and Fox; copies are available, respectively, in the film and television archives at UCLA, the sound archives at the National Archives and Records Administration in College Park, Maryland, and the news film library at the University of South Carolina at Columbia. For poetry, try Todd Moore, *The Name Is Dillinger* (Erie, PA: Kangaroo Court Press, 1987); for fiction, John Sayles, *Dillinger in Hollywood: New and Selected Short Stories* (New York: Nation Books, 2004). The rapper Das Dillinger and the punk band Dillinger Escape Plan are best traced on the Internet.

13. The Indiana Division of the Indiana State Library (ISL) in Indianapolis has an

excellent genealogy of the Dillinger family, including birth and marriage certifi-
cates, as well as printouts from the federal census, in the Dillinger Genealogy file.
The Mooresville Public Library (MPL) also has a file of materials labeled "John
Dillinger," which includes clippings from the Mooresville *Times*.

14. Tracing Dillinger and his family before he went to prison is not easy. Neither
Indianapolis public school records nor tax assessments are available. The family shows up in various years of the *Indianapolis City Directory* (Indianapolis: R.L.
Polk and Company), 1892, 300; 1897, p. 314; 1900, p. 352; 1903, p. 376; 1907,
p. 417; and 1913, p. 504. Vital records and manuscript census materials can be
found in the Dillinger Genealogy file, ISL. Another interesting source on these
early years, in which John Dillinger Sr. told his story to reporter John Cejnar,
is an untitled manuscript, Mrs. John Cejnar Collection, LL29, box 1, folder 7,
pp. 1–7, ISL. Dillinger's biographers have pieced together the outlines of the outlaw's early life. Probably the least embellished—and most accurate—is Robert
Cromie and Joe Pinkston, *Dillinger: A Short and Violent Life* (Chicago: Chicago
Historical Bookworks, 1990), 6–10. John Tolland, *The Dillinger Days* (New York:
Da Capo Press, 1995), 5–8, has extensive interviews by journalist Tolland with
those who knew Dillinger, but the author uncritically repeats every sensational
tidbit. Also see Dary Matera, *John Dillinger: The Life and Death of America's First
Celebrity Criminal* (New York: Carroll and Graff, 2004), 9–20; and Bryan Burrough, *Public Enemies* (New York: Penguin, 2004), 136–37. Dillinger's discharge
is discussed in his FBI file, memo from Washington, May 17, 1934, Dillinger file,
no. 62-29777-145. The FBI file on the Dillinger gang is over 36,000 pages long.

15. News stories from the Mooresville *Times*, September 19, 1924, and October 17,
1924, Dillinger file, MPL. Also see Dillinger Sr. interview with Cejnar, 9–17, as
well as an interview that Cejnar conducted with Dillinger Sr. and Audrey Hancock
(John Dillinger's sister), in Cejnar Collection, L29, box 1, folder 6, pp. 21–30, IPL.
A sidelight on sources: Joe Pinkston, a chronicler of Dillinger's life, was also an
avid collector of memorabilia. He made much of his collection, available in the
private museum he founded and operated in Nashville, Indiana, until his death
in the early 1990s. Those materials have since been moved to Hammond, Indiana, where a new Dillinger museum opened in the Indiana Welcome Center, just
across the Illinois border on Interstate 80/94. It is a very nice museum, but one
of Dillinger's heirs has filed a lawsuit against it, claiming that all of the materials
Pinkston collected are rightfully Dillinger family property. Until the litigation is
settled, the museum's small cache of papers is unavailable. Most of these items,
however, have been reprinted or quoted extensively elsewhere.

16. The Dillinger Gang's Papers and Packets files, housed in the Indiana State Archives
(ISA), Indianapolis, consist of four boxes of materials. Dillinger's records are
available in case no. 14395. Included are his records from the Indiana State Reformatory, which were transferred to Michigan City in 1929. The papers are bound in
large binders. Item no. 44, for example, is a brief summary of Dillinger's disciplinary record from 1924 to 1929 at the state reformatory; item no. 54 is an April 10,
1929, memo informing reformatory officials of Dillinger's divorce; item no. 49,
dated July 15, 1929, is a copy of Governor McNutt's executive order (no. 4519)
transferring Dillinger to the state prison.

17. Executive order no. 7733, signed by Governor McNutt, paroling Dillinger, item
no. 43, May 10, 1933; William's letter to the Indiana Parole Commission and
Clemency Board, March 14, 1933; the petition for clemency was addressed to

"His Excellency Paul V. McNutt, Governor of Indiana," February 23, 1933; all in record group no. 14395, ISA.

18. The literature on the 1920s and 1930s is enormous, but see, for examples, Lynn Dumenil, *The Modern Temper: American Culture and Society in the 1920s* (New York: Hill and Wang, 1995); and David M. Kennedy, *The American People in the Great Depression: Freedom from Fear* (New York: Oxford University Press, 2003).

19. For New Carlisle, see "3 Escape with $10,000 Loot," *Mansfield* (OH) *News Journal*, June 21, 1933, 1; for the thread mill, "Attempt to Rob Thread Mills," *Monticello* (IN) *Herald*, June 29, 1933, 1; for Daleville, see the *Muncie* (IN) *Evening Press*, July 17, 1933, 1. Telling the Dillinger story requires a range of sources. My brief synopsis relies mostly on local records and newspapers, as well as previously published books about him. After the beginning of 1934, the FBI became increasingly involved in the case, and their Dillinger dossier contains internal memos, newspaper clippings, field reports, and so forth. The entire dossier is available under the Freedom of Information Act, and workers at the Bureau were kind enough to give me a full copy on ten CDs (case no. 62-29777).

20. From among the many books on John Dillinger, the story of these early years is most reliably told by Burrough, *Public Enemies*, 21–23, 63–65, 94–97; and Cromie and Pinkston, *Dillinger*, 68–69. Also see Tolland, *Dillinger Days*, 74–77; G. Russell Girardin with William J. Helmer, *Dillinger: The Untold Story* (Bloomington: Indiana University Press, 1994), 28–34; Matera, *John Dillinger*, 31–35. For Mary Longnaker, see Ellen Poulsen, *Don't Call Us Molls* (Little Neck, NY: Clinton Cook Publishing, 2002), 37–42. Poulsen ably tells the story from the point of view of the women associated with the gang.

21. Burrough, *Public Enemies*,134–44; Cromie and Pinkston, *Dillinger*, 68–78. The breakout story was covered well in prominent local newspapers: "10 Shoot Way from State Prison," *Indianapolis Star*, September 27, 1933, 1; "All Trace of 10 Convicts and Kidnapped Sheriff Lost," *Post-Tribune* (Gary, IN), September 28, 1933, 1; and "10 Felons Flee Indiana Prison," *Chicago Tribune*, September 27, 1933, 1. For Sarber's death, see "Sheriff Is Slain in Jail Delivery," *Bluffton* (OH) *News*, October 14, 1933, 1.

22. Poulsen does a wonderful job of describing Dillinger and Billie's attraction to each other, and of detailing how wives and girlfriends played a key role in the gang's activities (*Don't Call Us Molls*, 72–74). For Greencastle and Racine, see "Eight Men Hold Up Indiana Bank and Flee with $70,000," *Chicago Tribune*, October 24, 1933, 2; and "Bandits Rob Bank at Racine," *Sheboygan Press*, November 20, 1933, 1. Also see Cromie and Pinkston, *Dillinger*, 83–86; and Burrough, *Public Enemies*, 143–44, 162–66.

23. Matera is especially good on the techniques and technology of the gang's heists (*John Dillinger*, 140–41). G. Russell Girardin was a Chicago advertising man who wrote a manuscript about the Dillinger gang based on extensive interviews with the robber's attorney, Louis Piquette. William Helmer found the manuscript, located Girardin, and together they published the book as *Dillinger: The Untold Story* in 1994. The book is especially strong on the gang's time hiding out in Chicago, which is where they spent most of fall 1933 (35–46). Helmer's notes and afterword are amazingly detailed and comprehensive. Also see Burrough, *Public Enemies*, 153–61.

24. Cromie and Pinkston, *Dillinger*, 131–32; Burrough, *Public Enemies*, 178–82; Matera, *John Dillinger*, 168–69; R. L. Shivers, FBI field report, Jacksonville office, April 9,

1934, p. 9, Dillinger file, no. 62-29777-424; R. A. Alt, memo to the FBI Chicago office, April 2, 1934, pp. 2–3, Dillinger file, no. 62-29777-293; "Dillinger Gang Named as Chief Public Enemies," *Chicago Tribune*, December 29, 1933, 1; "Outlaws Rob Bank, Kill a Policeman," *New York Times*, January 16, 1934, 4; "Notorious Bandits Escape," *Times* (Hammond, IN), January 16, 1934, 1.

25. J. Edgar Hoover to Attorney General Homer Cummings, January 31, 1934, p. 3, FBI, Dillinger file, no. 62-29777-70; "Salesmen Identify Leaders of Gang," *Tucson Citizen* January 26, 1934, Dillinger clipping file, Arizona Historical Society (AHS); "Dillinger Caught on Fireman's Tip," *New York Times*, January 26, 1934, 1; "Tamed Dillinger and Gang," *Chicago Daily News*, January 27, 1934, 1; "Speed Extradition of Dillinger Gang," *New York Times*, January 29, 1934, 1; "'I'll Kill You Yet You Dirty Rat': Pierpont," *Arizona Star*, Dillinger clipping file, AHS; "Speed Dillinger to Lake County," *Post-Tribune* (Gary, IN), January 30, 1934, 1; "Tucson Sighs as Gangsters Leave Arizona," *Arizona Star*, January 31, 1934, 1; "Dillinger's Three 'Stooges' Tucked Safely Away in Their Old 'Alma Mater,'" *Chicago Daily News*, February 1, 1934, 1; Cromie and Pinkston, *Dillinger*, 136–41; Burrough, *Public Enemies*, 199–205.

26. "One Happy Family," *New York Times*, February 2, 1934, 16; "Jail Will Keep John Dillinger in Crown Point," *Chicago Tribune*, February 13, 1934, 6; "Dillinger Escapes Jail Using a Wooden Pistol," *New York Times*, March 4, 1934, 1; Melvin Purvis to J. Edgar Hoover, March 3, 1934, FBI, Dillinger file, no. 62-29777-89; "Toy Pistol Fashioned from Old Washboard," *Times* (Hammond, IN), March 5, 1934, 1; Cromie and Pinkston, *Dillinger*, 154–66. For wire service coverage, see the United Press story "Dillinger Breaks Out of Bastille," *Helena* (MT) *Daily Independent*, March 4, 1934, 1; and "Dillinger Vanishes 'Into Air,'" *Nevada State Journal* (Reno), March 5, 1934, 1; Burrough, *Public Enemies*, 206–9, 234–42.

27. Rather suddenly, it seemed, J. Edgar Hoover became interested in John Dillinger. He wrote a sharp memo to Melvin Purvis, special agent in charge of the Chicago office, complaining that Purvis had failed to cultivate the snitches needed to reveal Dillinger's whereabouts. Committing the Bureau to the hunt, Hoover reasoned that Dillinger was hiding in Chicago, and he told Purvis to develop "channels of information into underworld sources." J. Edgar Hoover to Melvin Purvis, March 6, 1934, FBI, Dillinger file, no. 62-29777-93NR1. The Gary (IN) *Post-Tribune* gave the "man on the street" angle: "'Dillinger's escaped,' cried a breathless, hatless patron as he burst into a downtown saloon. . . . 'He walked right out of the country jail after locking up all his guards!' 'More power to him!' remarked the bartender, polishing his glasses'"; "Dillinger a Robin Hood to Boys in Backroom; They're Glad He's Loose," *Post-Tribune* (Gary, IN), March 10, 1934, 1. For the Houdini comparison, see, for example, the United Press story "Dillinger Opens Fire to Halt Trailing Car," *Sheboygan Press*, March 10, 1934, 1.

28. Burrough, *Public Enemies*, 244–57; Girardin with Helmer, *Dillinger*, 113–19; "Thugs Get $46,000, Kidnap 5 in Bank," *New York Times*, March 7, 1934, 2; "Machine Gunmen Rob Sioux Falls Bank of $46,000," *Chicago Tribune*, March 7, 1934, 8; "Outlaw Seen as Chieftain of New Gang," Associated Press (AP) story, *Mansfield* (OH) *News Journal*, March 14, 1934, 1.

29. "St. Paul Police Find Dillinger Fingerprints," *Chicago Tribune*, April 2, 1934, 9; "A Fast Moving Life," *Newark* (OH) *Advocate*, April 3, 1934, 4. The widely distributed AP coverage can be found, for example, in "Bold Bandit Once More Foils Dicks," *Helena* (MT) *Daily Independent*, April 1, 1934, 1. The Saint Paul part of the story

is covered in Paul Maccabee, *John Dillinger Slept Here: A Crook's Tour of Crime and Corruption in St. Paul, 1920–1936* (Saint Paul: Minnesota Historical Society, 1995), 213–25. Also see Burrough, *Public Enemies*, 266–72. For the Mooresville trip, see Dillinger Sr. interview, Cejnar Collection, L29, box 1, folder 7, pp. 41–50, 68–71, ISL; and "Dillinger Given Warm Welcome in Home Town," *Chicago Tribune*, April 20, 1934, 1. For Billie's arrest, see report of V. W. Peterson, May 6, 1934, pp. 5–6, FBI, Dillinger file, no. 62-29777-1222; Girardin with Helmer, *Dillinger*, 139–40; "Dillinger's Girl Friend Held on Federal Charges," *Chicago Tribune*, April 13, 1934, 1.

30. The most thorough coverage of Little Bohemia can be found on the front pages of the *Rhinelander* (WI) *Daily News*, April 23–25, 1934; also see "Four Others Hurt as Web Is Drawn on Famed Badman," *Bismarck* (ND) *Tribune*, April 23, 1934, 1; "Dillinger Escapes Posses after Two Running Fights; Two Killed, Five Wounded," *New York Times*, April 23, 1934, 1; "Hunt Dillinger; 2 Die, 4 Shot," *Chicago Tribune*, April 23, 1934, 1; "Department of Justice Makes Report on Dillinger Escape," *Elyria* (OH) *Journal Telegram*, April 23, 1934, 1; Burrough, *Public Enemies*, 299–333; Alston Purvis, *Vendetta: FBI Hero Melvin Purvis's War against Crime and J. Edgar Hoover's War against Him* (New York: Public Affairs, 2005), 101–25.

31. Clair Bond Potter, *War on Crime: Bandits, G-Men, and the Politics of Mass Culture*, (New Brunswick, NJ: Rutgers University Press, 1998), 138–68; "Crime Bills Sped by Dillinger Hunt," *New York Times*, April 25, 1934, 3; "Outcome in Dillinger Case to Affect Anti-Crime Bills," *Mansfield* (OH) *News Journal*, April 30, 1934, 4; "Charge Stupidity in Attempts to Nab Elusive Outlaw," *Reno* (NV) *Evening Gazette*, April 25, 1934, 1; J. Edgar Hoover to Homer Cummings, April 26, 1934, National Archives and Records Administration (NARA), Department of Justice (DOJ), Record Group (RG) 60, 95-57-8, box 14022, file 2, part 2.

32. "Rewards for Dillinger and Nelson," Justice Department press release, June 24, 1934, NARA, DOJ, RG 60, 95-57-8, box 14022, file 5 (the Federal Reward Bill was called "An Act to Authorize an Appropriation of Money to Facilitate the Apprehension of Certain Persons Charged with Crime"); "U.S. Offers $10,000 to Get Dillinger," *New York Times*, June 24, 1934, 1; James Menaugh, "Jesse James/John Dillinger," *Chicago Tribune*, June 24, 1934, G1; "Dillinger Head of Fatal Bank Raid, Say Police," *Chicago Tribune*, July 1, 1934, 1; Poulsen, *Don't Call Us Molls*, 330–33; Girardin with Helmer, *Dillinger*, 167–77; Potter, *War on Crime*, 152–54. On film, see Leonard J. Leff and Jerold L. Simmons, *The Dame in the Kimono: Hollywood, Censorship, and the Production Code* (Lexington: University of Kentucky Press, 2001); Thomas Doherty, *Pre-Code Hollywood* (New York: Columbia University Press, 1999); Jonathan Munby, *Public Enemies, Public Heroes* (Chicago: University of Chicago Press, 1999); and Gregory D. Black, *Hollywood Censored* (Cambridge: Cambridge University Press, 1994).

33. Girardin with Helmer, *Dillinger*, 215–21, 303–6; Burrough, *Public Enemies*, 388–402; Poulsen, *Don't Call Us Molls*, 329–37; "Indiana's Police Launch Quiz on Dillinger Death," *Chicago Tribune*, July 30, 1934, 3; "Dillinger a Gay Boy on Parties, Says Companion," *Chicago Tribune*, July 26, 1934, 5.

34. Poulsen, *Don't Call Us Molls*, 337–47; Burrough, *Public Enemies*, 402–16; Girardin with Helmer, *Dillinger*, 222–30; Dillinger Sr. interview, Cejnar Collection, box 1, folder 7, pp. 73–74, ISL.

35. The coverage lasted for days, beginning July 23. Try, for examples, "Story of Purvis, Leader in Long Desperado Hunt," *Chicago Tribune*, July 23, 1934, 1; "Cum-

mings Says Slaying of Dillinger Is 'Gratifying as Well as Reassuring," *New York Times*, July 23, 1934, 1; "Bandit Carries Photo of Indian Sweetheart," *Lima* (OH) *News*, July 23, 1934, 1; "Jealousy Set Dillinger Trap," *Chicago Tribune*, July 24, 1934, 1. Burrough does a fine job with the days immediately after the shooting (*Public Enemies*, 409–16). Also see Purvis, *Vendetta*, 157–68.

36. Many of these letters are available at the National Archives, DOJ, RG 60, 95-57-8, box 14021, files 1 and 2.

37. Paul Kooistra, *Criminals as Heroes: Structure, Power, and Identity* (Bowling Green, OH: Bowling Green State University Press, 1988). Also see Graham Seal, *The Outlaw Legend* (Cambridge: Cambridge University Press, 1996).

38. Richard Gid Powers, *G-Men: Hoover's FBI in American Popular Culture* (Carbondale: Southern Illinois University Press, 1983).

39. Potter, *War on Crime*, 106–95.

40. David Ruth, *Inventing the Public Enemy* (Chicago: University of Chicago Press, 1996), 63–86.

41. Newspapers often were torn between condemning Dillinger and marveling at how he came out of obscurity to "astound the world with his deeds of depredation," at how "no other criminal in American history ever so captured the imagination of the public." "Dillinger Legend Born of His Daring Deeds," *Chicago Tribune*, July 23, 1934, 1. He loved life on the edge and laughed at danger: "It was the bread of life to him to walk in disguise into night clubs and amusement places, flaunting his presence, in the hottest spots in the country. He couldn't leave the cities and night life alone. . . . Every 'coup' of Dillinger's was just one more joke on the world." Joseph K. Shephard, "Dillinger Expected Such a Death: Sense of Humor Kept Him in Trouble," *Indianapolis Star*, July 24, 1934, 3.

42. Mrs. W. B. Grant of Butler Tennessee wrote Eleanor Roosevelt that an unjust legal system made Dillinger an outlaw: "If he holds up a bank, what of it? Hasn't most of the bankers them selves been crooked, that is how they became wealthy." W. Guyer Fisher of Redlands, California, wrote to Attorney General Cummings about the businessmen who "fleeced the rank and file out of more of their hard earned cash" than did all the John Dillingers of the world. Fisher deplored the "wholesale thieves that use a sharp pencil" to rob a bank or steal a public utility and argued they were no better than those who got rich quick with a machine gun. W. B. Grant to Eleanor Roosevelt, May 4, 1934, and W. Guyer Fisher to Homer Cummings, April 30, 1934, both in NARA, DOJ, RG 60, box 14021, file 2, part 1.

43. See, for examples, James Finan, "Our Foot-Loose Correspondents," *New Yorker*, May 19, 1934, 67; "Dillinger Family Seeks Peace at Farm," May 18, 1934, and "Dillinger's Father Seeks 'Justice' for Son," June 9, 1934, *Indianapolis Star*, NARA, DOJ, RG 60, clipping file in box 14022, section 3.

44. Poulsen, in *Don't Call Us Molls*, does an admirable job of tracing the lives and speculating on the motives of the women who ran with the gang.

45. The morgue photos were printed in the *Chicago Daily News* of July 23, 1934, as well as in other papers. At least two witnesses said Dillinger was shot at almost point-blank range; see, for example, "Witness Tells How Dillinger Went to His Death," *Chicago Tribune*, July 23, 1934, 3; on the missing brain, see, for example, the AP story, "Dillinger's Brain Is Destroyed, Says Doctor," *Gettysburg* (PA) *Times*, August 3, 1934, 5. The autopsy report was found decades later: "Long-Lost Report on Dillinger Is Found," *Indianapolis Star*, March 25, 1984, 1.

46. Norman Mailer, "The White Negro: Superficial Reflections on the Hipster," *Dissent*, Fall 1957; reprinted in Mailer, *Advertisements for Myself* (New York: Putnam, 1981), 299–320.

47. "Dillinger Defied Capture for Year," *New York Times*, July 23, 1934, 10; "Women Figured Prominently in Dillinger's Life," AP story, *Zanesville* (OH) *Times Recorder*, July 24, 1934, 1; "Clear up Dillinger Mystery," *Chicago Tribune*, July 25, 1934, 1; "Jealousy Set Dillinger Trap," *Chicago Tribune*, July 24, 1934, 1; clipping from *Martinsville* (IN) *Republican*, no title, Dillinger file, MPL.

48. For a fascinating discussion of the allure of the underworld, see Jack Katz, *Seductions of Crime: Moral and Sensual Attractions of Doing Evil* (New York: Basic Books, 1988).

SIX

Behind Shirley Temple's Smile: Children, Emotional Labor, and the Great Depression

JOHN F. KASSON

Shirley Temple's smile is familiar, perhaps cloyingly so. Through much of the 1930s, it outshone even the smiles of Franklin Roosevelt, Dale Carnegie, and Louis Armstrong, and it lifted her to the position of one of the most popular Hollywood stars of the decade. In her numerous films she could easily be moved to tears, but her temperament was overwhelmingly sunny, and she persistently urged others to smile and laugh as well. Energetically cheerful, she frequently burst into songs, such as "Laugh You Son-of-a-Gun" (1934), "You've Gotta S-M-I-L-E to be H-A-P-P-Y" (1936), "Come and Get Your Happiness" (1938), and "Be Optimistic!" (1938). In the last she urged:

> Don't wear a long face
> It's never in style
> Be optimistic
> And smile![1]

Nonetheless, the nature of Shirley Temple's smile in her films—and in the photographs, magazine illustrations, books, sheet music, dolls, and numerous other products that emerged from them—was deceptive. It was represented as a natural effusion of cheer, a distillation of childish innocence, and, in a time of great national hardship and worry, a welcome tonic and diversion. Certainly, that smile did not purport to be an object of trade, a commodity. The smile and the child who beamed it were adored, while the work used to produce it remained invisible and unacknowledged. To suggest that its effortless simplicity was in any way an artifice or illusion would have seemed a sacrilege. One of the few to hint at its status as an American fetish was Salvador Dalí, who in 1939 created a montage portrait of Shirley Temple as a sphinx, titled *Shirley Temple, the Youngest, Most Sacred Monster of the Cinema in Her Time*.[2] And indeed, on a number of levels the smile contained riddles. Most fundamentally, it asked, what kind of little girl was this, and what lay behind her smile? Why did she possess such great value at a time when financial fortresses had collapsed? What was the source of her emotional power and cultural centrality in the Depression?

To answer these riddles, we need to look more closely at materials so well known as to have attracted little interest among film or cultural historians.[3] Shirley Temple's early career provides a vivid instance of the power of the Hollywood film industry to create new child celebrities whose fame could exceed that of heads of state; it also exposes deep tensions in the place of young children in the American economy (or rather, as we shall see, economies), in how they were valued, and in what kinds of work they were expected to perform. Examining the terms of that career and the ways little Shirley fought the Great Depression on a number of fronts can tell us much about the emotional demands of capitalist society during one of its greatest periods of crisis and the effects these demands had on children as well as adults.

The Depression as an Emotional Crisis

By the early 1930s there was widespread agreement that, to lift the country out of the Great Depression, the sense of fearful anxiety needed to be routed. The famous phrase of Roosevelt's first inaugural address, "the only thing we have to fear is fear itself," delivered in the patrician accent that still marked the standard for cultivated speech, spoke directly to the need for reassurance in order to increase investment and spending. The term *Depression*, of course referred to the drop in prices, values, and wages in the United States and to the loss of vigor in the economy generally. At the same time, the word carried an additional meaning of lowered spirits and, more specifically, a description of a pathological condition. To illustrate this last sense, the *Oxford English Dictionary* provides a quotation from 1934 that is striking in its aptness to the feelings of many Americans at the time: "Depression . . . a mood of pronounced hopelessness and overwhelming feeling of inadequacy or unworthiness."[4] Such feelings gripped individuals without respect to age or gender; yet in the 1930s and to a large extent since that time, the psychological burden of unemployment placed on adult men received special attention. A distinguished psychiatrist, Nathan Ackerman, remembered more than thirty years later:

> I did a little field work among the unemployed miners in Pennsylvania. Just observing. What the lack of a job two, three, four, five years did to their families and to them. They hung around street corners and in groups. . . . The women punished the men for not bringing home the bacon, by withholding themselves sexually. By belittling and emasculating the men, undermining their paternal authority, turning to the eldest son. These men suffered from depression. They felt despised, they were ashamed of themselves.[5]

In this context, the 1934 tribute Roosevelt reputedly paid to the rising child star Shirley Temple is noteworthy: "When the spirit of the people is lower than at any other time during this Depression, it is a splendid thing that for just 15 cents, an American can go to a movie and look at the smiling face of a baby and forget his troubles."[6]

Fighting the Depression in *Stand Up and Cheer*

Roosevelt's (possibly apocryphal) endorsement of Shirley Temple is an example of life imitating art that was, in turn, imitating life. *Stand Up and Cheer*, Shirley's breakthrough film, released in April 1934, showed how the entertainment industry could save the nation from the gloom of the Depression. The fictional president in the film, speaking with Rooseveltian inflection and cadences, addresses a theatrical producer named Lawrence Cromwell (loosely modeled on Florenz Ziegfeld):

> Mr. Cromwell, our country is bravely passing through a serious crisis. Many of our people's affairs are in the red, and, figuratively, their nerves are in the red. But, thanks to ingrained sturdiness, their faith is not in the red. Any people blessed with a sense of humor can achieve success and victory. We are endeavoring to pilot the ship past the most treacherous of all rocks: fear. The government now proposes to dissolve that destructive rock in a gale of laughter. To that end, it has created a new Cabinet office, that of Secretary of Amusement, whose duty it shall be to amuse and entertain the people, make them forget their troubles. Mr. Cromwell, we are drafting you and your splendid talents into public service. And it is with confidence and pleasure that I offer you the Cabinet position of Secretary of Amusement.[7]

This premise, of course, was a transparent, if indirect, Hollywood self-justification. Amusement, the film implicitly contended, was not frivolous or superfluous in the face of the Great Depression but a necessary and vital force in combating it. The Hollywood film industry itself had troubles aplenty in 1934 and not a little fear. The studios, riding the wave of sound that surged after the success of *The Jazz Singer* in 1927, initially gloated that they were "depression-proof." Although the industry remained profitable as late as 1931, by 1933 nearly one-third of movie theaters in the country had closed their doors, Paramount had declared bankruptcy, RKO and Universal had fallen into receivership, and Fox was staggering, eventually to swoon into the outstretched arms of the smaller Twentieth Century Pictures.[8] As the industry slumped, moreover, religious, academic, and political critics pummeled it from all sides. In 1933–34 the National Legion of Decency, the Motion Picture Research Council, and legislators and administrators in the federal government converged to demand more wholesome family fare and an end to salacious and immoral films. As *Stand Up and Cheer* was released, the industry was still scrambling for moral cover, which it largely found in July 1934 under the revised Motion Picture Production Code.[9] But clearly, a *Fox Follies of 1934* (*Stand Up and Cheer's* original title) that imitated the studio's recent "smutty" *George White's Scandals* would not do.[10] Instead, hitching its wagon to Roosevelt's star, the film extolled innocent laughter as the best medicine for the economy and healthful amusement as one of the highest forms of patriotism.

Opposition to the patriotic work of the new secretary of amusement in *Stand Up and Cheer* comes from two quarters: conspiratorial businessmen reaping vast profits from the crisis and hidebound senators concerned with their sense of dignity rather than the needs of the nation. Ultimately, the progressive forces of amusement triumph over the gloom and lift the country out of the Depression, emotionally and economically, but not without a struggle. Just when Secretary Cromwell's efforts appear defeated, the news comes, like a deus ex machina, that the Depression is over: "There is no unemployment! Fear has been banished! Confidence is reborn! Poverty has been wiped out! Laughter resounds throughout the nation! The people are happy again! We're out of the red!" Special credit for this sweeping victory goes to the Children's Division of the Department of Amusement. The smiling faces of Shirley Temple and other children have evidently done the trick. The film concludes with the ultimate National Recovery parade through the streets of the nation, led by jubilant, reemployed workers and civic and military organizations: chorines, forest rangers, sailors, nurses, firemen, policemen, locomotive engineers, farmers, milkmen, housewives, office staff, miners, chefs, maids, school-girls, sanitation workers, postmen, men in kilts, soldiers, Marines, rail-road porters (led by Stepin Fetchitt in top hat and tails), Boy Scouts, and others. Shirley Temple appears twice in close up as, in different garbs, she leads portions of the marching throng. What's good for the country, the film suggests, is good for Hollywood, and vice versa.

The Little Girl Who Saved Fox

Stand Up and Cheer rightly ended with Shirley prominent in the grand parade, for she immediately captured the public's fancy and set off a craze that lasted throughout the decade. Even jaded critics found her irresist-ible: "Such a happy little face! With a dimple close to the laughing mouth. Such starry, friendly brown eyes!" the *Chicago Tribune* exclaimed. The *Boston Globe* agreed: "She has the most adorable smile and the most daintily poised charm of any little girl who has yet played in the talkies." And the critic for the *Louisville Courier-Journal* could hardly stay in his seat: "For once an infant prodigy appears upon the screen with such charm as to disarm any abhorrence of the usual nuisance. . . . Little Miss Temple is blonde, dimpled and all smiles but better than these attributes for picture taking she seems to know her power and it is very great right now. Not being overly tender about these matters I must confess nevertheless one wants to walk up to the screen and snatch her off it and hug her."[11] Soon trade publication writers hugged her too. "The chief topic of conversation at home, at the office, at the club and wherever you go is Shirley Temple," the *Hollywood Reporter* exulted, adding that she would "serve as an answer to many of the attacks that are being hurled at pictures."[12]

The diminutive discovery, in fact, had been awaiting this break-through for some time. Born April 23, 1928 (a year her mother and Fox Film Corporation reported as 1929 in hopes of lengthening her child film career), Shirley Temple began making films at the age of three and a half. Between 1932 and early 1934 she made eight shorts in the Baby Burlesks series and four in the Frolics of Youth series for Educational Films Cor-poration and played minor roles in several feature-length films, earn-ing only around a thousand dollars over more than two years before her appearance in *Stand Up and Cheer* lifted her to stardom, though not yet to riches. (For that film, she earned twenty-five dollars a day.)[13]

On the strength of her performance in *Stand Up and Cheer*, she imme-diately vaulted to major roles and feature billing, and soon developed a box-office draw of unprecedented power. Three more films followed in quick succession, and two of these, *Little Miss Marker* (Paramount) and *Baby Take a Bow* (Fox), proved among the most popular of the year.[14] Beginning with *Bright Eyes*, her last film of 1934, Fox began tailoring scripts especially for her appeal. When Fox merged with Twentieth Century Pictures in 1935, the new vice president and director of production, Darryl Zanuck, replaced Fox's Wilfred Sheehan as watchdog of the precious charge. In a characteristic memorandum, he noted: "Shirley is most effective when she asks the kind of questions to which there are no answers one can give a child, like 'Why is the Depression?'"[15] Selecting stories to accord with tested formulas, he frequently based her films on children's classics such as *Captain January*, *Rebecca of Sunnybrook Farm*, *Wee Willie Winkie*, *Heidi*, and *The Little Princess*. Shirley Temple made four feature-length films in each of the years 1935, 1936, and 1937, and three each in 1938 and 1939. Unquestionably the most famous and admired child in the world, for four consecutive years, from 1935 through 1938, she easily surpassed all other movie actors as most popular at the box office, according to annual polls of movie theater owners.[16] At the end of this tumultuous decade and extraordinarily energetic period of performances (which would continue at a lesser pace through the 1940s), she was still under the age of twelve.[17]

As Shirley Temple's popularity soared, so too did her earnings. On several occasions her parents renegotiated her contract with the studio, beginning in July 1934, when they agreed to $1,250 a week. Preserving the image of little Shirley as thoroughly engaged with her affairs, a *Newsweek* article showed her signing the contract and beaming at the camera as her parents smiled approvingly (fig. 6.1).[18] By 1938, the year she turned ten and had grown to over four feet tall, she received $307,014 from Twentieth Century-Fox. One of the largest salaries among Hollywood actors, it placed her right behind Cary Grant and substantially exceeded the salaries of Clark Gable, Greta Garbo, Fred Astaire, James Cagney, Spencer Tracy, or Ginger Rogers. Yet even this sum was but a small fraction of what she garnered from endorsements of Shirley Temple dolls, dresses, underwear, coats, hats, shoes, books, tableware, novelties, sheet music of her songs, and other products and endorsements. By one estimate, her income from these agreements amounted to fifteen times the money she received from her films directly.[19] Even Darryl Zanuck's salary was less than Shirley's, although he shared in the studio's profits,[20] so he had every reason to skip jubilantly to the bank. Her films had

Fig. 6.1 Gertrude, Shirley, and George Temple beam over a lucrative new contract with Fox. Reprinted from *Newsweek*, July 28, 1934; reproduced with permission of Corbis Corporation.

kept the studio afloat, earning an estimated twenty million dollars in the three years 1935, 1936, and 1937. (By the time Shirley's parents severed her contract with Twentieth Century-Fox in August 1940, her twenty-two films had earned the studio over thirty million dollars.[21]) The bankers had reason to skip too. The recovery of the former Fox studio buoyed the assets of the once sagging Chase National Bank, controlled by the Rockefeller family. As the *Illustrated Daily News* observed, the turnaround at Chase was "due almost entirely to the nimble feet of a cute little girl with a winning smile."[22] The Depression hung on, and not everyone was out of the red, but Fox, Chase, and the Temple family certainly were. The little girl with precisely fifty-six curls (set by her mother each night) had the Midas touch.

Work or Play? The Ambiguities of the Child Performer

Was this magic the result of hard work or easy play? The Fox studio provided an answer within the very storyline of *Stand Up and Cheer*. The cabi-

Fig. 6.2 Little Shirley wins the support of the secretary of amusement; Shirley Temple and Warren Baxter (with James Dunn in background) *in Stand Up and Cheer.*

net secretary of the Department of Amusement must decide whether little Shirley Dugan's performance in her father's song-and-dance act should be exempt from the department's ban on child actors under the age of seven. "Shirley doesn't really work," her fictional father protests. "She just sort of comes on at the finish, and she really loves it." Even here, however, his motives appear mixed. He explains that his wife, who used to be in the act, has died. "Besides I got to have her [Shirley] in the act with me," he insists. "She helps me over the rough spots. . . . And, look at her . . . she thrives on it" (fig. 6.2).[23]

This justification was a common, even thread-worn, defense by parents and producers of child performers,[24] and it was frequently invoked by Gertrude Temple, Shirley's movie-struck mother. "Motion-picture acting is simply part of her play life," Mrs. Temple wrote in 1935. "It is un-tinged with worry about tomorrow or fear of failure."[25] Indeed, similar words were put in Shirley's mouth by a journalist that same year, when she supposedly told him her "autobiography" as a seven-year-old: "[Acting]'s like playing a game of make-believe. That's the easiest game in the world to play. It is for me, anyway."[26] Such assurances constituted an implicit reply to an unnamable charge: that child acting, far from harmless play, in fact constituted a form of exploitative child labor.

The defense of child acting as a legitimate activity, separate and distinct from oppressive child labor in textile mills, coal mines, glasshouses, tenements, street trades, and the like, had been fought by theatrical interests and the children's parents for over half a century. The child actor was in the highly paradoxical position of fascinating audiences by the ability both to imitate adults and to portray the unique characteristics of childhood innocence. To heighten this paradox, in this latter capacity, as the sociologist Viviana Zelizer has observed, such actors "were child laborers paid to represent the new, sentimentalized view of children."[27] Even very young children could score phenomenal triumphs in such roles in that they seemed not to work but to play—and earned far more for their families than most adults. One of the first American child stars, Cordelia Howard (1848–1941), appeared on stage at the age of four in *Oliver Twist* and soon after performed the role of Little Eva in *Uncle Tom's Cabin*, a part for which she became famous. Kate Bateman (1842–1917) also began her acting career at age four in *Babes in the Woods*. A generation later, another professional child actress who made her debut at age four, Elsie Leslie (1881–1960), achieved two of her greatest successes in dramatic versions of Frances Hodgson Burnett's *Little Lord Fauntleroy* in 1888 and Mark Twain's *The Prince and the Pauper* in 1890. In the first decade of the twentieth century, spectacular Broadway productions featuring children reached their height, led by *The Wizard of Oz, The Little Princess, The Blue Bird, Babes in Toyland,* and *Peter Pan*.[28] Hollywood followed with its own waves of child performers: the first of which, surging through the 1920s, was led by Jackie Coogan and Baby Peggy Montgomery; the second, cresting in the 1930s, was buoyed by the new capacities of sound recording to integrate spoken words, laughter, sobs, song, and dance.

Nonetheless, in the late nineteenth and early twentieth centuries, defenders of professional child actors frequently battled reformers who made little distinction between child performers on the legitimate stage and those performing in circuses or saloons.[29] Gradually abandoning arguments for the economically useful child, which had acquired a mercenary taint, such defenders claimed the higher ground of acting's educational benefits for children as well as realization of the playwright's artistic vision and the wholesome pleasures that children's performances gave to the public. A pamphlet published in 1911 by the National Alliance for the Protection of Stage Children argued for uniform laws that would eliminate children's performances under hazardous, unhealthful, or indecent conditions while preserving their appearances on the legitimate stage. The authors sharply distinguished between "the few moments of mental effort of the stage child" and "the blind, constant and degrading toil of the little slave of the mill, whose drudgery dwarfs mind, body, and spirit." They spoke glowingly of "the emanation of the spirit of childhood; an emanation which only a little child can convincingly give forth." The pamphlet even leapt to the defense of stage mothers and fathers, elsewhere depicted as mercenary and demanding: "Parents of the child genius do not lose their parental solicitude by reason of their child's unusual talents." The wages that a child actor earned were entirely secondary, even though these children were "mostly little geniuses of the poor, or of those in moderate circumstances."[30]

Others objected, however, that the professionalization of child actors turned childhood itself into a commodity. "The idea of a professional child—a child in whose case simple childhood is the sole stock in trade," a writer protested, " is touched with sacrilege." Learning to perform childhood innocence, the child performer lost the unselfconscious spontaneity that was its essence: "one of the most inalienable and fatal attributes of the true show-child . . . [is that] it has learnt to watch itself, and will go so far as to make a study of its own emotions." Such critics feared, nonetheless, that the "capitalization of childhood's appeal" might be an irreversible trend.[31]

Arguments for the exceptional situation of child actors ultimately prevailed under the New Deal. The codes of the National Recovery Administration, one of the monuments of Roosevelt's first Hundred Days in 1933, which sought to place limits on child labor, made an exception for children in motion pictures, and in any case the Supreme Court struck down the codes as unconstitutional in 1935. The Fair Labor Standards Act of 1938 became the administration's most effective and enduring weapon against child labor, and it too made exceptions for children working for their parents outside of mining and manufacturing and for some occupations, including children less than fourteen years of age working in agriculture, newspaper distribution, or performing in motion pictures and the theater. Perhaps by coincidence, Shirley Temple briefly met with Roosevelt at the White House on the day before he signed this bill into law.[32] Her career as a child star depended on the success with which she

Fig. 6.3 Shirley Temple holds an autographed portrait of President Roosevelt, 1935. Reproduced with permission of the New York Times/Redux.

could convince moviegoers, as she evidently convinced Congress and the president, that her own distinctive "spirit of childhood" emanated naturally and effortlessly (fig. 6.3).

The Emotional Work within Shirley Temple's Films

What made Shirley Temple remarkable and won her immediate popularity in 1934 was her winning mixture of contrasting characteristics that spoke to the emotional needs of children and adults in the depths of the Depression. She combined innocence and precocity, self-sufficiency and vulnerability, emotional directness and mocking hilarity, optimism and trust. Her characters repeatedly teach adults lessons they have ignored, forgotten, or perhaps never learned. Her films must be read against the mood of the period, particularly the concern that the Depression threatened the integrity of the family. Shirley's characters are usually at least half orphaned, sometimes wholly so. The loss of one or both parents had long been a staple of children's fiction, drama, and film—and also a common experience in children's lives.[33] In the immediate context of the Depression, however, the loss of shelter around Shirley's characters became a way of representing a more pervasive sense of vulnerability as well as a means of setting in motion the need for a new or more devoted guardian and for the security that only an adult could provide. Her contagious spirit summons key adult figures—white men, especially—to regain their emotional balance and to resume the roles they had lost. Freely contributing her own emotional currency, she encourages others to do likewise and restores the sentimental economy.

The sunny spirit of her characters powerfully appealed to both children and adults. Even her early fan mail in 1934 included letters from girls and boys, women and men, who saw in her an adored sister, friend, sweetheart, or daughter. "I think you are very cute," a seven-year-old girl wrote," and I'd like to be like you. You dance so much better than I do." A grade-school boy mixed adulation with a dash of caution (shared by many, as we shall see) that Shirley might lose her unaffected innocence: "I think you're swell and when I grow up I'm going to marry you if you haven't been spoiled by then."[34] Understandably the delight of children, Shirley Temple was also the most popular actress among women moviegoers, many of whom had postponed their own childbearing due to the Depression, and articles about her became staples of women's magazines. But she was almost as great a favorite among men. Not only did many indeed see the smiling face of a baby and forget their troubles, but some responded powerfully to her appeals for paternal protection. A self-described "two-time loser" just out of the penitentiary in 1934 saw the film *Baby Take a Bow,* in which Shirley portrays an ex-convict's ineffably trusting daughter. "I knew it was hokum all the time I was looking at it, but Kid, you got to me," he wrote. "I just wanted to tell you you taught me a guy can go straight if he has got a reason for it, and you are going to be my reason from now on."[35] In addition to appealing to male protectiveness, as the perceptive critic Gilbert Seldes speculated, Shirley Temple may have also inspired admiration for her boldness. "Women may gasp at her charms, because it is traditional to care for the sweetness of all children," Seldes wrote, "but I take it that men have plenty of that in their homes, and their roar of approval is not for what is sweet, but for what is mocking and hearty and contemptuous."[36]

On the Cusp between Innocence and Flirtatiousness

In fact, Shirley Temple's early roles were perched ambiguously on the cusp between innocence and flirtatiousness, characteristics that clung to her film persona. In her very first films, Jack Hays's Baby Burlesks series, her position as a surrogate for an adult—and, frequently, a seductive—woman was explicit. In the tradition of earlier children's impersonations of famous adult actors, such as those that Baby Peggy Montgomery made in the early 1920s and, beginning at age three, Jane Withers performed as Dixie's Dainty Dewdrop on Atlanta radio in the late 1920s and early 1930s,[37] the shorts spoofed well-known feature-length movies, with young children caricaturing adult roles. Shirley burlesqued actress Dolores del Rio's role as Charmaine de la Cognac in *War Babies* (a satire of *What Price Glory?*), Marlene Dietrich in *Kid 'n' Hollywood,* and a strumpet bent on seducing a senator in *Polly Tix in Washington.* To heighten the absurdity of children mimicking adults, Hayes dressed the boys in costumes in which the lower half consisted of a huge diaper and giant safety pin. The intended humor of these shorts, which seems exceedingly strained to modern viewers, rests on the difference between adult knowledge, desires, motives, and pleasures and childhood innocence. The children literally go through the motions of adult characters without, presumably, comprehending anything about the drama they are enacting. Without this protective ignorance, their innocence would burst like a balloon, and they would be grotesque figures whose bodies were unequal to their knowledge and desires.

In *Stand Up and Cheer* Shirley Temple performs as a flesh-and-blood child rather than a cartoonish prop, but the musical number of her one big scene, "Baby Take a Bow," continues an important aspect of the Baby Burlesks in that Shirley is a child who takes on a seductive adult woman's role (fig. 6.4). In the Hollywood tradition of musicals, this number emerges fully formed without our witnessing any rehearsal or preparatory effort. As the film critic Jane Feuer has written, "We are never allowed to realize that musical entertainment is an industrial product and that putting on a show (or putting on a Hollywood musical) is a matter of a labor force producing a product for consumption."[38] The number begins as a tribute by Jimmy to a supposed fiancée, "the future Mrs. Hemingway," who is the source of widespread attention:

Fig. 6.4 James Dunn and Shirley Temple in the "Baby Take a Bow"
number from *Stand Up and Cheer.*

> Everybody's asking me,
> Who's that bunch of personality?
> I'm presenting you right now
> Baby, take a bow![39]

Wearing top hat and tails and carrying a walking stick, Jimmy sings and
dances, first, with a platinum blonde woman, then with a cluster of scant-
ily clad chorines. Recalling the much more elaborate dance sequences that
Busby Berkeley made for Warner Brothers, the camera moves to a series
of close-ups of the chorines' faces, then, disorientingly, to doll-like figures in frilly dresses that turn out to be their knees and legs. Prepared by
this miniature scale, we then see little Shirley, in a frilly short dress of her
own, emerging from her father's spread legs to become the new "baby"
who is the source of everyone's tribute. She returns the song's compli-
ment, singing, with her characteristic broad gestures, swaying shoulders,
and emphatic delivery, "Daddy, take a bow." The two then perform a tap
dance, and Jimmy scoops her up in his arms for a final embrace and kiss.
In the course of the number, eroticism has supposedly been supplanted
by cuteness, and the father-daughter bond is evidently sufficient protection from Shirley's flirtatiousness. Nonetheless, the "innocence" of her
performance depends on the audience's knowledge of an erotic adult
alternative. The sentimental economy exists uneasily alongside an unacknowledged sexual one.[40]

Little Miss Marker: What Is a Little Girl Really Worth?

Stand Up and Cheer gave Shirley Temple the break her mother had dreamed of, but the film that established her as a star was *Little Miss Marker*. Based on a Damon Runyon short story,[41] it revolves around the question, What is a little girl really worth? How should she be valued? Here again, Shirley Temple plays a motherless little girl, but this time she almost immediately loses her father as well. He appears toward the beginning of the film as a well-spoken but clearly desperate man, who, his money all gone, asks an off-track bookmaker to take his little daughter as security for a twenty-dollar bet. In the argot of bettors, she is his "marker," his I.O.U.

The bookmaker, who has the wonderfully Runyonesque name of Sorrowful Jones (and who is played by Adolphe Menjou), has already made it clear he is no sentimentalist—or so he thinks. He has flatly refused others' markers. As a worker in a ruthless black-market economy run by gangsters and fixers, he has learned that he must look out for himself. The film has already suggested that he has been disappointed in love. When he first passes the attractive nightclub singer Bangles Carson (played by Dorothy Dell), the mistress of the gangster and nightclub owner Big Steve, she greets him, "Hello, Tightwad," to which he replies, "Hi, Golddigger."

But the little girl, Marthy, played by Shirley Temple, instantly pierces his callous façade to see into his emotional depths. Looking intently at him, she says, "You're afraid of my daddy. Or you're afraid of me. You're afraid of something." She has identified fear as the chief obstacle to a healthy sentimental economy as Roosevelt did for the financial one. Sorrowful lifts her up and returns her searching gaze (fig. 6.5). "Take his marker," he tells his assistant. "A little doll like that is worth twenty bucks, any way you look at it." The clerk, nicknamed Regret, replies sardonically, "She ought to melt down for that much." The horse loses in a fixed race, and as a result, the little girl's father, instead of returning for his daughter, kills himself. Little Marthy, an unredeemed I.O.U., becomes Little Marky, punning on the word "marker."

A sweet little girl left in the custody of hardened men is a situation rich in comic possibilities. Sorrowful quickly wins his money back by joining in a betting pool in which each of his cronies guesses Little Marky's weight. As the men pass her around and heft her, the explicit comparison is with picking up and fondling a voluptuous woman. The "little doll" is thus also a marker for a grown-up one. But one might see this as an attempt to place Marky on the scales by which these men cus-

Fig. 6.5 Adolphe Menjou as Sorrowful Jones appraises Shirley
Temple as Marthy in *Little Miss Marker*.

tomarily determine value—in terms of money and, at times, sex, but not
sentiment. Sorrowful wins the bet when, on her own initiative, Marky
conceals a large saltshaker in order to confirm his estimate of her weight.
Then, reluctantly contemplating sending Marky to an orphanage, Sorrowful sees a way to get still more money from the girl: he makes her titular
owner of a racehorse, the true owner, Big Steve, having been temporarily
suspended from racing because of infractions.

Sorrowful might be said to be not just a bookie but a comic version
of the disillusioned, untrusting economic man of the Depression: with a
single worn suit, no family, and no woman on whom he lavishes gifts or
affection. Emotionally as well as financially, he is a tightwad.

In the course of the film, Little Marky, in melting his frozen feelings,
also loosens his purse strings. Bangles, who enjoys fashionable clothes,
expensive jewelry (when it's not in the pawnshop), and a stylish apartment, attended by a maid, is shocked by Little Marky's single torn dress
and orders her new clothes. When the bill comes to Sorrowful, he holds
up one of Marky's new frilly dresses and then pays for them without complaint. Soon, he moves out of his spare apartment (a "fleabag" in Runyon's
story) to a spacious new one with a modern kitchen, large living room,
and at least two bedrooms (we see only the one in which Little Marky
sleeps). Still later, he buys a new suit (Adolphe Menjou, who played Sorrowful Jones, had a reputation as the best-dressed man in Hollywood)

and makes a resplendent appearance. The economics of consumer spending and sentiment turn together.

In *The Runt Page* and, to a large extent, in the "Baby Take a Bow" number in *Stand Up and Cheer*, the "make believe" of Shirley Temple's characters had been in the service of adults. But in *Little Miss Marker* her capacity for make believe is part of her distinguishing childish innocence. Orphaned by her father's suicide, she is sustained by a book of Arthurian legends. She projects their Arthurian titles and attributes onto the raffish characters about her, with unintentional mock-heroic effect. The gamblers pin their hopes on Dream Prince and similar horses, or, like Sorrowful, Regret, and, Bangles, they no longer truly dream of anything. When Marky seems to be growing tough and disillusioned herself and to be giving up on her fairy tales, they avidly seek to restore her faith by arranging an elaborate Arthurian ball. These doubly depressed adults, the story suggests, need the emotional qualities of childhood every bit as much as children do. The plot contains still more twists and turns, but ultimately Marky repairs the broken relationship between Sorrowful and Bangles—and even turns the gangster Big Steve from a heel to a hero.

This work of emotional repair of adults' relationships, and especially the repair of the sentimental economy of men, became a strong and abiding theme in Shirley Temple's films in the 1930s. The trajectory is unmistakable in her next films of 1934 and 1935. Fatherless and, ultimately, motherless in the first film written especially for her, *Bright Eyes* (1934), she heals the broken heart of the aviator Loop Merritt as well as the flinty one of rich Uncle Ned. In *The Little Colonel* (1935), she repairs the rift between her proud, crusty grandfather (played by Lionel Barrymore) and her own parents. And in a second film of 1935, *The Littlest Rebel,* she not only transcends the death of her mother but courageously climbs up on President Abraham Lincoln's lap and arranges pardons for her Confederate father and his Union friend—implicitly healing the rifts of the Civil War as a whole.

The Work behind the Smiling Effects

Hard as she worked onscreen to heal broken hearts, face down fear, and prove the power of childish innocence, off screen little Shirley worked harder still. "I started in Baby Burlesk films at about three," Shirley Temple Black later said, "and worked for the rest of my childhood. The studio didn't control my life, but I went to work *every day*. . . . I thought every child worked, because I was born into it."[42] In fact, little Shirley

Temple and thousands of other child film actors were workers in two off-screen economies: financial and emotional. The interaction between these economies and the nature of the child actors' work remained obscure to the public and to themselves, for it was not in the interests of either the Hollywood studios or the children's parents to clarify them. Outwardly, the terms of their work bore no resemblance to the common and oner-ous forms of child labor. Instead of toiling long hours under often dan-gerous conditions on the lowest rungs of the industrial economy, they seemed enviably perched at its height. At a time of the greatest period of unemployment in the nation's history, their apparently effortless acts of "make believe" on movie sets cheered millions and potentially brought them fame and fortune. Although most remained, in fact, anonymous and poorly paid,[43] the most celebrated (of whom Shirley Temple was the supreme instance) earned staggering sums and lived in the lap of luxury. To have suggested that they were in any sense exploited seemed ludicrous.[44]

Nonetheless, as Budd Schulberg once observed, "Hollywood's a fac-tory town, only instead of motor cars or steel, we turn out cans of film."[45] With high production costs, studios relentlessly pushed all their workers hard to deliver a product in the shortest possible time. The special needs of children, even of infants, often received short shrift, despite growing regulation. Anxious for their children to succeed, parents generally com-plied. Children characteristically worked despite illnesses or injuries. They missed school, and the minimal instruction they received as a sub-stitute seldom provided a comparable education. Even infants at times put in arduously long days and worked in hazardous conditions.

We glimpse some of these demands in a letter Shirley's mother, Ger-trude Temple, wrote to Shirley's grandmother when the girl was only three and a half and making *The Runt Page*, her first film:

> Shirley started rehearsing for the first picture a week before Christ-mas . . . finished last Saturday night. Poor little Shirley was all in . . . had a raging cold for the last ten days. Last Thursday night she awaked with an earache . . . the hospital had to pierce her ear drum . . . a game little soul. I stayed with her all night.
>
> The worst part . . . they had to have her at the studio the next day. Mr. Hays, the producer, was almost crazy and so was I.
>
> To think that after all our trips to town for rehearsals, which we were not paid for, Shirley would not be able to be in the picture. They wanted her especially for the first picture because if this picture is a suc-

cess, they are going on with the rest of the series and star her through the whole thing.

I begged them to wait until today (Monday) to finish the picture, but it absolutely had to be finished Saturday. We didn't leave the studio until that night. She went through her lines as if nothing had happened.

In the studio eleven hours and a half. She had two naps there, which helped. This business of being mother to a budding star is no joke. I think I look ten years older and have lost quite a little weight.

But we all think the picture is going to be a big success. However, employment conditions here seem very bad. The stores seem almost empty, and have just a few clerks on each floor. George [Temple, Gertrude's husband and Shirley's father] is also very worried, as our financial condition is pretty bad.[46]

This letter is revealing in several respects. Gertrude Temple speaks more candidly than she ever did publicly of the sheer physical demands that film acting placed on her daughter. She also exposes more nakedly her own ambition and vanity. And she reveals, as she never did in public, the association between her hopes for Shirley's film career and the family's financial worries.

The set on which little Shirley worked on the Baby Burlesks was hardly a model day nursery. To threaten and punish uncooperative child actors, the director, Charles Lamont, kept a soundproof black box, six feet on each side, containing a block of ice. An offending child was locked within this dark, cramped interior and either stood uncomfortably in the cold, humid air or had to sit on the ice. Those who told their parents about this torture were threatened with further punishment. When, nonetheless, Shirley confided this information to her mother, Gertrude Temple dismissed her report as a fanciful tale.[47] Lamont was equally ruthless behind the camera. In a *Tarzan* film spoof, *Kid in Africa*, for example, he concealed a tripwire to fell the "savages" played by African American children. In filming another scene, a terrified ostrich pulling Shirley and another child in a surrey careened wildly about the set before crashing into a wall. "This isn't playtime, kids," she later remembered Lamont saying, "It's work."[48]

Indeed, work, not play, defined Shirley Temple's childhood. After the Baby Burlesks and Frolics of Youth series had run their course and Jack Hays's Educational Films studio declared bankruptcy, her mother pursued every glimmer of possible stardom until her daughter secured a long-term contract in 1934. Thenceforth, with few vacations, Shirley worked a six-day week that included spending long hours on the set and cramming three hours' worth of school lessons into short breaks. Her days ended at bedtime with her mother coaching her on the next day's scenes and curling her hair. Supposedly, child film actors were limited to five hours of work a day on weekdays and eight hours on Saturdays and school holidays, including summer vacations. In practice, her days were longer. Shooting schedules for her films generally ran six to seven weeks, and she made four movies a year through most of the decade. Between films, she was still obliged to work at the studio for six to seven hours a day, where she was fitted for costumes, gave interviews, and posed for publicity photographs, which appeared in newspapers, magazines, and advertisements at an estimated rate of twenty a day.[49]

Shirley Temple as an Emotional Laborer

In addition to the physical and temporal demands of Shirley Temple's work as a child actor, there were emotional ones. The concept of emotional labor has not been developed as has that of physical labor, and it has been especially neglected with respect to children. The sociologist Arlie Russell Hochschild brilliantly addressed the subject of emotional labor in *The Managed Heart*. Studying adults in the service economy, especially those employed in the overwhelmingly female job of flight attendant and the overwhelmingly male job of bill collector, she emphasized the ways in which emotions that we customarily regard as private and discretionary are in fact part and parcel of such workers' jobs. Such workers are required "to induce or suppress [their own] feelings in order to sustain the outward countenance that produces the proper state of mind in others"—comfort and safety in the case of airline passengers, intimidation and compliance in the case of delinquent creditors. As Hochschild noted in the twentieth-anniversary edition of her book, others have since extended her concept to a number of occupations and situations. Some researchers have distinguished between higher-paid emotional laborers and the emotional proletariat, including those in the growing "care sector," such as those who care for children, the ill, and the elderly. Others have extended the concept to unpaid emotional work and personal relationships. But none that she mentions has studied or considered children as emotional laborers themselves rather than the objects of adults' emotional labor.[50]

Yet child actors are emotional laborers of a special sort, both in the work they perform on stage or set and, characteristically, in their larger position with respect to their families. Emotions, of course, are the stuff of acting, and the simulation and evocation of emotional effects is a key job of the adult or child actor, even if for the child the standard is lower. When Shirley Temple began to make the Baby Burlesks, the acting demanded of her was only mimicry, the most superficial kind of emotional labor. And when Alexander Hall needed Shirley to cry in a scene for *Little Miss Marker*, he simply tricked her into shedding real tears by telling her, "Your mother is gone."[51] Gertrude Temple was furious not only because of the deception but also because she considered her daughter an accomplished crier. To be able to cry convincingly was a key ability for a child film actor in this period, boys and girls alike, in films that were frequently awash with sentimental drama.[52] By age eleven, when she needed to cry in *The Little Princess* (1939), she was delighted to discover that she could throw herself into hysteria.[53]

Still, for Depression audiences, who had watched a decade of Jackie Coogan and lachrymose Dickensian waifs, Shirley's winning smile, hearty laugh, and boisterous cheer were what they most wanted. The favorite injunction of Gertrude Temple, Shirley's most important acting coach throughout the 1930s, was "Sparkle." As Shirley later described it: "Arching eyebrows and rounded mouth in an expression of surprise was 'sparkling,' by her definition. So was frowning with an outthrust lower lip, or a knowing half-smile with head cocked to the side. Her verbal definition connoted more than posing. It was a word covering a total attitude, an emotional *stance*. When she said 'sparkle' it meant energy, an intellectual intensity which would naturally translate itself into vivid and convincing gesture and expression."[54] This concept of emotional acting was based on the techniques developed by silent stars such as Mary Pickford rather than those of Stanislavski. But for Shirley, it was not only a summons to tap her own emotional resources but also—what ultimately involved much higher emotional stakes—to gain emotional cues from her mother, and to verify her success by her mother's approval.

Beyond all the emotional labor involved in acting and satisfying directors and others on the set, Shirley Temple found that fulfilling her mother's ambitions was the source of her most intense emotional work. Stage and screen mothers are notorious for living through their children, their daughters, especially, and the most fiercely determined of them from the mid-nineteenth to the mid-twentieth century make a formidable roll call: Mary Ann Crabtree, mother of Lotta; Jenny Cockrell Bierbow (later Janis), mother of Elsie Janis; Charlotte Smith, mother of Mary Pickford; Rose Hovick, mother of June Havoc and Gypsy Rose Lee; Lela Rogers, mother of Ginger; and Ethel Gumm, mother of Judy Garland. Gertrude Temple was not ruthless or egotistical enough to rank in this list, but she was proudly and single-mindedly devoted to her daughter and keenly jealous of any rival for her success. Like some other mothers of child stars, she claimed virtually to have willed herself a daughter, and to have chosen the child's name and launched her career in the womb by exposing her to classical music, uplifting literature, great works of art, scenes of natural beauty, and romantic films.[55] Although when Shirley was born Gertrude Temple already had two sons, her daughter became not simply Gertrude's "pet project" but the vehicle of her own driving ambitions.[56]

Virtually every substantial description of Gertrude Temple's relationship with her daughter remarked on their close bond, Mrs. Temple's fierce protectiveness, and the emotional controls she demanded from her offspring.[57] "Shirley was the product of her mother, the instrument on which she played," the director Allan Dwan declared.[58] Even if her daughter was not her puppet, they were an inseparable team. As such, Gertrude Temple was hardly in a position to understand—let alone to critique—the emotional labor as well as the physical labor that Shirley performed. On the contrary, she had every incentive to minimize this aspect of Shirley's work and publicly to insist that Shirley's acting was all really play.

As a child eager to comply with her mother's wishes, Shirley readily agreed. Nonetheless, even in the journalist Max Trell's highly dubious construction of Shirley's "autobiography" as a seven-year old, qualifications emerge that suggest some of the emotional pressures that she felt:

> Mom and Daddy and most of the other folks who know me say, "Oh, Shirley thinks acting for the movies is like playing a game!" Well, I don't think it's *exactly* like playing a game. It's more like going to school—like learning to read and write. It's something you're supposed to do. I can tell that everybody— the director, Mom, and all the other actors and actresses—want me to sing, or dance, or speak my lines *just right,* not any old way. They're disappointed when I don't. I can tell it on their faces, even though they don't ever scold me or anything. I feel disappointed, too. I feel sorry they don't like me. But when I do things right—why, then they're all as glad as can be.[59]

Although the "play" that little Shirley performed so assiduously was entirely of adults' devising, Gertrude Temple and Shirley's directors and producers, no less than her millions of fans, cherished what they regarded as her unaffected innocence and sought to protect it as long as possible. They frequently worried aloud about her becoming "spoiled," fearing that her knowledge of her importance to their projects and the immense financial and emotional hopes that rested on her—those of her parents, the studios, the public—would warp her personality and performances. When Shirley first became famous and admirers began to seek her out, Gertrude Temple confessed, "I was afraid it was dawning upon her that those people adored her image and her acting. I was afraid she would begin to act for me." She added, "I want her to be natural, innocent, sweet. If she ceases to be that, I shall have lost her—and motion pictures will have lost her, too."[60] In a cover story devoted to Shirley Temple in 1936, *Time* magazine reported that the question that seemed to concern people most was whether Shirley was spoiled. The article reassured its readers that she was not, approvingly quoting Gertrude Temple, "Spare the rod and spoil the star."[61] At Fox even before the merger with Twentieth Century, studio executives took their own steps to keep Shirley's ego proportionate with her little body by separating her socially from cast and crew in her own cottage on the studio lot. "She can't get spoiled," the studio vice president and general manager Wilfred Sheehan had warned Gertrude Temple. "She gets spoiled, it shows in the eyes."[62]

The Transformation of the Temple Family's Economy

The desire to keep Shirley innocent and unspoiled, living blissfully in a child's garden of movies without ever tasting the apple of knowledge that might enlighten and transform her, preoccupied Gertrude and George Temple in their domestic economy just as it did the executives at Twentieth Century-Fox. The adulation Shirley received was overwhelming, including a torrent of letters that occupied a full-time secretary, a profusion of gifts (over 135,000 gifts and greetings for her birthday in 1936), prying visitors about the Temples' house, and unruly mobs when family members ventured out in public.[63] The kidnapping and brutal murder of another blond-haired child, Charles Lindbergh Jr., in 1932 haunted Gertrude Temple as it did countless others, and Shirley was protected by a bodyguard, first paid for by the studio and later by the Temple family directly. The Temples tried to keep the family in balance, but the terms of their daughter's career shook them like an earthquake. By the mid-1930s, the Temples, who a few years earlier had lived in a modest Spanish-style bungalow, resided in a luxurious house on four acres in Brentwood

Heights, with its own swimming pool, carousel, and roller coaster, and tended by a large staff. The parents as well as Shirley dressed stylishly. Her older brothers were now out of the house: one was in military school, the other in college—educational advantages made possible by Shirley's earnings. George Temple, who had worked as a bank teller and then a cashier, rose to branch manager on his daughter's celebrity and by 1936 was making ninety dollars a week, a comfortable salary for the time and a considerable increase over his wages a few years earlier. Asked how he felt now that his daughter was making a thousand dollars a week, a sum that did not include her still more substantial licensing income, George Temple replied, "Very foolish."[64]

Shirley had been her mother's full-time emotional concern ever since her birth. Soon she became her father's chief occupation as well. He quit his bank job to manage his curly haired goldmine's investments, placing the bulk of her earnings—so magazine articles repeatedly reported— in "sound securities."[65] In an astonishingly brief time, little Shirley had turned parental and child responsibilities topsy-turvy by taking on the role of breadwinner and lifting her family's style of living to giddy heights.

Like the parents of other child film stars, the Temples tried to keep Shirley "innocent" of her extraordinary financial power and the degree to which they had become hostages to her career. Even so, at a time when poor children dreamed of becoming Hollywood stars as a way of supporting their families, it is hard to imagine that Shirley remained wholly unaware of her centrality to all her family's needs and expectations.[66] Nevertheless, at age ten and a half in fall 1938, she proudly reported that she received an allowance of $5 every two weeks and had accrued a savings of $105, which she kept in a strongbox.[67] Among families of all classes, children's allowances had grown increasingly popular in the first decades of the twentieth century. Such payments acknowledged the historic transformation in the place of the child from a vital economic contributor to a helpful household member and fledgling consumer. Like the parents of such child stars as Jackie Coogan and Jane Withers, George and Gertrude Temple participated in this practice designed to teach how to save, spend, and give wisely. In this way, they sought to normalize their child's stupendous income and to neutralize its immensely transformative effects on their family.[68]

By rights stretching back to British common law, the Temples, as the parents of a minor under their roof, were entitled to every penny that Shirley made, but that situation was about to change. In a highly publicized case in 1938, former child star Jackie Coogan sued his mother and stepfather for the money he had made as a minor, an estimated four million dollars. After a bitterly contentious suit in which his mother tearfully testified that "Jackie was a bad boy, a very, very bad 20-year-old boy" who "couldn't handle money,"[69] the Coogan case established that a child actor deserved a portion of his earnings. It was a largely pyrrhic victory, however, as he recovered only a fraction of his fortune. The dispute prompted the California state legislature in 1939 to pass the Child Actors' Bill, the so-called Coogan Act, which required parents or legal guardians to put at least half of a child actor's gross earnings in a court-approved fund or savings plan until the child turned twenty-one, although the law contained loopholes that considerably weakened its enforcement.

The Temple family did not seem to need the Coogan Act to remind them of their obligations to their child. They had established a court-approved trust fund for her as early as 1934.[70] Yet Shirley Temple remained so innocent of the state of her finances that not until she was twenty-two years old and at last insisted on seeing her financial records did she discover how disastrously her father and his business partner had squandered her earnings from her films, licenses, and royalties. Of the $3,207,666 in earnings her family had received in her name, only $44,000 remained. Poring over the bound volume containing the complicated and depressing account of income and expenditures, she found how much her innocence had been exploited:

> Bank and brokerage accounts opened, multiplied, then vanished, while Little Shirley earned, paid, and supported. Baby bountiful from childhood, she purchased clothing, a parade of automobiles, every dog bone, golf ball, and diamond for seventeen years. This had been my domain: parents, brothers, twelve household staff, until death a demanding grandmother, and two paternal uncles, whom I vaguely remembered collecting handouts at our gate. Implacably generous, I loaned cash, interest-free, to penitent friends of my parents and faceless names like Hap Nutts and Fanny Sniff. Few repaid. Summing up, I did.
>
> . . . Whether siphoned off as expense or investment, my salary checks had ended up in other purses. Through all those hoary records one human theme pulsed loud and clear: keep dancing, kid, or the rickety cardhouse collapses.[71]

Yet the financial records contained a further twist of the plot and a more disturbing revelation of character. As Shirley checked the figures, she realized that not only had her earnings been freely, even prodigally spent, but also that her father had simply ignored the stipulation of the California superior court under the Coogan Act that half of her earnings after 1940 be placed in trust for her. Of her MGM earnings, "$312,000 had vanished." "The more I checked my figures," she wrote in her autobiography, "the more inescapable became confirmation of my gnawing fear. For years Father had flagrantly disobeyed the Superior Court order. Commencing in 1942 he simply ceased depositing anything to my trust, a delinquency continued for eight years."[72] Only briefly speculating about his motives even in her autobiography, Shirley as a twenty-two-year-old chose not to pursue the matter. She later likened George Temple to Mr. Micawber of Charles Dickens's *David Copperfield*, the chronically improvident, impecunious, feckless, and jauntily optimistic man who believed something would turn up. In a final twist of roles, she protected her father from the humiliation of publicity and, for the rest of her parents' lives, kept this discovery secret.

The Separation and Integration of Sentimental and Financial Economies

Shirley Temple's career in the 1930s was a supreme instance of the tightening integration of emotional and financial economies that has characterized modern consumer culture. The trade journal of film exhibitors, *Motion Picture Herald*, spoke for legions when, following the release of *Baby Take a Bow* in 1934, it declared, "For straight-away commercial purposes, Shirley Temple is the most salable asset. She is the value that good business sense dictates should be capitalized to the limit."[73] An anomalous child laborer, she performed demanding physical and emotional work that was consistently portrayed as play. Not only did she prove one of the greatest box-office draws of the decade; she also instantly emerged as an icon of conspicuous display whose every feature and fashion from top to toe could be purchased in the form of Shirley Temple permanent waves, hair bands, hats, coats, dresses, socks, shoes, dolls, and the like. Moreover, the very autonomy and direct expression of "natural" impulses that made Shirley Temple's persona so beloved also served as a model for the child as consumer, with a personality, preferences, and desires to be indulged rather than constrained.[74] No figure in the Great Depression was more deeply enmeshed in the commodification of childhood.

Yet Shirley Temple served as such an effective agent for the increased integration of the consumer economy into children's lives as well as for modern understandings of childhood precisely because she seemed so impervious to the immense consumer markets in which her image cir-culated. Off screen as well as in her films, in scores of articles and inter-views during the Great Depression, the overarching narrative of Shirley Temple was of an irrepressibly sunny, good-hearted, emotionally direct, and delightfully unaffected child. Showered like a fairy princess with adulation, wealth, and luxuries, she seemed supremely uncontaminated by them.

As Shirley Temple assumed the place of fairy princess, however, those most directly propelling her into the consumer market—her directors, producers, and parents—worked like alchemists to turn her ebullient child-spirit into gold, while leaving her "innocent" and unchanged. They implicitly testified to their sense of the high stakes and risks of the endeavor with each reassurance that she remained unaffected, despite the myriad potential profanations of the markets in which she was a prime mover. As powerful a draw as Shirley Temple proved to be, both for her films and for the larger industry of products attached to her name, she would break the spell if ever she awoke to a full realization of her immense economic importance. Those around her spoke repeatedly of her "unspoiled" nature, what they prized as the emotional and moral capital that children uniquely possessed, even as they sought to exploit that capital for its maximum financial return. They proved themselves to be both calculating capitalists and credulous sentimentalists. The separa-tion of the child from the world of market relations in the twentieth cen-tury was increasingly a myth, but it was a useful one, not only in the self-serving way it consoled people such as film producers Wilfred Sheehan and Darryl Zanuck and parents such as Gertrude and George Temple, but also for the reassurance it provided for the emerging consumer culture as a whole. It allowed both merchants of the child commodity market and parents of consuming children to sleep better at night.

NOTES

1. Walter Bullock and Harry Spina, "Be Optimistic," in *Little Miss Broadway* (film) (Twentieth Century-Fox, 1938).
2. The portrait is now in the collection of the Museum Boijmans Van Beuningen in Rotterdam.
3. For example, Shirley Temple receives only the briefest of mentions—and an implicit dismissal—in Andrew Bergman, *We're in the Money: Depression America and Its Films* (New York: New York University Press, 1971), 72. Virtually the only discerning essay on her significance to film history and to the culture of the

1930s is Charles Eckert, "Shirley Temple and the House of Rockefeller," in *American Media and Mass Culture: Left Perspectives*, ed. Donald Lazere (Berkeley and Los Angeles: University of California Press, 1987), 164–77; the essay was originally published in *Jump Cut: A Review of Contemporary Media*, no. 2 (July–August 1974): 1, 17–20.

4. *Oxford English Dictionary*, http://dictionary.oed.com (accessed February 11, 2008). The quotation is from Howard Crosby Warren, ed., *Dictionary of Psychology* (Boston: Houghton Mifflin, 1934), 73/1. On changing medical understandings of depression, see Edward Shorter, *A Historical Dictionary of Psychiatry* (New York: Oxford University Press, 2005), 78–89.

5. Studs Terkel, *Hard Times: An Oral History of the Great Depression* (New York: Pantheon Books, 1970), 196.

6. Shirley Temple Black, *Child Star: An Autobiography* (New York: McGraw-Hill, 1988), 59. This tribute has been cited by others, including George F. Custen, *Twentieth Century's Fox: Darryl F. Zanuck and the Culture of Hollywood* (New York: Basic Books, 1997), 199. I have been unable to verify the quotation, however.

7. All quotations from films are my own transcriptions.

8. Robert Sklar, *Movie-Made America: A Social History of American Movies* (New York: Random House, 1975), 161–62.

9. Thomas Doherty, *Pre-Code Hollywood: Sex, Immorality, and Insurrection in American Cinema, 1930–1934* (New York: Columbia University Press, 1999), 319–27.

10. Philip K. Scheuer, "Depression Laughed Off" (review of *Stand up and Cheer*), *Los Angeles Times*, May 4, 1934, sec. 1, p. 13.

11. Mae Tinee, "Slump Yields to Treatment in This Movie," *Chicago Tribune*, May 2, 1934, 17; "RKO-Keith's *Stand Up and Cheer*," *Boston Globe*, May 4, 1934, 41; Boyd Martin, "*Stand Up and Cheer*," *Louisville Courier-Journal*, July 5, 1934, 18.

12. "Shirley Temple a Sensation; 'Little Miss Marker' Cashes," *Hollywood Reporter*, May 29, 1934, 7.

13. Ann Edwards reports Shirley Temple's earnings from her films before *Stand Up and Cheer* as $1,135. See Ann Edwards, *Shirley Temple, American Princess* (New York: Morrow, 1988), 49; see also p. 52 for the terms of the initial Fox contract. Shirley Temple Black says her earnings on the Educational Films shorts and her early bit parts amounted to $702.50. For *Stand Up and Cheer* she says she received $150 a week with a two-week minimum (Black, *Child Star*, 31, 33).

14. Douglas W. Churchill, "Taking a Look at the Record," *New York Times*, November 25, 1934, sec. 5. Shirley Temple ranked eighth in the *Motion Picture Herald*'s 1934 annual survey, "The Ten Biggest Money Making Stars," for the period beginning September 1, 1933, and ending August 31, 1934, even though she appeared in major films only beginning in April 1934. See *1935–36 Motion Picture Almanac* (New York: Quigley Publishing, n.d.), 94.

15. Rudy Behlmer, *Memo from Darryl F. Zanuck: The Golden Years at Twentieth Century-Fox* (New York: Grove Press, 1993), 17.

16. The annual survey was conducted by the *Motion Picture Herald*; "Shirley Temple Heads Film List for Fourth Year," *New York Times*, December 23, 1938, 17.

17. In 1939 Shirley Temple slipped from number one in box-office popularity to number thirteen. Edwards, *Shirley Temple, American Princess*, 124.

18. "Just Pretending Nets Shirley Temple $1,250 a Week," *Newsweek*, July 28, 1934, 24; see also Black, *Child Star*, 80–81.

19. Leo C. Rosten, *Hollywood: The Movie Colony, the Movie Makers* (New York: Harcourt

Brace, 1941), 330, 342, 343. Sales of Shirley Temple dolls by Ideal Novelty and Toy Company alone accounted for gross sales of $45 million before 1941 (Black, *Child Star*, 85).

20. Rosten, *Hollywood*, 273.
21. Edwards, *Shirley Temple, American Princess*, 93–94, 138; Rosten, *Hollywood*, 330.
22. Black, *Child Star*, 141.
23. Hamilton MacFadden, dir., *Stand Up and Cheer* (Fox Film Corp., 1934).
24. For example, the mother of the silent film star Baby Peggy Montgomery told reporters, "She [Peggy] works—if you would call it work—four hours a day, never at night and never on Sundays. She considers her work play and nothing is ever done or said to let her feel otherwise." The former child star found this comment bitterly amusing. Diana Serra Cary, *Hollywood's Children: An Inside Account of the Child Star Era* (Dallas: Southern Methodist University Press, 1997), 92.
25. Gertrude Temple, "Bringing up Shirley," *American Magazine*, February 1935, 92.
26. [Max Trell,] "My Life and Times: The Autobiography of Shirley Temple, Part I," *Pictorial Review*, August 1935, 40. A *Time* magazine cover story echoed this assertion: "Her work entails no effort. She plays at acting as other small girls play at dolls." "Peewee's Progress," *Time*, April 27, 1936, 42.
27. Viviana A. Zelizer, *Pricing the Priceless Child: The Changing Social Value of Children* (Princeton: Princeton University Press, 1994), 95.
28. Susan Rae Applebaum, "*The Little Princess* Onstage in 1903: Its Historical Significance," *Theatre History Studies* 18 (1998): 71–72. In New York City, applications to the mayor's office for licenses for juvenile actors, which had been less than two hundred in 1896, spiked to over four thousand in 1903. See Benjamin McArthur, "'Forbid Them Not': Child Actor Labor Laws and Political Activism in the Theatre," *Theatre Survey* 36, no. 2 (1995): 70.
29. A particularly formidable critic was Elbridge T. Gerry, longtime head of the New York Society for the Prevention of Cruelty to Children. See McArthur, "Forbid Them Not," 66–67.
30. National Alliance for the Protection of Stage Children, *Stage Children of America* (New York: Times Building, [1911]), 5, 16, 8, 22.
31. I. A. Taylor, "The Show-Child: A Protest," *Living Age*, January 11, 1896, 113, 116; see also F. Zeta Youmans, "Childhood, Inc.," *Survey*, July 15, 1924, 464.
32. Black, *Child Star*, 232–33. Black notes that originally the bill made no exceptions with respect to age for children in films. She mistakenly states that Roosevelt signed the bill on the day of her visit, June 24, 1938; in fact, he signed it on June 25.
33. Steven Mintz notes that "as late as 1900, 20 to 30 per cent of children lost a parent by age fifteen." In addition, the number of desertions rose notably during the 1930s, leaving more children in single-parent households. See Steven Mintz, *Huck's Raft: A History of American Childhood* (Cambridge: Harvard University Press, 2004), 157, 237.
34. Robert Eichberg, "Lines to a Little Lady," *Modern Screen*, February 1935, 48, 74ff.
35. Ibid., 48.
36. Gilbert Seldes, "Two Great Women: Intimations of Tomorrow Rise on Seeing the Shirley Temple of Today," *Esquire*, July 1935, 143.
37. Tom Goldrup and Jim Goldrup, *Growing up on the Set: Interviews with 39 Former Child Actors of Classic Film and Television* (Jefferson, NC: McFarland, 2002), 21, 334.

38. Jane Feuer, *The Hollywood Musical* (Bloomington: Indiana University Press, 1982), 13.

39. Lew Brown (words and music) and Jay Gorney (music), "Baby Take a Bow" (Movietone Music Corporation, 1934).

40. Famously, Graham Greene insisted on making this sexual economy explicit in his 1937 review of *Wee Willie Winkie:*

> In *Captain January* she wore trousers with the mature suggestiveness of a Dietrich: her neat and well-developed rump twisted in the tap dance: her eyes had a sidelong, searching coquetry. Now in *Wee Willie Winkie*, wearing short kilts, she is a complete totsy. Watch her swaggering stride across the Indian barrack-square: hear the gasp of excited expectation from her antique audience when the sergeant's palm is raised: watch the way she measures a man with agile studio eyes, with dimpled depravity. Adult emotions of love and grief glissade across the mask of childhood, a childhood skin deep. It is clever, but it cannot last. Her admirers, middle-aged men and clergy-men, respond to her dubious coquetry, to the sight of her well-shaped and desirable little body, packed with enormous vitality, only because the safety curtain of story and dialogue drops between their intelligence and their desire.

Twentieth Century-Fox, enlisting Shirley Temple's parents as coplaintiffs, sued Greene and his publication, *Night and Day*, for accusing them of "procuring" her "for immoral purposes" and won the suit decisively. See Black, *Child Star*, 184–85.

41. "Little Miss Marker" first appeared in *Collier's*, March 26, 1932.

42. Edwards, *Shirley Temple, American Princess*, 70.

43. Diana Serra Cary writes:

> When the child star craze was at its height—roughly between 1925 and 1945—an estimated one hundred children poured into the Hollywood marketplace every fifteen minutes. The ratio of those who in an entire year earned so much as a single week's expenses from movie work was reckoned at less than one in fifteen thousand. It is probable that at least half of those who arrived with dazzling dreams of stardom for their child were starved out and forced to return home at the end of the first two or three months. A small percentage, perhaps grubstaked by a husband's salary or a relative's nest egg to launch a more determined siege, might hold on for a year before giving up the fight. That left a small, fanatical corps of iron-willed survivors, women who preferred starvation and death to abandoning their dearly won positions before the very gates of fame. (*Hollywood's Children*, 149)

44. So ludicrous did the idea of Shirley Temple as a child laborer seem in the mid-1930s that it was the subject of a humorous imaginary interview between the child star and Secretary of Labor Frances Perkins, in which the child rejects the very notion that she works: "I don't work. I dance and sing and make faces." See Corey Ford (with illustration by Miguel Covarrubias), "Impossible Interview: Frances Perkins vs. Shirley Temple," *Vanity Fair*, September 1935, 33.

45. Bud Schulberg, review of *Despite the System: Orson Welles versus the Hollywood Studios*, by Clinton Heylin, *New York Times Book Review*, May 1, 2005.
46. Black, *Child Star*, 15–16 (ellipses in original).
47. Ibid., 22–23.
48. Ibid., 19.
49. Edwards, *Shirley Temple, American Princess*, 77–78; "Peewee's Progress," 38.
50. Arlie Russell Hochschild, *The Managed Heart: Commercialization of Human Feeling*, 25th anniversary ed. (1983; repr., Berkeley and Los Angeles: University of California Press, 2003), 199–207.
51. Black, *Child Star*, 48.
52. Gene Reynolds, a child actor five years older than Shirley temple, later recalled: "I realized that if I was going to stay in the business in those days, I had to learn to cry. That was one of the damn necessities at the time because they had all these scenes in which boys were losing their mothers or their dog" (Goldrup and Goldrup, *Growing up on the Set*, 249). See also Frank Coghlan, *They Still Call Me Junior* (Jefferson, NC: McFarland, 1993), 77–78.
53. Black, *Child Star*, 257.
54. Ibid., 20–21.
55. Ibid., 4. Among other future stage and screen mothers who began coaching their children in utero were Jenny Cockrell Bierbow (Janis) and Leila Rogers. See Cary, *Hollywood's Children*, 23, 169. Jane Withers's mother similarly planned her daughter's career long before conception. See Goldrup and Goldrup, *Growing up on the Set*, 33.
56. Black, *Child Star*, 59.
57. As a woman of sixty, Shirley Temple Black wrote of her mother, "She was no namby-pamby. In fact, my first spoken phrase—'Don't do 'at!' was probably in mimicry of what she said to me. Always inside that velvet glove was a hard hand, a symbol of linkage between command and obedience" (ibid., 7).
58. Dwan, who earlier had directed Mary Pickford and encountered her formidable mother, directed Shirley Temple in *Heidi* and *Rebecca of Sunnybrook Farm* (ibid., 205).
59. [Max Trell,] "My Life and Times: The Autobiography of Shirley Temple, Part II," *Pictorial Review*, September 1935, 52.
60. Temple, "Bringing up Shirley," 92.
61. "Peewee's Progress," 37.
62. Black, *Child Star*, 55.
63. Ibid., 138.
64. Ibid., 83.
65. See, e.g., "Peewee's Progress," 44.
66. See letters from children to Eleanor Roosevelt, beseeching her aid in their intention to become Hollywood stars, in Robert Cohen, ed., *Dear Mrs. Roosevelt: Letters from Children of the Great Depression* (Chapel Hill: University of North Carolina Press, 2002), 150, 184–87.
67. Constance J. Foster, "Mrs. Temple on Bringing up Shirley," *Parents Magazine*, October 1938, 23.
68. Zelizer, *Pricing the Priceless Child*, 97–112. Zelizer cites *Silver Screen*'s report in 1938 that Shirley Temple's allowance was $4.25 a week.
69. "Coogan a 'Bad Boy,' His Mother Testifies," *New York Times*, April 19 1938, 24.

70. Black, *Child Star*, 80–83.
71. Ibid., 485.
72. Ibid., 486.
73. Gus McCarthy, "Baby Take a Bow," *Motion Picture Herald*, June 16, 1934, 79.
74. Daniel Thomas Cook, *The Commodification of Childhood: The Children's Clothing Industry and the Rise of Consumer Culture* (Durham, NC: Duke University Press, 2004), 90–93.

SEVEN

Gimme Shelter:
Do-It-Yourself Defense and
the Politics of Fear

ELAINE TYLER MAY

We have nothing to fear but fear itself.

FRANKLIN DELANO ROOSEVELT, 1932

On the op-ed page of the *New York Times* of March 30, 2001, columnist
Thomas Friedman described a recent dinner table conversation he had
with his young daughters about the cold war: "I explained . . . that our
school had regular drills where we had to hide in the basement during
a simulated nuclear attack. Oh, my daughters said to me, we have those
kinds of drills, too. When I asked them to explain, it quickly became
apparent that the threat they were practicing for was not a nuclear attack,
and not just a bad storm, but an attack by an armed student or intruder
shooting up their public schools."[1] Friedman's comments suggest that at
the dawn of the twenty-first century, just months before September 11,
2001, fears of personal danger had shifted from distant external foes
with massive nuclear weapons to sinister internal enemies, in this case
young killers with guns hidden in school bags. How can we understand
this connection between the age of atomic attack drills and the era of
school shootings?

The obsession with security and the politics of fear so prevalent today
are part of the cultural inheritance of the early years of the cold war.
Although none of these trends emerged for the first time in the aftermath
of World War II, they gained a particular political edge and urgency in
the last half of the twentieth century. During the early years of the cold
war, Americans learned how to manage their fears. These fears came
from perceived new dangers: the atomic bomb, the power of the Soviet

Union, the potential spread of communism abroad, the rise of crime and juvenile delinquency at home. Although there was and remains considerable debate as to whether these were serious threats, there is no question that large numbers of Americans felt threatened and responded with an increasing concern for their safety and security. The cold war encouraged fearful citizens to protect themselves. Rather than calling for public solutions that would contribute to a safer world and minimize the dangers they faced, Americans turned to private security to insulate themselves from the public world they feared. Although the cold war ended nearly two decades ago, the preoccupation with privatized security lingers as cultural fallout across the national landscape.

Historians of the early cold war often see it as a self-contained era. My own earlier work is part of this scholarship.[2] But recent work has deepened our understanding of the cold war and its legacy. Much of this scholarship examines the unraveling of the widespread bipartisan support for cold war political and cultural norms in the 1960s, and the nation's subsequent turn to the right. A central theme in this literature is the reaction against changes in the urban landscape that began during World War II, especially the migration of large numbers of blacks into the cities and what many considered to be the excesses of liberal policies that extended the New Deal into the Great Society. Lisa McGirr points to conservative grassroots organizing and activism among southern California's middle-class suburbanites; Becky Nicolaides examines shifts in sentiment in working-class suburbs; Thomas Sugrue and Robert Self delve deeply into racial tensions that polarized postwar cities. Lizabeth Cohen points to increasing residential fragmentation and privatization in suburban areas, particularly the centrality of consumerism to citizens' political identities. Numerous scholars emphasize the social upheavals of the 1960s as a catalyst for a backlash against civil rights, feminism, and the counterculture. The Vietnam War looms large as a galvanizing event for both the left and the right. Andrew Bacevich sees the disaster of the war as the source of a new militarism in the nation that transcends political affiliation. Many of these scholars look to the late 1960s as a turning point, with conservatism capturing much of the mainstream during the following decade and flourishing in the Reagan era of the 1980s.[3]

At the heart of much of this scholarship is a recognition of a growing sense of fear and distrust that Americans felt toward outsiders and each other. Many scholars note this growing culture of fear but disagree on its sources and effects. Corey Robin and Joanna Bourke locate the roots of this fear deep in the Western political tradition, dating back centuries.

Michael Flamm considers the 1960s as a key moment in fear monger-ing, with politicians seizing on street crime and social unrest to fuel a national obsession with "law and order." Barry Glassner sees the culture of fear permeating everyday life in recent decades, fueled by a media that focuses excessive attention on the rarest but most terrifying crimes and dangers. Philip Jenkins sees an intense dread of domestic and interna-tional threats emerging in the late 1970s and early 1980s, pushing the nation to the right.[4]

This chapter builds on the insights of these scholars to examine how the culture of fear, the trend toward privatization, and the emphasis on consumerism came together in particular ways during the cold war era, leaving a legacy that continued beyond the cold war and into the post-9/11 national consciousness.

Do-It-Yourself Defense

In 1933, when Franklin D. Roosevelt told Americans that they had "noth-ing to fear but fear itself," he acknowledged the power of fear to affect the political landscape. Nearly a decade later, the Japanese attack on Pearl Harbor raised the level of fear and outrage to a fever pitch, launching a war-averse citizenry into near unanimous support for battle. Since that time, the fear factor in national politics has ebbed and flowed. The United States came out of World War II victorious, without the devastation on national soil and the civilian casualties that afflicted all other combatants in the war. Yet the coming of peace in the shadow of mushroom clouds over Japan gave victory an unsettling edge. The bombs that marked the end of World War II were also the opening shots of the cold war.[5] Fear was on the agenda of both major political parties as early as the presi-dential campaign of 1948. Republican candidate Thomas Dewey claimed that his party could best confront "a fearful world." Democratic incum-bent Harry S. Truman's view of the world was equally dire. In his inau-gural address in January 1949, he outlined the strategy of nuclear deter-rence based on mutually assured fear of overwhelming violence: "If we can make it sufficiently clear, in advance, that any armed attack affecting our national security would be met with overwhelming force, the armed attack might never occur."[6] But there were no guarantees that deterrence would work. Although national leaders claimed that the United States was a peaceful country, citizens knew that nuclear war could happen because it had already happened, and there was only one country that had waged it: the United States. If the ultimate good guys could drop the bombs, there was every reason to believe that the ultimate bad guys would do the same.

At the time, Communists were indeed perceived as the ultimate bad guys. Whether or not one believes that the nation was truly vulnerable to external or internal dangers half a century ago, people at the time surely did. There is no question that cold war anxieties seeped into the fabric of American life. Public opinion polls taken in the late 1940s illuminate the breadth and depth of anticommunist sentiment in the nation. The vast majority of those polled believed that members of the Communist Party in the United States were loyal to Russia, not to America, and that membership in the Communist Party should be forbidden by law. Nearly three-fourths of those polled believed that Communist Party members should not be allowed to teach in colleges and universities. Fully one out of three said that Communists should be killed or imprisoned. Only 16 percent believed they should be left alone. Americans expressed nearly as much hostility toward Communists in the United States after the war as they did toward Nazi leaders in Germany during the war. (One-third said Nazis should be executed, another third said they should be imprisoned, and 19 percent said they should be tried and punished.) In 1950, at the height of the anticommunist crusade in the United States, 90 percent of Americans polled believed that Communists should be removed from jobs in industries that would be important during wartime. When asked what should be done with Communist Party members in the event of a war with Russia, only 1 percent believed it was best to do "nothing, everyone [is] entitled to freedom of thought."[7] Although freedom of thought was one of the most cherished principles of the democracy that cold warriors were fighting to protect, most Americans in 1950 would deny this basic right to members of a small oppositional political party.

Fear of communism reached new heights in 1949 when the Soviet Union exploded its first atomic bomb. The Russians could ignite World War III, noted the young war hero and congressman John F. Kennedy, with an "atomic Pearl Harbor."[8] According to NSC-68, "the cold war is in fact a real war in which the survival of the free world is at stake."[9] Americans had to adjust to a time of not exactly peace but not quite war. In his first inaugural address in 1953, Eisenhower warned the nation that "forces of good and evil are massed and armed and opposed as rarely before in history." The struggle against the "divisive force [of] international communism" overshadowed the "preoccupations absorbing us at home . . . each of these domestic problems is dwarfed by, and often even created by, this question that involves all humankind. This trial comes at a moment when man's power to achieve good or to inflict evil surpasses the brightest hopes and the sharpest fears of all ages. . . . Freedom is pitted against slavery; lightness against the dark." Four years later the president's words were no less ominous: "We live in a land of plenty, but rarely has this earth known such peril as today."[10]

To combat this peril, Eisenhower relied on the nuclear arsenal. The "new look" he proposed for a more streamlined military would cut the defense budget by relying more heavily on nuclear arms and less on conventional land and naval forces. With nuclear weapons providing the main source of defense, any war that erupted would involve huge casualties. Relatively few soldiers would be exposed to danger, but millions of civilians would be vulnerable. Although deterrence was premised on the idea that massing nuclear weapons would prevent war, Eisenhower made it clear that he would not hesitate to use the bombs in battle. In a 1955 news conference he said that nuclear weapons might be used "just exactly as you would use a bullet or anything else" on "strictly military targets and for strictly military purposes." Critics like Senator Mike Mansfield warned that there was "very little assurance in the possibility of limiting an atomic war once it was started" and charged that Eisenhower's "dangerous new doctrine [of] 'limited' atomic war might lead to national suicide."[11]

Nuclear war was a real threat, and civilian defense was a serious concern. Public officials and political leaders debated the merits of various strategies to keep citizens safe, including publicly funded shelters and evacuation. Both strategies required advance notice and calm behavior, unlikely conditions in the event of a nuclear attack. Eventually, Congress defeated plans that called for significant public investment in civil defense. Administration officials and congressional leaders rejected the "communistic" idea of public shelters funded by Soviet-style big government programs.[12]

Instead of large publicly funded civil defense projects, official policy coalesced around a strategy of privatized protection. The government would provide the infrastructure, such as a national highway system that could move people quickly out of target areas. But homeowners would be responsible for sheltering their own families. They could construct and equip a shelter in the basement, or they could install one in the yard. They could even build "an all-concrete blast-resistant house," as advertised in the June 1955 issue of *Better Homes and Gardens*.[13] Civil defense planners had no advice for the one in four Americans who were poor in the mid-1950s or the one in three who were not homeowners, nor for the millions who were not living in single-family dwellings.[14] Atomic-age safety came in only one form: a nuclear family inhabiting a fortified suburban home.

Privacy by Design: The Fortified Family

Domestic security required adequate preparation of the house itself as well as the nuclear family within it. Few Americans in the early cold war era actually constructed fallout shelters, but the vast majority constructed nuclear families. With the marriage rate at an all-time high and the birthrate booming, families poured into expanding suburban developments across the country. These families symbolized the front lines in the ideological struggles of the cold war. Self-sufficient families would foster strong-minded citizens to soldier the task of keeping America free from communism.

Architects and designers advocated a new type of suburban housing to nurture these sturdy cold warriors. They believed that privacy was necessary to cultivate self-reliant citizens. In private spaces protected from public surveillance, citizens could develop the qualities of independence and autonomy necessary to resist un-American or collectivist ideas. One of the most outspoken advocates of this uniquely American style of privatized domestic space was Elizabeth Gordon, editor in chief of *House Beautiful* from 1941 to 1964. Gordon advocated a new style of American architecture that differed from the past as well as from contemporary European modernism. She was particularly hostile to the International style, typical of public buildings constructed after World War II, which used steel, glass, and modern design to signify breaks from tradition. The International style also emphasized openness—merging interior and exterior spaces. Some postwar housing, including multiunit structures as well as single-family homes, were built in the International style.

Gordon railed against the form:

> We don't believe the International Style is simply a matter of taste; any more than we believe that Nazism or Communism are matters of taste, matters of opinion. . . . Either we choose the architecture that will encourage the development of individualism or we choose the architecture and design of collectivism and totalitarian control. . . . The International Style . . . masses families together in one giant building so that relatively few, strategically placed, block leaders could check on all movements and conduct classes of ideological indoctrination . . . [it is] a design for living that we associate with totalitarianism.[15]

Gordon's hostility to the International style was widely shared by opponents of public housing. Realtors, many of whom were women in the years after World War II, campaigned vigorously against public housing.[16] City policymakers followed suit. In Los Angeles, for example, a 1952 ordinance, directed against "socialist projects," virtually outlawed public housing.[17] Unlike multiunit dwellings in the cities, American single-family homes in the suburbs exemplified the capitalist virtues of independence and self sufficiency. According to Gordon, privacy was the most important feature of American domestic architecture. Private homes should provide freedom from public surveillance in order to cultivate autonomy and independent thought. Interior spaces and gardens should require low maintenance and encourage leisure so that families could enjoy the fruits of capitalism at home. Ideally, families should never need to leave their property for fun and recreation, except to purchase the consumer goods to enjoy within it. The idea was to make the home "more exciting than anywhere else, canceling the need for seeking family pleasures in private clubs or public beaches."[18] Enjoyed within the home, leisure time would be wholesome and safe, removed from the corrupting influences of public life.

Privacy would allow the development of independence and autonomy essential for American national character.[19] Joseph Howland, the magazine's garden editor, agreed with Gordon:

> Good living is NOT public living. . . . We consider [privacy] one of the cherished American rights, one of the privileges we fought a war to preserve. Freedom to live our own lives, the way we want to live them without being spied on or snooped around, is as American as pancakes and molasses. . . . The very raison d'etre of the separate house is to get away from the living habits and cooking smells and inquisitive eyes of other people.[20]

According to *House Beautiful*, private leisure-oriented suburban homes would nurture the virtues of independence that defined American character. The magazine featured designs that offered privacy and a sheltered aesthetic, in contrast to the open and transparent look of the International style. To counter critics who saw her attack on modernism as old-fashioned, Gordon assured readers in 1946 that "*House Beautiful* . . . is as up-to-date as the atomic bomb, an achievement of which you may well be proud."[21]

Not only communist subversives, but the government itself, appeared to threaten American freedom. Several major companies, with a great deal to lose if the nation turned toward public ownership, published advertisements in mass circulation magazines warning of the dangers of governmental encroachment into personal life. These were the same corporate elites who railed against "creeping socialism" during the New Deal era; now the cold war gave their message an aura of patriotism. The symbols and images in these ads suggested that the government, like a dangerous intruder into the home, threatened families as well as freedom. The ads portrayed innocent children as particularly vulnerable. A 1950

You can get reprints of this advertisement, at no cost, by writing to this magazine.

Will you leave these to your children?

Men have died to leave you these 4 symbols of freedom:

A door key — your right to lock your door against illegal government force and prying.
(Fourth Amendment, U. S. Constitution)

A Holy Bible — symbol of your right to worship as you wish.
(First Amendment, U. S. Constitution)

A pencil — freedom to speak or write what you think, whether you agree with the government or not.
(First Amendment, U. S. Constitution)

And a free ballot — your right to choose the kind of government you want — your protection against government tyranny.
(Article I, U. S. Constitution)

These symbols have no meaning in countries where government controls everything—for there the individual man or woman has no freedoms.

"MEET CORLISS ARCHER" for delightful comedy. CBS—Sundays—9 P. M., Eastern Time.

But there are people who are trying to give the U. S. government more and more control over American life. "Let the government start," they say, "by taking over certain industries and services — the doctors, the railroads, the electric light and power companies."

Most of these people — like most Americans — *don't* want a socialistic U. S. A. They have other reasons for government control. But when government, moving step by step, controls *enough* things, you have a socialist government, whether you want it or not. *You'll* be controlled, too. Then what freedoms will you be able to pass on to your children?

* * *

We, the *business*-managed electric companies which publish this advertisement, are battling this move toward a socialistic government. We want to remind everyone how seriously it threatens *every* business — and *everybody's freedom*.

America's business-managed, tax-paying

ELECTRIC LIGHT AND POWER COMPANIES*

*Names on request from this magazine

Fig. 7.1. A 1950 public service announcement from the Electric Light and Power Companies warned of increasing government control. *U.S. News and World Report*, May 12, 1950, 25.

public service announcement from the Electric Light and Power Companies warned of increasing government control and assured readers that they were "battling this move toward a socialistic government." The ad pictured a small boy in front of a table holding four symbols of freedom: a key, a Bible, a pencil, and a ballot (fig. 7.1). The key symbolized "your right to lock your door against illegal government force and prying."[22] In 1953 an ad for Norfolk and Western Railway pictured a frightened boy at home at night in a dark hallway, with the caption: "You needn't be ashamed of being afraid in the dark, son." But it wasn't intruders who threatened. "The darkness is a hiding place for confusion, greed, conspiracy, treachery, socialism . . . and its uglier brother, communism. . . . In the U.S.A. you are free to become vigilant to see what's going on, informed to understand it, and vocal to express your opinion about it. . . . If you ignore this responsibility . . . what you lose in the dark may be your freedom."[23]

The Colors of Danger: Red and Black

By the 1960s, dangers seemed to threaten closer to home, and the family appeared unable to provide protection. The demographic indicators were dramatic. In the early 1960s, the baby boom came to an abrupt end. Men and women married later, or not at all. Most disturbing was the divorce rate, which, after leveling off for nearly two decades, suddenly skyrocketed. Women in increasing numbers abandoned the role of full-time wife and mother to enter the paid labor force. The characteristics of the family that had promised to contain the dangers of the age were dwindling, just when those familial attributes seemed essential for warding off social disorder. To make matters worse, internal dangers appeared to be proliferating as quickly as nuclear bombs.

Politicians, observers, and a wide range of experts made a causal connection, claiming that the decline of the nuclear family led to social chaos. Fear of communists and protesters, hippies and feminists, atomic bombs and muggers, "creeping socialism" and government intrusion coalesced in an exaggerated sense of personal and national peril. In the early 1960s, crime rates began to rise, and soon crime took center stage in the lexicon of dangers. Violent offenses, property crimes, and murder had all declined after World War II and remained low through the 1950s. But all kinds of crime increased in the 1960s and continued to rise into the 1980s, until dropping dramatically in the 1990s. Some observers blamed rising crime rates on the decline of the nuclear family and the emerging counterculture. Others pointed to deindustrialization, unemployment, and overzealous arrests of curfew violators in minority neighborhoods.[24] Whatever the cause, it is not surprising that rising crime rates created public concern. But the media fed a frenzy of fear. The popular press suggested that crime was much more prevalent than it actually was. Pundits and law enforcement officials focused on individual self-protection rather than on alleviating the social problems that led to crime.

Politicians were not far behind the press in capitalizing on the fear of crime. National political campaigns suddenly took up the issue. It had not always been there. From 1948 until 1964, there was no mention of street crime in any presidential candidate's acceptance speech, or in any inaugural address.[25] In 1964, law and order leaped into the center of political debates and stayed there for the rest of the century. Political protests, crime, violence, drugs, and the breakdown of the nuclear family merged with communism and nuclear nightmares as the flash points of political rhetoric.

Television campaign advertisements provide some of the clearest articulations of this transformation. In 1964, Democratic incumbent Lyndon Johnson used fear to attack his Republican opponent, Barry Goldwater, by suggesting that Goldwater would unleash nuclear war. In a famous television advertisement for Johnson, a little girl counts as she pulls daisy petals in a field of flowers. As a freeze frame captures her innocent face, a man's voice-over begins a countdown, followed by sounds of a blast and horrific scenes of a nuclear bomb exploding. Johnson speaks in an ominous voice-over: "These are the stakes: to make a world in which all of God's children can live, or go into the darkness. We must either love each other, or we must die." Goldwater responded with his own fear mongering, not about atomic war but about crime. Above scenes of crime, rioting youths, and ominous music are large bold words suggesting that Johnson was "soft" on the dangers facing the nation: "Graft! Swindle! Juvenile Delinquency! Crime! Riots! Hear what Barry Goldwater has to say about our lack of moral leadership."[26]

Although Johnson easily won the election, Goldwater set the tone for later campaigns. In 1968, both Republican Richard Nixon and American Reform Party candidate George Wallace focused on law and order. Nixon had a well-earned reputation as a fierce anticommunist; in 1968 he turned his attention to street violence. Nixon ran a television ad filled with scenes of raging urban riots, fire, and bloody violence, all presumably caused by angry political protestors. Over the scenes of chaos, Nixon says, "It is time for an honest look at the problem of order in the United States. Dissent is a necessary ingredient of change, but in a system of government that provides for peaceful change, there is no cause that justifies resort to violence. Let us recognize that the first right of every American is to be free from domestic violence. So I pledge to you, we shall have order in the United States." George Wallace also appealed to fear of crime and violence, especially the vulnerability of women on city streets. Echoing the emerging media onslaught warning of the alleged dangers women faced in public places, Wallace evoked scenes of urban terror. In one ad, viewers see images of a woman walking at night—with only her legs and high heels visible below the hem of her skirt. Suddenly the scene cuts to a streetlight shattering, and the announcer says, "Why are more and more millions of Americans turning to Governor Wallace? Take a walk in your street or park tonight." Wallace then states, "As president, I shall help make it possible for you and your families to walk the streets of our cities in safety."

Democratic candidate Hubert Humphrey was the only candidate to address crime as a social problem. In one ad Humphrey faces a huge audience and says, "When a man says that he thinks the most important thing is to double the rate of convictions, but he doesn't believe and condemns [me] for wanting to double the war on poverty, I think that man has lost his sense of values. You're not going to make this a better America just because you build more jails. What this country needs are more decent neighborhoods, more educated people, better homes. . . . I do not believe that repression alone builds a better society."

Humphrey in 1968 was the last candidate of either party to articulate an approach to crime that addressed its underlying causes. Although Nixon beat Humphrey by a narrow margin, the combined "law and order" votes of Nixon and Wallace came to 57 percent. The election results taught the Democrats a lesson. Four years later, Democratic candidate George McGovern embraced law and order and anticipated the War on Drugs later initiated by Republicans: "If you want to end crime in this country, it's going to take more than speeches. You're never going to get on top of crime in the United States until you get on top of drugs, because half of all the crime in this country is caused by the drug addict. They'll kill, they'll steal, they'll do anything to get that money to sustain that drug habit." From that time on, both parties embraced law and order and promised to be tough on criminals.

Politicians were not the first to fan the fears of crime. According to Michael Flamm, the cold war provided the context for the anticrime rhetoric that permeated public discourse. Flamm noted that "law and order" became "a mutation of anti-communism."[27] Throughout the 1960s, crime was consistently associated with racial minorities and linked to the communist threat. A writer for the *San Diego Union* noted, "Just as at another period, the Communist Party of the United States devoted itself to infiltrating the Negro population, so, for 1960, the program is youth. The Communist Party, which went underground during the early years of the cold war and peaceful competitive coexistence, is now coming out into the open again."[28] In Los Angeles, the fiercely anticommunist chief of police consistently pointed to black neighborhoods as the major sources of crime in the city and claimed that blacks were much more likely that whites to commit crimes. Along with dangerous blacks were the Mexican Americans in the barrios, who he described as "only one step removed from 'the wild tribes of Mexico.'"[29] Political protests fell into the same category as crime and urban riots, evoking atomic-age dangers. In 1961 the police chief warned that the "eruption of violence and disorder directed at society's symbols of authority could be more devastating to America's hopes for the future than rockets and the 100-megaton bomb."[30]

This racialized fear tactic reached new lows in 1988 with the infamous Willie Horton ad by Republican candidate George Bush, which featured a black man on parole who raped and murdered. The Democratic candidate, Michael Dukakis, responded not with a condemnation of the racially infused fear mongering but with a "Willie Horton" ad of his own, featuring a presumably Latino parolee from a federal prison who raped and murdered a woman during Bush's years at the helm of the CIA.

In 1996, bringing atomic-age fears full circle, a television ad for Republican presidential candidate Bob Dole began with the same footage of the little girl with a daisy, taken from the 1964 ad for Johnson. A voice-over intones, "Thirty years ago, the biggest threat to her was nuclear war. Today the threat is drugs." The scene then shifts from the little girl with the daisy to a huge newspaper headline, "TEEN DRUG CRISIS ," followed by scenes of young teenagers on streets and in city parks smoking and injecting various drugs, presumably crack cocaine and heroin. After the uproar sparked by the Willie Horton ad, the teens in this ad were white, even though the War on Drugs targeted mostly minority youth. The announcer continues, "Teenage drug use has doubled in the last four years. What's been done? Clinton cut the office of National Drug Control Policy by 83 percent. And his own Surgeon General even considered legalizing drugs. Bill Clinton said he'd lead the war on drugs and change America. All he did was change his mind. America deserves better." The ad ends not with nuclear bombs exploding but with a drug-using child swirling around to face the camera. A freeze-frame captures the child's anxious face.[31]

From Superbombs to Superpredators:
Women as Victims, Children as Enemies

Politicians were not alone in the campaign to ramp up fear of crime. By the 1960s, Americans were ripe for an escalation of fear. *U.S. News and World Report*, along with *Good Housekeeping* and other popular periodicals, joined a national chorus whipping up fears of crime. Many of these articles were directed toward women. The early sixties brought women's discontent into the open, with Betty Friedan's *The Feminine Mystique*, the publication of the President's Report on the Status of Women chaired by Eleanor Roosevelt, the founding of the National Organization for Women (NOW), and a stirring of women at the grassroots level as the feminist movement began to build momentum. Just when women were beginning to question their relegation to the private realm and increasingly going public, the media was suddenly choked with articles warning them that public space was dangerous. "First Scream, Then Scram," announced *U.S. News and World Report* in 1963, with a stark bold headline advising women how to respond to attacks in big cities, where "muggings, rapes and assaults have become common." The *Washington Post* warned women not to "walk around alone at night," to keep all doors and windows locked, and to install burglar alarms. Within a decade, the popular press saturated readers with the message that attacks on city streets were practically inevitable and that women were especially vulnerable. In 1972, for example, *Good Housekeeping* warned, "Women, either on the street or in their cars, are often subject to criminal attacks." The article offered twenty-one tips for women on how to protect themselves, including "Dress with discretion so as not to stimulate interest," and "*Always* check the back of the car for intruders." None of these warnings pointed out that women were much safer, statistically, out on the city streets in the middle of the night than in their own homes, where most violence against women occurred.[32]

Although crime was rising, attacks on women were neither "common," as *U.S. News and World Report* claimed, nor "often," as *Good Housekeeping* asserted. The rate of all violent crimes in 1965 was one-fifth of 1 percent. That meant that 1 in 500 Americans was a victim of violent crime during that year. The most likely victims, then as now, were men of color. The least likely victims were white women, and they were more likely to be harmed by family members in their homes than by strangers out in public. Nevertheless, the media focused on women as particularly vulnerable on city streets. As Susan Douglas notes, by the mid-1970s, when the backlash against feminism was already in full force, popular television shows depicted women in the public arena as particularly vulnerable to rape and other forms of violence, and needing men to protect and rescue them.[33] Not surprisingly, public opinion polls showed that women were most likely to fear becoming a victim of crime, even though they were least likely to actually be victimized.[34] Feminists responded to this growing fear by encouraging women to fend for themselves. No wonder martial arts classes, self-defense training, and target practice became popular among women as strategies of do-it-yourself defense.[35]

Fear of crime began to increase dramatically and became a problem in itself. As early as 1970, *Time* magazine noted the distinction: "Crime and fear of crime are ever-growing realities of the city streets."[36] In 1974, criminologist James Brooks noted that "the fear of crime in the United States is a fundamental social problem which has not yet received attention in proportion to its severity and which may well prove to be more difficult to treat than criminality itself."[37] By 2001, after a decade of plummeting crime rates, a study by three criminologists concluded that "fear of crime remains at record highs, and falling crime averages alone are unlikely to lower fear levels. These analyses indicate that fear of crime continues to be a paradox, with people exhibiting great fear of statistically rare events (e.g., being caught in gang crossfire) and much less fear of much more likely events (e.g. being killed by an abusive partner)."[38]

These fears began to change the meaning and representation of home security, especially in women's magazines. In 1964, when the crime rate had barely begun to rise, *House Beautiful* turned from privacy to security with a full-page illustration of a fortified house, with cannons, boarded-up doors and windows, alarms, guard dogs, locks, loud speakers, and a large sign announcing "Burglars Go Home."[39] *Ladies' Home Journal* followed suit in 1968 with an article featuring several gadgets that could be purchased to make the home more secure against intruders.[40] Companies that stood to profit from fear of crime did their best to whip up terror. In 1970, for example, General Telephone and Electronics took out a full two-page ad in *Time* magazine to promote their new intercom system. The device allowed residents to monitor visitors by connecting with them by an outside phone before answering the door. Such a device might be convenient for a number of reasons, security among them. But the advertisement focused on the fear factor. One side of the ad was a full-page photo of a man wearing a trench coat, face obscured by a hat. The facing page said in large bold letters, "Who's downstairs ringing your bell? A friend? Or the Boston Strangler?"[41]

"IF YOU CAN'T LICK 'EM, JOIN 'EM."

Fig. 7.2. In this 1970 cartoon from *Time* magazine, government intrusion is equated with criminal burglary. "A Response to Fear," *Time*, August 3, 1970, 10. A 1970 Herblock cartoon, copyright by The Herb Block Foundation.

Criminals were not the only potentially dangerous intruders. The government remained a prime suspect. *Time* magazine in 1970 carried a political cartoon depicting a house, labeled "individual security," with four gleeful men breaking the windows. Two were depicted as burglars, labeled "crime increase." The other two were portrayed as law enforcement officers, labeled "administration" and "no-knock, wiretapping, and preventive detention." The caption read, "If you can't lick `em, join `em" (fig. 7.2). In this case, the critics of the government were not conservative business elites railing against creeping socialism but liberals concerned about the erosion of civil liberties resulting from a controversial crime bill. Critics from all points along the political spectrum saw the government as dangerous—in this case, no different than thugs and burglars.[42] By the time the Watergate scandal unfolded in the mid-1970s, government officials had indeed become thugs and burglars. Trust in government dropped from 75 percent in 1963 to 25 percent in 1979.[43]

With fear of crime rising, and faith in public officials waning, do-it-yourself defense became increasingly draconian. In the emerging culture of domestic deterrence, the arms race shifted from missiles to pistols. Along with an increasingly armed citizenry came a growing acceptance of vigilantism. This tendency peaked in December 1984 when Bernhard Goetz, a white subway passenger, shot four black youths when they tried to rob him. Goetz quickly became something of a folk hero—the embodiment of do-it-yourself defense. According to a *Newsweek* poll taken in March 1985, 57 percent of respondents approved of Goetz shooting the youths, 70 percent said they believed race had nothing to do with it, 70 percent said vigilantism is sometimes justified, and 78 percent said they would use deadly force in self-defense. Half said they had little or no confidence in the police's ability to protect them against violent crime.[44] *U.S. News and World Report* was quick to comment with a telling image: a political cartoon depicting the inside of a subway car. All the passengers, including elderly women, are armed to the teeth with rifles, pistols, and ammunition belts. One of the passengers is reading a newspaper with a bold headline: "MUGGINGS DOWN" (fig. 7.3).[45]

In the 1990s, fear of crime increased even when crime itself declined. The expansion of gun clubs among women as well as men, and the pro-

Fig. 7.3. In 1985, *U.S. News and World Report* offers this editorial cartoon in support of citizens arming themselves. "Behind Tough Public Stance on Criminals," *U.S. News and World Report*, January 21, 1985, 60.

liferation of "conceal and carry" laws, reflected growing concerns that—just as they had to protect themselves in the face of the atomic threat—individuals had to take matters of safety literally into their own hands. Children—once portrayed as innocent and needing protection—had now become part of the problem, the new internal danger. Although the crime rate was declining, especially crimes committed by youths, the public had a vastly exaggerated sense of the danger. In 1994, official crime statistics showed that juveniles committed only about 13 percent of all violent crimes. But according to public opinion polls at the time, Americans believed that juveniles committed 43 percent of violent crimes—three times the actual proportion. Most of those polled wanted harsher punishment for young offenders.[46] No longer afraid *for* our children, we were now becoming afraid *of* our children.

In the post–cold war political climate, the new enemies were not foreign powers with nuclear bombs, nor communist subversives in our midst, but the nation's children. Experts warned not about "superbombs" but about "superpredators." In 1996, Princeton political scientist John DiIulio noted that by 2005 the number of fourteen- to seventeen-year-old males would increase by 23 percent and predicted that the crime rate would rise faster among black children than among white. Assuming that black male children would necessarily become violent teenage criminals, he coined the term "superpredator" and called the trend a "ticking time bomb" that would unleash "a storm of predatory criminality" on the nation.[47] Claiming that "superpredators" were "fatherless, godless and without conscience," he wrote in the *National Review:* "All that's left of the black community in some pockets of urban America is deviant, delinquent and criminal adults surrounded by severely abused and neglected children, virtually all of whom were born out of wedlock."[48] Critics who called DiIulio's warnings alarmist, racist, and inaccurate were correct. The crime wave he warned about never happened. Crime declined dramatically in the 1990s, and violent crime by juveniles dropped to its lowest point in twenty-five years. But the fallout from his false predictions fanned fears of allegedly dangerous black children. Michael Petit, deputy director of the Child Welfare League of America, using language more appropriate for describing bombs than children, said that "superpredators" are "literally being manufactured, programmed, hardwired to behave in a certain way." An editorial in the *Omaha World Herald* described these children as "killing machines."[49] Dire predictions about young black superpredators saturated the media during the very years that the crime rate dropped. Unfounded fears of rising crime, at a time when crime was declining and the nation was actually safer, may well have contributed to the building of more jails, draconian sentencing guidelines for young offenders, and the underfunding of public schools.

Locked Up: The Common Fate of Criminals and Suburbanites

By the late twentieth century, civic political will seemed to have shrunk to little more than do-it-yourself defense. Fear of crime had far outstripped actual crime rates, and public policies followed fear rather than fact. In the 1990s, as the crime rate dropped, the prison population soared— with a disproportionately high number of African American inmates.[50] At the same time, increasing numbers of nonincarcerated Americans locked themselves up in fortified homes with elaborate security systems, guarded by private security companies, or secluded themselves in gated communities. Rather than solve social problems, Americans increasingly retreated from them, walling themselves away from the public world.

Nowhere is the bunker mentality more obvious than in the rapid proliferation of gated communities across the nation's residential landscape. Gated communities have existed since the nineteenth century, but they were rare and reserved for the rich. In the 1960s the numbers of gated communities began to grow, increasing in the 1970s and skyrocketing since the 1980s. By the turn of the twenty-first century, in the West, the South, and the Southeast, more than 40 percent of new residential developments were gated. In southern California today, the majority of new housing units are in gated communities. Studies of gated communities and interviews with residents indicate that people move into gated developments for safety and also for status. Gates confer status because they symbolize exclusivity and offer a measure of conspicuous security. But perhaps the most significant feature of these communities is their self-contained, privatized government.[51]

Gated communities are private cities within public cities, where residents often own their own streets, pay for their own services and utilities, and provide their own security guards. Homeowners pay significant fees for their infrastructure and security, which are independent of public funding and oversight. Some gated communities have actually incorporated as cities to enable homeowner associations to function as city councils and levy taxes. Some have built their own schools. Not surprisingly, residents of these communities, who pay for their own infrastructure, resent paying taxes for the same services that are provided to the public. These fully privatized enclaves, cut off from the outside world, encourage residents to distrust and resent outsiders and support policies that favor low taxes and promote private enterprise at the expense of the public good.[52]

In many gated communities, however, freedom and security remain elusive. Homeowner associations develop policies that restrict residents' freedom to construct and decorate their homes as they wish, and enforce rigid behavioral codes as well. Even the most exclusive of these communities, home to some of the nation's wealthiest citizens, constrain residents' freedom to live as they please. In Beverly Park, for example, a gated community above Beverly Hills where 35,000-square-foot mansions sell for $30 million, a powerful homeowners' association tells residents what they can and cannot do. According to the *New York Times*, "The culture of Beverly Park is secretive, even paranoid, and a couple of residents who gave interviews urged caution and begged anonymity, so as not to arouse the wrath of the homeowners' association." One neighbor has already sued another for violating the rules imposed by the homeowners' association—in this case over a sculpture that some residents found offensive. The homeowners with the offending art discovered that barriers against the outside world could not protect them from vandalism. Given Beverly Park's security, they wondered, "who could have done such a thing?"[53]

Whether inhabited by the wealthy or those of modest means, gated communities sometimes actually heighten feelings of vulnerability. Residents often complain that security is lax and outsiders easily enter. An illusion of safety makes the wide streets more dangerous, because cars speed and children play without the wariness they gain when living on public streets. In some cases, privatization actually makes these neighborhoods less safe. Police and fire emergency vehicles have trouble entering these communities because access is restricted. Researchers report that children become fearful of strangers, especially strangers who look different from themselves. Service workers, often nonwhite, appear suspicious and alien in the homogeneous neighborhoods. Although there are gated residences in all areas, including inner cities, where crime tends to be higher and security important, the fastest growing gated communities are in remote areas, such as the outskirts of Las Vegas, where crime rates are very low.[54]

According to Edward J. Blakely and Mary Gail Snyder, who studied gated communities, "As families increasingly seek walled security communities as a refuge, they bring in their own teenagers who become a source, both directly and indirectly, of the problems they fled. The problems we face as Americans cannot be legislated, walled, or willed away.

If we are to be the democracy we set out to be, we have to do more to reach one another, not through walls or gates but across the street we live on." The real question, they ask, is why so many people feel they need to live behind gates and walls. "What is the measure of nationhood when the divisions between neighborhoods require guards and fences to keep out other citizens? When public services and even local government are privatized, when the community of responsibility stops at the subdivision gates, what happens to the function and the very idea of a social and political democracy?"[55]

Perhaps the perfect symbol of the trend toward disregard of the common good in favor of privatized protection is the sport utility vehicle (SUV). Although sales of SUVs have declined in recent years due to rising gas prices, for years they were among the most popular vehicles on the roads. In spite of the fact that SUVs endangered the environment, other drivers, and even their occupants, owners took comfort in the fact that the vehicles' bulk, weight and design rendered them dangerous to other motorists. Families often purchased SUVs believing that the women and teenagers driving them would survive an accident, even if the occupants of the other car would not.[56] Like residents of gated communities, SUV owners sought to insulate themselves by purchasing private forms of security—even if the dangers as well as the promise of security were largely illusory.

September 11, 2001: Echoes of the Cold War

The terrorist attacks of 9/11 shocked the nation into a new level of fear as nothing had since Pearl Harbor. As in December of 1941, the nation went to war. But rather than World War II providing precedents for a national response, it was the cold war that echoed most loudly across the post-9/11 landscape. Following atomic-age emergency procedures, the president remained mostly airborne and flitted from one small city to another, drawing widespread criticism for his apparent flight in the face of danger. The defense establishment retreated to "secured bunkers deep inside the earth," into fallout shelters constructed during the early years of the cold war.[57]

The villains seemed to personify the characteristics of the communist threat: foreigners who infiltrated the nation, studied our technology, and used our own power against us. They blended into society, plotting against us while enjoying the good life they professed to disdain. They turned our own proud monuments of postwar technological and consumer triumph, commercial airliners and towering skyscrapers, into the means of our destruction. The Bush administration responded in cold war fashion: increasing the defense budget by $48 billion (a sum larger than the entire defense budget of any other nation), and developing new nuclear weapons, according to a secret Pentagon report. The president also insisted upon continued funding for the Star Wars missile shield, which would be useless as a defense against terrorist attacks.[58]

In spite of government assurances that the War on Terror would keep Americans safe, do-it-yourself defense became the order of the day. No longer encouraging citizens to build shelters in their homes, the nation's leaders nevertheless recommended duct tape and plastic sheeting to keep families safe from weapons of mass destruction. Air-raid sirens did not sound, but red, yellow, and orange alerts kept the fear factor high. The Office of Homeland Security urged Americans to become "citizen-sentinels" and create a "national neighborhood watch" to become vigilant in spotting terrorist threats.[59] In July 2002, the Bush administration called for the establishment of the TIPS program, which would recruit volunteers among delivery people, utility workers, and others whose jobs brought them into people's homes to snoop on their fellow citizens.

Gun ownership reached new heights. In the first six months after September 11, the FBI conducted 455,000 more background checks for gun purchases than during the same period the previous year. The FBI also handled 130,000 more applications to carry concealed weapons. New groups became pistol packers. For the first time, the Second Amendment Sisters, a national women's pro-gun group, formed a chapter on a college campus. About fifty women at Mount Holyoke College joined the new chapter. One member boasted, "One of my guy friends said, 'you're a chick with a gun—I'm scared.'" Women's gun organizations proliferated, such as Mother's Arms and Armed Females of America.[60]

Consumerism once again became a patriotic duty. Unlike World War II, when the nation's leaders asked the people to make sacrifices to aid the common defense, after 9/11 President Bush called on Americans to do just the opposite: "Fly and enjoy America's great destination spots. . . . Get down to Disney World in Florida. Take your families and enjoy life the way we want it to be enjoyed."[61] Bush seemed to take a cue from Richard Nixon at the 1959 Kitchen Debate in Moscow, when he proclaimed that consumerism was the real stealth weapon that would trump the Soviets and win the cold war.[62]

Conclusion

The domestic culture that took root during the early cold war era taught Americans to rely on themselves—not their government—for safety, and to use the tools of capitalism for protection in a dangerous world. The front line against danger was the nuclear family, which held demographic dominance for two decades following World War II. But that short-lived family structure declined rapidly in the late 1960s, in the midst of social upheavals that gave rise to new anxieties. These developments fueled a politics of fear that led to an increasing national obsession with personal security. The politics of law and order fanned the fires of fear, heightened racial tensions, and pushed the nation to the right. In the process, citizenship shrank to little more than muscular patriotism, whereas concern for the common good withered away.

No longer protected by internally fortified families, Americans began to fortify their bodies, their houses, and their neighborhoods. They came to distrust and fear not only the nation's foes but also each other, and in response they retreated from any sense of the common good and locked themselves inside private spaces: suburban fortresses, gated communities, SUVs. Rather than trying to solve social problems by coming together, Americans sought protection from those problems by isolating themselves. As in the early atomic age, the illusion of security, if not security itself, could be found in the shelter of the home. At the dawn of the twenty-first century, remnants of the domestic cold war persist, especially the celebration of free market capitalism, private consumerism at the expense of the public good, and a muscular patriotism grounded in martial citizenship. These traits were quickly mobilized in the wake of September 11, 2001, and have fueled a quasi–cold war revival ever since.[63]

NOTES

1. Thomas L. Friedman, "Foreign Affairs; Code Red," *New York Times*, March 30, 2001, A23.
2. See Elaine Tyler May, *Homeward Bound: American Families in the Cold War Era* (1988; rev. ed., New York: Basic Books, 1999).
3. Lisa McGirr, *Suburban Warriors: The Origins of the New American Right* (Princeton: Princeton University Press, 2001); Becky M. Nicolaides, *My Blue Heaven: Life and Politics in the Working-Class Suburbs of Los Angeles, 1920–1965* (Chicago: University of Chicago Press, 2002); Thomas J. Sugrue, *The Origins of the Urban Crisis* (Princeton: Princeton University Press, 1996); Robert O. Self, *American Babylon: Race and the Struggle for Postwar Oakland* (Princeton: Princeton University Press,

2003); Lizabeth Cohen, *A Consumers' Republic: The Politics of Mass Consumption in Postwar America* (New York: Knopf, 2003); Andrew Bacevich, *The New American Militarism: How Americans Are Seduced by War* (New York: Oxford University Press, 2005).

4. Corey Robin, *Fear: The History of a Political Idea* (New York: Oxford University Press, 2004); Joanna Bourke, *Fear: A Cultural History* (London: Virago, 2005); Michael W. Flamm, *Law and Order: Street Crime, Civil Unrest, and the Crisis of Liberalism in the 1960s* (New York: Columbia University Press, 2005); Barry Glassner, *The Culture of Fear: Why Americans Are Afraid of the Wrong Things* (New York: Basic Books, 1999); Philip Jenkins, *Decade of Nightmares: The End of the Sixties and the Making of Eighties America* (New York: Oxford University Press, 2006).

5. See Martin J. Sherwin, *A World Destroyed: Hiroshima and Its Legacies*, 3rd ed. (Stanford, CA: Stanford University Press, 2003).

6. Thomas Dewey, acceptance speech, June 24, 1948, in *Campaign Speeches of American Presidential Candidates, 1948–1984*, ed. Gregory Bush (New York: Frederick Ungar Publishing, 1985), 14; Harry Truman, Inaugural Address, January 20, 1949, in *The Presidents Speak*, ed. Davis Newton Lott (New York: Henry Holt, 1994), 294.

7. George H. Gallup, *The Gallup Poll: Public Opinion, 1935–1971*, vols. 1 and 2 (New York: Random House, 1972), 339, 501, 639–40, 853, 869, 873, 916, 929, 933–34, 950, 1213–14, 1434.

8. Laura McEnaney, *Civil Defense Begins at Home: Militarization Meets Everyday Life in the Fifties* (Princeton: Princeton University Press, 2000), 14.

9. "United States Objectives and Programs for National Security" (NSC-68), April 14, 1950, as quoted ibid., 29.

10. Dwight D. Eisenhower, First Inaugural Address, January 20, 1953, in Lott, *Presidents Speak*, 301–7.

11. Eisenhower, as quoted in Lawrence Freedman, *The Evolution of Nuclear Strategy*, 3rd ed. (New York: Macmillan, 2003); "Mansfield Sees Danger in 'Limited Atomic War'—Doctrine Expounded by Dulles Might Lead to National Suicide, Democrat Says," *Los Angeles Times*, April 18, 1955, 25.

12. McEnaney, *Civil Defense Begins at Home*, 7.

13. Advertisement, Portland Cement Association, *Better Homes and Gardens*, June 1955, 3.

14. Stephanie Coontz, *The Way We Never Were: American Families and the Nostalgia Trap* (New York: Basic Books, 1992), 160–62.

15. Elizabeth Gordon, "The Responsibility of an Editor," manuscript for speech delivered to the Press Club Luncheon at the American Furniture Mart, Chicago, June 22, 1953, 14, 15, 21, as quoted in Dianne Harris, "Making Your Private World: Modern Landscape Architecture and *House Beautiful*, 1945–1965, in *The Architecture of Landscape, 1940–1960*, ed. Marc Treib (Philadelphia: University of Pennsylvania Press, 2002), 182.

16. See Jeffrey M. Hornstein, *A Nation of Realtors: A Cultural History of the Twentieth-Century American Middle Class* (Durham, NC: Duke University Press, 2005), esp. chaps. 6 and 7.

17. Mike Davis, *City of Quartz: Excavating the Future in Los Angeles* (New York: Verso, 1990), 63.

18. "Mark of a MODERN House—The Paved Terrace," *House Beautiful*, November 1952, 219, as quoted in Harris, "Making Your Private World," 197.

19. Harris, "Making Your Private World," 193.
20. Joseph Howland, "Good Living Is NOT Public Living," January 1950, as quoted in Harris, "Making Your Private World," 193.
21. "How We Did It in the Old Days," *House Beautiful*, December 1946, 250, as quoted in Harris, "Making Your Private World," 190.
22. Advertisement, Electric Light and Power Companies, *U.S. News and World Report*, May 12, 1950, 25.
23. Advertisement, Norfolk and Western Railway, *Newsweek*, September 7, 1953, 13.
24. Davis, *City of Quartz*, 277.
25. The only mention of crime in any of these speeches referred to organized crime and political corruption. See Bush, *Campaign Speeches of American Presidential Candidates;* and Lott, *Presidents Speak.*
26. All quotes and descriptions of television ads in this and the following paragraphs are from the Web site http://www.livingroomcandidate.org (accessed May 8, 2006), which includes the ads themselves and the voting outcomes of each election.
27. Flamm, *Law and Order*, 6.
28. As quoted in Mike Davis, *Dead Cities and Other Tales* (New York: New Press, 2002), 212.
29. As quoted in Davis, *City of Quartz*, 295.
30. *Los Angeles Examiner*, October 15, 1961, as quoted in Davis, *Dead Cities*, 213.
31. All quotes and descriptions of television ads are from the Web site http://www.livingroomcandidate.org.
32. "First Scream, Then Scram," *U.S. News and World Report*, April 1, 1963, which included excerpts from the *Washington Post*, March 17, 1963; "Street-Safety Precautions Every Woman Should Follow," *Good Housekeeping*, October 1972, 193.
33. Susan Douglas, *Where the Girls Are* (New York: Times Books, 1995), 209–11.
34. Data from on-line opinion poll, "Self Defense, Personal Safety—Public Opinion Polls," Lexis Nexis, Roper Center, University of Connecticut Public Opinion Online. For example, polls taken in 1981, 1990, 1995, and 1998 indicate that women are more fearful than men. On crime statistics, see Eric H. Monkkonen, *Murder in New York City* (Berkeley: University of California Press, 2001), esp. chap. 3, which discusses the fact that most violent offenders as well as victims are men; and chap. 6, which discusses the fact that black men are disproportionately victims of violent crime.
35. See, for example, Tia Gindick, "Self-Defense in Vogue: The Wealthy Prepare for Battle," *Los Angeles Times*, March 26, 1981.
36. "A Response to Fear," *Time*, August 3, 1970, 10.
37. James Brooks, "The Fear of Crime in the United States," *Crime and Delinquency* 20, no. 3 (1974): 241–44 (quotation from abstract).
38. Linda Heath, Jack Kavanagh, and Rae S. Thompson, "Perceived Vulnerability and Fear of Crime: Why Fear Stays High When Crime Rates Drop," *Journal of Offender Rehabilitation* 33, no 2 (2001): 1–14.
39. Full-page illustration, *House Beautiful*, July 1964, 100.
40. "Making Your Home Safe against Intruders," *Ladies' Home Journal*, no. 7 (1968): 66.
41. Advertisement, General Telephone and Electronics, *Time*, July 13, 1970, 60–61.
42. "Response to Fear," 10.
43. Kevin Diaz, "Cynicism Is Out, Trust in Government Is In," *Minneapolis Star Tribune*, October 23, 2001, A11.

44. David M. Alpern, "A Newsweek Poll: 'Deadly Force,'" *Newsweek*, March 11, 1985, 53.

45. "Behind Tough Public Stance on Criminals," *U.S. News and World Report*, January 21, 1985, 60.

46. *Gallop Poll Monthly*, September 1994, no. 348.

47. John DiIulio, "Lock 'Em Up or Else: Huge Wave of Criminally Inclined Coming in Next 10 Years," *Lakeland Ledger* (Lakeland, FL), March 23, 1996, A11; Joyce Purnick, "Youth Crime: Should Laws Be Tougher?" *New York Times*, May 9, 1996, B1.

48. Vincent Schiraldi, "Will the Real John DiIulio Please Stand Up" (editorial), *Washington Post*, February 5, 2001, A19.

49. "'Superpredators' Aren't Mere Kids" (editorial), *Omaha World Herald*, May 16, 1997, 12.

50. See, for example, Michael Tonry, *Malign Neglect: Race, Crime, and Punishment in America* (New York: Oxford University Press, 1995).

51. See Edward J. Blakely and Mary Gail Snyder, *Fortress America: Gated Communities in the United States* (Washington, DC: Brookings Institution Press, 1999).

52. For an insightful analysis of the privatization of public space, especially in suburban shopping centers, see Cohen, *Consumers' Republic*.

53. Sharon Waxman, "Paradise Bought in Los Angeles," *New York Times*, July 2, 2006, Style section, 1.

54. See Blakely and Snyder, *Fortress America*.

55. Ibid., ix, 3.

56. See Keith Bradsher, *High and Mighty: SUVs: The World's Most Dangerous Vehicles and How They Got That Way* (New York: BBS Public Affairs, 2002).

57. Rosie DiManno, "A Nation's Confidence Is among the Casualties after Unspeakably Bloody Attack on the Proudest Symbols of U.S. Power; U.S. Craves Revenge but Needs a Target," *Toronto Star*, September 12, 2001, B01.

58. Frank Rich, "The Wimps of War," *New York Times*, March 30, 2002, http://www.nytimes.com; Michael R. Gordon, "U.S. Nuclear Plan Sees New Weapons and New Targets," *New York Times*, March 10, 2002, 1A.

59. "Closing the Safety Gap" (editorial), *Christian Science Monitor*, October 11, 2001, 8.

60. Nicholas D. Kristof, "Chicks with Guns," *New York Times*, Friday, March 8, 2002, A23.

61. Peter Carlson, "America Gamely Stumbled Off to War," *Washington Post*, December 7, 2001, A01.

62. See May, *Homeward Bound*, esp. chaps. 1 and 7.

63. For one of many insightful commentaries on the new cold war, see Robert Scheer, "Bush Is Serving Up the Cold War Warmed Over," *Los Angeles Times*, July 5, 2005, editorial page. See also Elaine Tyler May, "Echoes of the Cold War: The Aftermath of September 11 at Home," in *September 11 in History: A Watershed Moment?* ed. Mary Dudziak (Durham, NC: Duke University Press, 2003).

EIGHT

"Be Real Black for Me": Representation, Authenticity, and the Cultural Politics of Black Power

WALDO E. MARTIN JR.

Our time, short and precious
Your lips, warm and luscious
You don't have to wear false charms
'Cause when I wrap you in my hungry arms

Be real black for me
Be real black for me

Your hair, soft and crinkly
Your body, strong and stately
You don't have to search and roam
'Cause I got your love at home

Be real black for me
Be real black for me

In my head I'm only half together
If I lose you I'll be ruined forever
Darling, take my hand and hold me
Hold me, hold me, hold me, hold me

You know how much I need you
To have you, really feel you
You don't have to change a thing
No one knows the love you bring

Be real black for me
Be real black for me
Be real black for me
Be real black for me

I want you to do that
Be real black for me
Be real black for me
Be real black for me
Be real black for me

Lord, have mercy
Be real black for me
Be real black for me*

"Be Real Black for Me," from the album *Roberta Flack and Donny Hathaway*, ROBERTA FLACK, DONNY HATHAWAY, CHARLES MANN (1972)

When you open the cover of the 1972 album *Roberta Flack and Donny Hathaway*, a casual and inviting portrait of the smiling and attractive couple greets you. With Flack seated above Hathaway's left shoulder and her arms circling his neck, her immaculately coifed Afro hairdo stands out. The image vividly captures the historical moment. They, especially Flack, look happy, and professionally speaking, they had every reason to be happy. As successful solo artists in the early 1970s, before coming together to do their duet work, both Flack and Hathaway, but especially Flack, already had had well-received and profitable singles and albums, and consistently played to enthusiastic and sold-out audiences. In 1972, when their jointly penned song (with assistance from Charles Mann) "Be Real Black for Me" appeared on *Roberta Flack and Donny Hathaway*, their celebrated album of duets and collaborative work, Flack (1939–) and Hathaway (1945–79) were highly acclaimed solo soul music artists at the height of their artistry and popularity. Their mellifluous duet "Where Is the Love" had shot to the top of the charts, subsequently winning the 1972 Grammy for Best Pop Duo Performance. And as a mega-hit, it contributed significantly to making the album a gold record.[1]

The year 1972 likewise saw Flack's mellow yet arresting interpretation of "The First Time Ever I Saw Your Face" (first released in 1969) win a Grammy as Record of the Year, in large part due to its inclusion in Clint Eastwood's successful directorial film debut, *Play Misty for Me*. Indeed like *Roberta Flack and Donny Hathaway*, two earlier solo albums by Flack, *First Take* (1969) and *Quiet Fire* (1971), also went gold in 1972. "Killing Me Softly with His Song," Flack's follow-up number one smash single, garnered recognition as Record of the Year in 1973.[2]

Hathaway, after earning an impressive and growing reputation in the late 1960s as an arranger and producer for the likes of Roberta Flack, Curtis Mayfield and the Impressions, and Woody Herman, emerged in the early 1970s as one of the most promising multitalented personalities on the music scene. He was now working with the likes of the queen of soul Aretha Franklin. *Donny Hathaway Live*, his 1972 gold album, featured the rocking and hard-edged hit "The Ghetto," a performance that remains fresh and vital today. In 1993, legendary producer of soul music Jerry Wexler, who worked with greats such as Ray Charles and Aretha Franklin, recalled: "I was certain that Donny was the next major artist after Aretha."[3]

Unlike the huge crossover hit "Where Is the Love," "Be Real Black for Me" is a different kind of song, a production that sensitively engaged the Black Is Beautiful sensibility that characterized the Black Power era.

Although nonblacks have enjoyed and related to the song, Hathaway and Flack clearly saw blacks as the song's primary audience. For Hathaway and Flack, as black cultural warriors themselves who were grappling with the meanings and consequences of Black Is Beautiful in their own lives, this song, manifestly an outgrowth of that grappling, was a significant musical contribution to the yeasty collective black project of giving meaning to the beauty of blackness. As such, Hathaway and Flack's appointed task was deceptively clear yet exceedingly complicated: As a people caught up in a radical yet shifting phase of an ongoing liberation struggle, how do we negotiate the complex terrain of self-definition and self-affirmation so central to the imperatives of Black Is Beautiful?[4]

Flack and Hathaway's charge to "Be Real Black for Me" signifies far more than a mere personal desire and choice; more important, it signifies a collective desire and choice. It is an invocation addressed in particular to a black national community, a "black public sphere," a black nation. On one level the mode of address is both public and personal. On another level it is affective and expressive as well as rational and logical. "Be Real Black for Me" is a plea issuing out of the black social imagination and emblematic of contemporaneous black cultural politics. The song pointedly asks that black people as a group as well as individuals embrace blackness: an interrelated and empowering emotional psychology and liberation politics. The "Me" in "Be Real Black for Me," therefore, represents all black people: the collective black "we."[5]

Not surprisingly, therefore, Flack and Hathaway's "Be Real Black for Me" found a harder to measure yet nonetheless hardcore and enthusiastic audience. "Be Real Black for Me" was never released as a single. Instead, it became an underground hit that has resonated deeply with a wide-ranging black audience since its appearance. Then and now, that particular audience has exuded much sympathy for the dominant Black Power culture of the late 1960s and early 1970s, from its moderate to militant expressions. That audience has likewise included fans of either or both Flack and Hathaway, especially those who enjoy their duet work, as well as fans of soul music.[6]

Perhaps most notably, the underground black audience for "Be Real Black for Me" has similarly encompassed those who enjoy message music, in particular popular black music that perceptively explored the exigencies of that exhilarating yet challenging historical moment. Iconic works such as Marvin Gaye's "What's Going On" (1971) and Stevie Wonder's "Innervisions" (1973) help to define the genre: popular black music in conversation with the Black Power movement. Even more pointedly,

"Be Real Black for Me," like other Black Power anthems, such as James Brown's "Say It Loud I'm Black and I'm Proud" and Nina Simone's "To Be Young, Gifted, and Black," spoke tellingly for greater popular black identification with the cultural politics of Black Power. Indeed, in *Everything Is Everything* (1970), Hathaway's first solo album, he offered a moving version of "To Be Young, Gifted, and Black."[7]

Notwithstanding their underground popularity, the powerful lyrics and performance of "Be Real Black for Me" function as a revealing cultural text, in large part precisely because of the song's potent yet unacknowledged and thus unexplored reach and resonance: its profundity. The song both encapsulates and represents the popular cultural expression of Black Power culture: a specific historical moment when Negroes became Black and the black freedom struggle moved from an emphasis on civil rights (1945–65) to an emphasis on Black Power (1965–75). Rather than reflecting the cultural imperatives of the assimilationist integrationism of the NAACP and the mainstream civil rights movement, "Be Real Black for Me" epitomized a searching black nationalism committed to community empowerment, best personified by the Black Panthers.[8]

Similarly, like Flack and Hathaway's "Be Real Black for Me," a significant slice of black expressive culture—notably poetry, drama, dance, and visual art as well as music—engaged directly the concurrent black freedom struggle. This popular cultural work was shaped by and sought to shape the Black Power phase of the struggle and its attendant black cultural politics. Spearheaded by forceful personalities such as Amiri Baraka (LeRoi Jones), Nikki Giovanni, Ron Karenga, Haki Madhubuti (Don L. Lee), and Sonia Sanchez, the Black Arts movement, most well known as a literary movement, functioned as a critical element of the cultural wing of the Black Power insurgency. In fact, the Black Arts movement (1966–80) was a sprawling, combative, and protean artistic, aesthetic, and philosophical undertaking whose aim was no less than to help create out of the political ferment of the era a viable black nation. A key goal of the movement was to develop an art that spoke to black experience as insightfully and effectively as did the best of popular black music. "Be Real Black for Me" epitomized that music. Indeed, one way to understand and appreciate the song is to hear it in antiphonal relationship to the Black Arts movement. A more inclusive view of the Black Arts movement would necessarily encompass the relevant popular black music, including songs like "Be Real Black for Me."[9]

The mode of analysis here is hybrid: part historical analysis of the song as prism through which to understand the cultural dimensions of

Black Power; part meditation on the ideological assumptions embedded in a particular notion of blackness. After framing that notion of blackness as a historical formation of the early 1970s, with its own ideological functions and elisions, I then use the song and its vision of blackness as a means to examine a broader historical development, namely, competing modes of "black cultural politics" during the late twentieth century. Many of the "readings" that follow, therefore, are provoked by the song and do not involve specific arguments about what Flack and Hathaway had in mind, or how the song was actually received in 1972.

"Be Real Black for Me," then, sheds important light not only on its specific historical moment, but also on its antecedents and its enduring legacy. The song's searching exploration of the historic imperatives of Black Is Beautiful speaks thoughtfully to enduring black battles around the politics of black beauty and black aesthetics that date back to the beginnings of African American culture. In the twentieth century, for instance, these concerns figured prominently in the racial nationalism of Garveyism and the cultural politics of the Harlem Renaissance.[10] The key distinction between these earlier moments of black cultural revitalization and that of the 1960s and 1970s was twofold. First, it was not until the latter period that there was a popular black embrace of the legitimacy and importance of black culture and its centrality to the ongoing black freedom struggle. Second, the mass black insurgency of the 1960s and 1970s shaped decisively the era's black cultural politics, giving that particular black cultural revitalization moment greater salience and a more substantive and enduring impact.

What made the moment of "Be Real Black for Me" substantially different from these earlier moments of black cultural revitalization, then, was the latter moment's radically altered historical context. On the one hand, "Be Real Black for Me" was part of a powerful and wide-ranging cultural revitalization of the continuing Black Is Beautiful struggle among blacks. In that sense, the song connected intimately not just to the civil rights movement but also to previous traditions and moments of heightened black struggle around this crucial issue. On the other, precisely because the song came out of a specific historical moment characterized by a mass and militant Black Power insurgency, the song's salience and appeal were due fundamentally to that charged and very different historical context. "Be Real Black for Me" thus reflected a black cultural politics at once continuous and discontinuous with earlier periods of black cultural politics. The song engaged and thus signifies an audacious and inspiring historical moment of black imagining, re-imagining, and nation building. In turn, the song illustrates the perils and downside as well as prospects and upside of such efforts. In the end, it showcases the fallibility as well as the necessity of the quest for authenticity in the politics of self-definition and representation.[11]

You've Got a Friend

When Flack and Hathaway combined their multiple talents on their 1972 album, the collaboration was a major aesthetic as well as commercial success. The fertile musical union showcased an aesthetic sensibility that irresistibly bursts forth, straight out of the dynamic black gospel and black church nexus so central to the best soul music. The work of Flack and Hathaway separately and together, and especially this project, exemplifies the mutual impact of down-home black church music on black popular music, especially classic soul. As a result, a mesmerizing rendition on the album of the classic hymn "Come Ye Disconsolate" fits perfectly with the secular numbers in aesthetic and tone. Understood in relation to the rest of the album, this hymn typifies the robust intersection and mutually enriching cross-pollination between African American traditions and practices, especially sacred and secular musics. It also illustrates the emphasis in both on related notions of love, hope, and transcendence.

Early on, Flack and Hathaway honed their musical talents in the uncommonly rich musical tradition of the black church. Hathaway had achieved notoriety in St. Louis circles before he even turned five years old as "Donny Pitts, the Nation's Youngest Gospel Singer," under the influence of Martha Cromwell, his grandmother and a well-known gospel singer in her own right. Flack grew up as the daughter of the church organist and early began piano lessons. Both became accomplished keyboardists, accompanying their equally accomplished vocals. They became friends in Washington, D.C., where both attended Howard University. Flack received her B.A. in music, whereas Hathaway, on a full scholarship in fine arts, left after three years to pursue his professional musical aspirations. Both also worked in the vibrant local music scene.[12]

Both were serious students of traditional Euro-American music repertory, theory, and performance, and their work, particularly *Roberta Flack and Donny Hathaway*, reflects this training. The classical bent of Flack's "Mood," an elegiac piano solo—the album's final track—as well as the string and horn arrangements throughout, some like those on "Be Real Black for Me" done by Hathaway himself, reflect this influence. Nevertheless, an even more deep-seated immersion in varieties of African American musics—notably spirituals, gospel, jazz, blues, and rhythm and blues—and various African American musical and cultural practices, notably improvisation, repetition, and antiphony, drive the album. The melding of African American and European forms and practices in addition to various American pop influences yields a characteristic hybridity throughout the album that has increasingly defined not only New World musics but also global musics more generally. This melding also reflected the clear intent of the album's creators that the project reach a wide and mainstream audience.[13]

A characteristic African American cultural emphasis on repetition drives the lyrics and performance of "Be Real Black for Me." The solemn and incantatory refrain of the song indeed frames this Black Is Beautiful anthem. Coursing throughout, the refrain accents and reiterates the song's central message: the urgent challenge of affirming black humanity and its beauty in the continuing war against white supremacy. This "lyrical, confident declaration of Black humanity," as Jacqueline Akins describes the song's message, is therefore a vital tactic in the all-out offensive against black dehumanization and antiblack racism at the root of white supremacy. The song's message is pro-black yet antiracist: at bottom both egalitarian and humanist. This set of positions has been a consistent feature of the enduring black freedom struggle and in particular reverberated deeply among innumerable African Americans in the context of the Black Power movement.[14]

"Be Real Black for Me" emphasizes the linked and expanding webs of self-love—not only love between two partners, but also black collective love as critical to the inextricable imperatives of Black Is Beautiful and Black Power. These particular varieties of love are also represented as crucial elements of an emergent black identification/identity or commitment to black unity or black solidarity.[15] The embrace of blackness as a means of self-definition, self-determination, and affirmation, all in the direction of advancing beyond the limitations of Negroness, similarly connected the song to its historical context. Put another way, Negroness signified a civil rights consciousness and practice seen as the past; blackness signified a Black Power consciousness and practice envisioned as the present and future.[16]

The challenge to "Be Real Black for Me," therefore, is the work's emotional as well as ideological center—not only its heart, but also the theme that structures and signifies a rich and complex set of ideas and practices. The title refrain is the framework within which those ideas and practices are explored as well as invoked. In addition, the hypnotic refrain signifies and extends the sense of urgency and importance: "Our time short and precious." By the song's conclusion, "Be Real Black for Me" has become a spiritual chant, a mantra—an open challenge pregnant with hope and possibility. Vocal and musical embellishments heighten the mood and emphasis. While Flack offers an emphatic series of "Whoa, whoa, whoa's," Hathaway waxes even more ecstatic in his melismatic plea "I want you to do that" and his devotional supplication: "Lord have mercy!"

In fact, a deeply moving sacred sensibility overspreads the album *Roberta Flack and Donny Hathaway* in its entirety, from the stirring rendition of "Come Ye Disconsolate" to the heartrending duet version of the love song "I (Who Have Nothing)" to the aching ethereality of Hathaway's solo interpretation of the love song "For All We Know." That overarching spiritual intensity similarly can be heard most compellingly in the work's robust vocal architecture. It can also be heard in the work's instrumental architecture, especially the elegant yet soulful piano and electric piano structures crafted by Hathaway and Flack. Particularly striking in the dynamic union of and interplay between her rich alto and his equally rich tenor is not only the strength and range of the singing, particularly the vocal pyrotechnics, but also the warmth and emotional depth that informs the vocals. This psychological power goes to the heart of the album's singular achievement: its artful marriage of spiritual and secular feeling and insight. Seen another way, it is an arresting exploration of that place where the flesh and the spirit become one: a probing exploration of the inextricable ties between them.[17] The overall effect is a masterpiece, an album of consummate beauty and resonance.

At its best, then, the album is a vigorous blend of the sacred and the secular—at once the sanctification of the secular and the secularization of the sacred. "Be Real Black for Me" is thus not just a moving soul love ballad, nor merely a touching and reverential Black Is Beautiful anthem. Equally important, it is an emotion-drenched and compelling secular hymn—a worldly praise-song to blackness suffused with the sacred. Indeed in structure and sensibility, "Be Real Black for Me" and "Come Ye Disconsolate" bear a striking resemblance. As heard in its opening, pacing, and feel, "Be Real Black for Me," of all the album's songs, is most like the album's only overtly religious tune, "Come Ye Disconsolate."

In this joint project, not surprisingly, Flack and Hathaway went with a tried-and-true formula for commercial success and emphasized love songs. Heavy on ballads, the album consists of several up-tempo numbers—including a country-inflected and infectious version of Aretha's big hit "Baby I Love You"—which balance the album's overall groove. Ostensibly an original soul love ballad, "Be Real Black for Me" clearly fits the album's overall design and mood. In its explicit black cultural politics, however, it starkly stands out. Whereas a more conventional ballad like "I (Who Have Nothing)" speaks of undying love, and a comparable ballad like "For All We Know" is an urgent love plea couched in life's utter unpredictability, "Be Real Black for Me" is a highly politicized soul love ballad addressed more explicitly to the larger imperatives of the historical moment.

"Be Real Black for Me" thus charts a related yet different direction from other "soul freedom fighters" such as Nina Simone, Aretha Franklin, James Brown, Marvin Gaye, and Stevie Wonder. Hathaway and Flack engaged the theme of love, in this case black love, in an especially heated moment of the Black Power struggle. In particular, the volatile issue of the putatively strained relations between black men and women was becoming increasingly public and politicized. Sociologically speaking, were black women the emasculating matriarchs portrayed in the Moynihan report? To what extent did Black Power perpetuate a tradition of male dominance in the Black Power movement and its representation? Unlike typical popular black love songs of the era, which obscure and evade these alleged contemporaneous tensions between black women and men, "Be Real Black for Me" grapples directly with those tensions, seeking to alleviate them through honest dialogue and affirmation.[18]

These kinds of hot-button issues were widely discussed in innumerable public forums and taken up throughout the Black Arts movement among poets, dramatists, visual artists, and musicians in particular. Perhaps most strikingly, contemporary poetry, such as Giovanni's popular *The Women and the Men*, and drama, such as Ntozake Shange's critically acclaimed yet highly controversial *for colored girls who have considered suicide/when the rainbow is enuf*, provocatively explored the powder keg of intraracial gender and sexual relations. As the inexorable logic and increasing ferocity of the Black Power challenge to white supremacy went forward, some of that critical vision and intellectual energy necessarily spilled over into other contemporaneous social movements, notably women's liberation and gay and lesbian liberation. The explosive terrain of black sexual politics thus went in many directions, including black feminist/womanist challenges to patriarchy and black lesbian and gay challenges to black homophobia.[19]

The Black Arts movement thus proved protean, diverse, and contentious, as it struggled with a broad range of pressing contemporary concerns, including ethnoracial diversity within the black nation and the role of the black political prisoner in the growing black insurgency.[20] Reflecting the affirmative yet relentlessly probing spirit of the times, "Be Real Black for Me" is a paean—a praise song, or tribute to joy, to triumph—but a paean with a critical twist. It goes deeper to both reflect and examine the growing concurrent black rhetorical emphasis on the imperative and logic of black love in a radical black social movement. In a related vein, late sixties black social scientists such as William Grier and Price Cobbs in *Black Rage*, echoing Frantz Fanon, reawakened and extended the swirling debate surrounding the deleterious effects of individual and structural forms of white racism on black minds, bodies, and souls.[21] A key motivation of these kinds of discussions was to move the black insurgency in particular and blacks individually and collectively to take seriously the sobering challenge of improving black mental and emotional health. The black freedom struggle depended on strong and balanced black women, men, and children. Problems between black men and black women, between black generations—notably between parents and children, the youth and their elders—as well as problems among black women themselves, men themselves, and youth themselves, had to be tackled head-on. It bears emphasizing, however, that psychic and physical health—indeed strong and even expanded self-esteem—does not and did not in and of itself translate into socioeconomic and political empowerment. These social, psychological, and emotional concerns were thus understood as fundamentally different although related aspects of the ongoing black freedom struggle.[22]

The Black Arts movement was likewise committed to delineating and to examining critically as well as affirming blackness in its diversity and complexity. Representative artists and cultural workers, Eugene Redmond's "cultural warriors," took up the challenge of being "Real Black for Me." That movement encompassed a widespread and striking series of black efforts—often contentious and debatable—to advance various notions of black cultural nationalism as well as various broader and less formal notions of black cultural politics. This movement included a diverse array of cultural warriors, many of whom, like the influential Amiri Baraka, obliterated the allegedly crucial distinction between politics and culture in their life and work, even as they embraced the distinction theoretically and ideologically.[23]

During this period, many groups and influential figures, such as cultural nationalist Ron Karenga and his US organization, and political nationalists such as the Black Panther Party, sought to draw firm lines between cultural and political struggle. Yet, as I have argued elsewhere, these lines proved exceedingly permeable in the context of the enduring black freedom struggle. The distinctions were particularly porous in a radical black insurgency in which such distinctions proved more apparent than real. This was so even within the Black Panther Party and Karenga's US, where the cultural was inevitably political, and the political was inevitably cultural.[24]

As a commercial form of popular entertainment, songs like "Be Real Black for Me" cannot be narrowly confined to the musical wing of the Black Arts movement. "Be Real Black for Me" circulated well beyond its core black audience, within a mainstream audience that listened to the album *Roberta Flack and Donny Hathaway*. The album sold exceedingly well—it went gold—and clearly reached a wide audience. One can infer that the mainstream response to "Be Real Black for Me" mirrored the general range of responses to Black Is Beautiful—positive, negative, and in between. The song appeals to a more broadly gauged sensibility that at once engages but also ranges beyond both the confines of the Black Arts movement and those of contemporary Black Power cultural politics. Ultimately, the song speaks perceptively to the timelessness of the universal quest for love and its far-reaching social ramifications.

The focus here, however, is the location and circulation of "Be Real Black for Me" within the contemporaneous black experience of the Black Power movement. Comparable songs like Marvin Gaye's "Inner City Blues (Make Me Wanna Holler)," the Staple Singers' "Respect Yourself," and Aretha Franklin's version of "To Be Young, Gifted, and Black" concurrently reflected and helped to shape popular black conversations and understandings of the historical moment. In July 1972 the Reverend Curtis E. Burrell Jr. identified Flack and Hathaway as part of a growing community of black bards. "The Bard," according to Burrell, "is not an artist for the sake of art, but for the sake of truth and the people." Committed to a "message of healing," these black bards promote critical individual and collective examination. Most important, for Burrell, "the Bards bring the people together." "Be Real Black for Me," therefore, reveals a broad initiative within black cultural politics to help make and to unify the black nation. [25]

Where Is the Love?

A central theme of so much of the impressive cultural work of the Black Arts movement was the centrality of black love in an age of black rebellion and revolution.[26] In moments of extraordinary sociopolitical flux and crisis, as in the Black Power era, virtually every aspect of life, including love, comes under growing scrutiny. In such moments, love itself becomes deeply politicized, as "Be Real Black for Me" posits. Here, the fact that certain popular cultural works, especially the black love song, become increasingly politicized vividly reflects the interpenetration of the political and the cultural within the dominant contemporaneous black cultural politics.[27]

One might ask, "What's love got to do with it?" In the context of the Black Power insurgency, being "real black" had a great deal to do with love. To be "real black," according to this view, demanded black love in its myriad manifestations, including love for one's black self and love for other black selves, or black people as a group. To paraphrase an often-repeated aphorism of the time: it was essential that one be true to one's black self. In order to "Be Real Black for Me," for one's partner, and by symbolic extension for the black nation, one first had to be black for one's own self. Blackness first and foremost had to be an individual's own choice before that individual could be "real black" for another.

Throughout "Be Real Black for Me" as well as the larger terrain of black cultural politics it reflects and contributes to, blackness is both racial agency (to "Be") and racial essence ("Real"); at times blackness is an uneasy conflation of both. On the one hand, blackness is racial choice, or what one does, with myriad meanings and consequences for the most public arenas such as political action as well as the most private ones such as intimate relations. On the other hand, blackness is a defining racial character, a natural essence: a racial "soul." The uneasy conflation of racial agency and racial essentialism masks not only the critical limitations of each position separately but also the compounded problems of conflating them. Indeed there is a tension between agency and essentialism both in the song and the broader black cultural politics that reflects the deep-seated and persistent challenges of racial identification and black nation building.[28]

In turn, self-love required self-awareness and self-criticism as basic to self-acceptance. Once you brought these interrelated capacities to bear, particularly in the context of a "love" relationship in the charged Black Power movement, as Flack and Hathaway acknowledged, "You don't have to change a thing." A popular expression of this omnipresent notion was to accept fully and completely your "natural" black self. On the one hand, this acceptance signified coming to grips with one's history and culture, notably the African origins and slave past of blacks. Yet such acceptance of one's natural black self simultaneously signified glorying in one's blackness. This acceptance found particularly potent expression in the valorization of what came to be represented as "classic" African features: dark skin, large lips, broad nose, tightly curled or "nappy" hair, wide hips, and all the rest. That many Africans, not to mention many American blacks, did not fit these criteria spoke volumes about the inherent limitations and growing problems of trying to structure a black cultural politics around these kinds of therapeutic yet exclusionary cultural projects.[29]

Nevertheless, the politics of skin color and hair texture proved particularly salient markers of a particular notion of an authentic blackness. Natural, unprocessed black hair—"crinkly," according to Flack and Hathaway—reflected not just an acceptance of one's inherent black beauty: it was also an unapologetic valorization of the Africanness of blackness. Chemical hair straighteners and relaxers—represented as assimilationist and self-hating—were out. In the context of an empowering black aesthetic, hair functioned as a viable and increasingly resonant symbol of the era's militant black cultural politics. Public fascination with the large and well-coifed Afro hairdos of Angela Davis, Kathleen Cleaver, Huey Newton, and Bobby Seale vividly epitomized the increasingly popular, mass-mediated fascination with Black Power style. Similarly, this complicated fascination reflected the resonance of black hair as a key visual and physical symbol of a militant black cultural politics: a militant Black Power culture.[30]

An equally, if not more important, visual and physical symbol of this construction of an authentic blackness was dark skin. The ongoing dilemma of the preference of the light complexioned over the dark complexioned, dating at least back to slavery, has served as a key battleground in the black beauty aesthetic wars. What Amiri Baraka referred to as "the old blackbrownyellowwhite phenomenon," or in the vernacular "being color struck," has historically constituted a vexed and persistent struggle. As one observer noted of the moment when dark skin came to signify Black Is Beautiful: "It was about time that the dark skin brothers and sisters got some play!" Or, as the popular folk aphorism framed the issue: "The blacker the berry the sweeter the juice!"[31] Thus when Hathaway and Flack sang of being "real black," in a most resonant sense they spoke to the enduring intraracial struggle to undo the perverse negativity associated with dark skin.

Seen another way, Flack and Hathaway represented black love as an emotional and psychological force shading indistinguishably into black self-esteem and self-empowerment—in fact, shading into black freedom.

Such individual and collective black love was seen as basic to love not just of one's black self and other blacks, but also of nonblacks, of "outsiders." Although the song's stated emphasis is decidedly nationalistic, it nonetheless implies an openness and flexibility, a sense of becoming, an overriding humanistic sensibility. What makes a "true love"? What does such a love look like? How does it feel? What does such a love ultimately mean? Even more to the point, once recognized, how can "true love" not only be sustained but also enhanced?

This celebration of love between the two halves of the authentic black self—a love between the "real" black woman and the "real" black man—reflected a normative heterosexuality. The completion of the black self necessitated a fulfilling relationship with one's soul mate. Hathaway thus praises his "beautiful and highly desirable black woman." After referring longingly to her "warm and luscious lips," he explains, "You don't have to wear false charms." Similarly, Flack praises her "beautiful and highly desirable black man," speaking longingly of his "body strong and stately." In fact, one of the song's most striking features is its sophisticated treatment of black intimacy.[32]

"Be Real Black for Me" and comparable works thus spoke to the urgent need to affirm blackness, especially black beauty, primarily as part of the making of the Black Power nation and secondarily as a necessary antidote to the poisonous impact of antiblack representations and assumption. To "be real black" demanded that one value blackness in its complexity and variety, notably the beauty of both the black female body and the black male body. Consequently, Flack sings lovingly of "Your hair soft and crinkly," and Hathaway responds with adoration for "Your lips warm and luscious." In response to the challenge issued by James Brown, the incomparable Soul Brother Number One—"Say It Loud, I'm Black and I'm Proud"—blacks, according to Flack and Hathaway, needed to do more than just speak self-love. They had to embody and practice it.

Another way of framing the issue is to understand that love—like freedom and equality—is an elusive yet powerful concept with potentially far-reaching, even transformative, meanings and consequences. Some have rightly seen these kinds of notions at the epicenter of radical social movements. "Freedom and love," suggests Robin D. G. Kelley, "may be the most revolutionary ideas available to us." Kelley explains, "once we strip radical social movements down to their bare essence and understand the collective desires of people in motion, freedom and love lay at the very heart of the matter."[33]

Especially in the context of the Black Power insurgency, strong black individuals, families, and communities, as well as black race pride and black unity, demanded black love. Put another way, black freedom required black love. A century earlier, Frederick Douglass had contended, "If there is no struggle, there is no progress." Flack and Hathaway, by contrast, would have put it somewhat differently: "If there is no love, there can be neither black struggle nor black progress."[34] Black love—black self-love, black love relationships, black collective love—is thus a prerequisite of, an expression of, a consequence of not only black struggle but also black hope. From this point of view, racial nationalism, and more precisely, black nationalism, were predicated upon a profound commitment to black love.

Thus when Hathaway and Flack asked "Where Is the Love," pairing that query with "You've Lost That Loving Feeling," they caustically evoked the emotional desperation and physical exhaustion that had already begun to eat away at the Black Power movement and concurrent radical social movements. In this sense, it is clear that Flack and Hathaway plainly understood that love had its limits. The assassinations of leaders of genius like Malcolm X and Martin Luther King Jr., and the increasingly murderous government repression of radical activism, especially of the Black Power movement, tempered any optimistic, or even naive, faith in the redemptive power of love. That powerful sensibility had been central to the civil rights movement led by Martin Luther King Jr., with its emphasis on the redemptive power of Christian love and forgiveness, particularly love for one's enemies. A similar ethos had contributed significantly to the interracial activism of the "Beloved Community" of the early Student Nonviolent Coordinating Committee (SNCC), before its turn to more radical Black Power politics.[35]

"Be Real Black"

Being "real black," of course, is anything but a simple entreaty—especially so in a nation where white supremacy still holds sway. To be black in a society that hates and fears black people, and the blackness they embody, presents a range of serious challenges. As Flack and Hathaway jointly acknowledge at one point: "In my head I'm only half together." Assessing the state of their own black consciousness and, by implication, that of their people, Flack and Hathaway contend that this consciousness is still evolving. It remains very much a "work in progress." Being real black, then, is a developmental process: a state of being and becoming, an interactive process of consciousness-raising and social action.[36]

In all of these respects, "Be Real Black for Me" pointedly addresses the exceedingly difficult questions of making and fixing an authentic blackness.[37] And during the 1970s, many of the internal fissures contributing to the decline of the Black Arts movement as well as the Black Power movement revolved around issues like "blacker than thou" prescriptions, competing notions of cultural nationalism, patriarchy, and homophobia. Indeed, as previously noted, the growing appreciation for the viability and strength of black culture that was a vital triumph of the civil rights–Black Power insurgency further intensified awareness of diverse and complex black experiences.

In its enthusiastic embrace of a holistic and affirmative view of black culture, John H. Blassingame's immensely popular 1972 work *The Slave Community* exemplified how the most influential African American cultural history of this period was inextricably bound up with the prevailing notions of blackness embedded in the era's cultural politics. Similarly, in 1977, as the Black Power and Black Arts movements were winding down, Lawrence W. Levine could write persuasively of historically coherent concepts of black culture and black consciousness. That compelling framework likewise encompassed similarly coherent, though more implicit, notions of historically grounded—and thus "authentic"—representations of blackness. With Deborah Gray White's important 1984 study *A'r'nt I a Woman: Female Slaves in the Plantation South*, the centrality of gender and sexuality, especially black women's experiences, to historical notions of black culture became manifest. In 1987 Sterling Stuckey offered a transatlantic historical conceptualization of slave culture. These conceptualizations retain descriptive and analytic power; indeed they help shape the perspective and analytic thrust of this chapter.[38]

Around the same time, however, and especially among an emerging and increasingly influential black British cultural studies school, these kinds of totalizing conceptualizations were vigorously and thoughtfully interrogated. The likes of Stuart Hall, Hazel Carby, and Paul Gilroy have insightfully emphasized the hybrid, fragmented, diasporic, and contested features of concepts such as blackness, especially as they evolved during the late twentieth century.[39] In 1993, however, Gilroy dissented from what he termed "a new analytic orthodoxy": "In the name of anti-essentialism and theoretical rigour it suggests that since black particularity is socially and historically constructed, and plurality has become inescapable, the pursuit of any unifying dynamic or underlying structure of feeling in contemporary black cultures is utterly misplaced."[40]

The essentialist/anti-essentialist debates of the 1980s and 1990s were a primary legacy of the black cultural politics of the 1970s. After all, it is only in the wake of self-conscious and strategic forms of racial essentialism like those deployed by Hathaway and Flack that the anti-essentialist turn becomes possible and, I would argue, necessary. During the Black Power and Black Arts movements, the search for the overriding commonalties and unifying forces that underlay black history and culture proved intellectually enriching as well as empowering. Yet the deconstructionist tendencies within the cultural politics of Black Power planted some important seeds for the apparent "new analytic orthodoxy" announced by Gilroy. But in the late 1960s and 1970s, the quest to represent an authentic blackness proved not only viable but also urgent, in spite of often-intractable problems.

In addition, the song illustrates the pivotal role of African American expressive culture and black popular culture in the creation of notions of authentic blackness during the Black Power insurgency. The song's concern with the question of black authenticity, of the truly black, is fundamental to a series of related issues raised in the song's lyrics. Several merit comment here. To paraphrase a popular song: What is this thing called "black"? Is it a newly minted, more appealing appellation for Negroes? Or, more to the point, is it a more politically correct ethnoracial designation for the highly charged moment of the Black Power insurgency? Something else? Something more? Highly reflective of the black cultural politics of the late 1960s and early 1970s, the song seeks to identify specific elements of what it means to be "black." Fundamental to this quest is the ferreting out and rejection of what Hathaway and Flack refer to as "false charms" of whatever variety—including the magical and the assimilationist. On the contrary, the point was the embrace and display of material and psychological elements that affirm black selfhood and black peoplehood and sustain the continuing freedom struggle.

In part, then, black in this instance is an innovative and increasingly popular contemporaneous self-ascribed reference to Negroes, as a people, as a "race." But it is that and much more. Black in this instance perfectly captures the interwoven cognitive and political leaps associated with the mid-1960s transition from civil rights to Black Power.[41] In this sense, "Be Real Black for Me" is an entreaty to accept the evolutionary tenets of Black Power and to shape one's personal/private life as well as one's public/political life accordingly. In other words, the challenge is to pursue a path of militant political struggle and the interrelated paths of love, desire, and social belonging that necessarily follow.

Equally important and telling, the designation "black" likewise refers

to the centrality of culture—Negro culture and, in turn, black culture—
to the ongoing historical process of defining and giving substance to
who African Americans were as a people at this particularly propitious
moment in their history. In other words, the contemporaneous cultural
roots and expressions of blackness in part illuminate the historical as
well as social processes of identity formation at the individual and group
levels. These identities are constantly being made and remade in dialectical relationship to the critical influences of the outside world, notably the
American state and its hegemony.[42] Similarly, these shifting identities
contribute to the making of social and symbolic boundaries—including
modes of expressive culture such as music—that help to demarcate black
culture as distinctive.[43] In effect, "black" in this context denotes race,
identity, and culture separately and together, in particular the synergistic
ties among them.

Seen another way, "real black" refers to the integral relationship
between the material and the conceptual. "Real black" refers to "webs of
meaning," building upon the influential cultural formulation of Clifford
Geertz, that define and substantiate someone or something as identifiably
black as defined by blacks themselves.[44] The issue of black authenticity
also possesses an inherently political dimension: a politics at once activist and historical. In this case, to be "real black" refers, on one level, to a
full identification with and active participation within the Black Power
phase of the continuing African American freedom struggle. On a related
level, to be "real black" demands an equal measure of identification with
African American history and culture, from its African roots to its most
recent manifestations. In this context, any effort to be "real black" must
come from a "black place"; it must engage the lived experiences and the
visions of African Americans across space and time, with special emphasis on this particular moment and place.

To speak of "real black" here is to speak not merely of cultural and historical claims of authenticity in terms of the actual, the factual, and the
material. Equally significant in this case is that "real black" refers to the
conceptual and the philosophical dimensions of experience and culture.
The notion of authenticity here springs from a shared sense of history
and culture. In addition, it encompasses the stunning diversity and complexity of black history and culture. This is a fundamentally descriptive
and inclusive rather than categorical and exclusionary notion of black
representation and black authenticity. This open-ended politics of representation and authenticity signified the best of the Black Arts movement,

the related Black Aesthetic movement, and the best and most hopeful reading of works like "Be Real Black for Me."

When Love Has Grown

In 1972, Abraham Chapman took note of the growing tension within debates surrounding black representation and black authenticity—between dogma and prescription, on the one hand, and openness and flexibility on the other.

> Today we are . . . witnessing a further "new breed" of Black writers who accept their Blackness thoroughly, organically, and naturally, and have gone beyond some of the original premises of the Black arts movement of the Sixties. They reject any prescribed definition of Blackness, they oppose dogmatism and attempts at the institutionalization of Blackness in any particular movement or organization which will try to tell the Black writer how he should write or what he may write about. They stress the importance of the individuality and originality of the Black artist.[45]

Although I dissent from Chapman's implication that dogma and prescription might be seen as a defining feature of the earlier movement, I accept the argument that elements of these tendencies were present from the outset of the movement and hounded it more and more over time. As so often happens in these kinds of movements, though, positions tend to rigidify over time, and such was the case with elements within the Black Arts movement.

There is a highly revealing tension in "Be Real Black for Me" between the work's own admittedly static and narrow representations of blackness and the historical and cultural reality of the stunning range and diversity of blackness. The omission is both understandable and telling. One song obviously cannot say everything. In both the song as well as in the Black Arts–Black Aesthetic movement, it was certainly strategically justifiable to valorize a black aesthetic rooted in affirming the Africanness of blackness. Strategic essentialism, in this sense, has been crucial to both black identity construction and the ongoing black freedom struggle.[46]

Nevertheless, cultural redress, not to mention racial essentialism, sometimes went too far, as in the shaming of light-complexioned blacks and those with more European-identified features. Such narrowness has proven exclusionary. For instance, it casts serious clouds over, if indeed it did not speak against, interracialism, notably interracial love. Probing the song, we ask in what, if any, ways might nonblacks be "real black"? As in virtually all love ballads, the song's normative gender politics reinforces traditional gender norms, necessarily excluding alternative gender norms. Similarly, the song's explicit hetero-normativity necessarily excludes alternative sexualities. To be fair, to the extent that the song implies gender and sexual equality, it can be read as a more critical and hopeful contemporary commentary on the period's gender and sexual inequality and the necessary struggles against both. However, in far too many ways far more egregious and exponentially more powerful than this song—such as in key institutions and structures—blackness has come to be represented as too narrow and stereotypically, such as the "folk." The excesses and errors of representational and authenticity politics must of course be resisted.

The question persists: Who and what is black? In effect, as Wahneema Lubiano has observed: "the resonances of [black] authenticity depend on who's doing the evaluating." Rather than give up, however, I agree with E. Patrick Johnson, who posits that "Blackness . . . is slippery—ever beyond the reach of one's grasp. Once you think you have a hold on it, it transforms into something else and travels in another direction. Its elusiveness does not preclude one from trying to fix it, pin it down, however—for the pursuit of authenticity is inevitably an emotional and moral one."[47] "Be Real Black for Me," like the best of the Black Arts–Black Aesthetic movement, epitomizes the inescapable lure of blackness. Precisely because the black freedom struggle persists, a related desire to fix and certify a unifying blackness persists, notwithstanding the protean nature and contested history of blackness as well as the anti-essentialist turn.

NOTES

For helpful critical responses to versions of this chapter, the author thanks respondents and audiences at the State of Cultural History conference, George Mason University, Arlington, Virginia, September 17, 2005; the Center for Race and Gender seminar, University of California, Berkeley, February 9, 2006; the Black Atlantic Seminar, Rutgers Center for Historical Analysis, New Brunswick, New Jersey, May 4, 2006; and the National Endowment for the Humanities Summer Institute, "African American Struggles for Civil Rights in the Twentieth Century," Du Bois Institute, Harvard University, Cambridge, July 14, 2006. For their extended and useful critiques, the author acknowledges Michael O'Malley, Lawrence Glickman, James William Cook, Donna Murch, Rebecca Hall, Jacqueline Akins, and two anonymous readers.

1. *Roberta Flack and Donny Hathaway* (album) (New York: Atlantic Recording Corporation, 1972); Irwin Stambler, *The Encyclopedia of Pop, Rock, and Soul,* rev. ed. (New York: St. Martin's Press, 1989), 786, 851.
2. Stambler, *Encyclopedia,* 785, 847, 227–28; Ralph Tee, *Who's Who in Soul Music* (London: Weidenfeld and Nicolson, 1991), 86–87.
3. Stambler, *Encyclopedia,* 283–84; Tee, *Who's Who,* 110–11; Jerry Wexler and David Ritz, *Rhythm and the Blues: A Life in American Music* (New York: Knopf, 1993), 259. Hathaway's promising career was cut short by a series of personal problems, notably depression, and ended by an apparent suicide in 1979.
4. For a useful overview of the Black Is Beautiful phenomenon, see William L. Van Deburg, *New Day in Babylon: The Black Power Movement and American Culture, 1965–1975* (Chicago: University of Chicago Press, 1992), 192–308; on cultural warriors, see Waldo E. Martin Jr., *No Coward Soldiers: Black Cultural Politics in Postwar America* (Cambridge: Harvard University Press, 2005), 44–139.
5. The Black Public Sphere Collective, eds., *The Black Public Sphere: A Public Culture Book* (Chicago: University of Chicago Press, 1995); Nancy Fraser, "Rethinking the Public Sphere: A Contribution to the Critique of Actually Existing Democracy," in *Habermas and the Public Sphere,* ed. Craig Calhoun (Cambridge: MIT Press, 1992); Michael Warner, *Publics and Counterpublics* (New York: Zone Books, 2002).
6. This judgment reflects an ongoing random survey conducted among a cross-section of multiracial audiences in the last several years and confirmed by the National Endowment for the Humanities (NEH) seminar "African American Freedom Struggles in the Twentieth Century," July 14, 2006.
7. For an extensive discussion of the complicated relationship between black music, especially soul, and the Black Power movement, see Brian Ward, *Just My Soul Responding: Rhythm and Blues, Black Consciousness, and Race Relations* (Berkeley: University of California Press, 1998), 339–415: Martin, *No Coward Soldiers,* 44–81. For a useful discussion that treats both the civil rights and Black Power movements and late twentieth-century developments, see Mark Anthony Neal, *What the Music Said: Black Popular Music and Black Public Sphere* (New York: Routledge, 1999); Donny Hathaway, *Everything Is Everything* (album) (New York: ATCO [Atlantic], 1970).
8. Peniel E. Joseph, *Waiting 'til the Midnight Hour: A Narrative History of Black Power in America* (New York: Henry Holt, 2006); Peniel E. Joseph, ed., *The Black Power Movement: Rethinking the Civil Rights-Black Power Era* (New York: Routledge, 2006); Jeffrey O. G. Ogbar, *Black Power: Radical Politics and African American Identity* (Baltimore: Johns Hopkins University Press, 2004).
9. James Smethurst, *The Black Arts Movement: Literary Nationalism in the 1960s and 1970s* (Chapel Hill: University of North Carolina Press, 2005).
10. Sidney Mintz and Richard Price, *The Birth of African-American Culture: An Anthropological Perspective* (1976; repr., Boston: Beacon Press, 1992); Robert A. Hill, ed., *The Marcus Garvey and Universal Negro Improvement Association Papers,* 10 vols. (Berkeley: University of California Press, 1983–2006), see esp. the introduction to vol. 1; Lawrence W. Levine, "Marcus Garvey and the Politics of Revitalization," in *Black Leaders of the Twentieth Century,* ed. John Hope Franklin and August Meier (Urbana: University of Illinois Press, 1982), 105–38; David Levering Lewis, *When Harlem Was in Vogue* (New York: Oxford University Press, 1981); Nathan Huggins, *Harlem Renaissance* (New York: Oxford University Press, 1971).

11. John J. Jackson Jr., *Real Black: Adventures in Racial Sincerity* (Chicago: University of Chicago Press, 2005), esp. chap. 1; E. Patrick Johnson, *Appropriating Blackness: Performance and the Politics of Authenticity* (Durham, NC: Duke University Press, 2003), esp. the introduction; Regina Bendix, *In Search of Authenticity: The Formation of Folklore Studies* (Madison: University of Wisconsin Press, 1997), 3–23.

12. Stambler, *Encyclopedia*, 227–28, 283–84; Tee, *Who's Who*, 86–87, 110–11.

13. Christopher Small, *Music of the Common Tongue: Survival and Celebration in Afro-American Music* (New York: Riverrun Press, 1987); Paul Gilroy, *The Black Atlantic: Modernity and Double Consciousness* (Cambridge: Harvard University Press, 1993), 72–110.

14. Jacqueline Akins to author, letter, July 15, 2006.

15. Tommie Shelby, *We Who are Dark: The Philosophical Foundations of Black Solidarity* (Cambridge: Harvard University Press, 2005), is a thoughtful, current philosophical treatment of black solidarity.

16. Van Deburg, *New Day in Babylon.*

17. Martin, *No Coward Soldiers*, 44–81; Lawrence W. Levine, *Black Culture and Black Consciousness: Afro-American Folk Thought from Slavery to Freedom* (New York: Oxford University Press, 1977), 136–202.

18. Michele Wallace, *Black Macho and the Myth of the Superwoman* (New York: Dial, 1979) .

19. Beverly Guy-Sheftall, ed., *Words of Fire: An Anthology of African-American Feminist Thought* (New York: New Press, 1995), 229–91; Johnson, *Appropriating Blackness*, 1–103. Dwight A. McBride, "Can the Queen Speak? Racial Essentialism, Sexuality, and the Problem of Authority," *Callaloo* 22 (1998): 432–60.

20. Lisa Gail Collins and Margo Natalie Crawford, eds., *New Thoughts on the Black Arts Movement* (New Brunswick, NJ: Rutgers University Press, 2006); see especially Margo Natalie Crawford, "Natural Black Beauty and Black Drag," 154–72; Cherise A. Pollard, "Sexual Subversions, Political Inversions: Women's Poetry and the Politics of the Black Arts Movement," 173–86; Lisa Gail Collins, "The Art of Transformation: Parallels in the Black Arts and Feminist Arts Movements," 273–96: Lee Bernstein, "Prison Writers and the Black Arts Movement," 297–316; Michelle Joan Wilkinson, "'To Make a Poet Black': Canonizing Puerto Rican Poets in the Black Arts Movement," 317–32; Rod Hernandez, "Latin Soul: Cross-Cultural Connections between the Black Arts Movement and Pocho-Che," 333–48; Smethurst, *Black Arts Movement*; Martin, *No Coward Soldiers*, 44–81; Nikki Giovanni, *The Women and the Men* (New York: William Morrow, 1975); Ntozake Shange, *for colored girls who have considered suicide when the rainbow is enuf* (1975; repr., New York: Scribner's Poetry, 1997); Paula Giddings, *When and Where I Enter: The Impact of Black Women on Race and Sex in America* (New York: Bantam, 1984), 354–57.

21. W. Grier and P. Cobbs, *Black Rage* (New York: Bantam, 1968); Frantz Fanon, *Black Skins, White Masks* (New York: Grove Press, 1967); Reginald Jones, ed., *Black Psychology* (New York: Harper and Row, 1980); Van Deburg, *New Day in Babylon.*

22. Philip Brian Harper, *Are We Not Men? Masculine Anxiety and the Problem of African-American Identity* (New York: Oxford University Press, 1996), 58.

23. Martin, *No Coward Soldiers*, esp. 1–9; Amiri Baraka, *The Autobiography of LeRoi Jones/Amiri Baraka* (New York: Freundlich, 1984); Baraka, *Selected Plays and Prose of Amiri Baraka/LeRoi Jones* (New York: William Morrow, 1979).

24. Scot Brown, *Fighting for US: Maulana Karenga, the US Organization, and Black Cul-*

tural Nationalism (New York: New York University Press, 2003); Kathleen Cleaver and George Katsiaficas, eds., *Liberation, Imagination, and the Black Panther Party: A New Look at the Panthers and Their Legacy* (New York: Routledge, 2001); Charles E. Jones, ed., *The Black Panther Party Reconsidered* (Baltimore: Black Classic Press, 1998).

25. *Chicago Defender,* July 13, 1972, 12, col. 2.
26. See especially the work of two of the most popular poets of the era: *The Collected Poetry of Nikki Giovanni, 1968–1998* (New York: William Morrow, 2003); and Haki Madhubuti, *Groundwork: New and Selected Poems, Don L. Lee/Haki R. Madhubuti, from 1966–1996* (Chicago: Third World Press, 1996).
27. Martin, *No Coward Soldiers.*
28. The critique of Lawrence Glickman was particularly helpful here. See also Johnson, *Appropriating Blackness,* esp. the introduction.
29. Addison Gayle Jr., ed., *The Black Aesthetic* (New York: Anchor, 1972). On this point more generally, see Johnson, *Appropriating Blackness,* 2–16.
30. Van Deburg, *New Day in Babylon,* 192–203, 17–18, 198, 201–2; Maxine Craig, *Ain't I a Beauty Queen: Black Women, Beauty, and the Politics of Race* (New York: Oxford University Press, 2002); Noliwe Rooks, *Hair Raising: Beauty, Culture, and the African American Woman* (New Brunswick, NJ: Rutgers University Press, 1996); Carolina Herron, *Nappy Hair* (New York: Knopf, 1997); Shane White and Graham White, *Stylin': African American Expressive Culture from Its Beginnings to the Zoot Suit* (Ithaca, NY: Cornell University Press, 1998).
31. Levine, *Black Culture and Black Consciousness,* 284–92; Baraka, *Autobiography,* 66; Fanon Che Wilkins, NEH Seminar, July 14, 2006. Wilkins observed: "It was about time that the dark skin brothers and sisters got some play."
32. Akins to author, July 15, 2006.
33. Robin D. G. Kelley, *Freedom Dreams: The Black Radical Imagination* (Boston: Beacon Press, 2002), 12.
34. Waldo E. Martin Jr., *The Mind of Frederick Douglass* (Chapel Hill: University of North Carolina Press, 1984), 124–25.
35. Adam Fairclough, *To Redeem the Soul of America: The Southern Christian Leadership Conference and Martin Luther King, Jr.* (Athens: University of Georgia Press, 1987); Clayborne Carson, *In Struggle: SNCC and the Black Awakening of the 1960s* (Cambridge: Harvard University Press, 1981). I am indebted to Doug Gilmore (NEH Seminar, July 14, 2006) for helping me to shape this view. Craig Werner, *A Change Is Gonna Come: Music, Race and the Soul of America* (New York: Plume, 1999), 172–73, makes a similar point.
36. Van Deburg, *New Day in Babylon,* 280–91.
37. For compelling critiques of the concept of black authenticity read as black essentialism, see Stuart Hall, "What Is This 'Black' in Black Popular Culture," in *Stuart Hall: Critical Dialogues in Cultural Studies,* ed. David Morley and Kuan-Hing Chen (New York: Routledge, 1996). This influential essay first appeared in Gina Dent, ed., *Black Popular Culture* (Seattle: Bay Press, 1992); Kwame Anthony Appiah, "Race, Culture Identity: Misunderstood Connections," in *Color Conscious: The Political Morality of Race,* ed. Kwame Anthony Appiah and Amy Gutmann (Princeton: Princeton University Press, 1996). See also David Lionel Smith, "What Is Black Culture?" in *The House That Race Built: Black Americans, U.S. Terrain,* ed. Wahneema Lubiano (New York: Pantheon, 1997), 192, 178–94. For a perceptive anthropological discussion of this issue, see Jackson, *Real Black,* 1–33.

38. John Blassingame, *The Slave Community: Plantation Life in the Antebellum South* (New York: Oxford University Press, 1972); Levine, *Black Culture and Black Consciousness;* Deborah Gray White, *Ar'n't I a Woman: Female Slaves in the Plantation South* (New York: Norton, 1984); Sterling Stuckey, *Slave Culture: Nationalist Theory and the Foundations of Black America* (New York: Oxford University Press, 1987).

39. Houston A. Baker Jr., Manthia Diawara, and Ruth H. Lindeborg, *Black British Cultural Studies: A Reader* (Chicago: University of Chicago Press, 1996); Morley and Chen, *Stuart Hall;* Hazel V. Carby, *Culture in Babylon: Black Britain and African America* (New York: Verso, 1999); Gilroy, *Black Atlantic;* Paul Gilroy, *There Ain't No Black in the Union Jack: The Cultural Politics of Race and Nation* (Chicago: University of Chicago Press, 1991); Paul Gilroy, *Against Race: Imagining Political Culture beyond the Color Line* (Cambridge: Harvard University Press, 2000).

40. Gilroy, *Black Atlantic,* 80.

41. Van Deburg, *New Day in Babylon.*

42. Michael Omi and Howard Winant, *Racial Formation in the United States from the 1960s to the 1990s,* 2d ed. (New York: Routledge, 1994).

43. For an insightful discussion of social boundaries, see Michele Lamont and Virag Molnar, "The Study of Boundaries in the Social Sciences," *Annual Review of Sociology* 28, no. 1 (2002): 167–95.

44. Clifford Geertz, "Thick Description: Toward an Interpretative Theory of Culture," in *The Interpretation of Cultures* (New York: Basic Books, 1973), 5. For a full exposition of this point, see Richard Handler, "Cultural Theory in History Today," in "Review Essay: What's Beyond the Cultural Turn," *American Historical Review* 107, no. 5 (December 2002): 1512–20.

45. Abraham Chapman, *New Black Voices: An Anthology of Contemporary Afro-American Literature* (New York: Mentor, 1972), 31.

46. Hall, "What Is This 'Black' in Black Popular Culture?"

47. Wahneema Lubiano, "'But Compared to What?' Reading Realism, Representation, and Essentialism in *School Daze, Do The Right Thing,* and the Spike Lee Discourse," in *Representing Black Men,* ed. Marcellus Blount and George Cunningham (New York: Routledge, 1996), 189, as cited in Johnson, *Appropriating Blackness,* 4; Johnson, *Appropriating Blackness,* 2; Bendix, *In Search of Authenticity,* 7.

NINE

Turning Structure into Culture: Reclaiming the Freeway in San Diego's Chicano Park

ERIC AVILA

"To you, Mexican culture means Taco Bell and the funny Mexican with the funny hat. . . . We gave you our culture of a thousand years. What have you given us? A social system that makes us beggars and police who make us afraid." Such was how one young activist addressed a reporter from the *San Diego Union,* explaining his involvement with a mass demonstration in the Barrio Logan neighborhood of San Diego.[1] On April 22, 1970, a crowd of approximately 250 people—mostly Chicano, mostly high-school and college-age youths—occupied a two-acre parcel of land that lay directly beneath a connecting overpass linking the recently completed Interstate 5 with the Coronado–San Diego Bay Bridge. Their intention was to block the implementation of a state project to build a station for the California Highway Patrol on that parcel of land and to demand the placement of a park in its stead. Shortly after state construction crews began grading the soil, community activists formed a human chain around the bulldozers, established a makeshift encampment, and occupied the site for twelve consecutive days. In that time, the demonstrators, with the help of local residents, planted shrubs, grass, and trees, anticipating the official establishment of Chicano People's Park.

This scene is familiar in the history of late postwar America: community activists standing up to bureaucrats and their bulldozers. From New York to Los Angeles, American cities witnessed a turning point in their development, in which decades of modernist city planning were interrupted by ordinary citizens who, in the spirit of the times, collectively sought to prevent the destruction of historic neighborhoods and streets that cultivated distinct and particular social identities across generations. City by city, Chinatowns, Little Italys, black and Jewish ghettos, Mexican barrios, mom-and-pop stores, tenement houses, and other red-brick

Fig. 9.1. *Parque Chicano* (mural), by Dolores Serrano, 1978. Photo by Eric Avila,
September 2005.

remnants of the industrial metropolis gave way to monumental civic
centers, corporate plazas, residential towers, and freeways, all of which
heralded the imposition of a new modernist, master-planned city clad
in concrete and glass. By the late 1960s, however, the moms, pops, and
children of the urban underclasses—at least those who did not, or could
not, move to the suburbs—had their say. From People's Park to Washington Square Park, neighborhood activists in cities throughout the country,
like those in San Diego's Barrio Logan, stood down the bulldozers and
blocked the ambitions of city, state, and federal authorities.

From a cultural historian's point of view, it was a remarkable moment,
for as the opening quotation suggests, it encompassed the striking clash
of two very different cultural perspectives. On the one hand, the modernist culture of urban design sought to eradicate, through planning and
architecture, the markings of particular sociohistorical identities upon
the urban environment and to implement a new landscape that transcended the historic manifestations of social and economic difference.
But, by the late 1960s, as Americans adopted a renewed appreciation of
difference and diversity, they looked on the efforts of the master planners
with growing suspicion. Especially in communities like Barrio Logan, a

Mexican American barrio galvanized by the energy of the Chicano civil rights movement, the antiwar movement, and burgeoning environmental activism, the disruptive work of state planners and engineers was seen as detrimental to not only community stability but also the very survival of Chicano culture and identity. This story is about one community making the best of an unfortunate situation: losing the fight against the encroachment of state infrastructure, then exploiting that loss to create a park of renowned beauty. Ultimately, the establishment of Chicano Park in San Diego in 1971 illuminates a community taking symbolic possession of the modernist-built environment and making itself at home in the modern world of traffic and sprawl.

————

In today's San Diego, the Interstate 5 freeway, completed in 1962, splits Logan Heights and Barrio Logan. Before the freeway's arrival, both communities were known simply as Logan Heights, one of San Diego's oldest neighborhoods, established toward the end of the nineteenth century and located less than one mile directly southeast of downtown San Diego. The neighborhood's location on San Diego Bay's waterfront, as well as its close proximity to the downtown core, made it important to transportation facilities as well as to local industry and commerce. With a streetcar line extended to the area in 1891, and the completion of a railroad line, terminating in Logan Heights, that linked San Diego and Los Angeles in 1907, the neighborhood developed as an industrial and manufacturing center of San Diego, and a growing number of working-class families settled in the area. Steel manufacturing, canneries and food processing, and shipbuilding were the area's main economic activities. In 1919 the city deeded ninety-eight acres of Logan Heights' land to the U.S. Navy for the building of a docking and fleet repair base, which was expanded in size over the following decades.[2]

As workers and their families sought quarters close to these industries, a residential neighborhood took shape, dominated by single-family dwellings built in the Craftsman, Queen Anne, or Colonial Revival architectural styles. From early in its establishment, the Logan Heights neighborhood sheltered a diverse pool of residents. Because the neighborhood was not "protected" by the restrictive covenants that other San Diego neighborhoods enforced, it sheltered a racially and ethnically diverse population. Mexicans, African Americans, Chinese, Japanese, and European "whites" shared the houses and jobs in the area, and depended on the growing presence of manufacturing and industrial plants for their livelihood. The 1920s, however, witnessed changes in the racial and ethnic profile of Logan Heights, as the growing adoption of the private automobile sanctioned an early form of white flight that granted older, primarily "white" families access to newer and more distant neighborhoods. As older homes in the neighborhood began to show signs of wear, people of color continued to converge on Logan Heights. Mexicans, fleeing the turmoil of the Mexican Revolution and taking advantage of a new railroad infrastructure in Mexico, accessed neighborhoods like Logan Heights, a mere eleven miles from the U.S.-Mexican border, and African Americans, seeking employment in the local shipbuilding industry, arrived in increasing numbers as well, particularly during and after World War II. By 1940, a WPA guide to San Diego described this corner of San Diego as "the residential section of the Negroes, Mexicans and Orientals." Also as far back as 1940, despite its racial and ethnic diversity, Logan Heights, with its numerical dominance of Mexicans in the neighborhood and 15 percent of San Diego's Spanish-speaking population, qualified as the West Coast's second largest barrio.[3]

After World War II, the military played an increasingly vital role in San Diego's development, as it did in other West Coast cities. The 32nd Street Naval Station greatly expanded its presence in Logan Heights throughout the 1940s and 1950s, blocking neighborhood access to the waterfront, where a pier and a beach had served as community focal points. At the same time, directly across the San Diego Bay from Logan Heights on Coronado Island, the North Island Naval Base also expanded its operations. The combined activity of these naval stations, and their growing stature within the regional economy, demanded the development of a new highway infrastructure, prompting city officials in San Diego to work with the California Division of Highways to devise a comprehensive solution to the growing transportation needs of the city. California experienced a boom in highway construction through the 1950s and 1960s, and cities like Los Angeles and San Diego, both of which emerged as vital centers within California's growing military-industrial complex, garnered an influx of federal, state, and municipal funds for the building of regional highway systems that had been envisioned by city planners as far back as the 1920s and 1930s. The martial impulse behind postwar highway construction is hard to underestimate, as it was plainly apparent in the names of such landmark pieces of federal legislation as the 1956 Interstate Defense and Highway Act, which unleashed a current of federal dollars into the efforts to build highways in and between major urban centers.[4]

In San Diego, two projects by the Division of Highways decisively altered the built environment of Logan Heights. First, construction of Interstate 5, financed by both federal and state monies, began during the mid-1950s; the route followed a north–south axis that sliced through Logan Heights and downtown San Diego on its way to Los Angeles from the Mexican border. This portion of Interstate 5, known then as the Crosstown Freeway, extended three miles, from Logan Avenue on the south, where it connected with what was then known as the Montgomery Freeway, to Market Street on the north, dividing an aging residential neighborhood established in the 1920s and occupied mostly by Mexican Americans. For highway planners, Logan Heights made perfect sense for the routing of the Crosstown Freeway. Because of the expansion of San Diego's downtown core during the 1950s, city officials had changed the zoning of Logan Heights from residential to industrial, inviting freeways and other enterprises that drastically altered the neighborhood landscape and the quality of life it sustained. During the latter half of the decade, as land was cleared to make way for the Crosstown Freeway, junkyards, called *yonkes* by the Spanglish-speaking residents of Barrio Logan, began to concentrate in the area, moving in alongside not only the burgeoning route of the coming freeway but also the neighborhood's established homes and schoolyards. Thus, highway planners found Logan Heights an "ideal" locale for their freeway-building efforts, as "its industrial and military character is well-suited for a new transportation corridor." With its proximity to the downtown core, as well as its importance to local military operations, the Crosstown Freeway was a vital link in an overarching "master plan" that called for some three hundred miles of freeway in San Diego's expanding urban region, incorporating the increasingly scattered centers of residence, commerce, and industry within a regional highway system.[5]

The second project implemented by the Division of Highways that would impact the landscape of Logan Heights was the construction of the Coronado–San Diego Bay Bridge. Throughout the 1950s, as highway planners were fleshing out the lines of an urban highway system, engineers serving the Division of Highways' District Nine, which encompassed the San Diego area, studied proposals for the construction of a bridge spanning the expanse of the San Diego Bay. As the community of Coronado developed rapidly around the growing North Island Naval Station, state and city officials recognized the need for a bridge connecting not only the city of Coronado with the city of San Diego but, more importantly, the North Island Naval Station with the 32nd Street Naval Station in

Logan Heights. State engineers, consulting with government and military officials, considered preliminary layout plans, profiles, and cost estimates for five underwater tube lines and four bridge lines running between the island of Coronado and various points along the San Diego side of the bay. A 1962 report issued by the Division of Highways concluded that construction of a four-lane bridge crossing would cost roughly the same as a two-lane tube crossing built under the bay and could carry approximately 2.5 times the traffic capacity of a two-lane tube. The remaining question was where to locate the bridge's terminus on the San Diego side of the bay. Of the nine proposals studied, six terminated along Crosby Street, between 10th and 11th avenues, right in the heart of Barrio Logan. Because that neighborhood had been rezoned as industrial, and because it met "a new cross town freeway skirting northerly and easterly of the San Diego downtown business district," the Division of Highways settled on that site for the bridge's arrival in San Diego. Engineers considered various bridge designs, deciding upon a four-lane girder-type structure built on concrete piers and footings. This design suited aesthetic considerations; it proved less obtrusive to military air and sea operations than other bridge proposals; and it provided for the easy extension of utility lines between San Diego and Coronado Island.[6]

The Crosstown Freeway and the Coronado–San Diego Bay Bridge momentarily incited a regional obsession with progress and civic development that saturated local channels of news and information. The *San Diego Union*, a fiercely conservative voice in the history of San Diego and leading booster of civic development, praised the Crosstown Freeway as "a vital link in our rapidly modernizing city." And it celebrated the opening of the Coronado Bay Bridge by declaring that "this bridge will stand as an icon of progress in San Diego, as the Golden Gate once did for San Francisco, and the Brooklyn Bridge did for New York. . . . Its cutting-edge design stands at the forefront of civic progress in mid-twentieth century America." The dedication ceremony for the Coronado–San Diego Bay Bridge on November 17, 1969, featured marching bands, beauty queens, and an array of civic officials, including mayors, councilmen, engineers, and state bureaucrats. These state and city officials stood behind Governor Ronald Reagan while he proclaimed, "this day belongs to San Diego and its future promise as a growing center of commercial wealth and industrial might."[7]

For the residents of Logan Heights, however, these lofty invocations fell short; their landscape was now very different from the one they had known before the arrival of junkyards, bridges, and freeway traffic. Where the residents of the neighborhood had once looked out on an undeveloped bay and the island of Coronado in the distance, now the massive concrete pylons that supported a highway interchange framed a view of junkyards and shipbuilding plants. The shadow of the Coronado Bay Bridge loomed over the neighborhood, and the noise and smell of freeway traffic infused the local climate. Moreover, the arrival of traffic and industry in the area precipitated a substantial decline in the residential population—from 20,000 to 5,000 between 1950 and 1970—leaving a community of mostly poor, Spanish-speaking residents who seemed without the means to resist the encroachment of industry and civic infrastructure.[8]

For the remaining residents of Barrio Logan, encroachments on the neighborhood had taken their toll. In 1967, a few assertive citizens of Barrio Logan demanded that the city develop a park beneath the highway-bridge interchange. Up to this point the citizens of Barrio Logan had quietly accepted that the imposition of infrastructure upon their community was the way things had to be. No one had considered petitioning the city council to express residents' opinions, nor had community members gathered to discuss the policies that affected their neighborhood. The local call for a park thus marked a change in the attitude of local residents, who grew more assertive in their response to city and state plans for development in the area. Two years later, their demands were met when the state of California agreed to lease the city a 1.8-acre parcel of land for a neighborhood park. The lease would run for twenty years, and the state would prepare the site for public use, while the city of San Diego would assume responsibility for maintaining and supervising the site.[9]

The city, however, stalled in its promise to deliver a park to Barrio Logan, and when bulldozing finally began on April 22, 1970, it was for the unannounced purpose of building a highway patrol station, not a community park. Furious by this discovery, a handful of local residents, joined by approximately 250 high-school and college-age youths, descended upon the site and formed a human chain around the bulldozers that had been grading the land earlier that day. They occupied the site for twelve consecutive days and nights, demanding that the state transfer the land to the city for the placement of a neighborhood park. "We're ready to die for this park," one protestor told the *San Diego Union*, and as the demonstration garnered more attention in the local media, it won the support of growing numbers of San Diegans, especially those who lived in Barrio Logan. Throughout the occupation, demonstrators and their supporters planted trees, shrubs, and grass to the site, in anticipation of a concession from the city and the state. Local residents supplied food and camping facilities for the demonstrators and aided in the effort to create a makeshift park. The Chicano flag, with its insignia of an eagle used by César Chávez and the United Farm Workers, was raised on a telephone pole, proclaiming the establishment of Chicano People's Park.[10]

This sort of confrontation, although unprecedented in this part of San Diego, had become commonplace in diverse urban centers during the 1960s. Almost exactly one year before this incident, students and community activists in Berkeley, California, had staged a major confrontation with authorities over an undeveloped acre of land owned by the University of California and near the Berkeley campus. Their strategy involved the spontaneous and unwarranted creation of a makeshift park, which incurred a heavy-handed response from state authorities, particularly Governor Reagan, who brought in the National Guard to maintain "law and order." Although these kinds of confrontations exploded throughout the nation with increasing regularity, this particular clash ensued over a parcel of land and marked one community's demand to maintain the peaceful and recreational uses of urban space.[11]

This effort is one aspect of the context surrounding the struggle to establish Chicano Park in Barrio Logan. Another is the emerging Chicano civil rights movement, which took shape in urban centers and rural areas throughout the U.S. Southwest during the 1960s and early 1970s. Poverty, the Vietnam War, police brutality, and the dearth of educational opportunity inspired this social movement, as did a much longer history of social, political, and economic disenfranchisement among Mexican Americans. But since the United States took over the vast parcel of land that includes today's California, Utah, Colorado, and Texas, the idea of turf has been a sensitive issue for Mexican Americans, particularly those living in southwestern urban areas, where during the 1950s and 1960s state and federal authorities often targeted barrio neighborhoods for massive urban redevelopment projects. Although it was the specific proposal to build a highway patrol station that sparked the protests that eventually led to the establishment of Chicano People's Park, the encroachment of junkyards, bridges, and freeways on Barrio Logan since the 1950s culminated in a concerted effort to protect the territorial integrity of San Diego's Chicano community.[12]

On the evening of April 23, 1970, a hearing took place at a local community center in which demonstrators voiced their demands before city and state officials, including City Councilman Leon Williams, District

Manager for the Division of Highways Jacob Dekema, and Captain Vincent J. Herz of the California Highway Patrol. City and state officials reiterated the state's ownership of the land but promised that construction for the proposed patrol station would cease until the issue was settled. They also promised that the city would aid the Highway Patrol in a search for an alternative site for the station, so that the community's desire for a park could be granted. If the state and the city could agree on an alternate site, officials promised, the city would lease the land from the state for the purposes of creating a park. Present at the meeting was local resident and artist Salvador Torres, who gave an impassioned speech outlining his vision of Chicano Park in which Chicano painters and sculptors would turn the bridge and freeway pylons "into things of beauty, reflecting the Mexican American culture." Born and raised in Barrio Logan, Torres had studied art at California College of Arts and Crafts in Oakland and returned to San Diego to immerse himself in the city's burgeoning art scene. In the late 1960s, he participated in two local Chicano art groups, Artistas de los Barrios and Toltecas en Aztlán, and in 1971 he established Congreso de Artistas Chicanos en Aztlán, an organization committed to the creation of art in service of Chicano community empowerment. He was the first to articulate a vision of murals painted on the concrete pylons. "They sent this freeway down the heart of our community and nearly killed it," Torres stated, "we did not want it. We hated the bridge and the freeway. But now that we have them, we have to deal with them creatively." Rebecca Castro, a Mesa College student and a demonstrator at the site, told a *Union* reporter of the plan to paint murals and place mosaic on the pillars, "This will make a great park . . . when the sun is right [under the freeway] it looks like a cathedral." Another resident saw the pylons as a kind of urban forest: "the area is cement, so the pillars are our trees."[13]

On May 1, 1970, the assistant city manager Meno Williams announced that an agreement had been reached with the state that would empower the city to begin negotiations for a land exchange between the city and the state, which in the end would allow the city to convert the site into a neighborhood park. After twelve days of occupation, the demonstrators vacated the site and negotiations began. On July 1, 1970, the San Diego Council authorized a $21,814 contract toward development of a 1.8-acre parcel of land for a park in Barrio Logan. City workers would grade and landscape the site and install sidewalks, a sprinkler system, and drinking fountain. Several months later, after city and state officials agreed on an alternate site for the construction of a patrol station, all the bureaucratic hurdles had been crossed. The California Highway Patrol transferred its deed for the land to the city of San Diego. The federal Department of Housing and Urban Development issued a letter approving a grant that covered most of the costs of constructing a community center on the site, and on April 26, 1971, almost one year to the day after the initial occupation of the site, the California state legislature voted 60 to 0 in an emergency session to approve the transaction between the city and the state. On May 23, 1971, Governor Reagan signed the bill into law, not a surprising move in light of his much-criticized handling of the People's Park incident in Berkeley, which had resulted in one fatality and scores of injuries. Shortly afterward, the residents of Barrio Logan held the first Chicano Park Day to commemorate the park takeover; more than a thousand people participated by attending cultural events and listening to political speeches.[14]

Although murals were an integral part of the Chicano Park vision from its inception, the first ones did not begin to appear until 1973. Enlisting the support of Victor Ochoa, a local artist who had attended the arts program at San Diego City College with Torres, and José Montoya, a graduate of the California College of Arts and Crafts and founder of the art collective Royal Chicano Air Force, Salvador Torres negotiated with bridge officials to obtain formal consent for the proposed murals. Torres was particularly inspired by a recent trip to Mexico City, where he had attended the inaugural ceremonies for the opening of the Siqueiros Polyforum, an elliptical building containing a 50,000-square-foot mural by David Alfaro Siqueiros, the last surviving member of Los Tres, the name assigned to Mexico's three master muralists: Siqueiros, Diego Rivera, and José Clemente Orozco. Torres noted the structural similarities between the Siqueiros Polyforum and the Coronado Bay Bridge, and recognized the local potential for a similar dynamic between aesthetic representation and monumental concrete architecture. By mid-1973, the San Diego Coronado Bridge Authority granted Torres permission to prepare and paint the surfaces of the freeway abutments and pylons. First, Torres and his crew brushed and sandblasted the concrete. Next they applied muriatic acid to the concrete surfaces to kill bacteria, followed by a white primer. The National Steel and Shipbuilding Company and San Diego Gas and Electric Scaffolding donated wire brushes and hard hats for the artists.[15]

The trained artists who led the fight for Chicano People's Park, however, were not the first to apply paint to the walls of the freeway-bridge interchange. In May 1973, the Chicano art group Toltecas en Aztlán enlisted the participation of approximately three hundred barrio residents to color the walls abutting the Interstate 5 freeway on Logan Avenue. Although this endeavor involved the community in creating what eventually became Chicano Park, it did not match the stated vision of trained artists and community activists. According to Torres, "the paints were all laid out. And there's this gigantic wall there, and all of us just looking at this wall. So we pour out the paint, took some rollers, and attacked the wall with the rollers. We put color everywhere. There were at least two or three hundred people there that all of a sudden were all over the walls. It was done spontaneously. We exploded on the walls."[16] Torres had recognized the need for community involvement in the early stages of the mural program, but other artists expressed concerns about the participation of so many nonartists. Guillermo Aranda, a muralist involved in the process of subsequent mural production in Chicano Park, recalled the disappointment of fellow artist José Gomez, who felt that mass community participation betrayed the mural concept. "But we haven't finished yet," Aranda replied to alleviate the concerns of his colleague. After this community event, the core artistic group returned throughout the following year to execute their more studied vision, decorating the concrete pylons with images of Mexican and Chicano history that echoed the platitudes and aspirations of the Chicano civil rights movement.[17]

It is important to understand that these artists painted the freeway within a broader political context of the Chicano civil rights movement, which emphasized the didactic role of art and the artist for generating aspirations toward social change. "El plan espiritual de Aztlán," a manifesto drafted in anticipation of the National Chicano Youth Conference in Denver in 1970, included in its call for community empowerment an emphasis on the cultural role of artists and writers to "unite and educate the family of La Raza." As a visual expression that found its home not in rarified spaces of museums and galleries but rather in everyday spaces of urban public life, muralism was well suited for the imperatives of the Chicano movement, which relied heavily on symbolic images that conveyed the historic struggles for survival among Indian and Mexican peoples. Chicano muralists like Salvador Torres, moreover, aligned themselves within the rich tradition of Mexican muralism as established by Rivera, Orozco, Siquieros, who emphasized the linkages between modern Mexican muralism and the murals found in the ruins of Aztec and Mayan civilizations. Thus murals flourished in the barrio neighborhoods of cities like Los Angeles and San Diego during the 1960s and 1970s, preserving a traditional form of cultural expression rooted in pre-Columbian civilizations.

After local residents had their chance to decorate one corner of the highway-bridge interchange, a group of eleven artists, including Salvador Torres and Victor Ochoa, began work in 1973 on the first mural of Chicano Park, *Quetzalcoatl*, which depicts the feathered serpent of Aztec mythology. That same year, a subsequent group of Chicano artists executed the *Historical Mural*, which depicts portraits of such Mexican revolutionaries as Miguel Hidalgo and José María Morelos, the early leaders in the Mexican War for Independence from Spain; the leaders of the Mexican Revolution, Emiliano Zapata and Pancho Villa; and the modern-day Chicano activists César Chávez, Reyes Tijerina, and Rudolfo "Corky" Gonzales. These two murals marked the inauguration of the artists' vision of Chicano Park, which emphasized the images that saturated the denouement of the Chicano civil rights movement during the late 1960s and early 1970s: scenes of Aztec deities that conveyed Chicano pride in its indigenous past; scenes of Mexican history that emphasized the revolutionary struggle for national sovereignty; and scenes from Mexican American civil rights activism, especially the steadfast determination of César Chávez and the United Farm Workers to end the exploitation of agricultural workers. All of these images played a conscious role in the Chicano movement throughout the Southwest, which emphasized the heroic struggles of Indians, Mexicans, and Chicanos to generate communal pride and solidarity.

Since the 1970s, and throughout the 1980s, Chicano and non-Chicano muralists alike have come to Chicano Park to enhance its murals program and to decorate the concrete pylons of the freeway. In addition to iconic references to Aztec and Toltec mythology, as well as to Mexican revolutionary struggle, the murals of Chicano Park feature portraits of the Virgin Mary, Frida Kahlo, and Ché Guevara. One prominent pylon, adjacent to a central kiosk decorated as a Mayan temple, features a scene from the Chicano Park takeover, depicting the residents' struggle to establish Chicano Park. Today, Chicano Park stands as an iconic pantheon of Chicano history, identity, and culture, and it is recognized as an official historical site by the city of San Diego. It is the largest outdoor display of murals in the world and marks one community's struggle to place itself within the restless landscape of American capitalist urbanism.[18]

Chicano Park, however, is more than an amassed collection of murals. It is also an occasional site for communal festivity and political expression. In April 2007, Chicano Park celebrated its thirty-seventh anniversary by hosting its annual Chicano Park Day, drawing a crowd of more than two thousand people. Since 1971, Chicano Park Day has commemorated the community's triumph in defeating official plans for the placement of a highway patrol station beneath the freeway-bridge interchange. The celebration features a variety of musical and dance performances, including the Ballet Folklórico of Mexico and Danza Azteca, which features indigenous dancing traditions of Aztec culture. Local activists deliver rousing speeches in the Central Kiosk of Chicano Park, and Chicano poets and writers share readings of their work. Community-based organizations set up booths and tables to advertise their nonprofit services available to San Diego's barrio community. The towering murals preside over this annual celebration, emphasizing the broader historical context of Chicano pride and political activism.

In a certain sense, therefore, the power of the Chicano Park murals rests on the ability of local artists, activists, and community-based organizations to act out the very themes that the murals portray: social justice, indigenous tradition, ethnic pride, historical memory, and communal integrity. That Chicano Park has become a focal point for Mexican American activism in southern California, a mere seven miles from the U.S.-Mexican border, illustrates the enduring pride that the murals engender and their ongoing ability to attract a diverse citizenry committed to preserving the cultural traditions and artistic expressions of San Diego's barrio. In fact, the act of painting murals on the surface of state infrastructure suggests the ability of Chicano artists and activists to reclaim urban space in the name of a community displaced by a military conquest some 120 years before the establishment of Chicano Park. To think of the murals as an act of reclamation resonates within the broader context of Chicano history, which to many historians began with the displacement of 100,000 ethnic Mexicans who owned land subsequently claimed by the U.S. government.

In their portraits of César Chávez, Ché Guevara, the Brown Berets, and Mexican revolutionaries, the murals of Chicano Park render messages of dissidence and social critique explicitly. Also important, however, is the way in which Chicano Park posits an urban mode of seeing that defies the visual culture of the freeway metropolis. One enduring critique of freeways, especially within urban communities of color, is that the experience of driving freeways promotes a selective, one might say edited, view of urban life, reducing the city's complexity and diversity to a highly simplified matrix of signs that only identify place, distance, and location. To travel from point A to point B on the freeway is to miss everything in between, as long as our eyes remain tightly focused on the road, as they are supposed to be. Especially when drivers are channeled along freeways that are depressed below the surface of the city, or elevated high above the landscape of daily life, there is little choice in what to see: freeways force their narrow perspective on drivers, diminishing our cognizance of who lives where and in what conditions they live. This experience, of course, marks a radical departure from that of riding subways and street-cars, a mode of transport that brought a previous generation of diverse city people into contact with each other and with scenes of urban life, forcing a heightened awareness of the city's intense diversity.

In the visual culture of San Diego's freeway environment, however, the murals of Chicano Park momentarily arrest the speeding views of freeway drivers and interrupt the lifeless scene of gray concrete and green signs. The broad faces of indigenous warriors and Mexican revolutionaries stare at drivers passing by, demanding a flickering distraction from the road ahead. The hot colors of red, pink, green, yellow, and orange bring life to the cold concrete surfaces of the freeway interchange, imposing the cultural palette of the barrio on the solemn modernist landscape and bringing scenes of Mexico City, Havana, or Caracas to a city that bills itself as "America's Finest City" (fig. 9.2). Murals often evade the attention of scholars interested in visual culture, who dwell on mechanical

Fig. 9.2. *Chicano Park Takeover* (mural), by Guillermo Rosete, Felipe Adame, and Octavio Gonzales, 1978. Photo by Eric Avila, September 2005.

and electronic modes of image reproduction, but as a central component of pre-Columbian visual culture, murals painted in the public spaces of American cities reflect the Latinoization of these cities, nourishing a pattern of transnational urbanism that is increasingly apparent in border towns like San Diego.

This narrative points to an unanticipated and usually unrecognized dialectic embedded within the post–World War II phase of urban modernization in the United States. City planners and state engineers in San Diego, working under the supervision of California's Division of Highways, were charged with a public mandate to facilitate the orderly circulation of vehicular traffic in an expanding urban region. They used scientific rigor and technological advancement to draft and execute plans for an integrated system of highways and bridges, while juggling the imperatives of cost-effectiveness, neighborhood impact, structural integrity, and aesthetic design. Their efforts also required the implementation of new models of surveillance and authority to enforce the orderly conduct of drivers in a new realm of urban public space. The highway and the highway patrol thus marked an unprecedented intervention of state authority into the landscape of urban public life, and they emerged as part of a new urban order that redefined the experience of the late twentieth-century American city.

The residents of Barrio Logan, however, not unlike the residents of other disenfranchised urban communities, bore the brunt of that intervention. During the 1950s and 1960s, their neighborhood witnessed the encroachment of junkyards, bridges, highways, and patrol stations, and that disruptive process culminated in an outburst of protest that galvanized a community against the execution of master plans crafted by distant bureaucrats in Sacramento and Washington, D.C. The nature of that protest deserves particular attention because it asserted the centrality of culture in the confrontation between city people and city planners. Artists like Salvador Torres won support for his vision of Chicano Park because he articulated a more pervasive perception that the cultural values of a specific social group were under siege. This vision resonated with a younger generation of community activists, who drew inspiration from the nationwide explosion of localized social protests, the sum of which issued a collective demand to defend communities against the assertion of state authority at home and abroad. The timing was right, in other words, to define a new vision of urban modernity that did not demand the sacrifice of neighborhood vitality, communal solidarity, and cultural integrity.

This new vision of modernity—issued from below, not above—insisted on the inclusion of diverse cultural expressions from diverse social groups, even as postwar urban policy bulldozed its way through the historic vestiges of that diversity. In the case of San Diego's Chicano Park, the city's Mexican American community won the right to add its own inflection to the master plan for infrastructural development and shifted the terms by which the modernization of the postwar American city took shape. The community did not ask for the placement of bridges and highways in its neighborhood; when these projects came anyway, the residents of Barrio Logan took advantage of their proximity to render conspicuous scenes of Chicano history, mythology, and identity. In doing so, the creators of Chicano Park personalized the impersonal structures of bureaucratic planning and reasserted a visual reminder of the complexity and diversity that remain at the heart of urban public life.

NOTES

1. "Chicano Takeover," *San Diego Union,* April 24, 1970.
2. Frank Norris, "Logan Heights: Growth and Change in the Old 'East End,'" *Journal of San Diego History* 26 (Winter 1983): 32.
3. Ibid., 33; Kevin J. Delgado, "A Turning Point: The Conception and Realization of Chicano Park," *Journal of San Diego History* 44, no. 1 (Winter 1998): 3. Patrick Barley and Michael Pearlman, *Barrio Logan and Western Southeast San Diego Historical Survey,* prepared for the City of San Diego Historical Site Board, June 1980.
4. Gerald Nash, *The American West Transformed: The Impact of the Second World War* (Lincoln: University of Nebraska Press, 1985), 60–61; Roger W. Lotchin, *Fortress California, 1910–1961: From Warfare to Welfare* (Champaign: University of Illinois Press, 2002), 45.
5. Jacob Dekema, "District IX Freeway Report: San Diego," *California Highways and Public Works* 36 (January–February 1957): 27–28; "San Diego Awaits Completion of Crosstown Freeway," *San Diego Union,* April 2, 1958.
6. "Report: San Diego: Coronado Highway Toll Crossing," Division of Highways, Department of Public Works, State of California, August 1962, 11. "Report on a Proposed Toll Highway Crossing of San Diego Bay between the Cities of San Diego and Coronado," Division of Highways, Department of Public Works, State of California, April 1957, 7.
7. "Crosstown Link Scheduled to Open Today," *San Diego Union,* November 18, 1969; "San Diego Celebrates New Bridge," *San Diego Union,* April 8, 1969.
8. Norris, "Logan Heights," 11.
9. "State Awards Land Lease Near Bridge," *San Diego Union,* July 24, 1969, B2.
10. "Chicanos Occupy Bridge Park," *San Diego Union,* April 23, 1970.
11. Terry Anderson, *The Movement and the Sixties* (New York: Oxford University Press, 1995), 321–34.
12. Rudolfo Acuna, *Occupied America: A History of Chicanos,* 2nd ed. (New York: Harper and Row, 1981). Juan Gomez Quinones, *Chicano Politics: Reality and Prom-*

ise, 1940–1990 (Albuquerque: University of New Mexico Press, 1990). David Gutierrez, *Walls and Mirrors: Mexican Americans, Mexican Immigrants, and the Politics of Ethnicity* (Berkeley: University of California Press, 1995).

13. "Chicano Park Occupation," *San Diego Union*, April 24, 1970. "Heavens Open Up to Aid Park Plan," *San Diego Union*, April 25, 1970; "City Hopes to Own Chicano Park Site," *San Diego Union*, April 29, 1970; "Chicanos Vacate Bridge Site," *San Diego Union*, May 1, 1970.

14. "Williams Vows City Gift of Park," *San Diego Union*, May 5, 1970, B3. "City Authorizes $21,814.96 for Coronado Bridge Park," *San Diego Union*, July 1, 1970, B3. Marilyn Milford and Mario Barrera, dirs., *Chicano Park*, with Marilyn Milford, prod. (Red Bird Films, 1988), 58 minutes (videocassette).

15. Pamela Jane Ferree, "The Murals of Chicano Park" (M.A. thesis, San Diego State University, 1994), 36. Eva Cockcroft, "The Story of Chicano Park," *Aztlan* 15 (Spring 1984): 82. Mitford and Barrera, *Chicano Park*.

16. Mitford and Barrera, *Chicano Park*.

17. Ferree, "Murals of Chicano Park," 51.

18. Ibid., 50–65; Cockcroft, "Story of Chicano Park," 86–88; Mitford and Barrera, *Chicano Park*.

PART III

Agendas for Cultural History

MICHAEL O'MALLEY

The four historians in this section, who review the course of cultural history and consider its trajectory and potential, come to cultural history with differing concerns—consumer culture, labor and gender history, the history of popular/mass culture, and Native American studies—and represent different generational cohorts. Agnew and Enstad, in their chapters, address how history can turn alterity into commonality and call for work that opens a path to empathy. Cook and DeLoria seek to integrate foundational modes of historical inquiry—political history and the critique of mass culture—with the insights made available by cultural history; they seek a cultural history that can take clear account of forms of material, political, and legal domination while also recognizing the fact that culture is itself discursive, contested, and rarely simply the product of top-down domination. In this sense, they encourage us to reconsider and ultimately reformulate traditional models of power running through the scholarship on empire, colonialism, and mass culture during much of the late twentieth century.

Cultural historians who worked in the discursive mode, this author included, grew suspicious of histories that tried to recover the voices of others or to speak for subaltern or neglected groups. If the term "American Indian" was itself a discursive formulation, then trying to recover the voices of "American Indians" perpetuated a kind of imperial fiction as if it were fact. Rather then writing about actual people, authors seemed to find it less problematic to write about the discourse of the American Indian. It's a familiar move—not writing about women but about "the discourse of gender," not writing about Chinese immigrants but about the discourse of race. The resulting histories tend to be long on thesis and interpretation but oddly bloodless (a word chosen deliberately) and short on actual human beings.

Philip Deloria's "From Nation to Neighborhood: Land, Policy, Culture, Colonialism, and Empire in U.S.-Indian Relations" aims to bridge the gap between discursive or "representational" accounts of Indians (his previous work as an example), ethnographical accounts of individual tribes, and political narratives of colonialism and imperialism. Opening with a demonstration of how political history and the construction of culture are embedded in even the most mundane acts, Deloria turns to the subject of land as it appears in four periodic iterations of Indian relations with the United States. Deloria's narrative combines the representational or symbolic with the ethnographic, the physical environment with the politics and culture made on and of it, including the blood spilled in its defense and acquisition. He begins with the complicated play of symbolic representation involved in simple acts like buying stamps and taking change in Sacajawea dollar coins, a transaction in which "structures of power are rehearsed and questioned at microlevels, macrolevels, and whatever it is that lies between." Deloria seeks "a more precise form of articulation between the cultural and the political, and requests an invigorated reading of national/imperial narratives."

In "The Return of the Culture Industry," James Cook also seeks a dialogue with other forms of analysis—in his case, Adorno's account of "mass culture" as a corporatized, homogenized product that infantilizes its public. The fantasy of a noncritical consumer, slack-jawed and credulous, has long been dear to the hearts of elites; indeed, as Cook points out, cultural history has done a great deal to undermine that fantasy by pointing to the contested, discursive nature of all culture. Cook notes that "Adorno's own position on the culture industry was far from static" and also reminds us that although culture may be discursive, not all parties have the same tools and resources at their disposal. Cook establishes that many of the institutional foundations and parameters of "mass culture" predate Adorno, but more importantly he demonstrates how, in the nineteenth century, "virtually every black performer to achieve a significant level of commercial success . . . did so by moving across national boundaries." Looking at the remarkable number of African American performers who spent much of their professional lives working in Europe, Cook concludes that "circulation across regional, national, and international markets was not simply incidental to these careers—it was the means by which something called black popular culture first became visible and ultimately sustained itself across the nineteenth century." Describing how "Juba" marketed essentialized notions of blackness as a commodity while also calling attention to their ambiguity, Cook sees a way to both acknowledge the capitalist nature of mass culture and to establish its permeability to influence, reinterpretation, and strategic movements across national markets.

Agnew and Enstad call strongly for a history open to the influence of feeling and the power of spilled blood, grief, and anger. Like Cook, Agnew in "Capitalism, Culture, and Catastrophe" reiterates the ways cultural history undermined elite theories about mass culture. Looking particularly at the career of Lawrence Levine, he ties cultural history to William James's pragmatism and his sense of empathy, the ability to see outside oneself. Agnew insists that empathy is transgressive—that it shatters convention and category and builds new forms of meaning, new paths for light. He notes that as cultural history grew more accepted in the academy, its transgressive qualities inspired attacks from the right. In the culture wars of the 1990s and into the present, Agnew writes, "culture was no longer just a resource; it had been weaponized." A cultural history that stressed the discursive resourcefulness of subalterns left itself open to charges that poverty or racism or sexism scarcely mattered because after all, everyone was making culture and had "agency" or multivalent power. Agnew insists on a cultural history that has room for the emotive force and shock of catastrophe, both the historical catastrophic shock of emerging capitalism described by Karl Polanyi and the present-day shock of 9/11, and more recently, the devastation of Hurricane Katrina. Agnew reviews and praises cultural histories that stress the power of catastrophe and the shock of empathy it provokes.

Nan Enstad insists similarly on the power of grief and the shock of empathy in "On Grief and Complicity: Notes toward a Visionary Cultural History." Enstad eloquently describes two "moments" in cultural history: the "visionary cultural history of subalterns," which began to take shape in the 1970s and early 1980s, and the "deconstructive cultural history of categories and hierarchies," which achieved a common currency during the 1980s and 1890s. Enstad adds depth and range to the categorical division of "empathic" and "discursive" modes suggested earlier and perceptively traces these moments in the work of major U.S. historians. While she celebrates the "visionary history of subalterns," with its emphasis on blood shed in noble (usually lost) causes, she also critiques its excessive reliance on "resistance" as a model. She argues that resistance tended to normalize the present and cast alternative strategies as de facto failures. It tended to imagine a realm of freedom from power, and from culture itself, that could never exist. When she calls for "telling new kinds of stories, not of resistance or oppression," she marks the influence of discursive cultural history but also the power of pragmatism Agnew describes. When she concludes that "we still need, as Lawrence Levine told us almost thirty years ago, to expand our consciousness through the pursuit of the craft of history," she insists on the power of empathy and durability of the human subject.

The essays ask similar questions—how does the cultural historian keep the blood spilled in catastrophe from becoming the essentialized blood that marked the difference between white and black? How can cultural history acknowledge disproportionate and biting forms of political and economic power in the past without "always already" reinstating those power relations in the present? Here Enstad and I might agree in seeing Foucault as an ally. For all his gloomy words about totalizing institutions, Foucault was essentially a pragmatist: John Dewey and Foucault, as Richard Rorty put it in *Consequences of Pragmatism*, are "two philosophers saying the same thing but putting a different spin on it." Seeing no possibility of escape from power, seeing power as an inevitable aspect of living and thinking and acting, Foucault instead focused on how men and women live in discursive relationships, webs of signification, which, in their give and take, themselves constitute culture, *are* what culture *is*. Imagining the commercial entertainment industry as having power and its audience as powerless clearly misses the mark; a better approach would, as Cook does here, document the interrelation of market forces and individual human aspirations. How did Americans work pragmatically with the tools available? And how did their work in turn make new tools available? Foucault arguably has had a greater influence in the United States than anywhere else, precisely because of his pragmatism, his egalitarian sense of how power operates. But Foucault also had a particular sensitivity to the ways that blood, pain, and grief can shock us into empathy.

We might also look again to the African American intellectual tradition, and especially to Ralph Ellison. Ellison consistently argued that African American culture *was* American culture, writ in bold capitals, and American precisely because it was hybridized, creolized, oppressed by politics, and shaped by inescapable commercial representations, yet capable of humor, beauty, intelligence, and grace; it mingled the comic and the tragic in equal measure. Ellison understood that popular culture in the 1950s, popular music especially, gave evidence of a different America than the formal, official political America of segregation and disfranchisement. In mass culture, frequently transgressive but never transcendent, we might find opportunities to "Change the joke and slip the yoke," as Ellison suggested in his essay of the same name. The striking last line of *Invisible Man:* "who know but that, on the lower frequencies, I speak for you?" derived its power from insisting that black Americans spoke for all Americans, that the underclass spoke for the overclass, whether the elite knew it or not, that culture was composed of many voices and that even the most superficially different members of American society "spoke for" each other.

TEN

The Return of the Culture Industry

JAMES W. COOK

For those of us trained as cultural historians during the final decades of the twentieth century, it was easy to perceive Theodor W. Adorno's landmark writings on the "culture industry" as out of synch with our own conceptual priorities. Where Adorno had emphasized the expanding scope and power of corporate producers, our primary concerns were the subjectivity and agency of individual consumers. And where Adorno had railed against a mass cultural landscape of "unending sameness," we set out to explicate more localized patterns of appropriation and refashioning. Starting in the mid-1940s, Adorno employed the phrase "culture industry" to exclude any notion of mass culture that "arises spontaneously from the masses themselves."[1] To our eyes, however, this notion seemed roughly equivalent to throwing the analytical baby out with the bath water. What Adorno's strict division appeared to foreclose were precisely the complex questions of use, meaning-making, and ideological struggle that had led many of us to study mass culture as a historical problem.

My point in elaborating these contrasts is not to suggest that our perceptions were somehow misguided. Even before I took my first cultural history courses during the mid-1980s, many of the field's leading voices were moving toward a far more contested notion of cultural commerce, one in which the agenda-setting powers of corporate producers operated in continuous, reciprocal tension with the creative choices of readers, listeners, and viewers.[2] This new conceptual framework sparked a "renaissance in the study of popular or mass culture" and quickly became the "opening move" for a wide range of pathbreaking essays and monographs.[3] It also signaled the gradual supercession of an older critical position (in many ways exemplified by Adorno's best-known work) that had postulated mass culture as "other."[4] For Adorno, it was still possible to imagine the culture industry as the debased antipode to an "autonomous art." Our concern, by contrast, was how to historicize—and ultimately transcend—the "fixed poles" of modernist and mass, high and low, inside and outside, dominant and resistant.[5]

Still, I found it hard to shake Adorno. What exactly were we losing, I wondered, in killing off one of the first and most rigorous efforts to engage mass culture as an object of critical analysis?[6] Did our own historiographical priorities make it harder to see and appreciate other important facets of this seminal project? My apprehensions here, I should explain, had less to do with Adorno's canonical stature (which, by the early 1990s, was in sharp decline among most Americanists) than my own desire to historicize and explicate mass culture as something more than a collection of localized phenomena. And on *this* score, especially, Adorno's essays had a kind of staying power that rewarded rereading. His broader vision of culture industry, that is to say, was never limited to this or that medium, nor even to the United States. Rather, he presented this industry as a global commodity system, just about as expansive as capitalism itself.

I also began to realize that Adorno's own position on the culture industry was far from static. Broadly speaking, his earliest formulations— for example, in the "mass deception" chapter of *Dialectic of Enlightenment* (1947)—were also his most severe, a pattern specialists have generally linked to three major developments: the rapid influx of American entertainment products in Weimar Germany; the subsequent rise of European fascism; and the broader shock experiences of wartime exile in New York and Los Angeles.[7] During the 1960s, by contrast, Adorno modified his "absolutist stance" on the culture industry in a number of important respects.[8]

In a 1966 essay for the newspaper *Die Zeit*, Adorno wrote in support of the "Young German Cinema" and expressed a more hopeful sense of the creative potential of alternative media practices and federal grant programs.[9] Three years later, he published an article in *Der Spiegel* praising long-playing records as both conducive to serious listening and more democratic than the "phony hoopla" of highbrow opera festivals.[10] And in a 1969 radio lecture titled "Free Time" ("Freizeit"), delivered shortly before his death, he ventured new forms of curiosity and optimism about the public's capacity for critical evaluation:

> What the culture industry presents people with in their free time, if my conclusions are not too hasty, is indeed consumed and accepted, but with a kind of reservation. . . . Perhaps one can go even further and say that it is not quite believed in. It is obvious that the integration of conscious-

ness and leisure time has not yet completely succeeded. . . . I shall refrain from spelling out the consequences; but I think that we can glimpse here a chance of maturity, which might just eventually turn free time into freedom proper.[11]

Significantly (and probably not coincidentally), I first became aware of these "self-revisions" around the same time that a second key development was taking shape, namely, the *return* of the culture industry as a widely invoked object of historical analysis.[12] This return, it is important to emphasize, was no simple recapitulation of Adornean positions (canonical or otherwise) in new scholarly contexts. Indeed, many of the best-known invokers were leaders of the very same projects that had made agency and contest first principles of the cultural turn.

Consider, for example, Michael Denning's introductory remarks from his well-known 1987 study of dime novels:

> I will argue that these popular stories, which are products of the culture industry . . . can be understood neither as forms of deception, manipulation, and social control, nor as expressions of a genuine people's culture, opposing and resisting the dominant culture. Rather, they are best understood as a contested terrain, a field of cultural conflict where signs with wide appeal and resonance take on contradictory disguises and are spoken in contrary accents.[13]

Or Eric Lott's 1993 formulation of the cultural politics of blackface minstrelsy:

> In contrast to both the populist and revisionist views, which sees minstrelsy's politics as univocal, my study documents precisely the historical contradictions and social conflicts the minstrel show opened up. . . . One of our earliest culture industries, minstrelsy not only affords a look at the emergent break between high and low cultures but also reveals popular culture to be a place where cultures of the dispossessed are routinely commodified—and contested.[14]

Or Robin Kelley's 1997 discussion of pleasure and profit on the post-industrial playground:

> What I am suggesting . . . is that the pursuit of leisure, pleasure, and creative expression is labor, and that some African-African youth have tried

to turn that labor into cold hard cash. Thus, play has increasingly become, for some, more than an expression of stylistic innovation, gender identities, and/or racial and class anger—increasingly, it is viewed as a way to survive economic crisis or a means to upward mobility. . . . In a nation with few employment opportunities for African Americans and a white consumer market eager to be entertained by the "other," blacks have historically occupied a central place in the popular-culture industry.[15]

Or Paul Gilroy's 2000 vision of black cultural circulation across the Atlantic world:

The black musicians, dancers, and performers of the New World have disseminated these insights, styles, and pleasures through the institutional resources of the cultural industries that they have colonized and captured. These media, particularly recorded sound, have been annexed for sometimes subversive purposes of protest and affirmation. The vernacular codes and expressive cultures constituted from the forced new beginning of racial slavery reappeared at the center of a global phenomenon that has regularly surpassed . . . innocent notions of mere entertainment.[16]

Particularly striking in these statements are the subtle reconfigurations of Adorno's concept to connote something other than straightforward manipulation or ideological domination. And one could point to many other prominent examples. From Miriam Hansen's work on silent film spectatorship to Janice Radway's analysis of the Book-of-the-Month Club to Mark Anthony Neal's discussions of transnational hip-hop: the popular and mass cultural "industries" now routinely referenced in much of the leading scholarship are clearly not operating on the same "totalizing" plan first sketched out by Adorno during World War II.[17] Yet this pattern begs a more basic question. Why reconfigure rather than *replace*? Now that the culture industry no longer serves as a synonym for social control, what exactly is it *doing* in so many of our texts?

Labels

Let me begin with the long-running problem of labels. Over the past three decades, most of us who work on cultural commerce have become far more careful and self-conscious about the adjectives we use. Few today would apply the term "mass" to cultural forms produced in a preindustrial setting or marketed to a single demographic. Fewer still would describe mass culture in the manner that so annoyed Adorno—as something "that arises spontaneously from the masses themselves." But what about the related questions of when and how mass begins? In his 1999 essay collection, *American Culture, American Tastes,* Michael Kammen offers one of the most careful and incisive arguments for restricting this term to cultural commodities produced after World War II. Simultaneous distribution and universal access, Kammen emphasizes, were not really possible before the advent of electronic media, national brands, and corporate franchising. Even McDonalds did not become "ubiquitous" beyond the middle-class suburbs until the 1970s.[18]

Yet the more one thinks about these complex questions of size, speed, and circulation, the harder it becomes to maintain strict categorical divisions. Two brief examples from my own research begin to illustrate some of the difficulties. In fall 1842, most U.S. commentators were positively dazzled by the pace with which Charles Dickens's *American Notes for General Circulation* moved across international markets. Within seventy-two hours, Dickens's widely anticipated travelogue (first published by London's Chapman and Hall) sold 50,000 copies in the United States alone. And within about a week, hundreds of newspapers in every part of the nation were running chapters—both in serial form and as special "extra" editions—with little regard for British copyright.[19] The very same year, P. T. Barnum became manager of New York's American Museum and quickly transcended older distinctions between local and national publics, firsthand observation in the exhibition hall, and secondhand evaluation through disembodied print media. Responding to the outrageous publicity stunts Barnum liked to call "humbugs," newspapers "throughout the country" regularly copied his press releases and exhibition reviews. Thus, he explained, was the "fame" of the American Museum "wafted from one end of the land to the other."[20]

One might object here, of course, that both of these examples point to historically specific senses of ubiquity—senses that were quickly superceded and recalibrated through the ongoing process of market expansion. What seems self-evidently large, fast, or far-flung at one moment may appear relatively modest, plodding, or circumscribed in another. But that is precisely my point: qualitative labels such as "popular" and "mass" inevitably refer to modes of production that are historically mobile and often vary from medium to medium. Perceptive critics sometimes respond to these dilemmas by adding a second adjective. In Kammen's schema, for instance, Barnum's antebellum shows are described as "commercial popular culture," which in turn gives way to "proto mass culture" around the turn of the twentieth century.[21] Other scholars employ the somewhat redundant phrase "mass popular culture" to distinguish between relative scales or stages of historical development.

Even these solutions, however, are plagued by a number of lingering problems. One involves the frequently nonlinear rhythms of cultural appropriation.[22] As most hip-hop fans know, the raw materials of their preferred musical genre first emerged during the mid-1970s, when a number of DJ's in the South Bronx began to employ older technologies of mass reproduction (records, turntables, and cassette tapes) for new strategic purposes (sampling, scratching, and localized distribution).[23] Here, as in many other cases of cultural recycling under capitalism, the dialectic between vernacular practice and mass production moves in multiple directions—sometimes, mass begets vernacular begets mass.[24] To describe the now global phenomenon of hip-hop as *either* vernacular *or* mass culture is to miss much of its social and historical significance.

The second basic problem involves the ongoing difficulty of lining up eras, products, and scales in any kind of fixed or finished way. As Kammen himself emphasizes, the corporate juggernaut known as McDonalds was far more *massive* in 1970 than in 1950. And it is hard to imagine that this category will ever stand still. Consider our Hollywood blockbusters that "open everywhere." In November 2003, the blockbuster film *Matrix Revolutions* achieved the largest international release in Hollywood history, opening simultaneously on more than ten thousand screens and in forty-three languages.[25] Yet as film distribution continues to move to wireless networks and the Internet, "everywhere" will quickly come to signify a far larger set of markets.[26]

In still other cases, the confusion derives from mass-distributed products, which in actual practice remain largely invisible. Lawrence W. Levine was among the first to draw attention to this possibility, noting: "not all mass culture was popular. Many mass-produced books went unread, many films unseen, many radio programs unheard by substantial numbers of people. This distinction is crucial: not everything mass produced for the American people was popular, even if a substantial percentage of what was popular by the 1930s was mass produced."[27] For Levine, the significance of this rhetorical slippage lay in unexplored consumer choices, the broader process of audiences "distinguishing between what they found meaningful, appealing, and functional and what they did not." But his insight also points to important questions of categorical cohesion and periodization. To describe the hundreds of unseen products in most local video stores as qualitatively more "popular" than, say,

Uncle Tom's Cabin, is to prioritize one category of measurement (distribution points) over others (such as resonance and impact) that are arguably more significant. The end result, as my students like to point out, is a pair of conceptual labels that sometimes confuse as much as they explain.

Culture industry, by contrast, conjures the image of a far more concrete historical entity whose specific organizational patterns and stages of development can be carefully tracked and explicated without unraveling the larger category. This capacity for historical differentiation is one of the built-in advantages of Adorno's catchphrase and may help to explain why so many recent scholars have reclaimed it: by moving the term "culture" from noun to adjective (mass *culture* to *culture* industry), we shift the conceptual emphasis from qualitative measure to mutable institution. This institutional category, moreover, poses fewer analytical difficulties in that it regularly shifts between literal and figurative meanings. It can refer to a specific business enterprise such as the late nineteenth-century vaudeville empire built by Benjamin Keith and Edward Albee, as well as to the larger process of syndication for which the phrase "Keith-Albee circuit" often serves as historical shorthand.[28] Much like the term "market," industry simultaneously signifies a microlevel site of production and a macrolevel system of circulation.[29] In his 1963 essay "Culture Industry Reconsidered," Adorno emphasized just this sort of analytical flexibility. "The expression 'industry,'" he explained, is "not to be taken too literally. It refers to the standardization of the thing itself—such as that of the Western, familiar to every movie-goer—and to the rationalization of distribution techniques. . . . It is industrial more in a sociological sense, in the incorporation of industrial forms of organization even when nothing is manufactured."[30]

This clarification points to a third major advantage. By its very design, Adorno's concept focuses more careful attention on the historical processes of standardization, distribution, marketing, and integration that ultimately connect Barnum's exhibitions and McDonald's burgers as systems of commodity production. Acknowledging this continuity, it seems to me, need not lead us to resuscitate older theories of economic determinism: the long-obsolete notion of cultural commodities as one-dimensional vessels of "false consciousness." Nor would I wish to endorse Adorno's troublesome habit of collapsing the distinction between commodity types for rhetorical effect—for example, his quip in "The Schema of Mass Culture" that "the Ford model and the model hit song are all of a piece."[31] Rather, what remains valuable in such quips is Adorno's stubborn refusal to consider questions of aesthetic form or ideological function *apart* from the mediating structures of capitalism. For Adorno, "the rationalization of distribution techniques" and "the incorporation of industrial forms" are not simply incidental context—they are the distinctive, inescapable features of modern cultural production that pervade his entire line of questioning.[32]

Massification

But how does one track something as large and abstract as "the rationalization of distribution techniques"? Where, in other words, might we look for key historical watersheds in the "production of the popular"—as industry, idea, and marketing category?[33] For the most part, our tendency has been to explore these questions of "massification" through regional or national studies of individual cultural forms.[34] One of the earliest and most sophisticated examples is Denning's *Mechanic Accents* (1987), which devotes an entire chapter to the reorganization of literary production during the second half of the nineteenth century. In the post–Civil War "fiction factories" of New York City, he explains, the "tendency of the industry was to shift from selling an 'author,' who was a free laborer, to selling a 'character,' a trademark whose stories could be written by a host of anonymous hack writers and whose celebrity could be protected in court."[35] In some cases, this meant that authorial brand names such as "Bertha M. Clay" long outlived the actual writers who first produced them. It also meant that the same authorial staffs who wrote "Bertha M. Clay" romances for women sometimes produced "Frank Merriwell" and "Nick Carter" adventures for men. These new forms of standardization, moreover, coincided with equally dramatic changes in corporate structure and distribution: "whereas the first wave of cheap books and story papers in the 1840s was often limited to the market of a single city and survived only a few years, the distribution monopoly of the American News Company made the post–Civil War nickel and dime libraries a national industry."[36]

In her 2002 study *The Circus Age*, Janet Davis charts a similar transformation in the late nineteenth-century exhibition trade, devoting the bulk of two early chapters to major changes in marketing, distribution, and labor.[37] Central to her story is the 1869 completion of the transcontinental railroad, a historical watershed that enabled the creation of more capital-intensive, three-ring spectacles and ever-wider national touring schedules. Yet, as Davis also makes clear, the structural transformation of the "railroad circus" was never simply a question of laying additional

tracks. In order to capitalize on the expanding reach of the new transportation networks, late nineteenth-century impresarios such as P. T.
Barnum, Adam Forepaugh, and James Bailey enlisted market researchers to analyze population patterns, weather conditions, competing summer resorts, factory rosters, even crop reports—anything, in short, to
identify the most profitable routes. They also added entire departments
of advance men to secure local contracts for fuel, water, animal feed,
and hotel rooms; bill posters to cover the public spaces of each new tour
stop; press agents to solicit promotional deals with local editors and merchants; and sledge gangs to erect and take down the traveling canvas
cities. As Davis concludes, "the relationship between the circus and big
business was more than metaphorical, because the circus *was*—relatively
speaking—big business at the turn of the century."[38]

One could go on like this for some time, mining leading studies of
individual cultural forms for evidence of additional changes. In his pathbreaking work on late nineteenth-century magazines, for example, Richard Ohmann has emphasized the symbiotic relationship between the
first national advertising campaigns of the 1880s and the emergence of
new nationally distributed periodicals such as *Ladies' Home Journal* and
Cosmopolitan, both of which strategized content, marketing, profits, and
distribution in direct relation to their ad buys.[39] In similar fashion, Janice
Radway has suggested that Harry Scherman's Book-of-the-Month Club
constituted an innovative response to one of the most basic dilemmas of
mass literature, namely, how to market new titles "widely, repetitively,
and continuously without devaluing the cultural itself as a status category." Part of what made Scherman's 1924 enterprise so successful, she
argues, was its ability to replicate some of the major "structural innovations of the Fordized economy" even as it recognized that "the relentless,
staccato pace set by the inexorable production of an increasing number of
goods and services caused great anxieties within the American population. With respect to the publishing sphere, this meant that the increase
in title output . . . presented readers with the daunting problem of how to
winnow the mass of books published to a reasonable collection of a few
titles to read."[40]

Collectively, it seems to me, these studies have provided a series of
important snapshots on much the same historical process: the specific
effects of corporate capitalism on specific cultural industries at specific
moments in time. But what about the even broader sense of culture industry first articulated in *Dialectic of Enlightenment*—a transnational "system
of capital," with multiple "branches," "media," and "sectors?"[41] Part of

what makes this wide-angle question somewhat trickier to answer is the polemical impulse running through much of Adorno's work. Precisely because he wanted to condemn the culture industry for its "totalizing" tendencies, he often engaged in obvious forms of hyperbole. "All mass culture," we are told, is "identical"—a calculated overstatement which immediately flattens the media-specific characteristics and year-by-year changes that concern most historians.[42] Adding to the problem is Adorno's preference for treating the culture industry as a fully formed contemporary menace. How, exactly, the menace came into being—or where we might mark the crucial turning points in its transnational expansion—never really surfaced as central questions in his larger body of work.[43]

This should not lead us to conclude, however, that wide-angle historicizing is simply impossible. Indeed, one of the more intriguing features of the culture industry over the past two centuries has been its tendency to generate published commentaries on its own historical development. The specific vehicles for such commentaries are familiar to most of us, although they more typically go by the name of trade papers—with titles such as *Variety, Publisher's Weekly,* and *Pollstar.* None of these titles offers perfect comprehensiveness, of course; most only survive a decade or two. And although some of the leading publications cut across multiple media, the vast majority focus on individual cultural forms.[44] Still, these periodicals constitute a badly underutilized resource for cultural historians, especially for those of us interested in connecting long-running investments in discourse, representation, subjectivity, and perception to much larger, macrolevel questions about market structures, institutional networks, distribution systems, and communication webs (those key words of twenty-first-century globalization studies).[45] More than virtually any other type of primary source, trade papers help us map the culture industry's tendency toward transnational "monopolization" and "bureaucratic expansion," a tendency that Adorno (channeling Marx and Weber) liked to assert but rarely explored in much specificity and detail.[46]

Consider two of the earliest and most important examples: the *Era* (published in London from 1838 to 1939) and the *New York Clipper* (published between 1853 and 1923).[47] One of the most striking features of these periodicals is their surprisingly broad and early articulation of international markets. During the 1850s, the *Era* ran regular columns on dozens of different cities across England, Ireland, and Scotland, as well as on a wide variety of "Foreign Theatricals" in New York, Boston, Philadelphia, Paris, Turin, Naples, Madrid, Berlin, Cologne, Vienna, Prague, and Saint Petersburg. By the 1860s, the paper's scope of foreign reporting was even broader, extending across most of the British Empire into Asia, South Africa, and the Pacific. The *Clipper* was a bit slower to push beyond the confines of Lower Manhattan, but starting in the 1860s, its weekly columns extended to openings in Britain and Canada. And by the 1870s, its "Foreign Show News" and "Theatrical Record" included reports from correspondents in France, Italy, Austria, Scandinavia, Cuba, South America, Hawaii, Australia, New Zealand, and India.[48]

My goal in assembling these lists is not simply to push for longer, transnational patterns of circulation—a move that goes back at least as far as Paul Gilroy's brief but rich discussion of the Fisk Jubilee Singers in the *Black Atlantic*.[49] The more important point, in fact, may be that trade papers such as the *Era* and *Clipper* were themselves instrumental in building the very networks of commerce and discourse through which early acts such as the Fisk Jubilee Singers became visible across vast cultural geographies.[50] Listen, for example, to the *Clipper* editors' description of their mission in the paper's first regular "Amusements" column of May 24, 1856:

> To the Profession—The Clipper is, perhaps, circulated over a wider extent of the country than any other journal in the United States. In view of this fact, we desire to make it as interesting to our theatrical friends as it already is in the sporting community. It is often the case that, owing to the changes occurring in the profession, actors and actresses are utterly unable to keep the "run" of each other. To obviate this difficulty, we have set apart a portion of our journal as a "Theatrical Directory," by means of which the whereabouts of our friends may be seen at a glance. In order to make this department as correct and complete as possible, we respectfully request those who take an interest in such matters to drop us a line, weekly, giving the movements of the disciples of "Thespis." Managers of Theatres, Circuses, Minstrels, &c., would perhaps consult their own interests by sending us a weekly "bill of the play," as such favors will always receive earliest attention.

What I believe we can hear in these lines is the culture industry becoming conscious of itself as a nonlocalized yet interconnected system of capital. Even as the system's self-appointed interlocutors acknowledge the relatively fragmented state of internal communication ("owing to the changes occurring in the profession"), they begin to imagine new methods for coordinating management, scheduling, and promotion across multiple markets. Over the next half century, this movement toward wider circulation and coordination registered most clearly in the papers' advertising columns. During the 1850s, the *Era* and the *Clipper* generally featured a page or less of ads, most of which simply announced the weekly offerings of individual theaters in London and New York. Around the turn of the twentieth century, by contrast, both papers regularly ran up to six full pages of ads, many of which promoted products (such as foreign booking agencies and steamship lines) specifically designed to facilitate the integration of performers, managers, and venues around the globe.[51]

On one level, then, trade papers such as the *Era* and *Clipper* help us to track the *longue durée* of capitalist expansion taking place across multiple decades, markets, and even hemispheres. Yet they also make it easier to see more localized shifts and political struggles occurring within different "branches" of this industry at particular historical moments.[52] Good examples can be found in the *Era*'s almost weekly coverage of British "singing saloons" during the 1850s.[53] Over the previous decade, these largely working-class venues had come to occupy a relatively secure position on one side of the institutional divide created by the Theatre Regulation Act of 1843. Simply put, this federal legislation forced British managers to make a choice: they could either show plays or serve alcohol but not both—a market-driven policy that increased the number of officially licensed "legitimate" theaters even as it created new forms of socioeconomic stratification.[54]

By the early 1850s, there were over a hundred singing saloons in Liverpool alone. But this explosion of extra-theatrical amusement mixed with alcohol did not go unchallenged.[55] Moral reform groups sought to curtail the trend by lobbying local governments and sponsoring alcohol-free "people's concerts" and "mechanics' institutes." Singing-saloon managers, by contrast, attempted to parlay their commercial success into more venues and broader clienteles. The typical pattern was to apply for a theater license with the profits from a singing saloon, thereby securing multiple sectors of a particular urban market. Theater managers, however, saw this maneuver as a potential encroachment on their interests and hired lawyers to fight the license applications of singing-saloon managers. The *Era* editors, hoping not to offend any particular constituency within their national readership, chose the safer option of blaming Parliament:

> It is the law that seems to be *the great* offender in this case. God forbid that there should be no restrictions upon public performances. At the same time, the public has a right to all the rational amusement it wants. So long

as there is no offence to morality, an Englishman is justified in demanding
to be permitted to listen to singing while he takes his beverage. . . . As for
singing rooms, let them be properly conducted, and who can reasonably
say that the Legislature should shut them up?[56]

I offer this brief episode from the mid-Victorian culture wars to support two broader conclusions. One is that the production of the popular
has never simply unfolded according to some inexorable logic of capitalist expansion. Rather, it always (simultaneously) runs through multiple
axes of competing products, shifting publics, and localized power struggles. For the most part, previous scholarship has cast these struggles as
relatively narrow conflicts between producers and consumers, with some
conflicts over access, others over behavior, and still others over the forms
and meanings of the representations themselves. Less well explored or
understood are the contemporaneous struggles that often take place
within and *across* culture industries. The British case we have just considered, for example, was as much a contest between competing entertainment sectors (licensed theaters versus singing saloons versus alcohol-free
peoples' concerts) and commercial interests (the rival managers who
produced and sold each type of product) as it was a struggle between
theater owners and their working-class patrons. In our own time, the
various forms and fronts of culture industry conflict have continued to
proliferate. Self-described "independent" film and music companies are
routinely celebrated, purchased, and then redefined as the niche markets
of multinational conglomerates; battles over file-sharing products such as
Napster make their way to the Supreme Court; evangelical groups uneasy
with society's prevailing norms produce their own cable channels, film
festivals, and concert tours.

A second key conclusion is that these battles within and across international mass culture frequently take on distinctive national characteristics. As some readers will have recognized by now, the singing-saloon
squabbles in Victorian Britain were virtually contemporaneous with
another, more violent eruption of culture industry stratification in New
York City—the notorious Astor Place Theater Riot of 1849, which left
twenty-two protestors dead in the streets.[57] In the United States, however,
there were no central regulatory mechanisms for distributing theatrical
patents, no federal laws about mixing alcohol and drama. Rather, in the
more laissez-faire cultural economy of antebellum Manhattan, licenses
and lawyers were replaced by brickbats and bullets.

The juridical contours of the antebellum show trade likewise varied from location to location. Some governing bodies (such as the states of Vermont and Connecticut, or the city of Lowell, Massachusetts) passed legislation banning "low theatricals," but many others did not. And the localized strictures often changed from year to year, a system that produced characteristically ad hoc patterns of domestic cultural politics. In London, the Lord Chamberlain's office read and approved or censored most of the new plays intended for the nation's stages. In most U.S. cities, by contrast, antebellum theater managers and publishers discovered they had pushed too far only when they found themselves targeted for boycotts, libel suits, or violence.[58]

Varieties of Conflict

At this point, it may appear that we have long since abandoned Adorno's top-down mode of theorizing. Nowhere in his culture industry essays, after all, do we find cases of internal struggle akin to the singing-saloon battles or the Astor Place riot. And on the rare occasions when he alludes to "the rebellious resistance" of low cultural forms, it generally comes in reference to some hazy moment in the pre-industrial past, when "social control was not yet total."[59] Still, I think it would be wrong to conclude that Adorno has nothing to teach us about how to theorize cultural conflict in a more rigorously historical framework.

Our current fascination with globalization is a good case in point. On one level, of course, Adorno's early essays seem to anticipate all-too-familiar arguments about the rise of corporate oligopolies and creeping Americanization. Yet his simultaneous focus on transnational systems of capital—rather than individual nation-states—also leads, somewhat more unexpectedly, to roughly the same analytical starting point adopted by recent theorists of black cultural politics such as Paul Gilroy, Stuart Hall, and George Lipsitz, all of whom have pushed for greater critical attention to the transnational circulation of cultural commodities (e.g., reggae and hip-hop records) as vessels of oppositional consciousness.[60] The intellectual lineage here is relatively straightforward but easy to miss: one cannot theorize mass cultural exchanges within and across diasporic communities until one has a transnational model *of* mass culture.

Adorno's emphasis on the interconnectedness of culture industry sectors and branches, moreover, helps us to think about how one form of market expansion might inadvertently reshape power relationships within another. Let me offer one brief example from my current book project. As I noted earlier, Dickens's *American Notes for General Circulation* (1842) was among the first mass-circulated texts of the nineteenth century. Less well known is that fact that its transatlantic popularity stemmed in part from one of the earliest published descriptions of African American dancing in a post-emancipation context. The key passage takes place at a Five Points dance cellar visited by Dickens during his March 1842 tour of New York City. It begins with an audience request:

> What will we please to call for? A dance? It shall be done directly, sir: "a regular breakdown." . . . Five or six couples come upon the floor, marshaled by a lively young negro, who is the wit of the assembly, and the greatest dancer known. . . . the sport begins to languish, when suddenly the lively hero dashes in to the rescue. Instantly the fiddler grins, and goes at it tooth and nail; there is new energy in the tambourine; new laughter in the dancers; new smiles in the landlady; new confidence in the landlord; new brightness in the very candles. Single shuffle, double shuffle, cut and cross-cut; snapping his fingers, rolling his eyes, turning in his knees, presenting the backs of his legs in front, spinning about on his toes and heels like nothing but the man's fingers on the tambourine. Dancing with two left legs, two right legs, two wooded legs, two wire legs, two spring legs— all sorts of legs and no legs—what is this to him? And in what walk of life, or dance of life does man ever get such stimulating applause as thunders about him, when, having danced his partner off her feet, and himself too, he finishes by leaping gloriously on the bar-counter, and calling for something to drink, with the chuckle of a million of counterfeit Jim Crows, in one inimitable sound![61]

Previous scholars have often presented this passage as a rare window onto black vernacular forms soon to be overshadowed by the rise of commercial minstrelsy (the first organized minstrel show in New York City took place only four months after *American Notes* was published).[62] Less understood are the broader historical impacts of Dickens's representational choices on the young black man at its center: the still anonymous "lively hero" whose climactic and "inimitable" laughter seems directed precisely at the commercial blackface industry ("a million counterfeit Jim Crows"). We now know a great deal more: that his real name was William Henry Lane, although he generally performed as Juba or Master Juba; that he began his career at least two years earlier, performing surreptitiously in blackface under P. T. Barnum's management; that soon after Dickens's visit he became the first African American dancer to perform in mainstream northern venues and headline touring companies;

and that he used this growing fame during the mid-1840s to forge a more lasting and successful career on the other side of the Atlantic, where he eventually appeared in almost every major theater and music hall across the United Kingdom.[63]

As I began this project, my instinct was to treat Lane's remarkable (and remarkably early) career as an exceptional case. Most antebellum black performers, after all, did not find their labors recorded for mass consumption by the world's best-selling author, a dramatically new form of cultural capital that Lane proceeded to leverage in multiple locations. Yet as I sat in the British Library pouring through hundreds of newspaper reviews across England, Scotland, and Ireland, I came to refine my initial appraisal in two key respects.

First, I found myself surprised by the sheer number of African American performers in Victorian Britain. From the dramatic performances of Ira Aldridge and the orchestral music of Francis Johnson to the operatic recitals of Elizabeth Greenfield and the panorama paintings of Henry Box Brown, virtually every black performer to achieve a significant level of commercial success before the Civil War did so by moving across national boundaries. This discovery led to a second round of rethinking about the structural parameters of black agency within early mass culture. Indeed, as I sorted through the peripatetic careers of other black pioneers such as Charles Hicks, the Fisk Jubilee Singers, James and George Bohee, Sam Lucas, Sissieretta Jones, George Walker, Bert Williams, and Aida Overton Walker, a much larger pattern began to crystallize. Strategic circulation across regional, national, and international markets was not simply incidental to these careers—it was the means by which something called black popular culture first became visible and ultimately sustained itself across the nineteenth century.[64]

Somewhat surprisingly, then, Adorno's early insistence on treating mass culture as a transnational industry made it easier to track larger patterns of subaltern struggle only partially visible in more recent and localized studies. But what of his much-better-known remarks regarding the culture industry's "regressive" effects on individual consumers? Here again it is important to be clear about Adorno's deep and abiding skepticism toward the very notion of an oppositional consumer consciousness. For most of his career, Adorno theorized mass consumption not as a domain of individual subjectivity or even play, but as something "administered" by the culture industry and its increasingly mechanized forms of spectatorship. "Rebelliousness," in this schema, was essentially a sham—

one of the culture industry's standard marketing angles (along with novelty and prudery) designed to seduce, distract, and pacify.

Even here, though, there are some important wrinkles. Recall, for example, Adorno's intriguing comments of 1969 (in "Free Time") about the ambiguous effects of culture industry immersion: the products and promotions that are only "accepted with a kind of reservation" and "not quite believed in." The empirical touchstone in this case was a 1966 study by the Frankfurt school of how the public perceived a royal wedding "broadcast by all the mass media." Initially, at least, the results only seemed to confirm the "familiar pattern." "Relevant, possibly political news" was "transformed into a consumer item," and most consumers parroted back the media hooks, describing the wedding as a "once-in-a-lifetime" event. In the same surveys, however, Adorno began to observe a curious commingling of "acceptance" and "disbelief"—especially when the questions focused on the "political significance" ascribed "to the grand event." He even detected "symptoms" of a broader "split consciousness," noting "that many of the people interviewed . . . suddenly showed themselves to be thoroughly realistic, and proceeded to evaluate critically the political and social importance of the same event."[65]

This notion of a "split" consumer consciousness—at once shaped by culture industry formulas and conscious of the shaping—has received relatively little attention from cultural historians.[66] Yet it may constitute one of the more important developments in the longer history of mass culture, an ideological pattern just about as old as the culture industry itself. As early as 1855, it was already creeping into Barnum's autobiography as a new managerial maxim—that "the public appears disposed to be amused, even when it is conscious of being deceived."[67] A decade later, it resurfaced in his 1865 essay collection *Humbugs of the World*, but this time in the form of a managerial complaint about the growing numbers of consumers who "humbugged themselves" by treating his most expensive, genuine wonders as possible fakes.[68] The problem, of course, was that Barnum had taught his audiences all too well. Thoroughly acculturated to the showman's bogus self-accusations and promotional shell games, many American Museum consumers now began to view *all* of his claims—even those that were entirely true—with a reflexive skepticism.[69]

In his recent work on the British music hall, Peter Bailey has identified a related species of mass cultural "knowingness" articulated between working-class performers and audiences—often at the expense of the more socially powerful. Particularly helpful is Bailey's insistence that the music hall's "knowing" aesthetic of double entendre and comic innuendo (the second-level "conspiracies of meaning" produced through winks, nods, and puns on stage) emerged not from some marginal or autonomous site of working-class struggle, but from within and through the ongoing processes of commodification, standardization, and combination that transformed the early singing saloons into a national industry. This industry, he concludes, "did not . . . generate an anti-language in the accepted sense of the term, but rather a resignification of everyday language which knowingly corrupted its conventional referentiality and required a certain competency in its decoding."[70]

Where might these arguments lead? Above all, I believe they push us to think beyond the well-worn questions of cultural industry manipulation (yes or no?) and cooptation (how much?). My point here is not simply that most culture industry products are ideologically contradictory, simultaneously shaped by producers as well as consumers.[71] Rather, I am suggesting that the longer historical process of culture industry expansion has generated new forms of self-consciousness (vis-à-vis its working methods) and expertise (vis-à-vis its aesthetic practices). In Barnum's museum, this process registered as an epistemological shift in the meaning of "curiosity." Although some viewers continued to debate the authenticity of the dubious wonders, others discussed how they were being manipulated *by* the debate itself, treating the showman's promotional tricks as an equally fascinating, second-level topic of moral and economic evaluation. In the British music hall, by contrast, knowingness crystallized as new forms of cultural competence, as the ability to resignify words and phrases increasingly subject to commercial standardization and government regulation.

Less clear is what *happened* to these new forms of market-driven savvy as they migrated (and cross-pollinated) beyond their historical points of origin. Bailey has urged caution in assuming a straightforward movement into oppositional politics: "it would be wrong to triumphalise. . . . the counter-discourse of music hall knowingness was limited to the infraction rather than the negation of the dominant power relationships and, as its echo of official idioms demonstrated, it was compromised between challenge and collaboration."[72] Much the same, I think, can be said about the rising tide of consumer doubt fostered by Barnum. By focusing more explicitly on the self-reflexive qualities of his public reception, we go a long way toward complicating the long-running stereotypes about Barnum and suckers. Yet as Barnum himself discovered, consumer skepticism in this context was a slippery thing. In some cases, it could produce a kind of critical distance: the ability to stand outside the system, explicate its working methods, and make new and different choices. But in other cases, it socialized its adepts to a more despairing and passive brand of cynicism: the conclusion that there was no outside of Barnum's shell games, or that the culture industry's long-running valorization of choice was nothing more than a fool's bet.[73]

Significantly, Adorno's final thoughts on these questions (issued less than three months before his death) were far more equivocal than most of his public statements from the previous three decades. Indeed, the closing lines of "Free Time" posed the problem of split consciousness in the form of an open question, one that still echoes into the present: "I shall refrain from spelling out the consequences; but I think that we can glimpse here a chance of maturity, which might just eventually help to turn free time into freedom proper."

NOTES

For their helpful comments on earlier drafts of this chapter, I thank Mike O'Malley, Larry Glickman, Paul Anderson, Rita Chin, and many of the individuals who attended the State of Cultural History conference in September 2005. My deepest debts here, however, are to Larry Levine. Although Larry had no great fondness for Adorno, he would have been open to the broader conversation this essay seeks to foster.

1. In Adorno's words: "the term culture industry was perhaps used for the first time in the book *Dialectic of Enlightenment*, which [Max] Horkheimer and I published in Amsterdam in 1947. In our drafts we spoke of 'mass culture.' We replaced that expression with 'culture industry' in order to exclude from the outset the interpretation agreeable to its advocates: that it is a matter of something like a culture that arises spontaneously from the masses themselves." Theodor W. Adorno, "Culture Industry Reconsidered," reprinted in *The Culture Industry: Selected Essays on Mass Culture* (London: Routledge, 1991), 98. This essay originally appeared in the form of a public lecture, carried by the Hessian Broadcasting System, in spring 1963, and was subsequently published in *Ohne Leitbild* in 1967. For helpful context on these issues, see Andreas Huyssen, "Introduction to Adorno," *New German Critique* 6 (Autumn 1975): 3–11.

2. Early examples of this pattern include the following: Gareth Stedman Jones, "Class Expression versus Social Control?" *History Workshop Journal* 4 (1977); Lawrence W. Levine, *Black Culture and Black Consciousness* (New York: Oxford University Press, 1977), esp. chap. 4, "The Rise of Secular Song"; John Kasson, *Amusing the Million* (New York: Hill and Wang, 1978); Frederic Jameson, "Reification and Utopia in Mass Culture," *Social Text* 1 (Winter 1979); Stuart Hall, "Notes on Deconstructing 'The Popular,'" in *People's History and Socialist Theory*, ed. Raphael Samuel (London: Routledge and Kegan Paul, 1981); Richard Ohmann, "Where Did Mass Culture Come From? The Case of Magazines," *Berkshire Review*

(1981); George Lipsitz, *Class and Culture in Postwar America* (New York: Praeger, 1981); Lewis Erenberg, *Steppin' Out* (Chicago: University of Chicago Press, 1981); T. J. Jackson Lears, "From Salvation to Self-Realization: Advertising and the Therapeutic Roots of the Consumer Culture, 1880–1930," in *The Culture of Consumption*, ed. Richard Fox and T. J. Jackson Lears (New York: Pantheon, 1983); Francis Couvares, "The Triumph of Commerce: Class Culture and Mass Culture in Pittsburgh," in *Working-Class America*, ed. Michael Frisch and Daniel Walkowitz (Urbana: University of Illinois Press, 1983); Roy Rosenzweig, *Eight Hours for What We Will* (New York: Cambridge University Press, 1983); Janice Radway, *Reading the Romance* (Chapel Hill: University of North Carolina Press, 1984); Warren Susman, *Culture as History* (New York: Pantheon, 1984); T. J. Clark, *The Painting of Modern Life* (New York: Knopf, 1985), esp. chap. 4, "A Bar at the Folies-Bergere"; Kathy Peiss, *Cheap Amusements* (Philadelphia: Temple University Press, 1986); and Elliott Gorn, *The Manly Art* (Ithaca, NY: Cornell University Press, 1986). My point here is not to suggest that the growing emphasis on cultural contest simply hardened into a unified position by the mid-1980s. Rather, as the preceding list demonstrates, scholars came to this position from a wide variety of disciplinary locations, which meant that they also argued for a "contested" model of cultural commerce with very different theoretical assumptions and priorities. Good examples of these competing priorities can be found in the occasionally heated 1992 *AHR Forum* on popular/mass culture featuring work by Lawrence Levine, Robin Kelley, Natalie Davis, and Jackson Lears, *American Historical Review* 97, no. 5 (December 1992): 1379–1430.
3. The quotations here come from Michael Denning, "The End of Mass Culture," in *Culture in the Age of Three Worlds*, by M. Denning, 97–120 (London: Verso, 2004), 97, 98. This important field critique first appeared as part of a special issue on mass culture in *International Labor and Working-Class History* 38 (Fall 1990).
4. Denning, "End of Mass Culture," 114.
5. Ibid., 98. To some extent, of course, these shifts were generational. Indeed, for those of us who had worked in college radio, played in bands, produced our own records, written for `zines, experimented with video, designed Web sites, or simply cared about the actually existing commercial landscapes we all inhabited, the most basic problem with Adorno's line of critique was not so much its ferocity as its inability to locate *any* creative activity in the cultural life of late capitalism. For my own part, casting mass culture as an unambiguous object of critical repulsion felt both disingenuous and unproductive.
6. The phrase "kill off" comes from Denning's afterword to "The End of Mass Culture": "Since my essay could hardly hope to kill off the capitalist culture industries, my more modest goal was to kill off the concept that is no longer particularly useful for mapping or understanding them" (115). I should note at the outset that Adorno was hardly alone in theorizing and critiquing mass culture during the mid-twentieth century. Other important interventions in the postwar mass culture debates included the following: David Riesman, "Listening to Popular Music," *American Quarterly* 2 (1950): 359–71; Leo Lowenthal, "Historical Perspectives of Popular Culture," *American Journal of Sociology* 55 (1950): 323–32; Dwight Macdonald, "A Theory of Mass Culture," *Diogenes* 3 (Summer 1953): 1–17; Gilbert Seldes, *The Public Arts* (New York: Simon and Schuster, 1956); Bernard Rosenberg and David Manning White, eds., *Mass Culture: The Popular Arts in America* (New York: Free Press, 1957); C. Wright Mills, "The Cultural Apparatus," *Listener,*

March 26, 1959; and Norman Jacobs, ed., *Culture for the Millions? Mass Media in Modern Society* (Princeton: Van Nostrand, 1961).

7. Adorno's *Dialectic of Enlightenment* (coauthored with Max Horkheimer) was first published in 1947 by Querido. Other key texts for the development of Adorno's conceptual apparatus include the following: "On Jazz" (1936); *In Search of Wagner* (1937–38, but not published until 1952); "On the Fetish Character in Music and the Regression of Listening" (1938); "The Radio Symphony" (1941); "On Popular Music" (1941); the early fragments of *Minima Moralia* (begun in 1944 but not published until 1951); *Composing for the Films* (1947, with Hanns Eisler); and Adorno's intense debates with Walter Benjamin, many of which are collected in *The Complete Correspondence, 1928–1940* (Cambridge, MA: Polity Press, 1999). For studies of Adorno's broader career and theoretical work on culture industry, see Martin Jay, *The Dialectical Imagination: A History of the Frankfurt School and the Institute of Social Research, 1923–1950* (Boston: Little, Brown, 1973); Jay, "Adorno in America," *New German Critique*, no. 31 (Winter 1984): 157–82, and Jay, *Adorno* (Cambridge: Harvard University Press, 1984); Eugene Lunn, *Marxism and Modernism* (Berkeley: University of California Press, 1982); Patrick Bratlinger, *Bread and Circuses: Theories of Mass Culture as Social Decay* (Ithaca, NY: Cornell University Press, 1983), 222–48; Andreas Huyssen, *After the Great Divide* (Bloomington: Indiana University Press, 1986); and Miriam Hansen, foreword to *Public Sphere and Experience: Toward an Analysis of the Bourgeois and Proletarian Public Sphere*, by Oskar Negt and Alexander Kluge (Minneapolis: University of Minnesota Press, 1993), ix–xli. See also Adorno's autobiographical essay, "Scientific Experiences of a European Scholar in America," in *The Intellectual Migration: Europe and America, 1930–1960*, ed. Donald Fleming and Bernard Bailyn, 338–70 (Cambridge: Harvard University Press, 1969).

8. I borrow the phrase "absolutist stance" from Hansen, foreword to *Public Sphere and Experience*, xx.

9. Theodor W. Adorno, "Transparencies on Film," first published in *Die Zeit*, November 18, 1966. This intervention, as Hansen has shown, was designed to support a 1965 federal grant program that subsidized the debut feature films of Volker Schlöndorff, Edgar Reitz, and Alexander Kluge. Miriam Hansen, "Introduction to Adorno, 'Transparencies on Film,'" *New German Critique* 24–25 (Autumn 1981–Winter 1982): 193.

10. Theodor W. Adorno, "Opera and the Long-Playing Record," first published in *Der Spiegel*, March 24, 1969, 169.

11. Theodor W. Adorno, "Free Time," in *Culture Industry*, 196–97. The first publication of this May 25, 1969, radio address appeared in *Stichworte* (1969). The title of the essay has also been translated as "Leisure Time."

12. This phrase comes from Hansen, "Introduction to Adorno, 'Transparencies on Film'" (190), which provides one of the earliest and most sophisticated treatments of Adorno's shifting positions. See also Andreas Huyssen's widely influential essay "Adorno in Reverse," *New German Critique* 29 (Spring–Summer 1983), which was subsequently reprinted as chapter 2 of *After the Great Divide*. Huyssen and Hansen deserve much of the credit for pushing U.S. scholars to reconsider Adorno's culture industry essays in more nuanced and historically contingent terms.

13. Michael Denning, *Mechanic Accents* (London: Verso, 1987), 3. Perceptive readers will note that Denning's use of "culture industry" in this passage stands in appar-

ent contradiction to his subsequent remarks about "killing off" Adorno's concept (in "End of Mass Culture"). In actual practice, Denning has been instrumental in reconfiguring (as opposed to eradicating) Adorno's catchphrase; it continues to appear in almost everything he publishes.

14. Eric Lott, *Love and Theft* (New York: Oxford University Press, 1993), 8.

15. Robin Kelley, "Playing for Keeps: Pleasure and Profit on the Postindustrial Playground," in *The House That Race Built: Black Americans, U.S. Terrain,* ed. Wahneema Lubiano (New York: Pantheon Books, 1997), x.

16. Paul Gilroy, *Against Race* (Cambridge: Harvard University Press, 2000), 130.

17. Miriam Hansen, *Babel and Babylon: Spectatorship in American Silent Film* (Cambridge: Harvard University Press, 1991); Janice Radway, *A Feeling for Books* (Chapel Hill: University of North Carolina Press, 1997); Murray Forman and Mark Anthony Neal, eds., *That's the Joint! The Hip-Hop Studies Reader* (New York: Routledge, 2004). Other prominent examples of this pattern include Paul Gilroy, *The Black Atlantic* (Cambridge: Harvard University Press, 1993); David W. Stowe, *Swing Changes: Big Band Jazz in New Deal America* (Cambridge: Harvard University Press, 1994); Richard Ohmann, *Selling Culture: Magazines, Markets, and Class at the Turn of the Century* (London: Verso, 1996); Michael Denning, *The Cultural Front: The Laboring of American Culture in the Twentieth Century* (London: Verso, 1997); Shelley Streeby, *American Sensations: Class Empire and the Production of Popular Culture* (Berkeley: University of California Press, 2002); Janet M. Davis, *The Circus Age: Culture and Society under the American Big Top* (Chapel Hill: University of North Carolina Press, 2002); David Suisman, "Co-workers in the Kingdom of Culture: Black Swan Records and the Political Economy of African American Music," *Journal of American History* 90, no. 4 (March 2004): 1295–1324;Victoria De Grazia, *Irresistible Empire: America's Advance through Twentieth-Century Europe* (Cambridge: Harvard University Press, 2005); and Karen Sotiropoulis, *Staging Race* (Cambridge: Harvard University Press, 2006). My own reworkings of Adorno's catchphrase can be found in James W. Cook, *The Arts of Deception: Playing with Fraud in the Age of Barnum* (Cambridge: Harvard University Press, 2001), esp. 28–29, 264–65, 274n56, and 308n11; and Cook, "Introduction: The Architect of the Modern Culture Industry," in *The Colossal P. T. Barnum Reader,* ed. J. W. Cook (Champaign: University of Illinois Press, 2005). On Adorno's conception of totality, see Martin Jay, *Marxism and Totality: The Adventures of a Concept from Lukacs to Habermas* (Berkeley: University of California Press, 1984).

18. Michael Kammen, *American Culture, American Tastes* (New York: Knopf, 1999). See esp. chap. 1, "Coming to Terms with Defining Terms," 3–26.

19. As Meredith McGill has demonstrated, this was only one major example of a much larger antebellum "culture of reprinting," which continued until the passage of an international copyright law in 1891. Meredith McGill, *American Literature and the Culture of Reprinting, 1834–1853* (Philadelphia: University of Pennsylvania Press, 2003). See also Ronald J. Zboray, *A Fictive People: Antebellum Economic Development and the American Reading Public* (New York: Oxford University Press, 1993).

20. P. T. Barnum, *Struggles and Triumphs* (Buffalo, NY: Warren, Johnson, and Co., 1872), 130. For examples of Barnum's rapidly expanding press coverage, see Cook, *Colossal P. T. Barnum Reader.*

21. Kammen, *American Culture, American Tastes,* 3–26. In fairness to Kammen, it should be noted that he mostly employs such labels to describe period-specific

tendencies rather than absolute qualitative differences. My goal in raising these issues is to suggest a way out of the analytical zero sum that pits qualitative specificity against the longer history of capitalist expansion.

22. For two early and sophisticated discussions of appropriation, see Hall, "Notes on Deconstructing 'The Popular'"; and Roger Chartier, "Culture as Appropriation: Popular Cultural Uses in Early Modern France," in *Understanding Popular Culture,* ed. Steven L. Kaplan (Berlin: Mouton, 1984). See also Chartier, "Texts, Printing, Reading," in *The New Cultural History,* ed. Lynn Hunt (Berkeley: University of California Press, 1989).

23. On these issues, see Tricia Rose, *Black Noise* (Middletown, CT: Wesleyan University Press, 1994); William Eric Perkins, ed., *Droppin' Science: Critical Essays on Rap and Hip Hop Culture* (Philadelphia: Temple University Press, 1996); Forman and Neal, *That's the Joint!*

24. We also know that this dialectic frequently moves in the opposite direction, as mass cultural commodities modeled on previously local songs, dance moves, fashion trends, and so forth, are *re*-appropriated on the other side of the commodification process by new groups of consumers with their own distinctive use patterns. It was precisely this complex circuit of re-appropriation that Lawrence W. Levine first made visible in 1977 when he described early twentieth-century blues records as "bearers and preservers" of folk traditions for rural African Americans thrust into motion by the Great Migration. Levine, *Black Culture and Black Consciousness,* 231. In Levine's powerful story, vernacular begets mass begets vernacular.

25. Editorial, *New York Times,* November 11, 2003.

26. Of course, much the same kind of argument can be made about pop songs, MP3 files, and the increasingly conventional practice of releasing music videos on the Internet.

27. Lawrence W. Levine, "The Folklore of Industrial Society: Popular Culture and Its Audiences," *American Historical Review* 97, no. 5 (December 2002): 1373.

28. On the Keith-Albee circuit, see Robert Snyder, *The Voice of the City: Vaudeville and Popular Culture* (New York: Oxford University Press, 1989); and Snyder, "Big Time, Small Time, All around the Town: New York Vaudeville in the Early Twentieth Century," in *For Fun and Profit: The Transformation of Leisure into Consumption,* ed. Richard Butsch (Philadelphia: Temple University Press, 1990), 118–35.

29. On the shifting meanings of market, see Jean-Christophe Agnew, *World's Apart: The Market and the Theater in Anglo-American Thought, 1550–1750* (Cambridge: Cambridge University Press, 1986), 41–42, 52–53, 55–56.

30. Adorno, *Culture Industry,* 100–101.

31. Theodor W. Adorno, "The Schema of Mass Culture," in *Culture Industry,* 79. This essay was originally written as a continuation of the "culture industry" chapter of Adorno and Horkheimer, *Dialectic of Enlightenment.* It first appeared in print as part of Adorno, *Gesammelte Schriften III: Dialektik der Aufklaerung* (Frankfurt am Main: Suhrkamp Verlag, 1981), 299–335.

32. An autobiographical footnote may be instructive here. For those of us who began to practice cultural history in the midst of the Reagan era "culture wars," Adorno's line of questioning often sounded disturbingly similar to the conservative jeremiads against mass culture echoing all around us. Rhetorically, at least, they had much in common. Where Adorno had described the "fun" of Hollywood movies as "a medicinal bath which the entertainment industry never ceases to

prescribe" (*Dialectic of Enlightenment*, 118), late twentieth-century conservatives such as Allan Bloom dismissed rock music as "a non-stop, commercially pre-packaged masturbational fantasy." Bloom, *The Closing of the American Mind* (New York: Simon and Schuster, 1987), 68–81. Rhetoric aside, however, these critiques grew out of very different analytical and political projects. As Andreas Huyssen first noted, Adorno's primary concern was neither the problem of "masses" threatening culture "from below," nor the "preservation" of a traditional "high culture" in the service of social and political "domination." Rather, the specific target of Adorno's mid-twentieth-century wrath was corporate capitalism's manifold impacts in ordering consumption "from above." Huyssen, "Introduction to Adorno," 8–9. See also Huyssen, *After the Great Divide*, 25.

33. This question of how the popular is "produced" has often been ignored or elided—even by leading cultural historians. Helpful discussions on this issue can be found in Hall, "Notes on Deconstructing the 'Popular'"; Clark, *Painting of Modern Life*; Denning, *Mechanic Accents*; and Richard Broadhead, *Cultures of Letters* (Chicago: University of Chicago Press, 1993).

34. The term "massification" is often used in studies of modern consumer culture. See, for example, James B. Twitchell, *Adcult USA: The Triumph of Advertising in American Culture* (New York: Columbia University Press, 1996); and Bill Brown, *The Material Unconscious: American Amusement, Stephen Crane, and the Economies of Play* (Cambridge: Harvard University Press, 1996).

35. Denning, *Mechanic Accents*, 20.

36. Ibid., 19. On this issue, see also Nan Enstad, *Ladies of Labor, Girls of Adventure: Working Women, Popular Culture, and Labor Politics at the Turn of the Twentieth Century* (New York: Columbia University Press, 1999), 17–47.

37. Davis, *Circus Age*, 15–81.

38. Ibid., 40. In many cases, Davis adds, the larger "logistical spectacle" performed by thousands of itinerant laborers proved to be just as fascinating to local audiences as the subsequent entertainment products exhibited under the big top (38).

39. Richard Ohmann, *Politics of Letters* (Middletown, CT: Wesleyan University Press, 1987), 135–51. See also Ohmann's revisions and expansions of these arguments in *Selling Culture*.

40. Radway, *Feeling for Books*, 169–70.

41. Adorno and Horkheimer, *Dialectic of Enlightenment*, 94, 105.

42. Ibid., 94–95. On Adorno's penchant for critical hyperbole, see Jay, *Marxism and Totality*; and Gillian Rose, *The Melancholy Science: An Introduction to the Critical Thought of Theodor W. Adorno* (London: Macmillan, 1978).

43. On Adorno's reluctance to explore the "crucial transition from the culture of liberal capitalism to that of monopoly capitalism," see esp. Huyssen, "Adorno in Reverse," 22–23.

44. In most cases, too, individual trade papers represent specific corporate and class interests, a pattern that necessitates careful cross-reading of a wide range of publications.

45. The list of major works in this burgeoning field is long and diverse. Those I have found particularly helpful include the following: Lisa Lowe and David Lloyd, eds., *The Politics of Culture in the Shadow of Capital* (Durham, NC: Duke University Press, 1997); Edward Herman and Robert McChesney, *The Global Media* (London: Cassell, 1997); Frederic Jameson and Masao Miyoshi, *The Cultures of Glo-*

balization (Durham, NC: Duke University Press, 1998); David Held, Anthony G. McGrew, David Goldblatt, and Jonathan Perraton, *Global Transformations: Politics, Economics and Culture* (London: Polity Press, 1999); Denning, *Culture in the Age of Three Worlds;* Pascale Casanova, *The World Republic of Letters* (Cambridge: Harvard University Press, 2004); Franco Moretti, *Graphs, Maps, Trees* (London: Verso, 2005); Donald Sassoon, *The Culture of the Europeans* (New York: Harper Collins, 2006); and Simon J. Potter, "Webs, Networks, and Systems: Globalization and Mass Media in the Nineteenth- and Twentieth-Century British Empire," *Journal of British Studies* 46, no. 3 (July 2007): 621–46.

46. These terms come from Theodor W. Adorno, "Culture and Administration," in *Culture Industry,* 109–10.

47. My thanks to Matthew Wittmann for his research assistance on these periodicals.

48. This international expansion of cultural circulation was aided by two mid-nineteenth-century technological innovations: the telegraph and the ocean-going steamship. For more on the early history of mass media, see Daniel Czitrom, *The Media and the American Mind: From Morse to McLuhan* (Chapel Hill: University of North Carolina Press, 1982); and Paul Starr, *The Creation of the Media: Political Origins of Modern Communications* (New York: Basic Books, 2002).

49. Gilroy, *Black Atlantic,* 87–96. For additional studies that devote significant attention to transnational cultural circulation before the twentieth century, see the following: Dale Cockrell, ed., *Excelsior: Journals of the Hutchinson Family Singers, 1842–1846* (Stuyvesant, NY: Pendragon Press, 1989); Joseph Roach, *Cities of the Dead* (New York: Columbia University Press, 1996); John Blair, "First Steps toward Globalization: Nineteenth-Century Exports of American Entertainment Forms," in *"Here, There and Everywhere": The Foreign Politics of American Popular Culture,* ed. Reinhold Wagnleitner and Elaine Tyler May (Hanover, NH: University Press of New England, 2000), 17–33; W. T. Lhamon Jr., *Jump Jim Crow* (Cambridge: Harvard University Press, 2003); Roslyn Poignant, *Professional Savages* (New Haven: Yale University Press, 2004); Cook, *Colossal P. T. Barnum Reader;* Robert Rydell and Rob Kroes, *Buffalo Bill in Bologna* (Chicago: University of Chicago Press, 2005); Daphne Brooks, *Bodies in Dissent* (Durham, NC: Duke University Press, 2006).

50. My thinking here has been influenced by Michael Warner's work on "publics" as simultaneously discursive and institutional entities. Warner, *Publics and Counterpublics* (New York: Zone Books, 2002).

51. Starting in 1874, moreover, the *Clipper* published an annual "almanac" featuring population statistics, railroad and steamship schedules, postage rates at home and abroad, distances between major cities, and seating capacities for "some of the largest theatres in the world"—everything, in short, for the managerial corps of a nineteenth-century "show trade" now redefining itself in more explicitly global terms.

52. In retrospect, it's easier to see that Lawrence W. Levine's widely influential *Highbrow/Lowbrow: The Emergence of Cultural Hierarchy in America* (Cambridge: Harvard University Press, 1988) was pushing in some of these same directions—that is, toward a more comparative historical analysis of socioeconomic stratification across multiple nineteenth-century cultural forms.

53. See, for example, the *Era* for December 7, 1851; January 2 and 9, February 20, August 29, September 5 and 12, and October 10, 1852; and January 2, 1853.

54. For further analysis of these issues, see John Russell Stephens, *The Censorship of British Drama, 1824–1901* (Cambridge: Cambridge University Press, 1980); Peter Bailey, ed., *Music Hall: The Business of Pleasure* (Milton Keynes/Philadelphia: Open University Press, 1986); Dagmar Kift, *The Victorian Music Hall: Culture, Class, and Conflict* (Cambridge: Cambridge University Press, 1996); and Jane Moody, *Illegitimate Theatre in London, 1770–1840* (Cambridge: Cambridge University Press, 2000).

55. For helpful discussion of similar stratification patterns in antebellum New York City, see Peter G. Buckley, "Paratheatricals and Popular Stage Entertainment," in *Beginnings to 1870*, vol. 1 of *The Cambridge History of American Theatre.*, ed. Don B. Wilmeth and Christopher Bigsby (Cambridge: Cambridge University Press, 1998), 424–81.

56. "Concert Halls and Singing Halls," *Era*, January 9, 1852.

57. On the Astor Place Riot, see Peter Buckley, "To the Opera House: Culture and Society in New York City, 1820–1860" (Ph.D. diss., State University of New York at Stony Brook, 1984); Levine, *Highbrow/Lowbrow*; and Robert Allen, *Horrible Prettiness: Burlesque and American Culture* (Chapel Hill: University of North Carolina Press, 1991).

58. On nineteenth-century theater riots and libel cases, see Bruce McConachie, *Melodramatic Formations, American Theatre and Society, 1820–1870* (Iowa City: University of Iowa Press, 1992); and Helen Lefkowitz Horowitz, *Rereading Sex: Battles over Sexual Knowledge and Suppression in Nineteenth-Century America* (New York: Knopf, 2002).

59. Adorno, "Culture Industry Reconsidered," 98–99.

60. See, for example, Paul Gilroy, *"There Ain't No Black in the Union Jack": The Cultural Politics of Race and Nation* (Chicago: University of Chicago Press, 1987); Stuart Hall, "Cultural Identity and Diaspora," in *Identity: Community, Culture, Difference*, ed. Jonathan Rutherford (London: Lawrence and Wishart, 1990); Hall, "What Is This 'Black' in Black Popular Culture," in *Black Popular Culture*, ed. Gina Dent (Seattle: Bay Press, 1992); and George Lipsitz, *Dangerous Crossroads: Popular Music, Postmodernism, and the Poetics of Place* (London: Verso, 1994).

61. Charles Dickens, *American Notes for General Circulation* (London: Penguin Classics, 1985), 138–39.

62. See, for example, Eileen Southern, *The Music of Black Americans: A History* (New York: Norton, 1971); Marshall Stearns and Jean Stearns, *Jazz Dance* (New York: Da Capo, 1978); and Shane White, "The Death of James Johnson," *American Quarterly* 51, no. 4 (December 1999): 753–95.

63. I examine this complex history in my current book project. On Lane's career, see Marian Hannah Winter, "Juba and American Minstrelsy" (1947), reprinted in *Chronicles of the American Dance*, ed. Paul Magriel (New York: Da Capo, 1978); and James W. Cook, "Dancing across the Color Line: A Story of Mixtures and Markets in New York's Five Points," *Common-place* 4, no. 1 (October 2003); and Cook, "Master Juba, King of All Dancers! A Black Dancer's Story from the Dawn of the Transatlantic Culture Industry," *Discourses in Dance* 3, no. 2 (2006).

64. This pattern, moreover, was never restricted to popular entertainment. Indeed, it was at this same moment, during the late 1840s and early 1850s, that black abolitionists, writers, and artists such as Frederick Douglass, William Wells Brown, and William and Ellen Craft first began to use British markets as oppositional

networks to raise capital, assert their ideological and political independence, and exert transatlantic leverage.

65. Adorno, "Free Time," 195–97. It's worth noting that the concept of split consciousness was not entirely new. In *Dialectic of Enlightenment*, for example, Adorno and Horkheimer described "the triumph of advertising in the culture industry" as the moment in which "consumers feel compelled to buy and use products even though they see through them." During the mid-1960s, however, this line of argument began to take a number of important turns. First and perhaps most important, Adorno began to treat the act of "seeing through" as a more ambiguous process, one in which the long-term ideological effects of culture industry immersion did not necessarily add up to collective "compulsion." He also began to express new forms of curiosity about the lessons of empirical research, especially as they related to the culture industry's historical evolution. In the final pages of "Free Time," Adorno made this relationship explicit. The Frankfurt school's study of the celebrity wedding, he now argued, was a "textbook example of how critical-theoretical thought can both learn from and be corrected by empirical social research." His reflections on the wedding also began with an intriguing moment of self-revision: "Let me say a little more on the relation of free time and the culture industry. Since Horkheimer and I coined the term more than thirty years ago, so much has been written about this means of integration and domination, that I should like to pick out a problem, which at the time we were not able to get a proper perspective on" (195–96). For helpful discussion of these developments, see also Hansen, "Introduction to Adorno, 'Transparencies on Film,'" 190–93; and J. M. Bernstein, introduction to *Culture Industry*, 12–16.

66. On this issue, see also Michael Saler's fascinating discussion of "ironic imagination" in two recent essays: "Clap if You Believe in Sherlock Holmes: Mass Culture and the Re-Enchantment of Modernity, c. 1890–c.1940," *Historical Journal* 46, no. 3 (2003): 599–622; and "Modernity, Enchantment, and the Ironic Imagination," *Philosophy and Literature* 28 (2004): 137–49.

67. P. T. Barnum, *The Life of P. T. Barnum, Written by Himself* (New York: Redfield, 1855), 27.

68. P. T. Barnum, *Humbugs of the World* (New York: Carleton, 1865), 55–56.

69. I examine the origins of this phenomenon in Cook, *Arts of Deception;* see esp. 1–29, 73–118, 259–62. See also Cook, *Colossal P. T. Barnum Reader,* 6–7, 85–102, 182, 227.

70. Peter Bailey, *Popular Culture and Performance in the Victorian City* (Cambridge: Cambridge University Press, 1997), 128–50. Bailey's work in this area first appeared as "Music Hall and the Knowingness of Popular Culture," *Past and Present* 144 (August 1994).

71. Denning, "End of Mass Culture," 98.

72. Bailey, *Popular Culture and Performance in the Victorian City,* 149–50.

73. For recent discussions of the problem of cynicism in mass culture, see Peter Sloterdijk, *Critique of Cynical Reason* (Minneapolis: University of Minnesota Press, 1987); Slavoj Zizek, *The Sublime Object of Ideology* (London: Verso, 1989), 1–53; and Timothy Bewes, *Cynicism and Postmodernity* (London: Verso, 1997).

ELEVEN

On Grief and Complicity:
Notes toward a Visionary Cultural History

NAN ENSTAD

[Not] only is life mostly failure, but . . . in one's failure, or pettiness, or wrongness exists the living drama of the self.

GORE VIDAL, *United States Essays, 1952–92*

In November 2000, the Chinese-born artist Xu Bing created an art installation called the Tobacco Project, in Durham, North Carolina, which made aesthetic use of his own grief and loss. Xu exhibited at two sites: Duke University, whose large endowment comes principally from its namesake, tobacco giant James Buchanan Duke, and the Duke Homestead, the birthplace of Duke which is now part of the North Carolina Tobacco Museum. In the early twentieth century, James Duke headed the American Tobacco Company monopoly in the United States, as well as the British American Tobacco Company, a multinational that sold cigarettes all over the world, including China. When I arrived at the outdoor part of the exhibit at the Duke Homestead on a drizzly and dark November evening, I followed signs to the refurbished Duke family tobacco farm. As the first tobacco barn became visible, I saw Chinese characters projected onto the old, rough-log wall. The characters, to me unintelligible, danced across the barn, and as the slides changed, a tape played a translation of their contents. Listening, I realized that I was seeing the medical charts of Xu Bing's father, recording his last days as he was dying of lung cancer.

Xu Bing's exhibit raises questions about the stories we tell as cultural historians. Xu's Tobacco Project haunted the old Duke homestead with what had been long denied. The ghostly Chinese characters traced their patterns over the earthy, restored wooden logs, interrupting the museum's heroic myth of success and prosperity through the tobacco industry with a specter of bodily vulnerability and personal tragedy. Xu's story disrupts the professionalized, modern historical narrative with illness, death, and grief. It bridges the national and transnational and asserts a connectedness written on the body. It invokes the intimate connections between an individual life and history: the way the self and the body take shape in intimate relation with large economic and medical institutions. It certainly implies culpability of the tobacco industry for the damage to his father's body. But even more importantly, it dramatically reveals the consequences of prior actions, so carefully occluded and denied by economics, politics, and a history that relies on the nation as its container. Proving culpability is the domain of law, but tracing the reasons and consequences of prior actions, revealing the links between people, their implications, and therefore the responsibilities we have to each other— this is the domain of the historian. Cultural history is currently at its most exciting moment of possibility, as well as perhaps our most dire moment of need. We cultural historians have a powerful and precious base to build on, and in envisioning our next moves we can take inspiration from Xu Bing's rendition of grief. Delving into grief has the potential to reveal the bodily and ethical connections between people and worlds, to reveal a shared history and therefore a shared future.

Revitalization may be critical. A number of people have noted that cultural history, or its cousin, interdisciplinary cultural studies, seems fatigued. In a *Journal of American History* article, Daniel Wickberg argued that social and cultural history should be seen as parts of the same paradigm, a paradigm that will soon play itself out. The turn in cultural history to studying normative categories of identity—what Wickberg termed the history of "whiteness, masculinity and heterosexuality"—is simply the "last gasp of the paradigm" that began as a social history of the oppressed in the 1960s. "Where will a new history come from, once social [and cultural] history has folded in on itself?" asked Wickberg. Interdisciplinary cultural studies critics also portend a change. Literary critic Michael Millner has pointed out that there is a pervasive "sense of exhaustion" around the issues of identity and power. Over the past fifteen years, scholars in a wide range of disciplines, including history, have created a vibrant body of work that deconstructs identity in order to challenge its naturalness and trace its construction in culture. Millner called this "post-identity" scholarship. Citing the frustrations of a number of diverse scholars with the work they themselves pioneered, including Terry Eagleton, Teresa de Lauretis, and Homi Bhabha, Millner questioned whether the idea of identity has a future, and what direction cultural critics might travel in a "post post-identity" era.[1]

I concur with Wickberg and other critics that cultural history is in flux, but our tradition of cultural history provides resources too rich for us to allow it to "fold in on itself." We need to understand where the political efficacy and intellectual excitement of cultural history came from in order to determine what to keep and amplify and what to shift and revitalize. To do so, I define and explore two key overlapping and interrelated "moments" of cultural history from the past thirty years, both of which made politically crucial interventions in scholarship and give us much to build upon. The first, which I call "visionary cultural history of subalterns," thrived especially in the 1970s and early 1980s. The second, which I name "deconstructive cultural history of categories and hierarchies," thrived in the 1980s and 1990s.[2] The first moment, I argue, constituted a fundamental epistemological challenge to modernist historical writing by asserting that historians and readers of history could learn from subaltern subjects of study. Rather than the historian illuminating the public, the practice of history would transform the practitioner. From the second moment, we gain the imperative of seeing power and ideology in more complex terms than did historians in the first moment. I will suggest that by investigating grief, and also complicity, we can draw on the resources we've inherited from the past thirty-five years of cultural history and create a new, visionary cultural history that will be relevant to our historical moment.

Cultural history of subalterns of the 1970s and early 1980s broke dramatically with an earlier tradition of intellectual and cultural history and transformed the ways historians conceptualized culture. Intellectual and cultural history previously had studied primarily the high culture of mostly Western civilizations. Cultural historians of the 1970s, in contrast, became concerned with two aspects of the cultures of nondominant people: they wished to reveal subalterns' "way of life," and they wished to understand subalterns' "consciousness" and its development over time. Historians were interested in the way of life of subalterns because they saw it as a central aspect of subaltern identity and heritage. As such it was crucial to developing alternate histories (African American, Native American, women's, working class, gay and lesbian, and so forth). Historians had a dual investment in seeing groups as partially autonomous, or having their "own" culture: intellectually, it would allow them to trace a group's own history through time, and professionally, it was important to the strategic construction of new fields of study.[3] Historians also studied culture to understand consciousness, particularly knowledges that arose outside the dominant society, and the process of politicization.

The deconstructive history of categories and hierarchies transformed the ways historians looked at culture again in the late 1980s and 1990s, due to the heightened concern with how power and ideology shaped experiences and identities. Cultural history grew dramatically as many social historians turned to cultural analysis to answer new questions. Historians of this moment were primarily interested in culture as the discursive site of meaning production that held clues to the construction of identities, both resistant and those corroborative with power. Cultural history participated in a larger, interdisciplinary conversation as well, drawing on as well as contributing to conversations about theory and method that reached across the humanities. Cultural history in this "second moment," because of the interest in ideology, also began forging a renewed link to the history of ideas—a field that itself was changing in interesting ways.

Although commentators have directed their attention to scholarship of the late 1980s and 1990s, in this chapter I spend more time on the 1970s because I believe that there are elements of the visionary cultural history of subalterns that we need to reclaim. It is commonplace to note that the innovations in social and cultural history in the 1960s and 1970s came from the response to social movements. I want to stress here that this response to activism was not simply an echo in the ivory tower of the actions taking place in the "real" world, but rather an active participation in the production of new forms of visionary knowledge. I call this knowledge "visionary" because this history (1) participated in a profound epistemological shift about the sources of knowledge and constituted the practice of history itself as a process of transformation; and (2) deployed the utopian rubric of resistance, which served to legitimate contemporary social movements by making them historically normative. Thus, by participating in change, the visionary cultural history of subalterns actively built new knowledges that generated a sense of hope about the efficacy of grassroots political action and the possibility of progressive political transformation.

In 1977, Levine wrote in *Black Culture and Black Consciousness:* "It is time for historians to expand their own consciousness by examining the consciousness of those they have hitherto ignored or neglected."[4] This remarkable statement posed a radical challenge to history's purpose and method. The conviction that subalterns had valuable knowledge disrupted entrenched modernist notions about the sources of knowledge.

Indeed, even today many historians would not accept the idea that people with Ph.D.'s have much to learn from people with little education or formal power. This epistemic shift was initially prompted by Marxism's theoretical elevation of the proletariat as the source of revolution and correct knowledge about class hierarchy. It first entered cultural historical discourse as an interest in wage workers' and slaves' political consciousness of their place in the means of production; for that reason, historians began to explore shop-floor culture and slaves' culture.[5] However, in 1977 we see Levine taking this in an even more visionary and open-ended direction. For Levine's was not an examination of culture for the tracks of a predetermined march to class consciousness, but a sweeping and open exploration of the intellectual history of the black "folk" and their shifting conceptions of freedom, to learn what their consciousness might be. This investigation had both a deconstructive and visionary aspect. Its deconstructive element was to unmask the hegemonic exclusions of traditional history as profoundly undemocratic. It deeply challenged modernism's elevation of professional knowledge by claiming not only that it left things out but that it did not lead, as the modernist project claimed, to a better society. On the contrary, modernist professionalism delegitimated local knowledges and established elite knowledge competencies as a requisite for gaining social power.[6]

This deconstructive element could not be separated from the visionary aspect. As Levine put it, "historians are the prisoners" of their impoverished sense of sources and historical subject matter. They have unwittingly colluded with the powerful. The question driving *Black Culture and Black Consciousness*, for example, was how the transition from slavery to freedom changed black thought. I want to emphasize that this was a study of freedom and its meanings, a central concern in U.S. history, rather than a study of a group designated as "marginal" or "powerless." The purpose here was not simply to study how "others" lived; it was to learn from African American people of the past lessons about freedom and democracy. Indeed, although Levine called the people he studied "folk" and drew upon insights in anthropology and folklore, he explicitly resisted conventions in those fields to compare folk to other folk, and thus to explore "primitive" cultures as a counterpoint to a reified "civilization." On the contrary, he called his work "intellectual history" and placed African American musicians and storytellers as bearers of American thought. The implication was that we require this history in order to change ourselves, whether one aims to build within African American communities or to transform dominant institutions. The history of subalterns, then, was the key to freedom, both as historians and as citizens. It was, as Levine noted, not just about studying consciousness in the past but about changing ours in the present.[7]

The visionary cultural history of subalterns also deployed the utopian rubric of resistance, which served to legitimate contemporary social movements by making them historically normative. The notion of resistance was utopian in that it was the key term in the effort to explore the limits of power and the capacities of human agency. This notion was a profound revision in the ways that historians and social scientists had thought about the cultures of subalterns. Established wisdom conferred cultural value on those art forms produced in contexts of freedom—freedom from slavery, freedom from market forces, freedom from the influence of mass culture. Levine, for example, explicitly rejected interpretations of the culture of slaves that saw it as simply a rudimentary coping strategy that could not carry profound beauty or a deep challenge to the institution of slavery. He wrote that "slaves' expressive arts and sacred beliefs were more than merely a series of outlets or strategies; they were instruments of life, of sanity, of health, and of self-respect."[8] Understanding culture and consciousness were crucial to discerning how people did not simply capitulate to power, how—in Levine's terms—legal slavery might not lead to "spiritual slavery." Cultural historians had a special role in this work because they not only studied rebellions, strikes, and protests but the forging of alternate knowledge that might lead to such formal resistance. The focus on resistance was closely related for cultural historians, therefore, to the broader epistemic shift of the focus on consciousness.

The focus on resistance created visionary knowledge because it served a legitimizing function for highly contested contemporary political action. It cast contemporary social movements as a normative part—or even as the culmination—of long traditions of revered activism, rather than as deviant actions of malcontents, as they so often appeared in the press. This move is partly why these histories served to inspire and instill hope. People came to history in order to change their consciousnesses: to learn from their "own" history or to learn from that of "others." If they associated with any aspect of the contemporary social movements, then they could find in historical study a powerful identification with legitimized resistance struggles of the past. The sense of hope and a new "pantheon of heroes" that came from the utopian rubric of resistance gained history, collectively, the widest audience since Bancroft's popular national histories of the nineteenth century, which had created history as a nationalist romance. Suddenly, some history classrooms were packed to overflowing, and history found new audiences outside the universities. The visionary cultural history of subalterns, then, offered people profound narrative pleasures: it allowed them to unmask power and challenge its limits, to transform their own individual consciousness, and to identify their political ideas and efforts with great traditions of resistance.

Grief and complicity played roles in the visionary cultural history of subalterns, although the move from grief to resistance was swift, and errors accrued mostly along the "dominant" side of the subaltern/dominant binary. While historians became attuned to "internalized oppression," a type of complicity in power, politicization released historical actors—and historians—from "false consciousness." As such, neither grief nor complicity was intensively interrogated. However, some of the power of this history came from its oblique attention to grief. The visionary cultural history of subalterns displaced the history of the United States as a story of progress and brought into central view fierce struggles that often came down to life and death. Histories of slavery, the labor movement, and women's struggle for reproductive freedom and autonomy, for example, all revealed that oppressive hierarchies, although lucrative for some, had high human costs. Learning about the poignancy of oppression and struggle allowed people to connect history to their own contemporary pain and to see how their pain was social rather than simply personal. However, because the project of the 1970s was to trace the limits of power, scholars rarely dwelled long on grief. Labor leader Joe Hill's famous 1915 exhortation, "Don't mourn, organize!" became popular on bumper stickers and T-shirts, and the same sentiment shaped historical narratives. In addition, the dichotomy between subaltern and dominant culture that characterized this work prompted historians to locate human error on the side of power. Indeed, even when historians "admitted" that nondominant people made errors, these errors were usually ones of power: for example, white working-class men organizing by using racist or sexist tactics. Complicity was rarely interrogated in a broader frame; indeed, when the subaltern and the dominant are diametrically opposed, it is hard to imagine how one would do so.

By the 1980s, the conceptual division between subaltern and dominant was breaking down, requiring a major shift in historical inquiry. By consolidating notions of "women," "African Americans," "Native Americans," and so forth, historians minimized differences, hybridity, and power differentials within each identity-based group. Although the consolidation of historical identities had seemed politically expedient, it proved to replicate hierarchies in the wider society. Despite some dramatically new epistemologies, much of African American history neglected gender, much of women's history occluded white women's participation in racism, much of labor history elevated a new "universal" ideal of resistance in the figure of the white male worker, and virtually all subaltern history outside the history of sexuality assumed a heterosexual subject and transhistorical heterosexuality. Furthermore, these were not simply omissions but silences inherent in promoting the project of writing histories of (at least partially) coherent subaltern cultures. This fact was both painful and intellectually exciting, as researchers struggled to implement new insights and theories about power and ideology to write new and improved histories. Now of concern were the ways that groups took shape within culture and the exclusions that they engendered. Attention shifted to the cultural construction of categories, hierarchies, and identities.

Nevertheless, I belabor the early moment of visionary cultural history more than I do the next stage because the contributions of this earlier moment are often simplified to the point of distortion, causing us to overlook the resources we need for our future. Most renditions of the historiography of the 1960s and 1970s emphasize the goal of including the excluded, and the effort toward "recuperation" of separate cultures in the past in order to trace one's own identity back in time. Recuperation was certainly an aspect of that scholarship, but it hardly expresses the whole of it; without further explanation, such renditions cast 1970s scholarship as naive and simplistic.[9] Some of this oversimplification comes simply from the fact that we are still working in the historiography built out of a critique of this era. Historians' subsequent focus on power and ideology lay precisely—and intentionally—in the blind spots of the earlier scholarship. Perhaps inevitably, this creates a new myopia in us as scholars.[10] However understandable, the lack of serious attention to the complexity of early contributions impoverishes us and unwittingly undermines our present project. By casting the 1960s and 1970s as a well-meaning but naively idealistic or simpleminded era, our historiography echoes widespread dismissals of the political movements of those eras. Whereas neoconservatives have created a history of that era that focuses on dangers of drugs, sex, and flag-burning, a wider range of people have come to see that time as simply silly.[11] When we participate in marginalizing our own legacy, we miss the opportunity to oppose this key rhetorical turn and lose access to learning from the achievements of history's past.

This second moment of our work, which I call the "deconstructive cultural history of categories and hierarchies," thrived in the 1980s and 1990s. The shift here was from studying subaltern cultures "on their own" to studying the historical development of lines that divide cultural categories. Work in this cohort revealed that binary oppositions that might seem like natural descriptions—highbrow/lowbrow, male/female, white/black, straight/queer, red state/blue state—create rather than reflect realities and have deep political ramifications. This inquiry entailed a more profound deconstruction of race, gender, and sexuality as categories rather than self-evident experiences, and included deconstructing and accounting historically for the normative and deviant sides of the binaries. Understanding how gender worked in society required understanding masculinity; understanding race meant understanding how whiteness came to confer privilege while remaining unmarked. Questions about how power and ideology worked also led to new cultural examinations of empire, often pursued through postcolonial or transnational studies. The best works of this broad cohort explored the interfaces between groups and cultures, the contact zones and borderlands where identities took shape. In recent years, a dynamic *multi*racial cultural history has emerged from the continuing development of Latina/Latino, Asian American, Native American, African American, gender, and sexual histories, from the challenges to the fixed nature of categories, and from notions of borders and empires as they shaped the identities of residents and migrants.[12]

I want to highlight two ways that this scholarship's focus on the culturally constructed nature of identity has radical implications that have not yet been fully realized: first, it has challenged a clear division between the subaltern and the powerful; and second, it has challenged notions of resistance and agency based in a liberal humanist subject. From this body of work we learned that we could not "discover" a separate subaltern culture; we needed to account for how it was constructed and differentiated from other cultural forms within an emerging matrix of power relations. While a subaltern group may have an identity with profound social implications, that identity itself is not natural or autonomous but forged in culture. As Stuart Hall wrote, "The fact is, 'black' has never been just there either. It has always been an unstable identity, psychically, culturally, and politically. It, too, is a narrative, a story, a history. Something constructed, told, spoken, not simply found."[13] Likewise, historians have shown that cultural forms and cultural memory can rarely be ascribed to a single group but come out of a myriad of interactions and exchanges. Work on the interfaces between groups has made clear the profoundly hybrid nature of culture in the United States, whereas work on consumer culture has revealed that discreet popular cultures, separate from the influence of the market—and therefore from the wider society—do not exist. For example, what might appear to be African American culture in vaudeville developed partly out of an economic need to match white racist preconceptions of African Americans popular in minstrelsy. Such cultural forms defy efforts to order history into dominant and subaltern "sides" as the visionary cultural history of subalterns tended to do, yet they reinforce our need to understand racialization and people's creative response to power relations. Thus the disruption of clear notions of subalternity poses a fascinating challenge to the study of culture.

The shift to seeing identity and categories of hierarchy as socially constructed has implications for the crucial conceptions of agency and resistance as well. If we have adopted a view of the subject as a product of culture, rather than as an autonomous individual standing in society and creating culture, then our notion of agency also must shift from celebrations of the free will of autonomous individuals to something else that acknowledges that people cannot fully extricate themselves from power. Likewise, the concept of resistance as the penultimate act of agency must be reconsidered. "Resistance" has operated in historical discourse as a utopian concept that imagines a heroic space separate from power. The counterpart to the concept of resistance is corroboration or domination— this binary tacitly undergirds all uses of the term. Thus, the concept of resistance that we have inherited articulates as an opposition—a morally loaded one at that—processes that are inevitably intertwined.[14] In the context of creating a historical narrative that served a legitimizing function for civil rights and feminist activism, resistance was the mark of the hero. Like most utopian concepts, resistance had a political utility in a particular historical moment. However, in our present moment this utopian concept keeps us tied to modernist visions of political purity, which seems to me to be dangerous.

Certainly, people's actions are not entirely determined by power and social hierarchies, but the utopian concept of resistance, ironically, can make it hard for us to see how creative response works. Some historians have tried to bridge the opposition between corroboration and resistance, and argued that historical subjects are constituted in power and both resisted and, sometimes in the very same actions, did not resist. The source of agency in such studies was not free will but the contingencies and contradictions of one's placement and statuses in the society.[15] However, such efforts have been only partially successful; the binary opposition between resistance and corroboration is difficult to dislodge. As Walter Johnson has noted, too often the concept of agency works to truck in liberal humanism despite our best intentions. Even work that is far more complex, for example, than whether slaves had agency or not is read and discussed for this question.[16] An endlessly broad range of identities, actions, impulses, ideas, cultural practices, and cultural products have been found to be "resistant." My problem with this assertion is not that it confers political significance too widely—I'm quite convinced that most human actions can have political meanings—but that it doesn't tell as much as we need to know, with the degree of nuance we require, about the incredibly diverse and conflicted and profound and surprising worlds that people make. The concept of resistance tends to render complex cultural forms in instrumental or functional terms; although this outlook has yielded many insights, much of expressive culture is left unexplored. Part of the efficacy of the concept of resistance was its moral vision; today, however, that same moral tone makes the ways we are made by power seem like failure, and that failure our downfall. In this way, we lose an opportunity to explore human creativity in the grip of history. Any revitalized notion of human action must deal with our complex understandings of subjectivities, power, and culture.

The deconstructive cultural history of categories and hierarchies focused more directly on exploring grief and complicity than did the visionary cultural history of subalterns, but like the first moment, it tended to posit as an antithesis (even an implicit one) a utopian space free of power. The deconstruction of identity revealed how power has shaped people's lives, both individually and socially, and traced complicity in the pain this causes. The new studies of whiteness, masculinity, and empire reverberated with lost opportunities and tragic errors. Interestingly, fewer studies of nonwhite or colonized groups participated in this narrative form. Furthermore, because resistance had not been retheorized, it continued to operate as a utopian rubric of purity—even when historians were criticizing the absence of it. This process can be seen, for example, in polemical calls for the "abolition of whiteness." Although the more nuanced critique of whiteness beneath this polemic is important, the rhetoric replicated the binary opposition between resistance and total power. That is, for both moments of cultural history, resistance—or creativity—did not emerge from inevitable conditions of complicity but remained its juxtaposed counterpart.

Can we write a visionary cultural history for our present moment that draws on the resources and challenges of the last two moments of cultural history? That is, can we create a history that has the kind of political efficacy and relevance of the cultural history of the subaltern, with the new understandings of power we gain from the deconstructive history of categories and hierarchies? We gain a model for how history can create visionary knowledge from the cultural history of subalterns of the 1970s. For many historians, the practice of history transformed the historian. The epistemic shift of this first moment meant that historians not only applied their professional expertise to their sources but themselves turned to history to learn new ways of being in the present. Many of them approached their subject matter expecting to find their imaginations stretched and their consciousnesses expanded. The first moment of cultural history also gives us a model of applying historians' tools to legitimating new political formations. The same social movements do not exist today, but historians can look to activists and artists who are engaging the contemporary context to explore how historical inquiries might help make new political futures imaginable.[17] I am not suggesting that historians passively echo artists or activists or simply recount their histories, but rather that we remember history's role as a political discourse that specializes in defining the possible.[18] In order to become (more) visionary then, cultural history might take from the first moment a readiness to be changed by our projects and a dynamic engagement with the ways that our histories interact with a wider political imagination. The second moment of cultural history provides us with profound challenges to thinking about power in dynamic and sophisticated ways. We know now that any cultural history that is going to be able to analyze power is going to have to move beyond the simple divide between subaltern and dominant, and is going to have to explore the construction of the subject in culture, as inevitably complicit in history. In addition, we have the great challenge of maintaining a historical discourse that supports the possibilities of social change while creating a more nuanced rubric than our present model of resistance. Our own moment is a remarkably fertile one; a plethora of ways to pursue cultural history's future are emerging and, if we are fortunate, will continue to do so. I spend the rest of this chapter suggesting just one.

To begin, I return to Xu Bing's exhibit in North Carolina in order to think about the analytical possibilities of grief and complicity. When Xu Bing projected his Chinese father's medical charts on a tobacco barn in North Carolina, he revealed that illness is social and that our very bodies are products of large historical processes that span national divides. Xu said in an interview, "Historically, American tobacco has a strong connection to China. I had done research and discovered that the Duke family brought tobacco and cigarette to China, before that China never had cigarette."[19] Few North Carolinians knew that the "golden weed" that gave them relative prosperity, and later, illness and premature death, had also shaped Chinese people's bodies, their lives and deaths. Xu Bing's exhibit clearly asserted the culpability of Duke and the tobacco industry. At the same time, however, the exhibit declared that stories that seemed half a world apart could be seen as connected. Some who saw the medical charts in Chinese on the old log wall must have had a moment of recognition similar to my own. Many of us have scrutinized medical charts outside of the rooms of loved ones, trying to decipher their mysterious glyphs that seem to hold the secret of life and death. Professional, medical lingo coldly expresses the most personal of journeys but is unintelligible to most in any language. So many people in the United States have lost loved ones to smoking-related illness, especially in North Carolina, where smoking rates are high. Xu Bing's father's story, though written in unfamiliar characters, challenges us to think about how we tell the bodily, lived history of transnational capital, its boundaries and its silences.

When we bring the cultural historian's tools to understanding Xu Bing's rendition of grief, we gain a glimpse into a cultural history method. In the nineteenth century, when a worker in France was injured, his co-workers would say, "the trade is entering his body." These workers knew that their bodies were products of the historical context they lived within, that their work would, quite literally, shape them. How does capitalism enter our bodies? How does globalization enter our bodies? Xu Bing does not tell this story by using his father's voice; rather he interrupts the modern narrative of capitalist progress with another modern narrative of official medical discourse. In this case, the confluence of the two, and the clear failure of the latter, exposes the limits of modernism. Medical sociologist Arthur Frank provides insight into why illness and grief might have such great epistemological potential. Under capitalism's reverence for and dependence on progress, according to Michel Foucault, the absence of work is rendered obscene. Illness and death, then, are even more obscene than the absence of work, and are a great challenge to the myth of progress and professionalism's triumph over nature. Frank notes that part of the professional role of modern medicine is to restore faith in progress challenged by illness. Doctors, through medical authority over the body, reform the body and restore it to productivity. In the process, professionalized medical knowledge alienates patients from their own experience of their bodies. The "sick role" under modernism is to accept these terms and defer to medicalized knowledge in order to get well. Most of us are more than willing to go along with this practice as long as it works. But recently, according to Frank, people have challenged progressive medicine's authority, particularly people for whom its promise has proven false. These people are reclaiming their own stories, mining their lives for new knowledges about their bodies and the society that made them. Much like the visionary cultural historians of the 1970s, Frank calls on us to listen to "wounded storytellers" for this new knowledge rendered in the "obscene" social locations of grief and illness.[20]

Political philosopher Judith Butler's writings on grief, likewise, point to its political potential for our time. Butler suggests that we see the condition of grieving as the foundation for a new political ethics. For in grieving we understand how profoundly interconnected we are: we not only become who we are in relation to others, but we are also unmade by losing them. We are dispossessed by grief, beside ourselves. Grief reveals our profound vulnerability at the level of the body. Our body's dependence on others' touch and our vulnerability to illness, violence, and loss are inescapable. Butler asks, "Is there a way in which the place of the body, and the way in which it disposes us outside ourselves or sets us beside ourselves, opens up another kind of normative aspiration within the field of politics?" This argument is not simply for the relational or culturally constructed self, but an argument about the political potential that arises when we recognize our common dispossession by our relations. Butler argues that this dispossession could be a foundation for political community: we might recognize and become responsible to this commonality rather than to fantasies of autonomy and mastery. Our shared vulnerability and grief might become the foundation for a political ethics that insists that all lives are grievable.[21] When Xu Bing projected his father's medical charts on the wall of a North Carolina tobacco barn, he insisted that his grief was part of North Carolina history. Suddenly, a bodily and ethical connection that few of us had imagined was brought into our consciousness. The vulnerable bodies of Chinese smokers, which many of us had never thought to grieve, resonated with our own loss and vulnerability to more loss. Our sense of the social and historical particularity that gave rise to North Carolina's tobacco industry required expansion to make room for a new story.

If we bring an attunement to history's role in legitimating new political discourses to Xu Bing's art, we can see that it calls for a new history, one that can explore heretofore hidden or denied affiliations across national boundaries. Although the export of cigarettes to China is no secret, histories have tended to tell the story of North Carolina tobacco as a state, regional, or national story. Business historians acknowledge the transnational web of tobacco, but they privilege high finance and powerful entrepreneurs in their tobacco histories and rarely venture into the realm of culture or daily life. Xu Bing, however, is an artist who has lived in both China and the United States; his art has been profoundly shaped by Chinese and international political events. Born in Chongqing, Sichuan Province, China in 1955, Xu gained prominence in China as one of the best New Wave artists of the 1980s. After the Tiananmen Square massacre, the increasingly constrained climate for artists prompted him in 1990 to accept a position as a visiting artist at the University of Wisconsin, and since then he has resided in the United States. Xu attributes the contributions of his generation of Chinese artists to the fact that "[we] went through ten years of socialist education, ten years of Cultural Revolution, ten years of open door policy, ten years of western influence. . . . These factors directly affect the way [we think and deal] with problems. Comparing with some western counterpart, we are rich with experiences."[22] The Tobacco Project makes discernable historical connections that may not have been visible to North Carolina tobacco farmers and cigarette factory workers—or, perhaps, to Xu's father—because concepts of nation and property obscured them. How might this new history change us? What might we learn when cultural history expands to create a story that can explain the loss signaled by characters on the tobacco barn, over one hundred years after the first North Carolina cigarettes arrived in China?

Furthermore, the practice of cigarette smoking suggests a way to move beyond a simple binary between dominant and subaltern and explore the inevitable complicity of the subject in history. While law says we must choose who is culpable, the tobacco industry or the individual consumer, history recognizes the bodily vulnerability that brings the smoker to smoke again. This is a highly personal, physical vulnerability, but elements of it are shared, that is, they are cultural, since personal desires and needs are refracted through social meanings of smoking as rebellion, as "modern," as "cool," that hold shifting but profound social and aesthetic value—even beauty. This personal and collective vulnerability leads the smoker to a failure that is deeply human: trivial in each instance of lighting up, devastating in its long-term effects. This complicity is not the end of the story but its precondition. As Gore Vidal has said, "[Not] only is life mostly failure, but . . . in one's failure, or pettiness, or wrongness exists the living drama of the self." How we deal with our failures, and the ways we find ourselves living out the ramifications of history in our daily lives, is the "living drama of the self," the individual formed in inextricable relation to power. By looking into our grief and our complicity, we have an opportunity to discover the unpredictable creativity of people's lives.[23]

My discussion of grief and complicity as ways to think about the future of cultural history is more epistemic and theoretical than a suggestion that we confine ourselves to particular topics. Certainly, a wealth of work has emerged in the past several years that directly engages grief and bodily vulnerability; work on trauma, torture, genocide, illness, memory, commemoration, and mourning has much to teach us, and the dramatic growth of these subfields is a reflection of shifting political exigency. I have learned a great deal from this work, and some of it moves beyond the subaltern/dominant binary and begins to redefine "resistance"—but this is not inevitably so. The model of grief implicit in both moments of cultural history is consistent with a figure of the innocent victim, standing outside of power and simply oppressed by it. The more complex view of the subject constituted in power bequeathed to us by the deconstructive cultural history of categories requires that we configure grief differently. My hope, then, in offering these thoughts about grief and complicity, is not so much to delineate a topic of study as to suggest a way to open our inquiries: looking into grief may not lead to a study that focuses on grief per se, but it may generate new questions in any number of fields. Xu Bing's artistic rendering of grief calls us to recognize a common history of tobacco and transnational capital though common loss, but that historical narrative would not be confined to recounting acts of mourning. But neither would it be a history of simple resistance and heroism.

Delving into grief and complicity can seem dangerous. The famous slogan "Don't mourn, organize!" serves an important function today just as it did when first uttered. Labor lore holds that Joe Hill wrote the line in a letter to Bill Haywood the night before he was executed by the state of Utah in 1915. Hill was convicted of murder, but many believed he was framed in order to discredit and discourage labor organizing. Haywood repeated Hill's famous line at his funeral because he knew grief could lead to immobilizing self-blame or despair. This insight seems especially important today, when devastating losses and political cynicism threaten to debilitate our will to continue the long effort for social justice.[24] Don't we need success stories of resistance in order to promote hope in political action? The visionary cultural history of subalterns built hope in part because it demonstrated that people had changed things before—social activism did in fact lead to social change. In the context of vibrant social movements that had made some undeniable gains, albeit suffered many losses, such recounting of success stories had political efficacy.

I contend, however, that it wasn't only the success of resistance or heroic agency in the past that was so inspiring about the visionary cultural history of subalterns. Stories of success resonated with the surge in social movements of the era; in our own very different times, stories of success can cut different ways, convincing students that activists are great people unlike themselves, or that charismatic leaders are needed but lacking. We need to distinguish between success and struggle in historical narratives' ability to inspire. Part of what engendered hope in that earlier historical narrative was the example of people endeavoring to create beauty in their lives—music, art, community, social change—despite their losses, their grief, and their errors. There is tremendous, life-giving power in this creative legacy. Indeed, there's more to the story of Joe Hill's death than we typically hear: despite the slogan "Don't Mourn, Organize," the International Workers of the World responded to Hill's execution by organizing through mourning. In his last letter to Haywood, Hill had asked Haywood to make sure he was not buried in Utah; in his last poem he wrote, "And let the merry breezes blow / My dust to where some flowers grow / Perhaps some fading flower then / Would come to life and bloom again." In response, the IWW coordinated memorials in every state and several other countries for May Day 1916. They mailed small envelopes with Hill's ashes to leaders organizing each ceremony, linking people across the country and globe by ritualizing the IWW's expansive vision of labor citizenship.[25] Thus, Hill was one of the most mourned labor activists of the twentieth century. The IWW knew that the act of mourning—if collective, that is, if made socially meaningful—would inspire activism rather than despair. Despite the fact that cultural history of subalterns did not directly interrogate grief and loss, its presence in those histories constituted part of their ability to inspire a sense of collectivity and purpose.

If cultural historians traditionally have been ambivalent about interrogating grief and complicity, grief and complicity are playing an even more fraught role in our current political culture. In the days after the September 11 attacks, the Bush administration worked diligently to turn our grief to anger at the terrorists. Grief asks, how could this have happened? Grief almost always asks, how was I involved? Do I bear some responsibility for this loss? But these were dangerous questions for the Bush administration. Attempts to understand the connections between people, and the consequences of our prior actions—the quintessential tasks of the historian—the Bush administration labeled unpatriotic. This tactic was just as politically intentional and strategic as the IWW's slogan. The Bush administration needed U.S. citizens to avoid criticism of U.S. policies, economies, and interventions that link us, without our daily knowledge, to the lives and suffering of others. It needed U.S. citizens to position themselves as aggrieved victims only, in order to forge a warrant for an escalation of the new right agenda in the Middle East and the rolling back of civil liberties in the United States. Complicity in subsequent, unfolding disasters was equally denied. Bush made catastrophic mistakes but admitted to none of them.

Human experiences so resolutely and obsessively and frantically denied—grief and complicity, vulnerability and death—must contain enormous power, and we need to interrogate them in our cultural history. Not just to expose the powerful as wrong but to explore the caches of meanings and knowledge there for all of us. At a time when fascism is on the rise in many nations—intolerance, assaults on civil liberties, and moral extremism are represented as godly, righteous, and unquestionable—it seems especially important for antifascists to remind us that vulnerability and failures make us human. If moral absolutism denies the ways that we are connected, the responsibilities we bear for each other, then historians have an opportunity to make a significant antifascist contribution.

Indeed, we are just gaining momentum, in my view, in the effort to create a visionary cultural history for our own historical moment. We're poised on the brink of telling new kinds of stories, not of resistance or oppression—at least not configured in those terms—and not about categories primarily, but ones that build on these resources we have inherited. I don't know what they will be, but I think they will fundamentally revise the utopian concept of resistance. I think they will further blur lines between subaltern and dominant; they will figure out what that hybridity and complicity means for our examination of culture and human action, and how we can envision justice utilizing such a critique. I think they will replace moralism, so rampant in our society right now, with moral vision. The unpredictable creativity of historical subjects can expand our own unpredictable creativity as historians. We still need, as Lawrence Levine told us almost thirty years ago, to expand our consciousness through the pursuit of the craft of history. If we do this, and who knows exactly how it would turn out, I am convinced we will write a visionary cultural history in new terms worthy of the amazing and precious tradition we have inherited, and relevant to the moment of danger in which we find ourselves.

NOTES

Many thanks to Dorothea Browder, Rachel Buff, Anne Enke, Dave Gilbert, Kori Graves, Brenna Greer, Wendy Kozol, and Stephanie Westcott, and the editors of this volume for helpful feedback, and to the National Endowment for the Humanities, which paid the bills during the period I worked on this chapter.

1. Daniel Wickberg, "Heterosexual White Male: Some Recent Inversions in American Cultural History," *Journal of American History* (June 2005): 136–57; I particularly benefited from Michael Millner's excellent essay "Post Post-Identity," *American Quarterly* 57, no. 2 (June 2005): 541–53.
2. Excellent work continues to appear in both of these scholarly veins. I periodize in this way not to signal completion but to mark the generative moments of intellectual excitement. In addition, I use tools of analysis and vocabulary from both moments to analyze cultural history's political efficacy. I use the term "subaltern" to describe the first moment because it is a useful way to aggregate the projects of writing history "from below." Whether or not we would now claim all of these historical actors as subaltern, they were studied at the time precisely as people excluded from dominant society and history. I also wish to signal that the U.S. project, inspired by the civil rights movement, which was in turn inspired by anti- and postcolonial movements, particularly in India and many African countries, bears resemblance to subaltern studies in its motivations, although it is certainly not identical to them. Finally, my analysis of these two moments is not meant to be a comprehensive review of the field but is selective and admittedly schematic to allow me to develop my argument about its future. My interest here is not to create new categories for historiography but to make claims about inherited resources and future directions. Both moments of cultural history that I identify, then, are strategically conceived for the purposes of this essay; I might represent the historiography differently in other contexts. For example, what I call the "first moment" of cultural history is obviously not really the very first. For a longer view, see my article, Nan Enstad, "Popular Culture," in *Companion to American Cultural History*, ed. Karen Halttunen (New York: Blackwell, 2008).
3. The degree to which historians thought these groups were entirely separate should not be exaggerated. Lawrence Levine, for example, notes that whites had a great influence on African American antebellum culture, but rather than focusing on hybridity, he argues that African Americans made aspects of Christianity, music, and folktales they learned from whites "their own." Gerda Lerner in 1975 called for attention to a separate "women's culture" but also acknowledged that it would bear the traces of "patriarchal assumptions." Subsequent critiques of this project should recognize that at least part of the effort to draw separate histories was strategic rather than simply essentialist. Lawrence W. Levine, *Black Culture and Black Consciousness: Afro-American Folk Thought from Slavery to Freedom* (New York: Oxford University Press, 1977), 25. Gerda Lerner, "Placing Women in History" *Feminist Studies* 3, nos. 1–2 (Fall 1975): 5–14.
4. Levine, *Black Culture and Black Consciousness*, ix. I use *Black Culture and Black*

Consciousness as my primary example in this section because the conference in Levine's honor for which this chapter was originally written gave me the occasion to look back at his early work in depth. The passion and political eloquence I found there inspired me to think about the visionary qualities of the first moment of cultural history. The reader should be advised that Levine was only one of many historians who participated in this moment and that historians contributed to that moment in their own particular ways, with disagreement playing as important a role in the development of the field then as always.

5.   Many historians participated in the development of this insight. E. P. Thompson saw "class experience" as rooted in material conditions of production, but he saw "class consciousness" as "the way in which these experiences are handled in cultural terms; embodied in traditions, values, systems, ideas, and institutional forms." The study of culture, then, was always integral to what is often called the "new social history." Herbert G. Gutman extended Thompson's innovations and argued that the rise of industrialization required a change in "whole cultures" as well as in labor structures. Historians came to see culture as a field of struggle between capitalist requirements and people's own interests. George Rawick argued that slaves' cultural practices, including African traditions, became resources for adapting to and resisting slavery. Once ordinary people's culture was seen as a resource for resistance for historical subjects, its value for political actors resisting in the present was evident. Carroll Smith-Rosenberg, for example, uncovered a "female world of love and ritual" in the nineteenth century that exceeded in some way the kinds of intimacy that women of the present could experience. This was significant new knowledge for feminists trying to reimagine both sexual and nonsexual relationships between women. E. P. Thompson, *The Making of the English Working Class* (London: Victor Gollancz, 1963); Herbert G. Gutman, "Work, Culture and Society in Industrializing America, 1815–1919," *American Historical Review* 78 (1973): 531–88; George P. Rawick, *From Sundown to Sunup: The Making of the Black Community* (Westport, CT: Greenwood, 1972); Carroll Smith-Rosenberg, "The Female World of Love and Ritual," *Signs: Journal of Women in Culture and Society* 1, no. 1 (1975). A flood of work, too voluminous to cite fully here, followed and pursued these questions in a range of ways and in a variety of subfields.

6.   Many historians associate postmodernism only with scholars steeped in European theory and juxtapose it with this moment in social and cultural history. However, a fundamental aspect of this history was postmodern in the sense that it levied a profound critique of modernist epistemology and the role of the professional. Women's historians participated centrally in the critique of traditional history as a professional discourse, and also critiqued medical and other professionals and their modernist authority to define and regulate gender. See Barbara Ehrenreich and Deirdre English, *For Her Own Good: 150 Years of the Experts' Advice to Women* (Garden City, NY: Doubleday, 1978); Carroll Smith-Rosenberg, "The Hysterical Woman: Sex Roles and Role Conflict in Nineteenth-Century America," *Social Research* 39, no. 4 (1972).

7.   Levine, *Black Culture and Black Consciousness*, xi. The idea of raising one's consciousness through historical study was held by both people of color and whites, by women as well as men, and people sought it out whether they worked on more nationalist projects within historical subfields or envisioned a transformed "U.S." history. Although standpoint epistemology (a reductive outgrowth of these epis-

temological challenges, laced with modernist notions of authority) emerged in the 1980s, few assumed in the late 1960s and 1970s that an identity category automatically generated a political position. Rather, people were alert to the ways that, in the language of the time, people "internalized their oppression."

8. Ibid., 80.

9. An example of this is Wickberg, "Heterosexual White Male," which simplified 1970s history to a single concept of "recuperation." He explores the nature of that project in only a few sentences before describing later critiques of it in great detail. He then characterizes the shift from the 1970s to the 1980s as one "from recuperation to critique," casting earlier historians as naively uncritical.

10. I noticed the effects first when trying to teach books from this era in my graduate seminars. Because students' critical acumen has been developed by post-1990 scholarship that directly responded to flaws in earlier work, students discerned those flaws with dramatic clarity, but the contributions were less visible to them. And although I was fluent in helping them articulate their critiques, I found myself struggling to explain to them what I found valuable in the work they had just eviscerated, not just as a pathway to something else but for us today.

11. See George Lipsitz, "Dancing in the Dark: Who Needs the Sixties?" in his *American Studies in a Moment of Danger* (Minneapolis: University of Minnesota Press, 2001), 58–72.

12. Work in this second moment is likewise too vast to cite comprehensively. Significant contributions include, however, works such as Joan W. Scott, *Gender and the Politics of History* (New York: Columbia University Press, 1988); David Roediger, *The Wages of Whiteness: Race and the Making of the American Working Class* (New York: Verso, 1991); Evelyn Brooks Higginbotham, "African-American Women's History and the Metalanguage of Race," *Signs* 17 (Winter 1992); George Lipsitz, *Time Passages: Collective Memory and American Popular Culture* (Minneapolis: University of Minnesota Press, 1990); Jonathan Ned Katz, "The Invention of Heterosexuality," *Socialist Review* 20 (January–March 1990): 7–34; Gail Bederman, *Manliness and Civilization: A Cultural History of Gender and Race in the United States, 1880–1917* (Chicago: University of Chicago Press, 1995); Philip Deloria, *Playing Indian* (New Haven: Yale University Press, 1998). One should not assume that the two moments were pursued by entirely different groups of historians. The work of Levine, Carroll Smith-Rosenberg, and Joan W. Scott bridged the two moments. See Levine, *Highbrow/Lowbrow: The Emergence of Cultural Hierarchy in America* (Cambridge: Harvard University Press, 1988); Smith-Rosenberg, "Hearing Women's Words: A Feminist Reconstruction," in her *Disorderly Conduct: Visions of Gender in Victorian America* (New York: Knopf, 1985).

13. Stuart Hall, as quoted in Joan Scott, "The Evidence of Experience," *Critical Inquiry* 17, no. 4 (Summer 1991): 773–98.

14. Several scholars have tried to introduce the Gramscian concept of hegemony into the conversation precisely because it suggests that the legitimation of power occurs through cultural struggle and is never complete. However, hegemony repeatedly morphed in historians' works into a concept of total power, and one often hears a phrase that would make no sense to Antonio Gramsci: "total hegemony." I suggest that this problem was rooted in the already entrenched binary of resistance and domination, and particularly the political/intellectual work performed in the 1970s by the utopian concept of resistance to imagine limits to power. By imagining power as total, historians found myriad examples of resis-

tance, but missed how power was working more dynamically in societies and selves. For an example of the debate about hegemony, see the forum by Leon Fink, Jackson Lears, John P. Diggins, and George Lipsitz, in *Journal of American History* 75, no. 1 (1988): 115–50.

15. Scott, "Evidence of Experience."
16. Walter Johnson, "On Agency," *Journal of Social History* 37, no. 1 (2003): 113–24. My own earlier work was concerned with trying to create a notion of agency and resistance that matched the more complex notion of the subject developed in the 1990s. I found the opposition between corroboration with power and resistance difficult to bridge. Despite my best efforts, most read my work as a celebration of my subjects' use of consumer culture, a consumer culture and a usage I was in fact deeply ambivalent about. And I think they are right: in tracing various kinds of informal and formal resistance, I made my critiques of corroboration more difficult to discern. Whatever nuance I managed to infuse into the work is often flattened out in conversations about it. "Are dime novels liberatory?" is a question I hope never to be asked again. We all struggle with the inevitable shortcomings of our work, but in this case I think my experience is emblematic of a moment in cultural history.
17. I have been influenced here by George Lipsitz, "'Facing Up to What's Killing You': Urban Art and the New Social Movements," in his *American Studies in a Moment of Danger*, 213–34. See also Robin D. G. Kelley, *Freedom Dreams: The Black Radical Imagination* (Boston: Beacon Press, 2002).
18. I am pleased to find my choice of language echoing the title of the important volume *"We Specialize in the Wholly Impossible": A Reader in Black Women's History*, ed. Darlene Clark Hine, Wilma King, and Linda Reed (Brooklyn, NY: Carlson Publishing, 1995). Power works to define certain actions as impossible or unintelligible, but as the field of African American women's history shows, historical actors regularly exceeded this. Both moments of cultural history have taught us about the efficacy of historical actors, but the role of history as a political discourse that renders these actions intelligible and undeniable in new, contemporary arenas is less discussed.
19. Xu Bing, interview by eChinaArt Web site, New York City, August 24, 2000; http://www.wchinaart.com/interview/xu_bing/int_xubing.htm (accessed October 24, 2003). The interview was conducted in Chinese and translated into English. Stan Abe, art historian at Duke University who curated the exhibit, and Dale Coats of the Tobacco Museum assisted Xu in learning about tobacco growing and production in North Carolina's past.
20. Arthur Frank, *The Wounded Storyteller: Body, Illness, and Ethics* (Chicago: University of Chicago Press, 1995).
21. Judith Butler, *Precarious Life: The Power of Mourning and Violence* (New York: Verso, 2004), quotation at 26.
22. Xu Bing, interview by eChinaArt. Xu gained international fame for his 1988 exhibition Book of the Sky, which used invented Chinese characters. In 2004 he exhibited Tobacco Project: Shanghai at the Hushen Gallery in Shanghai. He has exhibited all over the world and in 1999 received a MacArthur award.
23. The term "unpredictable creativity" is David W. Noble's. See Noble, *The End of American History* (Minneapolis: University of Minnesota Press, 1985). See also Lipsitz, *American Studies in a Moment of Danger*, 29. Gore Vidal, *United States Essays, 1952–92* (New York: Random House, 1993).

24. I make a distinction here between melancholy, in the Freudian sense, and grief. Melancholy references an unwillingness to let go of a loss or the identification with the lost object. Unlike grief, it does not consciously address the loss but displaces it, leading to self-blame and/or nostalgia. See Joan Scott's compelling argument that historians need to avoid melancholy in relation to feminist history's past, in Scott, "Feminism's History," *Journal of Women's History* 16, no. 2 (2004): 10–29.
25. Http://www.spartacus.schoolnet.co.uk/USAhillJ.htm (accessed August 6, 2006).

TWELVE

From Nation to Neighborhood: Land, Policy, Culture, Colonialism, and Empire in U.S.-Indian Relations

PHILIP J. DELORIA

Put a twenty dollar bill into a stamp machine at the post office and punch the button to purchase a small packet of first-class stamps. If all goes well, you'll get your stamps and a fistful of change, and you'll have participated in an act of culture.[1] In such transactions, texts are produced, distributed, and consumed; meanings are exchanged, challenged, reinforced, and transformed; institutions police and are policed, produce and are produced; and structures of power are rehearsed and questioned at microlevels, macrolevels, and whatever it is that lies between. Such acts—and their connections to institutions, social structures, and power—are the stuff of cultural analysis.

Contemplating your encounter with the stamp machine, for instance, you may find yourself considering abstract questions, such as the nature of machine transactions, or the ramifications of a national postal system, or the nature of money itself. You'll likely begin by focusing on the immediate and the textual, however, dwelling first on the form of the machine, or the architecture of the post office, or the iconography of stamps and bills. There is a good chance that your stamps (to follow this particular example for a moment) will be loaded with nationalist imagery, perhaps the Statue of Liberty with torch prominent and a flag unfurling in the background. Your fistful of change will likely come in the form of copper-colored one-dollar coins, emblazoned with the image of an American Indian woman named Sacajawea. It is a small irony, but the original twenty dollar bill that brought you the stamps and the Sacajaweas bore the image of Andrew Jackson, primary political architect of the policy of Indian removal. Jackson's removal policy codified and institutionalized the practice of displacing Indian people (including, eventually, Sacajawea's) from their land, thus clearing the continent for U.S. expansion.

Your Sacajaweas will direct you more precisely to recall the young Sho-shone mother who helped Meriwether Lewis and William Clark "open up" the West to American explorers, settlers, and commercial interests. The intertwined acts of Indian removal and western exploration proved critical not simply to the formation of the United States but to the expressions of "the nation" that you now find on your stamps. And we could go on, triangulating the imagery found on bills, stamps, and coins, and reading these things in relation to a collection of interlocked histories. A simple purchase of stamps demonstrates exactly the kinds of interplay among texts, institutions, actors, histories, and power relations that have characterized some of the most familiar methodological achievements of cultural history.[2]

The example, as you have surmised, was not chosen accidentally. Saca-jawea, who haunts both American coinage and history, guides us to the place where cultural history might be seen to meet up with Native Ameri-can studies. There, we might consider cultural history in relation to the broader imperatives of ethnic studies, to distinct genealogies of social and political history, and to specific contemporary interests in questions of empire and colonialism. Each of these has something to say to the present and future of cultural history. I begin by quickly tracing three sets of "Sacajawea questions" that point to established historiographies in cultural history, all of which have engaged the problem of situating multiple, colliding peoples on the ground of "culture." Then, I turn more specifically to ethnic studies and Native American studies genealogies, hoping, first, to illustrate how disparate such "cultural" histories can be and, second, to complicate the already complicated trajectory of cultural history writ large. I spend the majority of the chapter outlining a skeletal narration of Native/American history that suggests a more precise form of articulation between the cultural and the political, and requests an invigorated reading of national/imperial narratives.

Genealogies and Possibilities

For a long time, scholars and critics have productively asked how Sacajawea—and by extension, how Indian people in general—have cir-culated through something called American culture as (borrowed) repre-sentations, how those representations have changed over time, and what those representations say about particular moments in American history. From Roy Harvey Pearce to Robert F. Berkhofer Jr. and beyond, one might reasonably situate this engagement in relation to an American studies tradition concerned with the ongoing cultural production of a national imaginary of the collective self.[3] In much of this writing, particularly its earliest manifestations, culture exists as something of a bounded system, roughly congruent with American "society," and emergent over the course of a series of literary, social, and political struggles to imagine national community.[4]

A second set of questions have turned not on her image but on Sacajawea herself and on other indigenous people. How was Sacajawea positioned as a social actor? How, and under what conditions, did she conceive of her own identity as a Shoshone, a woman, a captive, a slave, a wife, a guide, a sister, or something else entirely? What kind of subjectivity could emerge out of the dizzying array of worlds she was forced to inhabit? And what of her son, taken by William Clark to be raised in St. Louis? What kinds of possibilities and restrictions would be open to him? How would the son of Sacajawea be able to place himself in the world? And how do such questions open up the experiences of other Indian people in similar situations? Such issues have been frequently treated in ethnohistorical research, most particularly in terms of informant biographies and "as-told-to" narratives. At the same time, they have also been questions central to the theoretical and historical work sometimes categorized under the name colonial or postcolonial culture studies.[5]

A third set of issues emerges out of the effort to move from individual lives and subjectivities to the structures of encounter between Indian and European worlds. In what ways can we see the individual experiences of Lewis and Clark and Sacajawea as being emblematic or representative? Were they part of a fleeting "middle ground" moment in which the power relations between Indian people and competing empires remained balanced enough to force individuals to embrace new orders of social and cultural creativity? Should we name Lewis and Clark as a baseline moment in the United States' imperial development, a moment in which Americans would lay down most of the tropes and techniques later applied in seemingly more visible manifestations of empire? Or, as carriers of a Jeffersonian vision of commerce and agrarian settlement, are they better named as both the continuation and the opening foray into new/ old patterns of settler colonialism along a western frontier?[6]

Taken together, these genealogies—for shorthand's sake, let us label them ideology, subjectivity, and power—have offered rich opportunities for exploring complex and overdetermined fields of cultural encounter involving multiple groups of people under conditions of struggle. In that sense, they serve as guideposts for the complex engagements between cultural historians and those concerned with the ethnic studies dimensions of such scholarship. Such guideposts, in my view, are necessary. Distinct in their motives, genealogies, and epistemologies, ethnic studies and cultural studies have not always found one another natural partners. Cultural history may well claim a wide cross-disciplinary purview, but the frequent tilt of ethnic studies' interests—particularly in the field's foundational years—toward sociology, law, political science, psychology, and economics produces very different forms of self-consciously interdisciplinary practice, forms arising from a political history centered in the late 1960s and early 1970s. The 1968 Third World liberation strikes at San Francisco State University and the formation, in 1969, of the College of Ethnic Studies at SFSU, for example, are central to an ethnic studies genealogy, while largely invisible in the narratives of cultural history.

Ethnic studies is structurally and intellectually bound to negotiate a wide range of internal difference. Asian American studies began with a solid social science orientation, for example, whereas Native American studies was from the beginning deeply rooted in law and politics. Latino/a studies took folklore seriously, as did African American studies, although it did so in a unique combination that featured innovative connections between the literary and the social sciences. These are the crudest of descriptions; greater precision actually proliferates the genealogies. Asian American studies, for instance, has been complicated by the emergence of Pacific cultural studies. Within Pacific studies, a more specific field of Micronesian studies might point to an interdisciplinary genealogy in twentieth-century Pacific ethnography and cold war area studies. And within Micronesian studies, Chamorro studies would insist on adding in the local knowledge found on Guam, particularly in the form of indigenous practices, which might as easily be seen as explicitly antidisciplinary.[7]

Historical experiences—colonization and military conquest, immigration and forced work regimes, slavery and diaspora, U.S. military occupation—have produced distinct communities with distinct questions and distinct ways of assembling disciplinary knowledge. Many ethnic studies scholars will not hesitate to point to the community-based origins of their operative questions, epistemologies, methodologies, and reporting structures. Ethical issues stand at the forefront of much inquiry, ends and means are sometimes inseparable, and political utility and efficacy, although not compromising the scholarship, matter in explicit ways. From this perspective, the cultural turn taken by social historians as a means of telling history from the bottom up can seem disengaged, characterized by a methodology that fails to question adequately the power structures underlying its own production of knowledge, and perhaps characterized by a politics with something less immediate at stake.[8]

This particular can of worms, though now open for your consideration, is simply too large to accommodate, however, and so I return to Native American studies as a suggestive case. Read in historiographic terms, Native American studies almost inevitably leads us to take seriously legal and political history not as the bases for superstructural culture studies but as critical contexts that require the establishment of numerous systematic and structured points of articulation.[9] Among the trajectories one might use to trace Native American studies historiography, there looms large a policy strand, characterized by detailed studies of the origins and implementations of federal Indian policy and jurisprudence.[10] For a long time, policy and law served as the starting point for at least two other analytical strands: the image or ideology historiography referenced earlier, which sought to untangle the shifts and persistences in representations of Indian people; and a tribal history tradition, which examined the relations between specific tribes and various invading newcomers. Even recent work, which has turned toward histories of Native American cultural innovation and production, contest and struggle, finds it difficult to escape law and policy. One important new direction in Native cultural history has been the engagement of cross-group relations (most notably African–Native American relations); another has come as an effort to place Indian people back into the story of Indian representational politics.[11] And perhaps most visible has been an engagement with tribal pasts that has emerged out of a new figuration of social/cultural history.

The familiar genealogy surrounding bottom-up social history is generally read in terms of the 1960s and the move, first, to quantification and later to "culture" as ways of gaining access to those generally left unrepresented in the master historical record. From a Native studies perspective, Indian people might be said to have been *overrepresented*— and certainly *mis*represented—in that earlier master record, invoked constantly through ethnography (which built a significant portion of its methodological authority in Native North America), military and western history, and popular frontier history. The turn to social history in Native studies, however, is of recent vintage (circa 1980s), has been exemplified by a new move to particularistic community and tribal studies, and has been driven, at least in part, by the growth of a cohort of American Indian and non-Indian scholars who feel accountable to Native communities.[12] It has been characterized by new models of social and ethnohistorical sophistication (which can be seen to distinguish it from the earlier tribal studies) and by a willingness to interpret culture against ethnographic sensibilities. The turn to this brand of social history should not be seen as a belated effort to revisit bottom-up history but as a strong reaction against *both* the political and cultural strands of Native studies historiography—and as the intellectual expression of new Native sovereignty movements.[13] In other words, community-based social history has arisen precisely because of the limitations of cultural history and of political history. Both the political and cultural strands of Native American studies scholarship tended to privilege non-Indian histories, either those of federal policy or of non-Native cultural production. It is easy to see how tribal nationalist studies willfully cut against this grain by turning to the local and the specific.

At the same time, however, these tribal studies threaten to function methodologically in the manner of classic ethnography, inviting readers to move from one discrete case study to the next, with theory emanating from particularistic examples and developing organically and laterally. Those seeking broader synthesizing pictures of Native American history have turned to new devices, and in particular to the critique of colonialism as a generalizable practice aimed most directly at Indian lands and Indian cultures, languages, and religions. Where once federal Indian policy—often, but certainly not always applied to tribes across the continent—seemed to offer a point for the synthesis of multiple Indian experiences, now that synthesis is likely to be seen in terms of the shared experiences of colonization. This synthetic and theoretical structure has often relied on analyses of cultural practice—forced transformations of language, religion, everyday practice, material culture, and subsistence, for example, or complex internal cultural change within Native communities. This particular form of cultural history—inflected by oral history, ethnography and the politics of knowledge production, ethnic studies genealogies, and a range of other influences—has been accompanied by calls for new cultural transformation, in particular the possibilities for "decolonization" and "indigenization."[14]

Although this particular strand of inquiry has much to contribute to new sensibilities in cultural history scholarship, I plan to move in almost the exact opposite direction—toward a reincorporation of policy. It is curious to me that this move to colonialism in Native American studies has been paralleled by the turn, in cultural studies and cultural history, to new questions surrounding the concept of empire, seen particularly in terms of the transnational. Given the distinct field genealogies at play, it is perhaps not surprising that the two foci—colonialism and imperialism—have failed to intersect practically in ways analogous to their theoretical overlaps and their material coproductions.[15] Cultural historians have been deeply interested in what we might call the new cultural studies of empire, examining "empire" for its internal contradictions, its modes of surveillance and production, its cultural politics and struggles. And yet despite Amy Kaplan's call to think about U.S. empire in terms more capacious than 1898 and after, twentieth-century global empire has still received relatively more attention than nineteenth-century continental empire, which has meant that American Indian histories of empire—which might include more focused attention to the practices of colonialism—have been relatively deemphasized in this particular sector of cultural history scholarship.[16] At the same time, Native American studies' emphasis on decolonization has led to a relative inattention to the question of empire. This disregard is understandable, since the metropolitan valences associated with the production of empire—cultural and otherwise—tend to point back to a center focused on federal Indian policy, that point of synthesis we have only recently left behind.

Yet it seems to me that each of these inquiries could benefit from more traffic—that cultural histories of empire and transnationalism may be invigorated by closer attention to their political interlockings with colonial practice, and that Native American studies' fascination with colonial encounter may require a return examination of imperial policy. Indeed, even in the midst of Native American studies' insistence on the importance of colonial encounters, "colonialism" itself has seemed in danger of losing its analytical precision, becoming too often simply "bad stuff that has happened to indigenous people."[17] Mohave scholar Michael Tsosie has been so bold as to suggest that colonialism actually does not serve as a particularly accurate description of all Indian experience and that it ought to be used with greater caution—at least as a generalizing or synthetic tool.[18]

In what follows, I ponder again what it means to name something "colonialism" in North America—and then, by extension, what it means to name that history as belonging also to the study or practice of empire. In that sense, I take a few risks in pointing not only to moments when imperialism and colonialism both describe the "same" process or historical moment, but also to times when, analytically, it might be productive to weight one over the other, or even to speculate on shifts in their relative centrality in understanding crossed culture and its production. In the structure that follows, I try to look, in broadly synthetic terms, at colonial and imperial practices existing historically in the relation between culture and politics, law, and social history.

To maintain some semblance of concrete grounding, I turn to the land itself—the object of imperial expansion and colonial settlement, and the root of Indian resistance, persistence, and political and cultural identity. I want to use land—broadly conceived from a cultural geography perspective—to put American colonialism and imperialism in dialogue from a Native cultural studies angle, taking seriously not only changes in ideological formations but also in federal Indian policy. I build four big temporal categories—moments, modes, or practices of U.S. imperialisms—and I ask you to come along for the ride, realizing, of course, that the categories are crude, full of variation, overlap, contradiction, and imperfection. As with all categories, building them may be a useful exercise; taking them apart can be equally useful. Indeed, I invite you to dismantle them—it is fairly easily done—and hope that you find both the categories and their dismantling to be revealing. In the end, I suggest that such categories deserve a place in the frameworks through which we tell new cultural histories of the continent and of the unevenness of its human history.

Frontier/Colony/Treaty

There are any number of ideological formations and practices one might use to delineate categorical moments of imperial/colonial Indian policy. In framing a first moment, I choose three in particular: first, a belief in the omnipresent possibility of Indian violence and thus the necessity for self-defense as a cultural mode of expansion; second, the spatial metaphor of the Frontier as key to a specific kind of Othering; and third, the possibility of treaty making as a recognizable political framework for negotiation.[19]

I have argued elsewhere that one can see visible shifts, during the mid- to late nineteenth century, in the ideologies surrounding Indian violence. These shifts help outline three of the four imperial/colonial moments I discuss. In an American colonial imaginary, for much of the eighteenth and nineteenth centuries, one found, if not actual and widespread fear, then a powerful discourse of Indian violence ("If you were to meet an Indian warrior in the woods, you would surely be attacked and killed"). This discourse functioned even though, as scholars have observed, peaceful interaction in many places was more common than actual violence.

At midcentury, these expectations changed in relation to newly created spaces of removal and reservation. New ideologies assumed the containment of still-dangerous Indians. Reservations—restricted spaces, but also thoroughly Indian in nature—created an ambivalent mix of confidence and nervousness about possibilities of Indian containment.[20]

By century's end, this second expectation had given way to one far more confining. In fairs, exhibitions, memoirs, and the naming of "last" battles such as that at Wounded Knee, South Dakota, U.S. citizens naturalized a notion of pacification ("Indians had not simply been defeated militarily, but also disciplined and subjectified within the bounds of the nation-state, so that there could be no possibility of a warlike attack; at best Indians might commit violent crimes, the same as anyone else"). In other words, the material fact of military domination was read back onto the bodies and essential natures of Indian subjects: they had been pacified; therefore they were peaceful. These changing ideologies positioned ideal Indian subjectivities in a shifting series of imperial relations: abject outsider; colonial subject-in-the-making; subaltern, quasi-citizen of the empire.

The first of these ideologies proved well suited to a military imperialism built around conquest. It insisted on a frontier dividing line between American territory and Indian territory, and it focused human imaginative energy on that particular line of difference, fixing Indians as savage Others prone to violence and thus deserving the same in return.[21] It naturalized American conquest as something that was always already an act of self-defense. Frederick Jackson Turner may have popularized the concept of the frontier in 1893, but its true power to shape culture and politics was active in the United States over a century earlier. The categorical distinctions created by a frontier ideology, and the linked concept of Indian violence, made American expansion seem a natural and inevitable thing, the common sense that underpinned claims to a national culture.[22]

In the earliest years of the United States, then, Americans delineated both material and imagined borders for the nation, and they placed Indian people on the outside. They confronted Indian people, however, who insisted on establishing their own borders—and often in similar ways. The result was a continuation (and, indeed, a substantial increase) in the negotiation of nation-to-nation treaties. Until it was abolished in 1871, treaty making served as the single most significant political act binding the United States together with Indian people—while at the same time assuming their mutual opposition. It was, in other words, a fundamental condition of empire.[23]

For both Indians and non-Indians, treaty making served as the political analogue to the cultural practices of difference. Treaty making's codification of difference established Indian peoples as nations (in a Western, legal sense) and brought them, through article 6 of the U.S. Constitution, into formal political relation with the United States.[24] Many, if not most, treaties were viewed by American citizens and negotiators as temporary expedients—temporary in large part because of a widespread belief that Indian people were vanishing. Still, the fact that treaties were so easily disregarded, altered after negotiation, or repudiated altogether might have thrown the United States into constitutional—or at least moral—crisis. That it did not, one might argue, established an early precedent for subsequent violation of negotiated agreements with other nations when it suited the needs of empire.[25]

Treaties were almost always negotiated from a position of power, which made their expediency more apparent. Native people attempted to negotiate in good faith, taking seriously the notion of diplomacy and political equivalence. As Dorothy Jones has observed, however, "One of the marks of colonialism is that it bends traditional diplomatic structures to exploitative ends. This is because accountability is not built into the diplomatic system. The only check is the assumption of countervailing force. When that is absent, as it invariably is in situations of colonialism, the whole treaty system becomes a weapon in the arsenal of the stronger power."[26]

In the early republic, treaty making fell into a wide array of patterns. By the 1830s, however, the understanding of white-Indian incompatibility was in ideological ascendancy, and these more complicated histories became increasingly difficult to imagine. See if you recognize a sequence like this, one that knits together ideological and colonial practice around familiar narrative tropes: White settlers (often bringing with them slaves) transgress the national border that separates their own nation from an Indian nation. They found settler colonies and establish market relations with the United States. Co-invasive species transform Indian environments. Land clearing, market hunting and trapping, control over water resources, creation of transportation corridors and networks, introduction of trade and new technology—all these factors (and this list is by no means exhaustive) impinge upon and transform Indian subsistence. Eventually, they produce conflict. Any act of Indian violence, retaliatory or otherwise, is taken as an attack and becomes the occasion for war. The colonizing settlers raise militias, which terrorize Native people but which are unable to win a decisive conflict. They call on the military resources of the U.S. government, which then transgresses its own national boundaries in order to attack Indian people in wars that are at once retaliatory, preemptive, and imperial. Having forced Indian people to negotiate for peace, Americans insist that treaties of peace also double as treaties of land cession, and so at the end of most Indian wars—and, as Donald Fixico has pointed out, there were 1,642 official military engagements between Indian peoples and the United States—vast tracts of land are given up, which are then newly eligible for incorporation into the U.S. empire.[27]

My sketch is a general one—a caricature in some ways—but one that captures many of the various elements present in a number of conflicts, negotiations, and cessions across the breadth of the continent. These situations, seen in retrospect, came to seem to Americans as if the United States had been defending its own territory all the time. Almost every gesture in this sketch had an accompanying set of cultural meanings that made each new move sensible: the desire for "elbow room," the assumption that Indians were nomadic, the ethos of frontier localism and community, the insistence that Indians were violent (which justified preemptive strikes), the demand for protection on the part of a federal government. Likewise, for Native people: the assumption that land rights were use based more often than property based, the ethos of young men searching for status through warfare, a general unfamiliarity with total war. The inevitabilities of a hyperfamiliar trope such as "manifest destiny," in other words, were produced culturally, politically, environmentally, and structurally through particular histories of imperialism and colonialism.

The practice of imperial consolidation of land should be seen in relation to critical pieces of policy developed in the early years of the republic. Explicitly imperial and colonial policies—the Land Ordinance of 1785 and the Northwest Ordinance of 1787, for instance, which established settlement practices and political trajectories for the Northwest territories—were, in a real sense, Indian policies. And nominally "Indian" policies—the Trade and Intercourse acts of the 1790s, for example, which laid out the nature of boundary activity between the United States and Indian nations—were simultaneously imperial in nature.[28]

The key legislative pieces that enabled American colonial settlement and imperial growth grew directly out of the redefinition of Indian lands as new spaces of empire. The 1785 Land Ordinance, for instance, established the structure of American colonial settlement on the basis of the grid system. In doing so, it also created a mechanism that allowed absentee citizens to anticipate the commodification of, and speculation in, Indian land from a distance, and it laid down the template for new imperial and colonial strategies of land division that would be put into practice a century later. It reflected and codified an imperative for order and measurement that would define the culture of settlement up to the present day.

The Northwest Ordinance recognized Native presence and claims, even as it established imperial policy for dealing with opened lands, the demography of settlement, and the coming of political order. At the same time that the ordinance proclaimed a policy of treating Indian people "with utmost good faith," it also created the structure that transformed former Indian lands into colonial outposts of empire, tested democratic abilities at the territorial level, and then brought such outposts into statehood and full membership in the nation. Demographic colonization of Indian space served as the precondition for political semiautonomy and eventual incorporation.[29]

It is worth quickly revisiting the Northwest Ordinance and its three phases of political development. In the first phase, control over the land was vested in an imperial metropole. Congress appointed governors and other officials, and approved lower-level appointments. These men enforced a series of laws and principles enumerated by the federal government. Once 5,000 free white male colonists occupied a territory, it might move into the second phase, which included elections and a representative assembly with local lawmaking authority—subject to the approval of the imperial governor. The territory's future was predestined: incorporation into the United States. Residents were liable for taxation and were allowed to have a debating (but not voting) representative to Congress. Territories existed under this kind of imperial governance until they acquired 60,000 free white male citizens, at which point they were eligible for statehood.

Statehood and incorporation, then, demanded vast amounts of Indian land for large numbers of settlers, which meant not simply military conquest but also policies of Indian clearance and containment, as well as cultural imperatives to move westward into what would later be defined as free land. The powerful tropes of "manifest destiny" and "vanishing Indians" both emerged in relation to this particular form of colonial settlement. The Land Ordinance—with its donations of school parcels and reserved federal sections—ensured that such settlement would use the bulk of the land available and that scattered frontier settlements would, in the near future, be replaced by an orderly, efficient, and connected landscape of small towns and settled farms.[30]

The Indian Trade and Intercourse acts of the 1790s made sure that the localism that had characterized the original colonies was eliminated in favor of the centralized control of the imperial state. The 1790 act forbade states, corporations, or individuals from entering into land cession agreements with Indian people. (Certain important Indian land claims— particularly the Passamaquoddy/Penobscot claim of the mid-1970s—rest on cession treaties in clear violation of the Trade and Intercourse acts.) In this sense, the 1790 Trade and Intercourse Act—like the Land Ordinance and the Northwest Ordinance before it—codified the particular mode of expansion that characterized the culture and practice of U.S. empire in its earliest manifestation. Even as the engine of colonial settlement continued generating conflicts, treaties, and cessions, the Trade and Intercourse acts also insisted that those cessions would be negotiated by the agents of empire rather than colony.[31]

The 1796 Trading House Act (later renewed in 1802) sought to link the state with the market, placing them together at the center of imperial Indian policy. The creation of the Indian "factory system" planted federal traders among Indian people, facilitated the opening of market routes into prime Indian lands, and created a vehicle for generating Indian debt (thus leveraging additional land sales). The factory system marked the beginnings of the state-capital linkage that would underpin so many reservations throughout the nineteenth century. Imperialism not only produced capital for settlers—in the form of cheap Indian land—but it also injected capital—via the goods, contracts, and wages dedicated to the trading/reservation/agency system—into Indian spaces, thus making them attractive for other kinds of colonialisms.[32]

This first moment of colonialism and empire, then, concerned itself with enormous divisions of land, boundaries conceived as national, demographic outposts that would begin small and then rapidly grow. In their small beginnings, such colonial footholds in Indian territory would face inevitable danger, articulated both in terms of the reality of Native resistance strategies and in the ideologies associated with Indian violence and frontier settlement. On one side of the coin was a picture of violence and a justified conquest, followed by treaties of peace and land cession, supported by ideologies and cultural productions that naturalized American expansion and Indian disappearance. On the other side was environmental transformation, the division of Indian land into parcels, the establishment of political and market incentives for demographic colonization, and the mechanism that allowed settlers to transcend colonial status and join the imperial nation-state.

Region/Reservation/Agency

Both of these sets of elements came together in the Indian Removal Act of 1830, which codified practices already in operation. Treaties of peace that were also treaties of cession were, whenever possible, followed by "voluntary" or forced relocations and the clearing of Indian lands, which were then subdivided, distributed, speculated, and settled. The Cherokee Trail of Tears is the most famous of these removals, but the forced movement and spatial consolidation of Indian peoples reflect a colonial practice that became standard in many places for much of the nineteenth century. The Indian Removal Act goes hand in hand with the so-called Cherokee decisions, three cases decided by the Supreme Court that gave legal imprimatur to the new political relationships that would quickly supplant the nation-to-nation distinctions performed in treaties. Most often quoted of the three cases is the line, penned by Chief Justice John Marshall in the 1831 case *Cherokee Nation v. Georgia,* which named Indian people's political status as that of "domestic, dependent nations."[33]

"Domestic, dependent nations" introduces a radically different concept to this story, and in it we can mark a breakpoint and a transition. The phrase contains in three words all the ambiguities inherent in subsequent imperial/colonial modes, which focused not on the conquest of distinct nations and the incorporation of their lands but on the shifting of "the Indian problem" from a foreign policy question to a domestic affairs one. Turner would lament the passing of a demographic frontier visible in 1890, but one might argue that it was in fact the midcentury political and cultural shift to Indian containment and possible domestic incorporation that marked the end of the material conditions that had accompanied America's earliest frontier ideologies.

Americans often imagined that the vanishing Indians being cleared from the eastern landscape naturally died out or simply "went west" somewhere. Quickly, that somewhere proved to be a bounded territory, a shrunken (if still relatively large) division of land that would, in the nineteenth century, take shape in practice and in the imagination as "Indian Territory," a region full of the smaller spaces named familiarly as "reservations." Although the idea of reserve territories could be found in early nineteenth-century treaties, the pairing of removal and reservation, and the sheer proliferation of small reservation spaces mark a new kind of practice. Not all Indian people were removed to the Indian Territory we would today recognize as Oklahoma, of course, but it marks the broad array of what we should properly view as radically new forms of Indian landholding, forms that spread both east from California and west from the seaboard metropole, eventually forcing a shrunken form of contained regionalism upon Indian peoples who had previously negotiated national borders with Spain, Mexico, Great Britain, and Canada.[34]

The space of the reservation, then, marks a second moment or practice of U.S. empire and colonialism, one reflecting the problems of dealing with incompletely conquered peoples in the midst of expanding territorial settlement. By containing Indians spatially, the reservation enabled the imperial structure laid out by the Northwest Ordinance and the Land Ordinance to function effectively. With Indians contained, regional-level space was effectively opened to a settlement that was relatively safe and that invited, say, 60,000 non-Indians to move in. The containments of the reservation regime enabled a new kind of colonialism, a shift from speculative frontier settler societies to those based on the speculative town building and agrarian resettlement envisioned in the Land Ordinance of 1785.

Here, too, the relations between Native cultures and North American environments proved critical. If Indian people were to be fixed on small, contained parcels, they would have to give up seasonal rounds, multiple subsistence strategies, and land management practices such as burning. The game-rich no-man's-lands between many Native groups would have to be eliminated. Here, we can see a political, legal, and economic relation to the cultural production that insisted on framing Indian people—even agriculturalists—as nomads needing to be "settled." In order to realign landholding, all Indian people, regardless of their subsistence past, would be forced into new European-American agrarian practices.

At the same time that it more or less protected settlers at a regional/territorial level, the reservation also functioned as a space of surveillance and reeducation designed to bring Indian people within the bounds of American national domesticity. It aimed to fix Indian people in place, to curtail their mobility, and to create new subjectivities. Indian people were named and renamed, recorded on lists—agency rolls, church rolls, baptism rolls, school rolls, and the like. The assault on Indian children, already under way, intensified as reformers and educators tried to "educate" Indian children out of their languages and cultures and thus transform entire social bodies, wiping away those things that defined Indian distinctiveness and foreignness. At boarding schools, uniforms, hair-cuts, and forced domestic, agricultural, and craft labor aimed to trans-form Indian hearts and minds, forcing the creation of a large cohort of culturally mixed individuals. In the West, Indian police were recruited and trained to take over self-administration, and they were put to work guarding the borders of reservations, many of which were fenced, so as to ensure the purity of the space both inside and out. (At the same time, reservation boundaries were necessarily more permeable than the older nation-to-nation frontier lines, simply because Americans who believed in the power of their culture had to allow Indian people to experience it, both inside and outside reservation spaces.) In effect, the reservation had multiple functions: it was often (though not always) a relocation camp for displaced people, a concentration camp for the containment of dan-gerous people, and a reeducation camp for the transformation of human subjects.

As numerous scholars have pointed out, resilient Indian people rapidly transformed these spaces into Native homelands. Many students return-ing from the schools found ways to put their skills to use, serving as trans-lators, cultural brokers, and producers of transformed and transforma-tional Native cultures. Key aspects of contemporary Native cultural life, including the powwow circuit and the Native American Church, emerged out of these new contexts. So too did new economies, including cattle and horse raising, migratory labor, and performance in sports, theater, music, and Wild West shows. In many places, Indian people transformed Christian religious practice into culturally resonant and meaningful ritu-als. Nonetheless, one might easily name U.S. policies of the latter half of the nineteenth century as interested not only in regional kinds of land sifting but also in a particularly Foucauldian brand of social relation.[35]

It should come as no surprise, then, that the most potent ideological charge, from midcentury through the massacre at Wounded Knee, did not concern the omnipresent likelihood of Indian violence across the landscape but rather the possibility that they would *escape* the contain-ing boundaries of the reservation and, maddened by their mistreatment, exact a terrifying revenge. The Minnesota Uprising of 1862 in which starv-ing Dakotas did exactly that made these fears palpable. Older keywords, which reflected white American fears of being surrounding or "forted up" by large groups of Indians, gave way to new worries, expressed in the lan-guage of Indian "outbreak," "uprising," "escape," "flight," and "rebellion." Iconic Indians like Tecumseh—figured as a racialist/nationalist leader and thus dangerous because he might have united disparate Indian peoples—

gave way to new icons such as Geronimo, Chief Joseph, and Sitting Bull, famous for their refusal to be contained, dangerous as the leaders of outbreaks. In the heaps of cultural production surrounding these figures—newspaper reportage, dime novels, public performances, the reproduction of famous last speeches, and the like—we can see older ideas of Indian violence and disappearance being refigured, through new mass-culture industries, in light of changing imperial and colonial practices.

The reservation policy grew up around a number of realities: that it was cheaper to feed Indians than to fight them; that concentrating Native people together would make feeding and reeducation easier; that containing Indians inside a bounded space *within* a newly forming American territory would allow that territory to successfully recruit settlers and thus fulfill its imperial destiny; and that the need for a small federal bureaucracy and the continual resupply of food and goods made reservations economically valuable in colonial (and thus imperial) development.

Spatial segregation proved critical to this more finely grained kind of colonial practice. The United States' colonial territories were no longer outposts and footholds contesting for Indian land. Now the situation was reversed. Indian lands were remnant outposts, tightly bounded and patrolled spaces that existed within the state and territorial system of the U.S. empire. Settler colonies surrounded those spaces, and the future—continued depletion of Indian land in the face of settlement—seemed self-evident. No wonder so many people believed that Native Americans were slowly vanishing and the frontier was either fading or moving someplace else.

But if reservation colonialism concerned itself with containment more than conquest, in its focus on reeducation it also gestured anew toward the dream of both past and future epochs—the survival and incorporation of Indian people, as a subaltern class, into the nation. The so-called peace policy of Ulysses Grant looked toward this goal, mingling a belief in uplift and social developmentalism with an impulse to reform the patronage system by putting upright churchmen in charge of reservations. It should come as no surprise that these particular colonial practices, especially the notion of social development and eventual integration of Indian people, went hand in hand with new forms of racialization.[36]

The conquest and violent removal of dangerous oppositional Indians, so characteristic of the "frontier" moment, suggest a particular kind of racial project, one emphasizing negative difference, savagery, and disappearance, and largely rejecting the possibility of social or cultural commensurability. Containment, uplift, development, and incorporation, however, suggest a racialization resting upon a notion not of equality necessarily but of commensurability and similarity. If, as developmentalists argued, Indians were what Americans had once been, then Indian people could rapidly evolve into something approaching (though never reaching) whiteness and modernity, while developing a love for freedom, democracy, and the market. Variations on the idea ranged from Jefferson's early hint that Indians could be transformed through amalgamation with whites to Richard Henry Pratt's often-quoted statement, about his Carlisle Indian Industrial School, of aiming to "kill the Indian and save the man."[37]

Indeed, this killing and saving was perhaps the critical goal to be played out on the field of cultural encounter that characterized reservations and schools. It aimed not only at the dispossession of additional lands but also at the making of Indians into effective subalterns, to be at once subjected and subjectified. It is this moment in particular, I suspect, that has led Native studies scholars to drift away from questions of empire and toward an emphasis on the colonial—and an expanded notion of the colonial at that. For it was here that the practices of colonization and domination turned to new projects designed to reshape the spaces not simply of Indian land and environment but of Indian cultures—body, psyche, spirituality, memory, kinship and home life, languages and epistemologies.

Imperialism and colonialism offer two interlocked but distinct lenses: the first is directed roughly toward the metropole and its practices and policies; the second toward the human relations proceeding from on-the-ground situations. Although one would be hard-pressed to separate these two concepts, one might argue that these first two particular moments—a nation-to-nation "frontier," on the one hand, and on the other a "domestic dependent nations" situation focused on regional space—suggest the possibility of a differential weighting of the ideas. In the first moment, Americans established the structures of imperial expansion, and empowered those structures in relation to both settler colonialism and the Indian people who would bear the losses of American expansion. In the second, they focused more precisely on the colonized—on geographic containment and on social transformation. Although the spatial segregation of the reservation regime allowed orderly imperial expansion, perhaps one might imagine a slight shift in emphasis, from practices weighted as *imperial*/colonial to those more easily visible—at least to Native American studies scholars—as *colonial*/imperial. (Of course, these moments are at once descriptive *and* chronological, and in truth, the thematic and descriptive elements I have described appeared in uneven and overlapped ways across chronological, historical time.)

Neighborhood/Allotment/Market

The notion that Indian people might ascend a developmental trajectory into modernity was predicated on a shift from "nomadic" life to agrarianism. Teaching farming and then demanding its practice would come to occupy Indian agents on most reservations. Here too, however, the question of Indian land seemed to get in the way. Even in the reduced form of the reservation, Indian landholding supported Indian cultural persistence and the Native refiguring of established practices and beliefs. We can trace a third distinct form of colonial/imperial practice, then, through yet another approach to the acquisition and management of Indian land, most particularly the policy innovation known as allotment and expressed in the Dawes or General Allotment Act of 1887.[38] A key premise behind the allotment act was that communal landholding—perpetuated by the fenced-in, segregated reservation—actually hindered Indian people from developing as yeoman farmers. The individualizing of Indians could be more effectively enforced in terms of individual landholding.[39]

Thus the allotment act provided for agents, following the lead of the 1785 Land Ordinance, to survey and divide reservation spaces into a grid of parcels—40, 80, or 160 acres—that could be allotted to individual Indian people. Assuming that families would take allotments together, the Dawes Act envisioned the creation of yet another new, and radically different, form of Indian landholding, one that would replace the communal, federally administered territory of the reservation with something resembling the individual family farm. Blithely confident that Indians would either disappear or assimilate, policymakers saw no reason to hold back Indian lands for future generations, and so the leftover "surplus lands" were opened to American settlement.[40]

The landholding picture that reformers envisioned was that of the neighborhood. From huge nationally conceived pieces of land, won through conquest, the Indian estate had been carved into small regional chunks of reservation territory, which were then gnawed and nibbled away over time and through subsequent treaties and agreements. Now the reservations themselves were to be disaggregated and desegregated, turned into checkerboarded landholdings on a grid. There a new class of white colonizers might live among Indian people, serving as role models and technical advisers in the development of a Native market agrarianism and a concomitant transition to citizenship within the imperial nation. Allotment—at least in many places—concerned itself not with white settler outposts, or segregated reservations within still-forming imperial territories, but with close, neighborhood relations in which any semblance of Indian space or collective landholding might be thoroughly disarticulated. In this sense, the Dawes Act represented a finer grain of colonial practice, and it functioned to sift out still more Indian land at exactly the level appropriate to the remaining Native estate.

Not surprisingly, this particular land policy lived in relation to shifting cultural practices and ideological formations among non-Indian Americans. The first concerned the possibility of oppositional Indian violence, and it is hard not to see the Wounded Knee massacre of 1890—just three years after the Dawes Act was passed and coming about the time of its first implementation—as being key. Wounded Knee marked a high point in the discourse of "outbreak." Newspapers reporting on the personalities and events leading up to the massacre puffed up the consequences of outbreak, providing a justification for the violent campaign. Everything about the buildup to Wounded Knee—and the justifications after the fact—emphasized the dangers of Indian escape from colonial containment.

At the same time, Wounded Knee made it abundantly clear that worries about uprisings and outbreaks were obsolete. In the largest mobilization of troops since the Civil War, the quickly moving army, drawing on railroads and nearby posts, easily surrounded and outgunned the Lakotas. The bloody decisiveness of the slaughter, and the mass parade of force as the troops withdrew—and their explicit threat to reprise the massacre if they were called to return—taught deep lessons about the impossibility of outbreak. Within a few years, non-Indians came to accept a new (and false) premise: that Indian people had been pacified not simply militarily but in terms of their very subjectivities.[41]

The growing nostalgia for the passing frontier, given voice in Buffalo Bill Cody's Wild West, Frederic Remington's paintings, Turner's thesis, and Theodore Roosevelt's writings, helped confirm the sense that times had changed. If Cody built his show, for instance, on the premise that America became America through violent struggle with Indian people, those same Indians now seemed completely safe, performers in one of the nation's preeminent mass culture spectacles. If Remington had started his career painting brilliant sunlit canvases full of white-Indian violence, he later turned to nostalgic Indian nocturnes and writing that longed for "the old days." These cultural meanings proved essential to the project of desegregation that was so critical to allotment. Settlers seeking land could move safely into checkerboarded reservation spaces, fearing nothing from tamed, dispossessed, and bitter Indians who were separated from them not by regional boundaries but by neighborhood property lines.[42]

Americans became suddenly interested, as well, in giving Indians "freedom." The Dawes Act was, according to Theodore Roosevelt, "a mighty pulverizing engine to break up the tribal mass," and it would enable individual Indians to break free of their old social bonds and find new destinies. The allotment act suggested that such futures would be found on individual landholdings, with Indians developing the small-scale market agrarianism proving so problematic for other American farmers at the end of the century. Crossed with this developmental and prescriptive belief, however, was an insistence that Indians ought also to be freed from the burden of reservation oversight, which was surely restricting Native ability to set their own direction. Indeed, Roosevelt went further, suggesting that "we should now break up the tribal funds, doing for them what allotment does for the tribal lands; that is, they should be divided into individual holdings."[43] These particular readings of freedom, however, were less about Native liberty and more about removing the last safeguards for protecting Indian land, resources, and labor power from the new forces of the market. At this point, the distinctions between familiar colonial practices and the equally familiar exploitation of an internal—perhaps colonial—class begin to blur.

Many reservations would be parceled up, and Indian people would make their choices or be assigned allotments. As Emily Greenwald has shown, these did not always correspond with the economic rationales underpinning allotment. Many people, for example, chose allotments that contained funerary or other important spiritual sites. Others used land to maintain social and cultural continuities, picking allotments in relation to family and kin groups.[44] What remained of an allotted reservation was then opened up to white settlement, with the fees generated from land sales going into the tribal accounts Roosevelt sought to eliminate. Individual Indian people received patents to their land but were prevented from selling that land for twenty-five years. The process of allotment did allow Indian people to claim U.S. citizenship. Twenty-five years is a long time, however, and it wasn't long before reformers began to worry that Indian people were being "enslaved" by their land, unable to sell it to make other capital investments. "Freedom" to control land—including the freedom to sell land, if so desired—seemed a completely logical next step, made reasonable and commonsensical through the (mis)invocation of powerful tropes like slavery and freedom.

A series of early twentieth-century modifications empowered the commissioner of Indian affairs to allow "competent" Indians to claim their titles and dispose of their lands as they wished. The result, especially in the early teens, was a series of "competency commissions" that traveled the country certifying—usually on the basis of blood quantum—the racialized "competency" of innumerable Indian people. Many Indians were certified competent against their will, and even those who desired competency were the victims of lawyers, swindlers, and crooks. In one final orgy of dispossession, land flowed like water out of Indian hands. Agents and reformers felt bad about this, but they regarded it as a necessary liberation: landlessness, they said, might well have to be a precondition for freedom, since land itself tied Indian people to their old lives. Landlessness, of course, liberated them to the extent that they could be welcomed into American modernity as bottom-rung wage workers in the marketplace.[45]

In 1924, even as immigration quotas were being set on foreign immigrants, Indians were extended the ultimate recognition of their own final incorporation into the empire: the Indian Citizenship Act, which dictated citizenship to Indian people across the board (and was rejected by a number of Native groups, who continued to claim the right of national citizenship in tribal terms). The payoff represented by citizenship makes clear that American imperialism had, at last, figured a solution to the nagging question that forces itself upon all empires: how to incorporate subordinate people. A range of colonial practices sought to produce new subaltern subjects willing to embrace such a solution. In this context, however, Indian refusals of citizenship and continued assertions of tribal citizenship reveal the continuity of indigenous sovereignties—and their existence prior to the contemporary vocabulary that struggles to describe them.

These practices of continental imperialism, which mingled the foreign, the domestic, and the colonial, had of course been accompanied by other kinds of global and hemispheric imperialisms in Mexico, Latin America, the Caribbean, and the Pacific. All of these forms maintained continuity across the century break and the marker year 1898, and their practices and techniques were necessarily characterized by interplay among a range of continental and global locations. It is important to note, too, that there are innumerable examples of resistances, breakdowns, and unanticipated consequences of these different practices. Indian people remade reservations into homelands. They constantly petitioned Washington, appealing to U.S. law and American values. They played cultural politics in efforts to educate and win over average American citizens. They refused citizenship. I don't wish to downplay these things. But it is also true that by the turn of the twentieth century, Indian population numbers were at their lowest ever—about 250,000 people, according to many demographers. Nations had been whittled to territories, then to reservations, then to checkerboards, then to even smaller remnants and footholds of Indian-held land, as allotments were themselves fragmented by death and inheritance, then reworked as economically viable aggregates of parcels, assembled by the Bureau of Indian Affairs and leased to outsiders.[46]

Self-Government/Dependency/Sovereignty

The United States had, from this bird's-eye perspective, run an extremely efficient exercise in colonization and empire. That exercise had helped produce the American nation-state through the effective claiming, settling, and incorporating of Indian land and the spreading of American demography and democracy across the continent. Minimized in a number of ways, Indians had been rendered almost meaningless politically, even as they maintained significant power in American cultural imaginations as figures of both nostalgia and modernist primitivism. In 1903, the United States Supreme Court showed little compunction in declaring that Congress had "plenary power" over Indian people, even to the extent of disavowing treaty commitments. Even if Native nations had wished to claim a degree of political autonomy in subordinate relation to the United States—empire in a classic sense—the United States had now laid the groundwork for a denial of even that possibility. According to the Supreme Court, Indian peoples had been fully incorporated into the national domestic body, losing—or potentially losing, at the will of Congress—even the kinds of limited authority possessed by territories and states. (Here again, one can see the resonance of the concept of colonialism, rather than imperialism, for Native people.)

So why reverse course, as New Deal Indian commissioner John Collier did, in 1934? The so-called Indian New Deal was anchored by the Indian Reorganization Act (IRA), which ended the policy of allotment and "allowed" and encouraged Indian people to set up tribal governments based on a U.S. constitutional model. The IRA not only stopped the flow of Indian land but encouraged tribes to shore up communal landholding and to reacquire land whenever possible. A revolving credit fund was created to assist with economic development, and an Arts and Crafts bill helped regulate a craft-based Indian "culture industry," itself an important exercise in primitivism, universalist aesthetics, and imperialist nostalgia. Today, a significant proportion of tribes are run by IRA governments, which have mingled the legal rationales for federal obligations outlined in treaties with the possibilities for semisovereignty and self-determination implicit in the Indian New Deal.[47]

These kinds of adventures in nation building and economic development have the appearance of something progressive, and of course, in relation to what preceded them, they were. The Indian New Deal was not a decolonization, by any means. It was *something*, however, and may well be seen in some future year (if not in the present) as an important moment in a larger and longer decolonizing struggle. It is also the case, however, that there are usually multiple motives for nation building and economic development, and there are consequences—anticipated and unanticipated—of such activities. In that sense, one might argue that, at least in the short term, the IRA simply introduced yet another set of new imperial and colonial practices to Indian peoples.

Tribes were asked to vote about whether or not to adopt the IRA and to set up a government. Those elections, in many places, forced into visibility a number of existing fault lines within tribes: distinctions between families and factions, generational differences between older and younger people, ethnic divisions between differently identified "tribal" groups on shared reservation space, racial divisions among "mixed bloods" and "full bloods," and, in Indian Territory and the Southeast, between descendents of freedpeople and those claiming greater proportions of "Indian" in their bloodlines. Established political leaders, often associated with churches or grassroots communities and often closer to older forms of Native governance, lost ground as elections insisted on new forms of collective decision making. Some elections split almost down the middle, splits that often masked three-part divisions: those voting in favor, those voting to oppose, and those who chose to demonstrate their opposition by not voting at all.

Just as allotment had echoed the 1785 Land Ordinance, the Indian Reorganization Act echoed the imperial provisions of the Northwest Ordinance, allowing tribes to draft their own constitutions but making the documents subject to approval by the secretary of the interior.

Tribes were allowed to create certain governing and policing structures, but these did not displace the supervisory presence of Indian Office employees on reservations. It soon became apparent that one of the main reasons for creating tribal councils was the need for central authorities to negotiate and approve business or governmental initiatives. Councils, according to the federal government (if not always the majorities of their constituencies), had the political and legal power to negotiate and sign deals for resource extraction or further land cessions. If we are thinking—analytically—about the relative weight accorded practices of empire and colony, then we might describe yet another shift: what had initially seemed an *imperial*/colonial dynamic—an empire consolidating power over both its colonies and independent Indian people—had given way in the nineteenth century to an imperial/*colonial* weighting— in which colonial subjects were produced on the contained reservation spaces some have referred to as "internal colonies." Now, in 1934, such a weighting might be reversed again, with the reestablishment of imperial political relations. Indeed, those relations—between tribal governments and the federal government—can be seen to demonstrate how U.S. imperialism might work in the twentieth century and beyond: nominally independent governments, largely dependent on the United States, overseen by imperial agents, with a divided populace subject to new forms of exploitation of land and resources. No longer domination, conquest, and dispossession, per se, but now semiautonomy and limited empowerment under the banners of "self-determination" and "freedom."[48]

It is also the case that this last category or moment relies as heavily on a culture- and subject-based understanding of policy formation, as do the previous three. In the wake of representations that layered upon and shifted from "violent" to "contained" to "pacified," the twentieth-century sense of Indian people as authentic remnant primitives in relation to modernity produced the cultural fascination visible in figures such as Mabel Dodge Luhan, who first invited John Collier to Taos. Collier's personal narrative demonstrates well the ways that cultural and political history articulate in compelling ways. After a modest career as a civic reformer, Collier found his life's new purpose in relation to a primitivist desire for Indianness. His lifelong fascination with Indians—who, he argued, were the last hope for the development of authentic, healthy personality— carried him into national political activism in the 1920s, and then to a dominating presence in the federal Indian bureaucracy, which allowed him to push through the reforms of the Indian New Deal.[49]

Empire, Indigeneity, and Cultural History

At different historical moments and in different tribal situations, then, it may be more or less useful to think of Native people as being putative subjects of empire, colonized subjects (or at least, subjects-in-the-making), national citizens, abject outsiders, and, of course, members of indigenous political collectivities—tribes, bands, villages, councils. Figuring a location for any individual or group amid these overlapping and conflicting statuses would require a precise understanding of the complex relations among multiple forms of Indian resistances, multiple American ideological formations, the trajectory of environmental transformation and patterns of landholding, and the range of origins and implementations that characterize the United States' Indian policy initiatives. Those policy initiatives functioned as simultaneously imperial and colonial, though we might explore the ways they shifted over time in degree, balance, and proportion. Specific practices in specific moments produced a wide array of colonial/imperial projects, each with a special genealogy for the present, and perhaps with a specific set of demands for decolonization, on the one hand, and for cultural studies scholarship, on the other.

It's not just that we ought to recognize that the conquest of Native North America was part of a wider history of imperialism and colonialism, but that it matters that we have a broad picture of particular moments and modes in that relation as they articulate across American history and the broader circuits of global empire. The industrial education given Indian children, for example, had its roots not in the United States but in the British empire, and one can chart a trajectory from South Africa to Hawai'i to the Hampton Institute, which threw Indian prisoners among black students, to the famous Carlisle Indian Industrial School. At the same time, we should also note the centrality of Indian experiences and federal Indian policy in the development of the practices that reverberated across these circuits. The use of the treaty system and the redefinition of communal and private landholding proved critical to the acquisition of the Mexican southwest. And it is a commonplace that the reservation administration system honed techniques and trained personnel for imperial/colonial adventures post-1898. The Indian Reorganization Act might well be seen as a kind of rough draft for certain recent, and even contemporary, imperial projects of the United States.

It is important to emphasize again that the history I've just narrated never worked according to plan. Although generally dominated, Indian people always managed to transform their situations in unexpected ways. They frequently did so on the ground of culture, particularly as it articulated with politics. Indeed, for Native people, the maintenance of political autonomy has required the continual refiguring of cultural differences, which serve as the visible and necessary analogue to a politics centered on sovereignty and distinctiveness. Nowhere is this dynamic more apparent than in the moments following the imperialisms and neocolonialisms of 1934 and after. In the 1960s, Indian leaders learned how to maneuver successfully within the bureaucratic apparatus of the Great Society state, and they borrowed the rhetoric and political reality of global decolonization. In the 1970s, they demanded governance by treaty and a reopening of the treaty relationship, while constructing a protest politics reliant on explicit cultural difference. In the 1980s, they reanimated tribal sovereignty simply by exercising it, not only in terms of gaming but also through law enforcement, regulatory actions, and assertions of legal jurisdiction. In the 1990s, Native intellectuals began arguing for true self-determination outside the U.S. and Canadian political systems altogether.[50] Across this entire sweep, North American Indian people began developing a global political consciousness and laying the groundwork for moral and political claims based on aboriginality and indigeneity, which were themselves the global products of long imperial and colonial histories that (sometimes) bind Native North Americans to Maori people, Ainu people, Saami people, Aboriginal people in Australia and Latin America, and the peoples of the Pacific, Asia, Africa, and elsewhere.

Indeed, it has become apparent in recent years that whatever form imperialism or empire now takes, national (and extra-national) political and cultural systems are being pushed to come to terms with a range of indigenous peoples contesting histories that run—or are running, as we speak—in lines that sometimes parallel, in various ways, the colonial/ imperial histories outlined here. Claims and strategies for decolonization, indigenization, sovereignty, or autonomy outside colonial systems will require—on the part of both aboriginal and nonaboriginal peoples—thorough understandings of such histories. Those understandings must acknowledge the specificity of particular genealogies of colonialism and imperialism, while also recognizing the breadth and depth of their structures.

These issues matter to cultural historians. For a long while, Sacajawea fit best into a cultural studies frame emphasizing the various tropes used to manage and produce "American" identity. She belonged, in symbolic terms (and along with Pocahontas) to a surprisingly singular kind of inquiry, one that tended to position her as one of the "mothers" of the American nation. Sacajawea also found herself treated in biographical terms as a heroic or multicultural figure, a kind of bridge between distinct societies. It has become apparent, however, that Sacajawea actually dares us to ask far more complicated questions: about her place as a subject within interwoven social fields; about the complex political and social structures in which she—and her descendents—found themselves; about the relations between these structures and the cultural fields in which Indian people and others have made and exchanged meanings; about the ways culture needs play into an analysis of dominative practices, particularly within the frames of the colonial and the imperial.

Within the framework I have outlined here, I do not spend a great deal of time considering actual cultural histories embedded within the narrative. And yet it seems to me that cultural studies questions are to be found everywhere within it. Although I have emphasized moments of policy practice, for instance, my intent is also to open up questions central to a cultural history of the meanings that exist in relation to figurations of land and place. "Place," in this sense, can take us in a number of directions: to the theoretical dialectics of space and place, to the material histories of place making, to ancient and longitudinal histories that do not shirk the moments of colonization and land loss, and to a flexible interpretive tool, akin to a biologist's conception of "ecosystem," which can be expanded or contracted in size to meet the demands of an analysis.[51]

A focus on empire and colonization is also meant to suggest synthetic narrative structures that exist in productive and angular relation to other key narratives in U.S. cultural history. Traditionally dominant among these has been the movement from slavery to freedom that forms the spine of the first half of most U.S. History survey classes. Other narratives include the formation of mass culture industries, new histories of emotion and experience, transformations of gender and power, sexuality and medicalization, everyday life. As Patricia Limerick once suggested in relation to the American West, the material fact of continental conquest, its practices, and its legacies must necessarily occupy a critical place in the writing of these other histories.[52]

These angular relations to other narratives necessarily reanimate the position of cultural historians in relation to social and political histories. Tiya Miles's *Ties That Bind: The Story of an Afro-Cherokee Family in Slavery and Freedom*, for example, demonstrates in painful and beautiful detail how the core narratives of African American slavery and Cherokee removal complicate one another across the fields of politics, culture, and social relations. The emerging practices of ethnic studies—comparative, to be sure, but also work that crosses and integrates—will offer historians opportunities to consider anew how to situate multiple peoples in relation on the ground of culture. Even as varied practices of domination infuse those relations, cultural meaning and exchange flow across social and political boundaries. In that sense, cultural history always complicates a policy narrative, even as policy and politics remind us that the sphere of meaning making and exchange—or however we choose to conceptualize culture—is always articulated with material exercises of power.[53]

This question of articulation, it seems to me, is crucial to a consideration of agendas for cultural history. Typically, hammers and wrenches lifted from the social historian's interpretive tool kit—race, class, and gender, to be precise—have served as key points of articulation among analytical fields. That is, one cannot successfully analyze racial formation (or gender, or class, or sexuality) without recourse to law, politics, economics, social relations, and, of course, culture. These tools continue to function effectively in analysis, but they have also been augmented and complicated by emergent interdisciplines—performance studies, queer studies, disability studies, and new figurations of ethnic studies, among others—each of which also offers possibilities for knitting together interpretation across traditional field categories. Indigeneity studies, linked to colonial, postcolonial, new imperial studies, ethnography, local knowledge, and Native epistemologies, is reasonably seen as one of these emergent practices.

Indeed, as scholars of U.S. empire and culture consider the transnational flow of politics, social relations, and cultural goods and meanings, it is worth keeping in mind not simply continental empire but more particularly the existence of domestic dependent nations—literally internal trans-nations—within the boundaries of (and willing to transcend the boundaries of) the United States. Even as globalization pushes us to consider a particular version of "the transnational," cultural historians might also keep an eye out for the longer timeframes and comparative opportunities to be found in internal transnationalism, continental empire, and multiple colonialisms.[54]

Finally, within these complex rubrics, cultural historians may find themselves returning to the immediate and textual in the form of biography and studies of subjectivity. Sacajawea, for instance, may seem a more alluring figure for cultural analysis when viewed from the perspectives of land and place, conquest and colonialism, empire and policy, social relations, identity, and subjectivity, and nation and transnation. It is perhaps worth lingering at the stamp machine next time around, then, considering for just a moment the questions raised by three immediate texts—your twenty dollar bill, your fistful of Sacajaweas, and your icon-drenched stamps. If these point you toward some of the questions central to the cultural histories that have shaped the field, they may also contain within them questions that structure the stories that are yet to be told.

NOTES

1. There is no act, of course, that is *not* identifiable as an act of culture. To accept this capacious assertion, however, requires an equally capacious understanding of culture as a set and system of meanings, constantly placed in motion and into contest and uncertainty through specific practices, each of which simultaneously reproduces and transforms those meanings. The power of cultural history (and the joy in its practice) comes from separating such acts out from the constant stream and holding them up for analysis. Paradoxically, that separation then requires a detailed reconnection—of cultural act both with historical change over time and with a rich context that recognizes articulated spheres of activity (and analysis) in economics, politics, law, social relations, and other fields of possibility. A rigorous definition of "culture" is far beyond the scope of this chapter. The introduction to this book, however, offers an excellent tracing of certain genealogies of "culture," which may be more useful and practical than a definition.

2. For excellent short- and long-form examples of this methodology in practice, see Mary Niall Mitchell, "'Rosebloom and Pure White,' or So It Seemed," *American Quarterly* 54, no. 3 (September 2003): 369–410; and Carlo Rotella, *Good with Their Hands: Boxers, Bluesmen, and Other Characters from the Rust Belt* (Berkeley: University of California Press, 2002). Among the many recent achievements in this form of cultural history, see Penny Von Eschen, *Satchmo Blows Up the World: Jazz Ambassadors Play the Cold War* (Cambridge: Harvard University Press, 2004); Melani McAlister, *Epic Encounters: Culture, Media and U.S. Interests in the Middle East, 1945–2000* (Berkeley: University of California Press, 2001); Laura Wexler, *Tender Violence: Domestic Visions in an Age of U.S. Imperialism* (Chapel Hill: University of North Carolina Press, 2000); Anthony Lee, *Picturing Chinatown: Art and Orientalism in San Francisco* (Berkeley: University of California Press, 2001); John Kuo Wei Tchen, *New York before Chinatown: Orientalism and the Shaping of American Culture, 1776–1882* (Baltimore: Johns Hopkins Press, 1999); and James Cook, *The Arts of Deception: Playing with Fraud in the Age of Barnum* (Cambridge: Harvard University Press, 2001).

3. See, for example, Roy Harvey Pearce, *Savagism and Civilization: A Study of the Indian and the American Mind* (1953; repr., Berkeley: University of California Press, 1988); Leslie Fiedler, *The Return of the Vanishing Native* (New York: Stein and Day, 1968); Robert F. Berkhofer Jr., *The White Man's Indian: Images of American Indians from Columbus to the Present* (New York: Knopf, 1978); Brian Dippie, *The Vanishing American: White Attitudes and U.S. Indian Policy* (Middletown, CT: Wesleyan University Press, 1982); Richard Slotkin, *Regeneration through Violence: The Mythology of the American Frontier, 1600–1860* (Middletown, CT: Wesleyan University Press, 1973); and Richard Slotkin, *The Fatal Environment: The Myth of the*

Frontier in the Age of Industrialization, 1800–1890 (New York: Atheneum, 1985). More recent work in dialogue with this historiographical strand includes Leah Dilworth, *Imagining Indians in the Southwest: Persistent Visions of a Primitive Past* (Washington, DC: Smithsonian Institution Press, 1996); Renée L. Bergland, *The National Uncanny: Indian Ghosts and American Subjects* (Hanover, NH: University Press of New England, 2000); Susan Scheckel, *The Insistence of the Indian: Race and Nationalism in Nineteenth-Century American Culture* (Princeton: Princeton University Press, 1998); Alan Trachtenberg, *Shades of Hiawatha: Staging Indians, Making Americans, 1880–1930* (New York: Hill and Wang, 2005); Steven Conn, *History's Shadow: Native Americans and Historical Consciousness in the Nineteenth Century* (Chicago: University of Chicago Press, 2004); Joel Pfister, *Individuality Incorporated: Indians and the Multicultural Modern* (Durham, NC: Duke University Press, 2004); Michael Pisani, *Imagining Native America in Music* (New Haven: Yale University Press, 2005); Shari Huhndorff, *Going Native: Indians in the American Cultural Imagination* (Ithaca, NY: Cornell University Press, 2001); Philip Deloria, *Playing Indian* (New Haven: Yale University Press, 1998); and Deloria, *Indians in Unexpected Places* (Lawrence: University Press of Kansas, 2004).

4. One of my concerns is to steer away from the notion of culture as a self-contained analytical category—named as American culture, or Native American culture, or even Shoshone culture, for that matter. These sorts of formulations of discrete cultures, while not entirely false, have never done justice to the complex inter-locked realities of cultural and social encounter. All too often they rely on the mapping of a culture concept over more visible group identities defined in the stricter realms of the social, the legal, and the political. "Shoshone," in other words, is made visible as a group politically; the texts, objects, and meanings "they" produce then delineate the thing we name as Shoshone culture. In fact, as numerous studies have demonstrated, culture is a permeable field of exchange, operating as the ground for shared cultural production, perhaps most visibly at moments when social exchange is circumscribed and when political and legal segregations are framed in stark terms. See William Sewell, *Logics of History: Social Theory and Social Transformation* (Chicago: University of Chicago Press, 2005), 156 and passim.

5. Standard historiographic markers for such ethnographic biographies include Anthony F. C. Wallace, *King of the Delawares: Teedyuscung, 1700–1763* (Philadelphia: University of Pennsylvania Press, 1949); Peter Nabokov, *Two Leggings: The Making of a Crow Warrior* (New York: Thomas Crowell, 1967); John G. Neihardt, *Black Elk Speaks* (1932, repr., Lincoln: University of Nebraska Press, 2004), which should always be read in tandem with Raymond DeMallie, ed., *The Sixth Grandfather: Black Elk's Teaching Given to John G. Neihardt* (Lincoln: University of Nebraska Press, 1984). More recent work includes the popular, as for example, Mary Crow Dog, with Richard Erdoes, *Lakota Woman* (New York: HarperPerennial, 1991); the theoretically self-reflexive, for example, Greg Sarris, *Mabel McKay: Weaving the Dream* (Berkeley: University of California Press, 1994); and the literary-historical, as in Robert Warrior's reading of William Apess, in Robert Warrior, *The People and the Word: Reading Native Nonfiction* (Minneapolis: University of Minnesota Press, 2005). Among the many texts dealing with ethnohistory as a field, and in relation to Indian people, see Kerwin Lee Klein, *Frontiers of Historical Imagination: Narrating the European Conquest of Native America, 1890–1990* (Berkeley: University of California Press, 1997); and Judith Daubenmier, *The Meskwaki and Anthro-*

pologists: Action Anthropology Reconsidered (Lincoln: University of Nebraska Press, 2008). For historical examinations of particular identity formations, see Alexandra Harmon, *Indians in the Making: Ethnic Relations and Indian Identities around Puget Sound* (Berkeley: University of California Press, 1998); and Eva Marie Garroutte, *Real Indians: Identity and the Survival of Native America* (Berkeley: University of California Press, 2003). The literature on postcolonial subject formation and apprehension is vast. Native American studies scholars have found particular resonance in Linda Tuhiwai Smith, *Decolonizing Methodologies: Research and Indigenous Peoples* (New York: Zed Books, 1999); and the works of Gayatri Chakravorty Spivak, particularly her essay, "Can the Subaltern Speak?" in *Marxism and the Interpretation of Culture*, ed. Cary Nelson and Lawrence Grossberg (Urbana: University of Illinois Press, 1988). The ethnohistorical strand of writing was part of the larger trends in New Social History to practice scholarship from the bottom up and to introduce missing lives, perspectives, and struggles of subaltern subjects. One could argue that, although later in time and framed differently, postcolonial studies also shared this impulse. At the same time, each of these three genealogies—ethnohistory, social history, and postcolonial studies—are distinct in their origins, touchstone texts, and methodologies. Pertinent here is Gayatri Chakravorty Spivak, *A Critique of Postcolonial Reason: Toward a History of the Vanishing Present* (Cambridge: Harvard University Press, 1999), in which she claims a trajectory "from colonial discourse studies to transnational cultural studies." It is also worth noting the absolutely crucial place of (contesting) indigenous theoretical traditions around the question of subjectivity and culture, particularly those found in Gerald Vizenor, *Manifest Manners: Narratives on Postindian Survivance* (Lincoln: University of Nebraska Press, 1994); Louis Owens, *Mixedblood Messages: Literature, Film, Family, Place* (Norman: University of Oklahoma Press, 1998); Donald Fixico, *The American Indian Mind in a Linear World: American Indian Studies and Traditional Knowledge* (New York: Routledge, 2003); Jace Weaver, *Other Words: American Indian Literature, Law and Culture* (Norman: University of Oklahoma Press, 2001); the more directly political writings of Elizabeth Cook-Lynn, *Anti-Indianism in Modern America: A Voice from Tatekeya's Earth* (Urbana: University of Illinois Press, 2001), and the contributors to Devon Mihesuah, ed., *Natives and Academics: Researching and Writing about American Indians* (Lincoln: University of Nebraska, 1998); and to Devon Mihesuah and Angela Cavender Wilson, eds., *Indigenizing the Academy: Transforming Scholarship and Empowering Communities* (Lincoln: University of Nebraska Press, 2004). A useful recent survey and critique is Jace Weaver, "More Light Than Heat: The Current State of Native American Studies," *American Indian Quarterly* 31 (Spring 2007): 233–55. Finally, although I do not list individual works, no note on this subject is complete without mentioning the enormous influence of Vine Deloria Jr.

6.   See, for example, Richard White, *The Middle Ground: Indians, Empires, and Republics in the Great Lakes Region, 1650–1815* (Cambridge: Cambridge University Press, 1991); Daniel Richter, *Facing East from Indian Country: A Native History of Early America* (Cambridge: Harvard University Press, 2001); Anthony F. C. Wallace, *Jefferson and the Indians: The Tragic Fate of the First Americans* (Cambridge: Harvard University Press, 1999); Karen Ordahl Kupperman, *Indians and English: Facing Off in Early America* (Ithaca, NY: Cornell University Press, 2000); Alan Taylor, *American Colonies: The Settling of North America* (New York: Penguin, 2001); David

Weber, *Bárbaros: Spaniards and Their Savages in the Age of Enlightenment* (New Haven: Yale University Press, 2005).

7. For my gesture to Pacific, Micronesian, and Chamorro studies, I am indebted to conversations with my colleagues Vicente Diaz, Amy Stillman, Damon Salesa, and Susan Najita. See Vicente Diaz and J. Kehaulani Kauanui, "Native Pacific Cultural Studies on the Edge," *Contemporary Pacific* 13, no. 2 (2001): 315–342; and Vicente Diaz, "To P or Not to P: Marking the Territory between Asian American and Pacific Islander Studies, *Journal of Asian American Studies* 7 (October 2004): 183–208.

8. This characterization may be unfair, and is not meant to suggest that cultural history does not have a pressing politics, but simply to note that the origins and practices of such politics are visibly distinct from those of ethnic studies. For one Native American studies perspective, see Philip Deloria, "American Indians, American Studies, and the ASA," *American Quarterly* 55 (December 2003): 669–680. See also, for example, Craig Womack, *Red on Red: Native American Literary Separatism* (Minneapolis: University of Minnesota Press, 1999); Fixico, *American Indian Mind in a Linear World*; Sandy Grande, *Red Pedagogy: Native American Social and Political Thought* (Lanham, MD: Rowman and Littlefield, 2004).

9. In invoking the metaphoric language of base and superstructure, I do not mean to dismiss economic factors from consideration but rather to suggest that, from a Native American perspective, the contexts established by treaties demand a different configuration of the articulations between cultural spheres of analysis and other spheres. Economics, while critical from an "American" perspective, has seemed perhaps to carry less potential analytical power for Native scholars and critics. The politics of economic development, however, have been central to U.S. policy, and analysis of Indian labor and capital systems has become increasingly important. See, for example, Alice Littlefield and Martha Knack, eds., *Native Americans and Wage Labor: Ethnohistorical Perspectives* (Norman: University of Oklahoma Press, 1996); Colleen O'Neil, *Working the Navajo Way: Labor and Culture in the Twentieth Century* (Lawrence: University Press of Kansas, 2005); Brian Hosmer, *American Indians in the Marketplace: Persistence and Innovation among the Menominees and Metlakatlans* (Lawrence: University Press of Kansas, 1999); Colleen O'Neil and Brian Hosmer, eds., *Native Pathways: American Indian Culture and Economic Development in the Twentieth Century* (Boulder: University Press of Colorado, 2004); Alexandra Harmon, "American Indians and Land Monopolies in the Gilded Age," *Journal of American History* 90, no. 1 (2003): 106–33.

10. See, for example, Francis Paul Prucha, *The Great Father: The United States Government and the American Indians* (Lincoln: University of Nebraska Press, 1984); Wilcomb Washburn, *Red Man's Land/White Man's Law: A Study of the Past and Present Status of the American Indian* (New York: Scribner's, 1971); Ronald Satz, *American Indian Policy in the Jacksonian Era* (Lincoln: University of Nebraska Press, 1975); David Wilkins, *American Indian Sovereignty and the U.S. Supreme Court: The Masking of Justice* (Austin: University of Texas Press, 1997).

11. On tribal histories, see, for example, R. David Edmunds, *The Potawatomies: Keepers of the Fire* (Norman: University of Oklahoma Press, 1978); Roy T. Meyer, *The Village Indians of the Upper Missouri: The Mandans, Hidatsas, and Arikaras* (Lincoln: University of Nebraska Press, 1977); Edmund J. Danzinger Jr., *The Chippewas of Lake Superior* (Norman: University of Oklahoma Press, 1979). On African/Native

American relations, see Tiya Miles, *Ties That Bind: The Story of an Afro-Cherokee Family in Slavery and Freedom* (Berkeley: University of California Press, 2005); Claudio Saunt, *Black, White, and Indian: Race and the Unmaking of an American Family* (New York: Oxford University Press, 2005); Circe Sturm, *Blood Politics: Race, Culture, and Identity in the Cherokee Nation of Oklahoma* (Berkeley: University of California Press, 2002). On representational politics, see P. Deloria, *Indians in Unexpected Places*; L. G. Moses, *Wild West Shows and the Images of American Indians, 1883–1933* (Albuquerque: University of New Mexico Press, 1996); Paige Raibmon, *Authentic Indians: Episodes of Encounter from the Late-Nineteenth-Century Northwest Coast* (Durham, NC: Duke University Press, 2005); Michael McNally, *Ojibwe Singers: Hymns, Grief, and a Native Culture in Motion* (New York: Oxford University Press, 2000); Jacqueline Shea Murphy, *The People Have Never Stopped Dancing: Native American Modern Dance Histories* (Minneapolis: University of Minnesota Press, 2007); Andrew Denson, *Demanding the Cherokee Nation: Indian Autonomy and American Culture, 1830–1900* (Lincoln: University of Nebraska Press, 2004); Mary Lawlor, *Public Native America: Tribal Self-Representation in Museums, Powwow, and Casinos* (New Brunswick, NJ: Rutgers University Press, 2006).

12. See, for example, Jean M. O'Brien, *Dispossession by Degrees: Indian Land and Identity in Natick, Massachusetts, 1650–1790* (Cambridge: Cambridge University Press, 1997); Melissa Meyer, *The White Earth Tragedy: Ethnicity and Dispossession at a Minnesota Anishinaabe Reservation, 1889–1920* (Lincoln: University of Nebraska Press, 1999); Frederick Hoxie, *Parading through History: The Making of the Crow Nation in America, 1805–1935* (Cambridge: Cambridge University Press, 1995).

13. The impact of sovereignty arguments on Native scholarship over the last twenty-five years can hardly be underestimated. On sovereignty, see Vine Deloria and Clifford Lytle, *The Nations Within: The Past and Future of American Indian Sovereignty* (New York: Pantheon, 1984); Russell Barsh and James Henderson, *The Road: Indian Tribes and Political Liberty* (Berkeley: University of California Press, 1980); Robert Williams, *The American Indian in Western Legal Thought: The Discourse of Conquest* (New York: Oxford University Press, 1990); Wilkins, *American Indian Sovereignty and the Supreme Court*. See Robert Warrior, *Tribal Secrets: Recovering American Indian Intellectual Traditions* (Minneapolis: University of Minnesota Press, 1995), for one of the first explicit calls for an intellectual sovereignty that would parallel political sovereignty movements. See also Warrior, *The People and the Word*; Womack, *Red on Red*; Craig Womack, Robert Warrior, and Jace Weaver, *American Indian Literary Nationalism* (Albuquerque: University of New Mexico Press, 2006).

14. On colonial relations and indigenizing, see, for example, Mihesuah, *Natives and Academics*; Mihesuah and Wilson, *Indigenizing the Academy*; Donald Fixico, ed., *Rethinking American Indian History* (Albuquerque: University of New Mexico Press, 1997); Taiaiake Alfred, *Peace, Power, Righteousness: An Indigenous Manifesto* (Don Mills, Ontario: Oxford University Press, 1999); Cook-Lynn, *Anti-Indianism in Modern America*; Haunani-Kay Trask, *From a Native Daughter: Colonialism and Sovereignty in Hawai'i* (Monroe, ME: Common Courage Press, 1993).

15. The two words may be seen to connote processes seen as (1) parallel, (2) overlapping, (3) mutually constitutive, and (4) roughly identical, although emphasizing different aspects: "imperialism" describing metropolitan power, or the will to it, and political (and generally economic and social) subordination; "colonialism" describing settlement, but also on-the-ground subjugation, accommodation,

resistance. The categories are intertwined, coproduced historically, and more complex than this short working definition suggests. See, in particular, Frederick Cooper and Ann Laura Stoler, eds., *Tensions of Empire: Colonial Cultures in a Bourgeois World* (Berkeley: University of California Press, 1997); Laura Stoler, ed., *Haunted by Empire: Geographies of Intimacy in North American History* (Durham, NC: Duke University Press, 2006); Mary Louise Pratt, *Imperial Eyes: Travel Writing and Transculturation* (London: Routledge, 1992). Among the classic texts on empire, see William Appleman Williams, *The Tragedy of American Diplomacy*, rev. ed. (1959; repr., New York: Norton, 1972); William Appleman Williams, *The Contours of American History* (Chicago: Quadrangle, 1966); Walter LaFeber, *The New Empire: An Interpretation of American Expansion, 1860–1898* (Ithaca, NY: Cornell University Press, 1963); Walter LaFeber, *The American Age: United States Foreign Policy at Home and Abroad, 1750 to the Present*, 2nd ed. (New York: Norton, 1994); Michael Hardt and Antonio Negri, *Empire* (Cambridge: Harvard University Press, 2000).

16. Amy Kaplan, "Left Alone with America," in *Cultures of United States Imperialism*, ed. Amy Kaplan and Donald E. Pease (Durham, NC: Duke University Press, 1993). Among the many noteworthy exceptions are Shelley Streeby, *American Sensations: Class, Empire, and the Production of Popular Culture* (Berkeley: University of California Press, 2002); Amy Kaplan, *The Anarchy of Empire in the Making of U.S. Culture* (Cambridge: Harvard University Press, 2002).

17. "Decolonizing" might in fact require a fairly precise understanding of the specific colonial practice to be undone, lest the word simply turn into a new-century synonym for "agency" or "resistance." The explicit calling out of colonialism can be found in numerous writings. For theoretical treatments, including an accompanying call for decolonization, see Mihesuah, *Natives and Academics*; Mihesuah and Wilson, *Indigenizing the Academy*; Fixico, *Rethinking American Indian History*; Alfred, *Peace, Power, Righteousness*; Cook-Lynn, *Anti-Indianism in Modern America*; and Trask, *Native Daughter*. It is worth noting the complications inherent in making "colonialism" and "decolonization" categories that claim a certain purity, and thus a position of (false) authority from which to offer critique. Consider, for example, the array of coffee mugs, barbeque aprons, license plate frames, pins, and bumper stickers proclaiming the virtues of decolonization via the virtues of Internet capitalism.

18. Michael Tsosie, "Kicking the Habit: Colonialism," paper presented at the University of Michigan, May 2005, 9–11.

19. In what follows, readers will find a great deal of law and policy. I begin, however, with ideological formations as central descriptors for the categories I attempt to delineate. In my view, one of the critical methodologies (and achievements) of cultural history has been the historical description of the material formations of ideologies and discourses. That is, cultural historians have not been content to pluck single texts—be they stamps, coins, or bills—from the flow of cultural production and hold them up as evidence for the existence of the cultural formations we might name "ideology," "discourse" (or, in my own usage, "expectation"). Rather, cultural history has insisted on assembling constellations of multiple pieces of textual evidence, which can then be read collectively for their generic similarities. These, in turn, can be used to trace the production and consumption patterns, all of which allows a concrete historicizing of shared (and contested) meaning. My naming of various ideologies—Indian savagery, manifest destiny,

vanishing Indianness, pacification—is meant to place cultural history in a structuring dialogue with the policies described. For my own reading on ideology and discourse, see P. Deloria, *Indians in Unexpected Places*, 7–11.

20. See James Merrell, *Into the American Woods: Negotiators on the Pennsylvania Frontier* (New York: Norton, 1999); P. Deloria, *Indians in Unexpected Places*, 20–21, 48.

21. I am focusing on this particular ideology in order to emphasize the dominative aspects of the relation. Certainly, as I've argued elsewhere, ideological practices involving Indian people were far more complicated. See P. Deloria, *Playing Indian*, for this earlier argument.

22. See Priscilla Wald, "Terms of Assimilation: Legislating Subjectivity in the Emerging Nation," in Kaplan and Pease, *Cultures of United States Imperialism*, 59–84. On Turner, see David Wrobel, *The End of American Exceptionalism: Frontier Anxiety from the Old West to the New Deal* (Lawrence: University Press of Kansas, 1993); Richard White and Patricia Limerick, *The Frontier in American Culture*, ed. James Grossman (Berkeley: University of California Press, 1994).

23. See Vine Deloria Jr. and Raymond J. DeMallie, *Documents of American Indian Diplomacy: Treaties, Agreements, and Conventions, 1775–1979* (Norman: University of Oklahoma Press, 1999); Charles Kappler, comp. and ed., *Indian Affairs, Laws and Treaties* (Washington, DC: GPO, 1904; 2nd ed., New York: AMS Press, 1971); and Francis Paul Prucha, *American Indian Treaties: The History of a Political Anomaly* (Berkeley: University of California Press, 1994). Deloria and DeMallie frame their compilation with a useful short history of treaty making. See *Documents of American Indian Diplomacy*, 6–15, for early treaty making, and 233–248 for an accounting of the 1871 end of treaty making, including a lengthy excerpt illustrating the complexities of the congressional debate. The meanings and practices of treaty making shifted in relation to the degree of power Indian people were able to bring to the table. In the few instances (and these almost all took place in the early republic) in which Indian military power remained substantial, negotiations might take on more of the dynamics characterized by Richard White as a "middle ground." As White has shown, however, power became rapidly unbalanced in U.S.-Indian relations, making treaty making a political manifestation of both difference and inequality. See White, *Middle Ground*. For a detailed treatment in relation to land, see Stuart Banner, *How the Indians Lost Their Land: Law and Power on the Frontier* (Cambridge: Harvard University Press, 2005).

24. Article 6 of the U.S. Constitution reads: "All treaties made, or which shall be made, under the authority of the United States, shall be the supreme law of the land."

25. I take a macroperspective here, including not simply the moments of negotiation and ratification but also the subsequent histories of treaty interpretation. As V. Deloria and DeMallie suggest and show, "we cannot assume a priori that Congress always acted antagonistically toward the Indian tribes. Some treaties and agreements were not ratified by Congress because its members believed that they would be harmful to Indians. The historical record is far more positive than most people would believe. Federal and state courts, however, in an effort to reconcile the interpretation of treaties and agreements with prevailing public sentiments of the time, often twisted language beyond its natural meaning to fit predetermined results. The Supreme Court has been notoriously guilty of violating Indian rights in that respect" (*Documents of American Indian Diplomacy*, 5).

26. Dorothy V. Jones, *License for Empire: Colonialism by Treaty in Early America* (Chicago: University of Chicago Press, 1982), xii.

27. Donald Fixico, "Federal and State Policies and American Indians," in *A Companion to American Indian History*, ed. Philip Deloria and Neal Salisbury (Malden, MA: Blackwell, 2002), 381.

28. All of these acts—the Land Ordinance of 1785, the Northwest Ordinance of 1787, the Indian Removal Act of 1830, and the 1790 (and subsequent) Trade and Intercourse acts—are available online through the Avalon Project. See http://www .yale.edu/lawweb/avalon/statutes/native/namenu.htm (accessed February 10, 2008). The original Trade and Intercourse Act of 1790 defined boundaries and proscribed a range of boundary-crossing activities. It expired after two years, so a subsequent series of renewals occurred in the years leading up to 1802, when a permanent act was passed. The final Intercourse Act (1834) was the first to lay out a legal definition of "Indian Country" as that land west of the Mississippi but not including Missouri, Louisiana, or Arkansas territory. See Francis Paul Prucha, *American Indian Policy in the Formative Years: The Indian Trade and Intercourse Act, 1790–1834* (Cambridge: Harvard University Press, 1962).

29. See Northwest Ordinance, sec. 14, article 3, at http://www.yale.edu/lawweb/ avalon/nworder.htm.

30. In many places, particularly the Midwest, mixed-blood Indians chose to remain, often making a claim to whiteness and even U.S.—or territorial—citizenship on ancestral lands. These claims to *national* or pre-national status paralleled—and often intersected with—those of anticipatory "white" citizens in the territories. And in many places such claims stood, since the agents of U.S. empire worried about the allegiance of Indians who remained able to move between the still-indigenous spaces claimed by both the United States and British Canada. I am indebted for this observation to Michael Witgen, who is currently at work on these issues.

31. Here, it makes sense to note the tensions between structures such as these, which reflected the broad interests of the empire, and those that advanced the local and regional interests of colonies and later territories. Strongly characteristic of this moment, however, was the effort to assert not simply a Hamiltonian agenda of federalized power but an explicitly imperial template as well.

32. See An Act for Establishing Trading Houses with the Indian Tribes, 1796, at http:// www.yale.edu/lawweb/avalon/statutes/native/na028.htm.

33. On removal and the Trail of Tears, see Satz, *American Indian Policy in the Jacksonian Era*; Anthony F. C. Wallace, *The Long Bitter Trail: Andrew Jackson and the Indians* (New York: Hill and Wang, 1993); Grant Foreman, *Indian Removal: The Emigration of the Five Civilized Tribes of Indians* (Norman: University of Oklahoma Press, 1953). On the Marshall decisions, see Lindsay Robertson, *Conquest by Law: How the Discovery of America Dispossessed Indigenous Peoples of the Their Lands* (New York: Oxford University Press, 2005); Tim Alan Garrison, *The Legal Ideology of Removal: The Southern Judiciary and the Sovereignty of Native American Nations* (Athens: University of Georgia Press, 2002); John Wunder, *"Retained by the People": A History of American Indians and the Bill of Rights* (New York: Oxford University Press, 1994), 24–29; Wilkins, *American Indian Sovereignty and the Supreme Court*.

34. Despite the fact that many reservations are land "reserved" from aboriginal holding (as opposed to serving as landing places for removed peoples), the sta-

tus under which Indian reservation landholding took place was fully under the sway of American power. On reservations, see George Phillips, *Indians and Indian Agents: The Origins of the Reservation System in California, 1849–1852* (Norman: University of Oklahoma Press, 1997); Robert Trennert, *Alternative to Extinction: Federal Indian Policy and the Beginnings of the Reservation System* (Philadelphia: Temple University Press, 1975). For an excellent treatment of the implementation of reserves in Canada, see Cole Harris, *Making Native Space: Colonialism, Resistance, and Reserves in British Columbia* (Vancouver: University of British Columbia Press, 2002).

35. P. Deloria, *Unexpected Places*, 26–27; On Indian police, see William T. Hagan, *Indian Police and Judges: Experiments in Acculturation and Control* (New Haven: Yale University Press, 1966). The literature on boarding schools is voluminous. See, for example, David Wallace Adams, *Education for Extinction: American Indians and the Boarding School Experience, 1875–1928* (Lawrence: University Press of Kansas, 1995); and K. Tsianina Lomawaima, *They Called It Prairie Light: The Story of the Chilocco Indian School* (Lincoln: University of Nebraska Press, 1994). The cultural histories surrounding Indian transformation and persistence are compelling. See, for example, Peter Iverson, *When Indians Became Cowboys: Native Peoples and Cattle Ranching in the American West* (Norman: University of Oklahoma Press, 1994); Tara Browner, *Heartbeat of the People: Music and Dance of the Northern Pow-Wow* (Urbana: University of Illinois Press, 2002); Raymond DeMallie and Douglas Parks, eds., *Sioux Indian Religion* (Norman: University of Oklahoma Press, 1987); Luke Eric Lassiter, Clyde Ellis, and Ralph Kotay, *The Jesus Road: Kiowas, Christianity, and Indian Hymns* (Lincoln: University of Nebraska Press, 2002); and Paul Steinmetz, *Pipe, Bible and Peyote among the Oglala Lakota: A Study in Religious Identity* (Knoxville: University of Tennessee Press, 1990).

36. On the peace policy, see Francis Paul Prucha, *American Indian Policy in Crisis: Christian Reformers and the Indian, 1865–1900* (Norman: University of Oklahoma Press, 1976); Norman Bender, *New Hope for the Indians: The Grant Peace Policy and the Navajos in the 1870s* (Albuquerque: University of New Mexico, 1989). On racialization, I am using the vocabulary of Michael Omi and Howard Winant, *Racial Formation in the United States, from the 1960s to the 1990s*, 2nd ed. (New York: Routledge, 1994), although emphasizing that these particular forms of racialization required significant cultural work, knit together with law and policy structures.

37. I have tried to explore these points elsewhere: ideological complexity in *Playing Indian* (see n. 21); developmentalism and changing racial formations in *Unexpected Places*, 84–88, 143–47. For the Pratt quote and a detailed exploration of the views of this important educational reformer, see Adams, *Education for Extinction*, 51–55, esp. 52.

38. As with other policies, allotment too had been foreshadowed in previous negotiations. The Ottawa Treaty of 1855, for example, contains an allotment provision. Thanks to Greg Dowd for reminding me of this chronology and offering the Ottawa example.

39. This was the argument of the Indian Rights Association, a late nineteenth-century cross between an NGO and a Washington think tank. The Allotment Act succeeded not only through the influence of the group but also through the lobbying efforts of land-hungry westerners, an evil alliance of greed and do-gooder policy wonks if ever there was one.

40. On allotment, see Wilcomb Washburn, *The Assault on Indian Tribalism: The General Allotment Law (Dawes Act) of 1887* (Philadelphia: Lippincott, 1975); Leonard Carlson, *Indians, Bureaucrats, and Land: The Dawes Act and the Decline of Indian Farming* (Westport, CT: Greenwood Press, 1981); Emily Greenwald, *Reconfiguring the Reservation: The Nez Perces, Jicarilla Apaches, and the Dawes Act* (Albuquerque: University of New Mexico, 2002); and Frederick Hoxie, *A Final Promise: The Campaign to Assimilate the Indians, 1880–1920* (Lincoln: University of Nebraska Press, 1984).

41. P. Deloria, *Unexpected Places*, 34–35.

42. See Alexander Nemerov, *Frederic Remington and Turn-of-the-Century America* (New Haven: Yale University Press, 1996); and Frederic Remington, *The Collected Writings of Frederic Remington*, ed. Peggy Samuels and Harold Samuels (Garden City, NY: Doubleday, 1979); on Cody, see Louis Warren, *Buffalo Bill's America: William Cody and the Wild West Show* (New York: Knopf, 2005), 198–204, 406–16; P. Deloria, *Unexpected Places*, 45–51.

43. Theodore Roosevelt, First Annual Message, December 3, 1901, as collected at http://www.digitalhistory.uh.edu/native_voices/voices_display.cfm?id=92 (accessed August 28, 2005).

44. Greenwald, *Reconfiguring the Reservation*, 39–41, 59–89.

45. An excellent account of competency commissions and the destructive land loss of the allotment policy is Janet McDonnell, *The Dispossession of the American Indian, 1887–1934* (Bloomington: Indiana University Press, 1991).

46. Kaplan, "Left Alone with America"; and Kaplan, *Anarchy of Empire*, 1–18. On demography, see Russell Thornton, "Health, Disease and Demography," in P. Deloria and Salisbury, *Companion to American Indian History*, 69, 74; Russell Thornton, *American Indian Holocaust and Survival: A Population History since 1492* (Norman: University of Oklahoma Press, 1987); and Nancy Shoemaker, *American Indian Population Recovery in the Twentieth Century* (Albuquerque: University of New Mexico Press, 1999), 1–5. Even a 160-acre allotment could be easily fragmented by the death of the owner. Complicated inheritance patterns split parcels into pieces of land so small as to be of little or no economic value. At this point, the Bureau of Indian Affairs often stepped in, assisting non-Indians by assembling these fragments into viable parcels and leasing them out. The ever-finer sifting of Indian landholding thus continued even beyond the level of the individual parcel.

47. Among the many writings on the New Deal, see, for example, V. Deloria and Lytle, *Nations Within;* Lawrence Kelly, *The Assault on Assimilation: John Collier and the Origins of Indian Policy Reform* (Albuquerque: University of New Mexico Press, 1983); Kenneth Philp, *John Collier's Crusade for Indian Reform, 1920–1954* (Tucson: University of Arizona Press, 1977); Thomas Biolsi, *Organizing the Lakota: The Political Economy of the New Deal on the Pine Ridge and Rosebud Reservations* (Tucson: University of Arizona Press, 1992); Donald Parman, *The Navajos and the New Deal* (New Haven: Yale University Press, 1981); and Laurence Hauptman, *The Iroquois and the New Deal* (Syracuse: Syracuse University Press, 1981). The origins of the Indian New Deal may be found in an effective political mobilization of post-frontier "imperialist nostalgia," genuine dismay and subsequent efforts to reform the policies surrounding allotment and forced assimilation, and the curious political skill and commitment of John Collier and a number of other reformers.

48. On new forms of practice and a shift from imperialism to empire, see Hardt and Negri, *Empire*.

49. See Philp, *John Collier's Crusade*, 1–54; Kelly, *Assault on Assimilation*, 103–40; and Collier's autobiography, *From Every Zenith: A Memoir* (Denver: Sage Books, 1963), 115–35.

50. For an excellent synthesis of recent history, see Charles Wilkinson, *Blood Struggle: The Rise of Modern Indian Nations* (New York: Norton, 2005). For work that moves beyond sovereignty, see Alfred, *Peace, Power, Righteousness*; and Alfred, *Wasáse: Indigenous Pathways of Action and Freedom* (Peterborough, ON: Broadview Press, 2005).

51. On place, see Karen Halttunen, "Groundwork: American Studies in Place," *American Quarterly* 58, no. 1 (2006): 1–15; Philip Deloria, "Places Like Houses, Banks, and Continents: An Appreciative Reply to the Presidential Address," *American Quarterly* 58, no. 1 (2006): 23–29. See also Henri Lefebvre, *The Production of Space*, trans. Donald Nicholson-Smith (Cambridge, MA: Blackwell, 1991); Laurie Hovell McMillin, *Buried Indians: Digging up the Past in a Midwestern Town* (Madison: University of Wisconsin Press, 2006); and Harris, *Making Native Space*.

52. Patricia Nelson Limerick, *The Legacy of Conquest: The Unbroken Past of the American West* (New York: Norton, 1987), 17–32.

53. Miles, *Ties That Bind*.

54. See, for example, Kevin Bruyneel, *The Third Space of Sovereignty: The Postcolonial Politics of U.S.-Indigenous Relations* (Minneapolis: University of Minnesota Press, 2007); Michelle Stephens, "Uprooted Bodies: Indigenous Subjects and Colonial Discourses in Atlantic American Studies," in *Imagining Our Americas: Toward a Transnational Frame*, ed. Sandhya Shukla and Heidi Tinsman (Durham, NC: Duke University Press, 2007), 190–213; and Walter Mignolo, *Local Histories/Global Designs: Coloniality, Subaltern Knowledges, and Border Thinking* (Princeton: Princeton University Press, 2000).

THIRTEEN

Capitalism, Culture, and Catastrophe

JEAN-CHRISTOPHE AGNEW

Those having lamps will pass them on to others.

PLATO, *The Republic*

Whether we regard the practice of American cultural history as new, old, or merely of a certain age, the genre itself is enough of a hybrid that no two practitioners would be likely to draw up the same family tree. Count the rings, trace the roots, scan the foliage of any particular tree—or read the book into which it has been pulped—and the results produced would likely strike us as but marginally related to the intellectual genus and genealogy that we understand as U.S. cultural history. Each of us comes to the field, such as it is, with our own exemplars and our own canonical historians in mind. We may be drawn to the field by the light of their inspiration, or we may find ourselves propelled there by the shocks to which we have been witness in our own lives. Perhaps both. Like a stand of trees, each generation of historians leaves a legacy that records its slow growth toward the light while at the same time displaying the scars and blight of its own time. So it will be with this volume, and so, of course, with this chapter.

My point of departure here is one such exemplary historian—Lawrence Levine—to whom this volume has been dedicated and to whom I am deeply indebted intellectually, even down (in this instance) to my choice of metaphors. The last time I caught a glimpse of Larry, he was striding, staff in hand, through Muir Woods. I saw him from a distance then, and in the pages that follow I try to sustain that same distance as I do two things. First, I attempt a sketch of Levine's model of cultural history as quite literally a thing of light and shadow, or rather

384 / Jean-Christophe Agnew

of light *against* shadow. Levine grew up during a period of history when
(according to Warren Susman) the culture concept came to function in
middlebrow discourse as a rhetorical homing device: a figure of thought
capable of imaginatively repatriating a generation of Americans that had
been emotionally and physically dislocated by years of depression and
war. The American Way of Life, as it was called. Like many historians in
his generation, Levine was brought up within earshot of this upbeat and
up-market jingle of an idea and of its more heroic and collective versions
in the New Deal and Popular Front. But even later, in graduate school,
where he was reeducated by consensus historians to detect the culture
concept's darker, more ironic undertones, Levine remained unpersuaded
by the claim of homogeneity: *the* American Way of Life. For him as for the
historians who shared his vision, it was always the American ways of life.
He heard other music and, as I try to show, saw other lights.[1]

Yet, as I am also suggesting, these flashes of illumination in Lawrence
Levine's cultural history—these other ways of life—have almost always
arrayed themselves against the darkness, by which I mean the injuries and
indignities he associated with exploitation and exclusion, nativism and
racism. Here again the historiography of Levine's generation may be seen
to bear the marks, the scars, of the Great Depression as the single greatest
shock to the capitalist system in U.S. history. The American Earthquake
the critic Edmund Wilson called it, and so it seemed. The Great Crash
was the primal scene for Levine's generation of historians, and no less so
for its having been filtered, framed, and reimagined through the stories
told by family and friends. The capitalist crisis of the thirties was the sup-
purating wound, to borrow once again from Edmund Wilson (and his
parable of Philoctetes), that paradoxically empowered the magical bow
of culture—culture, that is, understood as both art and weapon.[2]

My second purpose in this chapter, then, is to tease out this more
somber and shadowy side of Levine's cultural history and cultural history generally: namely, the traumatic or catastrophic moments of life in a
capitalist society and culture. Levine did not write about the open social
wounds of those years—the shame and stigma of eviction, unemployment, and hunger—until his 1985 essay "American Culture and the Great
Depression," but I believe that these collective memories formed the
experiential touchstone for his generation's cultural historical explorations into the slow-motion cataclysms of slavery and Jim Crow. In the last
half of this chapter, I show how a number of younger cultural historians
have returned in their own circuitous ways to this point of departure—a

specifically market-based trauma—and how this generational odyssey is already producing epics, models, exemplars of its own.[3]

———

"Writing," Lawrence Levine once wrote (quoting Laurence Sterne), "is but a different name for conversation," and everything that he wrote in his long and rich career honored this conviction. Personable and direct, Levine's prose—his essays above all—invite the reader to join the discussion that is American history and, in the process, to appreciate its many rhythms and accents.[4] And in keeping with Levine's intellectual and personal temperament, his perspective was almost always panoramic, encompassing, and inclusive. The reach of *Black Culture and Black Consciousness* (1977) was and remains breathtaking. The perspective of *Highbrow/Lowbrow* (1988) and of the essays collected in *The Unpredictable Past* (1993) is similarly broad, and so—in spirit and scope—is his history cum manifesto, *The Opening of the American Mind* (1996). True, had it not been for Allan Bloom's best-selling screed on popular culture a decade earlier, one can scarcely imagine Levine's having reached for a phrase like the "American Mind." Too Hegelian by half. Yet he never shied away from the hybrid singularity of American *culture*—culture, that is, in the lowercase, the popular case, the folkloric case.[5]

Or the hard case. Consider, for example, Levine's first book, *Defender of the Faith: William Jennings Bryan, 1915–1925* (1965). Could there have been a less auspicious example of the open-minded American than the figure of William Jennings Bryan sloping toward the Scopes "monkey" trial? Not only had Bryan's progressivism been summarily dismissed by Richard Hofstadter, Levine's dissertation adviser, but Bryan's piety had been mocked for ten long years in the various productions of *Inherit the Wind* that appeared on Broadway, in film, and—in 1965—on television's *Hallmark Hall of Fame*. Where others had found in the late Bryan a mind shuttered against modernity, however, Levine discovered Bryan's boundless and unshakable confidence in the judgment of ordinary men and women. *Defender* looked beyond or behind Bryan's moral absolutism to find the democratic faith—at once political and pious—that had underwritten the Great Commoner's life-project. These were the "enduring threads," as Levine put it, that ran "throughout Bryan's career."[6]

Some of these same threads ran through Lawrence Levine's career as well. Everything he wrote after 1965 might be said to have reenacted the democratic opening that his first book had identified with Bryan's abiding democratic faith. The depth and durability of that faith had surprised Levine, and he in turn made it a surprise for his readers. But as he also came to see things, Bryan's democratic hopefulness had as much to do with the collective belief system of the rural America in which he flourished as in the facts of his private life. Bryan had had no interior life, as far as Levine could make out, and it was just this lack of introspection that opened the Great Commoner to a social and cultural reading rather than a psychoanalytic one.[7]

Accordingly, what Hofstadter had written off as Bryan's backwater provincialism, Levine salvaged as a "rural reform tradition," an "antipathy to urbanism that was cultural as it was anything else." What Hofstadter had disparaged as Bryan's opportunism, his hypocrisy, his "incurable vulgarity," Levine redeemed as his "compulsive optimism." What looked like vulgarity to urban cosmopolitans—the upbeat, almost promotional language of nineteenth-century "social Christianity"—was but the evangelical vulgate, the lingua franca of heartland America. Looking back at Bryan's "last decade," Hofstadter and Levine agreed that the Great Commoner's moral insularity had blinded him to twentieth-century "realities," but teacher and student were miles apart when it came to the tone and tenor with which this judgment was delivered. Hofstadter's essay— "The Democrat as Revivalist"—was written as an epitaph; it aimed to close the book on an American democratic tradition. Levine, on the other hand, wished to reopen and reread that same book. More than that, I suspect, he meant to show that as a chapter in the larger epic of democratic culture, Bryan's last decade—his last stand, if you will—was neither ethnographically inaccessible nor politically irrelevant to the children and grandchildren of Al Smith, no matter how urban, or urbane, they might be.[8]

Retrospect permits us to see how *Defender of the Faith* turned an act of interpretive closure into a point of departure for a quite different kind of historical inquiry into American democratic culture. Considered as an exercise in sociological or anthropological empathy, *Defender of the Faith* looks very much like a rite of passage—securing Lawrence Levine's entry into the historical profession and, at the same time, licensing his own transformation from the biographer of a single mind to the genealogist of much broader and more complex forms of democratic consciousness and culture. No less important, *Defender* implicitly asserted Levine's democratic *right* of passage into a life-world—a cultural landscape—that Bryan's residual nativism, not to mention that of the historical profession, would have denied him. *Defender* thus effected a doubled act of inclusion in the

conversation of American history: of William Jennings Bryan and of Lawrence William Levine.[9] By 1962 enough of Levine's generational cohort of
immigrant sons had received their naturalization papers from the American Historical Association for its president, Carl Bridenbaugh, to lament
their arrival as part of what he called the Great Mutation and to disparage
the history produced by these "products of lower-middle class or foreign
origins" as the work of mere technicians.[10]

Olympian as this dismissal may have seemed at the time, it was Levine
and his other lower-middle-class comrades who managed to enlarge our
vision of the past and to amplify and multiply the voices we were able
to hear. Fortunately, the accumulation of sights and sounds in the work
that Levine produced after *Defender*—the thickening of what he called
"expressive culture"—never overwhelmed the story or stories he was telling. "Heterogeneity and variety," he wrote, "do not necessarily connote
chaos and loss of meaning." Although free blacks in church and white
groundlings in the theater pit may twist and shout in his books, there is
none of the cacophony of which high modernist critics complain. To the
contrary, it was really the static generated by high modernist canoneers—
the "Guardians of Culture" and "Keepers of the Flame" as Levine called
them—that amounted to so much white noise. By contrast, Levine's narrative never missed a beat, his interpretation never dropped a stitch, as
his history wound its way seamlessly from the folk culture of slave society
to the folklore of industrial society, from the intimate, firsthand world of
a hush arbor to what C. Wright Mills called the "second-hand world" of a
mass-mediated society.[11]

To mention C. Wright Mills is to evoke the pragmatist sensibility that
informs, indeed infuses, the work of Lawrence Levine: a pragmatist sensibility that sometimes toggles between the approaches of John Dewey
and William James. Experience had long been the grounding for Levine's
cultural history, so I am not at all sure he would have accepted my borrowed distinction between firsthand and secondhand knowledge worlds.
"It is a mistake," he once wrote, "to divide the world up too easily into
reality and representations of reality. . . . Rather, the entire setting con-
stitutes an important form of reality in which many essential things are
realized: lessons are learned, values enunciated and repeated, modes of
behavior scrutinized, social institutions and their effects explored, fantasies indulged." Likely as not, then, he would have insisted with William James that for *his* historical subjects—slaves, workers, jazz lovers,
and moviegoers— "knowledge of sensible realities comes to life inside
the tissue of experience" and that "it is *made;* and [re]made by relations

that unroll themselves in time." To speak as one might today of the irre-
ducibly discursive *construction* of that experience would be (to recur to
James) to evoke the image of "the dog dropping his bone and snapping at
its image in the water."[12]

True, individuals can be obdurate, oblivious or, like James's dog, narcissistic. William Jennings Bryan, for example. But for Levine, social
groups or collectivities—especially subaltern or subordinated ones—
must be adaptive, attentive, absorptive in order to survive. As a spokesman for the rural democratic tradition, Bryan was merely a vehicle for
an expressive culture, what Lawrence Goodwyn would later call a "movement culture," that had been generated around him; his authority was but
the gift or endowment of those whom he represented. Thus when, during
the late 1960s, Levine turned from the life of the Great Commoner *in
particular* toward the life of the slave *as such*, he was leaving behind a conventional historical figure whom he acknowledged to be "the *creature* . . .
of his culture" and, in his place, taking up a composite historical figure
whom Levine could show to be the *creator* of his culture. Here, it should
be said, Levine's pragmatism was more Deweyan than Jamesian, more
social than individuated. As he saw things, no matter how idiosyncratic
or individuated a particular cultural expression might appear, both its
structure and its improvisatory power sprang from the shared or social
handling of a common historical experience. All expressive culture was
in some respects secondhand, and the cultural historian was there to certify it as previously owned. For all its formulas, expressive culture was
also and in other respects experimental, open-ended.[13]

Openness was once again the keynote. Just as Levine rejected Stanley M.
Elkins' model of slavery as a closed system that sucked the air out of black
culture, so he rebuffed the notion that twentieth-century Americans
inhabited a one-dimensional ideological universe shaped and stamped
by the culture industries. "There is no cultural product," he wrote in "The
Folklore of Industrial Society," "no book or symphony or film or play or
painting—so overwhelming, so complete that it binds the audience to
a single interpretation, a single angle of vision, a single meaning." The
slaves did not submit to the slaveholder's Bible, nor did Depression audiences necessarily buy the Hollywood ending. American culture, American cultures, are at every point hybrid, creolized, coauthored.[14]

So let us try to sort out some of the meanings of this personal and, in
many respects, generational commitment of cultural history to the openness and open-endedness of collective experience, especially when pitted
against the traumatic closures or foreclosures of life we intuitively asso-

ciate with the systems of chattel slavery and Jim Crow. Having worked through these meanings, we can then turn to the role of the catastrophe as a fact and figure of thought deployed by cultural historians (and their co-workers in the social sciences) as they have moved from slavery into the industrial and postindustrial contexts of a global capitalism. Culture and catastrophe, light and shadow. At a moment beset by its own imagination of disaster, I would like to ask how cultural historians might bring these opposed thematics together to reconsider the questions that Lawrence Levine posed as he turned his historian's eye from the "hard rock" of slavery to the hard times of capitalism.

———————

Even as Levine's topical interests changed, he held onto his model of popular culture as open, as experiential, as experimental, and as collaborative. Meanwhile, those axioms quickly became articles of faith—a kind of low or demotic modernism—for a generation or more of American cultural historians. Emboldened by this faith, they revisited the concept of tradition, free of the elegiac mood and mode of high modernism and the patronizing attitude of high rationalism. Reading widely across the social sciences, they readily adopted a more ethnographic, eye-level perspective of collective habits, treating them as a patterned repertoire of improvisations, as a kind of craftsmanship—the artisanship or bricolage of life: bounded, yes, but scarcely brainless. No more Unit Ideas or Great Books. Not "thoughts" either but rather, to paraphrase the Berkeley colleague whom Levine repeatedly quoted, the visual and aural record of people "thinking."[15]

Under this new intellectual dispensation, tradition looked less like an unreflective deference to authority, more like a tactical response to power, to the brute facts of coercion and constraint. Tradition, too, now lived *inside* the "tissue of experience" as so many informal rules of thumb or working hypotheses: time-tested as much, if not more, than time-honored. Tradition understood as a thing of shreds and patches was good; tradition as an ideology scissored out of whole cloth was, well, not so good. Yet in both instances, tradition—culture—appeared as instrument, as resource, as (in Kenneth Burke's phrase) "equipment for living." "The slaves' expressive arts and sacred beliefs," Levine concluded, "were more than merely a series of outlets or strategies; they were instruments of life, of sanity, of health, and of self-respect." There was the wound, yes, but there was the bow too.[16]

Anyone familiar with the work of the new labor, social, and cultural historians of the early 1970s will recall how powerfully these statements of cultural agency reverberated at the time. It was not just the "Elkins thesis" that Levine's work challenged but the complex of assumptions undergirding contemporaneous debates about the social sources of totalitarianism, the psychic operations of colonialism, the "culture of poverty," and the "pathology" of the black family. And again, Levine was scarcely alone in this challenge. Herbert Gutman's *The Black Family in Slavery and Freedom* (1976) appeared a year before *Black Culture and Black Consciousness* as an avowed riposte to Stanley Elkins, E. Franklin Frazier, and the "bitter public and academic controversy surrounding Daniel P. Moynihan's *The Negro Family in America*" (1965).[17] So the policy implications of these debates were significant from the outset, and they grew ever more fraught as the years passed.[18] Yet it does not diminish the intellectual or political significance of Levine's challenge to say that this artisanal model of folk and popular culture resonated, subtly but forcefully, with the sense that left and left-liberal historians in the 1970s had of their own work culture, their own magpie approach to theory, and their own regulated improvisations in the archive.

Perhaps the most vivid formulation of this approach had been framed (again) by C. Wright Mills, in the appendix to *The Sociological Imagination* (1959), published shortly before Mills penned his famous "Letter to the New Left." Writing in the voice of a mentor speaking to a young graduate student (the essay was titled "On Intellectual Craftsmanship"), Mills advised the young scholar both to "use your life experience in your intellectual work" and to develop "the capacity to shift from one perspective to another" and thereby "build up an adequate view of a total society and its components." The panoramic view again, but one assembled and turned in kaleidoscopic or prismatic fashion by the sociologist—or historian—operating, in Mills's words, as a "mature workman."[19]

Mills's sociological imagination, like the cultural historian's imagination to which it was kin, was an *immersive,* at times even oceanic imagination. "You do not have to *study* a topic you are working on," Mills advised; "for once you are into it . . . it is everywhere. You are sensible to its themes; you see and hear them everywhere in your experience, especially, it always seems to me, in apparently unrelated areas. Even the mass media, especially bad movies and cheap novels and picture magazines and night radio, are disclosed in fresh importance to you." How often have students or colleagues been heard to describe the experience of their topics in this way? How often have we felt and said as much ourselves? And how often do we detect this same intersection of biography and history—this same experiential nexus—in Lawrence Levine's own work, not least of all in his treatment of American popular culture of the 1930s and 1940s, the tissue of his experience as a child growing up in a lower-middle-class Jewish household in Manhattan?[20]

Yet what might strike us now as a perfectly appropriate insider's account of the cultural historian's research experience might just as easily impress a less sympathetic outsider as a narcissistic compulsion: a *topical* disorder in every sense of the word. What could be more self-indulgent, after all, than the desire to pass off local, ephemeral, and superficial cultural forms and practices as some sort of "deep play" and portentous history? Levine confessed to feeling qualms of his own in 1990 when preparing the first lecture version of his "Folklore of Industrial Society" article. "*I* was the most obvious audience for this piece," he wrote later; "I had to convince myself that I could make an intellectual case for what I believed was true from my own experiences, observations, and values." His own "experiences, observations, and values." Just so.[21]

Not surprisingly, when the "Folklore" article appeared two years later in the pages of the *American Historical Review,* it was accompanied by comments from Robin D. G. Kelley, Natalie Zemon Davis, and Jackson Lears, each of whom represented a different intellectual current (cultural studies, women's studies, and consumer culture studies) in the gathering wave of the New Cultural History. Suspicions of superficiality (and Philistinism) have long dogged historians of popular culture, suspicions emerging at first from the precincts in which cultural history had been born—social and intellectual history—but over time extending to political, diplomatic, and even military history, as the so-called culturalists invaded *their* borders and took what were believed to be *their* jobs.[22]

But this impression of encroachment was in many respects true, wasn't it? It could be seen in the new editions of textbooks then coming out; it was visible in the syllabi of the new history surveys; it was heralded as well in the countless review essays, symposia, and anthologies of the time that remarked on "the cultural turn" in historiography. And lest we forget, when Lawrence Levine delivered the lecture that was to become, three years later, *The Opening of the American Mind,* he did so as the president of the Organization of American Historians (OAH).[23]

Now the OAH may not be Lenin's version of the "commanding heights," but it was—in April 1993—a forward position in the cultural wars then being fought in the press and on countless national, state, and local curriculum committees. And as Levine acknowledged in the collection of essays that appeared that same year under the title *The Unpredict-*

able Past, he still felt on the methodological defensive on the subject of mass popular culture, defensive in a way that he had never been made to feel on the subject of black folklore. Mass popular culture, critics insisted, was a fun house mirror in which the historian, like Mills's master workman, everywhere found confirmation of his or her "topic."[24]

The essays collected in *The Unpredictable Past* provided a characteristically patient and tactful response to this criticism. But what initially struck me when revisiting these pieces was Levine's own return to a passage in an essay of William James that he had invoked a decade and a half before in *Black Culture and Black Consciousness* and that he foregrounded again in his OAH presidential address that same year: a passage from James's essay "On a Certain Blindness in Human Beings," published in 1899. James's essay is largely a pastiche of observations taken from poets and other writers, but the first passage that interested Levine was from William James himself. Thinking back on a trip he once took through the hardscrabble backcountry of North Carolina, James recollects the aesthetic revulsion he first felt when coming upon the ulcerated squalor of clear-cut woodland valleys peopled by poor whites eking out a subsistence living among the charred stumps, pigs, and chickens.[25]

A shocked James asks one of these untouchables why his clan feels the need to "denude" the land and is told, in turn, of the pride the mountaineers feel in getting the country "under cultivation." Instantly James realizes that the mysterious obscurity—the opacity even—of this backwoods culture is an artifact of *his* blindness and of the parochialism peculiar to *his* "strange indoor academic ways of life at Cambridge." The log "cabin was a warrant of safety for self and wife and babes," so that what had seemed to him "a mere ugly picture on the retina . . . was to *them* a symbol redolent with moral memories and sang a very paean of duty, struggle, and success."[26]

James's ripe literary metaphors express his newfound conviction that the backcountry landscape is a text as moral and as aesthetic in its meaning to the farm families standing before him as the landscapes conjured up by William Wordsworth's "magnificent . . . morning" and Whitman's "Brooklyn Ferry" are for the imagined schoolteacher readers of James's own essay. Levine saw James's epiphany as a standing reproach to ethnocentrism, and he returned to it again and again, I would venture to guess, because ethnocentrism—a certain blindness—was for him a chronic condition of mankind, historians no less than others. William James's North Carolina anecdote served as an implicit rebuke to those who would see the plunge into folk or popular culture as a *self*-indulgence rather than a self-critique. To the contrary, James's ethnographic epiphany provides its own mythic charter for cultural historians to explore moral landscapes—moral "neighborhoods"—other than their own.

But how far and how deep into that landscape should they go? One can hardly imagine a contemporary environmental or gender historian passing over James's Blue Ridge parable without some comment on its "paean" to the domestication of land and women. A culture's *insensibilities*, as James called them, are rank-ordered; they cut across the grain of society in different directions and at different depths, and the scars that obliviousness leaves behind are never equally distributed. James, not surprisingly, is silent on this point of privilege, but the fact remains that the disadvantaged, the disenfranchised, the oppressed bear a disproportionate share of the costs imposed by that "certain blindness in human beings." Call this rank order of the visible in society a structure of *unfeeling* or an indifference curve. Call it what you will, but to see it at work is to appreciate popular culture, folk tradition, or "moral memories" as at times an *endangered* resource, a *blunted* instrument, or an *expropriated* tool. With the mountaineer as with the Great Commoner, culture cuts both ways—empowering and imprisoning.

Different historians have responded differently to this doubled dimension of culture—to its myopias and its illuminations. Some have looked to the darker side of the divide, tracking the cultural construction of ethnocentrism (or racism or misogyny, and so forth) and its payoffs, which is to say: the social contracts affirmed, the powers ratified, and the psychological wages taken home by the beneficiaries. Other historians have kept their eye on the brighter side of the divide—on the social and psychic space cleared, shared, and warmed by means of expressive culture—asking how ordinary men and women rekindled, renewed, and relayed its light. In their own way these cultural historians, Lawrence Levine not least among them, have become Keepers of the Flame.

The image of light brings me to the second passage, the second anecdote, in "On a Certain Blindness" that Levine borrowed to represent the kind of culture that traditional history had been unable to see. It is James's allusion to Robert Louis Stevenson's essay of 1888, "The Lantern Bearers," an autobiographical fragment in which Stevenson recalled the exhilaration of a late-summer game of his youth. The boys in his school would light tin bull's-eye lanterns, hitch them to their cricket belts, and hide them under their coats as they walked across the "links," meeting one another in the dark and offering the password: "Have you got your lantern?" "The essence of the bliss," Stevenson confessed, "was to walk by yourself in the black night . . . a mere pillar of darkness in the dark; and all the while, deep down in the privacy of your fool's heart, to know you had a bull's eye lantern at your belt, and to exult and sing over the knowledge."[27]

James draws from this anecdote a lesson about the "vital secret" that every individual protects, a secret that cries out for recognition and sympathy but that at the same time deadens the person to the secrets of others. But Levine rightly caught the social and collective dimension of Stevenson's little tale: the boys are thrilled by the freemasonry of their rites—the exchange of passwords, the mutual revelations, the sharing of light *against* the darkness. Stevenson himself recalled that the bull's-eye lanterns mimicked those worn by the local constables, but he confessed that "we did not pretend to be policemen" but rather burglars. The secret of the lanterns is a communal and transgressive secret, and it is *that* secret which animated *Black Culture and Black Consciousness* and the history that the book has, in its turn, inspired. "The black folk," Levine wrote in its epilogue, "are only one of the groups of people who have walked through American history with their cultural lanterns obscured from the unknowing and unseeing eyes of outside observers."[28]

If I were to single out a work that attempted not just to historicize but to theorize the lessons of the lanterns—the lesson, that is, of Lawrence Levine, John Blassingame, Herbert Gutman, E. P. Thompson, and others in the first generation of the new cultural or sociocultural historians—it would be James Scott's *Domination and the Arts of Resistance.* Published in 1990, the book offers a compendium of tales by lantern light and candlelight, tales of subcultural resistance to the insults and indignities of oppression, many of them taken from the work of cultural historians. Scott's new lexicon—"hidden transcripts," "the theater arts of subordination," "the infrapolitics of subordinate groups" —was in many respects a return gift; it gave back to cultural historians a new tool kit, one calibrated to that elusive dynamic by which cultural politics volatilizes into saturnalia or crystallizes into a political or movement culture. Robin Kelley was among the first historians to use Scott's approach to move American cultural history deeper into the politics of the twentieth century than many of the earlier generation had been disposed to go. Indeed, as a participant in the 1992 *American Historical Review* round table "The Folklore of Industrial Society," Kelley had both welcomed Levine's manifesto for the study of popular culture and urged its author "to push his analysis further, to insist on an even wider incorporation of cultural studies methods."[29]

Kelley's move toward politics and contemporary culture was but one of many encounters and convergences between second-generation cultural historians and second-generation cultural studies scholars. Throughout the late 1980s and the 1990s, cultural history entered into an intense, if sometimes stammering conversation with poststructuralism, new historicism, gender and queer theory, critical legal studies, critical race theory, new social movement theory, cultural geography, postcolonial theory, and other intellectual movements. The list seems inexhaustible. Historians, however, are not, and so it has seemed at times that the oceanic feeling of victory has somehow emptied cultural history of its insurgent energies: that because we all now *speak* cultural history, like so many *bourgeois gentilhommes*, our very fluency feels glib. The linguistic turn passed some time ago; is it culture's turn now?[30]

Hardly. If anything, the intellectual and political stakes have been raised over the past decade and a half. *The Opening of the American Mind* (1996) had been delivered as a broadside in a *national* culture war; Levine's historical and anthropological horizons remained those of the nation-state. By the end of the decade, "culture" had become part of a debate over globalized futures (and pasts) as neoconservative and neoliberal theorists mused about the role of social capital, cultural values, and civil society in the marketization of the world and Left theorists ruminated about stateless empires and the local, diasporic, and transnational cultural insurgencies ranged against them. Pundits debated Samuel P. Huntington's prediction of a "clash of civilizations," while bookstore tables displayed titles like his *Culture Matters*. Modernization theory had returned, it seemed, with a vengeance. Culture was no longer just a resource; it had been weaponized.[31]

But if "culture" ruled the waves, it also seemed to have lost its moorings as historians and anthropologists alike contemplated the accelerated global flow of labor, capital, information, and identities. "The Folklore of Industrial Society"—a proposition that had once to be argued (however belatedly) to a roundtable of historians in the pages of the *American Historical Review*—now seemed intuitively true to students wired to the Internet and reading about the imminent dissolution of modern national culture (itself an "imagined" community) into countless "deterritorialized ethnoscapes," "financescapes," "technoscapes," "ideoscapes," and "mediascapes."[32]

Looked at dispassionately, the attacks on the World Trade Center and the Pentagon would seem to have confirmed these globalist premonitions: a mass-mediated spectacle of diasporic, faith-based, nonstate actors weaponizing the classic icons of modern tourism in order to destroy the equally "branded" vehicles of global capital and state power. All the bases of postmodernity touched. Of course, to encapsulate the event in this way does little more than reduce it to a cultural studies or policy studies caricature—half allegory, half algorithm—as if the "global disjunctures" between all the "scapes" could somehow sculpt themselves into the forms of twisted steel and shattered concrete.

Yet there was more than a little such self-caricature in the aftermath of 9/11 as cultural commentators strove to theorize the first draft of history. Barely four days after the event, for example, the social philosopher and cultural critic Slavoj Zizek composed an on-line essay titled "Welcome to the Desert of the Real" in which he concluded that the "shattering impact of the bombings [could] only be accounted for" by the "notion that the two WTC towers stood for the center of . . . VIRTUAL capitalism." The violence was a shock to the system of First World, digitized, financial capitalism, which had for so long thought itself insulated "from the sphere of material production" in the Third World. And, he added, even though the towers had fallen, the structure of feeling within which Americans were processing the disaster remained intact, having been fashioned by innumerable Hollywood scenarios of terrorist paranoia—the folklore of *post*-industrialism. "America got what it fantasized about," Zizek wrote, "and this was the greatest surprise." Thus, weeks before rescue workers had dug their way into the ruins of the World Trade Center, at least one cultural theorist had managed to tunnel his way out by retrofitting the event, now framed as the culture's own gothic presentiment (or pre-sentiment) of trauma, into the intellectual machinery of political economy and film history.[33]

To be fair, few of the immediate pronouncements about 9/11—its cultural sources and significance—have withstood the test of time; written before the smoke had cleared, they were at once the symptom and the improvised solution to the shock of the event. That the collapse of the towers felt "just like a movie" to so many television viewers registered something more than its having been watched on screen. As a folk artifact of industrialism, the movies still serve us as the closest experiential analogy to the out-of-body sensations that shock produces. Our reflexive resort to the film analogy expresses our trauma and protects against it, so it is tempting to see the filmography that Zizek so quickly assembled not just as food for thought but as comfort food—a recipe for disaster. In 1992 Robin Kelley had urged Lawrence Levine to push his analysis further to "an even wider incorporation of cultural studies methods." Here in 2001 was cultural studies, here indeed were most of us, at the limit.[34]

———————

Given the ominous unfolding of world events since 9/11, it easy to forget how many of the first generation of cultural historians identified a specific catastrophic experience—slavery, dispossession, exploitation—as the historical crucible of their story. In the face of disaster and, in James Scott's fine phrase, in the teeth of power, subordinate cultures mobilized to transform or transmute that experience into a blueprint for regeneration, recognition, and reparation. "Upon the hard rock of racial, social, and economic exploitation and injustice," Lawrence Levine wrote in 1977, "black Americans forged and nurtured a culture." Fourteen years earlier, in 1963, E. P. Thompson had closed his famous chapter on exploitation by observing that "it is perfectly possible to maintain two propositions which, on a casual view, appear to be contradictory. Over the period 1790–1840 there was [in England] a slight improvement in average material standards. . . . By 1840 most people were 'better off' than their forerunners had been fifty years before, but they had suffered and continued to suffer this slight improvement as a catastrophic experience." *The Making of the English Working Class*, Thompson added, was an exploration of "this experience, out of which the political and cultural expression of working-class consciousness arose."[35]

Reading over these passages recently, I was reminded of an even earlier work on England in the period of early industrialization: Karl Polanyi's *The Great Transformation* (1944). Completed toward the end of World War II, Polanyi's book had an enormous influence on economic and political anthropologists writing in the teeth of modernization and rational choice theory. The book has more recently had another life in the hands of Fred Block, Margaret Somers, and other writers on globalization. Like Marx before him and Thompson after him, Polanyi began with two apparently contradictory propositions. "At the heart of the Industrial Revolution of the eighteenth century," his first chapter opens, "there was an almost miraculous improvement in the tools of production, which was accompanied by a catastrophic dislocation of the lives of the common people."[36]

Polanyi's words were chosen carefully: neither immiseration nor exploitation in any purely calculable sense but rather "dislocation" taken in the broadest, deepest, or "substantive" sense: namely, an unraveling of the institutional web of social meaning, obligation, and entitlement within which an economy—a society's mode of self-provisioning—ordinarily lies "embedded." Where Marx had treated the noise of the marketplace as deafening one's ear to the steady drip of surplus-value extraction at the point of production, Polanyi worried that the concept of exploitation, whether measured in a liberal or Marxist metric, obscured the cataclysmic social and cultural impact of an unregulated market economy and its "lethal injury" to the collective tissue of experience, or to what Levine, writing of slave culture, called "the instruments of life, of sanity, of health, and of self-respect." The result of this "economic earthquake," as Polanyi called it, was (among other things) "the loss of self-respect."[37]

A half century later, James Scott would readily admit that his analysis of domination likewise privileged "the issues of dignity and autonomy" over "material exploitation." Exploitation may well be the purpose of domination, he acknowledged, but the "very process of appropriation . . . unavoidably entails systematic social relations of subordination that impose indignities of one kind or another on the weak," and it was against the public performance of these indignities that "insubordinate" cultures nursed themselves—rehearsed themselves—into carefully dissembled existence.[38]

Polanyi's argument imagined a similar dynamic or dialectic at work within and across capitalist societies. He called it the "double movement," by which he meant the various class, coalition, or statist "countermovements"—from Chartism to the New Deal—that emerged to protect societies against the utopian liberal (and now neoliberal) project of full marketization. By Polanyi's lights, that project was doomed to failure because "no society" could survive the "crude fictions" of an unrestrained market economy. Among these "fictions" he ranked the commodification of labor, land, and money as the most damaging. "Robbed of the protective covering of cultural institutions," Polanyi warned, "human beings would perish from the effects of social exposure." As the "middle classes were the bearers of the nascent market economy," it was left to the "laboring people" to represent the "common human interests that had become homeless." Thus, the countermovement.[39]

James Scott's intellectual debt to Polanyi was plain enough, and one could plausibly argue that Edward Thompson's concept of moral economy—like his concept of exploitation—owed something to *The Great Transformation*. But the genealogical case is much harder to make for the first generation of American cultural historians, notwithstanding the family resemblances I've mentioned. Years ago social and economic historians debated the existence of a self-sufficient or "moral" economy in late colonial and early national America, and faint echoes of that once noisy controversy are still detectable in Timothy Breen's recent *Marketplace of Revolution*. More to the point, perhaps, was Thompson's approach to the encounter between traditional work cultures and new factory-disciplines; it had a visible impact on the so-called new labor history of the 1970s. But as narratives of *transformation*, these new accounts of late nineteenth-century American work culture or subculture were far more influenced by Marx or by modernization theory than by anything written by Polanyi and his heirs in economic and cultural anthropology.[40]

When U.S. historians did draw close to Polanyi's catastrophic notion of social and cultural dislocation, they were more likely to be writing about the Trail of Tears, Ellis and Angel islands, and the Middle Passage than about, say, the market revolution in antebellum America or the black migrations of the twentieth century.[41] Of the three dislocations— conquest, migration, and slavery—slavery, and above all, the slave trade, has so far provided the single most powerful example of an American market formation to exemplify Polanyi's double movement. On the one side stood the social and cultural calamity of a market in human beings, and counterposed to it the reparation and resistance—the "theater arts" and "freemasonry"—that John Blassingame, Leon Litwack, Ira Berlin, Steven Hahn, and Lawrence Levine (among others) have identified with African American culture and consciousness.[42]

A sharp foretaste of that catastrophism appeared a little more than a decade ago with Nell Painter's disturbing essay "Soul Murder and Slavery," an analysis that drew on a generation of feminist and psychoanalytic reflection on sexual trauma to highlight the psychic damage wrought upon slave families (and the wider society) by "child abuse, sexual abuse, sexual harassment, rape, battering" across the color line. Painter broke down the damage into familiar therapeutic categories like "depression, lowered self-esteem, and anger," but the bottom line of "soul murder," as she described it, was the extinction of personal identity and the brutalizing replication of patriarchal violence across the generations.

One could scarcely underestimate the boldness of this essay since, as Painter herself acknowledged, she could easily be seen as resurrecting the Elkins thesis—the infamous armchair exercise in slave psychologism that had sent Lawrence Levine and his generation of cultural historians to the archives. Painter cited that generation's work on slave resistance, slave communities, and slave culture as reason enough to reject Elkins' "closed system" and its implications of irreparable damage. On the other hand, she suggested that the revisionists had avoided and in some instances "positively resisted the whole calculation of slavery's psychological costs" in their haste to prove the resilience of the slave community.[43]

History being what it is, such matters hardly lend themselves to precise and final moral probate. All the more intriguing, then, that throughout an essay on soul murder, Painter should have insisted on what she described as bookkeepers' metaphors: the "calculation" or "toll" of slavery, "most notably the tragic overhead costs that were reckoned in the currency of physical abuse and family violence." The essay itself was subtitled "Toward a Fully Loaded Cost Accounting." Was this imagery a discreet gesture toward Elkins' institutional argument, often forgotten, that slavery owed its peculiarly brutal form in the United States to "the dynamics of an unopposed capitalism?" To the "mode of economic organization which was taking on a purity of form never yet seen?" Here, it may be worth recalling the question Elkins posed to his readers in 1959. "What happens," he asked, "when such energy meets no limits?" His answer: an "unmitigated capitalism" was free to become an "unmitigated slavery." Fifteen years after the publication of *The Great Transformation*, Elkins' argument in *Slavery* was as close as any U.S. historian had come to Karl Polanyi's idea of a disembedded market economy, and the surprise of it was that he had located it in the ostensibly traditionalist American South.[44]

Today, a half century of scholarly debate later, neither Elkins' notion of an "unmitigated capitalism" nor Polanyi's nightmare of a "disembedded market" have survived intact. Southern historians have painstakingly filled in the complex social and cultural matrix—the rites, roles, and codes—that underwrote and oversaw the plantation economy, while, for their part, economic sociologists have come to believe that *all* markets, even the most volatile and virtual financial exchanges, are institutionally born and bound. In fact, by the time Elkins published his thoughts on "unopposed capitalism," Polanyi himself had moved toward a view of modern markets as always, already embedded.[45]

Still, Polanyi never backed away from his catastrophic view of the free market as a utopian project. Classic liberalism's (and, again, neoliberalism's) threat to selfhood, society, and culture sprang for Polanyi from its promotion of the false or "fictitious" commodities of labor, land, and money, by which he meant the marketing of that which had not been produced for sale. "Labor," he wrote, "is only another name for a human activity which goes with life itself" and which cannot "be detached from the rest of life, be stored or mobilized." To the contemporary ear,

Polanyi's intimations of inalienability evoke the socialist humanist indignation associated with the early Marx, and there is an elective affinity between them. Perhaps that is why Polanyi took pains to distinguish fictitious commodities, which he saw inflicting symbolic violence of their own upon social and cultural life, from the phenomenon the later Marx labeled "commodity fetishism," understood as the mystification of socially produced value by means of the naturalization of exchange value. Classical liberalism, laissez-faire, the free market—what was for Marx a kind of ideological rapture was for Polanyi a sociocultural rupture, a fundamental disorientation or dislocation.[46]

In this way *The Great Transformation* rewrote Marx's materialist dialectic as a moral, at times allegorical, epic of the double movement—let us call it "Marketization and Its Nemeses"—with the vice figures played by commodified labor, land, and money. Most contemporary culturalists, not to mention most materialists, would dismiss the explanatory weight of Polanyi's "fictitious commodities." But Polanyi was not arguing against the operational reality of the markets in land and labor, especially if that reality were judged pragmatically, by its effects. To the contrary, he was arguing that the most incongruous and invidious of those effects sprang from the functional indifference, the inbuilt blindness, of the market principle to social and natural ecologies alike. Nell Painter's "fully loaded cost accounting" of chattel slavery quietly underscores that same incongruity and invidiousness; her deadpan metaphors subtly perform, as a matter of rhetoric, the arbitrary and indifferent violence that the chattel principle inflicted on slave families and communities. Sojourner Truth's parents, Painter writes, "were chronically depressed as a result of having sacrificed their [ten] children to the market, one after the other." One after the other—the phrase quietly translates a simple statistic into a protracted catastrophe.[47]

Nowhere has this approach to the "fictitious commodities" of the slave South been more effectively carried forward than in *Soul by Soul* (1997), a gripping revisionist history written by Painter's former student, Walter Johnson. Like Lawrence Levine before him, Johnson turned the historian's prism once again in order to see slavery anew, moving the action of his story away from the familiar terrain of the plantation and its quarters. Even more jarringly, *Soul by Soul* literalized the sardonic accounting metaphors of "Soul Murder" by treating the slave market as the abolitionists had: as "a part of slavery that could be used to understand the whole of the institution." There, in the slave marts, one could find "slavery reduced to the simplicity of a pure form: a person with a price." There, too, one could find the institutional figuration of a whole way of life and livelihood—albeit with an important difference. Unlike the traditional cockfights, horse races, and duels that historians have interpreted as ritual enactments of the Southern social order, Johnson singled out the slave market as the one public place where that order was explicitly fused to its political economy and where, as a result, its capital—material and symbolic—was not just on display but on offer. Paternalism thus made for a thin institutional constraint upon the slave trade precisely because it was, as Johnson put it, "something slaveholders could buy in the slave market."[48]

So "life in the antebellum slave market"—the subtitle of *Soul by Soul*— was both shaped and volatilized by this cold fusion between a racialized paternalism and the fictitious commodities of the chattel principle. "In the slave market," Johnson wrote, "the central tension of antebellum slavery was daily played out as slaveholders invested their money and their hopes in people whom they could never fully commodify." Spectators came to see a high-stakes, improvisational drama—"acts of sale" as Johnson called them—in which social life and social death were at once enacted and transacted. Over time slaves were relocated from the upper South to the lower South, but the substantive impact for families and communities was, to borrow Polanyi's terms, one of social and existential dislocation: one after the other.[49]

"Slaves in the market could not avoid being pushed out of any stable self-definition and into the space between person and thing," Johnson reminded his readers, and it was in the "boundary-blurring doubleness" of this experience that one could appreciate "the obscenity of the slave market: people forced to perform their own commodification." What Lawrence Levine called the "hard rock of racial, social, and economic exploitation and injustice," Johnson in *Soul by Soul* compressed to the dimensions of the New Orleans auction block, if only then to crack it open and read as evidence of a catastrophic event.[50]

———

More than three decades separate *Black Culture and Black Consciousness* from *Soul by Soul*, but the historiographical distance between them is not as great as the passage of time suggests. True, where Levine's book is panoptic, Johnson's is intensely focused. Where Levine's voice is ethnographic, Johnson's is philosophical. And where Levine looks beyond the Elkins thesis, Johnson, in his own oblique way, returns to it. But that said, Johnson returns neither to reaudit the damage wrought by slavery nor to reassess the regenerative and resistant powers of slave culture; *Soul by Soul* is, if anything, a book that takes those social and cultural resources as a given. A "majority of slaves," Johnson wrote, "spun transcendence out of everyday activities." They gleaned practical wisdom as well, steeling one another against the indignities—the exposure and abjection—of the slave sale. And finally, Johnson argued, they used their experience of the slave trade to create "a type of knowledge about the nature of slavery that was indispensable to its critics."[51]

And indispensable to the historian, too. By excavating and reassembling that practical knowledge of slavery at its "leading edge"—the slave trade—Walter Johnson was able to work his way back and out to the broader culture and economy of the antebellum South. By these means, he was able to revisit and revise Elkins' claim of an unmitigated or unopposed Southern capitalism from a different economic vantage-point: the point, that is, of exchange. Tiny as the New Orleans slave market may have been when set beside the broad array of antebellum slave institutions, its pens and coffles projected terror and enforced discipline across the South by means of the simple but "terrifying contingency of lives put up for sale." And indeed the slaves of *Soul by Soul* inhabit a landscape irradiated by the threat of commodification: alienated from their bodies, their sense of "time and space . . . bent around the ever-present threat of sale," and "every social relation" holding "within it the threat of its own dissolution."[52]

Americans have long been accustomed to think of slavery and waged labor as polar opposites, an opposition that racialization has made that much easier to embrace. So it is all the more startling to find in Walter Johnson's landscape—his social and cultural "morphology" of the slave trade—such a striking resemblance to Karl Polanyi's catastrophic account of the arrival of a "free" market in land and labor in England. The broad and many-sided phenomenology of the slave sale that *Soul by Soul* patiently reconstructed seems fitted precisely to Polanyi's notion of the fictitious commodity: an inherently contradictory status whose indignities (and exploitation) threaten the broader social fabric and the natural environment as they rend the tissue of experience.[53]

What are we to make of these metaphorical and morphological affinities between Johnson's account of the American slave economy and Polanyi's account of the English industrial economy? Might we take these two interpretations of fictitious commodities to be speaking to and about a market principle whose pure form ("a person with a price") epitomized without in any way exhausting the variety of impositions, indignities, and isolation present in the labor and capital markets in the North? Post–Civil War campaigns against wage slavery, debt peonage, and bankruptcy raise comparisons like these, and social and cultural historians exploring the Gilded Age have accordingly challenged the slave/free polarity, offering in its place a more graduated spectrum of market coercions and constraints together with their corresponding scenarios of subjection and abjection.[54]

From the side of capital and consumption, for example, Scott Sandage has looked at the "extinction of identity" in nineteenth-century bankruptcy, whereas Lendol Calder has highlighted the disciplinary powers of twentieth-century consumer credit. From the side of labor, Amy Dru Stanley and Todd DePastino have shown how threatening was the specter of the "free" and unencumbered worker to postbellum elites in the North. To paraphrase Walter Johnson on resistant slaves, post–Civil War hoboes and tramps turned their own commodification—that is, the relative liquidity of their own labor power—against the forces of capital and, in the process, forged their own solidarities, built their own hobohemias, and invented their own folklore. A countermovement, so to speak, at the leading edge of the free labor market.[55]

Much as slave pens had operated as the icons of the chattel principle, so tramp armies and hobo encampments operated for some sixty years as a visible sign of the dislocations and dispossessions experienced under the free-labor principle after the Civil War. Today, though, in a postindustrial, globalist, consumerist age of virtual finance, the United States has outsourced its imagery of outcast labor power as it has outsourced its industry. The same may be said for the imagery of the market as such; everywhere we find the spectacle of consumer goods and the satisfied customer but almost nowhere an image of a factory, an assembly site, or an actual market transaction. And so, Slavoj Zizek tells us, the spectacular destruction of the World Trade Center breaks through the bubble of virtual capitalism like some return of the repressed, shocking yet somehow anxiously anticipated, not to say illicitly entertained, by a long list of Hollywood screenwriters.[56]

Too Freudian by half? Maybe. Still, Zizek's grim, postindustrial fairy tale points to a few themes and interests common to several generations of historians who rounded the cultural turn. First, there is the abiding interest in the popular "knowledge of sensible realities" as it "comes to life" inside the collective "tissue of experience," especially as that fabric is seen to have been torn upon the "hard rock" of violence, exploitation, and injustice. Two decades of feminist debate over sexual and domestic trauma, coupled with a renewed interest (pace Elkins) in Holocaust memory, have sustained the significance, if not the authority, of the experiential in the face of poststructuralist doubts. "Soul Murder" builds deliberately on those traditions, whereas *Soul by Soul* draws on the archive to imaginatively reconstruct a vividly detailed social and historical phenomenology of the chattel principle. "Soul" is scarcely a word one would expect to find in a posthumanist glossary, yet Painter and Johnson freely use the word to capture the creatural integrity of each slave ("one after the other") as well as the slaves' shared understanding of their own condition, their "hidden transcript" or "freemasonry," as it were. Humanism, then, is part of what binds Walter Johnson and Nell Painter to Lawrence Levine and his generation: it generates the warmth as well as the illumination in their writing. They are all still—in Levine's special sense—lantern bearers.[57]

Second, there is a continuing interest in the relation of culture to capitalism. Even the recent, transnational turn in history and cultural studies bespeaks a familiar (Marxist? Weberian? Polanyian?) desire to think capitalism and culture together under whatever sign: chattel, property, capital, labor, commodity, or simply market. To read Lawrence Levine's or, for that matter, Warren Susman's marvelous essays on the thirties and forties is of course to recall how keen they were to puzzle out the response of ordinary Americans to the greatest systemic crisis of capital in living memory. Yet for all their interest in the question, both of them had to make—and remake—the scholarly case for the history of popular culture to skeptical or dismissive readerships. Susman's essays revolved around the discovery and defense of the cultural concept itself, whereas Levine, embroiled as he was in the culture wars, settled for "The Folklore of *Industrial* Society" (emphasis added) as the title of his principal essay. As for the folklore of *capitalism*, that has remained—from Thurman Arnold to Thomas Frank—an exercise in ideological critique, most often written to puncture the market mythologies of the moment.[58]

Thanks in no small part to the pioneering work of Lawrence Levine and his generation of historians and, no less important, thanks to their willingness to defend their collective project, we—their students and colleagues—no longer have to defend the same terrain. We are already looking "beyond" the cultural turn to discover what we should "bring back in." All of which means that we have been freed to press forward on the challenge first raised by Levine and Susman and Montgomery and others: to think capitalism and culture together. Their students, many but by no means all of whom I've referenced, have already done so, as have many other historians unmentioned here. Needless to say, cultural studies scholars have been a critical part of that cultural front, too.

But when it comes to the systematic description of market experience—the phenomenology or lived theory of markets—historians have much to learn as well from economic sociologists, cultural anthropologists, economic geographers, and historians of the social sciences, many of whom could properly be said to be working in the tradition of Karl Polanyi. To be sure, Karl Marx, Max Weber, and Georg Simmel had all commented in one place or another on the impersonality of the market principle and its solvent effect on traditional institutions, but it was Polanyi who detached marketization as such from modernity as such and identified it instead as a historically bound utopian project: a Euro-American (perhaps Austro-American?) ethnocentrism that mistook its own hypostasized market formalism for fairness rather than, in William James's terms, a "certain blindness."

I was reminded of the continuing force of that blindness when completing the first draft of this essay, for I was interrupted—the nation was interrupted—by the devastation left by Hurricane Katrina: a natural disaster transformed into a national catastrophe by a state blinkered, so to speak, by that same market triumphalism. How ironic, it seemed to me at that moment, that thanks to one of the most catastrophic exercises in laissez-faire, floodwaters were sweeping through the ancient slave pens and slave exchanges that had once housed—indeed, "embedded"—the chattel principle.

It had all happened before, of course, and not just as a Hollywood film. In 1927 the Mississippi River broke through the levees. Then it was the Agrarian poet Will Percy in the public spotlight: evacuating the whites to Vicksburg and, at the behest of his father, keeping 7,500 black Mississippians in a tent colony, in the rain, on the levee, where Percy had been wont to jot down fragments of poems. Race was written all over this gesture, to be sure, but the brute fact was that the labor was wanted by the local planters. Some four decades later, thousands of black Louisianans were herded into the Superdome precisely because their labor was not wanted. The same racism, the same market insensibility, the same blindness.[59] Percy put matters a bit differently when he later reflected back on the events of 1927, but the echoes of his words could still be heard on cable and talk radio in 2005. "No race probably ever had less knowledge of its own past, traditions, and antecedents," Percy wrote in 1941.

"The American Negro is interested neither in the past nor in the future, this side of heaven. He neither remembers nor plans. The white man does little else."[60]

William Alexander Percy set these observations down as what he called "fieldnotes" and titled them *Lanterns on the Levee*. Between Will Percy's lanterns and those of Lawrence Levine, though, there is a world of difference, and thanks to that difference we—his students and colleagues— have seen the light.

NOTES

I thank the editors of this volume, especially Mike O'Malley, for their criticism and suggestions, and the *Journal of American History*, in which an earlier and briefer version of this chapter appeared. My deepest debt, though, is to Roy Rosenzweig, who shepherded this piece from its inception, as he did most everything I have written.

1. Warren I. Susman, "The Culture of the Thirties," in *Culture as History: The Transformation of American Society in the Twentieth Century*, by W. Susman (New York: Pantheon, 1984), 150–83.

2. Edmund Wilson, *American Earthquake: A Documentary of the Twenties and Thirties* (Garden City, NY: Doubleday, 1958); Wilson, "The Wound and the Bow," in *The Wound and the Bow: Seven Studies in Literature* (Boston: Houghton Mifflin, 1941); Wilson's argument perfectly allegorizes the aesthetic and strategic—formalist and functionalist—approaches to culture treated in proposition 3, in the introduction to this volume.

3. Lawrence W. Levine, "American Culture and the Great Depression," in *The Unpredictable Past: Explorations in American Cultural History*, by L. Levine (New York: Oxford University Press, 1993), 206–55.

4. Lawrence W. Levine, "The Folklore of Industrial Society: Popular Culture and Its Audiences," in Levine, *Unpredictable Past*, 306–7.

5. Lawrence W. Levine, *Black Culture and Black Consciousness: Afro-American Folk Thought from Slavery to Freedom* (New York: Oxford University Press, 1977); Levine, *Highbrow/Lowbrow: The Emergence of Cultural Hierarchy in America* (Cambridge: Harvard University Press, 1988); Levine, *The Opening of the American Mind: Canons, Culture, and History* (Boston: Beacon Press, 1996).

6. Richard Hofstadter, *The American Political Tradition and the Men Who Made It* (New York: Random House, 1948), chap. 8; Lawrence W. Levine, *Defender of the Faith: William Jennings Bryan: The Last Decade, 1915–1925* (New York: Oxford University Press, 1965), 358–65; for a similarly sympathetic but full-length biography, see Michael Kazin, *A Godly Hero: The Life of William Jennings Bryan* (New York: Knopf, 2006).

7. Lawrence W. Levine, "The Historian and the Culture Gap," in *Unpredictable Past*, 27; Levine, *Opening*, 150.

8. Hofstadter, *American Political Tradition*, 202; Levine, *Defender*, 359.

9. Levine has written about his early resentment at the assumption—most infamously expressed in Carl Bridenbaugh's 1962 presidential address to the Ameri-

can Historical Association—that historians of "lower middle-class or foreign origins" were ill equipped to understand the "Remote Past" of Anglo-Saxon America; see Levine, "Historian and the Culture Gap," 14–16; in *Opening*, Levine rejoices in the hard-won freedom of historians "to move into neighborhoods once blocked to scholars, teachers, and students" (146).

10. Carl Bridenbaugh, "The Great Mutation," *American Historical Review* 68 (January 1963): 315–31.

11. Levine, "Folklore," 319; Lawrence W. Levine, "Jazz and American Culture," in *Unpredictable Past*, 183; C. Wright Mills, "The Cultural Apparatus" (1959), in *Power, Politics and People: The Collected Essays of C. Wright Mills*, ed. Irving Louis Horowitz (New York: Ballantine, 1963), 405; William James, "A World of Pure Experience" (1904), in *The Writings of William James*, ed. John J. McDermott (New York: Random House, 1967), 200.

12. Levine, "Folklore," 312; James, "World of Pure Experience, 200, 202.

13. Lawrence Goodwyn, *The Democratic Promise: The Populist Moment in America* (New York: Oxford University Press, 1976); Levine, *Defender*, 363 (emphasis added).

14. Levine, *Black Culture*, 30; Levine, "Folklore," 312; see also Lawrence W. Levine, "The Historian and the Icon," in *Unpredictable Past*, 269. Elkins was a student of Richard Hofstadter; see Stanley M. Elkins, *Slavery: A Problem in American Institutional and Intellectual Life* (Chicago: University of Chicago Press, 1959); and Ann J. Lane, ed., *The Debate over Slavery: Stanley Elkins and His Critics* (Urbana: University of Illinois Press, 1971).

15. The colleague was Joseph Levenson; see Levine, *Black Culture*, ix; Levine, "Historian and the Culture Gap," 23.

16. Kenneth Burke, "Literature as Equipment for Living," in *The Philosophy of Literary Form*, by K. Burke, 3rd ed. (1941; repr., Berkeley: University of California Press, 1973), 293–304; Levine, *Black Culture*, 80.

17. Herbert G. Gutman, *The Black Family in Slavery and Freedom, 1750–1925* (New York: Random House, 1976), xvii.

18. Much has been written on this issue, but see especially Daryl Michael Scott, *Contempt and Pity: Social Policy and the Image of the Damaged Black Psyche, 1880–1996* (Chapel Hill: University of North Carolina Press, 1997); and Richard H. King, *Race, Culture, and the Intellectuals, 1940–1970* (Baltimore: Johns Hopkins University Press, 2004), esp. chap. 6.

19. C. Wright Mills, "Letter to the New Left," *New Left Review*, no. 5 (September–October 1960); Mills, *The Sociological Imagination* (New York: Oxford University Press, 1959), 196–97, 211; influential *annaliste* Marc Bloch's *Apologie pour l'histoire, ou le métier d'historien* (1949) was first translated into English as *The Historian's Craft* in 1962.

20. Mills, *Sociological Imagination*, 211; Levine discusses the connections in "The Historian and the Culture Gap," and in *Opening*, 133–37; for other examples of this experiential intersection (biography and history) in Levine's generation, see the interviews collected in Henry Abelove, ed., *Visions of History* (New York: Pantheon, 1993), though it was really the next generation of historians, those who grew up with television, who took up mass culture in earnest.

21. Levine, "Folklore," 291.

22. Lawrence W. Levine, "The Folklore of Industrial Society: Popular Culture and Its Audiences," *American Historical Review* 97 (December 1992): 1369–99; Robin D. G. Kelley, "Notes on Deconstructing the Folk," ibid., 1400–1408; Natalie Zemon

Davis, "Toward Mixtures and Margins," ibid., 1409–16; T. J. Jackson Lears, "Making Fun of Popular Culture," ibid., 1417–26.

23. The bibliography for this intellectual moment is immense, but I single out three books by Europeanists as announcing the arrival of cultural history: Roger Chartier, *Cultural History* (Ithaca, NY: Cornell University Press, 1988); Lynn Hunt, *The New Cultural History* (Berkeley: University of California Press, 1989); and Robert Darnton, *The Kiss of Lamourette: Reflections in Cultural History* (New York: Norton, 1990); on the American side, there was George Lipsitz's pathbreaking *Class and Culture in Cold War America: "A Rainbow at Midnight"* (South Hadley, MA.: J. F. Bergin, 1982); Richard Wightman Fox and T. J. Jackson Lears, eds., *The Culture of Consumption: Critical Essays in American History, 1880–1980* (New York: Pantheon, 1983); Roy Rosenzweig, *"Eight Hours for What We Will": Workers and Leisure in an Industrial City, 1870–1920* (Cambridge: Cambridge University Press, 1983); and the posthumously published collection of essays by Warren Susman, *Culture as History*; for a recent memoir and reflection on this extended moment on both sides of the Atlantic, see Geoff Eley, *A Crooked Line: From Cultural History to the History of Society* (Ann Arbor: University of Michigan Press, 2005); similar "cultural turns" were being announced in literary criticism, anthropology, sociology, and political science.

24. Levine, "Folklore," 291.

25. Levine, *Black Culture*, 441; Lawrence W. Levine, "Clio, Canons, and Culture," *Journal of American History* 80 (December 1993): 849; Levine, *Opening*, 144–45; William James, "On a Certain Blindness in Human Beings," in *Writings*, 629–45; James's essay originally appeared in *Talks to Teachers on Psychology: and to Students on Some of Life's Ideals* (1899).

26. James, "Certain Blindness," 631.

27. Levine, *Black Culture*, 441–42; Levine, "Historian and the Icon," 285–86; Levine, *Opening*, 149–50; James, "Certain Blindness," 631–34; Robert Lewis Stevenson, "The Lantern Bearers" (1888), in *The Lantern Bearers and Other Essays*, by R. L. Stevenson (New York: Farrar, Straus and Giroux, 1988), 226–35.

28. Levine, *Black Culture*, 442.

29. James C. Scott, *Domination and the Arts of Resistance: Hidden Transcripts* (New Haven: Yale University Press, 1990); Robin D. G. Kelley, *Race Rebels: Culture, Politics, and the Black Working Class* (New York: Free Press, 1994); Kelley, "Notes," 1408.

30. Signs of such a passage have already materialized not only in Geoff Eley's magisterial memoir but in the appearance of new anthologies that point "after" or "beyond" the cultural turn. The currency of the "turn" among publishers may be measured in the sequence of titles that used the phrase; for example: David C. Chaney, *The Cultural Turn: Scene-Setting Essays on Contemporary Cultural Theory* (London: Routledge, 1994); Fredric Jameson, *Cultural Turn: Selected Writings on the Post-Modern, 1983–1998* (New York: Verso, 1998); Victoria E. Bonnell and Lynn Hunt, eds., *Beyond the Cultural Turn: New Directions in the Study of Society and Culture* (Berkeley: University of California Press, 1999); Larry Ray and Andrew Sayer, *Culture and Economy after the Cultural Turn* (London: Sage, 1999); George Steinmetz, ed., *State/Culture: State-Formation after the Cultural Turn* (Ithaca, NY: Cornell University Press, 1999); Simon Naylor and James Ryan, eds., *Cultural Turns/Geographical Turns: Perspectives on Cultural Geography* (Englewood Cliffs, NJ: Prentice Hall, 2000); Douglas Bruster, *Shakespeare and the Question of Culture: Early Modern Literature and the Cultural Turn* (New York: Palgrave Macmillan, 2003); Don Kalb

and Herman Tak, eds., *Critical Junctions: Anthropology and History beyond the Cultural Turn* (New York: Berghahn Books, 2005); Dale B. Martin and Patricia Cox Miller, eds., *The Cultural Turn in Late Ancient Studies: Gender, Asceticism, and Historiography* (Durham, NC: Duke University Press, 2005); Margarita Dikovitskaya, *Visual Culture: The Study of the Visual after the Cultural Turn* (Cambridge: MIT Press, 2005).

31. Samuel P. Huntington, *The Clash of Civilizations and the Remaking of World Order* (New York: Simon and Schuster, 1996); Lawrence E. Harrison and Samuel P. Huntington, eds., *Culture Matters: How Human Values Shape Progress* (New York: Basic Books, 2000); Michael Hardt and Antonio Negri, *Empire* (Cambridge: Harvard University Press, 2000).

32. On these "global disjunctures," see Arjun Appadurai, *Modernity at Large: Cultural Dimensions of Globalization* (Minneapolis: University of Minnesota Press, 1996); see also David Harvey, *The Condition of Postmodernity: An Enquiry into the Conditions of Cultural Change* (Cambridge, MA: Blackwell, 1989); and Harvey, *Spaces of Capital: Towards a Critical Geography* (Edinburgh: Edinburgh University Press, 2001); the most compelling effort to rethink these developments and, with them, the history of cultural studies, is Michael Denning, *Culture in the Age of Three Worlds* (New York: Verso, 2004).

33. Slavoj Zizek, "Welcome to the Desert of the Real," *Re:constructions: Reflections on Humanity and Media after Tragedy,* September 15, 2001; http://web.mit.edu/cms/reconstructions/interpretations/desertreal.html (accessed July 27, 2006).

34. On the impact of 9/11 on cultural studies, see John Frow, "The Uses of Terror and the Limits of Cultural Studies," *Symploke* 11 (Winter–Spring 2003): 69–76; Levine himself noted that in "the culture of the 1930s past calamities could become didactic mechanisms for illustrating the ways in which people might triumph over adversity" ("Historian and the Icon," 281).

35. Scott, *Domination,* xiii; Levine, *Black Culture,* xi; E. P. Thompson, *The Making of the English Working Class* (New York: Pantheon, 1963), 212.

36. Karl Polanyi, *The Great Transformation: The Political and Economic Origins of Our Time* (1944; repr., Boston: Beacon Press, 1957), 33.

37. Ibid., 29–30, 157–59; Levine, *Black Culture,* 80; for Marx's view of the market as a theoretical distraction from the productive sphere, see Robert Brenner, "On the Origins of Capitalist Development: A Critique of Neo-Smithian Marxism," *New Left Review* 1, no. 104 (July/August 1977): 25–93; but see also Allan Megill, *Karl Marx: The Burden of Reason (Why Marx Rejected Politics and the Market)* (Lanham, MD: Rowman and Littlefield, 2002), chap. 3.

38. Scott, *Domination,* xi, 23, 111.

39. Polanyi, *Great Transformation,* 130–34, 73; Polanyi's title referred not to the industrial revolution but rather to the social democratic and social justice countermovements he saw released by the catastrophic experiences of world depression and war; needless to say, in 1944 he did not foresee the contemporary recrudescence of liberalism.

40. For Polanyi's discussion or moral economy, see *Great Transformation,* 186; Polanyi elaborated his ideas of socially and culturally "embedded" economies in "The Economy as Instituted Press," in *Trade and Market in the Early Empires,* ed. Karl Polanyi, Conrad M. Arensberg, and Harry W. Pearson (New York: Free Press, 1957); on James Scott's use of Polanyi, see especially Scott, *The Moral Economy of the Peasant: Rebellion and Subsistence in Southeast Asia* (New Haven: Yale Uni-

versity Press, 1976), 5n8; on Thompson's use of the concept, see E. P. Thompson, "The Moral Economy of the English Crowd in the Eighteenth Century," *Past and Present* 50 (1971): 76–136; and the responses gathered in Adrian Randall and Andrew Charlesworth, eds., *Moral Economy and Popular Protest: Crowds, Conflict, and Authority* (New York: St. Martin's, 1999); for a history of the concept of moral economy, see William James Booth, "On the Idea of the Moral Economy," *American Political Science Review* 88 (September 1994): 653–67; T. H. Breen, *The Marketplace of Revolution: How Consumer Politics Shaped American Independence* (New York: Oxford University Press, 2004); for the treatment of work cultures in the United States, see, for example, Herbert G. Gutman, *Work, Culture, and Society in Industrializing America* (New York: Knopf, 1976); and David Montgomery, *Workers' Control in America: Studies in the History of Work, Technology, and Labor Struggles* (Cambridge: Cambridge University Press, 1979); on the tension between modernization and Marxist theory, see David Montgomery, "Gutman's Nineteenth-Century America," *Labor History* 19 (Summer 1978): 416–29.

41. For example, when Herbert Gutman referred to the internal migration of 20 million African Americans between 1940 and 1970, he alluded suggestively to "a modern Enclosure Movement without parallel in the nation's history" and to its corresponding "Poor Law," but this was in a "brief Afterword" to his monumental study of black family life before 1925; Gutman, *Black Family*, xxiv, 466–68.

42. See, for example, John W. Blassingame, *The Slave Community: Plantation Life in the Antebellum South* (New York: Oxford University Press, 1972); Leon F. Litwack, *Been in the Storm So Long: The Aftermath of Slavery* (New York: Oxford University Press, 1979); Ira Berlin, *Generations of Captivity: A History of African-American Slaves* (Cambridge: Harvard University Press, 2003); and Steven Hahn, *A Nation under Our Feet: Black Political Struggles in the Rural South from Slavery to the Great Migration* (Cambridge: Harvard University Press, 2003).

43. Nell Painter, "Soul Murder and Slavery: Toward a Fully Loaded Cost Accounting," in *U.S. History as Women's History*, ed. Linda K. Kerber (Chapel Hill: University of North Carolina, 1995), 125–46; reprinted in Nell Painter, *Southern History across the Color Line* (Chapel Hill: University of North Carolina Press, 2002), 15–39; see esp. 16–17, 20–21, 24.

44. Painter, "Soul Murder," 16. Elkins, *Slavery*, chap. 2, esp. 43, 49; a footnote (43n23) faults Marx and Engels for failing to distinguish capitalisms according to the social and cultural institutions surrounding (or as Polanyi might say, embedding) them. Among the historians who have discussed this aspect of Elkins's work are Scott, *Contempt and Pity*, 114–18; and King, *Race, Culture, and the Intellectuals*, chap. 6. Louis Hartz's thesis of an absent feudal tradition in America could be said to have prepared the way for Elkins's argument; see Hartz, *The Liberal Tradition in America* (New York: Harcourt, Brace and World, 1955); of course, it was against views like these that Eugene Genovese built his own case for American slavery as lodged or embedded within a seigneurial and paternalist institutional setting.

45. The revision of Polanyi's embeddedness argument began in earnest with Mark Granovetter, "Economic Action and Social Structure: The Problem of Embeddedness," *American Journal of Sociology* 91 (November 1985): 481–510; but see also John Lie, "Embedding Polanyi's Market Society," *Sociological Perspectives* 34 (Summer 1991): 219–35; Bernard Barber, "All Economies Are 'Embedded': The Career of a Concept and Beyond," *Social Research* 62 (Summer 1995): 387–414; J. Rogers

Hollingworth and Robert Boyer, eds., *Contemporary Capitalism: The Embeddedness of Institutions* (Cambridge: Cambridge University Press, 1997); Greta R. Krippner, "The Elusive Market: Embeddedness and the Paradigm of Economic Sociology," *Theory and Society* 30 (December 2001): 775–810; Neil Fligstein, *The Architecture of Markets: An Economic Sociology of Twenty-First Century Capitalist Societies* (Princeton: Princeton University Press, 2001); Warren J. Samuels, "Markets and Their Social Construction," *Social Research* 71 (Summer 2004): 357–70; but Fred Block makes a persuasive case for Polanyi's own acknowledgment of the embeddedness of all markets and, at the same time, for the ambiguities on this point in *Great Transformation;* see Block, "Karl Polanyi and the Writing of *The Great Transformation,*" *Theory and Society* 32, no. 3 (June 2003): 275–306.

46. Polanyi, *Great Transformation,* 72; the debates over what Marx meant by commodity fetishism have been long and vexed, but one of the best accounts is still Norman Geras, "Essence and Appearance: Aspects of Fetishism in Marx's Capital, *New Left Review* 1, no. 65 (January–February 1971): 69–85.

47. Painter, "Soul Murder," 24; Painter's imagery was likely intended as a belated rejoinder to the econometric moment in the historiography of slavery, as emblematized by Robert Fogel and Stanley Engerman, *Time on the Cross: The Economics of American Negro Slavery* (Boston: Little Brown, 1974).

48. Walter Johnson, *Soul by Soul: Life Inside the Antebellum Slave Market* (Cambridge: Harvard University Press, 1999), 2, 111; see also 82–84, 246n56. Johnson's arguments on paternalist status (and power) as a consumer good are the least persuasive part of his argument; they depend in part on marginalizing the "work" and contest of paternalism in the fields and homes of the planters, which would have been their (Polanyian) protection against an unregulated slave trade among whites; slaves (and their paternalist cachet) were also bequeathed to others as gifts or inheritances. Still, see Gavin Wright's review in the *Journal of Interdisciplinary History* 31 (2001): 469–70, where he comments on the "chilling . . . banality of slaveowners' attitudes toward their chattel."

49. Johnson, *Soul by Soul,* 214.

50. Ibid., 16, 164; compare these statements to Levine, *Black Culture,* 114–15; the phrase "social death" is taken from Orlando Patterson, *Slavery and Social Death: A Comparative Study* (Cambridge: Harvard University Press, 1992).

51. Johnson, *Soul by Soul,* 195, 77, 219–20.

52. Ibid., 18, 64, 163, 23, 22.

53. For a sense of how Polanyi's concept of land as a fictitious commodity has played itself out in environmentalist scholarship, see Mitchell Bernard, "Ecology, Political Economy and the Counter-Movement: Karl Polanyi and the Second Great Transformation," in *Innovation and Transformation in International Studies,* ed. Stephen Gill and James H. Mittelman (Cambridge: Cambridge University Press, 1997), 75–89; for examples of thinking about the commodification of land and labor together, see especially Donald Mitchell, *The Lie of the Land: Migrant Workers and the California Landscape* (Minneapolis: University of Minneapolis Press, 1996); Andrew Herod, *Labor Geographies: Workers and the Landscapes of Capitalism* (New York: Guilford Press, 2001); and Gunther Peck, "The Nature of Labor: Fault Lines and Common Ground in Environmental and Labor History," *Environmental History* 11 (April 2006), http://www.historycooperative.org/journals/eh/11.2/peck.html (accessed July 28, 2006).

54. On the continuing spectacle of black subjection in labor, law, and literature, see

especially Saidiya V. Hartman, *Scenes of Subjection: Terror, Slavery, and Self-Making in Nineteenth-Century America* (New York: Oxford University Press, 1997).

55. Scott A. Sandage, *Born Losers: A History of Failure in America* (Cambridge: Harvard University Press, 2004); Lendol Caldor, *Financing the American Dream: A Cultural History of Consumer Credit* (Princeton: Princeton University Press, 1999); Amy Dru Stanley, *From Bondage to Contract: Wage Labor, Marriage, and the Market in the Age of Slave Emancipation* (Cambridge: Cambridge University Press, 1998); and Todd DePastino, *Citizen Hobo: How a Century of Homelessness Shaped America* (Chicago: University of Chicago Press, 2003). On the challenge to "wage slavery," see especially, David Montgomery, *Beyond Equality: Labor and the Radical Republicans, 1862–1872* (New York: Knopf, 1967); and Montgomery, *Citizen Worker: The Experience of Workers in the United States with Democracy and the Free Market during the Nineteenth Century* (Cambridge: Cambridge University Press, 1993); Lawrence Glickman, *A Living Wage: American Workers and the Making of Consumer Society* (Ithaca, NY: Cornell University Press, 1997); Gunther Peck, *Reinventing Free Labor: Padrones and Immigrant Workers in the North American West, 1880–1930* (Cambridge: Cambridge University Press, 2000); Robert Steinfeld, *Coercion, Contract, and Free Labor in the Nineteenth Century* (Cambridge: Cambridge University Press, 2001); Jonathan Glickstein, *American Exceptionalism, American Anxiety: Wages, Competition, and Degraded Labor in the Antebellum United States* (Charlottesville: University of Virginia Press, 2002). On turning commodification against one's owners, see Johnson, *Soul by Soul*, 164.

56. On the relative invisibility of the market transaction in popular culture, see Jean-Christophe Agnew, "Advertisements for Ourselves: Being and Time in a Promotional Economy," in *Cultures of Commerce: Representation and American Business Culture, 1877–1960*, ed. Elspeth H. Brown, Catherine Gudis, and Marina Moskowitz, 343–64 (New York: Palgrave Macmillan, 2006).

57. See, in this connection, Johnson's response to Joan Scott's critique of the place of "experience" in historiography (*Soul by Soul*, 226n25); Joan Scott's critique may be found in "The Evidence of Experience" (1991), reprinted in *Questions of Evidence: Proof, Practice, and Persuasion across the Disciplines*, ed. James Chandler, Arnold I. Davidson, and Harry Harootunian (Chicago: University of Chicago Press, 1994); see also Johnson's qualifications on the "humanist" model in "On Agency," *Journal of Social History* 37 (Fall 2003): 113–24. For an example of a post-Foucauldian treatment of the "soul," see Ian Hacking, *Rewriting the Soul: Multiple Personality and the Sciences of Memory* (Princeton: Princeton University Press, 1995).

58. Warren I. Susman, "Culture and Commitment" (1973), reprinted in Susman, *Culture as History*, 184–210; Thurman W. Arnold, *The Folklore of Capitalism* (New Haven: Yale University Press, 1937); Thomas Frank, *One Market under God: Extreme Capitalism, Market Populism, and the End of Economic Democracy* (New York: Doubleday, 2000). Each of these works still repays a close reading.

59. For a useful discussion of the disposition of "waste" labor and landscapes in modern capitalist economies, see Zygmunt Bauman, *Wasted Lives: Modernity and Its Outcasts* (Cambridge, MA: Polity Press, 2004); and Alan Berger, *Drosscape: Wasting Land in Urban America* (Princeton: Princeton Architectural Press, 2006).

60. William Alexander Percy, *Lanterns on the Levee: Recollections of a Planter's Son* (New York: Knopf, 1953), 22–23; on the Percys and the flood, see John M. Barry, *Rising Tide: The Great Mississippi Flood of 1927 and How It Changed America* (New York: Simon and Schuster, 1997).

PART IV

Epilogue

The Art of Listening

KAREN HALTTUNEN

A child growing up in American slave culture didn't hear one rabbit story, he or she heard hundreds of them in his or her lifetime.

LAWRENCE LEVINE, *Black Culture and Black Consciousness* (2007 ed.)

The point is simply that all history entails comprehending the other even if she or he seems familiar. These people are not us, and it takes patience and hard work to hear *their* voices instead of merely echoes of our own.

LAWRENCE LEVINE, *Black Culture and Black Consciousness* (2007 ed.)

In his preface to the thirtieth-anniversary edition of *Black Culture and Black Consciousness: Afro-American Folk Thought from Slavery to Freedom* (published posthumously in 2007), Lawrence Levine retraced his own path to the emerging field of U.S. cultural history. As a young assistant professor, while completing the revisions of his dissertation—a study of William Jennings Bryan—he became active in the Congress of Racial Equality, made the march from Selma to Montgomery, Alabama, in 1965, and decided to write his next book on black protest in twentieth-century America. But not long into his readings of civil rights leaders and black intellectuals, he realized that he was replicating the approach of his Bryan book by "allowing the leadership to speak for the masses" (xiii). "How," he wondered, "did one penetrate the thought and aspirations of people who left few written records behind them, especially in the era of slavery and the decades following emancipation?" (xiii). He began to read anthropology in an effort "to devise strategies to hear these voices that had been so effectively silenced by historical neglect. . . . People 'speak' in a myriad of ways, and my first strategy was to discern whether certain actions of African Americans constituted 'voices' that could speak to us and explain the attitudes that were the basis of those actions" (xiv). The first major step of this pathbreaking work in U.S. cultural history was thus a commitment to the art of listening. The slave child was enculturated to the world of slavery by listening to hundreds of trickster tales. Levine spent years in his Berkeley study trying to understand the worldview of slaves and their emancipated descendants by listening to those same tales, along with hundreds of songs, folk beliefs, jokes, reminiscences, and proverbs—a body of material that he called African American "expressive culture."

But what this volume's contributors call Levine's "empathic" approach to cultural history has drawn criticism from those who follow the "discursive" model, as Michael O'Malley observes in his introduction to part 2. This tension between the empathic and the discursive was generated by a pivotal shift in the practice of U.S. cultural history during the last decades of the twentieth century—a shift discussed in the introduction and part 3 of this volume. In the 1960s, 1970s, and early 1980s, some of the new social, labor, and cultural historians turned to an ethnographic concept of culture to shape their explorations of oppressed communities. Working-class people, immigrants, women, and people of color (among others) employed culture—values, beliefs, conventions, rituals—as a resource for resisting dominant social groups and asserting their own agency in the face of oppression. But in the late 1980s, cultural history took the "linguistic turn" and began to focus on denaturalizing categories and hierarchies of difference—in particular, race, gender, and sexuality—by exposing the historical constructedness of identities. Whereas the ethnographic historians tended to treat their subjects as creators of culture, discursive historians tended to treat them as creatures of culture, imprisoned in an endless web of representations. Of course, the distinction was never absolute: both approaches shared a common concern for historical subjectivities; many cultural histories approached subjectivities as mixtures of self-determination and discursive construction; and this shared enterprise helped bind together successive generations of historians as "cultural." But from the perspective of discursive purists, Lawrence Levine's ethnographic listening in *Black Culture and Black Consciousness* could be seen as naive for confusing culture with power, colonialist in purporting to speak for subalterns, and essentialist in treating "African American" as a single, objectively real social group.

The editors and contributors to this volume share the belief, expressed by James Cook and Lawrence Glickman in the introduction, that "the time is ripe for a broad assessment of U.S. cultural history." We stand at a critical moment in the development of the field, when some scholars predict its "impending obsolescence"—in part, ironically, because so many historians now regard themselves as culturalists that the field is no longer clearly bounded, and in part because discursive studies of identity and power have reached the point of exhaustion. Are we now in fact "beyond" or "after the cultural turn," as several book titles proclaimed in the (perhaps significantly) millennial year of 1999? And does that mean that the field of cultural history has played itself out? The essays gathered here clearly demonstrate that U.S. cultural history is far from moribund. Although we may indeed be "beyond the cultural turn"—beyond, that is, discursive history in its purest form—we are not witnessing the demise of the broader field of cultural history. Instead, we stand, as Nan Enstad observes in her chapter, "On Grief and Complicity," at what may be cultural history's "most exciting moment of possibility," as the culturalist approach flows out of its many tributaries into the main streams of historical practice. And in moving "beyond the cultural turn" we may be turning full circle to a recovery of some of the most valuable practices of the earlier ethnographic approach to culture, but within more complex frameworks for coming to terms with the social and political power of cultural representations, cultural production and reception, hybridity and transnationalism—to name just a few of the enduring contributions of the newer cultural history.

The chapters in part 2 of this volume, "Practicing Cultural History," owe a significant debt to ethnographic or "empathic" history in their creative approaches to the art of listening. Ann Fabian, in "A Native among the Headhunters," manages to hear the voice of William Brooks, caught as he was in a web of conflicting representations: as Flathead Indian, Methodist convert, and racial specimen whose skull was coveted by Philadelphia's race scientists. While keeping clear of any effort to define his essential cultural identity, Fabian provides access to the radical displacement of this young victim of American imperialism by reporting his hybrid critique (as Flathead and as Methodist) of "civilization." John Kasson's chapter, "Behind Shirley Temple's Smile: Children, Emotional Labor, and the Great Depression," examines a very different young person whose expressive agency was similarly entrapped in powers beyond her control. Shirley Temple's seemingly natural smile was the product of grueling child labor, and her exploitation reveals much about "the emotional demands of capitalist society during one of its greatest periods of crisis." Kasson's empathic move is to draw as close as he can to the child actress's experience of commodification and listen to her as a young adult discovering the extent to which her parents had first used her labor and then dissipated her hard-earned wealth.

Two chapters in this section owe a particular debt to Lawrence Levine's practice of listening attentively to popular song. Waldo Martin, in "'Be Real Black for Me': Representation, Authenticity, and the Cultural Politics of Black Power," offers one of the most intensive acts of listening in the volume, treating the lyrics and performance of a single song as an important cultural expression of "a searching black nationalism committed to community empowerment, best personified by the Black Panthers." Bridging the gap between ethnographic and discursive cultural histories, he argues that "Be Real Black for Me" "showcases the fallibility as well as the necessity of the quest for authenticity in the politics of self-definition and representation"—a defense he extends to cultural histories by Lawrence Levine and Sterling Stuckey, against charges from black British cultural studies that they were essentialist and totalizing. Michael O'Malley's "Rags, Blacking, and Paper Soldiers: Money and Race in the Civil War," although the most discursive essay in the volume (as the author acknowledges), illuminates the double-natured listening practices at the core of postmodernist "readings" of texts. A close reading of the song "How Are You Greenback?" uncovers overlapping debates about the authenticity of black soldiers and greenback dollars; during the crisis of the Civil War, both race and money pretended, he argues, to a solidity that was belied by their instability.

In "Re-membering John Dillinger," Elliott Gorn listens to both rural folklore and popular culture—what Levine controversially called "the folklore of industrial society"—to explore the history and memory of John Dillinger. That gangster's often-told story, Gorn concludes, provided something for nearly everyone in the context of the Great Depression: an arena for discussing economic fairness and social justice, a satisfying restoration of moral order and a policy victory for the newly centralized state, an opportunity to vent popular rage at financial institutions and celebrate the freedom of the open road, and, above all, a fantasy of untrammeled masculinity. "The Envelope, Please," by Shane White, Stephen Garton, Stephen Robertson, and Graham White, draws closer to ground-level conversations than any other chapter in this volume. The authors use criminal court records to eavesdrop on confidence games played in Harlem in the 1920s and argue that the creativity of these "small dramas" of the streets qualify them as vernacular expressions of the Harlem Renaissance. Gorn's enlistment of folklore and the Australian collaborators' close attention to African American expressive culture perhaps come closest to completing the return to Levine's model of ethnographic history in *Black Culture and Black Consciousness*.

The last pair of chapters in part 2 of this volume pursue a fundamentally empathic approach to U.S. cultural history, while extending that approach to include space, place, and the built environment—demonstrating the impact of cultural geography on recent work in the field. Elaine Tyler May, in "Gimme Shelter: Do-It-Yourself Defense and the Politics of Fear," traces a white, middle-class American pattern of fear and distrust toward both outsiders and one another from its cold war origins into the post-9/11 era. "Gimme Shelter" both listens to verbal expressions of these fears—in sources that include popular magazines, presidential campaigns, and social-scientific literature—and demonstrates their materialization in underground defense bunkers, fortress-like domestic architecture, gated communities, and SUVs. And Eric Avila, in "Turning Structure into Culture: Reclaiming the Freeway in San Diego's Chicano Park," pursues a similar combination of verbal expression—in his case, political protest—and the built environment. After Interstate 5 had physically divided the racially and ethnically diverse community of Logan Heights, community members requested that a park be built beneath the highway-bridge exchange; the city of San Diego initially agreed but then decided to place a highway patrol station there instead. After a political demonstration involving a human chain facing down the bulldozers, community members and artists covered the pillars of the structure with murals depicting "an iconic pantheon of Chicano history, identity, and culture," thus asserting "the centrality of culture in the confrontation between city people and city planners."

The acts of listening at the core of these eight chapters draw implicitly on the greatest strengths of the earlier, ethnographic practice of cultural history best exemplified in *Black Culture and Black Consciousness*. The four chapters in part 3 of this volume, "Agendas for Cultural History," argue more directly for a return to earlier theories and practices. James Cook's "The Return of the Culture Industry" returns to Theodor Adorno's culture industry concept, which has been extensively critiqued by cultural historians who affirm the agency of individual consumers and uncover their strategic appropriations of mass culture. What remains valuable about Adorno, Cook argues, is his "stubborn refusal to consider questions of aesthetic form or ideological function *apart* from the mediating structures of capitalism." Cook's current work on the transnational circulation of African American expressive culture owes much to Adorno's insistence on matters of production, marketing, distribution, and labor, and uncovers new transnational modes of subaltern struggle in the performances of Master Juba and other black artists. Nan Enstad's "On Grief and Complicity: Notes toward a Visionary Cultural History" similarly argues the need to "reclaim" certain elements of "the visionary cultural history of subalterns": the capacities of human agency; the legitimization of contemporary political action; the pursuit of history to transform our own consciousness. A new visionary cultural history, she argues, would combine the political efficacy of the earlier approach with new understandings of power derived from interdisciplinary cultural studies. And she sees recent scholarly work on grief and complicity—studies of trauma and illness, torture and genocide, memory and mourning—as playing an important role in generating new stories that will "fundamentally revise the utopian concept of resistance."

Jean-Christophe Agnew's "Capitalism, Culture, and Catastrophe" further develops themes from both Cook's and Enstad's chapters in calling for a new, "empathic" cultural history that takes account of the traumatic or catastrophic moments of life in a capitalist society and culture. Catastrophe, he argues, has played a major role in shaping the work of cultural historians, as their interests have shifted from an earlier focus on slavery to the current emphasis on contemporary politics and culture in the context of global capitalism. The field of cultural history is not moribund, he notes; "if anything, the intellectual and political stakes have been raised over the past decade and a half" of national culture wars, globalization, stateless empires, and local cultural insurgencies. In recent work by Nell Painter and Walter Johnson, Agnew finds a continuing interest in the relation of culture to capitalism, and observes, "We are already looking beyond the cultural turn to discover what we should bring back in. All of which means that we have been freed to press forward on the challenge first raised by Levine and Susman and Montgomery and others: to think capitalism and culture together."

The most dramatic return in this final section of *The Cultural Turn in U.S. History* is Philip Deloria's, in his ambitious chapter, "From Nation to Neighborhood: Land, Policy, Culture, Colonialism, and Empire in U.S.-Indian Relations." For Deloria's understanding of what we should "bring back in" stretches to include legal/political history, especially the shifting imperial and colonial (the distinction is central to his analysis) frameworks created by federal Indian policy and law. He sketches four major, overlapping periods in Native American history from nation formation to the present, each defined by a distinct form of colonial/imperial practice (treaty making, reservations, allotment, and federally circumscribed tribal "self"-government). And he uses this periodization to demonstrate that at different historical moments, native people may be usefully seen as imperial subjects, colonized subjects, national citizens, abject outsiders, members of indigenous political collectivities, and participants in a global political consciousness based on aboriginality and indigeneity. Any study of Native Americans that treats them solely as cultural representations, or ethnographic agents creating their own culture, or victims of encounter and imperial development, is necessarily partial; Deloria calls for an acknowledgment of the "ecological relation among the social, political, juridical, and cultural." He closes his chapter with an assertion of the inadequacy of treating a historical figure such as Sacajawea solely within a cultural studies or biographical frame. Sacajawea, he writes, "actually dares us to ask far more complicated questions: about her place as a subject within interwoven social fields; about the complex political and social structures in which she—and her descendants—found themselves; about the relations between these structures and the cultural fields in which Indian people and others have made and exchanged meanings; about the ways culture needs play into an analysis of dominative practices, particularly within the frames of the colonial and the imperial."

Does Deloria's essay expressly summon us to listen to Sacajawea? No, but it does offer a sophisticated understanding of what listening to her would entail in terms of the complex multiplicity of her subject positions. It also implicitly reminds us of the colonialist pitfalls of claiming to "recover" or, worse, "give voice" to previously inaudible or inarticulate groups in the American past. Michael O'Malley states this problem effectively: "Cultural historians who worked in the discursive mode . . . grew suspicious of histories that tried to recover the voices of others, or to speak for subaltern or neglected groups . . . [perpetuating] a kind of imperial fiction as if it were fact." But the resulting histories, he observes, are "long on thesis" and "short on actual human beings." At their worst, they substitute the single, loud voice of the historian for the many voices of those he studies—a single, loud voice that can itself be thoroughly imperialistic in its claims to unmask cultural constructions of identities, explaining that the dead weren't really who they believed themselves to be. Whatever the flaws of Lawrence Levine's *Black Culture and Black Consciousness*, the arrogant unmasking of the past was not one of them. At the core of his historical practice was his conviction that to study the past was to engage in conversation: "And so the slaves, their post-emancipation progeny, and I had a long conversation from which I benefited more than

I can express" (xx). And while valuing the theoretical insights of other scholars, he was intent on not overlooking his subjects' local knowledge: "Historians naturally enough bring their theories and hypotheses, and those of other scholars, with them to their areas of research. Good enough, so long as they don't forget that the people they're studying had *their* own theories and hypotheses" (xx). As a gifted practitioner of the art of historical listening, Lawrence Levine wanted mentally to enter the world of his subjects, to comprehend their cultures by listening to their voices until "slaves explained themselves to me" (xix). Cultural historians working after the cultural turn do well to listen, in turn, to Levine.

CONTRIBUTORS

Jean-Christophe Agnew is professor of American studies and history at Yale University. He is the author of *Worlds Apart: The Market and the Theatre in Anglo-American Thought, 1550–1750* (1986) and numerous articles on consumer culture and cultural history. Most recently he coedited, with Roy Rosenzweig, *A Companion to Post-1945 America* (2002).

Eric Avila is associate professor of Chicano studies and history at UCLA. His publications include *Popular Culture in the Age of White Flight: Fear and Fantasy in Suburban Los Angeles* (2004).

James W. Cook is associate professor in the Department of History and the Program in American Culture at the University of Michigan. His publications include *The Arts of Deception: Playing with Fraud in the Age of Barnum* (2001) and *The Colossal P. T. Barnum Reader* (2005). He is currently writing a book about African American performers and the origins of modern show business.

Philip J. Deloria is professor in the Department of History and the Program in American Culture at the University of Michigan. He is author of *Indians in Unexpected Places* (2004) and *Playing Indian* (1998) and coeditor of the *Blackwell Companion to American Indian History* (2002). His specific interests in U.S. cultural history include American Indians, environmental history, and western and midwestern regionalisms. In 2008–9 he will serve as president of the American Studies Association.

Nan Enstad is associate professor of history at the University of Wisconsin, Madison. She is the author of *Ladies of Labor, Girls of Adventure: Popular Culture and Labor Politics at the Turn of the Twentieth Century* (1999) and is currently working on a book titled *The Jim Crow Cigarette: Following Tobacco Road from North Carolina to China and Back*.

Ann Fabian is professor of American studies and history and dean of humanities at Rutgers University. Her publications include *Card Sharps, Dream Books and Bucket Shops: Gambling in Nineteenth-Century America* (1990/1999) and *The Unvarnished Truth* (2000). The University of Chicago Press will publish her new book on skull collecting.

Stephen Garton is Challis professor of history at the University of Sydney and author most recently of *Histories of Sexuality: Antiquity to Sexual Revolution* (2004).

Lawrence B. Glickman is professor of history at the University of South Carolina. His publications include *A Living Wage: American Workers and the Making of Consumer Society* (1997), *Consumer Society in American History: A Reader* (1999), and *Buying Power: Consumer Activism in America from the Boston Tea Party to the Twenty-First Century* (forthcoming).

Elliott J. Gorn is professor of history and chair of American Civilization at Brown University. He is author of *The Manly Art* (1986), *Mother Jones: The Most Dangerous Woman in America* (2001), and coauthor (with Warren Goldstein) of *A Brief History of American Sports* (2004). Gorn has also edited several works, including *Constructing the American Past* (1995), *The Encyclopedia of American Social History* (1993), *Muhammad Ali: The People's Champ* (1995), and *Sports in Chicago* (2008). He is finishing a book to be titled *Dillinger's Ghost*.

Karen Halttunen is professor of history and American studies and ethnicity at the University of Southern California. She is author of *Confidence Men and Painted Women: A Study of Middle-Class Culture in America, 1830–1870* (1982), *Murder Most Foul: The Killer and the American Gothic Imagination* (1998), and editor of *A Companion to American Cultural History* (2008). In 2005–6 she served as president of the American Studies Association.

John F. Kasson is professor of history and American studies at the University of North Carolina at Chapel Hill. He has written four books: *Civilizing the Machine: Technology and Republican Values in America, 1776–1900* (1976), *Amusing the Million: Coney Island at the Turn of the Century* (1978), *Rudeness and Civility: Manners in Nineteenth-Century Urban America* (1990), and *Houdini, Tarzan, and the Perfect Man: The White Male Body and the Challenge of Modernity in America* (2001).

Waldo E. Martin Jr. is professor of U.S. history at the University of California, Berkeley. His most recent book is *No Coward Soldiers: Black Cultural Politics in Postwar America* (2005). He is the coauthor (with Joshua Bloom) of a history of the Black Panther Party to be published in 2009.

Elaine Tyler May, Regents Professor of American Studies and History at the University of Minnesota, is president-elect of the Organization of American Historians and served as president of the American Studies Association in 1995–96. Her publications include *Great Expectations: Marriage and Divorce in Post-Victorian America* (1980), *Homeward Bound: American Families in the Cold War Era* (1988), *Pushing the Limits: American Women, 1940–1961* (1996), and *Barren in the Promised Land: Childless Americans and the Pursuit of Happiness* (1997). She is also coeditor of *Here, There and Everywhere: The Foreign Politics of American Popular Culture* (2000) and coauthor of a college-level U.S. history textbook, *Created Equal: A History of the United States* (2003).

Michael O'Malley is associate professor in the department of history and art history at George Mason University and an associate director of the Center for History and New Media at GMU. His publications include *Keeping Watch: A History of American Time*

(1990). He is finishing a book on money, value, and race. He was a student of Lawrence Levine's at Berkeley and a colleague of Levine's at GMU.

Stephen Robertson is senior lecturer in the History Department at the University of Sydney and author of *Crimes against Children: Sexual Violence and Legal Culture in New York City, 1880–1960* (2005).

Graham White is an honorary associate in the History Department at the University of Sydney and is most recently coauthor, with the unrelated Shane White, of *The Sounds of Slavery* (2005).

Shane White is professor of American history at the University of Sydney and is most recently coauthor, with the unrelated Graham White, of *The Sounds of Slavery* (2005).

INDEX

CPSIA information can be obtained
at www.ICGtesting.com
Printed in the USA
LVHW04s1821290918
591770LV00003B/17/P